Modern
American
Religion

A World War II poster from the Laymen's National Committee urging rededication to faith for the country. (Courtesy of the Moody Bible Institute, Chicago.)

Modern American Religion

Volume 3

Under God, Indivisible,

1941-1960

Martin E. Marty

The University of Chicago Press
Chicago and London

MARTIN E. MARTY is Fairfax M. Cone Distinguished Service Professor of the History of Modern Christianity at the University of Chicago. He is the author of numerous books, including *A Nation of Behavers,* also published by the University of Chicago Press.

The University of Chicago Press, Chicago 60637
The University òf Chicago Press, Ltd., London
© 1996 by The University of Chicago
All rights reserved. Published 1996
Printed in the United States of America
05 04 03 02 01 00 99 98 97 96   1 2 3 4 5
ISBN: 0-226-50898-6 (cloth)

Library of Congress Cataloging-in-Publication Data

Marty, Martin E., 1928–
  Modern American religion.

Bibliography: v. 1, p.
  Includes index.
  Contents: v. 3. Under God, Indivisible, 1941–1960
  1. United States—Religion—1901–1945.
2. United States—Religion—1945–
3. United States—Church history—20th century.
I. Title.
BL2525.M37   1996   291'.0973   85-16524

To the memory of Fairfax M. Cone and in friendship with
George B. Caldwell, whose names I carry everywhere
with my own.

Enough my meed of fame
If those who deign'd to observe me say
I injur'd neither name.

(3rd Lord Holland, 1733–1840)

"I pledge allegiance to the flag of the United States of America and to the Republic for which it stands, one Nation, indivisible, with liberty and justice for all."

The Pledge of Allegiance as adapted from Francis Bellamy, Baptist minister, written September 8, 1892, made a matter of law in 1942, and in use until June 13, 1954.

"I pledge allegiance to the Flag of the United States of America and to the Republic for which it stands, one Nation under God, indivisible, with liberty and justice for all."

The Pledge of Allegiance as adapted by the United States Congress, Flag Day, June 14, 1954.

Contents

Acknowledgments

The University of Chicago makes available to me research assistants who help provide access to library and archival material and who check all citations and notes. James P. Wind, R. Scott Appleby, Stephen Graham, Peter D'Agostino, and Gilson Waldkoenig, now all productive scholars on their own, have served as researchers during the writing of volumes 1 and 2 of this work, and Waldkoenig bridged into this volume. Craig Prentiss was assistant through most of the work on *Under God, Indivisible,* and performed heroically, especially after a glitch occurred in the referencing system. In the late stages Jonathan Moore joined the team and was responsible for final touches. Whoever has engaged in scholarship of the sort that issues in books like these will recognize how great is my debt to these skilled, patient, and creative associates.

For a third of a century my writing has grown out of seminar and classroom situations, and this book like all the others reflects what I have learned from a new generation of historians; I cannot name them all, but they know how much I profit from our exchanges and I hope they carry the spirit of collegiality engendered in our classes with them wherever they go. Similarly, conversations with colleagues serve as critical stimuli. Since 1949 Jerald C. Brauer and I have interacted as historians and friends with a scholarly intimacy that has to be rare. Dean W. Clark Gilpin, who, with his assistant Sandra Peppers, arranged much to make my work possible and pleasant, has been a coteacher who teaches me along with the students who have been in our joint classes. More recently, Catherine L. Brekus has joined our team at the Divinity School and brings welcome insight from a new generation.

Fred C. Beuttler, James P. Wind, my brother, historian Myron A. Marty, and my son, pastor Peter Marty, were among those who read the manuscript and made suggestions; I am indebted to them and to two anonymous referees for the University of Chicago Press. Barbara Hofmaier, my partner in editing at the Park Ridge Center for Health, Faith, and Ethics, was a manuscript editor whose style and accuracy were welcomed quality controls for me when my style lapsed and inaccuracy plagued, and I thank her for wielding the blue pencil. Alan Thomas and his team at the University of Chicago Press have cooperated in producing a book whose somewhat different format represents challenges to the publisher but have been welcomed by reviewers and readers, and I thank him and his associates.

Closest to home: Micah Marty, now a literary partner and collaborator in production of books and editorial works, used his computer know-how, his editorial sense, and his filial courage to be of help at all stages. And for her part, through proofreading of *Pilgrims in Their Own Land* and these three volumes, spouse Harriet Julia Marty has been a practical aid even as, more importantly, she brings music to my life and keeps reminding me that there is more to living than the writing of multivolume histories.

1

"The Binding Tie of Cohesive Sentiment"

This series of histories, *Modern American Religion,* began 1:1
with the story of an argument between people we called modernists
and countermodernists. In a period of decisive change they fought
over the spiritual and religious aspects of life in the United States
around the turn of the century and through World War I (1893–
1919). That first book turned out to be a study in historical irony.
The turn of the century was a period usually measured by terms
such as "modern," "liberal," and "progressive," and was intended
to be such by citizens of cosmopolitan outlook. Yet their persistent
and pitiless rivals, the enduring antimodern, antiliberal, and anti-
progressive forces were invented in precisely those same years.
These include Roman Catholic antimodernism, Conservative Judaism, movements of religious and ethnic particularism, and Protestantisms such as fundamentalism, premillennialism, and pentecostalism. With both sets of rivals on stage, the scene was set for a
second argument between the two World Wars.

The Noise of Conflict, 1919–1941, developed the story of the 1:2
arguments between these warring parties during a period designed
to be one of "normalcy." Later generations often looked back to
it in nostalgia, picturing the lost world of grandparental towns
whose centers were each marked by "a single white church and a
nearby red schoolhouse," symbols of harmony in a simpler age.
The sentimentalists argued that Americans back then "agreed with

each other on issues of faith and morals, values and ideals." Instead, according to the narrative in that second volume, "conflict ruled" between "original-stock Protestants vs. everyone else; '100 percent Americans' vs. Communists and Slavs in the Red Scare; old-stock Anglo-Saxons vs. Catholic or Jewish or Asian immigrants; the Ku Klux Klan vs. the same, plus liberals and blacks; white Christians vs. black Christians; conventional black churches vs. 'back to Africa' movements; Zionists vs. anti-Zionists; pro-labor Catholics vs. antilabor Catholics; Protestant Fundamentalists vs. Modernists; pro–Peace Pact movements vs. anti–League of Nations sorts; pro-Repeal wets vs. anti-Repeal drys; Protestants against a Catholic president vs. Catholics for a Catholic president; supporters of birth control vs. enemies of birth control; Depression demagogues of the Right vs. left-wing firebrands; Protestant liberals vs. Protestant realists; Catholic Workers vs. capitalists; pro–New Deal realists vs. anti–New Dealers; pacifists vs. 'preparedness for war' partisans; and more."

1:3   The contentions took the form of and remained an argument. We noticed that while "all of these conflicts were based in religious beliefs and passions or else included profound religious motivations," they did not lead to bloodshed, as such encounters usually do. As surprising as their religious aspect was, equally astonishing, then, was "the virtual absence of dead bodies as a result of these intense conflicts." The book concluded with some theoretical discussion as to why this was the case. For one thing, the various parties were not concentrated in areas: "If there is shooting, at whom would or could one shoot?" in a holy war. Second, the American constitutional pattern survived. For all its flaws and limits, it provided modes for arguing and adjudicating that were lacking in many societies. Third, the American people had too much at stake in what united them, their "*real* or more fundamental faiths such as the religions of nationalism or materialism." So, "why shoot at other sects or factions, if the act of doing so slows down or confuses the hopes for national stability and personal success?" Fourth, many Americans had developed "measures of tolerance based on conviction," often of a religious sort itself. There were "criss-crossings" of loyalties by citizens who belonged to a variety of movements, institutions, and causes; hence a "web of commitments" formed as they do not form among peoples who have a single center of loyalty in their tribe or religious organization.

1:4   The heirs of the characters in the first two volumes, and sometimes the characters themselves, survived to carry on the argument that is at the center of this third volume, *Under God, Indivisible, 1941–1960.* New events and new cultural needs and circumstances called forth a fresh pattern of response in this period. In 1940 Supreme Court Justice Felix Frankfurter heard a case that demanded conformity in the public-school ritual of saluting the national flag—a ritual perceived as religious and abhorrent by Jehovah's Witnesses. The justice claimed that "the ultimate foundation of a free society is the binding tie of cohesive sentiment." He saw such a sentiment "fostered by all those agencies of the mind and spirit which may serve to gather up the traditions of a people, transmit them from generation to generation, and thereby create that continuity of a treasured common life which constitutes a civilization." Leaders in the very "agencies of mind and spirit" who had themselves been agents of the conflict in the period between the wars, more often than not put their energies into the "gathering up" of common traditions, their transmission to new generations, and their attempt to create "continuity" and "common life." We shall take due note of this dissent and these counterforces, but the direction of energies in this time, among elites and significant popular elements, was now not centrifugal, as between the wars, but centripetal.

This centripetal tendency and argument produced institutions   1:5
and images that promoted convergence between the interests of the peoples who made up the United States in these two mid-century decades. Some critics spoke of (and were nervous about) "conformity" or "consensus" in national life and made them their main themes. But the centripetal impulse also produced worldwide movements in which Americans took leadership roles: the United Nations, United World Federalists, the World Council of Churches, the National Council of Churches, the prime of the National Conference of Christians and Jews, among many others. "We live by symbols," Frankfurter had said, and many new and appropriate ones appeared. Prime among these was the flag salute itself, when in 1954 the words "under God" were inserted to describe the nation's stance. Add to this the concurrent inventions or development of the idea of a "Judeo-Christian Society" or "Protestant-Catholic-Jew" version of the American Way of Life. The new civil rights movement stressed racial integration, in a trend symbolic of efforts to overcome segregation and hostility. During World War II, four chaplains—two Protestants, a Catholic, and a Jew—sang hymns as they went down with their ship; they became an icon. The notion of a "Christian Crusade against Atheistic Commu-

nism" was another such symbol, as were the Peace of Mind, Peace of Soul, and Peace with God advocacies through the revival of interest in religion in the 1950s.

1:6   Three distinct events and cultural complexes appeared in these two mid-century decades. First, from 1941 to 1945 the need for national unity and harmony during World War II became obvious; religious forces supplied much of these. Second, from 1945 to 1952, the Cold War developed, producing a need for common symbols and energies. Third, through the 1950s, with the suburbanization of so much of white America and with other drastic cultural changes, many citizens found that they had the luxury of choosing their styles, and they chose centripetalism, interfaith and ecumenical activity, the common life, and consensus. I had intended to end this book in the mid-sixties, precisely with the summer of 1965. The inauguration of President Kennedy in 1961 symbolized the end of "Protestant America" and his assassination bred a sense of chaos in a world of presumed control and coherence. But the commitment of troops to Vietnam and the burning of Watts, events that signaled the end of certain international and domestic dreams for Americans, demonstrated that the consensus was often superficial. The centrifugal pattern reappeared with a vengeance after the mid-sixties.

1:7   Periods do not break as easily into a centrifugal-centripetal-centrifugal patterning as these paragraphs might suggest. Thus some of the most important events of the mid-century decades were indicators that not all would converge. Prime among these was McCarthyism at the end of the presidency of Harry S. Truman and the beginning of that of Dwight D. Eisenhower. It was a movement of opposition to the internationalism, moderate liberalism, and standard way of fighting the Cold War. Senator Joseph McCarthy created divisive suspicion and engaged in demonization of American foreign policy leadership, all in the name of a higher level of conformity and in the form of his personal anticommunist crusade. Similarly, liberal Protestantism fought some last battles against Catholicism at the time when two presidents, ten years apart, attempted to name an ambassador to the Vatican and when a third one was campaigning as a Catholic. Formation also of rather militant neo-evangelical movements provided very significant countermotion to ecumenical Protestantism. Yet even these, often ironically, made their moves in the name not of a permanent dissent but as claiming that they were the proper custodians of the national consensus.

Similarly, new movements in culture tend to begin their vital   1:8
life in subcultural or, in metaphor, subterranean ways. Thus film
critic and feminist author Molly Haskell, attempting to account for
the absence of a militant women's movement in these decades,
since such a visible one emerged soon after them, wrote: "It was
as if the whole period of the fifties was a front, the topsoil that
protected the seed of rebellion that was germinating below. The
cultural disorientation had begun, but it had yet to be acknowledged." Similarly, Brandon French, also commenting later on
women in films of the period, looked back: "America in the fifties was on the verge of a revolution which challenged many of
the fundamental ordering principles of Western culture. Not only
male supremacy, but white supremacy, and an economic system in
which one sector of society benefits at the expense of another." But
both comments come with retrospects after twenty years, while the
rules of the game of my writing of this history call me to try to see
events from the temporal vantage of those who experienced them
as they occurred, without benefit of hindsight or regular vision below the topsoil.

Considerable acts of empathy are needed by American readers   1:9
who have no personal recall of life in the mid-century decades, if
they want to do justice to the period. I have taught courses dealing
with it, just as in more general expansive surveys I have taught
about ways of life in earlier periods. In my experience, it is easier
for students near the century's end to be able to imagine many
circumstances of life and to have empathy for their actors in, say,
1250 or 1650 than in 1950. How, some ask, could mother or grand-
mother have settled for the situation and status she seemed to
occupy then? Or why were not more voices of Native Americans
or Latinos and Latinas heard in the larger culture? So, one also
asks, where *are* the women in *Under God, Indivisible?* They made
up the majority of the religious citizens, and this is a story of religion, so they belong. Indeed, they do appear, in connection with
scenes in which they took part and were noticed by other women
(and men) in the course of the open and public argument that
makes up the current plot. It should be said that authors who would
wittingly *under*stress the role of women while writing in the 1990s
would demonstrate that they are not wise to markets or to the contemporary cultural scene; indeed, they would not be wise at all.

This is instead a period well described by historian William   1:10
Chafe as a time of a "paradox of change," and which Glenna
Mathews calls a "situation whereby there were millions more

women gainfully employed outside the home, albeit fewer Public Women than in the '30s." Mathews goes on: "That is to say, more women than ever before were leaving woman's sphere, but fewer of them were genuinely influential." She develops the concept of the "public woman," showing how in the 1950s that term meant not a woman in public argument but a prostitute. "While 'public woman' was an epithet for one who was seen as the dregs of society, vile, unclean, a public man was 'one who acts in and for the universal good.' " Mathews argues that "in order to understand the sudden reappearance of feminism, it is important to grasp how aberrant the '50s really were in the long sweep of American history." It seems myopic for someone to point to the small role women played in the mid-century religious argument—even though at that time there were only one or two tenured women on all of the nation's theological faculties, relatively few ordained women in mainstream Protestant denominations, and few women not confined to (the often powerful) auxiliaries, whether these were in the military, voluntary organizations, or religious institutions. A response to anyone who would criticize the teller for saying so little about "public women" is, that *is* the point. For all the courage, enterprise, ability, and achievement of the women who worked against all odds to be heard in the public forum, they had great difficulty finding a platform or being heeded.

1:11   Something similar could be said of this story about an argument in which various members of communities that make up what later has been called "the pentagon of peoples" were seldom heard. While four decades later one now takes for granted the self-consciousness and conspicuousness of three of these, the Native Americans, Hispanic Americans, and Asian Americans, voices from these sectors of the population were almost never then part of the recognized public argument. Only African Americans joined those of European descent in the widely noticed public discourse. So a critic could say that after introducing all these peoples in the first two volumes of this series, the author has forgotten or neglected them, or with conscious purpose asked them to wait in the wings for Act IV in a fourth volume. Again, their relative silence among the characters in the current plot is part of the point: anyone who consults indices of the then contemporary public debate, for example, in *The Reader's Guide to Periodical Literature,* will quickly find that they were seldom given a forum or cited. For me to have moved them to center stage would have been to tell untruths about the character of the debate and the assertions of power in this period.

The concentration on certain movements and characters and the   1:12 concurrent obscuring of others can lead to two further questions: What is the public of which we speak? Who makes it up? And what is the genre of the history that permits or forces one to say less about the citizens in what might be conceived of as subpublics or subcultures? We might speak of the characters in this book as addressing "the *public* public," which means a combined product of elites and those who address broad elements of popular culture. At mid-century, magazines like *Life* and *Look, Newsweek* and *Time, Saturday Evening Post* and *Collier's*, the *Ladies Home Journal* and *McCall's* aspired to speak for and to very wide cultural strands, in a semifictive and taken-for-granted "mainstream America." It is hard for descendants of their readers two generations later, in an era when highly specialized magazines and journals prosper, to picture the common universe of discourse to which these appealed. In the decade when television became the dominant cultural transmitter to the homes of citizens, NBC and CBS and ABC held virtual monopolies as they competed, using similar strategies to reach the same putatively universal market. Those who live in the era of cable and fiber-optic television, when scores of channels are available, have difficulty imagining the extent of cultural homogenization that could occur in the earlier period.

In politics as in popular culture, there were also impulses toward   1:13 convergence and signs of the centripetal pull. Far from demonstrating polarization in the McCarthy era, Democratic candidate Adlai Stevenson sounded like Republican opponent Dwight D. Eisenhower: "It is time for catching our breath," he said in 1955; "moderation is the spirit of the times." The premier commentator Walter Lippmann said, without disapproving what he observed, that "for the first time in history the engine of social progress has run out of the fuel of discontent." Often quoted is the comment of sociologist Seymour Martin Lipset: "The fundamental political problems of the industrial revolution have been solved [through the] triumph of the democratic social revolution in the west."

Decades later, the era of World War II, the early Cold War,   1:14 and the 1950s, so often regarded with nostalgia in the new more turbulent time is being explored for what was then going on in subpublics, countercultures, and the like. Titles like *The Way We Never Were: American Families and the Nostalgia Trap* would shatter the stereotypes of conformity. *Young, White, and Miserable: Growing Up Female in the Fifties* is a typical retrospect that suggests that not all was well, that there was at least quiet subversion in the world of young women. Books like *Deliberate Speed: The Origins of a Cultural Style in the American 1950s*, dealing with the Beat counterculture, the rise of rock 'n' roll, bop and jazz, will have numerous counterparts in the years ahead. They point to significant undercurrents. What is significant about them all, however, is this: the authors recognize that there was a dominant culture and that there is a predominating interpretation of that culture. They turn their attention to minority, dissenting subcultures and offer alternative interpretations of the way these interact with the larger culture. By contrast, dissenters in our own time have difficulty finding and describing a single culture in the face of what has come to be called multiculturalism. Against what does one rebel? Against what widely agreed upon interpretation does one offer counterinterpretations?

1:15   The choice of topic, the story of a set of arguments, in this case as always helps determine the sort of history one chooses to write. *Under God, Indivisible* is not a work of social history, though it pays attention to the social history that was current in the mid-century decades. If this were an example of social history, perhaps the dominant form of scholarship in history in our time, it would involve ethnographic research, interviewing, statistical analysis, and other instruments that would bring one closer to the "ordinary people" who are represented here as audiences, readerships, and congregants. Social historians are uncovering the very large roles played by women in American religion. They also hear the voices of those women who do not have well-known names. Their research leads them to visit the reservations of Native Americans or the ghettos of the African Americans who do not have a voice that the elites do. Nor is this an example of intellectual history, though it pays attention to intellectuals who were taking part in the public forum. Yet it does not exist fundamentally to trace the career of the ideas of philosophers in isolation from publics.

1:16   This is a work of cultural history which, as here conceived, does not concern itself only with elites and their audiences; there are true reaches into popular cultures. Figures like Billy Graham, Fulton Sheen, Joshua Loth Liebman, and Norman Vincent Peale receive attention alongside John Courtney Murray, Paul Tillich and the brothers Niebuhr, or Abraham Joshua Heschel, who aspired to reach significant elements in the Catholic-Protestant-Jew highbrow cultures. Indeed, such history observes leadership seeking, convoking, creating, and addressing publics and remarking on the degree of their successes or on the ways they were apprehended, since these tell much about the public. For the sake of a useful analogy, I am going to substitute the word "religious" for "artistic" and "religious-historical" actor for "art-historical" actor in a definition by art historian Thomas E. Crow. A public, says Crow, is "a commonality with a legitimate role to play in justifying religious practice and setting value on the products of that practice." Therefore, "a public appears, with a shape and a will, via the various claims made to represent it; and when sufficient numbers of an audience come to believe in one or another of these representations, the public can become an important religious-historical actor." In other words, the congregants, the converts-to-be, or those resistant to congregating or being converted, alike are actors in the historical drama.

If cultural history is again the genus of historical writing in this   1:17
book, the history of rhetoric is the species, as it was in the two earlier volumes. As this is the story of an argument about One Nation, *Under God, Indivisible,* one notes the classic themes of rhetoric: the *ethos* or character of the persuading arguers; the *pathos* or situation of those who are to be persuaded; the *logos* or substance of the arguments used for persuading. In a recent work on the rhetoric employed in the controversies over abortion in the recent past, Celeste Michelle Condit condenses the argument over argument in terms congenial to my enterprise. The term rhetoric, she reminds readers, reflects its origin in *rheo,* "to flow"; "public rhetoric is important because it is the most immediate source of the flow of social meanings, and all persons, as social beings, are destined to live in the world through meaning."

If one takes a determinist, especially economic determinist   1:18
view, a view which Condit describes as "declaring every rhetorical statement to be a simple product of a particular condition," she recognizes that "the *articulation* of social conditions *through rhetoric* is a substantively different artifact than those supposedly primary social conditions themselves." This means that "large-scale social forces cannot be directly dealt with or even experienced by governments, politicians, bureaucrats [insert: religious leaders], or individuals. They can be dealt with only through understandings of them, which are predominantly carried through a shared public vocabulary." This full determinist position is not held consistently by most. Those who admit that public discourse

has some roots other than economic ones—and most who study religion believe that this sphere has such—find that "the social force of rhetoric appears even greater." The public, be it noted, says Condit, "is not a simple entity, including all the people of the nation equally; it is rather the articulated element of the populace—dominated by national politicians, journalists, and big-business leaders but also including, at lower amplification, organized classes and interest groups." In our case these are religious in aspiration and character. The articulation, Condit reminds us and this book demonstrates, goes on in "public arenas of discourse—such as newspapers, magazines, the floor of Congress, presidential speeches, television programs, or bureaucratic hearings." In them, "rhetors advance claims on 'the nation' couched in terms of major values, suggesting that particular sentiments, policies, or laws are in the general interest." Exactly. And "to the extent that they are successful at convincing the public of this potential for general good, they are able to enact their will."

1:19   Condit introduces one more theme that is relevant to our purposes, one that she calls "the dominant controversy in contemporary social theory—the characterization of the contents of public discourse." One school of contenders is led by social critic Jürgen Habermas and rhetorical theorist Douglas Ehninger. It argues that "public consensus through rational argumentation processes is the necessary end goal of public deliberation and that it is, ultimately, a largely achievable goal." Over against this, political and social theorists such as Murray Edelman and Anthony Giddens think that these arguments represent "naive idealism"; therefore "in seeking to 'universalize' or call up 'condensation symbols,' public discourse necessarily seeks to get a particular interest misidentified as a general interest." Condit wisely says that "the former school provides a necessary ideal and the latter an equally necessary restraint." In the mid-century decades, both the rhetors and the theorists tended to favor the universalizing, condensing line that was later represented by Habermas and Ehninger. More recently, the particularizing understandings of Edelman and Giddens may come more naturally to rhetors and are privileged among theorists of multiculturalism in the "One Nation." Condit points out properly that because argumentation and persuasion have social characteristics, "most discourse must deal with both dimensions—this double articulation of rhetoric—simultaneously, *not* with one to the exclusion of the other." This notion of "double articulation," a coinage of Condit's, simply suggests that discourse can have "both a 'universal' symbolic dimension and a partisan, functional dimension." The interest component to a discourse "does not disqualify our attention to the public, universal components that may be served by the discourse." For that reason, we shall listen to Protestant, Catholic, Jewish, African American, and other spokespersons who express interests that show themselves to be seriously aspiring to convince a cluster of interests that make up a public, that their concerns are all being addressed.

Study of the rhetors and their audiences and readerships during   1:20
and after World War II through the fifties will reveal a world of living memory for the senior generation at century's end. Yet it might just as well be captured with a borrowed book title as *The World We Have Lost*. That world as a whole may be lost, but selectively its elements live on, whether as subjects of nostalgia (e.g., for "family values" or "the American Way of Life") and as models for contemporary life (again, e.g., for "family values" or "the American Way of Life"). Or they may serve to fabricate constructs against which some in the multitude of American cultures today can and must rebel (e.g., as against "family values" or as "the American Way of Life"). I hope readers will find the story to be intrinsically interesting as well as instructive and provocative. Having confessed that it is difficult to conjure up this world for the imagination of students three or four or five decades later, I may serve the reader well by describing something of my own attitude toward this scene, many elements of which I experienced. The temptation to trash its rhetors for their idealism and smugness is as strong among many intellectuals as is the temptation on the part of others to create an illusory story of that past and to develop false models from it.

First, let me describe a stance toward the characters, the rhetors   1:21
and audiences, who make up this story. There is no such thing as a narrative told without viewpoint; even the choice to tell one, and the choice of which one to tell, is a commitment of sorts. An overly moralized telling will turn out to have been predictable, condescending, ideological, and thus unavailing. If in this book there is criticism of those who preached the values of "One Nation, Under God, Indivisible," it will more likely appear in turns of phrase than in thunderings of judgment. Condescension toward past actors is epidemic in 1995, and strikes me as being destructive of narrative and understanding. Knox College English professor Douglas L. Wilson put into words what I would convey here: "The people of the historical past, whom we tend to regard as somehow benighted,

were at least as honorable and well-meaning as people today. The arguments intended to reveal the ignominy and perfidy of our forebears are, after all, suspiciously self-serving, for their invariable effect is to suggest the superiority and wisdom of the present generation." But, adds Wilson, "our only demonstrable superiority to our counterparts in the past is that we know something about their future. To use this against them comes with an ill grace, particularly when we consider that we know nothing on our own."

1:22   As for the introduction of characters and peoples from the margins in the 1950s to the center ever after, Wilson has important words: "What formerly seemed marginal about our past may suddenly appear central, and what seemed puzzling and obscure may become brilliantly clear." That fact is the source of most historical revisionism. But "while we are thus obliged to continually reinterpret the past, we need to do so with the full awareness that our new insights and understanding are directly related to Today." Today is what makes the past change every time we look at it. Meanwhile, there would be something judicious about a generation of historians refusing to condescend to people of the past: "Our superiority to people of the past is nothing more than the kind of superiority that future generations will have over us." This means that "unless we are prepared to grant that our own good-faith efforts and intentions will some day deserve to be looked upon with contempt, we would do well to recognize the time-bound efforts and intentions of the past for what they were, and not for what they would be considered now." One could wish that the women and men of the 1950s had spoken differently about the role of women in the public forum; that all people of good will in the civil rights movement had listened better when African Americans spoke up; that more attention had been paid to Native Americans; that the religion of the American Way of Life would not some day bear foul fruit in the Vietnam War. It is possible and may be necessary to criticize these people of the past for having failed. But if the only credential for the critic is the advantage of hindsight, of perspective gained by the accident of later birth, one will temper the criticism.

1:23   Second, on the specific point of the religion of "One Nation, Under God, Indivisible," I prefer to play by the rules that will apply to all the chapters that follow. On these terms I adduce viewpoints that I held in the period of the story, and confine myself to what I could have known and said—what I *did* know and say in that time. It happens that my first book appeared at the end of the 1950s and at what appeared also to be the end of the religious revival: *The*

New Shape of American Religion. The "revival of interest in religion" then seemed to have focused on "the God of religion-in-general" and the "depersonalized" human in false community, then known as the Organization Man. Meanwhile, "America's Real Religion" was seen as an attitude toward religion; "raised to religious ultimacy is the advocacy or support of official religion, an overarching nationalization" of "religion-in-general" or a "religion-of-democracy." Several chapters in *Under God, Indivisible* revisit such a scene.

More hopeful then about Protestantism than I would have been   1:24
later, I saw two Protestantisms or aspects of Protestantism developing. One expression had so blended with the environment that it lost particularity or distinctiveness and thus prophetic or saving power. The other was generating self-enclosed movements that resisted the pluralism and dialogue without which a republic could not survive. There were both theological and institutional resources, it seemed to me, for use by particular groups who would meet some of the challenges after that revival. From the Hebrew scriptures came the enduring theme that the human *"lives in a community,"* but the current national community as such did not measure up. Neither did the then widely propagated notion of "togetherness" as the ideal for more intimate bondings. In a time of religious compromise, the scriptural notion of the Remnant provided a clue for the life of the ecumenical (then Protestant) churches. The summary came with italics: *"On the one hand there is a full human identification with every aspect of life in the larger community; thus communication endures. On the other hand there is a sense of separation: here is the place for integrity, for commitment and vocation."* The religious forces, as then seen, belonged to the republic, but dared not give it their whole heart. They had to be distinctive, but their distinctiveness dared not separate them from each other in expressions of sectarianism, exclusiveness, or intolerance. That book also celebrated the congregating of believers in patterns whence they could undertake reform. The congregation was an imperfect but available form where the local and the universal came together.

Third, still remaining within the contexts of what was said then,   1:25
I called for "a culture ethic," again, for the Christian majority, basing it in their classic texts and the church tradition at its best. I am impressed—should I be embarrassed?—to see how today in a vastly different America and despite the passage of a third of a century my Lutheran and Niebuhrian (in both the H. Richard Nie-

buhr and Reinhold Niebuhr versions) dialectical views of religion in culture have persisted in my mind. Two fears colored my comment on strategy in *The New Shape of American Religion:* one, that the churches—again, I spoke only out of Protestantism—would become so accommodated to the republic and to its pluralism, that "morally and intellectually debilitating relativism" would threaten to sap religion. Conversely, at the opposite extreme, there was fear that "absolutistic claims" would appeal to other religious people who wanted security in the form of "pure doctrine"—soon again to be renamed fundamentalism.

1:26   "There are other alternatives." This time the Niebuhr who influenced the writing was H. Richard Niebuhr, for his "confessional" as opposed to "apologetic" view of faith. In that view, a believing community, in the present case elements of Protestantism, begins "with the proclamation of what is the truth *for us* and our community." It gets presented as "an option for the faith and hope of the world." In this perspectival view, "in place of dissipating relativism there can be witness to truth tempered by recognition of the incompleteness of all human vision." Yet there truth was held to, as opposed to its being dissolved in the current "generalized everything-true-nothing-true religion." Now, after the intervening decades of cultural and ecclesial change, I would not frame those alternatives without being mindful of all of Christianity, and not only of one kind of Protestantism; of Jewish and Christian interaction; of the presence of other religions; of a secular order that is less self-assured than it was then. In this dialectical vision one can tell stories about the pluralist republic, often in a positive and constructive spirit, without making an idol of it. I hope to tell one here. And one can view the past religious scene from the angle of participation in believing communities that have reasons for believing and acting, without claiming that these have an absolute hold on absolute truth. Something of that vision guides the implicit judgments in the story that follows.

Part One

"Indivisible" in the Second World War, 1941–1945

2

"Damn War! Damn Pacifism . . . !"

$\mathbf{A}$merica entered the war immediately after the surprise   2:1
Japanese attack of December 7, 1941. Through most of the decade
before that event, much of the religious leadership had turned its
face against war and preparation for war. The majority of the
leaders now had to turn suddenly, as if in response to a barked
order, "About-face!" Such a military command, heard often in
wartime, found an echo or a parallel in the voluntary turns made
by many other Americans who had resisted the call to arms. Between the armistice that ended World War I in 1918 and the Japanese bombing of Hawaii's Pearl Harbor in 1941 that marked the
beginning of American military response in World War II, various
peacemaking movements enjoyed a moment in which to state their
case, and during much of the interwar period pacifists could count
on public sentiment being on their side. As late as August 1936,
95 percent of Americans in a poll answered "no" when asked
whether the United States should take part in war if one broke out
in Europe. As war came, however, many pacifists about-faced, pivoting to look in the direction opposite to where they had just been.
So did the nation at large, eager as the citizens were to fight and
win a war together. Three days after Pearl Harbor a poll revealed
that 96 percent of the people approved the declaration of war by
Congress. Only Representative Jeannette Rankin, who had voted
against the war in 1917, opposed the move in roll call, but this time

with more mixed feelings than in the previous case. Notable among the peace-minded who had to do some pivoting, for example, were American Jews. They later came to have most at stake when it became evident that Hitler and the Nazis wanted to kill all European Jews. Thus during the decade before Pearl Harbor, the National Federation of Temple Sisterhoods and the National Council of Jewish Women promoted strong peace agencies and sentiments. All through the 1930s, while Italy, Japan, and especially Germany were building up forces for war, these women issued resolutions, often impelled by religious motives, never to encourage a war or bear arms.

2:2   The leadership among liberal Jewish men had joined the women in expressing such peaceful sentiments. The potent Central Conference of American Rabbis in the mid-thirties could summon a clear majority for motions never to "support any war in which this country or any country may engage." When war did come in 1941, Reform leader Stephen Wise became the most conscientious rabbinical chider of Christian clergy for their sin, because they lacked militancy in efforts to save European Jews. Only ten years earlier, relying on the wisdom of that quieter day, Wise remembered how he had watched clergy bless the banners of armies in World War I. Back then the New York rabbi had called such endorsement wrong and made it clear that he for one would "never again commit that sin." "Never again" was a resolve most leaders found they had to forget when armies once again moved banners forward to battle in World War II and clergy made an about-face to follow.

2:3   The agony of the European Jews and horror over the Nazi policies to kill them did help to change the minds of some leaders, Jewish and non- Jewish alike, as the prospect of war increased. But these emotions did not convince all pacifists to become supporters of the war. Indeed, many who refused to reverse themselves and would not fight a war spoke up for the victims of Hitler more passionately than did others who came to bless the banners of the armies. At issue for many of them was the possibility of a policy change. They wanted America to welcome the Jews who fled the Nazis or who were rescued from Hitler's murderers. Only 10 percent of the public favored such a new refugee policy. Peter Maurin, the eccentric pacifist figure in the Catholic Worker movement, radically opposed the war. But at the same time he urged that "America is big enough to find a refuge for persecuted Jews." It was not, or did not consider itself so to be. Similarly, socialist Norman Thomas, speaking out of that political minority of less than

10 percent, observed already before France fell in 1940: "I learned first hand how many Americans preferred to fight or have their countrymen fight for the rights of Jews in Europe than to give them asylum in America." America closed its gates.

The rescue of European Jews and the idea of creating refuge for   2:4
survivors in the United States were only two elements in the drama of war and the about-faces it occasioned. As that drama developed, many pacifists deserted their old cause or if they did not, were scorned by those who did abandon it. Thus Thomas himself looked back on peace movements and came to see how impotent pacifists seemed in wartime. He charged that they "had nothing to offer in the problem of stopping Nazism" except for a religious faith and a moral argument, and these clearly were not enough. A prominent Unitarian minister, Edwin Buehrer, shared Thomas's vision but went on to scold the pacifists. Their voices had become routine, their patterns ritualized. They kept saying "it is Christ's Way, it is the Way of the Cross." Yet behind what they said were "no historical reasons . . . , no empirical reasons, no logical reasons, no practical reasons"—in short, no reasons at all.

The agony of change among those who made an about-face of-   2:5
ten turned to sureness of purpose and the scolding of those left behind. Take, as first example, an individual: the most prominent Protestant thinker of the day, Reinhold Niebuhr of New York's Union Theological Seminary. Although he had been reluctant to support military preparedness before Hitler's rise around 1933, he became scornful of those who continued to oppose it as the Nazi threat grew. In 1940 this Protestant scholar of German descent argued that "modern Christian and secular perfectionism, which places a premium upon non-participation in conflict, is a very sentimentalized version of the Christian faith." The peacemongers, in their turn, treated Niebuhr as a general in the ranks of prowar moralists. Thus Harold E. Fey of the Fellowship of Reconciliation claimed in that same year that he had wanted to remain Niebuhr's friend. But having taken the turn toward promoting preparedness for war, Niebuhr seemed to him "to have more influence than any other man in leading the church into another repudiation of its mission in compromise with the state on the war issue." Fey properly sensed that his Fellowship was henceforth to be on the defensive.

A second example is the Federal Council of Churches, a pow-   2:6
erful organizational force in mainstream Protestantism at this time in the United States. The Federal Council of Churches thought of itself as, and was, the most organized voice of churches that

claimed to be working for church and national unity. Through most of the prewar years the council's leadership had opposed preparedness and the voices of belligerence. As late as 1939, after the war began in Europe, its executive committee was still unanimous in calling war "an evil thing contrary to the mind of Christ." But much of the leadership of such Protestantism was both pro-British and antifascist, so what had been "contrary to the mind of Christ" two years earlier now came to be part of a policy the council would support.

2:7   Third, on the opinion-shaping front: the top editor in the sort of Protestantism that sought and made most public impact, Charles Clayton Morrison, displayed to his readers the agony of one who was in the process of making a reluctant turn. Can people drag their feet while making about-faces? Morrison filled books and the pages of the weekly *Christian Century* to urge human unity based on a religious vision. His great hope was for a stalemate between European powers; then they could not successfully prosecute war. Even after the fall of France in 1940 Morrison was still full of dreams. "We have small hope," he wrote, but in his losing cause he could only cling faintly to the dreams; "hope must not be given up entirely." Morrison could attach many causes to each specific dream. At the moment he was envisioning the possibility that Hitler would be forced to "give the rest of the world a system of interrelationships better than the trade-strangling and man-exploiting system of empire capitalism." France, Morrison assumed, would soon again be free, and he thought that in its freedom that nation would be "swept clean of secularism." No friend at all of Catholicism, Morrison now was settling for religious second-bests to help produce human bests. After its recovery, there would be "at least a France with a faith—and a faith which is incompatible with the faith of nazism." Far superior to it in his eyes was the faith of Americans, which he had touted in 1937: "We have discovered that our goodness, our moralism, is in large measure the expression of our relative detachment." The doughty Chicago editor quickly qualified this: true, Americans "are no more virtuous than others"; their "difference is a difference of circumstances," but they could make the most of these.

2:8   Like so many other leaders caught between the conflicting forces of the day, Morrison mixed motives and causes as he made his own turns. In March 1941, months before America entered the war, the editor heard President Franklin D. Roosevelt claiming that America was united behind his interventionist policies. How could he assume this, and how could it be? The *Christian Century* editors knew and made a charge. American unity on this cause resulted from "machine dominated politics of the hysterical eastern seaboard states." And the midwestern Protestants, who wanted unity on other than interventionist grounds, knew very well who lived on the seaboard: "The states containing a large proportion of recent European immigration, the states ruled by munitions makers, the states controlled by federal patronage, . . . these are the President's united America."

Morrison could not deny, however, that the debate was also   2:9
religious. Already in January 1940, clerical leaders, many of them from that same seaboard, brought together thirty-two signers of a statement called "The American Churches and the International Situation." Reinhold Niebuhr's cosigners included colleagues from Union Seminary—President Henry Sloane Coffin; emeritus professor and liberal ecumenical leader William Adams Brown; former modernist and pacifist Sherwood Eddy; Niebuhr's partner in many ventures, John C. Bennett; and future Union president Henry Pitney Van Dusen. Van Dusen was now arguing that pacifists showed "resolute unwillingness to face known and indisputable facts." The signers, on the other hand, would face the facts.

As editor of a weekly journal, Morrison was called and poised   2:10
to monitor all the about-facing of the early war years. In 1942 he collected some of his own editorials in a book, *The Christian and the War.* The Christian pacifist received chapter-length notice. In this section Morrison let his instincts to promote the cause of national unity win out over his other interests. The war had become all-consuming. By then, Christian pacifists were coming to fight in it alongside the now nonpacifist majority. Morrison looked over the fence to observe the historic peace-minded and dissenting churches forgetting their old dissent. "There are no exceptions. The Quakers fight, the Mennonites and Brethren fight, the pacifist preachers fight—despite their vows never to support war again." No cause of Christ provided the impulse for them. "These all fight by virtue of their implication in the indivisible solidarity of their national community." Most pacifists, editor Morrison thought, did not try to escape the clutching of the vast military machine. Even the Fellowship of Reconciliation by then had taken "a belligerent position, not a neutral one."

There was no chance or danger at all that pacifists would bring   2:11
the war effort to an end, but they could undercut the military draft if too many chose the way of conscientious objection to killing and

thus to service. Legislation for Selective Service passed Congress on September 16, 1940, more than a year before America entered the war. If an objector thereafter could convince authorities that he merited objector status, he had to engage in some "work of national importance." This meant that his legal dissent could never be final and total, a break with the national effort as a whole, or he would face prison. The original administrator of the system, Clarence A. Dykstra, had been generous in enforcing the laws, but his successor, General Lewis B. Hershey, was harsh and even punitive in carrying them out. Hershey also began to spell out some theological boundaries for defining the God to whom all objectors were called to make an appeal. There had to be a "recognition of some source of all existence, which, whatever the type of conception, is Divine because it is the Source of all things." In such phrases Hershey was more theological than many theologians, more judicial than Supreme Court justices wanted to be about defining. But he held the power on this subject there and then.

2:12   In a nation of two hundred million people, the objectors never did count for much statistically. In all, 10,022,367 men—women were not then subject to the draft—received the order to be inducted. Of these, 42,973 received conscientious objector status. This number represented three times as high a percentage of those called up as held that status in World War I. In addition to these, 6,086 who were not legally classified as objectors were imprisoned. Three-fourths of these were Jehovah's Witnesses. They found themselves, for once in their lives, in ecumenical circumstances. Sharing life behind bars with them were a few members of the new and barely visible Black Muslim movement, Quakers, and principled politically radical Union Seminary students who did not make the about-face from pacifism that their professors did, or who turned to nonpacifist radical sentiments. In World War I there had been only 450 imprisoned for such reasons. But this war was more protracted. More people had time to shape their witness and take a stand than they did in 1917 and 1918. The number of open dissenters still does not expose to view much sustained opposition to the war effort on the part of the young men who had most at stake: their lives and not, as most who heard the debates might have said, merely their arguments.

2:13   The reference by Morrison to fighting Quakers, Mennonites, and Brethren was a half-disrespectful nod toward these historic "peace churches." They retained some measure of public respect because they had so consistently and so long opposed war. Statistics bore out observations that this war caused great strain on consciences of their members and on the unity of their churches. Only one in four Quakers stood steadfastly against the draft. Three out of five drafted Mennonites did take legal alternative service as conscientious objectors and so did not have to bear arms. But only one-eighth of the Church of the Brethren young men did the same. Pacifist leaders in all three denominations were distressed. They feared an erosion of principle, a growing worldliness, in their movements. These small denominations kept passing antiwar resolutions, in the spirit of Quakerism's most eloquent voice, Rufus Jones: "There must be amidst all the confusions of the hour a tried and undisturbed remnant of persons who will not become purveyors of coercion and violence, who are ready to stand alone, if it is necessary, for the way of peace and love among men." What had begun as a movement that would propose policy was quickly reduced to a witness that evidenced conscience.

Still, the voice of that witness could be both eloquent and dis-   2:14
turbing. Guy Franklin Hershberger of the Mennonites' Goshen College in Indiana was representative and compelling when he published *War, Peace, and Nonresistance* midway through the war. This large tract, commissioned by his church's Peace Problems Committee, was crammed with biblical verses and Mennonite arguments coupled with narrative. "One cannot be the state's hangman and obey the Sermon on the Mount. . . . The nonresistant Christian cannot wield the sword for the state." Hershberger contended that since the fourth century at least, Christians had been doing such wielding, often for the states they considered to be Christian. His heritage, called Anabaptism, wanted to get beyond those centuries of compromise, back to the beginnings, because those who believed as he did saw themselves as preservers of the message of Jesus' gospel. "When the state reaches into the realm of religion, conscience, and the home, and attempts to control these, it is demanding what does not belong to it." The modern totalitarian states did such reaching; dared democracy do the same? People in peace churches had their own way of serving, argued Hershberger. "Ultimately the Christian will render society a greater service by remaining politically aloof and living a life of genuine nonresistance, than by being politically active where sooner or later he must sacrifice or compromise this principle." Two world wars within three decades meant that nations were opposing the mind of Christ. "This world sadly needs the ministry of nonresistant Christians whose light, set on a hill, stands as a glow-

ing witness to the way of truth and righteousness." Only a minority, even within Mennonites, could take the stand and the path cut by the Peace Problems Committee and their man Hershberger.

2:15   Whatever they proposed, many members of these churches made good on commitments. Thus, out of meager resources, they came up with $7 million to pay conscientious objectors, who went unpaid by the government, for eight million man-days of work. There are stories of heroism in the cases of some volunteers within their ranks, who let scientists experiment on their bodies and with their lives. The destruction of war meant the outbreak of disease, and this left the military and other populations at risk. Some conscientious objectors took risks for everybody, as medics tried various forms of treatment. Some served by subjecting themselves to near-starvation diets. Others did menial work in mental hospitals. The few who noticed could see that such people were not motivated by cowardice nor were they looking for comfort. The Selective Service people often showed disdain by providing demeaning if not punitive forms of work. The objectors received no income at all, and some had to leave their families impoverished. But Selective Service theory held that if alternative service came to look mild and attractive, many fence-sitters would choose it instead of heeding the call to bear arms.

2:16   This sequestering policy kept most Americans from hearing the witness of dissent. The camps were in remote places. Selective Service did what it could to keep publicity from issuing out of them. And there were internal tensions in each outpost of conscientious objection or imprisonment. Some were objecting to war and national participation in it on humanist grounds. They could not understand religious motivations, nor could the religious come to terms with the humanists. One secular rebel said that secular rebels in most respects had "far more in common with certain nonpacifist radicals and progressives" than they did with the "more conservative, more quietistic pacifists." Another described what he called a "Jim Quake" policy. "One unique problem fraught with somber difficulty," he complained, "is the prospect of seeing, talking with, working with, and even eating at the same table with Quakers." He emphatically rejected the notion that "Quakers should be treated just like everyone else—even to the point of intermarriage." The nonreligious radicals went their own way. And one befuddled superintendent who had to deal with resisters spoke for many: "No one who has not been closely associated with them for a substantial period of time could believe that such people could exist outside an insane asylum."

Resentment was most fierce against two groups: those who op-   2 : 17
posed not only the war effort but who considered the nation itself to be unworthy of support, and those who came from traditions which had not opposed military service or war in the past. As for the first of these, no one was hated more than Jehovah's Witnesses. Their movement had taken shape before World War I, during which they suffered much for their stands. To them any earthly government was of the devil, was anti-Christ, and they dared take no part in its legal life. During the earlier war one Judge Ruther-ford, their second leader, had been sent to jail for his stand. No one could argue that their portrayal of God did not meet General Her-shey's terms. They expected to fight for the God they named Je-hovah at the final battle called Armageddon. The militancy of their language about that battle, their readiness to defend their own selves when attacked, and their willingness to work in munitions industries made them look inconsistent in the eyes of draft admin-istrators. And they all claimed to be ministers. Here General Her-shey surprised many, because he agreed that anyone who gave more than eighty hours a month to ministerial work was a minister. This made such a person eligible for a 4-D classification and a clerical exemption from service. Yet many draft boards did not act on Hershey's word and refused to permit alternatives to military service.

The Seventh-day Adventists were another group that many con-   2 : 18
sidered marginal in American life, but they were deemed more patriotic and more moderate than Jehovah's Witnesses. They were not pacifists, but they did insist on calling themselves "noncom-batants." They made clear that, short of taking a life themselves, they would cooperate with the government. Adventists had long specialized in health care and could offer many skilled medical personnel, so the government often found ways to put them to work in their cherished noncombatant but by no means undanger-ous situations. They made their stand on the basis of their literal reading of the Bible. As they understood it, they must support gov-ernment but never take a life. So they suffered less stigma than did Jehovah's Witnesses.

The other pattern of resentment was directed against those who   2 : 19
did *not* inherit a legacy of pacifism and who chose what some called a popular war against which to take a first stand. The most

visible of these were Catholic, whose church's doctrine had long implied that a "just war" demanded support of the believer. Catholic pacifists were new on the American scene, and few held to the cause after Pearl Harbor. Peter Maurin among them did, along with his colleague in the Catholic Worker movement, Dorothy Day. Their stand hurt their movement, and they were forced to find warrants for it. Maurin, Day, and others therefore reached behind just-war theorists to the canon of the scriptures. A month after Pearl Harbor the *Catholic Worker* editorialized: "We are still pacifists." On what grounds? "Our manifesto is the Sermon on the Mount, which means that we will try to be peacemakers." Such editorials led to the loss of half the paper's readership. The Catholic Worker outlets, many called Houses of Hospitality, lost support and some leadership. In three states there were camps where Catholic objectors could take alternatives to military service, but they were required to find funds for their own support. It was not forthcoming, and the leaders were defenseless when the Selective Service, acting for the United States government, closed the camps.

2:20   The most visible Catholic pacifist was Dorothy Day herself. She could hardly have foreseen the hostility she would provoke when, in the seasons just before the war, she declared: "we will expect our Catholic workers to oppose, alone and singlehandedly if necessary . . . the militaristic system and its propaganda." Day did not understand the speed with which former colleagues made an about-face or the zest other Catholics showed in supporting war when it came. The *Catholic Worker* lost 100,000 subscriptions after Pearl Harbor. Day kept support from most at Catholic Worker houses in Boston, Detroit, and Cleveland, but those at Chicago, Seattle, and Los Angeles were opposed. Her stand split the community of Workers at Milwaukee and Pittsburgh. St. Louis and Buffalo leaders found the topic to be so volatile that they simply ruled it out of bounds. Uncharacteristically harsh language was whispered against their founder: some accused her of using "dictator methods" and "violent" means to promote nonviolence. To keep the movement alive and together, Day had to back off. The best she could do was to insist that her paper be consistent with her views. Meanwhile, personnel shortages hit the Houses of Hospitality hard, and they suffered during the war.

2:21   While most Americans were calling for unity behind the war effort, the rhetoric one can still all but hear while reading the record was sundering the world of pacifist from that of nonpacifist. A year after the Japanese attack, the uniting slogan that rallied fervent

and laggard Americans alike was "Remember Pearl Harbor." The
Catholic Worker thereupon forged its alternative, "Forget Pearl
Harbor." Such a theme sounded sacrilegious and almost treasonous, as did the urging that Americans should "humbly apologize
and beg forgiveness for our past mistreatment of the Japanese
people." By 1942 such language was no longer considered merely
foolish. It was dangerous. The Federal Bureau of Investigation
found it important to listen, to read, and then to watch the movements of Dorothy Day. A line of a transcript of an agent's tele-
phone call on December 10, 1942, catches the flavor: "Say, listen,
I think this Dorothy Day has gone off the reservation again." He
spelled out examples. She was criticizing mistreatment of Japanese
Americans, who at that time were relocated in American concentration camps in the West. "Any Jap that seems to be up against it
in this country, they try to give him help. It's cockeyed. I don't like
it." Added the pious agent, "From my religious standpoint, I'm
getting pretty sick of it." He went on to express fear that this complete pacifism would include "stirring up a Negro question about
race equality and God knows, you know how bad that is!" FBI
director J. Edgar Hoover had these words called to his attention.
Given their premises, there was reason for him to agree with the
agent's conclusion: "I think the whole group should be put in jail
until the end of the war." But jailing was unnecessary. In the wartime climate, such pacifism was destroying itself. One House of
Hospitality worker put the case to Day in a letter: "Damn war!
Damn Pacifism and stands! . . . How I wish you weren't a heretic!
And sometimes I wish that I were one too. But to agree with you
means cutting off from a much larger world and that pain is one
you must know well, so that my anguish of separation is meager in
comparison."

Some Catholic literati kept the new pacifist flame alive. One of   2:22
the nation's most notable younger poets, Robert Lowell, a recent
convert and only briefly a Catholic, argued for conscientious objection, nonviolence, and pacifism on the newly formulated Catholic grounds for peacemaking. He was sent to prison for his views,
as was the young novelist J. F. Powers, a Minnesota Catholic
Worker who wrote for the movement's paper. Day tried to make
things more congenial for such radical dissenters. She invented a
Catholic Civilian Public Service Camp on the model of the "peace
church" camps, where they could pursue dissent and alternate service. Two experiments, at Stoddard and Warner, New Hampshire,
turned out to be failures. Only several score people ever were as-

signed to these unproductive, lonely outposts. The official Catholic church gave no backing at all. Some non-Catholics who were assigned there asked questions that disturbed the peace of the faithful. Far-right-wing Catholics like Father Charles E. Coughlin were irritants. The closing of these New Hampshire experiments was a favor to the campers and the Catholic Worker movement.

2:23   On the official church front, the chancery of Archbishop Francis Spellman, the New York hierarch to whom Dorothy Day felt responsible and a man on the way toward national preeminence as an impassioned defender of military policy, all but silenced her. When Day called for Catholics not even to register for Selective Service, Spellman ordered her to desist. Day had promised to be an obedient Catholic, so when the order came, she obeyed, but only because it was an order. Spellman, never a master of understatement, reached for bodily metaphors to describe American impulse and to justify such actions of patriotism on his part. Japanese treachery at Pearl Harbor had meant that "America's throat was clutched, her back was stabbed, her brain was stunned; but her great heart still throbbed." And Catholics would help keep it throbbing.

2:24   The prewar style of language in support of international Christian unity came to be replaced increasingly by calls for a new language of national unity, a pattern of discourse one expects when dissent and disunity come to be luxuries. Thus the Methodists, whose southern and northern churches had merged as recently as 1939, spoke out from their new posture of internal unity. Those who have an eye for about-faces would have to look for a slow-motion reenactment if they wanted to catch the Methodist motions. Only a year and a half after they had said they could never endorse war, their General Conference voted and announced that "the Methodists of America will loyally support our President and our nation." And most did. Thus also, looking on, Charles Clayton Morrison, having made his own more grudging about-face, turned back to look at the company he formerly kept. His *Christian Century* suffered some reversals as a result of his own reversal. He received between four and five thousand critical letters from subscribers, many of whom stopped taking the magazine. Morrison busied himself understanding the company he now kept as he looked back at the old crowd. He spoke with some measure of understanding and almost with favor of the "natural manhood" that led even most pacifists to prefer victory by their own country to victory for the enemy. Yes, it was true, pacifists might prefer a

negotiated peace in the midst of war, and they might have some
other nuances of policy to offer. But, he went on, "the pacifist has
no monopoly on the thesis that peace is better than war, that a negotiated peace is better than a knockout victory." Morrison and
millions of others held that view. Why, he kept asking, did even the
pacifist prefer victory and work for it? The editor answered his
own question: because the pacifist cherished the precarious but un-
ashamed hope that "the survival and some semblance of the continued independence of his own national community" would survive the war.

Pacifists had come down to uniting on only one continuing   2:25
moral theme: they distinctively refused to bear arms. Bearing arms
was a burden that fell only on young men of draft age in that time
of total war. Here Morrison posed government policy over against
the ways of Christ and saw militarism winning. He had to justify
or explain this circumstance somehow. The government clearly
was working to blunt the witness of those who acted in conscience
to oppose killing. On the other side, he realized, "the teachings of
Christ cannot be practiced in total war." The editor worked his way
out of the corner by saying that "war itself is Christ's judgment
upon us for our disobedience to the word he spoke to us from the
hillside." The pacifist's witness was therefore not entirely futile.
"God forbid!" that it be thought of as such. As quickly as he had
uttered this, Morrison had to qualify his endorsement by pushing
the theme of common guilt. "There are no righteous paths for the
Christian's feet." During wartime the language of national unity
turned out to be loudest. Christ had not left America, and God had
not forsaken it; the editor was sure of that. So he preached a little
sermon to the effect that both pacifist and nonpacifist believers had
to recognize that war was God's judgment for disobedience to his
righteous will. Now the two factions, one very large and the other
quite small, must stay together and somehow win the war.

Those who were all but hidden away in camps, hospitals, or   2:26
other out-of-the-way sites for alternate service or those in prison,
being out of sight, were largely out of mind. More visible were the
people on the religious front lines, in the trenches, the ministers of
congregations, especially in mainstream Protestantism. They were
expected to be custodians of the national tradition, interpreters of
its ways, defenders of American unity, patriots, and thus supporters
of the war effort. Some of them sounded almost as militant as had
their predecessors in World War I. The young Norman Vincent
Peale, preaching only a couple of miles from the tumult at Union

Theological Seminary, argued against the peacemakers that those who had "thought they were 'keeping us out of war' " were precisely those who had been keeping General Douglas MacArthur, on the Pacific battle scene, out of ammunition. In the kind of low blow one comes to expect in such tense times, Peale suggested that Hitler and his kind were looking on as this small dissenting community took shape in the 1930s. "Due to the popular feeling against war we allowed ourselves to get into such a position that we were totally unprepared, thus giving the Germans an opportunity to make this war."

2:27   The career of the Reverend Ernest Fremont Tittle demonstrates how full of stress was the life of a pastor who refused to make the about-face and remained pacifist through the war. He was minister of First Methodist Church in Evanston, Illinois, a flagship congregation in the largest Protestant denomination. In his time, such a pulpit gave him access to power beyond the sanctuary. Many members were people of influence, and Tittle was inevitably subject to press scrutiny. The pastor was past draft age, but he had to pacify a constituency that included many who were not, or who had family members in military service. Tittle returned from a family vacation in September 1939, right after war began in Europe. In his subsequent sermon "The Church in a World at War," he warned against what he saw forming: a "Great Crusade" in the name of Christ. For two years the preacher voiced a hope against hope that neutral nations could lure belligerents to conference tables, where they could end the war through a "peace without victory," but few church members went along with such a dream.

2:28   To show that his heart was not only in the right American place but that he had a humane impulse for the victims of war, Tittle got the General Conference of Methodism in 1940 to support his call for America to welcome Jewish refugees. In November of that year he preached "Should Europe's Hungry Be Fed?" a discourse moving enough to get the eye of Herbert Hoover's National Committee on Food for the Small Democracies. But the British government and the Roosevelt administration killed the idea, and the sermon did little more than draw fire from militant clerics. From Union Theological Seminary, Henry Pitney Van Dusen sneered: "Men cry for freedom and are given bread." Humanitarianism, van Dusen went on, could weaken the war effort. Tittle received some support from those who could be heard above the noise of van Dusen's critiques, but his humanitarian plans were all but overlooked in the time when prowar energies were amassing in the clergy and the churches.

Tittle was at home with Methodist conferences and bureaucra-   2:29
cies. He used the time between the European outbreak in 1939 and Pearl Harbor to get Methodist agencies to support his antiwar views. He drafted the statement for assembled Methodists in 1940: "We insist that the agencies of the Church shall not be used in preparation for war, but in the promulgation of peace." And the Evanston minister linked up with circumspect and suspect peace causes alike. On the left were procommunist and on the right America First opponents of American entry. The Ministers' No War Committee, founded in 1941, and the Churchmen's Campaign for Peace through Mediation were favorite fronts. Only gradually did he learn how many benign-seeming groups were fronts for communists or fascists. But he quickly withdrew support, for example, from the America Firsters, because he found few pacifists there and mistrusted their goals and preachments.

Down the street from Tittle, in nearby Chicago, the *Christian*   2:30
Century opened its pages to the popular pastor, now on the spot. The magazine asked him to address the theme "If America Enters the War—What Shall I Do?" Tittle discreetly wrote that he was convinced, along with a pioneering interchurch group, the Oxford Conference, that war was "a defiance of the righteousness of God as revealed in Jesus Christ and him crucified." War therefore inevitably had to defeat the ends of freedom and justice. Of course, if the United States became a belligerent party to the war, the pastor would contribute to the good of his country, but not to the support of the war itself. Again, of course, he affirmed, Hitlerism had to be overcome. "On this point American Christians are agreed." But how?

Tittle helped his congregation organize a Laymen's Board for   2:31
Conscientious Objectors, to give counsel to young pacifists as they searched their souls and planned strategies. He could remain a part of established church causes. He served under John Foster Dulles, a future secretary of state, on the Federal Council of Churches' Commission on a Just and Durable Peace. He foresaw the creation of a cooperative world community through such efforts. Tittle was stung by the critique of Reinhold Niebuhr: "If modern churches were to symbolize their true faith they would take the crucifix from their altars and substitute the three little monkeys who counsel men to 'speak no evil, hear no evil, see no evil.'" But Tittle stood reso-

lutely while others were about-facing, and in a letter of June 11, 1940, he could still write: "The churches, so far, are keeping their heads, although a number of outstanding clergymen are vociferously advocating all methods short of war." He found such advocacy incredible, but it was Tittle and his kind who were losing.

2:32   The Sunday after Pearl Harbor he summoned courage to preach to his people at First Church. *"We cannot deny the faith that is in us, to which heretofore we have borne witness. That would be cowardice, betrayal of trust, and indeed, spiritual suicide."* He was trying to hold together a by-now torn congregation. But he did not call for an end to antiwar talk. His biographer scanned the letters Tittle received; to some writers he was a "Nazi neurotic," a "spineless man," a "coward all through." With these saved letters was a note in the archives: "Filed at Mrs. Tittle's request; not seen by Dr. Tittle." It may be that her shielding fed illusions in him, or else he transcended difficulties. For all the profound differences he faced, the pastor could still say after a year: "I may add that, according to the testimony of some of our laymen, we have never had such unity as now exists in First Church, notwithstanding the fact that both of its ministers are, and are known to be, pacifists."

2:33   This man—accused of Nazi neurosis, spinelessness, and cowardice—survived with ingenuity. His congregation developed a nationally recognized program of support for service people and entertained Chicago area soldiers and sailors at the same time they supported conscientious objectors. Tittle did not let his church invest in war bonds, but it did display a plaque honoring men killed in service. At the Methodist General Conference his side lost by one vote on May 3, 1944, in an action through which the church refused to reaffirm its prewar antiwar position and, though without hawkishness, affirmed participation in the war, now in its late stages. The press overinterpreted the action: "Methodists Favor War." Tittle was bitter over this vote and refused to have breakfast with or to respond to a reconciling letter from Charles Parlin, a lawyer who had outmaneuvered the cleric at the General Conference and perhaps the best-positioned Methodist lay person in the country. This kind of response earned Tittle renown, in one critic's terms, as a "pacifist who was at once militant and combative." Yet it was his genius to be able to keep together the laity in an educated, powerful, and now tense congregation. Few other ministers were capable of being true to their prewar positions and their wartime consciences and congregations.

2:34   There were very few conversions to religious pacifism after the war began, except perhaps among some conscientious objectors who were vulnerable to the draft. Some token gestures, however, were visible. Thus Federal Council of Churches president George A. Buttrick, a prestigious preacher, took pains on the day after Pearl Harbor to sign up with the Fellowship of Reconciliation, for whatever that was worth. It seemed worth less than it might have in the prewar days of unambiguous stands by such groups. Now it became important for pacifists to distance themselves from America First movements and more clearly profascist agencies. The most notable pacifist of the day, Quaker A. J. Muste, worked to cut all ties and shun even the appearance of ties: "Actually to go to the ultranationalist and near fascist elements for support in a movement to end the war, seems to me to jeopardize the political effectiveness of pacifism in the profoundest sense." Muste, born in the Netherlands and able to draw on the conservative Calvinist roots he knew in Michigan, became a Quaker in 1918. He spent the interwar years promoting nonviolent and pacifist causes on explicitly religious bases. As years passed and as his frustration grew, Muste spoke acidly of churches and for a time lined up with the Trotskyite Workers Party of the United States. A two-year sojourn in Europe cured him of Marxist-Leninism, and in July 1936 he underwent a decisive conversion back to the broadly religious viewpoint. He promoted an integrative vision. Comradeship became "the law of human existence," because it derived from God, Love, the "basic reality." Muste thought he could convert both the American left and the Germans to see the validity of this view; no wonder he came to be dismissed as a Utopian.

Muste saw his young friends from Union Theological Semi-   2:35
nary go to prison in resistance, but progressively they repudiated religious pacifism, just as the seminary's professorial "realists" scorned Muste for his idealism. He found himself counseling individuals who made conscientious protest. The Quaker maverick began to draw on extra-Christian sources, as he organized a "Non-Violent Direct Action Committee" that operated through a "Harlem Ashram." Eventually, exhibiting the influence of India's Mohandas Gandhi, he called for "total pacifism." This would result in a "new revolution, in which we seek to transform society by the method of non-violent action." Yet the leadership was inept, and soon the movement dwindled. At the University of Chicago a similar group began to discuss ways to use Gandhi's nonviolent mode, *satyagraha,* to improve race relations. From this effort was born the Committee of Racial Equality, a movement that later

spread under James Farmer and in June 1944 became the Congress of Racial Equality, or CORE. Musteism might lack victories against those who prosecuted the war, but his influence spread into other areas.

2:36   Critics in the established churches were unimpressed. From the most highly regarded pulpit in liberal Protestantism, at Riverside Church, across the street from Union Theological Seminary, the Reverend Harry Emerson Fosdick warned Muste in April 1944 not to utter calls for the immediate end of the war before the Allies were in a strong position. To do so would "postpone the day of possible peace by the violence of the reaction it would arouse" and would "deprive the peace movement of a large part of the all too small influence it has today." Fosdick counseled strategic silence, except in the case of criticizing the Allies for bombing civilians in European cities. But Muste was relentless. He kept earning the title some had given him in 1939: "The Number One U.S. Pacifist." Competition for such a title grew ever more thin in a time when "Damn War" and "Damn Pacifism" presented such vivid and exhausting but unattractive alternatives. In the face of Hitlerism and the Japanese attack and in instinctive support of national unity during a war, it got ever harder to find a company lining up behind pacifists Number One, Number Two, or on down the line. Far more visible were the pivotings by adept and flexible moral leaders who found good reason to make an about-face in a time that allowed no good and clear alternatives.

3

"The Whole Moral Ambiguity of Warfare"

merican people and peoples had to come together dur-   3:1
ing World War II against a common set of enemies. The island of
Crete provides a metaphor for their kind of unity. Ancient Cretans
were notorious for fighting each other, the cities making constant
war of each against all. But when an external enemy threatened
their individual and group existence, they had no choice but to
unite. Their coming together was strategic, not based on profound
new agreements, though one must assume that by forming alliances they at least came to know each other better. As soon as the
menacing forces disappeared, the cities had the luxury of going
back to their private wars. Modern dictionaries often still make
reference to this history when pointing to the roots of the word
syncretism. Syncretism means the "reconciliation or fusion of differing systems of belief, as in philosophy or religion, especially
when the success is partial or the result is heterogeneous"; *syncre-
tize* is the verb form. The root is the Greek *syncretismos,* union,
from *synkretizein,* to unite in the manner of the Cretan cities. While
it has always been impossible to do more than sample American
varieties of belief, listening to the experience of several sets of the
peoples who made up the national mix in the 1940s throws some
light on the religious scene. As the dictionary would have it, when
they *did* come together against the Axis powers, "the success was

35

partial and the result was heterogeneous." When war ended, they went back, though partially changed, to their old ways.

3:2   Were this book an account of social history during the Second World War, it would include a story of the hard to chronicle yet decisive changes that occurred in the understanding of the role of women. "Rosie the Riveter" was one mythic reduction of a complex tale of women being needed and finding a place in the war-production factories. There would have to be notice of the changes in the sexual ethos of the nation, especially after servicemen had been uprooted from home and placed in highly varied circumstances marked by strange freedoms, around the world. What happened to the psyche of people who had not previously traveled but now felt at home in Algiers, Shanghai, or New Guinea is a valid subject for the social historian. But this is a story of a public argument, a narrative that listens for the use of rhetoric that would persuade citizens who were experiencing changes in the relations they had to one another as religious and ethnic or racial groups. So it demands careful attention to the voices—usually male, in this kind of history of public power—who tried to do the persuading. (Of course, there are many "publics" in the many subcultures that make up American culture. The Hispanic, or Latino-American, and the Native American peoples had their own publics, and they regarded what I have called the "public public" differently than did those who dominated it. Our sampling deals with some stories of those who were dominant, as well as those whose attitudes about this "public public" received wide notice in the war years themselves.)

3:3   By no means did all those who spoke up in the public spheres find themselves content with anything as pragmatic, strategic, momentary, or crass as the Cretan sort of alliance. There were visionaries who wrestled with the issues of the "reconciliation" or "fusion" of different religious beliefs as these were embodied in different peoples. Their words demand special notice in a time when there was a jostling of these peoples, if not "as never before," then at least in a new set of circumstances. Military chaplains, each of them grounded in and representative of particular religious communities, from Christian Science through Catholicism, were especially exposed to believers of other sorts than their own. Among them Chaplain Ellwood C. Nance gathered essays to present an understanding of the *Faith of Our Fighters* in the midst of the war years. He asked Vice President Henry A. Wallace, who was to become a presidential candidate from the maverick left in

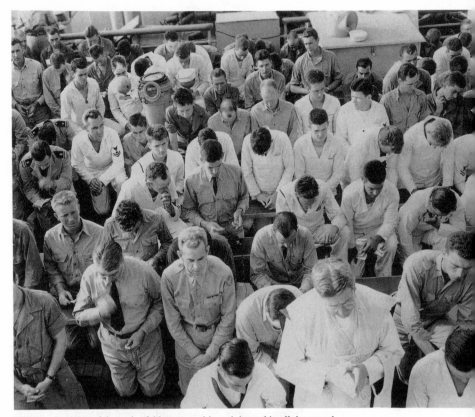

Military chaplains of the major faith communities ministered in all the armed forces with special intensity and effectiveness during World War II. Their achievements were often seen as vital contributions toward the war effort and had an incidental effect in stimulating interfaith tolerance during and after the war. (Reproduced from the Collections of the Library of Congress.)

1948, to describe such faith. Wallace wrote: "I am convinced that the world was meant eventually to be one world and to be a peaceful one." Its spiritual skein would be democracy; this was "the only form of government which harmonizes fully with the principles of the Bible." Wallace cited specifically Christian textual traditions and made explicit reference to the spread of the gospel. "The gospel we preach is the unity of free men and the unity of free nations." The vice president found this gospel confirmed in the doctrines of Thomas Jefferson, James Madison, and Abraham Lincoln: this was what Americans were fighting for, and what they found worth supporting. Such an understanding of "gospel," was, of course, far from any carried by Catholic, evangelical, or other conversion-minded missionaries past or present. But it accurately described a civil notion current around 1944.

3:4   A run of the finger along a library shelf of spiritual and patriotic literature from World War II would turn up many titles along the lines of *Faith of Our Fighters*. Chaplain Nance's typical venture issued from a religious publisher representing one English-speaking Protestant denomination, the Disciples of Christ. That group had been formed in the nineteenth century as an effort to be non-denominational, to transcend sectarian differences, so one might expect some generosity of spirit and outlook. But by 1944 little had occurred to reduce the hostility between the "Cretan" factions called Protestant and Catholic. Their representatives, however, could come to some sort of fusion of beliefs about the nation and its ideals against a common enemy. Thus New York's Archbishop Francis Spellman, the military vicar of the Catholic armed forces, would have been the enemy in any peacetime event of the Disciples of Christ. Yet here he was represented by a report that Protestant chaplain Nance called "inspiring." Spellman had come back after a six-month visit to the troops and pronounced them to be "like crusaders of old."

3:5   While members of the Disciples of Christ may have been no more or no less anti-Semitic than any other set of Gentile American Protestants—they left no particular record of anti-Jewish expression, living as most of them did in midwestern and southwestern nonmetropolitan America, where Jews did not cluster—it would have been exceptional for them in peacetime to be listening positively to a rabbi's voice. But not in wartime. Therefore Chaplain Nance welcomed the word of Rabbi Barnett R. Brickner of Cleveland. Brickner had logged 45,000 miles in his efforts to greet the troops. His word would have been reassuring to any Protestant patriot of generous sympathies: "Our fighting men are definitely more tolerant, racially and religiously, than people at home." The rabbi claimed that "when they live together, as our men do at the front, they think of each other as men, not as Protestants or Catholics or Jews, as Poles or Irish." Whether that was the true situation might be questioned; there was considerable segregation of African Americans, for instance, and close-up views might find all kinds of examples of bonding and rejection among the troops. What was important was the fact that Rabbi Brickner could be considered reassuring when he spoke of the overcoming of boundaries between peoples. Perhaps he went too far even for Nance or his editors and publishers. One of them introduced a note to remind readers of peacetime realities, preparing them for the return of the "Cretan" fighters to their eventual home bases: "Not that denominationalism is out, but rather that exclusive denominationalism is disappearing as men are sharing difficult experiences."

In a book that began to promote the tri-faith theme—Protestants, Catholics, and Jews were now making up the "one world" of American spirituality—Nance brought together voices that described the "parish" of the chaplain, the religion of women in uniform, the faith of generals, and confessions of faith from the battlefield. All were figurative Cretan brothers—and, now, sisters—who found it important to unite with each other as they stared at Hitlerism, fascism, and the Japanese war machine. To reinforce the general picture, Protestants like *Christian Herald* editor Daniel Poling pronounced on the moral fitness of the troops, in an account at whose naiveté and rosiness many sailors on shore leave would have laughed. On the syncretistic front, Chaplain William Barrow Pugh commented explicitly on the fusion of three faiths: "Behind this whole religious program are the chaplains of all faiths—Protestant, Catholic, Jew—who are laboring with unparalleled faithfulness and consecration." 3:6

Military chaplaincy itself presented problems for the church bodies that in peacetime or apart from the war effort embodied what the *Faith of Our Fighters* editor called "exclusive denominationalism." All the fundamentalist denominations, which defined themselves as "separatist" or "come-outers"—recalling a biblical injunction to believers to "come out" from others and "be separate"—belonged in this category. So did many of the evangelicals, who were moderates near the fundamentalist camp, having organized a National Association of Evangelicals in 1942. The Southern Baptist Convention, the Christian Reformed Church, and the Missouri Synod of the Lutherans were similarly in the "exclusive denominationalism" camp. These Lutherans had originally come from Saxony after 1839 to resist any "reconciliation or fusion of different belief systems," as these were being imposed by German governments. They abhorred the idea of communing or worshiping with anyone else, including other Lutherans, and called the practice of joint prayer or cooperation "unionism." In World War I they had resisted the idea of participating in chaplaincy because it might lead to commonness of expression and confusion in the ranks. They carried the burden now, though to a 3:7

lesser extent than in 1917, of Germanness—they were often nick-
named the "German Lutherans," a title hard to live with during
two wars against Germany—and therefore compensated with su-
perpatriotism. Their doctrine, in any case, demanded loyalty and
patriotism. Thus, in a tract, Louis J. Roehm counseled young men
of conscience who might be objectors to military service: "Your
government is instituted by God; therefore obey its mandate, and
you can have a good conscience." A Christian pastor should urge
church members to pray for government, to make themselves heard
through orderly processes, and "in time of national stress to uphold the government loyally, and to resist only when commanded
to sin." Military service as such could not be sin.

3:8   In tracts and magazine articles, some Missouri Synod Lutheran
pastors began to look for ways to transcend exclusivism. A notable
Illinois moderate, Otto A. Geiseman, joined everyone in saying
war was terrible, but he then found some compensatory factors.
The war effort was unifying the nation. It might help Americans join in producing future international concords. War showed
people how futile human action could be. Detroit's Louis B. Buch-
heimer reproduced some of the militancy heard in World War I:
"We must make the sword as keen as possible," since soldiers
were following "scripturalness" and wielding it, as commanded,
for government. God was guiding United States troops at Dunkirk
as God had guided affairs when the Spanish Armada was destroyed
while sailing against England. Editors of the Missouri Synod's *Lutheran Chaplain* endorsed the Maltese governor's view that "our
allies are motivated by the Spirit of Christ in their dealings with
the enemy and . . . they cannot become ruthless in their conduct
over against him." Citing no data, that governor, here favorably
quoted, said that "our warfare is tempered with compassion and
love." The fiercely anticommunist Lutheran church body even allowed its official periodical, the *Lutheran Witness,* to say good
things about the very Soviet Union it had recently seen as atheistic
and demonic. Now it was an ally. The editor speculated that Russia
must have changed its character; in fact, Russians were even permitting the opening of new churches in Germany, thus displaying
tolerance. When Soviets linked with noncommunist elements in
China, the editor asked: "Where are the Bolshevist hordes which
some of us saw rolling across China and engulfing in Red Communism all of Asia?"

3:9   Occasional controversy rose when a Lutheran would question
statements of patriotic fervor. Thus in the more moderate United

Lutheran Church, a minister disagreed with the thrust of a prayer in his church's own Army and Navy Service Book that read: "O Lord God of our Salvation, we beseech Thee to go forth with our Army, Navy, and Air Forces, and by Thy right hand and Thy mighty arm gain for them the victory." How, the pastor asked, could one square this plea with the spirit of Christ? Why consider it legitimate to ask God to be a warrior? He was given a Lutheran answer: no soldier was charged with "personal guilt" for his military actions; a Christian could fight with good conscience; why then should such a prayer be out of place? The questioner's question, appropriate in peacetime, found no hearing in time of war.

At the far end from the "exclusive denominationalist" orbit of 3:10 Missouri Synod Lutherans was the Federal Council of Churches, the voice of inclusive denominations of more liberal stripe. In a journal with wide academic circulation council executive F. Ernest Johnson, keeper of the ecumenical flame, made a midwar assessment titled "The Impact of the War on Religion in America." The "extremely heterogeneous character" of a nation with 250 religious bodies and the difficulty one had in gathering data and quantitative measures—Johnson was writing for sociologists—made it hard to generalize. He surmised that stability of belief and policy stood Catholicism in quite good stead. The Jewish community was "too closely bound by its sense of peoplehood to the democratic cause to experience any such shock in the outbreak of the war as has come to the Protestant churches," his council's constituency. Protestantism, however, had recovered from its hypermilitancy in World War I and made room for the "indubitably authentic movement" of pacifism between the wars. While Catholics had been ready for war, Protestants, pacifist or not, had offered little or no clear testimony in support of the war before Pearl Harbor. Therefore Pearl Harbor had a shattering effect on Protestant churches. Johnson collated material from hundreds of sermons and found in them great restraint of a sort not heard in 1917. There was now "very little of the note of belligerency" and "the old idea of 'manifest destiny' under God was absent. There was no glorified jingoism."

Ex-pacifists, Johnson noted, were now suffering "a mood of de- 3:11 pression and frustration" and needed ministerial care. He regretted that Protestantism of his sort was so individualistic that it could be of little help in group repentance or healing. At the same time, he presumed that many ministers were helping their members cope with individual stress in wartime. The executive reported on subtle trends. Some ministers, for instance, noted a rise in church attendance, though others missed the presence of a talented generation called to military service. The employment of women in industry and the need for a seven-day work week were factors limiting church attendance. The most cheering evidence of wartime activity was some growth of cooperation between Catholic and Protestant churches. This, Johnson thought, ought to lead "to the instigation all along the line of cooperative effort with appropriate machinery." He hesitated to prophesy that this would happen, perhaps out of an instinct that recalled the proverbial Cretan breaking of alliances after an enemy disappeared. His instincts did serve him well when he envisioned a postwar recovery. In some regions, churches might even have more money than they could spend. Still, he knew many would spend it on church buildings when materials were again available.

3:12   The leader of the Federal Council of Churches was one of the better reporters on the mentality of constituents. "The advent of war has deepened the religious mood of church people." The correspondents on whose opinions he drew thought this mood built on a trend that had begun during the late Depression. He quoted a cleric who reported that "the renewed interest in theology among clergymen is paralleled among the laity." Even formerly secular individuals were taking a new look. But Johnson's tone was always qualified, his voice cautious. He quoted and agreed with an Ohio church federation secretary: "I see nothing whatever to indicate that the general tone [in support of religion] has been raised. The secularization which characterizes our age is continuing at an unabated pace." Because the church was being sold to the public as the "bulwark of democracy," it might be experiencing some signs of growth in respect. The observer clearly agreed with a West Coast commentator who had written: "The government, rather than the Christian message and spirit, does our basic thinking for us, and gives the cue to the church in the war situation." Disturbing as the notion was, "action springs from secular demands, rather than from religious impulse." The war effort came garbed in "some sort of religious interpretation and justification, be it ever so thin and vulnerable." One slightly cheering sign for the Crete-like nation that was America: it "appears to be true of Protestant, Catholic, and Jewish groups alike" that "in the armed forces the evidence of religious interest is, according to reports, more marked than in the civilian community."

3:13   Johnson was trained in economics and informed about international development, so he pushed further than other executives might have, aware though he had to be that "contrasts and inconsistencies" characterized the religious scene. He was aware that the churches' foreign missionary activity had been curtailed during wartime. Yet Americans were now traveling all over the world, and "it is an axiom among church leaders that the foreign service quickens and vitalizes the home base." Therefore it was hard to predict what life in postcurtailment times might be. Closer to home the mission of the church was changing, thanks to the war. For instance, a "vast proportion of migrant populations," having been made migrant by the Depression and the needs of war-based industrial communities, represented "a kind of social change that has more than temporary consequences for organized religion." Never satisfied with the individualism or the mere organizationalism of the churches, Johnson here as elsewhere wanted to go deeper: the church "is a fellowship bound together by enduring sentiments which cannot be quickly built up." If wartime brought instability, Americans had better know that "it will take a long time to stabilize community life to the degree that normal, indigenous religious expression, particularly among Protestants, who constitute the religious majority, seems to require." The ecumenist in him was prompted to say that the new wartime situation might pressure religious denominations to "cease the competitive behavior which has so largely characterized the church life of the typical local community." However, "prediction would be premature." It was even possible that the anti-ecumenical forces might prosper. Here Johnson the reporter turned out to be the prophet: "From one of the nation's greatest urban centers comes the report that the pessimistic sects—small groups of Christians who look for an early end to this troubled world—are growing in strength!"

It was not the growing pessimistic and exclusivist denominations to which the custodians of the general public culture looked when they assessed Protestantism. They turned to the standard denominations that produced most of the people in *Who's Who in America* and held the allegiance or attracted the notice of those prominent in the mass media and circles of commercial or political power. Among these were the heirs of the colonial big three, Congregationalism, Presbyterianism, and Episcopalianism; or members of the frontier big three, Methodists, the Disciples of Christ, and the Baptists of the sort that made up the Federal Council of Churches. Debates within this cluster were believed to have more consequence than those in other religious circles. In their company

3:14

were many who would find Johnson too cautious, too self-critical of Protestantism, too qualified in his still evident patriotism. One of these who reached hundreds of thousands of Protestants through the periodical the *Christian Herald* and who had access to un-churched leadership was Daniel A. Poling, a moderately conservative mainstream Protestant. (The adjectives pile up as one tries to position those who were not exclusive denominationalists!) In 1943 this preacher-turned-editor could title his book *A Preacher Looks at War* and at once situate himself credibly in the midst of events. The dedication reads: "To our son Clark Vandersall Poling. . . . Missing in the North Atlantic, February 2, 1943," a minister, then a chaplain, "A man of peace."

3:15   In a foreword, Bucknell University president A. C. Marts re-minded readers that twenty years before, when pacifism had been in vogue, Poling was the only minister at a well-attended luncheon who dissented from a proposal to circulate a pacifist pledge among American clergy. "We know now that he was right," said Marts, who then rather meanly tried to settle old scores in new times: "We know now that if the seven thousand clergymen who signed that pledge had implemented their hatred for war in certain other mat-ters, it is possible that Germany and Japan might not have dared to plan and launch this present cruel war." That he pictured such power in the hands of seven thousand Protestant clergy was more a tribute to the clerical role than to Marts's understanding of power in religion and national life. "War is an evil which can be pre-vented," he went on, not spelling out how. He knew only that "there is no Christian virtue in pacifism under the circumstances which we are now witnessing."

3:16   Poling thought it necessary to make an apologia for defending the American way of prosecuting the war. He knew that clergy had been intimidated by the "horrific arraignment of the American pul-pit of the First World War" in pacifist Ray Abram's famed book *Preachers Present Arms.* Now many might fear that they would be similarly skewered after the war if their bolder wartime preach-ments were taken out of context and exploited. Too many pulpits were "often uncertain if not altogether silent" on war themes. His was a curious misreading of the popular opinion of 1943, when not to support the war would have been at best puzzling, in the mid-dling way a cause for suspicion, or at worst treasonous in congre-gations' eyes. Still, Poling felt he had to volunteer to represent the patriotic cause. "Is this then a holy war? No. War is not holy. Every hard thing said about war during the peace may in truth be said now." But there were holy causes, and the fight for freedom was one of these. He pronounced shame on clergy if they bestowed no blessings on their sons or their government.

Like the more liberal Johnson, editor Poling displayed an ecu-   3:17
menical instinct and opposed exclusive denominationalism, hoping it would disappear as a result of the wartime experience. People would "hardly return to the churches, when the war is over, if the churches fail now in their war-time ministry. Nor will they return to a divided church." In the crisis of war they turned to religion and felt they made direct contact with God. "But they are not interested in what keeps Baptists, Presbyterians, Episcopalians and Methodists apart." By this time they had found division to be "small and ridiculous," schism a "disaster," and sectarianism "sin." Ecumenical conferences would do less to bring about new concord than would proper pursuit of the wartime business of churches. Poling did not feel that the pursuit was going well. The Federal Council of Churches had attracted 370 leaders to Ohio Wesleyan University in May 1942 to discuss a "just and durable peace." The extremes of left and right were absent; some of the moderates between them who did come showed "courage and Christian statesmanship." But Poling sided with a woman who asked the committee there to "put a 'little religion' into the section on politics"; not one line of the document dealt with prayer. And the conference ducked even a mention of wartime needs. "Here its silence while the world burns is a failure tragic if not fatal." The editor faulted delegates for failing to discuss "the disastrous disunion of Protestant Christianity in the presence of a disintegrating civilization." Worst of all, the "major tragedy" of the conference was the passing of a resolution declaring that "the Christian Church as such is not at war." It was. "What does it mean to ten million men called to the colors and to their parents, wives, sweethearts, sisters, brothers, and friends? What does it mean to millions of Americans who believe they hear and follow Christ's call to them, in offering their lives and sacred honor to preserve freedom in the world and to win the peace?" The stinging question had to be: "Do we want America to believe that the Church is not in this war?"

The argument over whether the church was at war when the   3:18
nation was, exercised the most notable mainstream Protestant minister of the day, Harry Emerson Fosdick. It is hard to convey the sense of power such a minister once had. His congregation at Riverside Church on Morningside Heights above Harlem, well-

endowed (by John D. Rockefeller and others), was a Gothic preserve that signaled importance. His books, whether on popular interpretation of the Bible or the importance of individual life, were widely sold. Students from far beyond Union Theological Seminary across the street, and even seminarians far beyond the scope of his liberal Protestantism, observed and listened, taking lessons, as it were, on how to preach, whether on busman's holidays in his pews or by reading his books. Fosdick traveled widely and attracted large audiences. His "National Vespers" was the Federal Council's choice among radio shows, and networks donated time for it as a public service. The New York press, including that with a national readership, covered his moves and declarations. The minister possessed a charisma that attracted people to his opinions, whether they agreed with him or not. He loved to preach a soothing gospel, attractive to harried parishioners, but he was also regarded as a reasonably searching critic of national vices and follies. A leader against fundamentalism in the scrapes of the 1920s, Fosdick had signed on with the prevailing pacifists in the 1930s and became a leader among them, especially after an important sermon he preached in May 1934.

3:19   Being a pacifist took little courage that year. In one magazine poll, 12,904 ministers told the editors they would vow never to sanction war again. So Fosdick preached to the converted when at Broadway Tabernacle he chose to give "My Account with the Unknown Soldier." The *Christian Century*, almost always in his camp, called it the greatest sermon by Fosdick to date. He concluded: "I renounce war and never again, directly or indirectly, will I sanction or support another! O Unknown Soldier, in penitent reparation I make you that pledge." The preacher took that pledge on the road, drawing applause from campus audiences and seeing it reprinted in magazines and the *Congressional Record*. Throughout the decade, as Mussolini blustered and attacked Ethiopia, Japan built up its war machine and attacked China, and Hitler announced plans for war, Fosdick kept the pledge. This was not always easy to do, given his love of England, which was most threatened. In the mode of many mainstream Protestants, he could assert in a letter to a British friend after Britain declared war on Germany in 1939: "Sometimes I live more in Britain than at home, so keen my sympathies, so deep my apprehensions, so desperate my hopes." The new catastrophe, he went on, had "left in wreckage the things that I cared most for and worked hardest on in public life." But the present days were "among the darkest in my life." Not easily gotten down, however, Fosdick endured, claiming that he feared he might lose his pulpit because of unpopular stands he was taking.

The month the war in Europe began, September 1939, Fosdick   3:20
chaired a new Ministers' No War Committee, a clumsily named group that Union's "realist" critics like Reinhold Niebuhr found naive and worthy of derision. How could Fosdick and his colleagues hope to reach their goal of finding a negotiated way of peace? Riverside's minister picked up some support that the realists regarded as smelly or worse; America First paid the committee to distribute its literature to 90,000 ministers. America First included a variety of people who opposed alliance with England; some had a fascistic, others a right-wing American patriotic, and still others a mere isolationist bent. But taken together they were not the kind of company Fosdick would normally find congenial. He even permitted some of his writings to appear in America First's *We Testify*. When Congress was debating conscription, he took on Senator Burton K. Wheeler's prodraft position. "Conscription is the essence of regimented, totalitarian, militaristic autocracy," he could say as late as August 7, 1940. Fosdick had an answer ready in January of 1941 when the *Christian Century* asked him and others what they would do if America became involved in war. He said he would "not use my Christian ministry to bless war." Yet through the turn-of-the-decade years he began to moderate his "no war" stand. He also agreed to be a participant in the Federal Council of Churches' Commission to Study the Bases of a Just and Durable Peace, under the chair of John Foster Dulles.

Finding a just and durable peace with his Union colleagues and   3:21
other former pacifists turning to preparedness and making prowar sounds was almost as hard as envisioning postwar concord. The crowds were turning now to associate with old friends of his who were attracting a new generation while he often had to keep unlovely company off in the distance. Just as the realist faction found favor with communists, munitions makers, and militarists, Fosdick recognized that the right was too near and ready. His mail became nasty: "I see letters written by Christian pacifists to their nonpacifist brethren that for bitterness, acrimony, venom and dogmatism pass all decent bounds." But the man of balance also felt attacks from the other Christian side that "for scorn, misrepresentation, rancor and contemptuousness are appalling." The crossfire drama was being lived out in sanctuaries, seminaries, and editorial offices across the nation; Fosdick was merely the most visible actor. It was a measure of the man that he somehow held friendships

across the divide in Protestantism and the larger culture in the time between September 1939 and Pearl Harbor in December 1941. This was before the "Cretan" tribes in America formed their alliance against an external enemy who did not allow them any longer the luxury of mailing mean letters to each other.

3:22   The Japanese attack and America's entry into the war forced the alliance of previously uncongenial religious forces upon them. If Fosdick wanted to keep any hearing, or play any continuing part in shaping conscience, he had to be realistic, if not a member of the realist camp. He took to his pulpit the Sunday after the Japanese bombing and then aired his new views over "National Vespers" on the radio. The church dared not separate itself from the people and the nation; that was his new theme. Jesus had asked his disciples to be a leaven in society; how could the church suddenly become a sect, posturing in withdrawal? "We will not separate ourselves from our people. Their troubles are our troubles; their sins, alas, have been our sins too; their peril is ours." It was urgent that the churches keep America spiritually strong and—this became the new liberal impetus—that it put energies into working for a durable peace. Most emphatically, the churches should not help turn this into a blessed or holy war. Such a line had to antagonize people like Daniel A. Poling, who insisted that in the proper sense the church *was* at war. Explicitly, Fosdick put it in a radio sermon, the "church of Jesus Christ is not at war." This meant for him that the religious forces had to work against stimulation of hatred against Japan, which was itself a racist expression. Fosdick unashamedly used theological language: "Humility and penitence become us all, and if coming into the Christian church and kneeling before the altar of the Crucified, whom the world is crucifying afresh, we are not reminded of that, then the church has failed in its function." What was a pacifist-minded minister to do? He had to realize that pacifism was not practicable in wartime, yet he also had to "stand for and bear witness to a way of life and a means of combating evil utterly different from the violence his nation uses, practically unavoidable and relatively justifiable though it be." The pacific preacher announced throughout the war that the church is "a super-national institution, universal, catholic, ecumenical," so it dared not "echo nationalistic war cries."

3:23   Something of the old liberal optimism remained with Fosdick through the darkest war years. In 1944 he published sermons called *A Great Time to Be Alive*. He played with paradox: "This certainly is a ghastly time to be alive," and "an especially hideous generation for Christians." Yet it was "also a great time to be alive, and alike the personal and the public issues of it depend on whether we see that." While the church was not at war, the three major political forces of the day, fascism, communism, and democracy, were, and they made exacting demands on people of faith. The old preacher against the fundamentalists averred that it was a time to go "back to the fundamentals." He revisited the old battle scenes where he had been a warrior twenty years before. If he were preaching today to fundamentalists, the veteran pastor said, he would urge them to forget *their* fundamentals—"all this Biblical literalism, this insistence on the peccadilloes of tradition, this sectarian provincialism in the church, this belated theology," all together a travesty of Christ's gospel. At Thanksgiving in 1943 the Riverside pulpiteer was publicly worrying about the "strange things" war does to religion. "It makes some people fundamentalists," he said, as if looking over his shoulder at growing forces coming to crowd him. "Fundamentalism always has a revival in wartime," for obvious pyschological reasons. People turn "back to old ideas that seem familiar and stable" and thus seek "security where no real security is." Others, however, were driven to superstition, a religion of magic which proclaimed "no atheism in the fox-holes."

Present-day battles were now more important. Fosdick had heard three reasons for deserting Christian faith, all voiced by German General Ludendorf: "I reject Christianity because it is Jewish, because it is international, and because in cowardly fashion, it preaches peace on earth." Fosdick directly countered these; they were good reasons to accept the faith. "It is Jewish, thank God, rooted in the great Hebrew prophets of righteousness." It was international, "believing in one God and one human family." And it preached peace, knowing that humanity's suicide was the alternative. "Don't be a Nazi!" was his word to American anti-Semites.

Fosdick would go deeper than the surface syncretism of allied "Cretan" parties in the face of an enemy. These were good times to improve relations among races and religions. He even took lessons from wartime Germany, relying on the word of Swedish journalist Arvid Fredborg, who had come out of Germany and announced in surprise: "One must not lay too much emphasis on the differences between Catholicism and Protestantism [in Germany] for in the face of common pressure many barriers have fallen." There were reports that Catholic priests were preaching in Protestant churches and that expelled Protestant pastors were enjoying the support of Catholic funds that had not yet been successfully

3:24

3:25

plundered by Nazis. The American had to be awed, too: "Catholic priests preaching in Protestant pulpits and Protestant pastors living on Catholic funds is strange business, and doubtless it will not outlast the common peril, but it illustrates the theme." And the preacher thought of the United States and Russia, "strange bedfellows," showing that wartime was an occasion of unity as well as murderous division. Pastor Fosdick found domestic cheer on the race relations front (though not in the case of the imprisonment of Japanese Americans in western camps). To illustrate: in New York a black man had defeated a white in a race for a judgeship and had done so with white votes. "Then the defeated candidate gave a dinner to his successful Negro rival, and Catholics, Protestants, Jews and Negroes dined together in his honor." Fosdick kept promoting a postwar vision: "When once the world catches a glimpse of itself organized for peace instead of war, something happens that all the forces of darkness cannot prevent." When that occurs, "that vision becomes the standard of our judgment, the criterion of our endeavor, and short of it mankind will never be content."

3:26   Fosdick learned the importance of nonverbal communication during the war years. One day in 1942 the Riverside Church carillon chimed with the happy sounds of Franz Josef Haydn's "Glorious Things of Thee Are Spoken, Zion, City of our God." The carillonneur did not know or remember that to some Manhattanites who did not sing hymns the melody was that of the German military song "Deutschland Über Alles." But his minister kept finding ways to speak the glorious things. Fosdick consistently opposed the internment of Japanese Americans and the atomic bombing of Hiroshima and Nagasaki near the war's end. The aging pastor was of a mind to retire at sixty-five. But Riverside leaders feared that his leaving would look like defeat for his and their causes, and they kept inventing ways that the church could be of use to service people and others involved in the war effort, always in modes congruent with their minister's conscience. He may have been a critical and uneasy supporter of the war effort, but his church did not divide, and most members stayed faithful, even if many of them would have been happier had they heard an uncritical prowar message from Fosdick.

3:27   Little of the Fosdickian uneasiness marked the wartime career of his neighbor, Reinhold Niebuhr, who was to Protestant theology and public life what Fosdick was to preaching. If it is hard to picture the cultural power of the most notable Protestant pulpiteer, it is also not easy to recapture a sense of a theologian's, or at least this theologian's, potency. A co-inventor of "Christian realism," the Union Theological Seminary professor had left pacifism far behind and now scorned pacifists. Like Fosdick, a friend whom he admired in other contexts, Niebuhr was also on the Federal Council of Churches' Commission to Study the Bases of a Just and Durable Peace. He took on many committee assignments, assumed diverse political roles, and tirelessly spoke to church leadership during the war years, while interrupting the activity to complete his most nearly systematic theological work, the Gifford Lectures at Edinburgh. These became the second volume of a two-volume work, *The Nature and Destiny of Man.*

Niebuhr could fend off the left as successfully as the right or the   3:28
pacifist middle. He antagonized other leaders of the Socialist party, to which he belonged, when in 1940 he urged full support, short of entry into the war itself, of Allied activities. Party leadership tried to discipline him, so he resigned: "The Socialists have a dogma that this war is a clash of rival imperialisms. Of course they are right. So is a clash between myself and a gangster." But the professor spent more energy criticizing pacifists and liberal Christians. These had developed a vapid culture whose "will-to-live has been so seriously enervated by a confused pacifism, in which Christian perfectionism and bourgeois love of ease have been curiously compounded," Niebuhr argued, "that our democratic world does not really deserve to survive." It was Christian realism that faced the "barbarism" of the enemy and demanded toughness. Niebuhr wrote all this in *Christianity and Power Politics,* a book published to meager secular reviews, which he thought showed incomprehension. It also led to the decisive break with his old editor, Charles Clayton Morrison, at the *Christian Century,* who blasted the book but wanted to remain a friend. "You can get no moral advantage of me by generously claiming to be my friend when I saw a friendship is ended," was Niebuhr's brusque brush-off. "This whole business of covering up ugly realities with words is of no avail. The conflict between you and myself or between your side and mine is, in miniature, as tragic as the world conflict." The professor could love the editor as an enemy, as Christians must and might, but not as a friend.

Niebuhr's revenge was the founding, mainly with Union Semi-   3:29
nary colleagues, of *Christianity and Crisis.* It looked like a biweekly clone of Morrison's magazine but was marked by the Christian realism that the Niebuhrians favored. Not strong enough to counter or kill the *Christian Century,* it did lure readers from

some more radical but dying Protestant magazines. In 1941 he also led the new Union for Democratic Action. In the magazine, Niebuhr was more explicitly political than a Fosdick could be or would choose to be. He argued against some of the Roosevelt administration's bombing policies and the demand for unconditional surrender. He warned against seeking revenge, as the Allies had done after World War I, and looked ahead to the postwar world, which he hoped would be reorganized in ways that would limit national sovereignty. But as the war became more preoccupying, the editors had to postpone treatment of such concerns. In the face of liberals who thought they could help integrate the nations and peoples after the war, Niebuhr spoke out against their fallacy, because "governments have only limited efficacy in integrating a community." What was possible instead was some limitation of national sovereignty, which could make it possible for a measure of world community to appear.

3:30   Like Fosdick, Niebuhr had to be careful, poised as he also was between extreme camps. His view of prophetic Christianity meant that believers had to criticize their country, something that detractors on the right thought was subversive. Professional anticommunists helped prompt the Federal Bureau of Investigation and the State Department to keep their eye on him—a flattering notion for a theologian!—and it took highly placed people like Supreme Court Justice Felix Frankfurter and the State Department's own Sumner Welles to get these agencies off his trail. In any case, there was no reason to shadow Niebuhr, since his wartime leadership was so decisive that even those seeking revenge on old communists and socialists found their pursuit of him unproductive, and watched and protested elsewhere.

3:31   Fearing an Axis triumph and the death of democracy, Niebuhr refused to call the nation's polity "God's cause," but he believed it was generally defensible, and defended it. Popular though he was, Niebuhr found that secular critics as well-placed as philosophers John Dewey and Sidney Hook, or religious critics on right and left, found his language paradoxical, confusing. But he was clear on one point, which he shared with Fosdick: this was not a holy war. "It is not possible to achieve this pure holiness; and yet we must act. The Christian acts with an uneasy conscience both because of the ambiguity of his cause and the impurity of his weapons." So Niebuhr had to act, at least with his voice, even to defend bombing that took civilian life. His stand did not square with Fosdick's. Bombing cities was "a vivid revelation of the whole moral ambiguity of warfare," he wrote in the summer of 1943. Yet it was "not possible to defeat a foe without causing innocent people to suffer with the guilty." And it was not possible to engage "in any act of collective opposition to collective evil without involving the innocent with the guilty." There seemed to be resignation or defeatism in his observation that "once bombing has been developed as an instrument of warfare, it is not possible to *disavow* its use without capitulating to the foe who refuses to disavow it." Yet Niebuhr criticized some of the military policies and praised American pilots who could not in conscience bring themselves to receive the Lord's Supper before their flights. This was not a holy war; the Christian church was not at war. But it had much at stake in the outcome. The holy war at times seemed to be between various Protestant camps who were settling old scores and positioning themselves in new ways. But so overwhelming was the defeat of the old pacifists, so urgent the need for all to be supportive of the war effort, that the churches of the Johnsons and the Polings, the Missouri Lutherans and the Federal Council, the Fosdicks and the Niebuhrs, were so similarly pulled into alliances with Jews, Catholics, Negroes, and others that the generalization holds: wartime brought these factions into some sort of reconciliation and fusion in the face of the task at hand. They could remain divided on what appeared during the war to be lesser causes, could redivide when the threat was past, or find themselves part of a movement of centripetal forces pulled by the needs of their "one nation, indivisible," pulled finally, even, by religion.

4

"The Jewish Problem"

4:1   In 1917 and 1918, during the First World War, there was little talk of America being made up religiously of Protestants, Catholics, and Jews; of a society composed of Christians and Jews; or of the nation being "Judeo-Christian." In 1931, exactly ten years before Pearl Harbor, the United States Supreme Court could still speak of the United States as being a "Christian nation." It was the Second World War that found a nation in need of unity developing a new language and a new concern, one that had begun to be developed between the wars and had been encouraged by an interfaith movement. The need for national unity during the war, the contribution of Jews to the war effort, and a set of three events increased the perceived need to see Jews fully integrated into civil and spiritual life but also, sooner or later, complicated the transition of Jews from the margins to the center; from being outsiders to becoming insiders; from being a curiosity into becoming the nation's third faith, or even the third version of a single faith in "the American Way of Life." The first of these events, whose effects were largely felt a generation later by Jews and non-Jews, was the Nazi Holocaust, which brought forth the expression of a range of American attitudes toward the destruction and the rescue of European Jews. The second, the birth of the state of Israel, occurred soon after the war, and gave rise to American debates over support of Zionism and Zion. The third was the event of suburbanization,

54

the breakup of the urban ghetto and the dispersal of Jews to communities where they were a more diffused presence among non-Jewish neighbors.

The story of attitudes toward European Jews cannot be seen as   4:2
a major event in American consciousness during the war itself; its
effects came later. Yet the argument that began during the war became a large part of the debate over the place of Jews in that national consciousness. It occurred while Jews were debating the
ancient issue of universalism versus particularism, a controversy
heightened by the issue of Zionism during the rise of Hitler and of
Nazi anti-Jewish policies. If American Jews paid no attention to
Hitler or to the rise of Zionism, they would be cutting themselves
off from their people in a time of need and aspiration; they would
lose their spiritual hopes and time-honored commitments. If the
same Jews paid so much attention to the plight of Jews in Europe while everyone else was preoccupied with winning a war, or
showed too much devotion to the Israel that needed to be born,
their loyalty might be questioned. After the war had begun in Europe but before Pearl Harbor, the dispute within the Jewish community raged, most notably within the Reform movement. Reform
Judaism was the branch most exposed to public view and the one
most familiar to Christian leadership. In a 1939 lecture to the Central Conference of American Rabbis, Rabbi Samuel Goldenson,
voicing familiar concerns, urged that Reform should "emphasize
less and less the particularisms in our Jewish heritage, those particularisms that separate us from others, and stress the universal
concepts and outlooks more and more." Would not particularism
awaken charges that Jews held dual loyalties? Typical of the responses from the other half of Reform was Rabbi Julius Gordon's. He cited Supreme Court Justice Louis D. Brandeis, "whose
'Americanism' can hardly be questioned." Brandeis had said, "Let
no American imagine that Zionism is inconsistent with Patriotism.
Multiple loyalties are objectionable only if they are inconsistent."
Support of world Jewry was not inconsistent with Americanism.

Two years before, at Columbus, Ohio, the rabbis had gone on   4:3
record in new "Guiding Principles of Reform Judaism" as supporting a commonwealth of Israel. This was a reversal of Reform's
founding policies in changed times. Only aged David Philipson
among them had been present at the Pittsburgh Conference of
1885, which had condemned Zionism outright. Now he could
make the motion for change: "We affirm the obligation of all Jewry
to aid in [Israel's] upbuilding as a Jewish homeland by endeavoring

to make it not only a haven of refuge for the oppressed but also a center of Jewish culture and spiritual life." Five years after the Columbus meeting, the defeated anti-Zionist faction organized a militant American Council for Judaism, claiming that 90 percent of the laity opposed Zionism. The council's presence had to be debated at the 1943 conference: "Are Zionism and Reform Judaism Incompatible?" Young Rabbi David Polish spoke for the new day: "Jewish nationalism which is the hope for the restoration of a Jewish homeland in Palestine" had never been challenged until modern times. Whatever Reform had said from its beginnings until 1937, the time had now come to reaffirm the old hope. By a vote of 137 to 45 the conference rabbis asked the fledgling American Council for Judaism to disband, and most leaders deserted it. But the council did not disband: under the leadership of Rabbi Elmer Berger, a group made up largely of lay people continued the council's activities and gave very visible opposition to the Israel-to-be and to "particularism" in general.

4:4   The battles over particularism and Americanism moved quickly from the conference to the local scene. One contention that drew national notice occurred at prestigious Congregation Beth Israel in Houston. In 1943 German Jews in this congregation feared that new companies of Jews from Eastern Europe would overwhelm them, and they voted to establish two classes of members. New members would have to sign a statement: "We consider ourselves no longer a nation. We are a religious community, and neither pray for nor anticipate a return to Palestine nor a restoration of any of the laws concerning the Jewish state." The congregation found a rabbi to match their views. The Central Conference of American Rabbis dispatched its president, Solomon Freehof, to try to prevent the Beth Israel virus, which lingered long in Houston, from spreading. Reform's pioneer pro-Zionist, Stephen Wise, blasted the "Jewish Grand Inquisition" set up by that congregation. An "almost psychopathic local phenomenon" it was; he saw in it a "loathsome brand of cowardly anti-Jewishness."

4:5   Zionism and the rescue of Jews from Hitlerism were connected, because refugee Jews had nowhere to flee. The half million Jews in Palestine were eager to see their numbers grow, but the British held a mandate there and, fearing reactions by Arab allies during the war, refused to change policy. Refugee boats were turned back at the shores. In a late-night speech to a late summer meeting of the American Jewish Conference in 1943 at New York's Waldorf-Astoria Hotel, Rabbi Abba Hillel Silver convinced a majority to support the formation of Israel. It was the absence of a Jewish homeland that made Jews so vulnerable in Europe; this absence was "the principal source of our millennial tragedy." Silver asked: "Are we forever to live a homeless people on the world's crumbs of sympathy, forever in need of defenders, forever doomed to thoughts of refugees and relief?" Zionists won almost everything at the Waldorf-Astoria, though their victory led to further fissures in Judaism. Rabbi Joseph Rauch of Louisville, a holdout, charged that the move had "wrecked Jewish unity in the United States" just when it had been most needed and most promising. Prominent Rabbi Maurice Eisendrath concurred: "American Jewry has never been more bitterly divided than it is today." Rabbis Wise and Silver set out in 1944 to convince presidential candidates Thomas E. Dewey and Franklin D. Roosevelt to put the moral force of the United States behind Zionism. Roosevelt, however, when reelected, slowed the movement for support, fearing loss of Arab enthusiasm for winning World War II. The issue remained in suspense for four more years, while the story of the fate of Jews, denied existence in Europe or a homeland in Palestine, was revealed.

Solomon Freehof, after the experience with Beth Israel in Houston, tried to make psychological sense of things. Why did Jews oppose each other so vehemently at the moment when unity was both urgent and possible? He gave his analysis at the 1944 convention: "We knew that millions were going to their death and we were powerless to aid. We have failed our brothers at the time of their greatest need." The result? "All this induced in us a profound sense of frustration which has embittered us more than we can ever realize and is perhaps the cause, certainly it is the spur of our own wild fury at each other." Therefore: "We lash out against each other in the helpless rage typical of those who must admit their futility." 4:6

"We have failed our brothers." Freehof was referring, of course, to the experience of the previous ten years in Hitler's Germany and then expansively through much of Europe—the move toward the extinction of Jews. Hitler wanted a "Judenfrei" Germany, a nation free of Jews. He and his colleagues, moved by demonic passions, harassed Jews, deprived them of liberties, ruined their businesses, attacked their synagogues, rounded them up in concentration camps, and began the systematic program of killing them. The most visible incident before the war was Kristallnacht, November 7, 1938, which was an attack on Jewish property, espe- 4:7

cially synagogues. The Christian press was alert and commented for its readers. Thus the Swedish-American magazine the *Lutheran Companion:* "The recent brutal attacks on Jewish lives and property in Germany were described by Dr. Goebbels [Hitler's aide] as 'typical, spontaneous, popular demonstrations.' " The Lutheran editor disagreed: "We do not believe it. They bear the earmarks of official Nazi planning and constitute a deliberate act of government policy." Then came what later looked like wishful thinking: "They do not reflect the spirit of the German people."

4:8   The liberal *Christian Century* magazine, later much on the spot for having given more attention than any other outlet to the Nazi persecution of the Jews but failing to promote counteraction, editorialized at the same time: "Type will not carry the sense of horror and consternation with which the world reacts to the latest outburst of Nazi violence against the Jews." Like the Lutheran editor, it pondered what Kristallnacht revealed about the German people: "The Germans are not an undisciplined people. They riot only when they are instructed to riot." But the same editors, still stung by what they considered misuse of distorted atrocity stories about Germany in World War I and still eager to prevent American entry as World War II loomed, did not know what to recommend. "With respect to the specific Jewish problem created by German inhumanity, this editorial, therefore, seems to end in a blind alley." In "bafflement" they meandered on: "Meantime the solution of the deeper and universal problem of anti-Semitism rests, we hold, with the Christian Church, and with the Jewish people themselves. Democracy cannot solve this deeper problem. Perhaps religion can."

4:9   The situation for Jews only grew worse as Hitler attacked Poland in 1939 and the Allies responded. The "Jewish problem" became only one of many in the minds of the Allies. As one turns the pages of the secular and religious press, meanwhile attempting to empty the mind of knowledge acquired later about outcomes, it is almost eerie to see how editors reported, quietly at first and then with terror and numbness, on what was later seen as a horror beyond the scope of their imaginings. Charles Clayton Morrison of the *Christian Century* makes the best subject for observation. One year into the war he attempted a summary: "Beyond doubt, horrible things are happening to the Jews in Poland. It is even probable that the Nazis are herding all the Jews of Europe, so far as they can capture them, into Poland with the deliberate intention of exterminating them there." He remembered a Nazi leader telling one of the magazine's staff members in perfectly clear English that the Germans were planning the "humane extermination" of the Jews.

Some Christian groups paid for advertisements to draw atten-   4:10
tion to the evil and solicit support. As early as the week of Pearl Harbor, a Friends of Israel Refugee Relief Committee advertised in the *Presbyterian:* "FOR NINE MILLION JEWS LIFE APPEARS HOPE-LESS . . . LIFE FOR THE JEW IS IMPOSSIBLE under the NAZI regime." The Friends, who were raising money for refugees, added: "Thousands of Jews are in Concentration Camps dying inch by inch. Over One Hundred Thousand Committed Suicide. Over 200,000 Have Been Murdered or Died." Fundamentalist Protestants, friends of Zionism because they believed for their own reasons that Israel should become a state, also spread the word and made appeals. In 1942 the *Watchman-Examiner,* the very magazine that had chosen and, in effect, patented, the name "Fundamentalist" in 1920, reprinted a letter to the Baptist World Alliance from England's chief rabbi, J. H. Hertz: "Destruction, total and irretrievable, is overhanging Israel in Europe. A sentence of death has been pronounced upon the entire Jewish population on the Continent, and—by machine gun and poison chamber, by torture and famine—millions of my brethren have already fallen victims of the Nazi fury." He asked for sympathy, prayers, and support.

In April 1942, the United States and Great Britain held a con-   4:11
ference in Bermuda, ostensibly to discuss the issue of refugees but actually to relieve the growing pressure on both governments to do something, anything. Press coverage was limited, but after twelve days it was clear that neither nation had come up with much. As British delegate Richard Law saw it, the whole event turned out to have been a "facade for inaction." Jews were understandably angry. Rabbi Wise termed the event "sad and sordid." A Committee for a Jewish Army advertised in the *New York Times:* "To 5,000,000 Jews in the Nazi Death-Trap Bermuda Was a 'Cruel Mockery.'" Jewish commentators mourned the indifference and hardness of heart of the nations. Protestant thinker Reinhold Niebuhr and other Christians advised President Roosevelt that "wise and well informed" Jewish leaders had fallen into "deep pessimism."

In a bizarre turn, that autumn, in the *Christian Century,* Morri-   4:12
son resumed a feud with Stephen Wise as the rabbi was attacking the United States State Department for inactivity. It all began as a fight over numbers. Wise charged that Hitler was out to kill all

Jews in Nazi-ruled Europe within the year. The exiled Polish government meanwhile spread the word that only half the Jews of Poland were targeted during that time and that 250,000 had been killed through September. Morrison did not trust Wise's statistics or their source and did not agree with Wise's campaign for the total destruction of Germany. That notion did violence to Morrison's chosen policy of restraint in reaction to reports of atrocities, a follow-up to his earlier near-pacifism. The editor's flourish was aimed to end debate: "Dr. Wise's allegation that Hitler is paying $20 each for Jewish corpses to be 'processed into soap fats and fertilizer' is unpleasantly reminiscent of the 'cadaver factory' lie which was one of the propaganda triumphs of the First World War."

4:13   Wise was positioned to get inside information from a faction in the State Deparment who feared that the rabbi "might put up a kick" if they did not keep him informed. Undersecretary of State Sumner Welles phoned Wise with a request not to release unconfirmed inside information. The State Department was dragging its feet, lacking a policy for refugees and not wanting to have their plight overpublicized. But on November 24 Welles summoned Wise and handed over documents from the Swiss legation: "I regret to tell you, Dr. Wise, that these confirm and justify your deepest fears," and added, "There is no exaggeration." That day Wise held the press conference that inspired Morrison's reaction. Wise became furious about the *Christian Century*'s expression of doubts. "It would appear that you are more interested in seeking to prove that figures which I gave out in the name of five important Jewish organizations of America are inaccurate in respect to Jewish mass massacres in the Hitler-occupied countries than you are in making clear to American Christians how unspeakable has been the conduct of Hitlerism against the Jewish people." Wise accused the Protestant magazine of showing "a frankly or disguisedly anti-Jewish attitude"; was this part of "a personal Judeophobia on the part of the editor" or editorial board policy?

4:14   On one level, Morrison's approach can be seen as intervention in Jewish affairs. He sided with the Reform rabbis he knew well and favored, those who were forming the new American Council for Judaism, the nemesis of Wise. Wise, in turn, claimed to have discussed the feud with Christian ministers. They felt Morrison's article "reflected the subconscious desire not so much to express compassion for the victims of Hitlerism as to shield Hitler from the consequences of his crime." Then came a theological dig: why was

the magazine so "spiritually unconcerned about the tragic fate of
the people whose gift to the world you purport to revere and worship"? Morrison responded to only one feature of the attack. He
claimed he had checked with his sources in the State Department.
They had replied "not for publication" but "through an accredited
officer" that government files did not support Dr. Wise's contentions. It turns out that just as Jews and Christians were divided
within their own camps, so it was with the State Department,
whose differing elements had reasons either to maximize or to
minimize stories of Jewish suffering. Wise and Morrison broke relations. A month later the *Christian Century* editorialized: Americans stood appalled over reports of the atrocities, mainly against
Jews. But what should they do? "They feel that signing 'protests'
is too cheap and ineffectual a way to register their indignation;
many are taking out their sense of frustration by registering their
determination to see that punishment is meted out after the war to
those guilty of such barbarities." Otherwise there was not much to
do except to seek early victory over Germany, so that "this gigantic
crime can be stopped and the criminals punished." Morrison was
clear: "Extermination of a race has seldom, if ever, been so systematically practiced on a grand scale as in the present mass murder
of Polish Jews by the Nazi power."

All American Christians who spoke up seemed as baffled as   4:15
Jews were ("we were powerless," "we have failed our brothers")
and as Morrison was, but not all shared the latter's distracting concerns about World War I atrocity stories and the possible exaggeration of Jewish misery. Henry A. Atkinson, the general secretary of
the Church Peace Union, was calling on the American churches
"in the name of our Lord, our religion and suffering humanity" to
"denounce these crimes against the Jews as major crimes against
our common humanity." He urged quick acceptance of refugees
into the United States and Allied countries. The Federal Council
of Churches in its biennial meeting in December 1942 saw Germany's policy to be one of "deliberate extermination" and "incredible cruelties" and resolved "to do our full part in establishing
conditions in which such treatment of the Jews shall end." Christians should also work to improve relations with Jews at home. In
early 1943 "tangible evidence was given of genuine concern of
Christians to work with their Jewish fellow-citizens for justice for
all the people of Israel." But a council-called Day of Compassion
on May 2, 1943, was a total failure. The council sent letters to
70,000 ministers, urging support by their congregations. Notables

made proclamations and newspapers gave publicity to the venture, but in many cities not a single congregation responded. In New York it was a "complete fiasco," as a letter to the editor put it. One rabbi had occupied a Christian pulpit that day, and the writer's own little Unitarian church in Brooklyn had observed the occasion. The *Christian Century* that same spring did begin to urge action, citing Britain's chief rabbi as being "fully justified in pressing home on the British, American and Russian governments his demand that something shall be done." The British announced readiness to allow a contingent of 35,000 Jews, many if not most of them children, to move from the Balkans to Palestine. That was a start, but "only a start toward the full effort which will be required to save Europe's still surviving Jews from extermination."

4:16   The National Conference of Christians and Jews more than any other organization in the interwar period advanced the moves of Jews to become central in American religious life. Where was the conference now? asked Rabbi Israel Goldstein, president of the Synagogue Council of America. "How can an organization whose program is brotherhood, exclude from its sphere of concern . . . the dying gasp of European Jewry?" President Everett R. Clinchy responded that his conference's Religious News Service was giving the theme publicity and wanted to promote joint church and synagogue action but had not much more to offer than had the rabbinical associations, the Federal Council of Churches, or the pro-Zionist fundamentalists.

4:17   In the summer of 1944, when the Russians liberated the first of the camps at Majdanek near Poland's Lublin, thirty American journalists were invited to witness the scene. "No atrocity story of the year is likely to top the latest concerning the alleged killing of 1,500,000 persons at the German concentration camp near Lublin, Poland," wrote *Christian Century* editors. But they again downplayed the event because of what they saw to be its parallelism to First World War atrocity stories—even though the magazine had done extensive sympathetic reporting of events that made Lublin's 1,500,000 dead credible. The liberation of the major camp at Auschwitz occurred in January 1945, near the end of the European war; Buchenwald and others followed. The time had come to begin talking about rebuilding Europe. The *Christian Century* editors understood why surviving Jews wanted a voice: "The Jews have been so victimized, persecuted, knocked about that it is to be expected that they would wish in every possible way to protect their position in the postwar world." Finally editor Morrison found himself on the scene, after which he wrote "Gazing into the Pit." He found it "almost physically impossible to write" about what he saw. "What can be said that will not seem like tossing little words up against a giant mountain of ineradicable evil?" He had "found it hard to believe that the reports from the Nazi concentration camps could be true." The editor revealed much about a state of mind: "Almost desperately we have tried to think that they must be wildly exaggerated." He had resisted them as products of fevered revenge-seekers or atrocity-mongers. "But such puny barricades cannot stand up against the terrible facts. The evidence is too conclusive." Long would Morrison see in his mind's eye the pictures of naked corpses piled like firewood. "The thing is well-nigh incredible," yet it happened. This was "the horror of humanity itself when it has surrendered to its capacity for evil." He went on: we are "looking into the very pit of hell which men disclose yawning within themselves when they reject the authority of the moral law, when they deny the sacredness of human personality, when they turn from the worship of the one true God to the worship of their own wills, their own states, their own lust for power."

Protestant Fundamentalists, who backed Zionism, gave a theo-   4:18
logical interpretation of events that was friendly to Israel but that no Jew could accept. The *Watchman-Examiner,* three months after the end of the war, wrote on "the Jewish problem." The editor favored Palestine as the place for Jewish exiles and stated a rationale: "Jewish sufferings of the past few years will in the end prove divine compulsions driving an apostate people out of their ghettos in order that they might ultimately arrive in the land which God originally gave to their fathers." Concerning the Jew as apostate: "While he is out of his own land and unconverted, the Jew is a stumbling block to the Gentiles. It is the purpose of God, and not any international act of the Jews themselves, which has made Israel—as the nation which has most definitely rejected Christ—a token to other nations."

What could American Christians and Jews have done through-   4:19
out the war? No one argued against the notion that a quick end to the war would have helped most. But through it all there were questions about aid to refugees and places of refuge, with Palestine being both strategically and symbolically most valid. During the Depression before the war, and after the anti-immigration legislation of 1924, it was hard to promote successfully the cause of welcoming more Jews. During the war many feared the return of economic depression and unemployment and hence resisted

immigration. In 1939 two-thirds of polled Americans opposed a single exception that would have allowed 10,000 refugee children to exceed quota limits. In 1943 78 percent thought it a bad idea "to let more immigrants come into this country after the war." Politicians would have been hard pressed to get support for a change in policy, and church advocacy was too weak to build up any pressure.

4:20   Crying over spilt blood and mountains of human ashes was a natural and profoundly humane thing to do, but now the world and especially America, home to so many Jews, had to go beyond weeping and look for practical addresses to the situation. That meant, among other things, looking to Zionism. Christian fundamentalists were ready to support Zionism, but liberals were more ambivalent, when not hostile. The old issue of "particularism," among others, haunted them, as it always does those who do not notice their own particularisms or are convinced they see excesses in others. The *Christian Century* was typically in a quandary. Why should it be taken for granted "that all the Jews who are snatched from the grasp of Hitler and his tortures be taken to Palestine"? it asked in 1943. Even the most convinced Zionists should not want the lives of "these helpless ones to be used to prejudice the future adjudication of the Palestine question." But where then should the refugees go? The editors mentioned no permanent place, such as Israel would be. "There are many other temporary places of refuge available, in Russia, in the Near East and in North Africa" or, "at a pinch, perhaps even in the United States."

5

"The War Is Crucial for the Future of the Negro"

When the Reverend Harry Emerson Fosdick of New York 5:1
wanted to advertise improved relations between American peoples
in 1944, he described an event of reconciliation, a dinner involving
"Catholics, Protestants, Jews and Negroes." Most citizens then
regarded the first two of these as religious groups, the third as religious and racial, and the fourth as—what? Most African Americans—then called Negroes by those who would not insult them—
were Protestants, a few were Catholics, and some were religiously
unidentified. In daily life they were seen as a racial group, when
they were seen by others at all. Seeing by such others was difficult
because most were segregated in the rural and urban South and
in the metropolitan North. The war meant upheaval: millions of
blacks relocated, to be near war production sites and other urban
places that offered some opportunity. Many others served in the
military. If Jews had problems of "particularism" as they moved
toward the center of American life, blacks were not even permitted
much of a move in the first place. They were seen as doomed to be
nothing but particular in the eyes of nonblacks. Segregation pre-
dominated in the armed forces—that story belongs to military history more than religious—while moves toward civilian integration
of race in that wartime decade were few and frustrating. The story
of Negro community and religious life during the war is inade-
quately told in statistics of population change or chronicles of the

65

effects of mobility and migration. Fortunately, two major reckon-
ings from these years, one by a European visitor and another by
two Americans, provide a glimpse of life among the millions of
Americans who were regarded as outsiders, at the margins, exempt
from or to be thrown off by the centripetal forces that were pulling
"Catholics, Protestants, Jews" into wartime intercourse.

5:2   In 1944 sociologist Gunnar Myrdal, heading a Swedish team,
turned in a landmark two-volume report, *An American Dilemma:
The Negro Problem and Modern Democracy.* The classic was an
early warning signal of changes long overdue but not much addressed until the Supreme Court's *Brown v. Board of Education*
decision against "separate but equal schooling" that was handed
down in 1954, and the subsequent civil rights movement. Meanwhile, Myrdal and his team showed how separate but unequal the
life of the races in America had turned out to be. In a foreword,
F. P. Keppel of the Carnegie Corporation, which sponsored the
study, told of the report's prewar roots. Back in 1937 "no one (except possibly Adolf Hitler) could have foreseen that it would be
made public at a day when the place of the Negro in our American life would be the subject of greatly heightened interest in the
United States." The war had made it relevant; "the eyes of men of
all races the world over" were turned upon America to see how the
most powerful people of the United Nations were dealing *at home*
with the major problem of race relations.

5:3   Myrdal, writing in Stockholm in 1942, showed he had acquired
perspective on the United States and its history. After thanking
the many who had helped produce the 15,000 pages of typescript
that he had compressed, he reached for italics: *"Not since Reconstruction has there been more reason to anticipate fundamental
changes in American race relations, changes which will involve a
development toward the American ideals."* Conscious of the wartime scene, he knew that blacks were "not optimistic as to what its
significance for them would be. They knew that the democratic war
aims were not meant for them." Myrdal then cast the story inter-
nationally. "The democratic ideology stimulated by the War and
the heroic example of the colored peoples" of China, the Philip-
pines, and elsewhere "outweighed the emphasis upon 'wartime
unity and harmony' " and offered the Negro at least some attention
by whites in the North. "These same things made the Negro want
to protest more," so "Negro protest has risen higher than ever."
Then more italics: *"This War, when and if it is won, and its sour*

*aftermath will act like the First World War did—as a great shock
to the Negro people and as a stimulant to their protest."*
    At the end of the report Myrdal was still connecting its plot with   5:4
the war. "This War is crucial for the future of the Negro, and the
Negro problem is crucial in the War." No one could foresee the
details of the redefining that would follow. "Social trends" had to
do with *"what is in white people's minds,"* and these implied the
need for *"changes in people's beliefs and valuations."* An old
race-based caste system lingered after it had no ideological support among the informed. *"The gradual destruction of the popular theory behind race prejudice is the most important of all
social trends in the field of interracial relations."* And a warning:
*"America can never more regard its Negroes as a patient, submis-
sive minority."* In one of the most bitter as well as most honest lines
in the report, Myrdal pictured "a young Negro, about to be inducted into the Army," who said, "Just carve on my tombstone,
'Here lies a black man killed fighting a yellow man for the protection of a white man.'" Despite such understandable expressions of
bitterness, Negroes were loyal. The American Constitution meant
more to them than to their white compatriots. They were more
unreservedly antifascist. As races clashed meanwhile, the situation was grave, but "there is not going to be civil war, of course."
The conservative white Southerner himself could be won over to
equalitarian reforms, thought the Swede in a hopeful moment:
*"America is free to choose whether the Negro shall remain her
liability or become her opportunity."*
    "The Negro Church" interested Myrdal and company as it   5:5
would anyone who wanted to understand power in the black community, where it was a central creation, yet it was often seen by
restless and progressive leaders as a refuge from assertive roles.
Myrdal lumped church and school and press together, not as "agencies of power for the Negro caste" but as agencies "of importance
to the power relations within the Negro community and between
Negroes and whites," though they were often overlooked. Churches
brought blacks together for common causes and trained them
for concerted action, while providing an organized followership.
"These institutions sometimes take action themselves in the power
field" but also help Negroes relate with others "more directly concerned with power problems." These churches were run exclusively by blacks; they were "interracial institutions" as some secular ones were. They were products of the caste system, and as such

had become "one of the chief organs for the Negro protest." Myrdal hurried past the religious, educational, and cultural aspects of
their activity, subjects of interest to the social historian, to come at
once to our topic, "power and power relations."

5:6   In the South the Negro churches could not even by World War II
lead black opposition to the caste system, but they promoted solidarity and helped ease the worst sufferings. In the North, more
independently, they could work for freedom and find a place in
local politics. Myrdal pointed to Abyssinian Baptist Church in
Harlem, by far the country's largest individual Negro congregation, to show how some churches had "taken the lead in expressing
to the world the Negroes' needs and protest." Such congregations
countered the image of the black church as being otherworldly—
as many Negro churches were. Myrdal liked to speak of the Negro
as "the exaggerated American," since he or she had to adhere to
common American patterns and do better within them. "Americans generally are a religious people; Southerners are more religious than the rest of the nation, and the Negroes, perhaps, still
a little more religious than white Southerners." More females than
males, more middle-aged and old than young, more uneducated
than educated, more lower and middle classes than upper classes
attended the churches. Just as some young Jews abandoned synagogues, so many young blacks were left cold by the "backwardness" of their churches. Yet membership conferred respectability,
and many turned to them as the years passed.

5:7   Statistics were inaccurate, but still helpful. In 1936 black
churches had claimed 5,660,618 members while whites claimed
50,146,748. This meant that blacks attracted 44 percent of their
population, while whites held only 42.4 percent of theirs. In addition, a relatively small minority of blacks were members of
largely white denominations. "America as a whole is still predominantly Protestant in spite of the 'new' immigration; southern
whites and Negroes are even more Protestant." The "low church
denominations with less formalized ritual" like Baptists and Methodists prospered. For his European readers Myrdal had to note
that American religion was more emotional than European: "The
South is somewhat extreme in this respect, too, and the Negroes
still more so." Beyond the emotional cast, he found few distinctions. "God and the angels are ordinarily white to Negroes, as
they are to white churchgoers." Sung spirituals differed somewhat
from other hymns. Denominational and congregational organization among both peoples was similar, though "the split into

miniature congregations is driven nearly to its limit in the Negro world"—witness the storefront churches in Harlem. A study in Chicago in 1938 found that such groups averaged but thirty members apiece, yet the tiny congregations also met needs and fostered community.

One great fact marked everything these "exaggerated Americans" experienced: segregation. "There is astonishingly little interracial cooperation" between churches, South and North. This created the moral dilemma. Author Myrdal cited sociologist Edwin R. Embree: "Segregation in Christian churches is an embarrassment. In a religion whose central teaching is brotherly love and the golden rule, preachers have to do a great deal of rationalizing as they expound their own gospel." Blacks pointed this out. Southern Christians kept the challenge of religious brotherhood off their minds. And white ministers elsewhere were watched lest they "start to draw practical conclusions from Christian doctrine that would favor the improvement of race relations." Blacks had come to terms with segregation; they did not like it, but now they had a vested interest in their own churches and suspected that movements of interracial cooperation would deprive their ministers of influence. They need not have worried, thought Myrdal. Catholics, Quakers, Congregationalists, Episcopalians, Christian Scientists, and others had all made ineffective efforts to attract blacks. "The great majority of white churches, in the North as well as in the South, thus do not want to have a substantial Negro membership," and vice versa. So "as usual the caste separation has been fortified by its own effects."   5:8

Power was Myrdal's theme, and he found the Negro church, adept at using power inside its own structures, weak in relations outside it. Leaders like Howard University president Mordecai Johnson made strong public impressions; many such leaders were Baptist ministers. So, "potentially, the Negro church is undoubtedly a power institution." Yet it was on the whole "passive in the field of intercaste power relations." The church, relatively inefficient and uninfluential, was thus in a deplorable but unsurprising situation. "Christian churches generally have, for the most part, conformed to the power situation of the time and the locality." Schisms and competition afflicted black churches, while low salaries kept talented and educated leaders from emerging, though once upon a time the church had been their outlet. Now "upper and middle class Negroes deprecate the common uneducated Negro preacher," and, Myrdal added, it was "difficult to see how the   5:9

continuing decline of the minister's prestige and leadership can be stopped." Unless there was radical reform in ministry, people would expect ever less of it. And there was an ideological lag. Black community leaders complained of the "timidity and disinterest on the part of the preachers." Back to italics: "*The Negro church fundamentally is an expression of the Negro community itself.*" As one changed, so would the other. If blacks wanted to be escapist, the leaders would readily be "timid and pussy-footing," but when the Negro community changed, the church would also change. The Negro church was thus part of the whole circular process now moving some American blacks onward in their struggle against caste. In summary: some trends were "making the Negro church a more efficient instrument for amelioration of the Negro's position," even as, ironically, they were reducing the relative importance of the church in the black community.

5:10   Myrdal's rhetoric was designed to persuade Americans to confront the dilemma of race, to face new issues of power, especially during wartime. Almost coincidentally, the Works Progress Administration of the New Deal and the Julius Rosenwald Fund, which meant Sears, Roebuck and Company earnings, subsidized an equally important but localized study. St. Clair Drake and Horace Cayton published the most extensive study yet of a metropolitan black community, including its churches, *Black Metropolis: A Study of Negro Life in a Northern City*. Novelist Richard Wright, introducing the book, identified with the authors in their notion that "Chicago is the city from which the most incisive and radical Negro thought has come"; it was a place filled with "extremes of possibility, death and hope." E. Franklin Frazier and a host of social scientists had thrown light on it. But, urged Wright, remember the underside: "Do not hold a light attitude toward the slums of Chicago's South Side. Remember that Hitler came out of such a slum! Remember that Chicago could be the Vienna of American Fascism!" If Chicago could not change and if conditions remained hopeless, then "the liberals, the intellectuals, the artists, the students, Communists, Socialists, New Dealers, all who hope for life and peace will lose to war."

5:11   If Myrdal spoke of a dilemma, Wright described a schism in the American soul and conscience. "The apex of white racial ideology was reached when it was assumed that white domination was a God-given right." White philosophers as important as John Dewey and William James only tried to allay the anxiety of moderns, but African Americans wanted substantive change. The American black, "child of the culture that crushes him, wants to be free in a way that white men are free." Wright expected the Drake and Cayton book to shock. "American whites and blacks both possess deep-seated resistances against the Negro problem being presented, even verbally, in all of its hideous fullness, in all of the totality of its meaning." Like Myrdal, Wright looked at religion. "The church in America," he said, "had shied from presenting this problem to the American people from a moral point of view, for fear that it would place itself in a position of having to do something about it." While the political left gyrated and squirmed to turn race into a class issue, the right worked to keep the Jim Crow culture of segregation alive. Everyone tried to change the problem into something they could control. How, the novelist asked, could readers not be moved toward action? Did they expect the black to "continue, as he does today, saying Job-like to the society that crushes him: Though it slays me, yet will I trust in it?" In his most searching lines, addressed to church leadership, Wright said: "Perhaps for the first time, we can see how the Negro has had to take Protestant religion and make it into something for his own special needs, needs born of an imposed Black Belt existence." And he left with questions worth quoting: "To what extent has racial religion replaced Christian religion in thousands of Black Belt churches? And what is wrong with religion in America that it has turned its back upon the Negro and his problem?" One more: "And to what degree is religion in America officially and ideologically identified with the policy of White Supremacy?"

Drake and Cayton visited all the corners of the black metropolis, including in their book a seventeen-page section on "The Grip of the Negro Church," one of the best mid-century portraits. "Grip" was a carefully chosen word. In Bronzeville, the authors' name for Chicago's black ghetto, the church was ostensibly religious, but people also wanted it to "advance the Race." With 500 churches and 200,000 members in thirty denominations, it seemed poised to do this. Most members had almost no face-to-face relations with white fellow believers. So theirs was, indeed, a "Race Church," a concept that confined and liberated at once. This was as true of the standard-brand Baptist majority as of the small churches that made race a theme: the Temple of Moorish Science, the African Orthodox Church, the Christian Catholics, and often in others thought of as "cults"—Holiness, Spiritualist, and Community churches. Only 10 percent of the churches and an even smaller percentage of church members were affiliated with predominantly

5:12

white denominations. Most of the buildings had been purchased from white churches and synagogues whose members abandoned them as they moved away from changing neighborhoods. The new congregations were heavily in debt and full of resentment over the high prices they felt they were forced to pay in Depression times.

5:13   The authors made careful studies of the quiet side of black church life and noted the use of their buildings by everyone from

Varieties of African-American religious experience included a range of worship settings from the ubiquitous storefront churches in the poorest communities, at left, to formal contexts in liturgical churches, such as this one at an Episcopal church in Chicago, Easter, 1941. (Reproduced from the Collections of the Library of Congress. Photos by Russell Lee.)

communist organizations and left-wing labor unions to American Legionnaires. But even the black newspapers gradually ignored this quiet side of Bronzeville community life. By World War II, "churches and preachers seldom make the front page unless some sensational incident is involved." Drake and Cayton noticed, as Myrdal did, that these churches collected more funds than any other black voluntary organizations, a fact resented by many, and that at the same time they suffered competition from secular organizations. The coauthors brought up the grumblers' sometimes self-contradictory complaints: the church, said some, was a racket. There were too many churches, and they were too emotional. Ministers did not practice what they preached. Most of the criticisms had to do with finances and with preachers as fund-raisers and users. For all the rightful attacks on them, however, the clergy did retain loyalties in general, even though a good deal of switching between congregations and denominations took place. Drake and Cayton, with their reductionist worldview, found little religion or theology in church participation. People liked entertainment, the authors thought, along with good singing, good speaking, "restful and beautiful" worship. "Preachers who can flay sin in an original manner, who can denounce iniquity with a 'knowing' air and with some sexual innuendo, attract large crowds." So did concerts, pageants, plays, suppers, and other congregationally sponsored events. But the main reason for belonging—the authors did not say how they knew—was that it gave opportunity for "large masses of people to function in an organized group, to compete for prestige, to be elected to office, to exercise power and control, to win applause and acclaim."

5:14   Despite the best efforts of preachers, there was backsliding, discontent, indifference, and hostility; one section of the Drake and Cayton chapter spoke of "revolt against Heaven." "Bronzeville is in revolt against Heaven, and the rebellion centers in the lower class." The vitriolic attacks against ministers were "part of the general secularization of life in the urban, industrial society." No one was yet talking about a "revival of religion," but there was also little "frank and open atheism." The backsliders had several places to go. Some went "good-timing," others to racial causes which they turned into religion, still others to communism, and a fourth group to labor unions. Working to "get ahead" looked quasi-religious to Drake and Cayton. The presuppositions of the authors may have colored their conclusion that the rhetoric of religion often disguised the grand theme: "advancing the Race." But they did elevate a theme that had been neglected in earlier studies of the passive-looking black churches.

"Advancing the Race" was an important theme in World War II.   5:15
The authors spotted a few blacks who were so alienated that they were pro-Japanese; some of these were among the "Moors" who made racial identification with nonwhites. They called themselves "Asiatics" over against "Europeans." The vast majority joined the war effort, in the spirit of heavyweight champion Joe Louis: "There's a lot wrong with this country, but Hitler can't fix it." But they remained nervous: would blacks be better off for their patriotism, efforts, and sacrifice? The authors of *Black Metropolis* saw limits to revolt. They did not envision outbursts like the "Black Zionism" of Marcus Garvey's "Back to Africa" movement after World War I. Garvey had never been popular in Chicago, and during the war many ridiculed the notion of going back to Africa. "There ain't no boulevards in Africa!" said an interviewed lounger at a barbershop. During the war, Americans came to speak of the "Four Freedoms." Now blacks were helping liberate people "from Fascism abroad and they were expecting to be liberated from Jim-Crow at home. For them this was a Fifth Freedom as precious as the other four." The authors ended the book ominously: "The problems that arise on Bronzeville's Forty-seventh Street encircle the globe." Then: "A victory for Fascism in Midwest Metropolis will sound the knell of doom for the Common Man everywhere."

6

"A Jap's a Jap"

6:1   The wartime alliances within the nation of various races and religious groups against common enemies pulled ever larger numbers of people into confluence. Jews, long outsiders, were tugged in, even if uncertainties remained over questions like the settling of European Jewish refugees or support for Zionism. African Americans were needed and welcomed in the war effort, but residentially and religiously they remained largely segregated. They moved, as it were, in a track parallel to that of white Americans. The strategic alliances of war therefore were not of the sort that helped America complete the dream of those who wished to stress the "One Nation" motif. A similar case could be made concerning Native Americans or Hispanic/Latino Americans as well. They were people needed by the larger coalition of American peoples to prosecute the war, but this did not make them acceptable to the powers of the populace in the larger culture. But one set of people was forced to move entirely apart from all the others: Japanese Americans. The United States was fighting Germany and Italy, but Americans of German or Italian descent did not suffer rounding up and imprisonment. Yet while fighting Japan, citizens did little to protest a government policy that, in retrospect, came to be regarded as the most reprehensible on the home front in wartime, and led to the internment of 70,000 Japanese Americans in what they and their supporters called concentration camps, in the western states.

76

The public press by and large promoted the institution of such   6:2
camps and the incarceration of citizens of Japanese ancestry. Salty
Hearst columnist Henry McLemore on January 29, 1942, spewed:
"I am for immediate removal of every Japanese on the West Coast
to a point deep in the interior. I don't mean a nice part of the interior
either. Herd 'em up, pack 'em off and give them the inside room in
the badlands. Let 'em be pinched, hurt, hungry and dead up against
it." In case his subtleties were lost on readers, McLemore added,
"Personally, I hate the Japanese. And that goes for all of them."
Father Hugh T. Lavery of a Maryknoll Center orphanage in Los
Angeles asked how *Japanese* would be defined: what about children who were only one-fourth Japanese? A military officer in
charge of some of the operation, Major Karl R. Bendetsen, answered: "I am determined that if they have one drop of Japanese
blood in them, they must go to camp." And California attorney
general Earl Warren, arguing for the roundup, spoke in overtly racist terms: "We believe that when we are dealing with the Caucasian
race we have methods that will test the loyalty of them." Germans
and Italians were easily tested. "But when we deal with the Japanese we are in an entirely different field and we cannot form any
opinion that we believe to be sound."

If the Jewish scene can be covered by notice of rabbinical as-   6:3
semblies and magazine editorials, or the black circumstance addressed by recall of reports dealing with a metropolis, the less
familiar Japanese case is best opened by attention to the personal
hurt of two people. Josef Stalin said that the death of one person
was a tragedy; the death of a million, a statistic. A minister of
my acquaintance, the late Jitsuo Morikawa, through his biographical record, will serve as one of the two to represent this wartime
tragedy.

A third of a century before the war, in 1907, Jitsuo's father had   6:4
migrated from Japan via Hawaii to Vancouver Island in Canada.
Jitsuo was born in 1911 in British Columbia to a mother who
committed suicide when he was a year old. She was a victim of
postpartum psychosis and dread of exploitative bill-collectors. A
stepmother helped the family survive the Depression in rural Canada. Morikawa's biographer printed a picture of the farmhouse and
captioned it with words that matched the experience of tens of
thousands: "This is the farm and home with all its furnishings that
[Dad] and the family lost, a dream of a lifetime representing years
of sweat, tears and hard labor." What the Depression and the ex-
ploiters could not ruin, Canada did: "Everything seized, . . . every

hard earned earthly possession confiscated by the government of Canada following Japan's bombing of Pearl Harbor in Hawaii on December 7, 1941."

6:5   An order to "liquidate, sell or otherwise dispose of such property" was disguised under a label to the Custodian of Enemy Property, "For safe keeping." The senior Morikawa was too ashamed to admit how small the pittance for his property was. Jitsuo made his way to the United States, remembering his Buddhist family, living far from shrines. In the home had been a *kamidana,* a god-shelf where Buddhist and Shinto images reposed until a brother who craved assimilation removed it. Gradually the brothers made a move to Christianity, inspired by the example of admired adults. Jitsuo joined what would later have been called a fundamentalist Baptist church and was pressed toward ministry by a pastor he did not much admire. Surrounded by a community of non-Japanese, the young man learned to adapt and then wanted to convert others. His father and his Buddhist friends resisted this *baka* or fool of a son or companion that they had lost to *Yasoko,* a despised term for Christianity. But father and son worked in relative harmony as Jitsuo dreamed of the city. One evening the father blurted: "Jitsuo, I know you want to go to school. If that's still your wish you're free to go, but you must understand there will be no help from home." There was not. Morikawa headed for the fundamentalist Bible Institute of Los Angeles and thence to the giant Southern Baptist Theological Seminary in Louisville. He was ordained in 1937. At Louisville he became a friend of Clarence Jordan, later the founder of Koinonia Farm in Georgia, and others in the advance guard of seminarians who would improve race relations.

6:6   Morikawa acquired a United States visa in 1940, thanks to some pullers of strings who knew how to work around immigration restrictions that had been set against Japanese in 1924. Now he *belonged* in the United States, and he set out to minister in three American Baptist mission churches in Los Angeles. There he married Hazel Takii, who came from a more aristocratic line, indeed, from the *samurai* class. The couple had no time for a honeymoon after the September day in 1941 when they were married. Like so many other Japanese Americans, the Morikawas made a home in a West Coast America that was not eager to welcome them. Only seventy-seven days after the wedding, Japan, no more their country than was Ireland for the Irish Americans or Germany for the German Americans, bombed Pearl Harbor. The Morikawas were interrupted at a bridge on their way to church. Hazel remembered, "America was in panic, and we were abruptly made both perpetrators and victims." She read the situation: "Our lives were ruptured as repeated acts of repression came swiftly in relentless succession." At once they were branded pariahs. "In our own country we watched in utter disbelief our freedom and rights literally stripped from us." They felt the hate of governmental, business, and political forces; these "wanted to get rid of us."

Attorney General Earl Warren, with an eye on the governor's   6:7
chair, advanced the legal theory that "since not a single Japanese American had so far committed any disloyalty, this was proof that they intended doing so in the future," as Matsumoto phrased it. The Justice Department, instead of defending the people, pushed decision off on the military. The secretary of war did not mention religion or race hatred, just military necessity. On February 19, 1942, President Roosevelt issued Executive Order 9066. While 73 percent of the people subsequently rounded up were American citizens, now called "non-aliens," they were moved as aliens to an "Assembly Center" and thence to war relocation centers. The Morikawas all but memorized the testimony of General John L. DeWitt, who carried out the order, to a Congressional committee. "A Jap's a Jap. They are a dangerous element," and "there is no way to determine their loyalty." Of each, he added, "it makes no difference whether he is an American citizen; theoretically he is still a Japanese and you can't change him." Morikawa's church members were fishers who lost their licenses and were detained while their wives had to dispose of gear and goods to scavengers. But in that sad time Christian organizations, those of American Baptists preeminently, came forward to help, despite the presence everywhere of probing Federal Bureau of Investigation agents and a growing network of restrictions.

The Morikawas soon became Family No. 34412 and were sent   6:8
to a desert north of Phoenix, where temperatures would reach 120 degrees. They could take only what their hands could carry; everything was stamped No. 34412. At Poston, a Colorado River relocation center, they made their movements in the face of guns and were forced to take the fetal posture to show they were nonresistant. Block 35, Barracks 2A, a tarpaper shack, became their bare one-room home, where sand sifted onto their straw mattresses in an apartment where privacy was absent. There were no shower stalls or doors on women's toilets. Winter was cruel. "The consti-

tutional separation of church and state, because Poston was under
federal jurisdiction, made it necessary for Jitsuo to be compensated
by the denomination," he remembered, and he was paid $17 a
month for his ministerial service. But "being deprived of 'things'
brought greater meaning to spiritual values and made possible a
time of introspection and discovery," he also recalled. "Christians
found they could still pray and worship, and in doing so, found that
furniture and special buildings were not essential." They replicated
in miniature what people in military chaplaincy at large learned.
Denominational differences meant little, and Christians worked together as one. More than that, as Jitsuo later remembered: "The
Christians, together with the Buddhists, proposed conducting a
community-wide daily vacation school for all children," and 800
came to the Christian part in the summer's heat. So the war also
worked unitive effects among those cast aside. Hazel Morikawa
wrote years later: "Many have never since known the depth of this
profound desert experience."

6:9   Ministry was all-consuming for Morikawa and other ministers
who were Nisei, offspring of Japanese immigrants to America.
Despite government discouragement, Christians offered materials,
Bibles, and the like, and Baptist friends came through with bi-
cycles and a piano. "The reassuring love of the denomination
reached us all during our stay behind barbed wires giving us the
support we needed." No wonder the very independent-thinking
Morikawa remained a critical but consistently loyal member of the
American Baptist denomination throughout his life. As the war
progressed, he took part in efforts, sometimes successful, to see
that students were removed from the camp and placed in colleges.
A study leave took him to Minnesota, where he learned, while he
stayed with a denominational executive and his wife, that hate was
portable beyond the West Coast. The couple was harassed with
unpleasant calls from neighbors "accusing them of disloyalty for
entertaining a 'Jap.'" Such incidents left scars, what Morikawa
called a "repressed psychic wound," as "displaced persons kept in
darkness" came toward release and were having to look into the
bright light of day. After the war Jitsuo became part of a racially
integrated congregation on Chicago's South Side, where he was
soon preaching to students like John Cobb, later a preeminent theologian, and professors like Markus Barth, son of the great Swiss
thinker Karl Barth. For twenty years he also served American
Baptist National Ministries and was even an interim pastor at Riverside Church in New York, where Harry Emerson Fosdick had

Famed documentary photographer Dorothea Lange photographed the Manzanar
Relocation Center in California; her camera also captured the image of little girls
pledging allegiance at Rafael Weill Elementary School in San Francisco, April 20,
1942, shortly before they evacuated to camps like the one at Manzanar. (Courtesy
of the National Archives.)

once preached, before concluding ministry in Ann Arbor, Michigan. The "psychic wounds" of the war years marked him, but "the bright light of day" in cooperative ministries won out.

Toro Matsumoto, another camp survivor, got to tell his story the   6:10
year after the war in *Beyond Prejudice*. A Reformed Church in

America pastor, he had trained at Meiji Gakuin, a Christian school in Tokyo, and Union Theological Seminary in New York, before he was ordained in 1944. Interned for eleven months, he served on a Federal Council of Churches commission, a Committee on Friendly Relations among Foreign Students, and the Japanese Student Christian Association of North America. His book makes clear that Pearl Harbor was at least as traumatic an event for Matsumoto as it was for other Americans. He told of pastor Thomas J. Machida, who decided to preach at West Seattle Methodist Church on Pearl Harbor night, "as though nothing had happened." The topic was "Walking in the Light with Christian Brotherhood." But brotherhood ties suffered as Matsumoto and Machida and Morikawa and all the rest were rounded up. The Federal Council of Churches reacted with an appeal whose first paragraph had an ironic sound: "We are gratified to observe that the agents of our government are dealing with [the Japanese Americans] with consideration" during a time when church people had to maintain "Christian composure and charity." None of that helped when the federal government made its inconsiderate arrests.

6:11   Some West Coast non-Japanese Christians stood against the tide of prejudice and supported Japanese Americans, Christian or not. Matsumoto told of the Reverend Everett W. Thompson, ex-missionary to Japan, who reported that Christian grocers in Seattle had donated food. Those who spoke Japanese served as interpreters, and others helped with legal matters. A Protestant Church Commission for Japanese Service set up shop in San Francisco and tried to get the government at least to establish selective and more nearly fair evacuation policies. But General DeWitt was unmoved, and evacuation remained wholesale. Not until the damage had been done did Congressman John H. Tolan of the House Defense Migration Investigating Committee express regrets. He understood that the evacuation of citizens, the trampling on constitutional rights, disrupted the morale of vast groups of citizens and recent immigrants. He tried out the language of "One Nation": "America is great because she has transcended the difficulties inherent in a situation which finds all races, all nationalities, all colors, and all creeds within her borders. This breadth of vision must be applied to the present circumstances." Tolan did not win a hearing.

6:12   Matsumoto did record breakthroughs within the camps. At the Tulare Fair Grounds near Fresno, California, reported Charlotte and Royden Susu-Mago during internment, a Buddhist group asked the Reverend Raymond Schroth, a Quaker, to address them, and they then approached the Susu-Magos: might they not have a "union Buddhist-Christian service?" Elders were cautious, but the young leaped at the chance, and 2,500 people showed up, winning over the doubters. But Thompson also had to report the bad news: at "Camp Harmony" in Washington, "the Army made the rule that only three types of service would be held, Protestant, Catholic, and Buddhist, and asked the various denominations to cooperate to this end." The First Amendment constitutional clause on religious liberty was just one more of the terminated freedoms. As word spread, commuters between camps and the free world reported on confusions. Some young people were allowed to go to a summer camp, where one was asked, "Do you mean to say they put you, an American citizen, into a concentration camp?" She answered, "Yes, me and seventy thousand other American citizens." The Federal Council of Churches Home Mission Council tried to ease abrasions; at Christmas it sponsored "America's Biggest Christmas Party," and sent ahead 17,000 gifts. Matsumoto responded: "We know that the spirit of Christ lives on despite hatred and strife." That the Women's Federation, some of the Protestant churches in the area, and other Christian groups added their signatures to the response was not remarkable; that the minister of the Buddhist church signed on in thanks for "this expression of Christian brotherliness" was the novelty.

The Christian record contrasted with government policy, as   6:13 Matsumoto told of it. "Particularly restless was the Christian church. American Protestantism seldom speaks or acts as one body," but here "the churches agreed spontaneously and unanimously. Conservatives and liberals, pacifists and non-pacifists," and even "the *Christian Century* and *Christianity and Crisis* agreed!" on this one. The *Christian Century* spoke up almost weekly for Japanese Americans. The Federal Council of Churches talked up to the federal government: "Here in the United States," it charged, "we have an uneasy conscience because this policy savors of totalitarianism and discrimination," and enemies abroad could exploit the situation. Such agreements, editorials, and pronouncements were to no avail; America had a war to fight, even against its own. The effects of cooperative wartime action were felt more within the churches. At the Manzanar camp in California, according to the Reverend Abe, a Congregationalist, nine Protestant ministers, three Catholic priests, and four Buddhist priests formed a "federated church program" of a sort unthinkable outside the barbed wire. Government policy, of course, restricted the efforts to just three denominations. So Nichiren, Shinshu, Zen, and Kohya Buddhist bodies had to unite under War Relocation Authority, and this uniting contributed "to the harmony and morale of the camps." The groups held joint conferences and services for Nisei men killed in action—Nisei fighting for the country that was imprisoning their people. As for the future: "As we have maintained a federated church here at Manzanar, our members are ready to join a church of any denomination when they go out." Abe added an ecumenical flourish, the irony of which would have been noted by Japanese Americans: "How much freer we should feel if the churches in America were all united so that we could integrate fully into the life of the American churches!"

6:14   Thousands of stories parallel these two, all reinforcing the idea that even wartime could not make One Nation of one nation. Not only the government was at fault. The *Los Angeles Times* led the press battles, calling California after Pearl Harbor a "zone of danger." It asked "alert, keen-eyed civilians" to help spot "spies, saboteurs and fifth columnists," especially among Japanese Americans. So lofty a pundit as columnist Walter Lippmann came down from principle to pronounce the Pacific Coast a zone of danger and said he feared "a combined attack from within and from without." As a combat zone it could not tolerate anyone "who has not good reason for being there. There is plenty of room elsewhere for him to exercise his rights." As in an internment camp. And Edward R. Murrow, notable defender of civil rights for the Columbia Broadcasting System, told a Seattle audience on January 27, 1942: "I think it's probable that, if Seattle ever does get bombed, you will be able to look up and see some University of Washington sweaters on the boys doing the bombing!"

6:15   Morikawa and Matsumoto as Christians had enough difficulty in this climate; Buddhists were worse off, because their religion had often drawn subsidies from fellow believers in Japan. Their priests, often arrested first, were aliens and were regarded as such. The American Civil Liberties Union never lifted a hand to help, nor did the American Communist Party, which thought it was helping the Soviet Union by seeing Japanese Americans locked up. The Japanese American Citizens League lived in a momentary paradise of illusion because its leaders, intensely loyal to America, thought authorities would discriminate among Japanese Americans. They feared that dissent would make things worse, and they may have been right. They counseled meekness and might have helped ease steps toward reintegration after war. Buddhism survived. Just as in 1924 some non-Japanese Americans confused Buddhism with Shinto and "Mikado worship," now again guilt by association caused confusion, and ignorance hurt Buddhists. A California Joint Immigration representative in 1942 still contended that the religion of Japanese emperor worship kept them from adopting Americanism. And in Oregon a state senator further carried stigma over to Buddhists: "The Buddhist religion is looked on as a national Japanese custom," and that meant that "even among the children there isn't much social mixing between the Buddhists and the Christian children."

The North American Buddhist Mission tried to teach lessons   6:16 stressing separation of religion from race: "The suddenness and the unwarranted and inhumane attack upon these United States of America leave us, the Buddhists in America, with but one decision: the condemnation of that attack." Their condemning did no more good than their declaration of duty: "The loyalty to the United States which we have pledged at all times must now be placed into instant action for the defense of the United States of America." Their adherents destroyed Buddhist objects, hid family altars, and even burned some books, to no avail. The Oakland Buddhist Church spelled out what it was doing for the nation as it urged members to buy defense bonds and enroll in Defense Bond work or give time to the Red Cross. They gave parties when their sons were drafted and gifts to those in service. Some preached sermons on loyalty. They passed on a letter from the North American Buddhist Mission: "Respect the government of the United States and its laws and regulations; [strive] to hold fast to your religious faith in Buddhism and to be calm and collected at all times." Adherents should also "make all preparations within each Buddhist Church to be able to cope with problems arising from evacuation" and then prepare to evacuate.

Within Buddhism the war and camp experiences had unitive   6:17 effects. Various sects drew closer, and a Buddhist Brotherhood of America developed under the noses of the Lippmanns and Murrows. "Slowly but surely, a number of American students were absorbing Buddhist thought, and striving to practice the Buddhist philosophy in their daily living." No wonder that in a time of "stress and upheaval" they should unite "to carry the torch of Buddhism forward and on high. In this endeavor there can be no thought of discrimination in sect, race or color." And the Young Buddhist Association promoted an "all-sectarian" organization, as they worked to "diminish the identification of Buddhism strictly

with Japan." Buddhism had to learn American religious competition; thus the leaders had to notice events like one covered by
Newsweek—the baptism as Mormon of seven Nisei soldiers in the
U.S. Army. During resettlement Buddhists recaptured confidence
and in April 1944 organized a new Buddhist Churches of America,
drawing on six camps. That July at Salt Lake City delegates ratified
the plans and declared that there would be no ties with Japan. Here
was to be a fresh, attractive English-speaking Buddhism. Like
other ecumenical efforts, it did not win a clean sweep, but the Buddhist map was clarified, and a mission was ready for postwar
moves. In 1944, for instance, Chicago Buddhist Church and Midwest Buddhist Temple were founded in one city.

6:18   Outside the camps, some Christian leaders tried to shock. When
Congressman John H. Tolan's committee held hearings on the West
Coast as early as 1942, representatives of a number of hate groups
showed up, some of them urging extreme policies like sterilization.
In their face, Pastor Thompson of Seattle reminded the committee
of the Japanese American records of loyalty and spoke out against
the policies that were just beginning to be put to work: "In mass
evacuation we should be repeating the deed that Hitler perpetrated
against the Jews. Though our policy would be gentler than Hitler's
in many ways, the basic injustice would be the same." He pressed
further; if the policy continued, "we should be conquered by Hitler's spirit and methods even though not by his military machine."
Yet Thompson did not carry the day. In Los Angeles the president
of the local church federation was pointedly "too busy" to testify. In the Northern California Council of Churches, a million-
aire leader from Sacramento, Charles M. Goethe, became noted
for supporting Japanese-hating movements. And for all the more
friendly expression by other church leadership, the membership
blended into the general population. Either they favored the government policy and the concentration camps, or they gave a low
priority to the idea of trying to alter it. To them, evidently, whether
Christian or Buddhist, "a Jap was a Jap": these fellow citizens
were not to be trusted, were to be punished, and were not allowed
to be in the mix with fellow Americans. Healing would have to
come after the war.

6:19   In 1944, after many relocations and resettlements, the War Relocation Authority began to end the internment policies, largely
because of the distinguished military service given by Japanese
Americans. Department of the Interior Secretary Harold Ickes,
long a protestor against the government action, spoke up. He in-

Japanese relocation camp at Manzanar, California, photographed by Dorothea
Lange. (Courtesy of the National Archives.)

tended "to keep in mind the need of recognition of the rights of the
United States citizens regardless of ancestry," and particularly of
the Japanese. During 1944 some camps started to be phased out,
and on January 2, 1945, the evacuation orders were rescinded.
Now Ickes urged, as reentry began: "By our conduct towards them
we will be judged by all the people of the world." Such reentry
was difficult. At Hood River, Oregon, for instance, the American
Legion Post for a time removed the names of sixteen Japanese
American soldiers from the Legion's Honor Roll and warned them
against coming back to town. There were some terrorist acts but
no punishments. Matsumoto quoted a defense attorney: "This is
a white man's country." After twenty-four reported terrorist acts
Ickes spoke up, hoping for an "aroused national opinion," and
some clergy did help in the rousing. The Hood River Ministerial
Association had the courage to declare: "We consider it unjust,
unAmerican and unchristian" to deprive the servicemen of Japanese ancestry their honors. One of the sixteen never learned that
his honors were restored. He was killed at Leyte.

6:20   Matsumoto did not expect all citizens to follow clergy leadership. Social integration is "a slow process, and no scientific measurement can be applied to gauge its success." Push too fast, and individuals would become overly self-conscious, he warned. He knew of his nation that "the majority are living like any normal human being, seeking company with those of similar interest and congeniality." But even California came to have a new State Council of Civic Unity, made up, as Matsumoto noted, of membership that was "splendidly representative of all kinds of people: liberals and 'reactionaries,' church people and non-church people, workers and industrialists, and Negroes, Mexicans, Orientals, and Caucasians." He closed with "the unfinished part of our business," as he called it. This was "to render out of date any reference to a group of people as 'Japanese Americans.'" This was the same kind of business he thought the church must take up "everywhere in the United States and, for that matter, throughout the world—making real the divine plan of God, the unity of the human race."

7

"The Christian Church Is Reintegrating"

Although most American religious leadership had not called for war, when it came they supported it with varying degrees of enthusiasm. At once, however, they began to envision postwar order. Among the more enthusiastic on both fronts were public figures in American Catholicism, a body whose involvement in the war effort helped propel it toward the center of American argument. Catholics represented up to one-fourth of the American people, so their voice had to be heard, but how? While any number of bishops, editors, and theologians made the Catholic case, none exceeded Monsignor Fulton J. Sheen in popularity, eloquence, representativeness, or reach beyond Catholicism. Sheen was a fresh voice for two reasons beyond his mere and predictable Catholic patriotism. First, he was almost obsessively concerned to help provide a moral base for the forthcoming era of peace and to be sure that Catholic thought would have its place. So he had to attack what he called the immoralism, the secular or godless pattern that he contended prevailed among the American elites. One hears something of his voice in two wartime books: *Philosophies at War,* from 1943, and *Seven Pillars of Peace,* published in 1944. No newcomer to writing, he could list thirty-five books before these two. Five had the word *Communism* in the title, and *war* was now in three. Sheen hoped to reveal a theologian's mind in addition to his journalist's eye as he told "not only why [something] hap-

7:1

pens, but also what matters." If one looked at the war through the eyes of God, said Sheen, "then the war is not meaningless." So, not bothering to hear how presumptuous it sounded—no one ever accused the handsome and charismatic cleric of humility—he claimed that his approach came "from the divine point of view." The war was not a mere political or economic struggle "but rather a theological one."

7:2   Sheen wanted at once to shift the ground from the questions "How can we get rid of Hitler?" or "Who will win the war?" to "Who will win the revolution, the battle of ideologies for postwar dominance?" There were three competitors: totalitarianism ("anti-Christian, anti-Semitic, and anti-human"), secularism, and Christianity, "which grounds the human and the democratic values of the Western world on a moral and religious basis." The priest included Jews in this third moral framework. Secularism preoccupied him; it was humanistic and democratic, but it identified morality with self-interest instead of the will of God. If totalitarianism abroad was "hard" barbarism, secularism at home as well as abroad was its "soft" counterpart. Secularism would remain most at home in the Soviet Union, where communism and socialism combined amounted to "rival religions" and "pseudo-mysticisms." In contrast, the Christian Middle Ages, for which Sheen had nostalgia, stressed that humans were "one because there was one Lord, one Faith, one Baptism"—all of them now rejected by barbarisms. At this point the cleric dug at Protestantism for having shattered that blissful unity. Protestant reformers promoted the Bible until "every man became an infallible interpreter of the Book" and "there were as many religions as heads." Sheen's rhetoric has to be reproduced word for word if one is to catch its strange combination of cleverness and bluntness: "Once the Book was detached from the Board of Editors which guaranteed its inspiration, and from a Supreme Court which interpreted it, it became rather the basis of discord than of harmony." Come back to the Catholic Board and the Papal Court.

7:3   Still, secularism more than Protestantism was on the agenda. Harvard's Pitirim Sorokin gave a name to its fruit: a "sensate culture," which for Sheen was the "staff that will pierce our hands." For all his linguistic dazzle, the monsignor did build on a reasonably sophisticated analysis, asserted polemically. Secularization to him meant the separation of parts of life from the center, which is God. For secularism, each department of life was autonomous. "Secularism affirms an absolute irrelevance of the moral to the secular, denies a religious culture, and, if there were one, denies it could be superior to an anti-religious culture." The French Catholic journalist Charles Peguy gave Sheen the perfect aphorism: "Never has the temporal been so protected against the spiritual; and never has the spiritual been so unprotected against the temporal." Millions of Christians and Jews in America lived in close union with God, but let them try to put religious or moral training into public schools, and one would soon learn how little influence they had. To make his case on these themes, the priest adduced ecumenical quotations from the American Institute of Judaism, a Church of England conference, the Federal Council of Churches, and the Eastern Orthodox philosopher Nicholas Berdyaev.

Sheen was also ecumenical when listing his secularist villains,   7:4
"barnacles on the ship of democracy." Among them were Bertrand Russell, who "should now fall into a hellish despair"; H. G. Wells, quoted as an authority by "Fascist intelligentsia"; John Dewey in America, who claimed that science was "the sole authentic mode of revelation." The monsignor favored capital letters for his additional horsemen of the apocalypse. To match Secularism there was the superstition of Relativism: "Whatever the majority decides is right, and a Gallup Poll is the best way to find out." Pragmatism: "Ideas thus were regarded as instruments of power." Materialism: Americans "want to be whole again. They are sick of being thrown into a Darwinian pot to boil as a beast, or into a Freudian stew to squirm as a libido, or thrust into the Marxian sandwich." License: perverted freedom, simple self-interest. "What moral standards are the Japs violating?" he asked of those who used relativism or pragmatism as measures. Yet, he complained, "our journalists, our educators, our movies, our best sellers, our forums, and even some of the Churches have been sniping away for years at the moral law." He knew it was wise to cite America's war heroes—Colin Kelley, Edwin O'Hare, the five Sullivan brothers, and others— who, Monsignor Sheen was sure, "had no 'opinion' about America's cause" because they were not subjectivists. "They believed in an absolute distinction between right and wrong, our cause and our enemy."

After predictable attacks on divorce, birth control, and progres-   7:5
sive education Sheen got serious about a new order of Peace, which he capitalized, as he capitalized Secularism. Pius XI had said that "the sacred rights of natural and divine law" had to be at the basis of peace moves and treaties. Yet repeatedly almost no national

leaders were ready to admit to the table the Holy See, an "unarmed, responsible, supranational moral force" that could serve as "custodian of a fixed concept of justice." To illustrate, Sheen sniped at an American president. When Pope Benedict XVI had made peace proposals, France's Ambassador Jusserand had called President Woodrow Wilson, affirming the proposals. Wilson: "Why does he want to butt in?" That had been long ago. In the present chaos the question the president should ask would be, "Why does not your spiritual authority have more authority?" Sheen had his own picture of how the centripetal impetus of spiritual authority was now to work. Somehow he pictured that after the war previously distant nations would acknowledge the pope: "The world drove away the shepherd and his sheep and then complained that it had no wool." Sheen could make a general suggestion appear to be credible. He could say that "nations must abandon the idea of their absolute sovereignty in order to give some sovereignty to the international order" and then add incredibly that there must be something or someone to be "recognized an authority above the nations." He did not leave people guessing who or what this was. This must be the papacy, the arbiter of the absolute, the setter of norms, the authority to whom parties in conflict would appeal. What non-Catholics, non-Christians, and nonreligious people would do about such a proposal he did not try to picture.

7:6   Aware of the limits of a purely pragmatic union of the sort we have called "syncretic" after the pattern of ancient Cretan cities who allied only against a common enemy, Sheen called for more in his *Seven Pillars of Peace:* "A common hatred can make nations *allies,* but only a common love can make them neighbors." At an international conference at Teheran dealing with postwar planning, President Roosevelt had talked of the people of "good will." Sheen assumed that 90 percent of the people belonged in that camp; the Holy Father had called them "the great majority." They had had to unite, thinking of the Axis, "because *there is a common enemy.*" But they had to probe more deeply in matters of the spirit. For that quest, the priest quoted the pope: the difficulties, anxieties, and trials of the present hour "make all believers in God and Christ share the consciousness of a common enemy." Their common love was religiously grounded. Curiously, Sheen's postwar America and even the United Nations included no sense that there were Muslims or Buddhists or people of other faiths. But the author did find ways to transcend the old, lesser patterns of divisiveness in American life. "A few decades ago Christianity's struggles were more in the nature of a civil war; that is, religious rivalries and contentions existed between Methodists and Presbyterians, Lutherans and Anglicans, and in a broader way between Jews, Protestants, and Catholics." Prematurely but decisively Sheen announced: "Today that simple condition no longer prevails." Christians no longer engaged "exclusively in a civil war"—one flags that qualifying word *exclusively*—because they were now faced with an invasion, an incursion, by forces opposed to all religion, all morality, "whether they be Jewish or Christian."

Some of this language sounded fresh, coming from a Catholicism that was no longer speaking only to its figurative ghetto. "Imagine a Catholic and a Protestant in a forest attempting to settle the problem of Infallibility, not by argument but by muscular Christianity." A lion attacks them. They will interrupt their controversy to do battle against the common enemy. So it was now during the war. Previously, he said, the antimoral forces had been united, while people of goodwill were divided. The new vision was not born simply of a fear that the "Church or religion is in danger," though, of course, they were. God had promised that evil would not prevail against them. "It is not the sanctuary that is in danger; it is civilization." Then came the sharp Catholic distinction on which the papacy insisted and which Sheen blithely promulgated. The unity Sheen pictured was not proposed at all for *religious purposes.* As a Catholic, he said, the priest had no interest in what is "commonly called union of Churches" on lines "broad and vague enough to be acceptable to all" but manmade, "purchased in compromise to truth and misery." The priest promoted unity only for *social purposes.* This approach would leave theology untouched; it "unites religious people rather than religions." Sheen insisted that "outside of the faith, where we are divided, there is a common ground where cooperation between men of good will is necessary and possible." Starkly, he posed against each other "the forces of good and evil, the seed of the Woman and the seed of the Beast, the City of God and the City of Satan, the Army of God and the Army of Anti-God." 7:7

When he set forth the basis for social unity, Sheen showed that he thought he was universalistic, but he sounded only and particularly Catholic. The new order, he contended, had to be united on "the moral law," on "a participation or indwelling of the Eternal Reason of God in nature and in man." He did try to argue that "it makes no difference if one be a Jew, a Protestant or a Catholic, a Hottentot, a Mohammedan, Hindu, German or Japanese." 7:8

All shared or could share the moral law. Too bad, he went on, that language about that moral law was now being challenged in American courts; judges all too typically had said that "man must no longer search for God in law." Over against this Sheen reached into history for more profound examples, to Cyrus of Persia, Alexander the Great, and Cicero, the last of whom had said that "the universe is to be regarded as a single commonwealth, since all are subject to the heavenly law and divine intelligence of Almighty God." And the Bible advanced and clarified this language about "the whole earth." "The only alternative to One World based on One Lord and one moral law is to have many worlds and many lords, where each nation is its own law, its own god." If mid-century times were a time to promote convergences of peoples and ideas, Sheen has to be seen as a master. But he could also resort to hyperbole to bring things back to his own stable ground. The last three lines of the book were: "A new crime is arising in the world today; be prepared for it. The crime of being a Christian. The crime of believing in God."

7:9   In the war years other Catholics joined Monsignor Sheen in offering visions of life in the face of what he called barbarism and the continuing competition for the soul of America and the world. But these all came down to the theme that international relations, if they were to advance justice and peace, had to be grounded in "natural law" or "the moral law." This the articulators then connected with the idea of truth as expounded by the Catholic church and under the authority of the pope. Many non-Catholics agreed on the need for some sort of consensus based on a law of nature, a law stamped into conscience, but none would defer to the Catholic magisterium, the teaching office, or the papacy to be its custodian. Opponents of Sheen's vision, he argued, dared not be content merely to confront it. They had to offer alternatives. The monsignor's dreaded "secularists" saw themselves best poised to propose some, assuming as they did that they were the possessors of the universal language and that the religions only complemented it, lived off it, or, when Catholics insisted on the teachings of their popes or scriptures, obscured it. Clyde Eagleton, who was involved in debates over a future world order, spoke for this secular mainstream and specifically pointed to scientists: "No group has a greater appeal to the public and none has greater potentialities for producing change in public opinion." This community had invented weaponry and developed the atomic bomb; now within the scientific company there were increasing numbers speaking against the use of that weapon and promoting globalism and peace through international organizations in which scientists had a prime role.

For all the awe with which religious communities regarded   7:10
scientists, their leaders did not permit talk of peace and moral order to be a secularist monopoly. Matters of spirit and soul and heart, all central to international life and in American energy, were somehow their preserve. Not only Catholics and secularists struggled with these themes. The Protestant majority through its leadership during the war poised themselves to present alternatives. Even groups close to the prewar pacifists organized. The voices of the Women's International League for Peace and the Fellowship of Reconciliation may have been muffled or discredited to some extent because their leanings toward pacifism had been unpopular. But in November 1943, E. Raymond Wilson and other Quakers formed "the first Protestant lobby." Using the slogan "Win the War, Win the Peace," they pleaded for a shortened war, including negotiated peace and then an end to demands for unconditional surrender. And they wanted a just scheme for reconciliation after the war. Out of such impulses came the more centrist Commission to Study the Bases of a Just and Durable Peace, a coalition of world federalists, many of them being of Protestant background. These federalists were much involved in a Dumbarton Oaks conference in Washington in 1944, where visionaries drafted plans for the forthcoming United Nations organization. A new phrase became popular in these seasons, after former Republican presidential candidate Wendell Willkie in 1943 published the volume *One World*. No nonfiction book had sold more copies more quickly in all American history. It was clear that dreams of peace and plans for postwar international order were not the concern only of elites gathered at Dumbarton Oaks. What we can see as a vortex pulling disparate forces together was evident in all these moves.

The Federal Council of Churches' Protestantism was poised to   7:11
be most specific about blueprints, and it got off to an early start. One of the most clear scripts appeared already in 1941, when war had not started but seemed inevitable. The author was Roswell Parkhurst Barnes, who had moved from fashionable Presbyterian pulpits to leadership in the council and was the man on the spot when issues of chaplaincy, refugee and relief work, and peace conferences came up. *A Christian Imperative: Our Contribution to World Order* was his Protestant program which in its typicality matched Sheen's for Catholicism. "The Christian Church offers more hope for the rehabilitation of international society than any

other institution in the world." Such a bold claim for the situation of only three out of ten people in the world matched Sheen's. So did Barnes's critique of the major liberal alternative. Barnes placed himself in the company of those who were "disillusioned about the possibility of saving the world through secular liberalism." Like Sheen he thought pragmatism was insufficient for world order. The nation and the world had to speak in "terms of principles believed to be intrinsic in the Christian understanding of the world and of history." The world needed "a common ethos," which for Barnes as for Sheen meant "a recognition of universal moral law and of a transcendent sanction of that law," something Russia, Germany, and Japan lacked but which lived on in some Western nations. To the ears of generations that are alert to religious pluralism and competing secularisms, liberal or not, such language sounds sectarian and triumphalist, but in 1941 the Christian communities still felt they could get a hearing for it. Barnes told of the time a year before at a European conference when an American diplomat held up an identifying card with Barnes's name on it. He covered up all the words except the title "Reverend," and said, "That is the most important part of your name for your work in this terrible crisis. There are many things that you can do as a minister of the church that I cannot do." The Federal Council official said he was resolved to see his clerical status as an asset in international work.

7:12   With Sheen he looked at the chaos around the world and empathized with those who began to wonder "whether the gods have not made us mad." Part of that madness was the result of "absolute" national sovereignty, the bugaboo of all internationalists. With many citizens then turning into hyperpatriots, it became ever more difficult to remain credible or popular while criticizing nationalism, but Barnes was quite representative of conciliar elites when he said that "nationalism has become a religion" and thus a rival to historic faith. He pointed in America to the Fourth of July, Independence Hall, the Capitol, and the Liberty Bell as parts of a complex of civic shrines and altars, creeds and rituals, public symbols and holy days. With Sheen he scored public education—liberal Protestantism then was still largely backing broad-based religion in the schools—for having "prepared the way for nationalism to supplant the teachings of the Church as the inspiration for noble life and the source of moral standards and social ideals." The United States Supreme Court had not yet entered debates about the subject, to say nothing about deciding to rule religion out. The distancing had occurred on voluntary grounds. Children learned more about nationalism than Christianity, which had become "an elective in the curriculum of life; one can 'take it or leave it,' as he likes." They obviously had to "take" nationalism, the rival.

How Barnes the realist and his colleagues could speak so confidently of church influence at the same time that they complained about the decline of support for religion was not clear. Barnes assumed, against meager and conflicting statistical evidence, that there had been a decline in religious participation in recent decades in America. One New York official told him that only 10 percent of the population in the city had more than a nominal attachment to church or synagogue. Even for this tenth, the base was weak because the churches had become so secularized. Council leader that he was, Barnes went one step further to deplore churchly weakness by addressing "a divided and faltering church." How could Christians preach world unity in their division, he wondered: "Denominationalism sometimes displays many of the provincial and selfish aspects of nationalism." Something of the old liberal optimism, however, lived on in Barnes, who, despite what he saw in his surroundings, made a bold claim: "At the very moment in history when our world is disintegrating politically, the Christian church is reintegrating." He coupled this view with what also had to be a statement of faith: "Politically the nations come to have less and less in common; religiously they come to have more and more in common." In neither Barnes's nor the other major proposals was there ever much concern about what nations with Muslim, Buddhist, Hindu, or secular populations would think of Christian primacy and grounding, or how Sheen's Catholicism and Barnes's Protestantism, themselves given to division and "petty wrangling," in the council leader's own words, could reintegrate themselves enough to integrate the world.

7:13

Decisive Protestant lay leaders emerged with realist visions of international order and just peace, and some of them were to have roles in postwar diplomacy. None stood out more than Presbyterian lawyer John Foster Dulles, who had been involved in 1937 with a meeting at Oxford that helped plan the postwar World Council of Churches. The year before the war Dulles was writing for the *Federal Council Bulletin:* "We want America to stay out of the war," but "we cannot be content that America should stay out of peace." He came to chair the Commission to Study the Bases of a Just and Durable Peace for the nascent World Council; everyone thought of him as the prime lay person in that sphere. The commission's handbook on the theme of a just and durable peace reached 450,000

7:14

readers; it was followed by a steady stream of Christ-centered reflections on world affairs. Dulles took one of these, "The Six Pillars of Peace," to President Roosevelt in March of 1943. Governor Thomas Dewey, who challenged Roosevelt the next year, spoke favorably of these booklets of Christian reflection, as did senators and other officials. Niebuhr found them "increasingly realistic," which meant they were satisfying to him. In the Niebuhrian magazine *Christianity and Crisis,* Henry Pitney Van Dusen patted Dulles's back: the commission was offering "the briefest, clearest and soundest agenda for post-war order which has yet been forthcoming from any source, within or outside the churches." From his New Jersey bastion, however, Presbyterian dissident Carl McIntire, who was tending the lingering fundamentalist fires, demurred: "All this brings out into the open the real Communistic nature of the controlled world order desired." Pacifists thought the proposals too hard-line, but after leaders like A. J. Muste had spoken their critical piece, many fell into line.

7:15 Throughout the war, "World Order Days," meetings in Britain, at Bretton Woods in New Hampshire and Dumbarton Oaks in Washington, and in denominational conferences everywhere promoted this "realistic" approach in support of what became the United Nations. When the U.S. government began to plan its participation in the San Francisco United Nations Conference of April 1945, Dulles, appointed a counsel, was strategically placed to advocate his version of Christian realism, disguised as a moral-law approach to moral order. One cannot say that conciliar Protestantism invented the United Nations, but its leadership did help bring church people of their sort into line and helped them summon enthusiasm for it. Of course, Dulles would not sell Presbyterianism or Protestantism or even explicit Christianity as a base for the world organization or order. He too agreed with Sheen and Barnes: "We believe that moral law, no less than physical law, undergirds our world. There is moral order which is fundamental and eternal, and which is relevant to the corporate life of men and the ordering of society." But to people like Dulles, this general moral law and moral order demanded and would receive explicit Christian support. Christians tried to "view all problems of world order in the light of the truth concerning God, man and God's purpose for the world made known in Jesus Christ." Dulles was traveled enough to know that non-Christians would not explicitly draw on this truth, even though God in Christ was the source of the moral law and the power to make it effective.

Through it all, Dulles was as concerned as were Sheen and   7:16
Barnes about the thrall of nationalism as a religion and, more, over
the "lack of impelling faith," the failure of Americans to draw on
"the propulsion of a deep faith and high sense of mission in the
world." Without these, how could the United States overcome the
primitive emotions evoked by war; how with a spiritual vacuum
could the nation counter Germany and Japan, with their abhorrent
faiths? "We, too, need a faith, a faith that will make us strong, a
faith so profound that we, too, will feel that we have a mission to
spread it through the world." Years after the United Nations was
founded, after it became a forum for competing nationalisms and
an exemplar of wild spiritual pluralism, it is hard to recapture the
sense of credibility that came with the confession of a founder like
Dulles: Americans can "be confident that in following Christ we
are not jeopardizing the welfare of our nation." And in the lineage
of an earlier Presbyterian statesman, Woodrow Wilson, Dulles
argued on. The broad principles put to work in internationalism
"grow out of the practice by the nations of the simple things Christ
taught." The diplomat could even sound hopeful in a dire time:
"As our national faith thus grows and is made manifest by works,
its influence will be contagious throughout the world."

How would a Christ-centered order attract non-Christians, be-   7:17
ginning with the well-poised Jews in the United States? Everett R.
Clinchy, who worked with the National Conference of Christians
and Jews, had to take up that issue. "Protestant Christians are
not the only ones who desire peace, nor the only ones who are
taught by their religion that to seek peace is a duty imposed on
them by God." Clinchy reached even beyond Catholic and Jewish
sources and quoted Islam, Taoism, and Hinduism, since, he recognized, "the forces of religion are divided." He reminded Protestants, Catholics, and Jews that, however homogeneous their cluster
looked from a distance, they represented only "unity in diversity"
and "cultural pluralism" up close. So he was drawn, with Sheen
and Barnes and Dulles, to the place where he proposed the idea of
a "moral order." As he spelled this out, it remained creedal, theistic, and patriarchal: "In sum, then, in the area of natural religion,
that is, in the belief in the Fatherhood of God and the Brotherhood
of Man, people of varying religious groups can meet together,
speak unitedly and act in concert." Work for world peace was in
that category. When it came to supernatural revelation, Clinchy
said in addressing pluralism: "We may continue to worship sepa-
rately, compete in our separate claims, and carry on a rivalry in

excellence." Even he did not really depart from the notion that world order could follow an American "Conference of Christians and Jews" model, and he did not reckon with what this would mean for a framework of world organizations that would include hundreds of millions of Taoists, Hindus, Buddhists, Muslims, and people with no explicit faith.

7:18   The Protestant council leaders were not the only Americans who thought they could universalize their particular vision or faith. In the spirit of the times Henry Luce, founder of *Life* and *Time* and *Fortune* magazines, offered his own triumphalist picture: this was to be "The American Century." But some of the church leaders were critical of that term. Thus Walter Van Kirk, the colleague of Barnes at the Federal Council of Churches, responded in *Religion and the World of Tomorrow,* "This is not 'The American Century,'" nor the British, German, or Japanese century. Christians had to join others in asking what kind of world they wanted in such a century. But he linked up with Sheen and his fellow Protestant leaders in decrying what secularists wanted. Chiding church leaders for emulating King Canute of Denmark, who had commanded the tide to recede, Van Kirk said they had "sought to pacify a turbulent world by the magic of rhetoric." They were earnest, "but the evils of a pagan secularism could not be exorcised by ecclesiastical pronouncements." They and he had been failures through sixteen years of life in a futile peace movement. They had not gone deep enough to oppose the spirit of anarchy, and now they had to reach further. "There is no denying that the followers of Jesus are, in principle, internationalists." They had to accept their duty and opportunity with other Americans in "the most powerful and vital nation in the world," and exert upon the world the full impact of their influence. He pointed with favor to the British churches, the praying pope, the chief rabbi in England, and the dean of Canterbury to show how all would fight off the spirit of pagan secularism, of which Hitler was "only a particularly offensive form."

7:19   Four years after Pearl Harbor and his earlier book, after the Bretton Woods and Dumbarton Oaks conferences and with the United Nations being born, Van Kirk also sounded triumphal. Now, he said, "the basic presuppositions of geopolitics" had been demonstrated. "The world is one." The interconnectedness of political and social phenomena was evident to anyone aware of the speed of air travel and radio. "To geopolitics the world is not only one world with its accompanying interconnectedness of land and sea spaces; it is a dynamic world." Van Kirk saw geopolitics to be "but a belated recognition of the fundamentals of the Christian gospel." And he looked back at the apostle Paul as geopolitician: "What global strategists these early Christians were!" But today was today, a time of new opportunity and potential triumph. Those who found an answer "in the religion of the Galilean preacher" saw "that the world is one." But Van Kirk shared everyone else's complaint: "Secularism is everywhere in the ascendancy and Christians are in retreat on many fronts" until one could no longer draw meaningful lines between Christian and pagan nations. He decried a recent massacre of blacks in a Detroit race riot but then looked for subtler signs of decay: "Within the academic world, religion is not infrequently regarded as an 'extra'. God is tolerated, if at all, as a theological hangover from an age that was both superstitious and unscientific." No wonder crime rates rose. But "God's war against secularism" could not be won by Christians whose forces were "sundered by the ecclesiastical leftovers of an age that is forever gone." The language of triumph turned uncertain as Van Kirk looked inside the churches. Could there ever be a "united global strategy of Christian conquest as between the Roman and non-Roman churches, the Protestant and Eastern Orthodox churches, and within the Protestant community itself?" For most readers the question answered itself: no. But Van Kirk could hope for little more than joint or parallel actions by Christians who would redeem secular society.

Because the mainstream Protestant churches were soon to give up their attempts to keep the public schools religious, Christian, or, as they really had preferred, generally Protestant in ethos as they had once been, it is startling to hear how frequently the council leaders in wartime still looked to schools as a battle line, even as they were already being abandoned as religious redoubts. Yet the Protestant conciliarist could ask: how could American Christians integrate the world if they turned secular, and how could they not turn secular if they were not educated in faith and morals? "Religion was driven out of the public schools of America not by its enemies but by its friends," in their intolerance of each other, Van Kirk argued. "Hence the complete secularization of education. Hence the ignorance of American youth of the fundamentals of religion." And the Federal Council man asked for countering action, for aggression. Catholics could put the heat on, he observed, but Protestants lacked a strategy of public relations just as they possessed an inferiority complex. They must "stop their crying and get down to the more important business of studying the sci-

7:20

ence of public relations and developing a strategy that would more effectively register the total strength of the Protestant churches upon the public mind." If they strengthened the home front, the "non-Roman churches of the United States will be giving powerful aid to the forces of Christendom on the world front."

7:21   The language of conquest was consistent. "The time has come for Christians to sound the trumpets of advance on the world front." Imperialism was on the way out in East Asia, Africa, and the Middle East. "Are the Christian-thinking people of our country spiritually awake to this fact? No." Low support of Christian missions was positively shocking. Van Kirk coined a new hyphenated word to describe provincialism: "Here, within the Christian community, there is an Atlanto-centric attachment which is a denial of the spiritual outlook of Jesus." War had not yet fundamentally changed the horizon of Western Christendom. There was no united "world strategy of Christian conquest." But he was as sure as Sheen and Barnes and Dulles had been that there was "latent in the hearts and minds of humans a sense of yearning for divine comradeship that reaches far above and beyond the statistical charts of denominational yearbooks." There was yet no strategy by which Christendom could make this yearning operative in the world of nations. In the world that was disintegrating, the church should be reintegrating. Was it? Would it be? Geopoliticians had to leave their readers with the questions.

8

"Here Ceaseless Vigilance Is Required"

The advocates of reintegrated Christianity and friendly interfaith relations increasingly, indeed, conventionally, used a neat and innocent three-faith model. They consistently spoke of the need for Protestants, Catholics, and Jews to fight off secularism and to provide the basis for world order and peace. That model was far too simple. There were as many people of Eastern Orthodox Christian outlook as there were Jews, but they were seldom mentioned. Voices of African American Christianity regularly reminded the larger public that their churches were kept on a separate track, segregated from and unrepresented by almost all of white Protestantism and Catholicism. But one other fissure, overlooked in the three-faith talk, sundered Protestantism and made much of the ecumenical talk sound hollow. This was the divide between the Protestants, sometimes called mainstream or established, represented in the Federal Council of Churches, and the fundamentalists, evangelicals, and pentecostals who had never shared denominational life with council types or had gone their own way after bitter Fundamentalist-Modernist controversies within American denominations in the 1920s. Out of mainstream sight, they were expected to be out of mind of the larger public. Of course, most Americans were aware that in the back country there were hillbillies, rednecks, holy-rollers, tent revivalists, Bible colleges, and evangelistic radio stations and publishing companies. But these

8:1

were segregated in the Bible Belts of the Midwest and especially the South. They did not count for much, especially since their vision of the public order usually seemed negative. They disapproved of worldliness and immorality, but one seldom saw them approaching the halls of secular power to make their case. They were not much at home in the higher academy. Since they were out of step with modernity, they were expected increasingly to disappear. Certainly they were beside the point in an age of cooperation, reduced to grumbling whenever the council's Protestants spoke up on world order and national unity.

8:2   Almost unnoticed—the secular press all but ignored them and the religious press outside their own hardly noticed—was the regrouping and revitalizing that went on among these recalcitrant Protestants who just would not go along with the larger trends of the time. Most notice came when these conservatives put energy into sniping at every ecumenical move that mainstream Protestants made. The fundamentalists were isolated, people who responded to biblical commands to "come out and be separate," as they were—even from each other. They attacked moves toward church unity because these initiatives, they believed, were prudential and pragmatic, not born of common conviction. Not many observers noticed that during the war years most of these independents found reason to cluster in either of two new families and, indeed, new organizations. One might say that ironically the anti-ecumenicals turned out instead to be paraecumenicals who were organizing in order to know each other better, to speak with a united voice, to explore common concerns. Since neither they nor the denominations in the Federal Council gave up any part of their autonomy, and since in both organizations all member churches could live by their separate convictions, the conservative organizations were more like the moderate and liberal ones than either side or the public commentators then saw them to be. And they forced the ecumenists into rear-guard actions involving public relations.

8:3   The Federal Council of Churches, formed in 1908, aspired to speak for all Protestantism, or would have liked to make others forget that it did not. The council gained influence during the war as it helped monitor the military chaplaincy program, assigned network radio time, addressed mass communicators, set forth programs, and reflected its presumed place as the dominant voice of religion in the culture. But millions of Protestants were not in member denominations and were resentful of them and the council. A reactionary Disciples of Christ minister, James DeForest

Murch, gave an insider's account of one of the organizations opposed to the council, the National Association of Evangelicals. His voice quite accurately reflected the language of countless magazines, tracts, radio programs, and sermons that attacked liberal Protestantism. Murch's book deserved notice decades after publication. As he and the self-named evangelicals saw it, the council was theologically too broad, nondescript, generous, and wishy-washy; this to them meant faithless and false to Jesus Christ. Murch claimed that by 1940 the council had become unacceptable to 176 out of 200 Protestant communions. That figure was distorting, because with two or three exceptions, the standoffish groups were very small compared to most constituents of the council, but citing it was not entirely beside the point.

Newsweek magazine had said that the Federal Council pos- 8:4
sessed a "virtual monopoly" in Protestantism; such statements gave ammunition to Murch and his companions. In their eyes the council was trying to play the same game that Catholics were: to dominate and speak for those they did not represent. Second, it welcomed Eastern Orthodoxy, which Murch found abhorrent. When the council met in Cleveland in 1942, a metropolitan of a member church had not been criticized by the Protestants present for invoking in prayers "our all-immaculate Theotokos and ever Virgin Mary" or when he went so far as to call Catholicism a "sister communion," which it could never become. Third, the council was politically liberal, and it slighted economic conservatism. Murch quoted a Michigan newspaper to the effect that in 1945 the Federal Council of Churches was stopping "just short of proclaiming the allegiance of the church to a socialized economic system for America instead of the democracy of free enterprise." Fourth, ecumenical Protestantism had been too friendly to pacifists before the war, and this alienated the more military-minded evangelicals. The list of charges was long: where, in addition to everything else, asked Murch, was the energy in council-related churches comparable to that of the nascent evangelical organizations Youth for Christ or InterVarsity Christian Fellowship, for working among the young? Where did the mainstream missionaries go when they disappeared from foreign fields? Why did no one notice the evangelical best-sellers, which outsold mainstream Protestant books? Businesspeople crowded evangelical prayer breakfasts but shunned ecumenical ones. It was time to make evangelicalism visible.

At precisely the time it was working to do so, evangelicalism 8:5

was almost eclipsed by another association, this one headed by
Carl McIntire, an even more vehement enemy of the Federal Council, who patented his own American Council of Christian Churches
in 1941. To the more moderate conservative evangelicals this move
looked like a publicity stunt, a largely preemptive move. McIntire
knew that the National Association of Evangelicals was on the
drawing board; association leaders had even been conciliatory
enough to invite him to a meeting in Chicago. But McIntire declined the invitation. He relished what others would have called
bad publicity. The fundamentalist flaunted a release of the International Council of Religious Education in 1945. It said, among
other things, "Probably we can dismiss the American Council of
Churches with the evaluation that it is not likely to become very
strong nor significant." His council was dismissed as a movement
"dedicated to bitterly attacking the Federal Council," but it had
also recently turned on the National Association of Evangelicals
"with like bitterness." Anyone who knew McIntire had to know
how he could enjoy two "bitters" in one day. The release the fundamentalist quoted went on: "The National Association of Evangelicals is quite different"; while it too was critical of cooperative
agencies, "its best leadership does not waste time in destructive
criticism." Destructive criticism was precisely what the Federal
Council merited; to make it, McIntire and *his* council were called
into being.

8:6   Carl McIntire was in the middle stages of a stormy career. He
had followed Presbyterian leaders who split from the main body
in the mid-twenties and then led his own separation from their
separation. His move, in short, was from the Presbyterian Church
in the U.S.A. through the Orthodox Presbyterian Church to the
Bible Presbyterian Church. His anti-ecumenical ecumenical cre-
ations were then both the American Council of Christian Churches
in 1941 and the International Council of Christian Churches in
1948. Too extreme to prosper, he attracted a small but loyal set of
followers in a small but loyal set of churches. His mark in history
is as an opponent of ecumenical organizations; he would be "militantly pro-Gospel and anti-modernist," he announced when the
American Council formed. McIntire's strongest case against the
National Association of Evangelicals was in protest against their
willingness to allow churches or units to belong to both their organization and the Federal Council of Churches.

8:7   Against his negativism, 147 evangelical leaders went ahead
with plans for a conference in St. Louis in 1942. "There is a

widespread desire to bring together the various evangelical groups within the United States into a voluntary fellowship for purposes common to all." The association would be "purely voluntary and operated democratically"; also, like its counterparts, it would "in no wise conflict with nor interfere with the rights and prerogatives of member bodies." Allowing the autonomy of church bodies was the price all councils, federations, and associations had to pay for support. Still, "millions of evangelical Christians in this country," the founders said, felt that they had "no corporate means of making their wishes known in matters common to all." Its founding committees could not resist a more vigorous swipe: "We realize that in many areas of Christian endeavor the organizations which now purport to be representatives of Protestant Christianity have departed from the faith of Jesus Christ." Much bad history, resentment, and wounded pride went into the choice of the verb "purport": the evangelicals saw themselves as custodians of the main Protestant tradition from which, they were sure, moderates and liberals had departed.

The gathering gave birth to the association which by May of 1943 in their meeting in Chicago could claim to represent various parts or the whole of some fifty denominations, and three years later it had attracted twenty-two full denominations, with a membership of 1,000,000—still small by Federal Council standards. Biblical literalism became the association's mark, but the evangelical leadership put some energies to work at once in the public sector. They went out of their way to attack the decision by President Roosevelt to name a representative at the Vatican. They put their views of church and state into a statement. Government "should not use any public funds for the benefit of any sectarian institution." In both cases the impulse was anti-Catholicism, a spirit that made the evangelicals in no way distinctive, since the same impulse motivated the mainstream Protestant ecumenical forces. Almost at once the leadership attacked the policies of radio networks to give time to Federal Council bodies, while the council itself worked to have the networks refuse even to sell air time to evangelicals. Clearly in this case the Federal Council had overplayed its hand, and reaction was merited. The association went on to organize a National Religious Broadcasters group; in open competition it soon left mainstream Protestants fumbling with their dials and their viewpoints, as evangelicals drew larger audiences. By 1944 the association was also challenging the Federal Council monopoly as the endorsing body for Protestant chaplains. The edi-

8:8

tors of the *Christian Century* were nettled enough to say that the association was "giving sectarianism a new lease on life" and encouraging "reactionary and dissident wings of the great Protestant denominations" which remained active in the Federal Council. By war's end it was becoming increasingly clear that the American religious mix was Catholic, Jew, Protestant, *and* Protestant.

8:9   The one position on which the two largely white Protestant clusters agreed during the war was anti-Catholicism. They might be a part of strategic alliances against totalitarianism to win a war. But for all the friendly if condescending sounds made by a Fulton Sheen or the council leaders, the bargaining for position on the home front continued. No incident did more to fuse the energies of the Federal Council denominations and their evangelical and fundamentalist counterparts than the appointment by President Roosevelt of representatives to the Vatican. In 1939 he sent Joseph P. Kennedy to attend the elevation of Pius XII, a perfectly normal diplomatic courtesy in the eyes of the president. The Southern Baptist Convention called this act of representation a "dangerous tendency toward the union of church and state." But more ominous still was the effort by Roosevelt to establish diplomatic relations with the papal state. Vatican City saw itself as a state among the states and enjoyed such relations with many nations, including the United States until Congress cut off ties in 1867. Roosevelt needed to be in touch with the Vatican, which was poised between the Axis and the Allies. He clearly did not anticipate the intensity of the furies that his appointment of a personal representative meant in still-Protestant America.

8:10   Although Roosevelt was rankled by the pope's studied efforts to remain neutral when Germany attacked Russia in 1941, he still worked for alliance with the Vatican. Good news came when the president received word that the pope would support the Atlantic Charter. Roosevelt played up the religious theme in his instructions: "The objectives are based on the teachings of the New Testament, and call for spiritual leadership in opposition to the extremely pagan views and objectives of the Axis Powers." Yet the Vatican found itself isolated between sets of powers after Pearl Harbor, unwilling to take sides and unable to be truly above the battle, and therefore ineffective. The pope was also reluctant to back Roosevelt's move for "unconditional surrender." Roosevelt's man Myron C. Taylor, not a Catholic himself, spent wartime energies helping to keep Rome an "open city," exempting it from bombing in the rest of the war. For that, he won the Vatican's

Myron C. Taylor, a Protestant, was President Roosevelt's personal envoy to the Vatican after 1939; he was kept in the post until 1951 by President Truman. The presidents wanted to be represented at the Vatican, wishing to use it as a diplomatic listening-post during and after the war. Protestants and other Americans vehemently opposed efforts to appoint Taylor or anyone else as formal ambassador to a diplomatically recognized Vatican. Taylor is pictured with Pope Pius XII. (Photo: National Council of the Churches of Christ in the USA.)

thanks and favor. The pope's fixed point through the worst years was the preservation of Rome's churches and their treasures. The city fell into German hands in the summer of 1944 and had to be liberated twice. For the part they played in protecting Rome, the pope found reason during both the Roosevelt and Truman presidencies to recognize increasing bonds with the United States.

Truman asked Taylor to remain in Rome as his representative,   8:11

even though the president could not name him ambassador, fearing Protestant backlash. The Catholic versus Protestant debates over whether there should be a representative had to go on among people who could not be told about, and therefore acted in ignorance of, all the services Taylor had performed as a shuttle diplomat. The very Protestants who talked of "One World" and "One Church" were most ardent fighters on the front where Catholics threatened the Protestants' hold in American politics and culture. Catholicism was making advances and growing. By 1944 it numbered 21,403,000 members and had more churches than any other denomination in 38 of the 50 largest American metropolises, where they often got to have much of their political way. This flexing of power inspired Harold E. Fey, formerly of the Fellowship of Reconciliation but now of the *Christian Century,* to issue a wartime report in a series of articles titled "Can Catholicism Win America?" which eventually became a book. This was part of what the journal called a "Protestant Reorientation." "American Protestantism is striving to reorient its forces," wrote the editors, acknowledging as the "source of pressure" the "growing power of Roman Catholicism in the political and social life of the nation."

8:12   Fey voiced the concern of liberals and fundamentalists alike: "Unlike members of nearly all other churches, these millions of American citizens are subject to the spiritual direction of an Italian pontiff who represents a culture historically alien to American institutions." While Protestants were aware of Catholic action in the social sphere ever after the Bishops' Program for Social Reconstruction was set in 1919, now Catholic leaders, he wrote, "for the first time [have] begun to plan and function *as a unit* on questions which affect the status of the church in our national life." He charged that they had "cast off the inferiority complex which naturally characterizes an alien minority and have begun boldly and aggressively to assert their power." Fey saw Catholicism "mobilizing powerful forces to move this nation toward a cultural unity in which the Roman Catholic Church will be dominant." That gave one more reason to promote a Protestant-based ecumenical movement.

8:13   Clearly, the wartime alliance on the model of the ancient Cretan cities, a working together against a common foe, had not served the purpose of seeing the "one nation, indivisible" overcome religious hostilities. Protestants in their two great parties were more divided after the war than before. The World Council of Churches, which had many supporters in the United States, was put on hold as the churches in Axis and Allied countries blessed the cannon against each other's sides. The Federal Council met challenge from the National Association of Evangelicals. Relations between many Jews and Christians were strained because non-Jews did not come up with much by way of help for Jews seeking refuge from Hitler. In the rhetoric of Catholic and Protestant alike, the secularist was a great threat to moral law and republican values. Most of all, the two clusters of Protestantism could never come together for positive reasons and allied only negatively, against Catholicism. The rhetoric of a spiritually informed "one nation" sounded hollow, superficial, contrary to fact. Yet some still voiced dreams for something deeper, richer, more long-lasting. An example of such an attempt to give substance to the idea of convergence came in the final work, posthumously published, of a veteran ecumenist, William Adams Brown, emeritus at Union Theological Seminary in New York.

Brown had been stranded in Lisbon in 1942, waiting for a plane   8:14
home on his way from the enthronement of William Temple as archbishop of Canterbury. He spent his time there setting forth his vision once more and came back to work further until his death in 1943. Then Samuel McCrea Cavert, his heir in ecumenical reflection and a Federal Council of Churches executive, finished *Toward a United Church.* Brown wrote for "plain Christians" who were trying to make sense of what theologians and ecclesiastics, who did not need the book, were doing. "No one can say with certainty when the first meeting of the World Council will be held or under what conditions it will meet," he wrote, but it was time to prepare spiritually. He had to explain the word *ecumenical,* which meant "world-wide," but was now given new meaning. It referred to the fact that the *official* church leadership "of the larger Christian communions, Eastern Orthodox and Old Catholic as well as Protestant," were the initiators. The "as well as Protestant" phrase was a nice Brownian flourish, since for most Americans ecumenism was a Protestant venture. But it was another Brownian touch then to put Catholicism gently in what he regarded as its place. "The Church of Rome, the largest as well as one of the oldest of the Christian communions, still holds aloof." The phrase "one of the oldest" was quietly insulting, because Rome yielded to none in its claims for priority.

How could one talk about the "One Church" without touching   8:15
the biggest element? "When one touches the Church of Rome," Brown noted, "one is confronted by a whole group of unanswer-

able questions." It would not likely abandon its claim to exclusive authority and take its place among the churches. But that did not mean there could be no change in the way it expressed authority. "What concerns the Ecumenical Movement more immediately is the degree of cooperation which Rome will permit in the different areas in which that movement is functioning." Brown pointed to applied ethics, possibly common prayer, and religious liberty as areas for breakthrough. On the last point, "all Protestants and not least those of the Churches in the Ecumenical Movement will have to keep alertly on guard." "On guard" was no doubt the way the strategically united factions of Crete fought against their common enemy. For all his good spirit and dreams, even Brown had to leave his readers with a word of warning that suggested how little had been achieved to fulfill the dreams of "One World," "One Church," "One Nation" by war's end: "Here ceaseless vigilance is required."

Part Two

"One Nation" Early in the Cold War, 1945–1952

9

"The Vital Center"

holy war it had not been, but the conflict involving the   9:1
United States between 1941 and 1945, the Second World War, had
summoned the spiritual energies of religious forces backing their
"One Nation" against Germany, Italy, Japan, and their allies. However much these forces insisted upon their independence of each
other, however much they displayed religious varieties seldom if
ever seen in one nation before, however much they reserved the
right to snipe at each other on a variety of issues, they largely
agreed that the enemy represented such a demonic assault on civilization that it had to be stopped. What has sometimes been called
"the last popular war" waged by the United States led Protestants,
Catholics, Jews, and others to present a united front. If the presence
of external foes served to push or pull together Americans and their
religions in common purposes, while they remained separate and
often antagonistic to each other on many other fronts, in 1945 one
might well have asked what was going to happen now that those
enemies, in defeat, offered no more such challenges. A futurist in
May and August of that year, after the conquest by the Allies of
European and then Asian enemies, might well have wondered what
or who might serve as the external catalyst for unity when the guns
were silent. The answer came almost at once: the Soviet Union
(or the Russians, as most Americans spoke of their allies-turned-
enemies) loomed instantly. What soon became the Cold War did

not end the cool wars between religious forces in the matter of doctrines and denominational positionings and posturings. But it did become the magnet that attracted many of the energies religious people devoted to public life, and attitudes toward it and the new enemy became standards for measuring who belonged, or who most belonged, in this One Nation, Indivisible.

9:2   Wartime president Franklin D. Roosevelt hoped he could somehow work with the Soviet Union to assure postwar peace. But experiences at several conferences of allies and various aggressive actions by the Soviets warned him that he had to keep his guard up. The president had to oppose the territorial ambitions of Josef Stalin, the wartime dictator in the Soviet Union, when Stalin began to make clear that he would grab portions of Poland and would not stop with that move. During the war President Roosevelt dared not risk alienating this mighty ally who was helping bring down Germany. Somehow, the president reasoned, he must help keep alive the "Grand Alliance," in a flexible pattern of cooperation with the Soviet Union one day and confrontation the next. The story of the origins of the Cold War and of the Roosevelt administration's policies is highly controversial; it belongs to political more than religious history. But the response of churches and synagogues and the interpreting of events by theologians and lay diplomats came to be the central theme of American religion as it affected the public order, even through the presidency of Harry S. Truman and beyond. Truman succeeded Roosevelt upon the latter's death in April 1945, and after a surprise election victory in 1948 he led the country until the Democrats yielded to Dwight D. Eisenhower and the Republicans in 1952. Truman wanted to continue Roosevelt's policies, but he soon saw that his own had to include "getting tough with Russia," and he took some risks in dealing with aggressive Soviet leadership.

9:3   By the time of the founding of the United Nations in April 1945, a move long favored by moderate and liberal religious groups, "getting tough" meant recognizing how opposed were most interests of the two new antagonist nations. A check of periodical literature would turn up hundreds of parallels to the assessment of *New Republic* writer Vera Micheles Dean early in the summer of 1945; she saw "the tendency to believe that a conflict between the United States and Russia is becoming inevitable." Poet Archibald MacLeish, then serving in the State Department, concurred, warning that "explicit reference to the possibility of a war with Russia is becoming more common in the American press from day to day." Another liberal, broadcaster Raymond Gram Swing, watched U.S. representatives at San Francisco during the founding of the United Nations "engaged in building up a logical record which would give us a clear and unarguable *casus belli* in a war which never ought to occur and which clearly could be avoided." Whether avoidance was possible, however, itself became an issue that posed religious groups against one another and blurred the outlines of the One Nation theme.

The religious leadership of the nation had been unprepared to   9:4 deal with the qualitatively different element in total warfare that came with the dropping of atomic bombs over Hiroshima and Nagasaki, Japan, in August 1945. Only years later, after the development of the hydrogen bomb and the awareness that the Soviet Union also had nuclear destructive capabilities, did the churches and synagogues take up the subject systematically and make it a part of their ethical discourse. Still, there were some thoughtful early reactions mingled with stunned response muffled because of the louder affirmations of victory that August. Already on August 9, 1945, John Foster Dulles and Bishop G. Bromley Oxnam, speaking out of the Federal Council of Churches context, bid for "a temporary suspension or alteration of our program of air attack on the Japanese homeland," and some Protestant clerics were immediately vocal as they expressed revulsion. When the pope attacked the atomic attackers, so did American Catholic editors, while Federal Council Protestants increased the vehemence of their response seven months after the bombings: "As American Christians, we are deeply penitent for the irresponsible use already made of the atomic bomb," which was "morally indefensible" and an evidence that the nation had "sinned grievously against the laws of God and against the people of Japan." Through the Cold War years to follow, the shadow of the bomb colored religious and cultural language and was often credited with having helped produce "the Age of Anxiety."

World history and the play of national forces entered a qualita-   9:5 tively new period after the use of atomic weaponry against Japan in 1945, and as America became aware that the Soviet Union was developing nuclear capabilities. The new weapons, sober scientists, alarmists, and moralists alike warned, could create such devastation that civilization and the human race were in jeopardy. Some Americans were suspected of passing atomic science secrets to the Soviet Union, and some of these, acting on their own prewar procommunist commitments or on whatever motives, without doubt did. But in such a climate many innocent people also came under suspicion. Religious and political leaders for a time could gain by rendering others suspect. It was a time when the One Nation theme was both demanded because of the Cold War and tested in a climate of easily exploitable distrust of citizen by citizen. The House Committee on Un-American Activities, reactivated under John E. Rankin of Mississippi, became an instrument for pursuing people who did not seem "tough on Russia." The world of religion did not lack people who knew how to apply various toughness tests.

9:6   The presidential administration had no motive to enter the contest of citizen versus citizen and had reason instead to seek unity among the people. Every move the United States made on the world scene now when prewar styles of isolation had become obsolete had to be motivated by thoughts of checking the spread of communism and of concern for the future of the United States. President Truman had to sound as tough as Congressman Rankin: "Unless Russia is faced with an iron fist and strong language another war is in the making. Only one language do they understand—'how many divisions have you?'" Hence, a postwar arms buildup was necessary. A Truman appointee, Averill Harriman, told secretary of the navy James Forrestal in the spring of 1945 that "the outward thrust of Communism [is] not dead; we might well have to face an ideological warfare just as vigorous and dangerous as Fascism or Nazism." Catholic and Protestant churches alike, moved by an awareness of the atheism of the Soviet regime, the devastation it was working against Eastern European churches, its dangerous defensiveness and menacing aggressiveness, instinctively joined in tough talking. Only a small minority of left-tending religious voices spoke up for dealing with the new enemy on more flexible terms. They were easily and quickly branded "soft on communism" by those on the right who wanted to take advantage of the climate of uneasiness.

9:7   *Containment,* a term invented by George F. Kennan, who was to become chairman of the State Department Policy Planning Staff, came to be the policy pursued against the Soviet Union. A theologically informed diplomat, Kennan charged that the Russians were acting with a "sense of insecurity" and displaying a "particular brand of fanaticism, unmodified by any of the Anglo-Saxon traditions of compromise." Accordingly, they were "easily persuaded of their own doctrinaire 'rightness,'" and they habitually "insisted on the submission or destruction of all competing power." Long before such an assessment became commonplace, Kennan noted that the aggressive impulse was the obverse of the "concept of Russia as in a state of siege, with the enemy glowering beyond the walls." Kennan knew that a nation acting thus could not be reined in by restrictions of either "God or man." He cast the conflict in doctrinal terms; the dogmas of Marxism and Leninism fueled the Soviets' "instinctive desire," because these afforded "pseudo-scientific justification for their impatience." The United States therefore had to employ a policy of "long-term, patient, but firm and vigilant containment of Russian expansionist tendencies." At Kennan's side was theologian Reinhold Niebuhr, an ex-Marxist himself who in January 1947 helped form and then chaired a liberal anticommunist group, Americans for Democratic Action. In *Life* magazine in October 1946, Niebuhr had written that "Russia hopes to conquer the whole of Europe strategically or ideologically." Niebuhr scorned the vestigial optimism and latter-day pacifist proclivities of some fellow believers as he tried to pull them into line or push them off: "It has been the unfortunate weakness of both liberalism and liberal Christianity," he charged, "that they have easily degenerated into sentimentality by refusing to contemplate the tragic aspects of human existence honestly." Only toughness would do.

A "Truman Doctrine," announced on March 12, 1947, in which   9:8 the president declared that the United States would back Greece and Turkey against Soviet aggression, and the Marshall Plan for the rebuilding of Europe, announced on June 5, 1947, and to be headed by war-hero general and now secretary of state George C. Marshall, were two major responses. They were designed to help prevent a European void from developing, one that the Soviet Union could fill. Truman contrasted the Soviet and the American or free-world systems in drastic (theologians would have said Manichaean) terms. Every nation at the present moment had to choose, though the choice was too often not freely made, between two ways of life. One nation was distinguished by free institutions and "guarantees of individual liberty, freedom of speech and religion," while the other relied on terror and oppression "and the suppression of personal freedoms." The United States had no choice but to support those who chose the former. When the Soviets broke the terms of postwar agreements and blocked highways to Berlin in 1946, Truman responded with an airlift to help the free parts of the city survive, an action that gave him a reputation for anticommunist leadership. But soon his energies had to be directed to

China, where the United States, with Marshall as agent in a futile task, had tried to prop up Nationalist forces against the communists. The communists were victorious in January 1949, and as Nationalist leader Chiang Kai-shek fled to Taiwan and Mao Tse-tung (as his name was then spelled) proclaimed the "Communist People's Republic," the United States in a "China White Paper" faulted Nationalists for failure. Arguments over "who lost China" grew intense in American politics.

9:9   Hostilities between communist and anticommunist powers broke out in Korea on June 25, 1950, as North Korean forces crossed the thirty-eighth parallel in that divided nation. Five days later President Truman committed U.S. forces with others from the United Nations to defend the South. Containment had become a global policy; Truman noted that communism was no longer merely subversive—it used armed invasion and war to gain its ends. The Korean "police action" was never a declared war, and the rhetoric of the time revealed little of religious interest that was independent of general contentions over who was tough or soft on communism. Truman, a personally pious man who ordinarily cooled the often heated voice of religion in war, could say now and then, as he did in 1950, "We are on the right track, and we will win—because I think God is with us in that enterprise." But most of his energies went into tactical and practical activities. The liberal lay Catholic journal *Commonweal* tried to find high ground: "At a time when the world wavers on the verge of the most hideous slaughter imaginable, we submit that the Truman-Acheson policy of exhausting every honorable means of defeating the Soviets without provoking a general war is the only position a Christian can take in good conscience." A critic of Truman's policies was John Foster Dulles, the prewar lay ecumenical leader who brought moralistic language to the anticommunist military campaigns. Containment for him was now insufficient; America must "liberate" nations. Dulles's approach was supposed to mark the new administration of Dwight D. Eisenhower who, during his campaign in 1952, promised to end the Korean action. But Eisenhower, too, had to settle for containment, a policy that frustrated the right-wingers in the churches, who kept talking about aggressive liberation.

9:10   Church leadership was prominent in such debates. The Jesuit magazine *America* advocated having American troops cross the thirty-eighth parallel and fight to liberate North Korea from communism, as it must aid "free peoples" in Indo-China, Formosa,

Yugoslavia, and elsewhere. The Catholic editors of *Columbia,* for the Knights of Columbus, also took the hard line. In their eyes, the United Nations offered little hope. America should enter into "a new covenant of nations, drawing a new charter," these editors proposed, "which will exclude from the society a government that blatantly and persistently impedes the program of peace." Thus the United Nations became part of the strategic debate and the support of it something that inspired name-calling. The evangelical *Christian Herald* supported similar policies, while charging that the U.S. government in the Truman era had been partly at fault for permitting "atheistic Communism to engulf China, to invade Korea and to threaten all other Asiatic lands," to use editor Daniel Poling's language. The more liberal *Christian Century* supported the Korean police action but started calling for worldwide programs of justice as the instruments for heading off communism. If the United States was to lead, it had to be just in its action at home and dared not fall into the "military obsession" that the editors saw developing. America, they charged, had acquired an "obsession with the idea that the way to handle the Communists and insure lasting peace is to spend hundreds upon hundreds of billions to build up gigantic armed forces." Many denominational periodicals echoed these sentiments, leaving only some small dissenting Protestant periodicals on the left to protest against containment as such. *Commonweal* promoted the longer-term moral theme: "It is still true that to overcome Communism we must feed the hungry, clothe the naked, and shelter the homeless." And *World Call,* the periodical of the Disciples of Christ, argued that the way to produce a more stable world was to set forth belief in "Christian teaching and love toward one's neighbor."

One year after Dwight Eisenhower's election a leading secular 9:11 liberal who was a friend of George Kennan and Reinhold Niebuhr, historian Arthur Schlesinger, Jr., tried to provide a midcentury vision of the life of One Nation. His book title served well then and serves now to show where all religious forces but those on the extreme left and extreme right were trying to head—to "the vital center." Centrism became a passion. In Schlesinger's book, religion was seldom mentioned; he touted a new "radicalism" of the center which held to "a belief in the integrity of the individual, in the limited state, in due process of law, in empiricism and gradualism." In works like his, progressivism and utopianism disappeared, and realism prevailed. Schlesinger was speaking up for the anticommunist liberalism of the Americans for Democratic

Action, but his title could as well have been appropriated by more
conservative types, who also wanted centrist policies, though
these would have been somewhat different from those Schlesinger
promoted. Jonathan Daniels, a journalist who admired Truman,
thought Schlesinger's book "may suddenly and clearly announce
the spirit of an age to itself." Meanwhile, only crusaders against
communism who were exploiting the uneasinesses of religious believers and other citizens would have pushed for the "vital right."
Journalist Leland Stowe gave a populist reading to the move into
the vortex of centrism. In *Target: You* he addressed "Mr. American
Middle Man," who was targeted by both "Big Capitalism" and
Communist Marxism. The American middle class provided the
"strong political Center" against extremes. "Keep in mind that the
crossfires of totalitarianism come from *both* the extreme Right and
the extreme Left; that they will continue, in one guise or another
throughout our lifetime." This meant that "free men must compre-
hend and combat *every* assault upon their freedoms from every
direction."

9:12   The theological voice that gained the most hearing during the
Cold War was that of Reinhold Niebuhr, whose outlook his critic
Morton White in the *New Republic* considered to be "part of the
canon of a new generation of American liberals and the spiritual
guide of those who are now revisiting conservatism." Of course,
no one spoke for American religion. Leftover old-style Protestant liberals and the more militant evangelicals lobbed critiques at
Niebuhr from both sides. Catholics and Jews, to whom he was
friendly, had their own outlets for expression. But the theologian
was personally close to State Department leaders and made consistent and sophisticated attempts to bring a theological viewpoint to
the Cold War. His midcentury statement, published in 1952, was
The Irony of American History. Henry Luce, while promoting the
idea of "the American Century," favored Niebuhr and gave him
space in *Life,* the popular and influential weekly magazine, for
theological interpretations that matched the ironic theme.

9:13   While fearing that Americans would try to impose their "religion" of libertarian democracy and laissez-faire capitalism on
Europeans, Niebuhr supported the Marshall Plan, "a turning point
in postwar history." When the most notable European Protestant
theologian, Karl Barth, charged that liberal Christians in America
were turning the gospel into a "Christian Marshall Plan," Niebuhr
replied. Barth, he thought, was taking too transcendental a view,
seeking a vantage and appeal above human history. It was "wrong

to preach this Gospel *sub specie aeternitatis* [under the aspect of eternity] as if there were no history with its time and seasons." Such realism impressed George Kennan and others in the State Department. The religious right was unimpressed. An American Council of Christian Laymen, which wanted to isolate people on the left and taint them, had produced a pamphlet in 1949, *How Red Is the Federal Council of Churches?* Niebuhr was in the front of their red ranks, belonging as he did, said the Laymen, to twenty-four "God-hating, unAmerican organizations." They, of course, were not seeking "the vital center."

Niebuhr intended his book to be called *This Nation Under God,*   9:14 but as he collected his lectures from a two-year period, he noticed that increasingly they dealt with the irony of the American situation, so he developed the theological motif of irony. The publisher suggested he call the work *The Irony of American History;* it became a landmark in his life, the last work completed before a stroke in 1951 began to slow Niebuhr for his remaining two decades. The term *irony,* for Niebuhr, was not used conventionally as it would be by literary analysts. Nor did it represent curious destiny. Instead—and this is what made it relevant for the Cold War—it was the perspective with which one best understood human actions when they took surprising, often contradictory, turns and when these were based at least in part on something the actors brought to the scene. Events in history therefore are not subject to mere fate; cause-and-effect relations can be established and responsibility does matter. Speaking of nations as he could of individuals, Niebuhr wrote: "If virtue becomes vice through some hidden defect in the virtue; if strength becomes weakness because of the vanity to which strength may prompt the mighty man or nation; if security is transmuted into insecurity because too much reliance is placed upon it; if wisdom becomes folly because it does not know its own limits—in all such cases the situation is ironic." In short, in the ironic situation "the person involved in it bears some responsibility for it."

To give background to his Cold War argument, Niebuhr began   9:15 at the beginning with America's sense that it was a covenant people with a divine mission, "called out by God to create a new humanity," a religious one. Out of this was born a sense of "unique innocency," which survived into the middle of the twentieth century. "Every nation has its own form of spiritual pride," he said, but America's was a peculiar version. America after World War II was strong as never before and knew it. Though the nation wanted to act upon its strengths, it always met limits. The "element of irony lies in the fact that a strong America is less completely master of its own destiny than was a comparatively weak America rocking in the cradle of its continental security and serene in its infant innocence." It was webbed into the destiny of many peoples and, while it could not control history, lived with "pretensions of innocency." The current age, Niebuhr thought, "is involved in irony because so many dreams of our nation have been so cruelly refuted by history." America thought it was and could remain virtuous, but it was not and could not. So it was, also, with innocence.

9:16   Niebuhr nevertheless sided with America in the struggle and saw the nation as crucial to the world's future. He was a frontline Cold Warrior. Communism and the Soviet Union were absolute evils, "demonically" motivated. Some secular critics considered Niebuhr an unironic Christian exclusivist when he wrote that only through religious faith could a nation have "an experience of repentance for the false meaning which the pride of nations and cultures introduces into the pattern" of history. Communism, despite its nominal atheism, propounded a messianic vision; "as a religion this faith generates what in Christian terms is regarded as the very essence of sin." It identified "the interests of a particular self or of a particular force in history with the final purposes of the God of history." Communism had "transmuted religious truths" into political slogans with "a noxious virulence of unparalleled proportions." Yet Niebuhr rescued his own vision with an ironic perspective that should not lead to pride and condescension, or to futility and folly, simply because whatever one tried would go at least partly wrong. No, "a divine judge who laughs at human pretensions without being hostile to human aspirations" governed the world and Niebuhr's vision.

9:17   Niebuhr as a professor, a churchly interpreter, and a journalist, for all his political involvements, sat figuratively on the sidelines while people in government advanced the realist vision. The most articulate of these in the crucial years was the stern and unironic moralist John Foster Dulles, who became Eisenhower's secretary of state. We have met him as a Presbyterian ecumenist; he was for a time an elder in a Presbyterian church in New York, where on occasion he preached lay sermons. The Commission to Study the Bases of a Just and Durable Peace, under his leadership, had stated a mission "to clarify the mind of our churches regarding the moral, political and economic foundations of an enduring peace." Dulles's group had also worked to mobilize "the support of the

At a conference at the White House in June 1954, prominent churchman John
Foster Dulles, now secretary of state, had opportunities to give expression to his
version of Christian realism during the Cold War. Here he meets with Winston
Churchill, Dwight Eisenhower, and Anthony Eden. (Papers of John Foster Dulles.
Public Policy Papers and University Archives. Photo: Department of Rare Books
and Special Collections, Princeton University Libraries.)

Christian people of all lands in the making of a peace consonant
with Christian principles." In the 1940s people in American state-
craft could speak congenially of the teachings of Christ, or of principles consonant with his, being influential in international affairs.
Dulles, respectful of theologians, "was always watching not to
let them get sentimental or superidealistic"; but he did so because
he regarded the message of Christ as being unsentimental and
realistic.

A sample of the commission's language provides a window on   9:18
Dulles's thought. Thus, "from [their] faith Christians derive the

ethical principles upon which world order must be based." These principles, it went on, seemed to be "among those which men of goodwill everywhere may be expected to recognize as part of the moral law." But to be effective in the non-Christian world, too, the document "first set out . . . those guiding principles which, it seems to us, Christians and non-Christians alike can accept." Its report was clear about the special responsibility of American believers. "Above all, we are impressed by the supreme responsibility which rests upon Christians. Moral law may point the way to peace, but Christ, we believe, showed that way with greatest clarity." Dulles also helped formulate "A Just and Durable Peace: Statement of Political Propositions," which was much discussed after 1943. After the dropping of the atomic bomb on Hiroshima on August 6, 1945, the Federal Council of Churches issued a statement signed by Dulles: "If we, a professedly Christian nation, feel morally free to use atomic energy in that way, men elsewhere will accept that verdict. Atomic weapons will be looked upon as a normal part of the arsenal of war and the stage will be set for the sudden and final destruction of mankind." Truman did not feel judged by this statement. The president wrote Dulles in November 1945 that he welcomed the "advanced position in international thinking" taken by the Federal Council of Churches. He was sure that "spiritual values are indestructible only as long as men are willing to take action to preserve them." Six years later his correspondence secretary, Matthew J. Connelly, added a gloss that had to infuriate evangelicals: "We have always considered the National Council of Churches [successor to the Federal Council] as the most nearly representative of all the Protestant Churches in this country."

9:19   Dulles, who early called for international control of atomic weaponry, revealed something of the closeness between diplomatic leaders and a certain kind of Protestantism when he spoke at the inauguration of his friend Henry Pitney Van Dusen as president of Union Theological Seminary in November 1945. "Out in Tennessee there is a plant," he said, "which turns out bombs. Here we have a plant which turns out ministers of the Gospel. The two seem remote and unrelated," Dulles mused, but he knew they were not. "Actually, the issue of our time, perhaps the issue of all human time, is which of the two outputs will prevail." Yet as Dulles commuted between both worlds he was sensitive to the criticism, and even claimed to agree with it, of churches as bodies in international affairs. There should be "no question of religious representation" involved. "I am, and always have been, strongly opposed to representation of the churches at any peace table." When Dulles had to defend controversial and compromising policies to the churches, he was always the realist, stressing that religious groups had to learn they could not win everything. "It seems to me that unless it be conceded that Christians in their capacity as citizens have the duty to choose what seems the lesser of two evils, then they are made impotent through their seeking to be perfectionists." And "while one never should compromise one's belief, it is often necessary to compromise one's action."

After 1945 Dulles increasingly deserted the nuanced positions he had previously expressed about nationalism and self-righteousness. As his moralism took a new turn in the face of the Soviet threat, he began to make uncritical defenses of America. By 1950 he confessed that his earlier, hopeful moves toward collaboration with the Soviet Union had been naive, unrealistic, and idealistic. Now on the other hand he had to ward off cynicism. In a *Life* article, he stressed a demand for "an affirmative demonstration that our society of freedom still has the qualities needed for survival." Now America had to show that "our free land is not spiritual lowland, easily submerged, but highland that, most of all, provides the spiritual, intellectual and economic conditions which all men want." He argued for religious affirmation more than military response. "The most significant demonstration that can be made is at the religious level. The overriding and ever-present reason for giving freedom to the individual is that men are created as the children of God, in His image." Thus the human personality is sacred, and "the State must not trample upon it." Dulles became ever more explicit about religion in world affairs: "The truth is that a society of freedom *cannot* persist, and probably *ought not* to persist, except as a religious society," he told fellow church members at the Presbyterian General Assembly. He even came to call for an old-fashioned "spiritual revival."

Almost no one except professional revivalists called for that at midcentury; it was not in the vocabulary of public officials, publicists, commentators, or reporters. Dulles, however, was explicit: "Western ascendancy," he wrote, had not been "so much the work of generals as it was of diplomats, merchants, and missionaries" in the past. Now America had to return to its old sense of mission. The older missionaries "had a sense of mission in the world, believing it their duty to help men everywhere to get the opportunity to be and to do what God designed." They had established schools and colleges and spread American ideals. In that speech of 1948

9:20

9:21

he continued: "It takes work to get religion and keep it, and no community will bear the imprint of righteousness unless the people get together in worship, to pray, to sing hymns, to hear the reading and preaching of the Holy Word and to plan to spread the truth." Otherwise "a society inevitably becomes rotten." Theologians were not using such language, but Dulles the layperson came to a rhetorical climax with the declaration that "what America needs now is a religious revival."

9:22   Reinhold Niebuhr saw the need for perspective on one's own nation, but this tended to be lost on his friend Dulles, who started complaining that historians and commentators found too many faults in the American past. The statesman asserted ideas to the effect that the American economic system had been ordained by God. Americans were "predominantly a moral people, who believe that [their] nation has a great spiritual heritage to be preserved." This heritage belonged to a society "of individuals who love God and their fellow man, and who fear only God and not any man." Dulles was setting forth what amounted to the ideals of mainstream middle America in the 1950s: Americans were individuals "who work hard as a matter of duty and self-satisfaction, not compulsion; who gain personal and family security primarily through ability and willingness voluntarily to earn and save." They were inclined toward not merely "physical growth and enjoyment, but intellectual and spiritual development." Where, Dulles's critics asked, had his realism gone?

9:23   Dulles was coming ever closer to the language that sounded jingoistic to critics like Niebuhr. It was more explicit, of course, from the pens of evangelicals and fundamentalists, for whom the "Christian America" thesis was most congenial. In *Moody Monthly,* for example, Luther J. Holcomb wrote that "Christian America" kept the position of "moral and spiritual leader in world affairs." Oppressed peoples now looked to America as the bastion of hope. Jews, secularists, and others need not apply as defenders of the bastion: "Whatever faith other peoples have in our country must be attributed to the fact that we are a Christian nation and that the ideals for which we strive are those which are consonant with the principles of Christian living." But Dulles himself was leaning toward such an interpretation. In 1950 he complained that "some of the denominations that are members of the Federal Council of Churches have representatives with the Federal Council who seem to me to be too far to the left." How did this come about? Many Protestant denominations had allowed church offices and appointments "too much to get into the hands of those of Left Wing and Socialist tendencies." That was "the real trouble," and "the Federal Council of Churches merely records the fact." Was it deserting the vital center, or had Dulles moved to the right?

In July 1949 New York governor Thomas E. Dewey named Dulles a senator to fulfill a term for four months, but he was defeated in November by Democrat Herbert Lehman, who, Dulles claimed, had communist support. The Truman administration named Dulles a State Department adviser during the Korean War, a post he used as a platform from which to praise the United Nations troops. He had become as explicit now as *Moody Monthly.* He told a radio audience in 1950, "We have borne a Christian witness. We need have no remorse. Also we need not despair. We have acted as God gave us to see the right." This meant that United Nations troops could be "pretty sure that they are fighting for a just cause." That July Dulles brought morality closer to home. Americans should not be afraid "to live sacrificially and even dangerously in a righteous cause." Dulles was a natural candidate to become secretary of state when Dwight D. Eisenhower was elected president in 1952 and took office in January 1953. As secretary of state, Dulles could plead for "a just and righteous cause," his version of the vital center. He was not alone, in either party or in the major religious bodies. Which element in American religion would determine what the "just and righteous cause was" and who, "under God," would articulate it and monitor its expression became the postwar issue.

9:24

10

"Can Protestantism Win America?"

10:1   **O**ne Nation" with three religious peoples, Protestant, Catholic, and Jewish: to think of it this way became a political convention during World War II. Smaller minority faiths beyond Judaism, other Christian sectors such as Orthodoxy, and various Protestant peoples such as African Americans numbered tens of millions. But they were not part of the conventional reckoning of religious powers by public figures, mass communicators, academics, and those who invoked common symbols of the society. As for the largest single cluster, the Protestantism that was dominated by white people, such an accounting of the whole usually overlooked the wide internal diversities. Of course, sometimes those who did the accounting gloried in these as exemplifications of American freedom, ingenuity, and tolerance. Or they reckoned that the differences between groups were of private but not public significance. In their distinctive groupings those with differing and peculiar allegiances had the luxury of doing irrelevant things together, such as worshiping, caring for souls, or arguing theology. They recognized the necessity of supporting the war effort or the Cold War cause as if the differences between faiths did not matter. If one looked at American Protestantism from a great, great distance, something of this vision made sense. But even the visionary person from afar, or the generalizer with a very broad sweep, had to notice that the Protestantism they were talking about was divided into two

130

large camps. Their leaders and laity had quite disparate views of the nation, its causes, their places in them, and the God who called them or the churches that gathered them. This meant that when Protestants contended for the right or privilege to continue to be the main contributor to and monitor of public life, their case was compromised from within and without. Still, there were good reasons for them to present their best face after World War II, over against Catholic and secular contentions, and independently of those of Judaism, which was less a rival.

How can we hear that Protestant case? The reader of religious   10:2 periodicals and observer of community rites can begin observing almost anywhere. But now and then a document turns up that consolidates and confirms impressions gained from wide reading and long familiarity. As revealing as anything one is likely to come across is a certain picture book. It dates from the era just before television began to preempt the role in image-making that photographs had previously held. Appropriately titled *The Protestant Panorama,* it was written by Clarence W. Hall, managing editor of the evangelical *Christian Herald.* He designed it to delight churchgoers and to present as genial and open a picture as possible of the majority faith cluster. Hall clearly aimed it at "the vital center," to illustrate the safe, moderate middle way of the churches and their contribution to the American way of life. Former Federal Council of Churches president and lawyer Charles P. Taft introduced the book, thereby imparting a kind of Good Churchkeeping seal of approval by conciliar and ecumenical Protestants. Dust-jacket copy and book subtitles are not always to be trusted, but in Hall's case they perfectly condensed the plot. He intended the book to answer negatively and emphatically two questions posed on the jacket: "Are the churches dying? Is religious faith ebbing away in modern times?"

In assembling his book, Hall could not answer these questions   10:3 for all churches, but he was sure about Protestantism and its place. A clear equation made the point designed to elbow non-Protestants aside: "The American heritage *is* the Protestant heritage" (the whole phrase was italicized in the book, so these italics are mine, but the emphasis is Hall's). This declaration informed the presentation of "America's majority faith." The same emphasis also colored the way that faith was finally seen in the mid-century context. For this equation meant that Protestantism was "inevitably cast for the role of chief adversary of communism." The pictures in the book would hardly have stirred the hearts of Protestant re-

At mid-century denominational and interdenominational magazines, here panoplied, served to represent the varieties of Protestantism and, in their abundance and reach, to suggest something of Protestant influence around 1950. It was estimated that 950 periodicals reached fifty million subscribers. (Photo: The Christian Herald Association.)

formers four centuries earlier or of the pioneers who had brought the faith from Europe three centuries before. If Protestantism meant prophecy or protest, if it implied critique or radical reconstruction, one would not learn it from Hall's panorama. The subjects, be they children or servicepeople, parishioners in pews or at committee meetings, all tended to be posed in neat and orderly rows and classes. Taft must have sensed the limits of the safe approach: "The tough fibre of Protestantism must be recovered from much of the soft sentimentality that has sometimes engulfed us."

The Protestant Panorama was written in a mode that a later 10:4 time would call triumphalist; yet whoever compares it to contemporaneous writings will find that its mode and tone were typical. The author piled on his claims, and we do best by figuratively turning the pages with him, liberally using quotation marks to reproduce a midcentury voice. Protestantism, Hall wrote, was not a church; it was "an idea, a spirit. It is a way of thinking God's thoughts after him," especially about freedom. "Protestantism, pure and undefiled, is the most democratic thing on earth today." To the author and, he hoped, his readers, it was not surprising that "Protestants came to America, settled America, made America after the likeness of their own ideal." Nor, in the advertising climate of the Cold War, would many find it astonishing to read that Protestant America sparked the ideal of freedom in the "minds of little people everywhere, starting them on the march to self-realization, God-realization." Hall ended his prelude with recall of the "prophetic vision" of a "new 'nation under God,'" the vision which led some to the *Mayflower.* On this Pilgrim ship some Puritans brought "The Big Idea" of freedom across the Atlantic. Hall did have to deal with the presence of Catholics who were here before this Protestant ship came in. But Catholics, he claimed, failed to bring freedom because they were part of "systems, governmental and ecclesiastic, which were forever alien to this new land." How did he explain Maryland, which Roman Catholics founded and in which religious tolerance was early promoted? That colony did right on this issue because it was "influenced by the prevailing Protestant spirit" of the times and the surroundings.

As is often the case in promotional material aimed at masses, 10:5 historical accuracy was not a prime concern. In his search for roots, Hall saw the Protestant spirit surfacing at a climactic moment when Benjamin Franklin called for prayer at the Constitutional Convention of 1787. "The weary delegates arose and cheered. The motion was unanimously approved and voted." In fact, the convention ignored Franklin's request; its members did not rise, cheer, approve, or vote favorably. They seemed a bit embarrassed until someone muttered that there were no funds for a chaplain. Never mind: "Is it strange that from that moment onward progress was rapid in the framing and the adoption of The Constitution of the United

States?" Hall used the term *separation of Church and State* for the action taken two years later to assure legal support for religious freedom and then went on to stress that such separation had never meant renunciation of religion. Then came a true sentence, "Our national culture is permeated with religion," coupled with a compromising bit of evidence and the trumpeting of a connection: "Witness the legend 'In God We Trust' on your coins placed there by a Protestant Secretary of the Treasury."

10:6   The rest of the book elaborated the America = Protestantism thesis in pictures and prose. The United Nations was new enough still to elicit some support from a middle America that also criticized it, thus: "When it seemed the new United Nations was making space for everything but religion, Protestant laymen almost drowned the UN with demands for a chamber for prayer and meditation, also for a period of reverent silence at the opening of each UN Assembly wherein each delegate could commune according to his faith; they got both." More predictably popular was Hall's gallery of national heroes. "Run your finger down any list of American great[s], past and present, and see there the towering totality of Protestant men." (Women were in auxiliaries, in Hall's and much mainstream elaboration at mid-century.) No one should be baffled that so many of America's "great creative minds in all fields have been Protestant. The unshackled mind is the only truly creative mind." The unshackling of minds was most evident in the American capitalist order, a system that was being "pilloried by every pink from Moscow to Manhattan." Protestant reformer John Calvin, according to Hall, was responsible for what began as an imperfect system. But it had a "Christian basis in this land," and the current generation was being called to "labor ceaselessly to further Christianize it." This Christianizing was evident in the stewardship practices of such wealthy Protestants as "Andrew Carnegie, the Rockefellers, Andrew Mellon, Henry Ford—to name just a few." (Carnegie in fact had been an open agnostic who was derisive of most kinds of faith.)

10:7   Women, so often neglected in mid-century portrayals of public Protestantism, received their own chapter, "Ten Million Church Women." That figure was far too low, but Hall was counting only those who counted, in organizations that struck his kind of Protestant as being most approved, especially the United Church Women. "Only a fool—usually a male fool—ever apologizes for the preponderance of female influence and representation in Protestant church life." Woman, after all, "achieved her first liberty within its precincts, her fullest liberty in response to its ethic," and the greatest outlet for "her urges to self-expression." Hall then asked, *Cherchez la femme?* and answered: "That's easy. Survey your church, your community, your nation"; wherever there would be evidences of reform "you will 'find the woman.'" Christianity gave her most of the "equality and dignity she enjoys." Not just any old Christianity did this; "*Protestant* Christianity lifted her to her feet and set her on the long march toward full emancipation." Hall noted that Quakers had first recognized women "preachers on an equal basis with men" but observed also that the Disciples of Christ had "a cordon of able women preachers." True, women had not yet won complete equality as ministers—a gross mid-century overstatement—but Hall had a ready explanation: "The reason probably is that not enough of them want it. Let the hankering arise on a wide enough scale, and you can put it down that universal ordination will be theirs." As they had made their way in other realms, he advised, expect great things to be forthcoming for women on the women religious front.

Nationalism ruled in books like *The Protestant Panorama.* 10:8 "The United States today, with its more than fifty million [adult] Protestants, is the largest and most virile Protestant nation on the face of the globe." Hall explained away the presence of 28,470,092 Catholics by pointing out that their number included infants and children. "Protestant membership gains consistently have been higher than those of any other faith in America." In 1950 alone there had been a net gain of 3 percent by Protestants against a population gain of only 1.67 percent. Hall did not analyze which parts of Protestantism were doing the growing. Was there uniformity? Was the mainstream expanding, or was the often overlooked fundamentalist and evangelical sector beginning its surge? Yes, Protestants were divided among themselves, but "far from being something to carp at," this division to him was "Protestantism's glory." In Hall's portrayal, the profusion of denominations represented a "spiritual free enterprise" to match the economic version in which Americans gloried. With an implied swat at American Catholics and European critics, who dismissed Protestantism in the United States as divided and divisive, the author dismissed them as carpers "who have yet to be imbued with the spirit of democracy and religious liberty." While critics scorned what he called "our 'vast proliferation of sects,'" what disturbed them, he observed, was a lack of *uniformity,* a lack that Protestant founders cherished.

In the midst of the ecumenical era, an evangelical like Hall who 10:9

said he favored ecumenism was typical of a generation that poised
the uniting impulse of Protestantism in One Nation against the
diversity that gave the public options. Something to cheer was
the presence of 250,000 congregations to "fit the yearnings of
ultraconservative, ultraliberal, and all between." If people thought
about this range, "jeers may turn to cheers." After the cheers, Hall
still spent time justifying. American Protestantism was not inco-
herent, he maintained: over 95 percent of all Protestants were in
one-tenth of the 250 denominations. Protestants were not, as cari-
catured, "so many embattled pups, huddling jealously over their
respective bones of contention, and growling ominously at others
over theirs." Most Protestants had taken lessons from "Theodore
Roosevelt (Dutch Reformed)," as Hall chose to identify the former
president, that " 'there are plenty of targets to hit without firing into
each other!' " Had no one noticed that Catholics with their religious orders and national groupings showed "quite as much, perhaps even more, bitter rivalry" within their own camp? "That
Catholic dissensions do not get to the public is due to the hierarchy's ability to enforce silence when they become too vitupera-
tive." To be praised were Protestant sects of the past "who fought,
when they did fight, out in the open, with no holds barred and no
shades drawn," while Catholics, more divided than they, fought
"behind the scenes." At last Hall took time to recognize the fateful
division, the one between liberals and conservatives, "the only major wall separating Protestants from each other." Other walls kept
tumbling. "Not only has schism virtually ceased within denominations, and the multiplication of new sects has almost come to
a standstill, but churches formerly separated have been rushing
back to the remarriage altar." The author saw signs of "organic
consolidation" everywhere, as unions of churches kept being con-
summated.

10:10   If Hall's rhetorical jumble seemed bewildering, it must be said
that the author had no monopoly on confusion. Did the public want
a divided religious force to assure freedom? Protestantism was just
that, in the writings of many besides Hall. Did the One Nation need
a uniting spiritual force in order to ensure unity? Protestantism was
best qualified. Did the people seek both division-with-unity *and*
coherence? Protestantism was not as confusing as it looked. The
many writers and promoters who had to advertise the values of
Protestantism for the One Nation could draw on apparently conflicting if not contradictory tendencies when putting it forward. So
it was also with interfaith relations; Hall, himself hardly tolerant of

Catholicism, credited Protestants with having worked more than
any others for "brotherliness between Protestant, Roman Catholic
and Jew." Ecumenism was fine, but few sought "organic union of
the *whole* of American Protestantism," he said, "however passionately some Protestants may yearn for it." Here he may have read
public opinion better than some ecumenists did: Americans did
fear bigness, monopoly, uniformity, and amalgamation of machinery; they cared only for "the 'communion of saints.' " Hall discerned less maturity in "splinter groups," even though their members were pious, loyal, and ready to defend their spirituality; "only
the religious snob would deny them a place, and a suitably prominent one, in the total Protestant picture."

The *Christian Herald* and its editors were moderately conser-   10:11
vative evangelicals who intersected with moderately liberal mainstream Protestants. So Hall, representing them, performed a service by calling attention to the revivalists and evangelists. His
timing was right: "From their ranks largely have arisen such significant movements as 'Youth for Christ' and such phenomenally
successful evangelists as Billy Graham," who was just then coming to true national prominence. Now their more conservative
camp was making strides toward united action through a new National Association of Evangelicals, founded in April 1942. The
main action in Protestantism, however, remained with "the majority wing," which in November 1950 had just "put the capstone
on their steadily arising arch of Christian co-operation by the creation of the National Council of Churches." Friendly to the council, he surmised that its invention would accelerate the growth of
"unity within diversity." It would also cut down on overhead and
duplication and "make for increased influence of American Protestantism through its 'united front.' " Hall sounded as if he pictured
every member of the constituent denominations simultaneously on
their knees on Sunday, December 3, 1950, the first Sunday in the
council's life, when 31 million Protestants "went to their knees,"
being thankful for "this newest and biggest 'coming together' in
American Protestantism's history." The author's final flourish on
that scene: Protestants had "a way of making their dreams come
true," and their new dream matched the spirit of Christ's prayer
" 'that they might be one!' "

Protestants were good for much in society, as the major force   10:12
for reform, social reconstruction, welfare, and mercy. "Walk into
the background of almost any project to alleviate human woe, religious or secular, and you cannot avoid bumping into Protestants

all over the place." But remedy was not enough; "the present Protestant mood, strong and growing by the hour," was "that rescuing brands from the burning [was] a necessity, but putting out the fire makes more sense." Now as never before, he thought, Protestantism was "tackling the unclean spirits" that caused so much distress in the world, and, "mark this," said the author, Protestants "have never approached any social task with a Protestant ax to grind, a Protestant profit to accrue, a Protestant interest to serve." Thus they simply promoted education; the American educational system "is the child of American Protestantism"; that fact was a byword with historians. Then Hall uttered one of his scolding cautions: in setting up the public schools, Protestants insisted that "*public funds were to be expended only on schools under public authority* and that no religious sect should share in any way in such funds." This theme Hall accompanied with the most predictable line on the subject: of course, "there was no separation of *religion* from education." The Bible was always prominent in public education.

10:13   *The Protestant Panorama* was almost entirely sunny, but now a cloud came. American education had reached a peak in efficiency, but "something has happened to its heart. Protestants are facing this curious anomaly: religion, which has founded the public schools, made them free, has largely been elbowed out." This elbowing out induced parents and educators to fling epithets at schools: "Godless! Secular! Pagan!" What had happened? Was the "unreligious influence" of pioneer educator Horace Mann at fault, or the pragmatism of the public school's modernist philosopher John Dewey? Could it have been the "'growing godlessness' of science?" All of the above, plus the fact that the "dereligioning of public schools" began a century earlier? Mann and Dewey were "not the irreligionists their detractors claim," said Hall, who had to part with detractor claims to make his own italicized charge: "*The schools began to lose their religion when the Protestant belief in free public schools was met head-on by the designs of the Roman Catholic clergy against them.*" Look at the record, he advised. Immigrant Irish and German Catholics in the nineteenth century swarmed into the cities and demanded public funds for their parochial schools. Failing to get what they wanted, the hierarchs attacked public education by claiming to see the King James Version and the reciting of a longer version than theirs of the Lord's Prayer as evidences of Protestant sectarianism. So the Bible and the Lord's Prayer got dropped from classrooms, whereupon Catholics called the schools godless and pressed for government support of their own institutions. Protestants tried to restore religion through "released-time" practices, but an atheist challenge and the United States Supreme Court had recently struck even that down. Yet in revised form the teaching of religion was coming back, ready to assure that in this form faith but not any form of sectarianism was promoted. This innovation would help rescue "the Christian faith from the limbo into which misguided interests and religious intolerance have forced it."

American Protestantism was not yet perfect, agreed Hall, but it   10:14
assured an "eventual 'going on toward perfection' " because of its readiness to admit failures. Was Hall providing an example of such admitting? The main flaws, in his reading of the situation, were sectarianism, middle-class smugness, failure to appreciate the Protestant heritage, and Protestants' being "tardy in the employment of their powers." Despite these flaws, Protestantism had a compensating strength for such an hour as this, in the Cold War: "Protestantism has been inevitably cast for its role as chief adversary of Communism." Methodist bishop G. Bromley Oxnam—who, ironically, was to be scored by the Protestant right for being too soft on communism—had recently pointed out in *Look* magazine that it was precisely in Protestant regions like Scandinavia and the rest of northern Europe that communism had made little headway. Meanwhile Italy, 99 percent Roman Catholic, "was but recently in danger of Communist revolution." Poland, Czechoslovakia, Hungary, and Austria, Catholic countries all, were in the Moscow orbit—Oxnam did not stop to explain why—while France was seriously infiltrated; Catholic Spain was not communist, but only thanks to a bloody civil war and a fascist dictatorship. The United States, Oxnam said, was in no danger of accepting communism. Rural areas in the Protestant West or the Protestant South were least tempted to turn left. Finally, even the "Universal Declaration of Human Rights," passed by the United Nations in December 1948, "was largely authored, sponsored, and piloted through the General Assembly" by Protestants. Could anyone doubt that the time had come for Protestantism's great idea, freedom, to break forth?

In one terse phrase Hall, whose book we now close, had men-   10:15
tioned a topic that merited book-length notice: "the only major wall separating Protestants from each other"; it was "the division between liberals and conservatives." How, one asks, did people on both sides of that division advertise Protestant readiness to meet the needs of their One Nation in Cold War times and midway

through "the American Century?" Many different kinds of advocates spoke up within divided Protestantism. But the statement of the case made in two works by editors of the *Christian Century* is as credible as any other. That weekly, subtitled a bit belligerently "undenominational," was friendly to the denominations of the Protestant mainstream. Protestant clergy especially sought out the magazine for expressions of congenial views. Though Hall represented middle-brow, middle-of-the-road, middle-class Protestantism, he did not deviate at all in his cultural depiction of Protestant glories from the viewpoints expressed by editors Paul Hutchinson, a Methodist, or Charles Clayton Morrison, a member of the Disciples of Christ, both of whom stepped away from their editorial duties long enough to promote the Protestant case at book length. If Hall was always sunny, except when he made his dark polemical swings, the works of these editors qualified their praise of Protestantism with shadows in the form of a more self-critical, even threatening note.

10:16   Paul Hutchinson wrote *The New Leviathan* as the war was ending, while citizens were contending over the meanings of state, nation, and nationalism. The Allies were defeating totalitarianisms, but the spiritual threat of these remained. What should one say about the "increasing tendency to look to the state for the ordering of all of life and every life?" asked Hutchinson. There were dangers closer to home than Italy, Germany, Japan, or the ally that was turning enemy and certainly was a totalitarianism, Russia. One could promote the idea of America as One Nation to the point that people might lose direction and liberties and see that idea realized in ominous forms. Then what? Hutchinson had watched churches in enemy lands capitulate to the all-consuming nation. Might they here? Hall had not worried about such specters. Yet, Paul Hutchinson knew, they haunted "the ostensibly democratic nations," including the United States. To bring back a popular phrase of the times: it can happen here!

10:17   In the heady moments of victory in 1945, not many citizens remembered, or perhaps cared to revisit, old domestic battles. But to show the danger of Leviathan, Hutchinson had to remind people that an instance of the "complete rule of the state in the realm of conscience" could be cited from as recent a year as 1931. That case demonstrated that the good citizen now "must accept the voice of Government as the voice of God." He pointed to Yale theology professor Douglas Clyde Macintosh, who had served honorably in the Canadian and American armies in the First World War and, while in the process of migrating to the United States, had to state his views on conscientious objection. No pacifist, Macintosh declared he would bear arms only in wars approved by his own conscience. The Supreme Court by a 5–4 vote ruled against citizen Macintosh, or, better, ruled against citizenship for Macintosh. Hutchinson winced to recall the reasoning: a citizen could not put "his allegiance to the will of God above the allegiance to the government." The Christian, Hutchinson proposed, had to read the next sentence repeatedly to let it sink in. "Unqualified allegiance to the nation and submission and obedience to the laws of the land, as well those made for war as those made for peace, are not inconsistent with the will of God." Not only immigrants from Canada had to learn this; it applied to all. "One Nation" stood higher in conscience than "One God," and that for Hutchison was blasphemy and heresy. He cited other cases that had been decided against Jehovah's Witnesses but did not need more than the decisive one against Macintosh to make his point. (That Court ruling, by the way, was the last to call America a "Christian nation.")

Ah, but that was long ago; fourteen years later America had   10:18 won a victory for freedom and had done so by fighting a war— Hutchinson often heard the injunctions and the boasts— "repentantly." To urge repentance and to claim that it had occurred when it had not was to "prostitute a great word in the vocabulary of religion." Repentance meant turning from past sin. "It is a perversion of the truth to say that Christians in any significant numbers fought the Second World War repentantly," even though many did fight reluctantly, skeptically, and with moral revulsion over what they had to do and how they had to do it. The United Nations Charter at war's end, charged Hutchinson, expressed the interests of the Great Powers. The idealist, antimilitarist, anti-imperialist United States was now turning imperial in the mode of the Great Powers. Russia and the United States would dominate at the expense of the colonized peoples. A believer in Christian missions, Hutchinson became skeptical as he heard denominations announce plans to raise money for "a period of greatly expanded missionary activity." Missionaries today and tomorrow would not be accepted, because they would be agents of imperial and colonialist America. How would representatives of the nation that had used the atomic bomb be welcomed?

As for nonrepentance over evils on the domestic front, lib-   10:19 eral Protestant Hutchinson was disturbed by the idolatry of free-enterprise economics. He quoted his friend Halford E. Luccock's satirical dictum: "Thou shalt not upset the applecart." Not that Hutchinson was for socialism; indeed he called in two unlikely sets of allies to support his own case against an encroaching state. One was Friedrich A. Hayek, whose *Road to Serfdom* was rallying conservatives. Along with Hayek, two others—Albert Jay Nock and Ludwig von Mises, not ordinarily *Christian Century* favorites— were warning against the managerial state in economic life. The other set of surprising witnesses were the modern popes, ordinarily despised by the likes of Hutchinson, popes who in 1891 and 1941, in the letters *Rerum Novarum* and *Quadragesimo Anno,* had pointed to a "third way" in economic organization.

10:20   As quickly as he picked up the popes in economics, Hutchinson dropped them in politics. They represented, abroad and at home, the new Leviathan. A quick world tour of Catholic Spain, Portugal, and Latin America gave him a horror show with which to frighten non-Catholic Americans. He cited the famed textbook *Catholic Principles of Politics,* by John A. Ryan and Francis J. Boland, a bugaboo book to Protestants in those years. In effect it told Protestants who worried about the coming of Catholic authoritarianism, "it can't happen here!" and featured a plea for such Protestants not to worry, "until a point has been reached at which, by virtue of the preponderance of Catholics in the population, it has become too late for Protestants to worry!" Protestantism in some forms could also encroach on liberties in its support of the One Nation. So, most of all, could secularism. Liberals fought secularism in 1945 with fervor to match that generated by evangelicals ever after. With virtually all expressive Protestants, Hutchinson saw public schools as the battleground. "Democracy, in the final analysis, is a religious idea." Secularism instead saw the human "as nothing more than a creature of earth" and thus readily a slave to the Leviathan. The Judeo-Christian religion—the phrase itself, one recalls, was a new coinage—offered instead a concept of the worth of all humans, under God. Schools without the "under God" motif, Hutchinson feared, would become America's "most prolific sources of cynicism, self-regarding egotism, indifference as to morality in public affairs and the worship of state power."

10:21   What to do was clear; how to do it was an issue that befuddled Hutchinson, because America was growing religiously illiterate. The religious background of older generations had disappeared. In colleges, religion was belittled. The diversity of "melting pot" America made it hard to provide coherent readings of texts, and the result would be a loss of community. Parochial schools drove "deep fissures through the community," so they were part of the problem and not of the solution. If they prevailed, "that process of amalgamation on which rests the future of such a country as this" would end. "Released-time" programs (in which students would be released from school to attend religious education classes at their respective churches) did not work, and in practice they created invidious distinctions among students as some children headed from a common school to different churches while others did not attend the programs at all. What Hutchinson proposed would have astounded advocates of parochial education just as it showed how ready liberal Protestants were to hold on to power by setting the terms for religion in public education. He quoted his colleague Charles Clayton Morrison, who argued that America was now past sectarian rivalry, thanks to both the liberalization of the churches and the growth of objective techniques in education. Hutchinson argued that teachers could and should be "objective" in presenting religion and should not turn schools into churches. "Religious education is the gaining of knowledge, true knowledge, *about* religion." The editor was starting an argument that would continue indefinitely, and he was aware of uneasinesses around him. He had to ask, for and with his fellow citizens: Whose knowledge was true knowledge? How would agreement be reached on what Morrison called the "common subject matter of religious faith?" Where were teachers who could handle it? Would this plan not match those of European nations which, if anything, secularized their nations further? Citizens had to be on guard lest the omnipotent state, the new Leviathan, exploited and preempted religion for its purposes. At the crucial point, Hutchinson could do little more than mumble.

American Christians had always been "too ready to lean on the   10:22 secular arm, without realizing that the secular arm was encircling the church and throttling it." So Christians now must "proclaim the end of the world of nationalism and the necessity for the transformation of our existing national loyalties into a globe-encircling loyalty to one world state." As for the churches' role working for the cause of One World, Hutchinson carried on the *Christian Century*'s ecumenical crusade: "certainly everything that savors of clinging to old denominational sovereignties and sectarian factionalisms is a hindrance to any effective proclamation of the goal of a world state." A world state! The cry "unite or die" applied to churches as much as to nations. Hutchinson did not seem to worry about the potential Leviathanism of the one-world state and the one-world church.

10:23   Three years after his book was published, the vision of Hutchinson had not advanced at all, but the great threats to it, secularism and Catholicism, had. So Charles Clayton Morrison brought out a collection of articles with a title designed to astonish: *Can Protestantism Win America?* Had not Protestantism shaped the United States and had it not "won" the nation centuries before? How could this vision of America be squared with the one that had given Hall his evidence in *The Protestant Panorama?* Morrison saw those things as part of an "illusion of progress and strength" that resulted from the "parochial habit of measuring Protestantism in terms of local or denominational successes," of which there must have been some. It was the forces surrounding Protestantism that were growing, that were "carrying American society away from Protestantism." In the face of weakened churches and the low morale of their leaders, Morrison wrote: "If I could state it all in a sentence," this book was "a plea for Protestantism to be itself, that is, to be truly, consistently, unitedly, and militantly Protestant."

10:24   Morrison was as sure as Hall had been that Protestantism was now tempted to become falsely tolerant or sentimental. Protestantism "regards itself as the carrier of a universal principle of reality and of the ultimate meaning of human existence. The missionary spirit is of its essence." The definite article before the word *carrier* sounded imperial, and was intended to. Morrison heard such a claim as well from two rivals, Catholicism and secularism, each of which was also "determined to mold the character of American culture" and "out to win America if it can." And they were gaining, at Protestantism's expense. Now he sounded like Hall. Until recently there had been no competitors to Protestantism as "the ascendant faith of the American people." In long gone horse-and-buggy days, things had been different. Now there was decline. Less ready than Hall to believe the statistics of selective Protestant growth, Morrison knew that even if they were accurate, they indicated nothing about the depth or quality of the movement and the churches.

10:25   For Morrison as for Hutchinson and other Protestant liberals, the best evidence for the decline was the change in public schools, preserves of their kind of Protestantism in days past, but now lost, or nearly lost, to secularism. The losses were too large and stunning for anyone to realize the full effects. The change resulted from a misinterpretation of the principle of the separation of church and state. It had led many Protestants to go along with the notion that religion had to be ruled out of general education. The public was consequently so far from an understanding of the role of religion that it was developing a blind spot concerning it. Many citizens did not even notice the millions going to church, did not ask why they went, what they did, what impact they had. "The public school does not know that there is such a thing as religion in American society," though its own leaders and teachers may well have been privately religious. In public life, religion had become insignificant and marginal. Morrison joined Hutchinson in his belief that teaching "about" religion would improve the situation. For now, "if Protestantism is to win America it must take up the religious education of its children with the same seriousness which characterized its churches before the public school came into existence." Just how and why non-Protestant America would step back and permit this "winning" to go on, Morrison did not state.

"If Protestantism is to win America from secularism," Morrison went on, "it must win science," which did not mean "win America from science." This was Morrison's second line of counterattack. In the new atomic age, scientific knowledge, everyone knew, could end the world. Only a world community and universal education would counter the dangers of that happening. But scientific secularism, because it lacked a transcendent dimension, could not produce these. The absence of transcendence led to the idolatries of nationalism or, in America, to "a religion of humanism which, largely under the influence of science, denies the Christian God, and sets up a god of its own whose name is Man." Only Christianity could create a humane "world community, a universal *modus vivendi.*" It is hard to recapture the heady and uncalculating sense expressed by liberal Protestantism in the early days of the United Nations and in those ripe years for proclaiming One World over against One Nation. Morrison certainly retained enough pacifism not to picture the less than 30 percent of the world that was nominally Christian, and the less than half of that group that was Protestantism, uniting in an army for military conquest. With Hutchinson at his side, Morrison certainly cannot have pictured missionaries turning aggressive in their attempts to convert people. So he was reduced to abstract advertising: "Christianity is the only religion which has the dynamic of universality, the spiritual resources, the adaptability, and the inherent sense of moral responsibility for the character of civilization which world commmunity requires."

10:27   When Morrison said Christianity, he meant only Protestantism. By page sixty he was complimenting Catholicism for its "bold and highly intelligent strategy" to win America, but it was a compliment marked by fear. *Christian Century* editors pictured the bishops and theologians sitting around in cabals and conspiracies, plotting how to take over, using winsome and persuasive "forward preachers" to do the task. These Catholic strategists no doubt felt secure in their position in American society, as they watched Protestantism "becoming less and less militant." The Romanists were observing "the cultural drift away from Protestantism, and, within Protestantism, into secularism" and spotting the opening for their own advance. Hierarchical and authoritarian though it was, Catholicism was appealing to two types of secularists, thought Morrison, as Protestantism was not: "the sophisticate among the intelligentsia, and the unreflective person representing the great mass whose capacity to think upon the ultimate meaning of life has been shrunk by an absorbing preoccupation with secular interests." While inauthentic, Catholicism could address the void in the lives of such people at the fonts where wisdom, reverence, and faith normally had their source.

10:28   If Hutchinson was moderate and discreet, Morrison was a street fighter who used any weapons at hand to stigmatize the enemy. It was certainly inflammatory, early after World War II, to see Catholicism as "the perfect embodiment of the principle of fascism," with the pope as the counterpart to or prototype of "the fascist or nazist or communist 'party' with the dictator at its head." Catholicism was totalitarian, "a monarchical and feudal institution," operating on a principle "exactly opposite to that embodied in our democracy and in Protestantism." One hears the preemptiveness of the word *our:* as the Roman Church—even the choice of that term, which omitted the word *Catholic* to suggest foreign control, is significant—extended power, it would "profoundly transform our culture and institutions." Catholicism's "degree of solidarity unknown in Protestantism" gave it a political advantage which Morrison claimed it used in bloc voting. Catholicism was targeting Negroes for future growth. Its laws against mixed marriage and opposition to birth control helped its population grow. There was no hope for the reform or redemption of Catholicism. "The Roman Church is thus an exotic and alien ingredient in the social and political life of America," and it existed now "as an already perfected dictatorship" within the nation.

American elites, even if they were Protestant, Morrison feared,   10:29
now saw Protestantism to be only a survival of a past era, never as "a formidable entity." It failed because it was not "corporately oriented." The elites had to be retaught. They had to "get rid of the notion that Protestantism ever did *win* America. By and large, it *was* America from the beginning." The map now led to a new conclusion: "The naked truth is that American society was once predominantly Protestant and is no longer." To argue with Catholicism was a waste of time. *"The true task of Protestantism is to win the very America which Catholicism is out to win."* Never subtle about strategy, Morrison reached for more italics: *"Protestantism must now confront the contemporary scene as if the Christianization of America depended, under God, upon it alone."* And only one kind of Protestantism would serve. The camp that lay over the wall described by Hall was too conservative, too orthodox, too fundamentalist, and thus too isolated and withdrawn to be in the battle. Only one kind of Protestantism would serve, claimed Morrison, and it was drifting into secularism. "Thus liberalism played into the hands of secularism by offering it a Christianity which was itself secularized."

Hall's triumphalism was foreign to Morrison. The editor instead   10:30
saw Protestantism being victimized by false tolerance. Yes, there was room for interfaith movements with Jews and Catholics, but, the author noted, Catholics had taken only a "minor, and what seems like grudging, part" in them. And in such movements, Protestantism was always expected to step back, in a spirit of *noblesse oblige,* while others advanced. And it was too divided. "America will never be won by a sectarianized Protestantism," hence ecumenism was important for it. Though Morrison came from a group that stressed congregational autonomy and localism, he now believed that Protestantism was too localized, a victim of "undisciplined, relatively irresponsible, atomistic parochialism." Preachers had to invent specialties, entertain and tantalize members, or produce "sterile religious fanaticism" to keep their congregations alive. They could never unite to help "win" America. Protestantism, Morrison said in the face of rivals who must have been surprised to learn this, *"has lacked the will to be strong"* and has chosen to make a virtue of its weakness. True, there were 43 million Protestants to 23 million Catholics, and a "wide populational

periphery surrounding the Protestant churches" swelled that number. True, membership en masse was wealthy, and the members were often generous. But the giving of funds largely supported irrelevant institutions. Certainly, the laity had to be dissatisfied with this situation, but it was unaroused. How could one rouse them? "There is a way. There must be a way. And Protestantism, if it is to win America, must find it."

10:31   There was one way out of the present malaise: "*The only alternative to a sectarianized Protestantism is an ecumenical Protestantism.*" Ecumenism, however, did not mean the involvement of all Christians; it meant something that was "inclusive, intentionally and potentially inclusive, though not necessarily at its beginning actually inclusive, of the whole non-Roman Christian community." The church unity movement must be "*Protestant:* in the sense that it rests upon the ecumenical basis of the sovereignty of Christ," as Catholicism could not. It must become a *church:* "not a 'council' of 'churches,' nor a 'federation' of 'churches,' nor yet

The rarely photographed Executive Committee of the Federal Council of Churches in session in 1945. Bishop G. Bromley Oxnam is presiding while a report is being read. (Photo courtesy of the National Council of the Churches of Christ in the USA.)

a mere 'invisible church,' but the actual, empirical, functioning *church of Christ* on earth." Of course, Protestantism must begin with "*cooperation on a federal basis,*" as in the Federal Council, which meant it would develop a cautious, limited "*agency,*" a "*contrivance,*" and not a church. Second, there must be "*reduction of the number of denominations by mergers.*" Then there would follow an overcoming of denominations, which were still successful at producing the "*illusion of distinctiveness.*" Such a vision, Morrison knew, could itself look parochial, local, and limited, since he was using America and Protestantism as his base, while, he knew, "neither America nor Protestantism can any longer be taken for granted." In a collapsing world, people must urgently take the whole human future into consideration. One had to begin somewhere working toward a new, reformed "ECUMENICAL CHURCH OF CHRIST." "Only such a church," Morrison argued, "can win the America that now is or the America that is to be, to the Christian faith," and "only upon this faith" could an "enduring order of mankind" be built "in America and in the new world that is struggling to be born."

Such mainstream Protestantism, from its side of the wall, paid   10:32 no attention to those who would "win" America through revivals and evangelism. For instance, Harvard Divinity School dean Willard L. Sperry, in *Religion in America,* the first notable book-length assessment of religion in America after the war, explained this to British readers. Evangelical revivalism was in his eye a thing of the past. Sperry paid respect to the ways in which "for nearly two hundred years, a tried and proven device," the "revival," had worked. But a once noble line that ran through revivalists like Dwight L. Moody in the nineteenth century had degenerated in the twentieth into ventures like those of Billy Sunday. He was crude, sensational, commercial, shrewd, high-pressure, theatrical, and calculated. Sunday "discredited the tradition in which he stood" and represented "the final degeneration of what had been one of our major religious institutions." Such revivalist instruments and evangelical churches, thought Sperry and more like him, could not help win or hold America.

The British had heard of the Oxford Group Movement, founded   10:33 in the 1930s by the American Frank Buchman and eventually called Moral Rearmament. Some were then looking at this very different approach with hope for revival. But, sighed Sperry, "with us, Buchmanism, for all its apparent novelty, was an old story. We are tired of religious revivals as we have known them in the last half century." The theology of revivals was foreign and incredible to him and his class, its applied psychology emotionally danger- ous, the influence of revivals ephemeral, the permanent residues too meager, the evangelistic mechanisms too obvious, and the commercial instincts too highly developed to be of help for the American future. Yet the end of revivals also presented problems. "The passing of the religious revival from the American scene has deprived our churches," thought Sperry, "of what has been for at least a century the one most familiar means of recruiting the ranks of members, both young people and lapsed adults."

10:34   "The passing of the religious revival": many were in position to ask, who said it was past? Evangelicals and evangelists asked that. Harvard deans and liberal magazine editors could be wrong, or shortsighted, or dismissive, failing as they did to look at the contemporary world across the wall of division between Protestant camps as Hall had described them. Billy Sunday may have become a disgrace, but he was certainly not the end of a line, and by 1945 and 1948 when Hutchinson and Morrison wrote, a new Billy—this one named Graham—was making his way among urban youth and on the revivalist trail. Soon this one would break into national prominence, the leader of a new generation of conservative evan- gelical leaders who would reshape American Protestantism and, through it, America. Morrison's question, "Can Protestantism win America?" received an affirmative answer from Graham and the evangelicals. But they did not mean to win chiefly by exerting in- fluence in Congress, the universities, or the media—winning there might come later. Instead, they would recruit new souls for Christ and thus win and save America as a righteous place, One Nation that would serve divine purposes. Morrison had devoted a few friendly lines to Graham and to Youth for Christ, but to most of liberal Protestantism Graham would have been seen as at best a mutation, a momentary phenomenon.

10:35   In the manner of southern Protestants, young Graham had to be "born again"—a phrase hardly known in other precincts—which meant that he had to be converted personally after reaching the age of decision. He was converted in 1936; radical fundamentalist and racist Mordecai Ham was the agent of that conversion. After some meager schooling at the fundamentalist Bob Jones University, and a Bible college in Florida, Graham attended Wheaton College in Illinois. There he met and then married Ruth Bell, the daughter of an evangelical medical missionary. Ever after, she helped him de- fine his mission and stand firm for the evangelistic cause. Graham

took on a pastorate, mastered radio preaching, and helped lead
Youth for Christ. On May 27, 1944, he showed his crowd appeal
at Chicago's 3,000-seat Orchestra Hall. By October he had to use
the 30,000-seat Chicago Stadium. Graham became the first "field
representative" for Youth for Christ, where he linked up with
another boy wonder, Chuck Templeton. Templeton remembered:
"We were just these dynamic, handsome young guys, you know,
full of incredible energy, full of vitality, and we were totally committed . . . every one of us. We really thought we were involved in
a dramatic new resurgence of revivalism over the country." Templeton later left revivalism and the faith, but he was right about the
new resurgence at the time.

"Can Protestantism win America?" For all the talk of rescue   10:36
from the world, Graham and his colleagues made much of the
American part of that world. One of the team, Torrey Johnson, led
a Memorial Day rally at Chicago's Soldier Field as the European
war ended. With red, white, and blue as the featured colors, and
"God Bless Our Boys" the hymn, the crowd heard Taps, purchased
more war bonds, and unveiled the sign "Jesus Saves." Technically,
the revival leaders were "premillennial dispensationalists," which
meant they believed that Jesus would come again soon and that the
world would get nothing but worse before then. Yet that night,
as so often, the congregation affirmed the world that was, which
meant especially the America that had become God's instrument.
According to Torrey Johnson, the Hearst newspapers in Los Angeles chose to "puff YFC" and give Graham a soft press instead
of the satirical working over he might have expected. *Time* magazine also took notice. On the road for rallies, Graham tried to convert
people, but he also kept remembering how popular Cold War themes
were in his crowds, how favored anticommunism was among them,
how important to God they thought America was, how dangerous
the enemy. In 1947 in Charlotte, North Carolina, Graham preached:
"There are Communists everywhere. Here, too, for that matter."
And "unless the Christian religion rescues these [other] nations
from the clutches of the unbelieving, America will stand alone and
isolated in the world." One Nation was becoming *the* one nation.

On either side of the Protestant dividing wall were ecumenists   10:37
and evangelicals, but for a time Graham straddled. He was an
official observer in 1948 at Amsterdam as the World Council of
Churches was formed. His theology did not match the council's,
but he had precedents. Before him, giants like Dwight L. Moody
and John R. Mott had tried to keep ecumenism and evangelism

together, and so would he. He called Amsterdam "one of the most thrilling experiences of my life up to that moment." Good-bye, Mordecai Ham and Bob Jones, he was saying; he could never be cooped up within stereotypical fundamentalism and had already made his decisive move into moderate neo-evangelicalism, as it was then called. But Graham could be as grudging as the liberal Protestants about uncongenial faiths. He spoke of "how Communism and Catholicism are taking over in Europe; how Mohammedanism is sweeping across Africa and into Southern Europe." These were signs to Graham that the end was near, which is why revival had became ever more urgent. Several years before sociologists, theologians, and broadcasters were using the word *revival* to describe a move of apparently greater religious interest in America, Graham was predicting a revival, meaning Protestant evangelism, that would break forth from the Bible Belt and become nationwide in scope. For early signs, Graham pointed to the sales of Bibles and religion books, the many new postwar churches, many radio ministries, and growing attendance at revivals. One evening under the heavenly sign of the aurora borealis he told friends: "I want the Lord to come, but I sure would like to do something great for him before he comes." Graham effectively employed nostalgia for the horse-and-buggy days in order to evoke revival. "I am also convinced that the only hope of preserving our way of life, the only hope of preserving our present culture, is an old-fashioned, heaven-sent revival," he told Los Angelenos in 1948. America was "on the verge of a great national revival."

10:38   Russia tested the atomic bomb while Graham was campaigning in Los Angeles. The weaponry spelled a threat that communism would increase, even though it was, said Graham, a movement that had decided "against God, against Christ, against the Bible, and against all religion. Communism is not only an economic interpretation of life—Communism is a religion that is inspired, directed, and motivated by the Devil himself who has declared war against Almighty God." The preacher then located evils close to home, as revivalists do. "The Fifth Columnists, called Communists, are more rampant in Los Angeles than any other city in America," he preached, and foresaw judgment about to fall on the nation. How did he know about the numbers or even the presence of communists in that metropolis? Where did he get his credentials for knowing? "Let me tell you something; when God gets ready to shake America, He may not take the Ph.D. and the D.D. God may choose a country boy." Graham devotees knew which one he had chosen. "The only reason that America escaped the ravages and destruction of war was because God's people prayed," he said, with an implication that England did not pray. "Can Protestantism win America?" had to be asked and answered again. "Many of these people believe that God can still use America to evangelize the world." And Americans were "living at a time in world history when God is giving us a desperate choice, a choice of either revival or judgment."

The Hearst people had said "Puff YFC"; now it was said that 10:39 William Randolph Hearst himself sent a new message: "Puff Graham." Whether he sent it or not, they did puff the evangelist. Media focused on him. Celebrity conversions followed: movie stars, athletes, crime syndicate figures professed faith at Graham rallies. In Boston the crusader preached an unsophisticated dispensational premillennial message about the Rapture, a forthcoming event in which God, revisiting the world in the second coming of Christ, would "rapture," which meant seize and take away, the elect. Graham was exuberant about the prospect: "Wait till those gravestones start popping like popcorn in a popper. Oh Boy! Won't it be wonderful when those gravestones start popping?" This he uttered not too far down the road from Harvard Divinity School, where Sperry was writing about religion and writing off revival. So prominent did Graham become that his team got him an audience with President Harry S. Truman at the White House on July 14, 1950. Graham botched the event and his relations with Truman by making an embarrassing show of public piety. It was the last president with whom he botched things, and the evangelist became a confidante of every subsequent president.

Paradoxically, this preacher of an exclusive Gospel—Jesus 10:40 Saves! meant *Only* Jesus Saves!—came to be seen as an inclusivist who could figuratively wrap his long arms around Protestant-Catholic-Jew, around black and white, male and female America. The fate of the whole nation, in no matter what vicissitudes, was at stake. The Korean War gave Graham new reasons to preach for revival. It showed again how aggressive atheistic communism had become abroad, but Graham spent as much time scoring immorality at home. In a Washington crusade in 1952, to which Truman turned down an invitation, the evangelist came away with a consolation prize. Virginia Senator A. Willis Robertson, father of a little boy who would grow up to be televangelist M. G. "Pat" Robertson, gained unanimous Senate approval for an endorsement of the rally along with the prayer that "God may guide and protect our nation and preserve the peace of the world."

10:41   To promote his program for saving America, Graham risked stepping into politics. In 1951, before many others foresaw the potential in any politically conservative evangelical movement, Graham warned or promised that "the Christian people of America will not sit idly by in 1952." Charles Clayton Morrison, across the Protestant wall of division, had worried about Catholic bloc voting; Graham threatened that it would now be done by Protestants. They were "going to vote as a bloc for the man with the strongest moral and spiritual platform, regardless of his views on other matters," said Graham, and added, "I believe we can hold the balance of power" in the nation. Bloc members would listen to "the instructions of their religious leaders." Graham engaged in political prognostication. In the spring of 1952 he prophesied, "there's going to be the Jewish bloc, there's going to be the Roman Catholic bloc, there's going to be the labor bloc, there's going to be the Negro bloc, there's going to be the Polish bloc, there's going to be the Irish bloc." They would all exert tremendous pressure in the political process. "Why should not Evangelicals across America be conditioned and cultured and instructed until we, too, can make our voice known?" In a rare moment of frontal hubris, Graham flexed his revivalist muscles: "If I could run for President of the United States today on a platform of calling the people back to God, back to Christ, back to the Bible, I'd be elected. There is a hunger for God today." In fact, "if the country ever comes close to Communism," he teased in 1952, "I will offer myself in any capacity to lead the Christian people of this country in the preservation of their God-given institutions." There things stood on the eve of the Eisenhower presidency and what many came to see as the One Nation's revival of interest in things religious.

10:42   Graham was in the advance guard of the new evangelicalism, but the movement also needed more systematic and scholarly support. This it got from leaders like journalist-turned-theologian Carl F. H. Henry, the foremost of the company. In 1947 he published a rallying book, *The Uneasy Conscience of Modern Fundamentalism.* Henry sensed that a new moment had arrived. Even his friends all thought "nobody should 'perform surgery' on Fundamentalism just now," with things so tense on the religious scene. Why wait? Without revival, renewal, and rebirth, "Fundamentalism in two generations will be reduced either to a tolerated cult status or, in the event of Roman Catholic domination in the United States, become once again a despised and oppressed sect." Henry was aware of the ways universities and both secular and religious colleges constantly assaulted what he called "our position." But "we" who had been called fundamentalists, he confessed, had "needlessly invited criticism and even ridicule." They, "we," had failed to apply "the genius of our position constructively to those problems which press most for solution in a social way." He would not let liberalism (which he called modernism) and humanism have their way, but he still tried to reach across the Protestant wall. He had a few friendly things to say about the new World Council of Churches which was being born as he wrote. "The studied Fundamentalist avoidance of, and bitter criticism of, the World Council of Churches and the Federal Council of Churches of Christ in America" were examples of fundamentalist refusal to come to terms with social necessity. Fundamentalists, he charged, were good at treating individual sin, but they now had to address social evils.

As readily as Hall and Hutchinson and Morrison and as urgently as Graham, Henry addressed the moment. He had moved far from the straight-out effort to save souls and confine evangelistic work and evangelicalism to that task. "We must confront the world *now* with an ethics to make it tremble, and with a dynamic to give it hope." He looked at his compatriots, on their side of the wall: "The evangelical uneasiness is one of the most promising signs of the times," Henry declared, because it might issue in a formula for providing a "twentieth-century reformation within Protestantism and leading to a global renaissance within modern secularism." He could seem heady as he spoke of the need for Christianity to "compete as a vital world ideology," with its evangelicalism projecting a "solution for the most pressing world problems." It would have to "offer a formula for a new world mind with spiritual ends, involving evangelical affirmations in political, economic, sociological, and education realms, local and international." Henry would not go along with Morrison; Christianity in its evangelical form could *not* provide a whole "future world culture" that could be "identified fully as a Christian civilization." It could not preach "imminent utopia"; even liberalism was discarding that. But it also need not share the view "found both in neo-supernaturalist and higher liberal circles" that the human as sinner could achieve nothing. Instead, he reassured readers, he approached the future with a "sober optimism."

In 1947 Henry could still find enough Christian clarity and vigor in ecumenical forces to picture some reaching by Protestants across the walls and boundaries they had chosen. Not all association with nonevangelicals would be tainting. "For Fundamentalist

10:43

10:44

churches in no liberal association whatever are often as socially
inactive as others." He was bold enough to picture ententes like
those that occurred between factions described in the biblical book
of Acts. He pictured an evangelical and fundamentalist united
front; "it remains true," he said, "that evangelical convictions
need a united voice; the force of the redemptive message will not
break with apostolic power upon the modern scene unless the
American Council of Churches and the National Association of
Evangelicals meet at some modern Antioch, and Peter and Paul are
face to face in a spirit of mutual love and compassion." Henry then
dreamed of an accompanying organizational power. "If, as is often
remarked, the Federal Council of Churches is the voice of Protestant liberalism in America, Protestant evangelicalism too needs a
single voice." And "when such a unity comes, the present competitive spirit of evangelical groups shall be overruled to the glory
of God and the furtherance of the Gospel witness." Other groups
that were or would be acting in the name of a unity that was not
profound would wither.

10:45   Fearful of Catholic domination, disgusted by secularism, dismissive of Protestant liberalism, Henry touted evangelicalism as
the single force that could properly shape national and world culture. This goal did not mean that evangelicalism could shape national and world culture; nor should it turn progressive or utopian. Personal rebirth was still the primary focus of the gospel. But
cultural contexts did matter. The "sub-Christian" environments of
America were at least preferable to those contexts marked by an
"atmosphere almost entirely devoid" of the redemptive aspects
that somehow survived in pluralist America. It was easier, the editor thought, to represent the gospel in a climate that he described
as idealist—and America in part fit that description—than in a
thoroughly naturalistic one. Of course, argued Henry, neither idealism nor liberalism was to be "identified with the kingdom of
God." Still, Anglo-Saxon democracy was a "relatively better atmosphere by far than German totalitarianism, and what made it
better [was] the trace of Hebrew-Christian ideology that lingers
in it." Can Protestantism win America? Evangelicalism, reformed
and awakened, could win much of it, thought Henry, and along the
way the nation would see the turning of "the uneasy conscience
of modern evangelicalism into a new reformation—this time with
ecumenical significance."

11

"Stating the Catholic Attitude with Every Frankness"

Catholics had been in the hemisphere since the fifteenth century, on the continent since the sixteenth, in the colonies since the seventeenth, in the nation since the eighteenth, in place as the largest denomination since the nineteenth, and still on the defensive through the first half of the twentieth. Catholicism was and remained a religious minority when posed against Protestants en masse. But the massing or surface uniting of Protestant forces occurred only when it came time to attack Catholics or, as in the case of World War II, to give religious support to the United States as the distinctive and set-apart One Nation. While for 23 million Americans, Catholic life had its own integrity, moves by non-Catholics and anti-Catholics also shaped life in what many in 1945 thought of as a Catholic ghetto. While non-Catholics could point to no acts of disloyalty by the Catholic church or its members, anti-Catholics always raised the question of their loyalty to America. Because Catholics were governed by a foreign pontiff who since 1870 had claimed infallibility, and as the vicar of Christ on earth could make final claims of authority on believers, it was asked what they would do if Roman commands contradicted American interests. Along with that peak issue came countless subordinate ones, and tensions were exacerbated in incidents and emotions of the sort that develop when there is mistrust between people, between neighbors. If tension between Catholics and others was

11:1

157

chronic, it became acute near the middle of "the American Century," while various elements contended that they best supported the idea of the One Nation. That very contention, ironically, increased the difficulty of supporting the claim that there *was* One Nation.

11:2   Catholicism was well poised to support its own claims in the early years of the Cold War because anticommunism was popular and because the Church was anticommunist. The presence of an atheist system that persecuted Catholics in Europe and the fear that it was encroaching on the United States and the rest of the free world, Catholic or not, removed the temptation for Catholics to be anything but alert in the face of the communist menace, whether real or presumed. But while being free of the charge that they were "soft" on communism, Catholics had to defend themselves against the notion that they were communist-like, because their system was accused of being totalitarian and aggressive. In every generation, some attack prevailed over others, and some frontline attacker of Catholics emerged to make the case. If one measures the space given one nominee in reviews and counterattacks or in recorded mentions among Catholic folk, pride or shame of place at mid-century has to go to Paul Blanshard.

11:3   Blanshard, an ordained Congregationalist minister who came from a family of ministers, and who eventually identified himself with Unitarianism, was glad, he said, to be called an "anti-Catholic bigot," because he wanted to be seen as obsessive in pursuit of his cause. He was everything Catholics advertised themselves not to be: an eventual atheist, someone given to marital infidelity, a socialist, a critic of all church institutions, and thus, in the mores and ethos of the time, hardly a character with whom pious non-Catholics would identify nor one to whom pious Catholics need respond. Yet many enemies of the Church did identify, and even more responded. Blanshard could count on the support of secular notables at a time when anti-Catholicism was respectable in some intellectual circles. He claimed that one night after a lecture at Princeton a slippered old man stood up to express his gratitude "to a man who is fighting the abuses of a powerful organization." When the Catholic press criticized the old man, who happened to be the physicist Albert Einstein, he replied: "I am convinced that some political and social activities and practices of the Catholic organization are detrimental and even dangerous for the community as a whole, here and everywhere," especially on issues like birth control in an overpopulated world. America's most influential philosopher, John Dewey, also endorsed Blanshard, calling Catholicism a "powerful reactionary world organization promulgating principles inimical to democracy."

British philosopher Bertrand Russell, who spent much time in the United States, received a gift copy of Blanshard's *Communism, Democracy, and Catholic Power.* He responded with a crude parody of Lewis Carroll's "The Walrus and the Carpenter," calling it "The Prelate and the Commissar." Along with it came a note from Russell: "May you have all success, or, alternatively, not live long enough to be burnt at the stake!" If a pact between anticommunist zealot Senator Joseph McCarthy and communist leader Georgy Malenkov were ever concluded, Russell went on, "you and I will be stood up between the two armies and co-operatively shot as proof of perfect harmony." The philosopher remembered hearing an audience first gasp and then applaud as Blanshard attacked Catholicism: "I felt that they were living under a reign of terror and were enjoying the breath of freedom from abroad." 11:4

Paul Blanshard later remembered the midcentury years as the time of "the greatest struggles over the separation of church and state in our history," which had compelled him to lobby actively against Catholic interests. It was in 1951, during the peak of the McCarthyism that was named after Joseph McCarthy, when anticommunists were most zealous, that Blanshard published *Communism, Democracy, and Catholic Power.* Its thesis is condensed in the paragraphs Russell remembered having heard the accuser deliver: "It is dangerous error to think that the evils of communism can be combatted by Catholicism." All the evils—"adherence to a rigid and static system of doctrine," some of which was doubtful and some false, "persecution as a means of enforcing orthodoxy," a belief that True Faith was the exclusive property of one agency, the use of this power "to secure an undue share of wealth for the priesthood at the expense of the rest of the population," and the like—were "exhibited by the Catholic Church when it had power." As for the present, it was irrational, thought Blanshard, to suppose "that much would be gained if, in the defeat of communism, Catholicism were enthroned in its place." 11:5

Some lectures by Harvard historian George La Piana gave Blanshard ammunition because they pointed to the "impressive parallelism of theoretical principles and of institutional features in a totalitarian church and in a totalitarian state." Blanshard saw both the Vatican and the Kremlin as "dictatorships" aspiring to mind control. The two patterns of power "occupy the opposite extremes 11:6

of our moral universe but they represent the same type of intellectual climate." One of them, Blanshard went on, "is fighting on our
side in the east-west struggle, and the other is fighting against us."
But "the Kremlin and the Vatican are far more conspicuous in their
similarities than their differences." In America, communism was
"so weak that it cannot elect a single congressman, senator, governor, mayor, or city councilman in the whole nation." Even misguided Henry Wallace, though a former vice president, "could not
poll 3 per cent of the national vote" in what Blanshard called "the
days of his unfortunate left-wing honeymoon." But Vatican power
in America was "pervasive and substantial," outnumbering communist power in membership by about 490 to 1. Ominously, it was
now inextricably entangled with "the tradition of American freedom which protects both good and evil against attack if they happen to wear a religious label." Who would dare to counterattack,
"because Catholic power makes cowards of more men in public
life than we like to think?"

11:7   Blanshard would, first by breaking the taboo against frank talk.
He knew this talk risked making one sound antireligious, but, seeking the support of non-Catholic religionists, he made clear that it
was not religion he was talking about. No, Catholicism was "a
foreign government with a diplomatic corps; an agglomeration of
right-wing clerical parties and fascist governments; a cultural imperialism controlling a world-wide system of schools; a medieval
medical code with comprehensive rules for personal hygiene," and
more. As a civil libertarian who drew support from others who
cared about civil liberties, Blanshard insisted that he would not
deprive the Vatican of any *right* in the United States, nor would his
antagonism to *political* Catholicism degenerate into *religious* anti-
Catholicism. No, Americans had to fight specific political aspirations and ties, like the idea of having a United States representative
at the Vatican. Conclusion: "We have been thoroughly aroused to
the necessity of defending our freedoms against one form of totalitarian power; we have been astonishingly apathetic concerning the
perils of the other." Such arousals made Blanshard's books big
sellers in rectories, where they confirmed the presence of an anti-
Catholic menace and provided agenda for counterattack. And they
were bought and quoted by civil libertarians, in secular and Protestant communities alike.

11:8   Fortunately for Blanshard, such incidents as President Truman's
move in 1950 to establish diplomatic relations with the Vatican
seemed to reinforce his case. But then a domestic incident involv-

ing the best-known woman and the most discussed prelate in America further drew attention to it. Blanshard pointed to the incident involving Eleanor Roosevelt, widow of the former president but long well known for her own opinions and causes. Her antagonist was New York's Francis Cardinal Spellman, a man with a gift for attracting headlines. For Blanshard the story showed how difficult it was for even the most highly placed to make political criticisms of Catholicism without being charged with anti-Catholicism. As background to the incident one must know that a Supreme Court decision in 1948 implicitly allowed the use of public funds for auxiliary services in private and parochial schools, including, many contended, the provision of some kinds of texts and permission for parochial students to ride on state school buses. So Catholics moved to render such support explicit, assured, and generous. North Carolina Representative Graham Barden wanted to check such moves, so he offered a bill in Congress to rule out this support. Mrs. Roosevelt, then writing a daily newspaper column, gave space on one June day to support of the Barden bill and criticism of the cardinal, who pressed for textbooks and bus rides: "Those of us who believe in the right of any human being to belong to whatever church he sees fit, and to worship God in his own way, cannot be accused of prejudice when we do not want to see public education connected with religious control of the schools, which are paid for by taxpayers' money."

Yes, you can be accused of prejudice, replied Spellman, who   11:9
used characteristic bluster as he played and then overplayed his hand. He took Mrs. Roosevelt's charges personally, saying she had condemned him "for defending Catholic children against those who would deny them their constitutional rights of equality with other American children." Did they have such a right? many asked. So far, the Court only *permitted* some funding. Yet Spellman spoke of Mrs. Roosevelt's "misinformation, ignorance or prejudice," because she supported the now "famous, infamous" Barden bill. Accusing the columnist of anti-Catholicism, he invoked patriotic themes. America's Catholic youth had helped fight to save Americans from oppression and persecution, and now, he implied, Mrs. Roosevelt's attempt to keep Catholic children off free public buses desecrated their memory: "Their broken bodies on blood-soaked foreign fields were grim and tragic testimony" of their sacrifice. Now, he charged, the president's widow would deny their children equal rights, after two bitter wars. So overreaching was Spellman's move that public outcries forced him to apologize. Blanshard

had comment ready: "Not many persons were deceived. Cardinal Spellman has no authority to alter the world policy of the Vatican which demands public money for Catholic educational enterprises." No one was in position to make Blanshard apologize for his overreaches.

11:10   It would be false to suggest that Catholicism was always on the defensive. Many members were ready in editorials, speeches, town hall arguments, and books to state the case for Catholic contributions to the One Nation, Indivisible. As in the Protestant case, the best way to hear the sustained argument is to turn the pages written by, in one example, a typical, and, in another, an advance-guard articulator. The former was Francis E. McMahon, a layperson, and the latter, Father John Courtney Murray of the Society of Jesus. I do not suggest here that folk piety and parish practice, by which most Catholics lived, are directly represented by two scholars; most people do not mark their days debating nuances of public life. But both authors were highly conscious of being responsible to the church with its 23 million American members. And when pressed to consult sources and authorities, lay leaders and priests would turn to figures like these. Both were grounded in the natural-law philosophy which they thought could undergird life in a pluralist society. Both were intellectuals, one so representative that he evoked little controversy within the church, the other so experimental that he suffered setback and near suppression. McMahon was a University of Chicago philosophy professor who in 1945 wrote *A Catholic Looks at the World.* Fortunately for those in search of the larger picture, the author worked to set a mature Catholicism in a global context in the very years when the United States was finding its way in the global society during what was being called "the American Century."

11:11   McMahon was not a polemicist, and he did want to please. "The strictures contained in the book, whether against my fellow-Catholics, the Protestants, or the Liberals, are not animated by a desire to offend." The professor said he only wanted to help build a better world, "to assess the gap between what is and what ought to be." Writing as one who was "Catholic in religion, American in nationality, Irish in ancestry," the Chicagoan thought back to his years as a student in Nazi Germany. McMahon quoted Adolf Hitler's *Mein Kampf* to show how worldviews were at issue in the grand struggles of the day. Hitler had written: "The program of a *view of life* means the formulation of a declaration of war against an existing order, against an existing condition, in short, against an existing conception of life in general." The conception in this case was that of the free world, the West, or America. Americans, McMahon knew, did not often think on such a scale: "We are quite blind even to the meaning of culture. Who spontaneously thinks of himself as a member of Western culture in conflict with the forces of barbarism?" He urged that citizens learn so to think. In the spirit of a time when many hoped for the convergence of individuals and groups and spoke in terms of centripetal movements in history, McMahon was anything but a Catholic sectarian. "We are members of one civilization because of a certain conception of life, a common scale of values, a common idea of man and the universe." His America did not reflect the presence of non-Europeans, though nothing he wrote was designed to exclude them. After citing the Greeks, the scholar used the newly current hyphenated description of religion in the culture: "Above all, the Judeo-Christian religion has given form and shape to our lives" and produced "a particular moral and intellectual climate." At root was the concept of *natural rights,* "which no person or institution could violate for any purpose whatsoever."

McMahon was ready to locate Catholicism congenially in the United States, but he did not think the state dared be the end-all of existence. He quoted Mussolini to suggest the horror of the notion that the state could play such a role: "Nothing outside or above the State, nothing against the State, everything within the State, everything for the State." From such concepts came totalitarianism, a modern invention, "a novelty in our history, if not in the history of all mankind," for the way it denied "all that is sacred in cultural and religious values." Totalitarianism was ecumenical in its attacks: "Protestantism and Catholicity alike have suffered," but the slaughter of five or six million Jews showed that they were worst off; "they died simply because they were Jews." Racism also moved Japan, but "there is a bit of racism in our blood," the professor reminded his readers, referring to anti-Asian prejudice. Why, then, devote more attention to Europe? Because "the crimes of Japan have been those of a nation outside Christianity," whereas the German criminals "had seen the light of high Christian principle and had rejected it." A war against such offenders had been worthwhile. It had not been "a 'holy war,' a war fought formally in defense of religion," but a war to preserve civilization and involving the fate of religion itself.   11:12

The unholy war for good causes was produced by "a world hell-bent for destruction" because of three forces: "exaggerated nation-   11:13

alism, economic disorder, and spiritual bankruptcy," the first and third of which concern us here. Over against these McMahon saw two defenders of what was left of civilization in 1945, Christianity and liberalism. Although he criticized the Vatican for having kept friendly ties to the totalitarianisms it condemned, he gave positive readings to the papal teachings on the social order after 1891 and the Bishops' Program of 1919 in the United States. He had reason also to criticize fellow Catholics for going along with the existing order instead of paying attention to such church teachings. But exaggerated nationalism disturbed him most, as his chapter-length critique made clear. And McMahon was also self-critical, recalling how as late as 1940 in arguments at Notre Dame and elsewhere he had failed to see that Europe's war was "our war." Across the religious wall of Protestantism, he saw the *Christian Century* being "as myopic on this question as any Catholic paper." Yet articulate and responsible Catholics, not the "America First" fringe, he said, were guilty of having held back. Evidently they had not realized what was at stake: "the spiritual foundations of the American way" and the fact that "the Catholic Church has never been so free to prosecute her Divine Mission as in these United States." A few communicants had been pacifist, some were anti-Semitic, more feared alliance with Russia, and most were simply passive, thus failing "the high vocation which history has imposed on them."

11:14   McMahon's critique of liberalism was a conventional liberal Catholic analysis of secularism, but his mind was more fixed on issues of faith: "Religion is not something accidental to a culture. It is not a mere reflection of economic processes, as the Socialist or the Communist maintains." With Christopher Dawson, the British Catholic whose writings were then in vogue, he stressed that religion is "*the very life-blood of culture itself.*" This liberalism was too narrow to see, because for many "devotion to and support of a completely secularized way of life" in which "religion does not matter greatly" prevailed. Americans asked, "We are getting along fine without it, aren't we?" Apparently "we are," McMahon answered, "with our twentieth-century concentration camps, torture chambers, exterminations of whole peoples, and total wars!"

11:15   With liberal and conservative Protestants alike, McMahon developed the argument against secularism. which he saw to be "characteristic of the modern world." It was exceptional in history, but it often went unrecognized: "When a culture loses its religious basis it is doomed to decline." To show how slippery things had become, McMahon did not lack secular voices to criticize, but he began by noting the defense of relativism given by former Supreme Court Chief Justice Oliver Wendell Holmes, Jr., and the horror of "absolute truth" that then marked Holmes's life. That horror may have come in reaction to past intolerance and persecution. "Catholic and Protestant vied in former ages in trying to crush each other," but, trusting that "we are through forever with those unfortunate periods," McMahon hoped they would ally against a common enemy. Others feared clericalism, but he defended the priests for their moral concern, not clericalism, as they asked their flocks to stay away from immoral movies or to join their "fight against the spread of contraceptive information." In 1945 liberal Catholicism still lined up in support of laws prohibiting such a spread and such information. "If Mr. X., a Protestant Liberal, can fight for their repeal, why cannot Mr. Y., a Catholic, fight for their retention?" Was it "clerical interference" when popes tried to prevent the exploitation of laborers? In a few pages the professor sneaked in a full defense of Catholic social policy, some of which policy angered liberal secular and Protestant citizens, but some of which they too supported.

In the debate within the One Nation, Indivisible, McMahon   11:16
argued that Catholics rightfully had a central political place. "It might satisfy some if the Catholic Church were to disappear tomorrow. But it is not going to." What about its political power? "One could argue that question until doomsday without getting anywhere." But why worry? In an age when physical power was the last word, the church had no physical power. And "so far as her spiritual penalties are concerned, they simply do not register greatly in a climate that has become de-spiritualized." Liberals also usually failed to notice how the Catholic church possessed internal variety, composed as it was of "all sorts of political and social streams." A few liberals admired communist collectivism, but most had to cast their lot with democracy. "Some would like to forget or ignore it," he wrote, "but it is a historical fact that the democratic ideal of human dignity had its roots in the Christian religion." And McMahon could play the ironist: "believe it or not, we have had the paradox of an authoritarian Church—the Catholic Church—throughout the ages proclaiming the natural equality of all men, the rule of justice under the law, the inherent dignity of the human personality, the autonomous character of the state under God," and more.

By page 154 McMahon came to the point of confronting the   11:17
conflict of the times: "I know it is the fashion today to identify

Protestantism with democracy and Catholicity with dictatorship."
But Catholic authoritarianism was dated, and accounts of it were
distorted. Did Protestantism, on the other hand, deserve "all the
credit it currently gets for being the immediate source of modern
democracy"? Hardly; mainstream Reformation movements were
generally undemocratic. The professor did not buy the "Luther to
Hitler" descent that some traced, but he attacked the Lutheran record of ambiguity about natural law, an "irrationalism" that "came
down to the acceptance of the *status quo* in a world of darkness
governed by force." So people had to know that there was "a split
in the Protestant world on this question of democracy," and some
of the roots of Nazism were to be found in "the theological dis-
putes of the sixteenth century." Since all Christians were on the
same playing field, McMahon could risk handing Protestants the
ball. Yes, the Catholic church was authoritarian, "because Christ
made it that way" by handing over the authority of God Himself,
by founding a hierarchical church, and setting over it "His vicar,
the Pope." But in the temporal order, "the Law of Nature holds in
all its fullness," as it does in democracy, so Catholicism could support democracy. It would not, he would not, impose religion on
anybody. McMahon knew that a problem remained, but, he said,
"it is the problem of the collective conscience realizing that religion is not something that can be accepted or rejected as one is
inclined."

11:18   Tit for tat. If the Catholic tendency was toward authoritarianism, the Protestant version tilted toward secularism, and some parts
of Protestantism had already succumbed. Looking at local practices, the Chicago professor wrote, "I submit that the primary purpose of the corner church is the worship of God in His Majesty and
in His glory." Therefore, to do what many Protestants did, "to turn
the church into a forum for the discussion of social problems might
please the agnostic humanitarian." But, McMahon reminded those
who stayed with him, "it won't satisfy the demands of an age that
needs both social betterment *and* spiritual inspiration, both democracy *and* religion." Except for a few Protestant and Jewish groups,
he thought, it sometimes seemed as if Catholics might be alone "in
defending the primacy of the spiritual in the emerging world," the
"One World" described by Wendell Willkie.

11:19   So it was that for the expansive Catholic, One Nation had to
relate to One World. Now no country was self-sufficient, and "culturally the world is interdependent. Ideas cannot be confined to
certain geographical areas." Literature and art spilled over all bor-

ders; so did "X-ray, television [not yet a common instrument], the radio"; only "outmoded nationalism" kept the world from political integration. "Because of their common origins, their common nature and their common destiny, men everywhere on the globe have always constituted a single family, a world society." With old barriers gone, that had become obvious. "The family of nations is no longer a dream. It is a living actuality." Now "Humanity First" was replacing "America First" as a slogan. There had to be a world organization, McMahon wrote in the year the United Nations charter was signed. In the new order, whatever the past record of Catholicism had been, "religious liberty should be guaranteed. Before God and the truth there is, I believe, but one true religion, but before man and the state everyone has the right to worship according to the dictates of his own conscience."

The Chicago Catholic was impressively self-critical about   11:20
America; he also criticized the racism present within the "single family" of world society or the One Nation. He had recently been asked by the editor of the *Negro Digest* to write on the topic "If I Were a Negro," and this he had done, thus reminding himself of how far the nation still had to go on this front. Religious tensions "disfigured the face of America." Anti-Semitism was growing. "In the foxholes and in the B-29 bombers, Jews, Catholics and Protestants," he observed, could "work together in the common cause. The war has united these fighters. It is different on the home front." There was, he knew, no earthly hope for reforming the professional anti-Semites, but "millions of gullible Americans" might change; they should hear Pope Pius XI, who said in 1938, "Spiritually, we are Semites."

Toward the end of his book, McMahon treated the postwar "re-   11:21
surgence of anti-Catholic feeling." He did not see it as part of the old "Know-Nothingism" or "Native Americanism," which would have been ineffective after the war, now that the Catholic had demonstrated "beyond question his loyalty." Indeed, "no 'defender' of American principles could hope to succeed by a frontal attack." Now the attack had to center on elites, on the hierarchy. Anti-Catholics cultivated the myth that the hierarchy was united and had a single strategy. In reality, he asserted economically, "there are bishops who are progressive, and there are others who are conservative." Despite the picture, "the Church is not an army, where the command of the Pope is carried out with military precision." No, the hierarchy was supporting democratic values and was doing so also in its battle against moral relativism. "There is not a shadow

of conflict between the mission [Catholics] have as Americans and the temporal mission outlined for them by their spiritual mother, the Church." Yes, McMahon reminded, "we Catholics, on the whole, are a sensitive lot," too ready to take offense. "There is often a note of hysteria in our replies to attacks," analogous to the hysteria of certain branches of Protestantism. "We are a clannish lot," stand-offish at times, "not very cooperative on matters of a social and civic character." "We are a bit arrogant," he added, and unready to join with the pope and other people of good will to address social problems. "We are a bit arrogant," often failing to notice much good outside of the church. "We are a prey to political extravagances." Having shown he was a good Catholic by confessing, McMahon observed further that "our virtues, however, are strong, and vitally important for the preservation of Western culture and American democracy."

11:22   Well aware of the *Christian Century*'s voicing of Protestant fears that Catholics would win America, he again affirmed: "There is no doubt that the Catholic Church would like to see America Catholic," just as every Protestant would like to see his faith prevail. But Catholics intended to work only by persuasion, and it would be "a long time before the Church could ever dream of amending (if it wanted to) the Constitution of the United States," the way—and here was the dig—rural American Protestantism had done in passing the Eleventh Amendment, Prohibition. However, just suppose that down the road, safely away in 5648 A.D., this country should become Catholic. With the *Christian Century* McMahon asked, "Would religious liberty cease?" In 1945 the answer was still somewhat ambiguous because of what was on the books in Rome. "Theoretically the Church insists upon special recognition in a predominantly Catholic state. But such recognition takes on an indefinite variety of modes," and, McMahon added in his least reassuring line to non-Catholics, "it is a pure fantasy." For now common devotion to democracy was the issue. "Religious differences should be discussed, but not quarreled over. Protestantism, Catholicity, and Judaism, moreover, have a common foe in secularism. Why, then, should they battle with one another?" McMahon ended optimistically, affirming those who spoke of "the American Century." "Those who know America for what she truly is will be certain she will not fail either humanity or herself."

11:23   The one line of McMahon that could still chill non-Catholic hearts had to do with the theoretical insistence by the church "upon special recognition in a predominantly Catholic state." That kind of sentence gave anti-Catholics their best ammunition. It also was an unnecessary leftover or imported stand, argued another American. That one was eventually to do more than any other to help world Catholicism change its theory and thus reassure people everywhere about its practice in modern times and in the future. Unknown to most non-Catholics (though noticed in one line of Charles Clayton Morrison), he was a young Jesuit, John Courtney Murray, a teacher at the Jesuit Woodstock College in Maryland. Murray was just then beginning to test the religious liberty scene with some probing and controversial journal articles. While his impact on America and world Catholicism would come later, Murray was beginning to plot ways for Catholic intellectuals and political figures to make their way in a society that he and others were beginning to call pluralist. He came on the scene after a half century of relative passivity in American Catholic thought, the theologians having been rendered timid after the condemnation of modernism by the pope in 1907. Yet in 1939 a new *Catholic Biblical Quarterly* began to show stirrings, and in 1940 the new Jesuit *Theological Studies* began to push further. In 1946 both a Catholic Biblical Association and a Catholic Theological Society took shape. The editors of the retrogressive *American Ecclesiastical Review* were busy watching all these, and, in the new theological ranks, young Murray, on whom they reported to Rome.

When the Jesuits prevented Murray from becoming a military 11:24 chaplain during the war, he took an interest in university student life and race relations. But it was in 1945 that he found his focus. Some hierarchs asked him to meet with them and some Protestants on a Joint Committee on Religious Liberty. This was an agency of the Federal Council of Churches and the Foreign Mission Conference of North America. "As you know," Murray wrote a superior, "our Protestant brethren are very excited over the issue of religious liberty." The Jesuit knew that he was not on friendly soil, having criticized a Protestant "Statement on Religious Liberty" that spring in *Theological Studies*. But inspired by this new mission, he began writing journal articles with such devotion that he even overworked and risked his health. In 1947 at the Catholic Theological Society meeting in Chicago he read a tentative but well-worked-out paper on the "governmental repression of heresy." One of his two main nemeses, Francis J. Connell, C.S.S.R., editor of the *American Ecclesiastical Review* and the society's president, found parts of the paper "out of harmony with the traditional belief and attitude of the Church for many centuries."

From those lines on, Murray never had peace again in this part of
the Catholic house.

11:25   Connell had been carping about interfaith statements since
1941, when he wrote that some Catholics "in their laudable efforts
to be broadminded and charitable toward the members of non-
Catholic religious bodies" were becoming "unduly tolerant toward their doctrines." He charged that the Catholic pendulum was
swinging "from bigotry to indifferentism" in the "interfaith" or
"three-faith" meetings, such as those of the National Conference
of Christians and Jews. Murray was to be at least implicitly in his
target range, for he had drafted the Catholic section of that conference's document of 1943, "The Catholic, Jewish, Protestant Declaration on World Peace," a statement that created some wartime
stir. Murray both instinctively and strategically quoted popes; that
time it was Pius XII, who had recognized that "whether we like it
or not, we are living in a religiously pluralist society at a time of
spiritual crisis; and the alternatives are the discovery of social unity
or destruction." And Murray claimed the backing of Pius XII for
permanent interfaith structures, because the pope had wanted cooperation to be "institutionalized in an international organization,
that will function as a sort of collective conscience and be able to
enforce its imperatives."

11:26   Murray agreed that Connell, when on the attack, had to support "Catholic exclusivism" in matters of truth, but he wondered
whether almost anyone could offer proof for Connell's charges
about indifference and false tolerance. Murray kept pressing the
point, as had McMahon, that the world and America were a single
scene, a "concrete, total situation" that needed a coherent approach. "There is room for an exploration of the dangers to human
life, national and international, involved in the failure of Catholics
to cooperate with non-Catholics in the sphere of social reconstruction—dangers so great as to create a necessity for such cooperation." But Connell kept on tagging the interfaith movement, even
if to score he had to reach all the way back to 1893 and the World's
Parliament of Religions, when Leo XIII showed disapproval. Had
not the war also led to indifferentism, asked the intransigent priest,
thanks to the "attitude toward a diversity of religious beliefs engendered by conditions existing in our armed forces" and because
of "the emphasis that is nowadays laid on one of the 'four freedoms,'—freedom of religious worship?"

11:27   Murray joined the Hutchinsons and Morrisons and Grahams in
Protestantism and the McMahons in Catholicism in a critique of

"the Secularist Drift" for its manifest illiberalism. If that kind of critique was one day to become a preserve of religious conservatives, those who were marked as liberals isolated it and counterattacked first on the intellectual level. Murray saw a drift "toward an atheism that consciously sets out to be 'positive, organic, constructive,' a dynamic anti-Christianity and anti-theism, bent on destroying the traditional concept of man, and setting in its place a positive new ideal—a humanism without God." He thereupon responded to the "New Nativists" such as humanist Blanshard and sundry militant Protestants. The Old Nativism had been simply Protestant, said Murray, but "the newness of the Nativism is revealed by the fact that it is *not* now Protestant but naturalist." Therefore in the humanist camp "the primary accusation is that Catholicism is anti-American because America is a democracy and democracy is necessarily based on a naturalist or secularist philosophy." Aware of the charge, Murray added a second front to his life mission; he must point to a theist basis for a pluralist republic that also aspired to be One Nation, Indivisible.

While most of Murray's early work was sheltered from view in theological journals and verbal brawls with the likes of Connell in rectory back rooms, now and then public light fell on his ventures. *Time* magazine in 1949 covered an encounter between the Jesuit and Professor Walter Russell Bowie of New York's Union Theological Seminary. The raucous *American Mercury* magazine had asked them to state their varying cases against secularism and sectarianism. Bowie led off by rounding up the usual suspect statements that put fear into non-Catholic hearts. There was, he began, a "clearly stated Roman Catholic purpose 'to make America Catholic,'" and thus to jeopardize "the religious and civil liberties which have been the glory of Protestant countries and of Protestant culture." Nonsense, said Murray. Bowie "does indeed have his few scattered bones" of the sort from which "the Sunday-supplement archaeologist constructs the museum-piece prehistoric monster." Dismiss them with sarcasm he might, yet Murray knew he had to reckon with those scattered bones, and he did. He tried to move beyond Catholic-Protestant battle lines, which he thought had become an irrelevance because "the peril of a 'Catholic America'" was a chimera. The real enemy was Blanshard's style of secularism, which was hung on "a philosophical armature which they call evolutionary scientific humanism." In those lines Murray pointed to the field where he would rather do battle, among intellectual elites. In 1951 he became the first Catholic priest to be a guest professor at Yale University. For a time he moved out of the gunsights of Father Connell and his other tormenters, to develop views on religious liberty that would change Catholicism around the world scarcely more than a decade later.

11:29   The efforts to present the best face for Catholic America in the early Cold War years came not from wars in theological journals but on the popular front. There Fulton Sheen presented the Catholic edifices on the new instrument of television. On the same front any number of Catholics were inventing new ways of commending the faith and the church to the public. In those ways they would reassure other Americans that Catholics were responsibly contributing to the One Nation, Indivisible. Typical of these, as well as the best known and most successful, was a movement called the Christophers, founded by Father James Keller. Born at the turn of the century, the priest, as handsome as Sheen, knew how to exploit mass media and appeal to people of power in the broadcasting and publishing industries. Forget Blanshard and Connell and, for that matter, Murray, his manner seemed to say: notice what Catholicism is and what Catholics are doing to fortify America and change lives.

11:30   Keller paid his dues to the system by joining the Maryknoll order of missionary priests, for whom he raised funds by working his magic on well-off Catholics. He then used the same magic to attract young men to Maryknoll and other places for pursuing religious vocations. For four years in the thirties he also worked for the Society for the Propagation of the Faith but found that task limiting and somewhat distasteful. On October 18, 1945, in a letter to a superior, Keller charted his future work. "It had long been my hope that Maryknoll would be able to take some active interest in the enormous work to be done in this country in saving the Christian tradition that seems to be fast disintegrating with the breakdown of Protestantism." Not many were yet noticing or admitting such a breakdown, but the insecure voices of some leaders suggested that they were haunted by what they saw beyond the facades of postwar prosperity. Keller thought that the hour had come for Catholics to strike.

11:31   The Maryknoller traded on the self-assured outlook of colleagues who profited from a revival of the thought of Saint Thomas Aquinas. These Thomists believed in natural law, in the congruence of Catholic faith and human philosophy at its ordered best, and in the Catholic church as the possessor of the truth. Devoted utterly to the American constitutional tradition, Keller himself believed with McMahon and Murray that Catholic teaching best guaranteed human liberties. But he avoided both theology and politics and aimed for the heart. He could consort, for instance, with the Grace family, made wealthy by their shipping lines, while staying close to Dorothy Day as she worked with the poor. A special friend of the Joseph P. Kennedy family, he claimed that his approach to life had helped influence John F. and Robert Kennedy to participate in politics. An index to his memoirs would replicate the listings of names in celebrity phone books. But even as he enjoyed the hobnobbing, Keller kept his missionary context in mind. Of the influential, he said, "While only an occasional one will become Catholic, yet it is quite possible to dispose them towards the great fundamentals of religion."

The Maryknoll superiors were made uneasy by Keller's free-   11:32
wheeling, so he developed ties to other clerical leaders. Archbishop John Timothy McNicholas consulted him about how the church could achieve a "more effective penetration of Catholic ideals into American life and opinion." Keller specialized in seeking that. His charter came from an article in *Catholic Mind* by journalist Michael de la Bedoyere. He quoted: "The force of Christianity as a world-ordering influence can only be restored in the end if millions of Catholics throughout the world are fully instructed in regard to Catholic teaching on the State." And then they would have to be "led by the example and instruction of their pastors to effect the immense revolution that would result from genuine fidelity to that teaching." Through the ages, through de la Bedoyere and now Keller himself, Catholicism failed whenever ordinary believers were not able to articulate an understanding of "what is involved in the Church's teaching about citizenship and public affairs." Keller drew up and announced plans to help the articulators. He chose the conservative *American Ecclesiastical Review* in which take out his patent on the idea of what he would call the Christophers. In a decisive article at the end of World War II the priest asked, "What About the Hundred Million?" According to his reckoning, that many Americans had no connection with organized religion. They were, he feared, letting slip away the "great Christian fundamentals that make possible their present way of life." The article was a sensation. Bishops asked for thousands of reprints, thus signaling an awareness that his innovation was welcome. Keller was doctrinally safe. He spread his propagandizing wings with a small Maryknoll book, *The Priest and the Hundred Million*. His superiors, with their interest in foreign mis-

sions, found this theme distracting and naive. One member of the Maryknoll Council, Father Thomas Kiernan, delivered an appraisal that Keller's denigrators then and since liked to make: his "writing and thinking on problems of this nature" was "superficial, immature and on the emotional side." Keller, he judged, lacked "the intellectual capacity or experience required to be an apostle of this kind." The superiors started raising psychological questions: was the priest in midlife compensating for frustrations he had developed during the years he did promotional work?

11:33   Keller resisted when Maryknoll wanted to farm him out to Japan or other foreign fields. Though elected to attend as a representative a meeting of the Maryknoll general chapter in 1946, Keller could not keep his mind on the order's affairs. His plans sped ahead as he put energy into his idea of the Christophers, and he received encouragement from Cardinal Spellman in New York. In the *Catholic World* Keller told how the master of ceremonies at a huge patriotic rally in Los Angeles had turned off all lights and then asked the 100,000 attendees each to light a single match. The audience gasped as its members realized the power of the individual. This empowering became Keller's theme, which he always connected to the mission of America. Recalling Christopher, the saint who was a "Christ-bearer," Keller said to any and all, "You can be a Christopher." His primary source for quotation here as often was a Luce publication, this time *Fortune* magazine, which had referred to America as "the leading practical exponent of Christianity" in the world. He enjoyed having his ideas confirmed as he read that "the basic teachings of Christianity are in [America's] blood stream." Today, in the battle of ideals and the defense of individual freedom, *Fortune* and Keller went on, "the American owes all this to the Church."

11:34   Well aware of Cold War symbolism, the priest promoted Mary's Day celebrations to upstage and put down communist May Day rituals. He wrote his new and more congenial superior, Father Raymond A. Lane, that his Christopher approach would help in "saving America from Communism." Could he have a leave of absence to promote it? Given such a leave, Keller found ways to advance *Christopher News Notes* and to infiltrate public media. A constant theme was anticommunism. Communists, he charged, were trying to control writers' associations, hoping to determine the message for radio and movies and to "throttle the literary work of non-Communists." Keller did not mention his contemporary Senator Joseph McCarthy, but he did generally buy into the idea that a domestic communist conspiracy had "started twenty years ago and is still going" and that it "has helped to shape our domestic and foreign policies." Only strong faith could counter it. America itself became a theme of Keller's Cold War faith and propaganda. Let McMahon quote the philosophers and Murray the theologians; Keller would cite crooner Bing Crosby, now a favorite in folk Catholicism: "It is the American way to believe in God. There can be no real brotherhood of man without the Fatherhood of God." Keller added his gloss: "For the present, at least, as America goes, so goes the world." When a Connecticut woman agitated for having the motto "In God We Trust" bannered in a junior high school in 1952, the head of the Christophers applauded: "She decided that if we Americans put 'In God We Trust' on our coins, the least we can do is put it in our schools."

Despite all the good works in his priestly life, Keller's former superior, Thomas S. Walsh, kept dogging him, warning that he might be watering down the Catholic message in efforts to advance Americanism. "Though we invite the cooperation of Protestants in combating Communism, we don't want to give them the impression that we have abandoned our distinctive position." Feeling himself stuck in the Maryknoll order, the loner set off to form his own Christopher world. He cultivated but was not close to New York diocesan leadership, which admired but did not fully trust his enterprise. Maryknoll could no longer control him, or he his impulses to leave the order. In his transition he wrote a book. Drawing on old news notes, the assistance of writer friends, and the counsel of Fulton Oursler of *Reader's Digest,* he produced the best-seller *You Can Change the World.* Father John McConnell, the Maryknoll censor, compared Keller's writing to that of Eleanor Roosevelt; it was "awful," but "powerful with many people for the same reason," because neither "flinched from repeating the same dull truism." Of course, the book was unscholarly. "You had always to be rescuing him from monstrous fundamentalistic statements."

Appropriately, given the nature of the times and its obsessions, the specter of communism haunted author Keller from line one: "Did you ever stop to think that the United States is being effectively undermined by less than *one percent* of the people of our country, of whom only a portion are Communists?" He had no data to back those statistics, but having evidence and being precise were never his strong suit. Convinced that he was replicating papal social teaching, Keller wanted to quicken other Christophers to promote America. What the world's people need and want, he af-

11:35

11:36

firmed, and "what they crave above all else is the spirit that makes America the great nation it is." That spirit, "above all else is God's truth proclaiming through the Declaration of Independence, the Constitution and the Bill of Rights that even the least individual as a child of God, has rights that no man or nation can take from him."

11:37   Friendly commentators like George Sokolsky and Bob Considine trumpeted the Keller book. The priest's regular charge that elements in the media had been taken over by procommunists was countered by the fact that the *New York Times, Saturday Review,* and the *Library Journal,* among others, gave positive reviews to the book. It was Catholic social critics who had trouble with it. The new Catholic magazine *Integrity* offered sour comment. Carol Jackson there found clichés and piousness in Keller. "The Declaration of Independence seems almost interchangeable with the Ten Commandments, and the defense of American democracy nearly synonymous with the defense of the Church." Where was comment on the sacraments, on Catholic social action? *Commonweal,* the lay magazine, also criticized Keller's "villain thesis of history" and the naive notion that an individual who was "a lone Christopher" could have much influence on the powers that be. Keller claimed that such criticism would "do us a lot of good." And Father Walsh, writing from Shanghai, liked the book "immensely," as did Walsh's Shanghai friend, "a very wealthy banker of Jewish race," who wanted to pass it on to friends. "What we both liked in it particularly was the spirit of charity that breathes in it" and "the care used to avoid offending sensibilities while stating the Catholic attitude with every frankness."

11:38   Keller was showing that if Catholicism was indeed still in a ghetto, its walls were by then quite porous. No Protestant apologist could match his list of celebrity friends and endorsers. A paging-through the records turns up names like Clare Boothe Luce, the Joseph P. Kennedy family, Gian Carlo Menotti, J. Edgar Hoover, Charles Lindbergh, Samuel Goldwyn, Walt Disney, Dinah Shore, Loretta Young, Ray Bolger, Irene Dunne, and Richard Nixon, all headliners in his time. Protestants and secular liberals by midcentury perhaps had less to fear from Catholic violations of the separation of church and state than from postwar Catholicism's access to the people of power and influence who would help shape the nation Protestants had once tried to monopolize.

11:39   Of course, there were still embarrassments, but the church was learning to take care of them. Every Catholic and informed Protestant, for instance, knew that since the third century Catholic doctrine held that *extra ecclesiam nulla salus,* which to the Catholic meant "outside the Catholic Church there is no salvation." In premodern Europe the church had the luxury of flaunting that teaching. Today, however, support for it would not go well, not in an America where others knew that Catholics thought they alone had the full truth of faith. They surmised as well that these Catholics also expected a loving God to allow some non-Catholics into heaven. Take such a doctrine literally in America and follow its consequences, and you would set back efforts by Catholicism to commend itself. Yet take it literally Jesuit Leonard Feeney did, at a no less visible place than Harvard. He developed an organization called the St. Benedict Center. Like his contemporary believers both Catholic and Protestant, Feeney found secularism at places like Harvard to be as distasteful as he found the faith tasteful. Catherine Clarke and other laypeople in 1940 helped him set up his center in Cambridge. It attracted students who later became influential, including Avery Dulles, son of John Foster Dulles. Avery was making his pilgrimage from Presbyterianism to Catholicism. Clare Boothe Luce, playwright and journalist, and Dorothy Day both spoke there. William Cardinal O'Connell and then Richard Cardinal Cushing, aided by the intellectual Auxiliary Bishop John Wright, gave the St. Benedict Center and Feeney their encouragement. At last, at least someone was effectively doing something in the face of secularism at a strategic place.

In 1945 the Jesuits moved Feeney from their Weston College   11:40
to pursue full-time work at the center. But while McMahon and Murray used lofty argument and Keller and Sheen reached for the heart, Feeney took a different and alienating (to all but an elite few) approach. Through the periodical *From the Housetops* and in regular meetings he propagated hard-line Catholicism and, with it, a negation of all secular and humanist thought, as he found it expressed among his Harvard neighbors. He swung just as wildly at non-Catholic and thus unsaved Christianity, as well as at softer-line forms of Catholicism itself. Feeney preached on the scandalous theme that outside the Catholic Church there was no salvation, and he prospered by winning some seekers who survived and even enjoyed high hurdles to faith. Dulles, who later acquired an ecumenical temperament, for a time sounded Feeneyite notes. In *From the Housetops* he could write, "Every culture which is not Catholic is in some degree anti-Catholic." Therefore, "the belief that one can with impunity consort constantly with heretics and

atheists, and casually exchange ideas with them, is a dangerous product of modern liberalism." Some Harvard students agreed with this and left secular Harvard. Where could they study? Feeney arranged that the St. Benedict Center could give accredited degrees and even be acceptable for veterans who would use GI Bill funds for study. The more emphatic and distancing Feeney became, the more attractive was his lure.

11:41   As Feeney began to show his anti-Semitism (and for other reasons as well), the Boston archdiocese grew uneasy. Cardinal Cushing liked to participate in forums with non-Catholics. Here, under his own nose, priests were criticizing such efforts. He and John Wright tried to limit the appeal of Feeney but at first had little effect. The famed British convert, novelist Evelyn Waugh, by visiting the center in 1948, called attention to it and showed how extreme it was. His reaction, however, surprised Feeney. While Waugh the convert had a high threshold of tolerance for outrageousness, often choosing to offend those who had not converted to Catholicism, in this case he found Feeney outrageous and the center's students "stark, raving mad." Waugh walked out on an event: "It seemed to me [Feeney] needed an exorcist more than an alienist. A case of demoniac possession and jolly frightening." As publicity about such impressions developed, the archdiocese had to react. By Christmas, Feeney was forbidden any longer to say mass. He responded by inventing his own religious order, the Slaves of the Immaculate Heart of Mary. *Time, Newsweek,* and *Life* found this religion story relevant and, for a moment, made Feeney a household name.

11:42   Cushing had to silence the obsessed priest and refused permission for any Catholics to receive the sacraments at the St. Benedict Center. That autumn the Jesuits dismissed Feeney, who was eventually excommunicated. The Slaves were reduced to being super-Catholics who were no longer Catholics at all. They had to find forums where they and their dwindling company of loyalists could gather. They turned out to be several centuries late in their choice of dogma. Yet as Feeney moved toward oblivion, he still struck at themes that critical Catholics raised against the Fulton Sheens and the James Kellers. Indeed, he struck one note with which serious theologians were not likely to have disagreed: "Here in America," he grumbled, "instead of religion we talk about 'good Americanism' and 'the Constitution of the United States.' Why, sometimes I believe that the people of this country believe Americanism is more important than religion!" Going down, he swung out once more at the postwar cultural reality by hitting the interfaith sphere. It was "a place where a Jewish rabbi, who does not believe in the divinity of Christ, and a Protestant minister, who doubts it, get together with a Catholic priest, who agrees to forget it for the evening." Despite the murmurings of super-Catholics like Feeney, in pluralist America it was the interfaith ethos and not an exclusivist ghetto faith that would serve the purposes of mainstream American Catholicism.

12

"That Each American Jew Become a Zionist"

12:1   Fᴏʀ American Jews the question of participation in the One Nation, Indivisible, was decisively different than it was for Protestants and Catholics. The concept that America, formerly a "Christian nation," was now made up of "Protestants, Catholics, and Jews" was greatly enhanced by Jewish contributions to national life in World War II. Ten years after the war, with the breaking up of the old urban ghettos and the diffusion of Jews into the general population through massive suburban moves, the language of "Protestant, Catholic, Jew" was confirmed, as in a popular book title by Will Herberg. But during the early years of the Cold War, roughly during the Truman administration and climaxing with the birth of Israel in 1948, Jews were on the spot with a particular issue. Were they *really* at home in the One Nation, or did their support of Israel divide their loyalties and make them part of "Two Nations?" Did their Zionism complicate their Americanism, not only politically but also spiritually? Would encouragement of Israel by the American government and by the Christian majority breach convention and set bad precedents by making too much of nationhood and peoplehood? These issues, as old as American pluralism and modern Zionism, and certainly not settled in 1948, brought drama to the early Cold War years and provided the main plot for Judaism in America at that time.

12:2   Enter Cyrus. Cyrus, king of Persia, had helped make possible

180

the return of ancient Jews from exile in Babylon to Zion, to Israel. In Second Isaiah the prophet, speaking for the Lord, called this monarch God's "anointed," or "messiah." "I surname you, though you do not know me," the prophet heard the Lord of Israel telling his commissioned servant Cyrus. In imagination, one leaps across the centuries. On February 22, 1960, the Jewish Theological Seminary in New York conferred an honorary doctorate on former president Harry S. Truman as "a man who contributed much" to the birth of modern Israel. According to legend—one does not find the quotation in his formal remarks or newspaper reports—Truman was said to have responded: "'A man who contributed much?' I am Cyrus, I am Cyrus!" That an American with Baptist loyalties should be honored by Jews and subject to such evidently legendary enhancement suggests how webbed and tangled religious histories in America can be.

As soon as Truman became president he began to find himself   12:3
in the crossroads of expectations concerning Israel. He could have heard a typical word of urgency on July 25, 1946, when the noted Cleveland rabbi Hillel Silver spoke for many: "For the Jews of Europe it is now Palestine or death; for the Jews of Palestine it is now liberty or death." Truman began his presidential career as no Cyrus. In fact, he singled out Silver as a special irritant. The president generalized: "The Jews aren't going to write the history of the U.S. or my history!" His predecessor, he was told, had understood the imponderables of Jewish feelings. Truman responded: "I am not Roosevelt. I am not from New York. I am from the Middle West. I must do what I think is right." Simply backing Jews against Arab claims to Palestine that July did not seem right. It looked as if under his administration Americans would go no further than helping settle European Jewish refugees.

"I am from the Middle West." The One Nation was made up   12:4
not only of many religions but also of diverse regions. Coming from where he did, Truman had less familiarity with Jews and experienced less prodding to support their causes. Born in Missouri in 1884, Truman attended a Presbyterian Sunday school where he met Bess Wallace, who became his wife. At eighteen he joined the Baptist church and remained an occasional attender throughout his life. He read the Bible early and often and cited it with ease. His Masonic lodge membership enforced his notion that biblical morality should undergird life. He liked to urge that the United States should live by the Sermon on the Mount as read in the Gospels. Ex post facto he did little to discourage notions that the Bible had

influenced his views of Israel. In 1959 he told an interviewer: "As a student of the Bible I have been impressed by the remarkable achievements of the Jews in Palestine in making the land of the Holy Book blossom again." But three months before he became president in 1945 he also confided in a private memorandum: "The Jews claim God Almighty picked 'em out for special privilege. Well I'm sure he had better judgment." Then he spelled out his civic faith. "Fact is I never thought God picked any favorites. It is my studied opinion that any race, creed or color can be God's favorites if they act the part—and very few of 'em do that."

12:5   Long friendship with business partner Eddie Jacobson, who belonged to a Reform temple in Kansas City, helped give Truman positive views of Jews but did not introduce him to Zionism. It was not a conventional part of the Reform credo or program. Jacobson helped his friend work past the conventional racist and anti-Jewish opinions of his time and place in the years when Truman the businessman was turning to machine politics, before becoming a senator and vice president and, after Roosevelt's death in 1945, president—precisely in the years when Zionist issues came into focus. As he took leadership, his Midwestern rootage disturbed some Zionists. The month Truman became president, David Ben Gurion, a pioneer of Israel, expressed worries: "Coming from the Midwest (Missouri) I doubt whether the President has any connection and relationship to Jews," as Roosevelt had. Would Felix Frankfurter, Henry Morgenthau, and Sam Rosenman, Israel's friends in Washington, now continue to have good White House contacts? Ben Gurion hoped that because "public opinion in the United States has gained in importance" and because Jews could help shape that opinion, they could indirectly influence the president.

12:6   Truman faced what was called "the Jewish problem" at once, since the issue of where to resettle European Holocaust survivors was pressing. In Chicago on April 14, 1943, he had made a rare comment on "the edict of a mad Hitler and a degenerate Mussolini" who were killing Jews. "Today these oppressed people, still with spirit unbroken look for succor to us, we people of the United States." Because the Nazis had planned "the systematic slaughter throughout Europe," so "today—not tomorrow—we must do all that is humanly possible to provide a haven and place of safety." Nations must open free lands for them. "This is not a Jewish problem. It is an American problem—and we must and will face it squarely and honorably." Yet as Senator Truman concentrated

on winning the war, except for helping constituents and friends
resettle a few Jews, he had little record of support activity.

During the war the senator and then the vice president chose to   12:7
see Palestine as a British concern. He could verbally affirm Jewish
interests, but he was procrastinating. In a letter of February 16,
1944, Truman wrote Jewish lobbyists that his "sympathy of course
is with the Jewish people," and "when the right time comes I am
willing to help make the fight for a Jewish homeland in Palestine."
During his vice presidential campaign that year he shared a Democratic platform that called for a "free and democratic Jewish commonwealth," but not much was being made of it. Rabbi Silver, who
had ties to fellow Ohioan Robert Taft, a Republican who always
nettled Truman, was so aggressive that Truman came to mute his
reference to the adjective *Jewish* in the platform phrase. As a candidate he agreed, Truman said, with anti-Zionist Jews: a Jewish
commonwealth would mean "a racial and theocratic state," which
he opposed. Eddie Jacobson, back at B'nai Jehuda congregation in
Kansas City, kept hearing and passing on word that Truman was
alienating Jews. Another congregation member and friend, Alex
Sachs, thereupon wrote Truman that "those to whom I have talked,
have only the highest commendation for you on your stand opposing a Jewish state—and for urging every assistance for the refugees to enter Palestine." But Sachs noticed that Truman's "opposition to a Jewish state will not be popular with the large group of
ardent Zionists who have already voiced their disapproval." Hearing of such conflicts, one could hardly have expected candidate
Truman, a Gentile, to solve an issue Jews could not resolve among
themselves. So he stood between counsels.

The counsel of Silver and Zionism was more forceful. But dur-   12:8
ing the final months of the war they got little hearing. Truman said
he feared that overt commitment to Israel would demand a troop
commitment of a half million American soldiers and could even
lead to World War III. When Rabbi Silver and the aged and tiring
Rabbi Stephen Wise approached Truman on October 2, 1945, the
president asked them to go slow, to exert less pressure. He was
getting pressure from Poles, Italians, and Jews alike, and would
support no religious state, "be it Jewish or Catholic." Yet during
the 1948 campaign, Silver worked to produce a "Jewish vote" for
Republicans, and Truman had to protect his Jewish flank.

The problem was, Truman saw two flanks within Judaism. Sil-   12:9
ver and Wise pitted themselves against strongly reactive Jews who
opposed what they called "theocracy." Keeping their eye on preju-

dice in the One Nation, Indivisible, that was America, they said they feared that support for Israel would increase domestic anti-Semitism and lead to credible charges that Jews in America held dual loyalties. The new American Council for Judaism was now the voice for this minority, a former majority. Council president Lessing J. Rosenwald was most clear as he addressed the third annual gathering: "Zionists *created a Jewish issue in the elections.* A vast, powerfully organized, unholy effort was made to introduce consideration for a so-called Jewish bloc vote, and a threat to use that bloc for punitive means." Zionism was "a fraud upon the public," he said, "one of the most evil and gravest injustices done to the Jews of the United States."

12:10   Most Orthodox Jews had considered Zionism to be a messianism that preempted the role of the true Messiah. Secular, socialist, and progressive-minded leaders brought the doctrine of progress to their Zionism. They came to see the religious side of Judaism as retrogressive and defeatist, the mark of Jews who only sought refuge in modern storms. Reform, the most public expression of organized Judaism in America, had opposed Zionism. But after jurist Louis Brandeis, just before World War I, began to support it, there was more enthusiasm for his dictum that "loyalty to America demands that each American Jew become a Zionist," and after the rise of Hitler, it was easy to think in such terms. The American Council for Judaism reacted against that trend and, through Rabbi Morris Lazaron of Baltimore, cultivated relations with Undersecretary of State Sumner Welles. It was Welles and his faction who downplayed the statistics of Jewish death and destruction under Hitler and reinforced the opinions of Christian anti-Zionists. Lazaron's colleague Louis "Cardinal" Wolsey argued that Zionists had "completely Nazified" Reform and wanted "to rule world Jewry," planning "to take everything from us, including our religion." Elmer Berger, a rabbi in Flint, Michigan, took up these themes and stayed longest with the movement and sentiment.

12:11   In August of 1942, long before Truman took office, a "Statement of Principles by Non-Zionist Rabbis" of the fledgling council expressed concern for Judaism's "growing secularism," which it saw in Zionism. Yes, Palestine was important for the Jewish soul, but not as a nationalistic feature. The accent instead should be on the "eternal prophetic principles of life and thought, principles through which alone Judaism and the Jew can hope to endure and bear witness to the universal God." This was the kind of language with which a Truman, who had friends like those from B'nai Jehuda back home, would feel most familiar. Rosenwald, son of the founder of Sears, Roebuck and Company, though not highly religious, also thought that Judaism was a spiritual not a political force. His friend Arthur Hays Sulzberger, publisher of the *New York Times,* agreed and saw the council to be working for "Americans of Jewish faith," not for those of national aspiration. *Life* magazine gave a voice to this anti-Zionist movement when on June 28, 1943, it published an article by Rosenwald to which Zionists vehemently reacted. All this was prehistory, but after the war Rosenwald was back, testifying in 1946 at hearings of an Anglo-American Committee of Inquiry, designed by President Truman and British foreign secretary Ernest Bevin to address the situation in Palestine. He said that Jews wanted no separate state, no special privileges. Zionism he compared to the "Hitlerian concept that the Jews are a race or nation." Rabbi Wise raged back, quoting Brandeis: "Let no one imagine that Zionism is inconsistent with American patriotism." Rabbi Elmer Berger stayed his course all the while, working and worrying the "Two Nations" theme. In *The Jewish Dilemma,* published one month after the war in the Pacific ended, he noted: "Isn't it a curious thing, and tragically ironic, that Zionists and extreme anti-Semites agree on the same solution—isolate the Jews in a country of their own."

How nuanced a view President Truman could have had of this conflict within Judaism it is hard to know. Had he listened in on Christian debates, however, he would have heard counterparts almost as noisy. Many liberals, in sympathy for Arab peoples who would be displaced by a partitioned land of Israel, or in the conviction that Zionism was a nationalism of the very sort they opposed for Christians, for Americans in general, or for any peoples, were anti-Zionist and became friends of the council. We have seen *Christian Century* editors in this company. Yale theologian H. Richard Niebuhr expressed anxiety over Zionism, and successive Union Theological Seminary presidents Henry Sloane Coffin and Henry Pitney Van Dusen favored the American Council for Judaism even up to 1948. By then it had itself become largely isolated within Judaism and could no longer attract the support of notables such as it had enjoyed only a few years before. 12:12

Had Reform and other now-Zionist branches of Judaism wanted to understand liberal Christians—fundamentalists were on their side, for Christian millennial reasons—they would have noticed that the universalistic element in the One Nation and One World theme dominated their thinking. The liberals tended to favor 12:13

melting-pot images of America. Jews could and should be Jews religiously, but their religion ought not include Zionism, because that meant tribalism, theocracy, and divided national loyalties. In 1945 a *Christian Century* editorial asked postwar Jewish survivors everywhere to decide "whether they are an integral part of the nations in which they live or members of a Levantine nation dwelling in exile." The words "integral part" served as a code for the approach of liberals who seldom asked what made up the integralism and who determined what it was. From Brandeis on, Zionists had a different interpretation of that very theme, namely, that one could be a citizen of one country and work zealously for the birth of another. But sometimes liberal Protestants reached for such hyperbole that they descended into offense. A month after Germany surrendered, the *Christian Century* expressed the hope that Germany in defeat not "become another Jewry. They have not lived long enough with their ideology of a unique and privileged race" as Jews presumably had for such a bad thing to happen. What had begun as an honest attempt to question religious nationalism came to be a scandalous dig at the victims of modern Germany.

12:14   H. Richard Niebuhr's brother Reinhold tried a third way between fundamentalism's uncritical supporters of Israel and liberalism's critical rejecters. As early as 1942 in the *Nation* he argued that Israel was a collective and "a collective survival impulse is as legitimate a 'right' as an individual one." Liberal Protestants were too tied to "individualist and universalist presuppositions and illusions" to see this. At the same time Niebuhr criticized many Zionist tendencies, including attempts to gloss over the traumas Israel would induce in the Arab world. "It is absurd to expect any people to regard the restriction of their sovereignty over a traditional possession as 'just,' no matter how many other benefits accrue from that abridgement." Asked to write a preface for *The Jew in Our Day,* written by his friend Waldo Frank in 1944, he drew back when the author linked modern Judaism with ancient Isaiah's "suffering servant." No, said Niebuhr, support for a Jewish homeland had to exist for promoting political justice, not religious nationalism. "There must be a political solution of the problem of the Jews without reference to the final religious problem." But he also did not see "how it is possible to develop this prophetic overtone of high religion in the Jewish community fully, if the nation does not have a greater degree of socio-political security." In other words, he wanted a homeland for Jews in Palestine precisely so that Jews could avoid the problem *Christian Century* editors and other liberals saw unfolding in nascent Israel!

The story of late-blooming liberal Christian Zionism is not a   12:15
distraction from the Jewish story of the rise of Israel. In America, the liberal Christian voice was the one most heard in the public sector and would then have been politically influential as American opinion was taking shape. So one notes that a Christian Council on Palestine, founded by Reinhold Niebuhr, refugee theologian Paul Tillich, and others, merged in 1946 with the American Palestine Committee. Subsidized generously by the American Zionist Emergency Council, this merger developed over a hundred chapters and attracted three thousand pro-Zionist Christian clergy. Carl Herman Voss, an old friend of Rabbi Stephen Wise and now secretary of the group, was not subtle: "We shall never be able to secure the wide-spread Christian support needed for the fulfillment of the Zionist aspirations unless we have the complete cooperation of Zionist groups in every community throughout the United States." Yet they pushed less for a Jewish state than a sort of binational state, a place of refuge. They wanted to protect themselves from both *Christian Century* and Niebuhrian charges that Jewish nationalism, if integrally bonded to a race and a religion, would represent the kind of idolatry that Judaism and prophetic Christianity alike opposed.

The Christian Council on Palestine had trouble keeping its own   12:16
ranks peaceful. In January 1946 it issued a political statement recognizing that leaders of its factions who promoted "spiritual" Zionism chafed in the company of aggressive "political" Zionists. They agreed that Zionism was essentially valid "as a political and moral ideal," but contending elements in the Christian Council were not "officially committed to any particular formula of the Zionist purpose." Its leadership admitted that the notion of a "Jewish commonwealth" divided their own camp. Niebuhr, meanwhile, moved toward the commonwealth idea. In his testimony before the Anglo-American Committee of Inquiry in Washington early in 1946, he said that "the Jews have survived as a people, so presumably they will survive even if they don't have a Jewish state." But "the spiritual and physical price is terribly high" if they do not; the physical price was clear in the fact that "they were almost liquidated" without a state of their own in the Hitler years.

Many Zionists were sensitive to the problems that both Chris-   12:17
tians and Jews had with the "Two Nations" theme. A front for

some of them was the American Christian Palestine Committee, founded in 1948. Its mission was to cultivate friendly Christian groups. Peter Bergson, who called himself Hillel Kook and led an American delegation of the underground Zionist liberation organization Irgun, in 1943 had also founded the Emergency Committee to Save the Jews of Europe. His was an endeavor that showed mindfulness of the problems of American Jews who feared being stigmatized as disloyal to America if they also promoted Israel. In April Kook and his colleagues wrote Chaim Weizmann, the scientist who had so much to do with Israel's founding, that he should distinguish between *Hebrews,* the Jews of Palestine and the refugees in Europe, and *Jews,* meaning all other Jews of the world. On these terms America's Jews were "Americans and wish to remain Americans. They are not now Hebrews but are Americans of Hebrew ancestry." He was fumbling his way through the maze of American ethnicities and religiosities. "Like all other Americans, they have a national extraction (Hebrew) quite apart from and in addition to their religious affiliation, which is Jewish." For example, Weizmann was acquainted with Rabbi Stephen Wise, "an American who practices the Jewish religion." The group headed by Kook, not large in numbers or influence, typifies the efforts of Zionists who ministered to many kinds of needs.

12:18   One would have expected to hear the voice of Arab Americans speaking up for the Arabs in Palestine. They were the people who, as Niebuhr reminded, could not possibly regard future restriction on their sovereignty as just and then welcome it. But one must try to picture how unorganized and muffled the voices of overseas Arabs then still were, and how few people of Arab descent were United States citizens. There were only about 350,000 in the United States, and they came from many nations with differing histories, religions, and outlooks, not all of them sympathetic to Palestinian Arabs. Still, a few efforts and voices were present, such as those of the small Princeton-based Institute of Arab American Affairs. Professor Philip K. Hitti, who headed it, feared that Zionism was leading America into a path of injustice to Arabs. Boston lawyer Faris S. Malouf, president of the group, saw to the issuing of a monthly *Bulletin* that was no match for Jewish publicity. No wonder Harry S. Truman regularly could say, had to say, that he had heard from few Arab voices and voters.

12:19   Absent a mass of Arab voices, there were interests that spoke up for them, notably the Committee for Justice and Peace in the Holy Land, formed in February 1948 by Rabbi Lazaron and others.

Committee members wished to foster "friendly relations among the peoples" of three faiths, Jews, Christians, and Moslems, in the Near and Middle East, and "throughout the world," and they opposed the United Nations Assembly's action of November 29, 1947, partitioning the Holy Land. The usual company of anti-Zionists was a part of this committee, including the former dean of Barnard College, Virginia Gildersleeve; an editor of the *Christian Century;* Theodore Roosevelt's grandson Kermit; liberal preacher Harry Emerson Fosdick; and American Council for Judaism members. Virginia Gildersleeve then as later criticized many of her fellow Christians. Eight years after the birth of Israel, in *Many a Good Crusade,* she still chided them for having advocated a "national home" for Jews. They had done so simply because "these unworthy Christians did not want to admit any more Jewish refugees into America." The committee attracted few politicians; most feared reaction by Jewish voters, while ordinary activists feared they might be seen as anti-Semitic if they did not support Israel. As Gildersleeve put it, "nearly all had a kind of 'guilt complex' in their emotions towards Jews because of the terrible tragedies inflicted upon them by Hitler." The committee remained important not politically but as an interesting voice that criticized nationalisms and as it expressed concern about disrupting the presumed integral fabric of America. Thus one month after Israel became a state in 1948 it warned that "American Zionists, Christians as well as Jews, gravely consider the great growth of feeling in this country against the extreme Zionist pressure here." The American Council for Judaism pronounced its verdict against Zionist "insistence on separate Jewish nationalism, as causing danger of disruption of our national unity and encouraging anti-Semitism."

Political and military historians conventionally treat most of the   12:20
story of the birth of Israel. But religious organizations and spiritual motivations are also part of that story, whether it deals with President Truman's attitudes, State Department maneuvers, or international relations. If American Jews and Christians both presented a confusion of arguments on the subject, one would hardly expect a busy politician to have made his way through the maze to find perfect consistency and direction. According to Henry Wallace, secretary of commerce and former vice president, Truman let some frustrations show at a cabinet meeting in July 1946 and in fury blurted about Zionists as Jews that "Jesus Christ couldn't please them when he was here on earth, so how could anyone expect that I would have any luck?" and, on theologically weaker ground, that

Jesus "had no use for them and didn't care what happened to them." Only slightly more discreetly he wrote Eleanor Roosevelt, "I fear very much that the Jews are like all underdogs. When they get on top they are just as intolerant and as cruel as the people were to them when they were underneath." Still he kept moderate Zionist Jews in his circle and welcomed Jewish support in his upset election of 1948. He told aide Oscar Ewing: "I have two Jewish assistants on my staff, David Niles and Max Lowenthal. Whenever I try to talk to them about Palestine, they soon burst into tears because they are so emotionally involved in the subject." Candidly, "So far I have not known what to do."

12:21   He had to do something. His State Department, keeping Arab interests in mind, opposed American support of the state of Israel. Under the example and influence of Dean Acheson, much leadership did not even want to back Truman in a program of resettling one hundred thousand European Jewish refugees in Arab Palestine. Truman appealed to the Jewish vote and interests, saying he had no counterpart of Arab supporters. Niles said to Lowenthal in the midst of these tensions that "people in State are bitching things up," which meant not abiding by executive decisions. This "bitching up," he knew, was motivated by American desires to please Arab oil interests.

12:22   "So far I have not known what to do." Deciding what to do on the basis of Jewish interests remained complicated. Increasingly the American Jewish Committee came to position itself between radical Zionists and interests such as the American Council for Judaism. It had begun as an anti-Zionist organization in 1942. In 1943 Judge Joseph Proskauer, its president, linked with New York judge Irving Lehman to draw up a "Statement of Views" for the committee. Unsurprisingly, it added glosses to the standard theme of One Nation: "In the United States as in all other countries Jews, like all others of their citizens are nationals of those nations and of no other." This meant emphatically that "there can be no political identification of Jews outside of Palestine with whatever government may there be instituted." He led the committee to have ties with the State Department, which had been more comfortable with the American Council for Judaism. Proskauer could see that the council was increasingly strident and unrepresentative, so he worked to establish a middle course. But to Zionists the American Jewish Committee also looked "traitorous, irreligious and anti-Jewish." When the State Department became open to partitioning Palestine, the committee finally moved toward moderate Zionism.

Nahum Goldman, a Zionist diplomat, confronted Proskauer: "You will fight the Jews in Palestine after Auschwitz because they want to have a Jewish state? You will be torn to pieces between your loyalty to America and your loyalty to the Jewish people." Proskauer kept his reservations about Zionism to himself and put energies into supporting refugee resettlement. The American Council for Judaism was left to stand alone, its power declining, still claiming to fight against "Jewish nationalism" and for Jews having a "single, indivisible, and exclusive allegiance to the United States."

Given the small quotas of immigrants allowed into the United States from anywhere and the absence of bids from other nations, there was little Truman could do to advance his cause of refugee resettlement. The council wanted America to open its doors, and Zionists wanted to invent Israel as their haven. On November 5, 1946, the council proposed a lobby, "a broadly based national citizens committee, composed of prominent Christians, and perhaps a few Jewish leaders from the ranks of the ministry, business, labor, education, and social welfare" for the refugee cause. It attracted Eleanor Roosevelt, Lessing Rosenwald, New York mayor Fiorello La Guardia, and Federal Council of Churches president Charles P. Taft, among others. The strategy was to mute specific support for Jewish refugees but to be more generous about immigration in general, and thus to include them. Truman knew he could not sell such a policy in a time when Americans were scrambling to get jobs in a tight postwar market. There were also fears lest immigration mean communist infiltration. The president found abhorrent the terms of an immigration bill proposed in Congress in March 1948, which, he thought, discriminated "in callous fashion against displaced persons of the Jewish faith." That was the "brutal fact" which could not be obscured "by the maze of technicalities in the bill or by the protestations of some of its sponsors." When it passed, Truman signed the bill with the urging of some Jewish leaders who saw clearly the irony of supporting a measure born to favor Jews but now virtually excluding them. They felt they had to consider any legislation better than none, but they only enraged and inspired Zionists to more aggressive action.

Pressure now was exerted on Britain, which since 1916 had held a mandate with respect to governing Palestine. In the early postwar years militant Zionists in Israel turned increasingly violent, thus provoking the British in 1946 to arrest Hagana and Jewish Agency figures in Israel. On July 22 Irgun bombed and destroyed much of the prominent King David Hotel in Jerusalem, taking 100 lives at

12:23

12:24

that British headquarters. The only way to make peace, Zionists said, was to invent the state of Israel. In America they won over Judge Proskauer and the American Jewish Committee. On Yom Kippur that year President Truman, with politics in mind, made a pro-Zionist statement designed unsuccessfully to be helpful to Democratic candidates in New York. Still, Truman set his course for 1947–48 to support Israel and prod Great Britain to go along.

12:25   As the Israeli cause worked its way through the United Nations, Truman remained an almost grudging supporter. He still desired a unified Palestine but knew that the United Nations would go for partition. Truman wrote Wise in August 1947 that "there seem to be two sides to this question. I am finding it rather difficult to decide which one is right and a great many other people in this country are beginning to feel just as I do." He named Eleanor Roosevelt and John Foster Dulles, among others, to a United Nations delegation, seeking bipartisan counsel and support. While all this dragged, old friend Eddie Jacobson, who had not originally been a Zionist, approached him in 1947. "Harry, my people need help and I am appealing to you to help them," he wrote. There were a half million Jewish refugees in Europe: "In all this world, there is only one place where they can go—and that is Palestine." To this hometown eloquence Jacobson added the reminder that Truman as "leader and spokesman for our country" should support the action. Truman responded that he could not be up front during United Nations debates: "I don't want to be quoted on the subject at all. When I see you I'll tell you just what the difficulties are." Among them was Truman's fear that the United States would have to back its support with troops and risk antagonizing the Soviet Union.

12:26   In the spring before independence came, American Jews took stock. In April 1948 the Community Service Department of the American Jewish Committee, for example, made a study. "We are certain . . . that as of today, the desire for a Jewish State based on the concept that the Jews will be at the mercy of every aggressor as long as they are 'homeless,' remained deeply imbedded in the minds of the most active members of the Jewish communities including rabbis, congregational leaders, Jewish community councils, board members, etc." Suddenly a maverick but powerful troubler came on the scene—Rabbi Judah Magnes, who before 1921 had been a New Yorker and after 1925 and 1935 chancellor and then president of the Hebrew University in Jerusalem. Magnes had long held a pacifist dream of finding ways for Jews and Arabs to coexist. The United Nations and the United States were thwarting it. Why not, at the last minute, sponsor a binational state in Palestine? Could Magnes not be the agent to help bring it about? Of course, Zionists would oppose him, but what religion did not have internal conflict? Magnes got through to see President Truman with ease. Some in the State Department looked to the grand old man as an ally who could help prevent partition and promote trusteeship. But while his visit caused some confusion in the Zionist cause, he did not prevail, and the United Nations moved along toward partitioning.

The partition plan failed to get the necessary two-thirds vote, so   12:27
Truman evidently began to work behind the scenes. No one knows for sure what moved him, but he was in frequent contact with old friend Eddie Jacobson, who made "off the record" visits along with another Kansas City loyalist, lawyer Abraham Granoff, a tutor to Jacobson in matters political. Truman remained noncommittal in the face of their mild appeals. When Zionists asked for a frontal approach, Jacobson knew better: "Harry Truman will do what's right if he knows all the facts," and, be assured, Jacobson would transmit them. By November he was ready to push for support of partition, which would pit the president against the will of the cabinet and the State Department. On November 26 he wired news of this risky policy to Truman, and two days later he heard from the president's secretary "not to worry." The Jacobson diary the next day has the words: "Mission accomplished." On November 29, 1947, the vote for partition won. The Kansas City petitioners stopped asking and started thanking. Granoff told an interviewer later, "And we two poor guys dug into our little bank accounts and went there. We were ushered in and stayed quite a while." When the time came, they said, "Mr. President, we came here once in our lives not asking you for anything. Just to say thank you and God bless you." Truman was glad to take credit for having swung several delegate votes and to savor a victory.

All too soon the savor was lost, because war was to break out in   12:28
Palestine. Arabs were in control from that November day through March, after which Israel began to prevail, until by Independence Day, May 14, 1948, they had drawn their map of choice. President Truman was busy with Cold War tensions and Soviet troop buildups, so he could not take much interest. He made clear that United States troops would not be engaged. And the president was also busy with his own reelection campaign and given almost no chance to succeed himself. It was during these months that all the lobbies, the Committee for Justice and Peace in the Holy Land and

the American Council for Judaism and people like Chaim Weizmann—who flew in from London and was forced to cool his tired
heels for weeks—all spoke up. Truman told Jacobson how impatient he had become, "how disrespectful and how mean Jewish
leaders had been to him," how they "slandered and libeled" him.
The "Keep Out" sign went up for Rabbi Hillel Silver, "who had
more than once raged into the office of the President of the United
States and pounded his fist on his desk and shouted at him." One
last time Jacobson had to risk everything, as he confronted Truman on Weizmann's behalf. Truman turned tense and grim and, as

Chaim Weizmann (1874–1955) was a Zionist scientist who was elected Israel's
first president in 1948. President Truman was slow to receive Weizmann and show
him courtesy, but in due course the two leaders came to respect each other. Here
Weizmann presents Truman a Torah scroll in May 1948. (Photo courtesy of the
United Jewish Appeal.)

Jacobson said years later, came as close to "being an Anti-Semite as a man could possibly be." But then Truman said, "You win, you bald-headed s.o.b. . . . I will see him." And thereafter tense communications and wary respect developed between Truman and Weizmann.

Fearing that the Soviet Union would embarrass the State De-   12:29 partment and the United Nations delegation by being the first to recognize Israel, and responding to Zionist appeals, Truman had the United States recognize Israel on its Independence Day. What convinced Britain and the United States more than anything else to do this was the sense that Israel could be a much-needed ally in the Middle East. While the president was given much recognition by Jews, he responded modestly: "I sincerely hope that the Palestine situation will eventually work out on an equitable and peaceful basis. Sincerely yours, Harry Truman." He also wrote that his sole objective had been "to prevent bloodshed. The way things look today we apparently have not been very successful."

Three years later the *Christian Century* fell into line. "The right   12:30 of the Jews to Israel is no longer the question. Whatever the rights or wrongs that accompanied its birth, Israel exists. It must continue to exist." In 1951 a new Friends of the Middle East came into being to spearhead criticism of Israel. Of course, Rabbi Elmer Berger was on its board. So were Lowell Thomas the newscaster, columnist Dorothy Thompson, former Democratic Party chairman James Farley, Yale idealist philosopher William E. Hocking, and Edward L. R. Elson, the Presbyterian pastor who would baptize the newly elected president Dwight D. Eisenhower one year later. Garland Evans Hopkins spoke up for the Friends, in the interest, he said, of contributing to balance between Jewish and Arab public opinion in the United States. Hopkins later told James Sheldon of the Non-Sectarian Anti-Nazi League what motivated him and what his fears were, in barely shrouded language that sounded like a threat: "If the American people ever find themselves losing in another war in the Middle East and begin to ask why, and discover what the cause has been [an inordinately strong Jewish pressure on the U.S. government], you will find the same thing happening here to the Jews as happened in Germany. I hesitate to think what might happen in New York." Yet there turned out to be no measurable increase in anti-Semitism, and in the next decade Jews found even more secure places in the scheme of what was then called the American Way of Life.

A religious issue did surface soon: that of access to places in   12:31

Jerusalem that were holy to three faiths. On November 29, 1947, a United Nations resolution had called for the city of Jerusalem to be a *corpus separatum* under an international regime administered by the United States. Israel, of course, wanted to control the whole of Jerusalem, whereas at that time it dominated only West Jerusalem. Most Protestant leadership, including the National Council of Churches, formed in 1950–51, as late as 1953 backed international control. The *Christian Century,* no longer anti-Zionist but still anti-Catholic, heard rumors that the Vatican sought a mandate over the Holy Places. The scene in Palestine, said the editors, was "forbidding enough without making it still worse by injecting this proposal to turn Jerusalem and Bethlehem over to the pope." The war in 1948 did not win all of Jerusalem and thus all of the sites for Israel, and Arabs controlled access there.

12:32   Through it all the theological theme of battle had been the central public issue of One Nation, Indivisible, and the dividing of loyalties by Zionists. In February 1949 former Union Theological Seminary president Henry Sloane Coffin, who was also a leader in the International Missionary Council, used the pages of *Christianity and Crisis,* the journal his colleague Reinhold Niebuhr had helped found, to make a last strong statement on "Perils to America in the New Jewish State." He saw in it a "resurgence of fanatical Jewish nationalism" and the "stimulation of anti-Semitism" in the United States. Then came the liberal Protestant charge: "Many of our Jewish fellow citizens will gain for themselves the suspicion of being hyphenates," which meant "half Israeli and only half American." This status would prove "a source of prejudice and be an added difficulty for all Christians eager to end the hideously anti-Christian feeling against Jews in many of our communities." There could have been "no greater blunder" than Zionism. But he was resigned: "For the present we can do nothing but accept the fact of this new nation." And then: "We can give our sane Jewish fellow citizens our hearty support in their effort to be members of our nation alone and to repudiate Jewish nationalism." He evidently had no program for "our *nonsane* Jewish fellow citizens" but was ready otherwise with the plural pronoun: "our nation alone."

12:33   The word of benediction in that round of controversy came from aged Stephen S. Wise, the pioneer battler for Zion in Reform Judaism. At a commencement at the Jewish Institute of Religion, which he had founded and which was merging with Hebrew Union College, he told a newly ordained group of Reform rabbis, "If

men . . . ask of you, 'Are you a citizen of the State of Israel?' or
'Are you a citizen of the American Republic and a teacher of its
people?' answer them, 'The memories, the traditions, the hopes,
the dreams, the sufferings, the sorrows of four thousand years have
not sundered me from the blood and the race of the people of Israel.
I am one of them.' " But also: " 'As a citizen I belong wholly to
America. America is my country and I have none other. To it I give
the utmost of my loyalty, the deepest of my love, the truest of my
service.' "

13

"A Religious Monopoly Which Has Ceased to Exist"

13:1   If there was to be convergence of peoples and faiths in their One Nation during the American Century, sooner or later they would have to settle some affairs on the battleground labeled "church and state." Neither the word *church* nor the word *state* appears in the sixteen-word charter for religious liberty that appears in the First Amendment to the United States Constitution: "Congress shall make no law respecting an establishment of religion, or prohibiting the free exercise thereof." But Thomas Jefferson borrowed the two terms from Europe, where they were more appropriate, encompassing usually only one church, established by law, and one state, *the* state. The third president spoke of a "wall of separation between church and State" and, ever after, citizens did their fighting over the meaning of "separation" between the churches and religion on one side, and the legal jurisdictions on the other. None of the three branches of the federal government was able to escape controversy over the subject, but one incident in the executive branch and a sequence of rulings in the judicial revealed how much unfinished business remained on the "separation" front. They demonstrated how hard it was for individualist and sectarian Americans to agree on what the concept meant or should mean, or how they should live together in church and state.

13:2   The executive occasion was in a way a reprise of the 1939 incident when President Roosevelt had named Myron C. Taylor his

198

"personal representative" at the Vatican, to advance causes of mutual interest with Rome as World War II began. Now in 1951 Roosevelt was long dead, replaced by Harry S. Truman. But Taylor was still on the scene doing his representing, and the president had an impulse to name him or someone not merely a representative but the Ambassador Extraordinary and Plenipotentiary to the state of Vatican City. For a second-to-last time in American politics Catholics were able to unite in support of a single cause. For a second-to-last time Protestants across the spectrum from fundamentalist through moderate and liberal to modernist were able to combine for an attack on a single front. (The presidential candidacy of Catholic John F. Kennedy in 1960 was the last event to draw widespread support of Catholics, often across political party lines, and to attract, though selectively, Protestant opponents who could momentarily forget their theological differences within their separate camps.)

Truman may have acted out of mixed motives, but he was   13:3
moved by Cold War interests. He seemed to have thought naively that an ambassadorship would now help bring religious groups together. After all, religious America was fighting a war against atheistic communism, and the Vatican was a valuable ally. Truman was a Baptist, but now in his presidential prime he got his first and most vehement lessons about religious passions from fellow Baptists. In Arizona the *Baptist Beacon* asked, "Since when did it become the function of the President of the U.S. to lead the churches into religious unity?" The Arizona editors were in fact Southern Baptist, and as such were standoffish from even Christian ecumenical causes. They knew that the president "could not get church people together in matters of theology," but they also saw that "he has gotten all Baptists and Protestants [Southern Baptists were not even sure they should be lumped together with Protestants in general!] together in their opposition to sending an ambassador to the Vatican at Rome." Nothing in the nation had ever "been so unanimously opposed by the non-Catholic population as the nomination of a Vatican ambassador." Now, it seems, non-Catholics had become like the partisans we have mentioned earlier, partisans in Cretan cities of old, brothers and sisters who could forget their separate interests and antagonisms when faced with a single, in this case fellow Christian, foe. The *Beacon* editors charged that Truman had "sowed the seeds of the worst religious prejudice campaign this nation has ever known," and they seemed to be helping prove themselves right. "This is church unity à la President," the

editorial went on to say; the gesture would "degenerate into religious hatred and persecution."

13:4   The National Council of Churches of Christ, newly formed in 1950, at the other end of the Protestant spectrum, prophesied that the appointment "would produce consequences both far reaching and disastrous to the national unity of the American people." Top New York clerics gathered to say that national unity was urgent, but now the president would "bitterly divide our people and do immeasurable harm." Glenn Archer of Protestants and Other Americans United for Separation of Church and State called the moment a "national emergency." Secular newspapers agreed; the Boston *Herald* said of Truman that "the hurt he has done to national unity detracts from the good he has done for the world's defense against communism." Years later the incident was seen as too trivial even to take up space in most books on politics, but it is easily revisited. Myron C. Taylor hoped to retire as the president's personal envoy, and Truman wanted to appoint a successor. The *New York Times* headline read: "GEN. CLARK NAMED FIRST AMBASSADOR OF U.S. TO VATICAN." The story had the usual subhead, in this case: "Anti-Red Gain Seen/White House Cites Rome Resistance. Calls Step in National Interest." But so complex was the issue that the story needed subsubheads: "But Criticism is Sharp—Action Arouses Protestants—Recess Appointment Likely—Congressmen Silent." They had reason to lie low as churches fired at each other.

13:5   Presidential press secretary Joseph Short released the news of the planned appointment on October 20. The president was acting "in the national interest," both for reasons of diplomacy and for "the amelioration of human suffering." It was good to have Vatican ties. "It is well known that the Vatican is vigorously engaged in the struggle against communism," so such ties, said Short, would help "combat the Communist menace." General Mark Clark, a war hero, certainly was a logical choice and should have been a welcome appointee. But the critical mail piled high in any case at the White House. French visitor André Siegfried, a veteran religion-watcher amid things American, saw the response to be one of "astonishing violence," as pastors denounced this "intolerable scandal, an insult to the Protestant character of the nation." Siegfried saw the point: "The depth of this reaction must not be misunderstood; it represented instinctive defense on the part of a religious monopoly which has ceased to exist."

13:6   Catholics enjoyed the appointment but feared the reaction to it.

When it came, John Cogley, an editor of *Commonweal,* saw that
"something has happened to Catholic and non-Catholic relations
in this country." Far from progressing, "they are not what they
were even a few years ago." World War II was already beginning
to look like the good old days. Where there had been "goodwill
and understanding, mutual forbearance and tolerance," now there
was "dissension, controversy, suspicion, and distrust." But Cogley
wanted to moderate by interpreting. He pointed out that to the
Catholic the reaction was simple "anti-Catholicism," while the
non-Catholic thought of it as "dealing with the Catholic problem."
But "call it whatsitsname or whatdoyoucallit or the Thing, call it
whatever you choose," mourned Cogley: it was tearing America
apart. The Reverend George A. Crapullo, a leader in Protestants
and Other Americans United for the Separation of Church and
State, saw in the response "a tidal wave of Protestantism such as
this country has not seen in years." But it remained for the progressive Jesuit Gustave Weigel, reviewing the scene a decade later,
to explain why the Thing produced such a wave. "I believe that
there is a double fear in American Protestantism." One was "the
fear of the death of Protestantism, a haunting awareness of its own
mortality," and this made Protestants nervously vigilant. The object of suspicion therefore turned out to be "not communism, not
nazism, not rationalism, not secularism, not naturalism, not neo-
paganism" but Catholicism. Second was the American Protestant
fear of "their possible loss of political and cultural dominance."
This fear was more easily recognized in 1961 than it had been in
1951; Weigel still had to note that "as a matter of fact this dominance is already lost, but so many Protestants are unaware of it."

Catholicism was one of two main challengers to that domi-   13:7
nance; secularism, as it was then named, was the other. During
the decade which opened with this dispute, Catholicism was to
grow from 27,766,141 members in 1950 to 39,509,508 in 1958, a
42 percent jump, according to *Official Catholic Directory* figures.
Meanwhile, according to the *Yearbook of American Churches,*
Protestant growth in the same years went from 50,021,960 to
61,504,669, an increase of only 23 percent. Catholics were claiming growth by a million people a year at the time of the Vatican
appointment, a rise not unnoticed by nervous Protestants. While
as many people as ever told the poll takers they were Protestant,
actual Protestant church membership was not keeping pace, thus
making it harder than before for leaders to claim a position of
dominance. The *Chicago Tribune* thought that in such a climate,

naming a Vatican ambassador was "the worst thing a president could do." It would "split the country on religious lines." The editors argued that America was already, or still, split and Truman had only widened the chasm. From 1946 to 1951 Protestant delegations had gotten the impression that Taylor would be the last of the Vatican representative line, but now something more irritating had come to pass.

13:8   New times called for new organizations, so a new one had come to the scene after 1948: Protestants and Other Americans United for Separation of Church and State. Its ostensible purpose was to protect the "wall of separation" from all transgressors, but in fact most of those in power were preoccupied only with Catholic intrusions or assaults on that presumed wall. Never known for moderate language, the organization's leadership called for the "immediate discontinuance of the ambassadorship to the papal head of the Roman Catholic Church," a not quite accurate representation of what Baptist Truman had in mind. Glenn Archer, acting for the Protestants and Other Americans United, contended that world peace would not be furthered "by enlisting the services of the Roman Church in a gigantic game of international espionage," since Catholicism represented a two-edged sword. Hitler, remember, had also used the Vatican for such purposes, against Allied troops in World War II. In an atmosphere to which Archer contributed poison, he added that "the Taylor mission has poisoned the atmosphere."

13:9   Did Baptist Truman not think that a Vatican ambassadorship would conflict with "our own doctrine of separation of church and state?" The president in reply did not even need a whole sentence: "Certainly would not." Did Truman not know he would be criticized? "You hear all kinds of criticisms." Had he not stirred up "more hullabaloo" than he had expected to? "No, not as much." Edward H. Pruden, Truman's own pastor, opposed the president this time but came to apologize for the vehemence of some responses, including one from the Baptist Sunday school people. Truman became pastoral: "Don't let the communication from the Sunday School bother you. I have stacks of petitions on that order every week," he said, "and it is simply a part of the Presidential office to listen to everybody's viewpoint." But the thick-skinned president must have been sensitive to delicacies when he made the appointment of Clark, a fellow thirty-third-degree Mason and thus a member of a secret fraternal order with an anti-Catholic reputation. Clark had been "the liberator of Rome" in World War II, the commander of the Fifth Army which retook Rome in 1944. Truman approached Clark with, "I'm looking for a fellow who's a Protestant and a thirty-third degree to make him Ambassador to the Vatican." Keep all this confidential, Clark was told, "because it is a controversial subject." As for the public, the president said, "I believe they will accept it." Clark reluctantly permitted himself to be nominated. The name went forward on October 20, 1951, the day after the war with Germany, which had effectively been ended over six years earlier, was declared officially over. The president wanted early and unanimous consent of the sort ambassadors usually get, but Congress was to adjourn that day and would not hurry the process.

Legislative candidates on the trail that fall tried to duck the issue, but Protestant leadership did not. Editors at the *Christian Century* led the charge against "the foxy politician from Independence, Missouri" who evidently wanted to guard "his own race next year from any Catholic defections." The Catholic *Commonweal* also watched the political front: "It is no secret that criticism of Mr. Truman's foreign policy and the charges of Senator Joe McCarthy have had their effect on large numbers of Catholic voters," but, the editors still asked, who knew why the president had acted as he did when he did? Charges that this proposal was pro-Catholic made little sense, since Truman had established no record of seeking Catholic favor, and the act by itself seemed too mild to please Catholics, while it antagonized Protestants, whose votes he needed desperately.   13:10

The notion of using the Vatican as a "listening post" was a common rationale, especially since Truman advanced the notion of the Cold War as a holy war. When he lit the White House Christmas tree in 1950 the chief executive had made a speech: "We are all joined in the fight against the tyranny of communism. Communism is godless." Only "the Ruler of us all" could produce victory, but Truman was an ally of this Ruler as he proceeded to elicit from the world's religious leaders a "common affirmation of faith." This affirmation, he said in the standard language that promoted convergences across religious lines, "would testify to the strength of our common faith and our confidence in its ultimate victory over the forces of Satan that oppose it." On September 28, 1951, at an interchurch peace occasion, a first annual Washington Pilgrimage of American Churchmen, the president also remarked that it was America's task to try to "preserve a world civilization in which man's belief in God can survive," a theme that made him   13:11

sound like more than a foxy politician from Independence, Missouri. In the face of communism, all churches of all creeds, he reminded hearers, were jeopardized. But when he included Catholicism, some militant Protestants thought he had gone too far. Methodist editor Emory Stevens Bucke did not lack company when he said that it would be a disaster if Truman included the Vatican and Rome in efforts to effect the "mobilization of the spiritual forces of the world." The General Board of the National Council of Churches thought that if Catholicism was already on the right side, it needed no diplomatic recognition or ambassador: "Eager allies in a common cause are not frustrated in their common efforts by considerations of protocol or prestige."

13:12   Truman, however, was beginning to assume a priestly role, with the presidency serving as the pulpit for the nation's public religion. And that role had to be ecumenical. Years later he was to call the roll of his contacts from these years. In 1948, he remembered, he had tried to interest "the religious leaders of the world" against communism. He mentioned Methodist bishop G. Bromley Oxnam, Samuel McCrea Cavert (later of the National Council of Churches), "prominent Jewish leaders," even some Muslims and the Dalai Lama of Tibet. The president called the leaders of the National Conference of Christians and Jews "my friends" and told them, "I am doing everything of which I am capable to organize the moral forces of the world" against communism. "I am trying to get all those people who look up and who know that there is a greater power than man in the universe to organize themselves to meet those who look down and who are strictly materialistic." Truman's private papers include a longer list of the looked-up: the presiding bishop of the Episcopal church; Athenagoras, who headed Orthodoxy; German Lutheran bishop Hans Dibelius; the pope; the archbishops of Canterbury and York; a Huguenot leader in France; the cardinal of Bonn, Germany; Jawaharlal Nehru of India; Chaim Weizmann and David Ben Gurion of Israel; Charles P. Taft for the World Council of Churches, and more. Two items stand out in his notes. One was a memo reminding that "Taylor couldn't get to Moscow" to penetrate Russian Orthodoxy, and that "Oxnam, Nicholas, and S. Baptists refuse to join," a reference to some reluctant American Protestants. In a speech in 1951 the president regretted that it had "not yet been possible to bring the religious faiths together for this purpose of bearing witness in one united affirmation that God is the way of truth and peace." Even Christian churches, he complained, had not made a common statement of their faith "that Christ is their Master and Redeemer and the source of their strength against the hosts of irreligion and danger in the world, and that will be the cause of world catastrophe." Truman still gave the cause priority and with a note of resignation said, "I have been working at it for years."

In the year of the Mark Clark appointment, it turned out that Truman paid more attention to the congressional calendar than to the church year. He had chosen the worst possible fortnight to make his move. This moment gave the Protestant churches just enough time to prepare for their then annual custom of having "Reformation rallies" near October 31. Designed to celebrate the positive side of Luther's and then other Reformations of the sixteenth century, these had often become anti-Catholic gatherings. Because of the Vatican appointment, crowds were larger than usual. That year a fire inspector in Savannah, Georgia, after turning away 3,000 people who would overflow the city auditorium said, "This is the first time I ever had to call a policeman to keep folks from going to church." Scorekeepers counted 9,000 rallying Protestants in St. Louis and more than that in Houston; 11,000 came to hear Bishop Oxnam in Cincinnati, while in Washington 10,000 gathered. The National Council of Churches reported that 800 local councils of churches were protesting. The NCC even smiled in the company or support of nonmember Protestants who were usually their foes: the National Association of Evangelicals, the Missouri Synod Lutherans, and the Southern Baptists. The NAE spent half a million dollars for a radio crusade. Churches began letter-writing campaigns to the White House and past it to Congress. Nothing in World War II, no ecumenical gathering, no crisis of the economy or issue of war and peace stimulated so much common action by Protestants; yes, here, ironically and for reasons Truman did not welcome, was "church unity à la President." But as one surveys the terrain of battle, a haunting question that might portend illuminating answers is in place: was the brouhaha an invention of Protestant leaders, as opposed to their rank and file? The Gallup pollsters were surprised to find that 60 percent of the people were aware of the issue, but they occasioned surprise, given the climate, when they reported their findings that large blocs of the population had not made up their minds or did not share the Protestant leaders' suspicions or rage. Among Protestants, only 35 percent clearly opposed the ambassadorship and the appointment.

Perhaps reflecting this breach between leadership and ordinary citizens, people on the secular front began reacting. Arthur M.

13:13

13:14

Schlesinger, Jr., a liberal historian and commentator, pronounced the Protestant leadership's reaction "a spectacular case of much ado about nothing." Catholics were happy with the appointment but not noisy about expressing any glee they may have felt. A few used political forums. Thus Representative John J. Rooney of New York used a comparison to rub salt in the wounds on the congressional front: "Of all the major powers, the United States and the Soviet Union are the only ones which do not maintain diplomatic relations with the Vatican today." Was it presumptuous to ask, he asked, "how much longer we are going to continue to be bedfellows with those atheists in the Kremlin?" But it was in diocesan papers and through episcopal voices that the Catholic response was most clear. New York's Francis Cardinal Spellman typified the lofty reach. Because the United States and the Vatican had "identical objectives of peace," it was "most logical therefore that there should be a practical exchange of viewpoints in the search for this peace so devoutly desired by all peoples, and especially 'little peoples.'" And St. Louis's archbishop Joseph E. Ritter considered Truman's move "a recognition of the moral influence that has been exercised in trying to restore peace and to combat the enemy of civilization—atheistic Communism." Daniel Lord, S.J., in the Boston *Pilot* tried to give things another twist: "As an American, I should like to see an Ambassador to the Vatican. As a Catholic, I and the overwhelming number of my Catholic fellow citizens are notably unconcerned."

13:15   A few courageous Protestants broke ranks. At Yale Divinity School, a young Lutheran historian of theology, George Lindbeck, sounded like Congressman Rooney: "On this side of the Iron Curtain, only Americans apparently find diplomatic recognition of Vatican City objectionable." Storm over the appointment was deplorable. "The apparent belief on the part of some Protestants that the mere appointment of a representative to the Vatican threatens a fundamental principle of American democracy reflects a disturbing lack of sense of proportion." Lindbeck foresaw as an outcome the "alarming consequence of leading us into a religious controversy unrelated to the central problem at stake." His fellow believers then demonstrated the "narrowness and defensiveness of the only issues on which Protestants can unite with vigor." Yet united they stood.

13:16   Don't get us wrong, some Protestant leaders protested. The General Board of the National Council of Churches did not want to play with fire. "As Christians and as Americans we repudiate prejudice against Roman Catholics and deplore religious dissension." And Bishop Oxnam urged Methodists to "reveal your true spirit. There is no anti-Catholic spirit among us. We are fighting the violation of an American principle by a hierarchy that is determined to secure political power." When Truman's pastor, Edward H. Pruden, joined with Oxnam to lead the clerical delegation meeting with his wayward parishioner, the pastor said it was wise for Truman to meet, "for all the heads of the major Protestant denominations, Negro and white, liberal and conservative, make up this group [who] desires to meet you." He knew of no matter on which there had been such unanimity of feeling among Protestants, and Pruden added, "as you probably know, a large segment of the Jewish community" was also critical. Yet anti-Catholicism did dominate, he contended. And the *Christian Century* kept talking about Truman's "surrender to the pope."

Could permanent Protestant-Orthodox ecumenism be built on   13:17
the purely defensive and negative cause? Church historian John T. McNeill observed that "the rising strength of Roman Catholicism with its example of solid unity," which Protestants then believed it had, might be what was forcing Protestants "unwillingly to clasp each other's hands." He granted that Protestants might be equally sincere in their belief that separation of church and state was a high priority, but they had never fought each other with such fury when a fellow Protestant group had tested the principle of separation in its practices. *Christian Century* editor Paul Hutchinson kept pressing the agenda as if posing the question for a formal collegiate debate: "Shall such an embassy at the seat of the Roman Catholic Church be established if it violates the principle of separation of church and state as that is embodied in the Constitution of the United States?" Some gadflies raised embarrassing questions: why had such a question not come up, asked a Minnesota Catholic educator, H. A. Rommen, in the case of recognition of ambassadorial appointments to the Court of St. James? After all, the king of England was officially and effectively both "head of the Church of England and of England," an appointment Rommen had never heard challenged.

Legal scholar Mark De Wolfe Howe of Harvard Law School   13:18
tried to sort out the legal issues and keep them pure and clear. He agreed with Justice Hugo Black's definition of *establishment,* stated in a decision as recently as 1947: "Neither a state nor the Federal Government can, openly or secretly, participate in the affairs of any religious organizations or groups and vice versa," and

in Howe's eyes the Vatican was a "religious organization." And
there would now be a showing of preference for one such organization. Within Protestant churches, Henry Pitney Van Dusen, now
a power at New York's Union Theological Seminary, elaborated:
"the so-called 'American principle of separation of church and
state'" had not signified indifference or neutrality toward religion,
but it did serve to oppose the "interlocking of church and government." The national founders "were especially opposed to any
church which took to itself the prerogatives of a state," as the papacy did for Catholicism. "The Roman Church has not altered its
policy" of attempting to "direct and dominate governments," and
this intention had to be countered. Less moderately, Winfred E.
Garrison, speaking at a Houston rally in 1951, said "it would be
an insult to the intelligence of an insane asylum to ask its inmates
to believe that the present proposal is to send an ambassador to
Vatican City State because of its importance *as a state.*"

13:19   Turn the issue on its head, some provocateurs suggested. A letter to the editor of the *Christian Century* put it formally: with this
policy, "the Vatican now has 300,000 unregistered spies in the
United States." How so? Because if the Vatican was declared a
foreign state, then its agents, American priests, would be on the
spot and have to surrender American citizenship. *Zion's Herald,*
speaking to and presumably for New England Methodists, published a similar letter. The writer was happy with the Vatican move,
because it was declaring Catholic schools to be foreign institutions. Bishop Oxnam presented the bottom line: basically, the issue
is *clericalism.* "This is a term our people must understand." To
him the ambassadorship was "the pursuit of power, by a religious
hierarchy, carried on by secular methods, for purposes of social
domination." The sin of power-seeking that Catholics had charged
against the Protestant clergy in America would now be their own.
John C. Bennett of Union Seminary did not disagree with the Protestant attackers but added a mournful note. Why could not the
Protestants unite similarly for positive causes? In *Christianity and
Crisis* he mourned the "sobering fact that in the memory of men
living there has probably never been an occasion on which the
leadership of American Protestantism has spoken with such spontaneous unanimity."

13:20   The incident ends not with high drama but with the quiet act of
Truman letting it slip from view during his five-week vacation. By
December, General Clark, who had not looked for the post or the
furor, was growing weary and feeling marooned. The two leaders

met and came to the conclusion that the appointment had been a good idea that had gone wrong. In the State of the Union address on January 9, 1952, Truman did not even refer to the plan that he had earlier thought would bring religious peace at home, because it would simplify fighting the Cold War abroad. On January 13 radio commentator Drew Pearson spread word of Clark's secret visit to the White House, so Clark insisted that the matter be brought to a head. That evening word went forth from the White House that the nomination "will not be resubmitted to the Senate," at the request of General Clark. The president still planned to name an ambassador at a later date, the press was told.

The *New Republic,* grateful that Clark had backed off, saw that 13:21 "one of the bitterest fights in modern Congressional history" had been avoided. "The Protestant Churches were organized to make every ounce of their influence count in voting on confirmation." This was the case because they had few "ounces" of influence left, and the whole fight now had been about retaining some of those that remained. The editors could have brought plenty of evidence. Stoddard Patterson, for example, of St. Paul's Protestant Episcopal Church in Milwaukee, preached in 1951 at a Reformation obser- vance: "We Protestants must interest ourselves in politics and we must vote for Protestants at the polls—and vote for Protestants who will uphold the traditions." The alternative was to go the route of lost freedom of worship, as Protestants had lost it in Spain, Italy, and Latin America. The *Christian Century* took out a patent on single-issue politics. When it was foreseen that Congress would have to vote, one of its editors wrote: "Unless we are greatly mis- taken, a senator's vote on this issue will weigh far more when he comes up for re-election than his vote on anything else that has come before Congress." Given the relative insignificance of one diplomatic appointment, that sounds shrill, but the editor revealed his motives. "Protestants are still in a majority in this country." They should be able to persuade the senators of thirty states to reject the Vatican appointment. "Many senators may be under the impression that Protestant tolerance is limitless. Now is the time to disabuse them of that idea."

An era was passing, and with it went a term, as a new one began 13:22 to come into fashion. In 1951 notable scholar of religion Arnold Nash published *Protestant Thought in the Twentieth Century.* It included a chapter on "America at the End of the Protestant Era." In it Nash made early use of the concept of "post-Protestantism." New words were characterizing new religious life in the One

Nation: *pluralism,* and now *post-Protestantism.* With its first front-cover usage, the one that brought the word itself and its new associations into public records and led off the entries of the word in the *Reader's Guide to Periodical Literature,* the *Christian Century* summed up the outlook of the waning Protestant establishment. It featured an editorial and bannered it on the cover: "Pluralism—National Menace."

14

"Religion Is Not a Civil Function or a Public Matter"

I f religious pluralism loomed as a menace to Protestant leaders in post-Protestant America, who would profit from its threat? Catholics would, thought such Protestants, because Catholics could challenge the dominance of the old and now thoroughly divided Protestant majority. But many Catholic, Protestant, and Jewish leaders, eager to use public institutions to advance their own religions, or to promote religion itself, saw themselves progressively yielding to a fourth force. Sometimes they called it Humanism, but more frequently they named it Secularism. Their chosen battleground for fighting it off was to be the American public school. There, they contended, ideologies of secularism dared not displace religious interests or teachings in any direct way. Meanwhile they saw religion progressively being assigned a place only in private life. As the American Civil Liberties Union lawyers put the growing conventional wisdom in a celebrated Supreme Court case of the time, "religion is not a civil function or a public matter. An education which includes religious teaching is a private matter and function." Such reasoning was designed to put all religions and nonreligion alike on a level playing field. Its advocates contended that if there was to be One Nation, Indivisible, divisive religious blocs and interests dared be given no chance to occupy privileged public space. They all had to content themselves working with the private lives of citizens. Those who had thought that

religion should have any public role might well have changed
the *Christian Century* cover headline of 1951 from "Pluralism—
National Menace" to "Privatism—National Menace." Secularism, by default, was becoming free to take over because it looked
organized and public, supported as it was by so many leaders in
higher education, literary and artistic elites, commerce, and government. The Supreme Court came to be the adjudicator in the case
of issues concerning religion in public life, especially in public
schools, and it increasingly assumed this role in novel ways toward
midcentury.

14:2   The Supreme Court decisions of this period did not first address
the issue of how religions of all sorts must confront secularism of
any sort. They were instead wartime judgments against Jehovah's
Witnesses, at a time when the court was fumbling for ways to be
neutral in matters dealing with religion. This posture was difficult
to maintain in the face of a religious group that appeared to be
hostile to everyone else's interpretation of the place of religion in
the nation. But the seeds of the secular growth to which we are
pointing were latent in the decisions involving the Jehovah's Witnesses. By the fourth case the Court showed that it was recognizing
the need to protect religion from state intrusion just as it would
later want to protect the state from churchly or religious intrusion.
In both kinds of cases the Court was showing how, in a certain
reading of the logic of constitutional development in the United
States, the realms of church and state, or religion and republic,
could be kept separate and autonomous—and church or religion
would in the final legal sense be seen as irrelevant. So the Jehovah's Witnesses cases and the public school instances were indeed
connected.

14:3   In the cases of the Witnesses, Felix Frankfurter, a recent (1939)
appointee of Franklin D. Roosevelt, was pivotal. The justice was a
man caught between eras. Frankfurter brought to his office a formidable intellect, credentials gained as a teacher at Harvard, faith
in his own ability to have his way through rhetoric and flattery,
friendship with Oliver Wendell Holmes and Louis Brandeis, a passion to make his mark and even to dominate. Frankfurter was also
a nonpracticing Jew who displayed an almost mystical patriotism
and a passion for public schools. Expected to be the prime defender of civil liberties, he was soon caught in the ambiguities of
national life and became a promoter of a sort of communal faith
for America while it was being tested in war.

14:4   Frankfurter's antagonists, nemeses, or at least agents of befuddlement were a religious group, the Jehovah's Witnesses, that had been formed in the late nineteenth century and had come to be known by its present name after 1931. The group spread its preachments by selling tracts and through aggressive door-knocking campaigns. The denomination was distinctive because it believed all others, along with the government of the United States, were from the domain of Satan. This belief led them to see the national flag as an idol, and they argued that to salute it was an act of idolatry that they must resist. A pamphlet gave *"Reasons Why a True Follower of Jesus Christ Cannot Salute a Flag."* The United States flag was "the symbol of National sovereignty and authority. Men speak of it in highly laudatory terms, and the very attributes of deity are ascribed to it." But "TO SALUTE THE FLAG WOULD BE A VIOLATION OF DIVINE COMMANDMENT STATED IN EXODUS 20:3–5," a prohibition against having any other Gods before God. Second, "THE SALUTE TO THE FLAG MEANS IN EFFECT THAT THE PERSON SALUTING THE FLAG ASCRIBES SALVATION TO IT, WHEREAS SALVATION IS OF JEHOVAH GOD." And third, "FLAG SALUTING IS PART OF A CREED OF A SECT OF SO-CALLED PATRIOTS, TEACHING A RITUAL OF PATRIOTISM AND FROM SUCH ALL TRUE CHRISTIANS ARE COMMANDED TO TURN ASIDE."

Unwelcome sentiments or doctrines at any time, these were 14:5 considered dangerous and even treasonous to many in wartime. Even before these flag-salute cases, the Jehovah's Witnesses had been subject to trials that had reached the Supreme Court, as few legal squabbles concerning church and state between 1789 and 1940 had ever been. Jesse Cantwell and sons loudly played a violently anti-Catholic phonograph record in a Catholic neighborhood of New Haven, Connecticut. They were arrested for a breach of the peace and for having failed to secure a "certificate of approval" for their broadcasting. When the *Cantwell v. Connecticut* 310 U.S. 296 (1940) case reached the United States Supreme Court, the justices for the first time clearly invoked the Fourteenth Amendment to support the First. The Fourteenth Amendment, adopted in 1868, prohibits all states from "depriv[ing] any person of life, liberty, or property, without due process of law." It was designed to protect ex-slaves, but now the Court would use its clause about "liberty" in cases involving religious liberty in every state. Justice Owen J. Roberts further invoked the notion of a "clear and present danger" to the republic for the first time in matters of church and state. He judged that the abrasive Witnesses were irritants, but they were not manifest dangers to the republic.

14:6   The majority decision of the Court, for Cantwell and against Connecticut, included words reminding citizens that "in the realm of religious faith, and in that of political belief, sharp differences arise." True, the justices agreed, Mr. Cantwell was resorting to vilification and even false statement. "But the people of this nation have ordained in the light of history, that, in spite of the probability of excesses and abuses, these liberties are, in the long view, essential to enlightened opinion and right conduct on the part of the citizens of a democracy." Nowhere, thought Justice Roberts, was there more need for a shield of liberties than "in our own country for a people composed of many races and of many creeds." Of course, there had to be *some* limits. Roberts spelled that out: "The danger in these times from the coercive activities of those who in the delusion of racial or religious conceit would incite violence and breaches of the peace in order to deprive others of their equal right to the exercise of their liberties" was being emphasized by events familiar to all. The reference was to Hitler's Europe. But, he was quick to say, the Witnesses in America raised no such menace.

14:7   After *Cantwell* came two far more volatile cases, subsequently shortened to *Gobitis* and *Barnette,* these again being the names of Witness families. The decisions involved religious issues associated with saluting the American flag. To make sense of these two cases one must locate the ceremony of flag-saluting in the public school tradition. The phrases of the salute were invented in 1892 by a former cleric in the religious magazine *Youth's Companion.* Congress took up a version of the words and authorized a national holiday. President Benjamin Harrison duly proclaimed such a day as the occasion to promote the saluting of the flag. Over thirty states passed laws to enforce saluting in public schools. The trend of the years, then, was from voluntary encouragement of the practice to a kind of nervous threat that there would be penalties against those who resisted pledging. In 1942 Congress passed a law stipulating that citizens must salute the flag with their right hand over their heart. An earlier stiff-arm version was now judged to look too Nazi. As for the words themselves, God was not mentioned in the pledge that had been written and used since 1892; the name of God did not appear until a secular Congress rewrote the pledge in 1954. But the quasi-religious character of the salute was clear before 1954. Patriotic organizations and particularists alike—from the American Legion, the Veterans of Foreign Wars, and the Daughters of the American Revolution to the Ku Klux Klan—championed the practice, opposing teachers who deplored the roteness of chil-

dren's recitation, complained of the boredom the ceremony induced, or bemoaned its failure to promote reflective patriotism as
they observed it. Open opposition, however, was slight.

A few religious groups were wary of all moves toward making   14:8
the pledge a matter of law and compulsion. For example, many
Mennonites complained, but they made no formal case of it. The
Jehovah's Witnesses were the group that chose to be scandalous
and to provoke counteraction. Their official literature claimed that
in 1935 the United States had imported the stiff-arm salute to imi-
tate "Heil Hitler!" and that the government wanted to embarrass
or harass Witnesses. They were also reacting to measures taken
against their fellow believers by Nazis in Germany. They feared
that the spirit of these repressions would spread. Jehovah's Witness
literature grew ever more explicit in denunciation. "To salute a flag
means, in effect, that the person saluting ascribes salvation to what
the flag represents," was one line of reaction. Since, as these religious believers taught, nations were ruled by the Devil, "the law
of the nation or government that compels the child of God to salute
the national flag *compels that person to salute the Devil as the
invisible god of the nation.*" Pennsylvania—from the beginning a
home to many dissenters—in the course of time expelled over
a hundred Jehovah's Witness children from school because they
would not obey the law and would not salute. In parts of the state
ruffians beat up on punished students. In 1938 a family named
Gobitis, whose children had been expelled, won a ruling by a federal judge that permitted them to return to school in Minersville.
Judge Albert B. Maris himself found "no religious significance"
in the salute but saw some reasons why Witnesses might. So he
ruled for them, and the case moved through the federal circuit court
of appeals to the United States Supreme Court. Everyone assumed
that the Supreme Court would go along with the lower courts in
supporting the Jehovah's Witnesses.

Observers had not reckoned with or read in advance the mind   14:9
of Frankfurter. His brief honeymoon with his colleagues on the
bench was over, and now he had to confront them and his own
conscience as *Minersville School District v. Gobitis* 310 U.S. 586
(1940) came before the judges. Frankfurter then surprised the pre-
dicters by reaching for resources he said he had inherited from
Holmes, as well as for psychological readings of the meaning of
civil life. He wrote Alexander Bickel: "You probably have heard
me quote Holmes's epigram, 'we live by symbols.' Marion [Frank-
furter's spouse] says I quote it so often that she wishes Holmes had

never said it, but I said I quote it so often because it is so often applicable." Notably, Frankfurter was speaking of common symbols for the whole nation. He evidently had erased from his mind, if it ever had been there, the notion of religion having a bearing in private as opposed to public life. The justice could not see why the Gobitis family should think differently than he did. Their religion was standing in the way of what he took to be their fulfillment as Americans. Because he was a civil libertarian, bias or interest should have led him to support the scrappy or grudging Gobitises. Frankfurter did say he recognized a "grave responsibility." Such a sense always developed when the "conflicting claims of liberty and authority" came into play. What should one judge, therefore, when "liberty of conscience" conflicts with the authority "to safeguard the nation's fellowship?" The issue grew tense, he knew, because "the manifold character of man's relations may bring his conception of religious duty into conflict with the secular interests of his fellow-men." So he had to ask, "when does the constitutional guarantee compel exemption from doing what society thinks necessary for the promotion of some great common end, or from a penalty for conduct which appears dangerous to the general good?"

14:10   Frankfurter's next eloquent phrases became classic, even among the many who disagreed with his decision against the Witnesses. Paradoxically, the judge argued, "to affirm that the freedom to follow conscience has itself no limits in the life of society would deny that very plurality of principles which, as a matter of history, underlies protection of religious toleration." His classic line: "The ultimate foundation of a free society is the binding tie of cohesive sentiment." The Court did not have to do all the assuring, he went on: "Such a sentiment is fostered by all those agencies of the mind and spirit which may serve to gather up the traditions of a people, transmit them from generation to generation, and thereby create that continuity of a treasured common life which constitutes a civilization." Then, without apologies to his wife Marion and with unacknowledged gratitude to Holmes, he added, one more time: "We live by symbols." The flag was "the symbol of our national unity," and that banner helped citizens transcend all internal differences. Public schools, then, had a right to promote "that unifying sentiment without which there can ultimately be no liberties, civil or religious."

14:11   In 1940 all but one of his colleagues agreed with Frankfurter's reasoning. To Justice Roberts it was "among the best ever prepared

by a judge of this Court." Justice Frank Murphy used a Christian
reference toward the Jew who had helped him through "a Geth-
semane." But, after all, he declared, the Constitution "presupposes
a government that will nourish and protect itself," so Murphy
would join Frankfurter. Only Justice Harlan Stone raised questions. What did *Gobitis* have to do with individual liberties, and
what would the limited exceptions for Jehovah's Witnesses harm?
"Here we have such a small minority entertaining in good faith a
religious belief, which is such a departure from the usual course of
human conduct, that most persons are disposed to regard it with
little toleration or concern." Why should the Court work to "secure conformity of belief and opinion by a compulsory affirmation
of the desired belief?" In the matter of the "relative weight of imponderables," he thought the Constitution tipped the scale in favor
of religion. Stone's kind of argument began to have increasing influence. When Frankfurter ran into Justice William O. Douglas on
summer vacation that year, Douglas reported that Hugo Black had
already changed his mind about *Gobitis*. Why, asked Frankfurter.
"Has Hugo been re-reading the Constitution during the summer?"
No, said Douglas, "he has been reading the papers."

The papers carried many reports of violence against Jehovah's   14:12
Witnesses by other citizens who were acting in fits of viciousness
during May and June of 1940. The American Civil Liberties Union
complained for these religious believers that sheriffs often refused
to protect Witnesses under attack. Members were arrested, were
imprisoned without charge, had their automobiles wrecked, and
saw their halls attacked. Maine saw six beatings. Citizens of a town
in Illinois assaulted a caravan of Witnesses' cars. In Wyoming a
roused populace tarred and feathered a Witness, and in Nebraska
one was castrated. Francis Biddle, solicitor general of the United
States, finally went on radio to say in June 1941: "Since mob violence will make the government's task infinitely more difficult, it
will not be tolerated. We shall not defeat the Nazi evil by emulating
its methods." Some in the religious press found the courage to
speak up. Thus the *Christian Century* found it "bitterly ironical
that a free government should inflict a penalty for refusal to salute
a symbol of freedom." While Witnesses had always been hard on
Catholicism, many Catholic editors also fought the Court's reading. Soon 171 secular newspapers attacked the decision. Some of
his old allies started to wonder aloud why Felix Frankfurter had
deserted the civil liberties cause. A liberal trio of Douglas, Black,
and Murphy began to form an informal bloc, and their common

thinking showed up in test cases over the next two years. Their growing opposition to Frankfurter's view showed up most forcefully in *Jones v. Opelika* 340 U.S. 584 (1942). In it, the Court majority declared that municipalities had authority to tax religious literature sales by this group. Now the three judges said they had changed their mind and must dissent, saying of their earlier stands in *Gobitis,* "we now believe that it was also wrongly decided." The Bill of Rights, they argued, committed the American democracy to "accommodate itself to the religious views of minorities, however unpopular and unorthodox those views may be."

14:13   This is the point where the three innovated and began to help set a precedent. The Bill of Rights back in 1789 talked about what *Congress* may or may not do about religious establishment and the free exercise of religion. Its First Amendment had nothing to say—perhaps because its backers had to seek ratification from the states—about what *states* must use to judge cases. The Fourteenth Amendment, from the Civil War era, however, could help the Court now, they thought. *Opelika* was reversed. By the time of *Martin v. Struthers* 319 U.S. 141 (1943), the majority came to support the Witnesses in their refusal to take out a license to circulate pamphlets door-to-door. An angered Frankfurter in a personal note told of lunching with Frank Murphy, the Catholic justice whom Frankfurter often called "The Saint." "The Saint said to me at luncheon that the reason for his vote and voice in *Struthers* was that he wanted always to err on the side of religion." Frankfurter wrote that he had said in reply, "as we are judges it is our business not to err on either side." Contempt started showing as Frankfurter mused further about Murphy: "This seemed a new thought to him. He made no reply but rushed out!"

14:14   Frankfurter believed that since he had long ago personally moved toward an agnostic position about his Judaism, he could be religiously impartial, as believers could not so successfully be in matters dealing with religion. In 1953 the justice recalled how as a child he had sensed hypocrisy developing in himself when he worshiped with people who believed, as he could not. "I left the service in the middle of it, never to return to this day." But Frankfurter was quick to add that "by leaving the synagogue I did not, of course, cease to be a Jew or cease to be concerned with whatever affects the fate of Jews." Frankfurter also continued to sharpen his theological interest by talking with Reinhold Niebuhr at their summer places in western Massachusetts. One story had him say, after he heard Niebuhr preach, "Reinie, may a believing unbeliever thank you for your sermon?" Niebuhr was said to have asked in turn, "May an unbelieving believer thank you for appreciating it?" Frankfurter would be "a reverent agnostic." Anti-religion was not his cause, he insisted, when he made religion secondary to the need for the state to support common values and "cohesive sentiment."

In 1943, a new case, *West Virginia State Board of Education v.*   14:15 *Barnette* 319 U.S. 624 (1943) brought a situation similar to *Gobitis* to the Court. This time Frankfurter's allies deserted the old cause. Justice Jackson, who had sided with him the first time, now stressed the opposite case: "One's right to life, liberty, and property, to free speech, a free press, freedom of worship and assembly, and other fundamental rights may not be submitted to vote; they depend on the outcome of no elections." To Jackson, "the compulsory flag salute and pledge requires affirmation of a belief and an attitude of mind." The Jehovah's Witnesses presented no "clear and present danger." For Jackson, "to believe that patriotism will not flourish if patriotic ceremonies are voluntary and spontaneous instead of a compulsory routine is to make an unflattering estimate of the appeal of our institutions to free minds." Then came Jackson's own classic phrase: "If there is any fixed star in our constitutional constellation, it is that no official, high or petty, can prescribe what shall be orthodox in politics, nationalism, religion, or other matters of opinion or force citizens to confess by word or act their faith therein."

Frankfurter as a Jew did not want to take such preachments   14:16 leaning back. "One who belongs to the most vilified and persecuted minority in history is not likely to be insensible to the freedoms guaranteed by our Constitution." He said he would also associate with the libertarian view, since, as always, he was impartial. But then Frankfurter came back to his favored Holmesian dictum: "We are told that symbolism is a dramatic but primitive way of communicating ideas. Symbolism is inescapable. Even the most sophisticated live by symbols." The Constitution drafters "knew that minorities may disrupt society" and had no interest in preventing that. By this point in his arguing Frankfurter's friends on the Court had deserted him, not because they rejected the notion of living by symbols but because they adjudged the symbols of national interest to be most secure when they were promoted by persuasion, not through coercion. *Barnette* was a reversal of *Gobitis,* and Frankfurter, in defeat, was left to nurture his symbols and find other ways to promote cohesive sentiment in the free society.

To match the four Jehovah's Witnesses cases there came three   14:17

notable rulings affecting public schools around midcentury, and these helped the Court do some further defining. Code-named *Everson, McCollum,* and *Zorach,* each provoked intense controversy, with somewhat different casts of supporters and opponents each time. By the time it decided the three, the Court had gotten into the custom of using the Fourteenth Amendment to put the First Amendment to work. *Everson* 330 U.S. 1 (1947) was of special interest to Catholics (and some smaller Protestant groups which operated parochial schools), because they wanted tax funds to be used to bus children to church-related institutions. Enemies of such proposals argued that such a busing program would represent an unconstitutional subsidy to religion. Before 1947 there had been only two Supreme Court cases in all American history respecting parochial schools. Neither of them found the Court using the Fourteenth Amendment to extend First Amendment rights to the states. The outcome of *Everson* was not radical, since the Court now actually permitted part of what the church school leaders and many others involved with religious education had been hoping for. The language used by Justice Hugo Black to define separation of church and state, however, was radical. We shall see why.

14:18   In 1941 the New Jersey legislature passed a law saying that when any school district provided for transportation of public school children to and from school from any point in an established route to any other, such a route "shall be supplied to school children residing in such school district in going to and from school other than a public school, except when such school is operated for profit in whole or in part." Taxpayer Arch R. Everson challenged this law. The New Jersey Supreme Court thereupon ruled that lawmakers had no authority to permit such an arrangement. Then the New Jersey Court of Errors and Appeals reversed that decision; no, it said, such legislation did not conflict with the New Jersey or the United States constitutions. So the case moved to the United States Supreme Court. Justice Black reviewed the charges, including a second objection: the statute and the resolution "forced inhabitants to pay taxes to help support and maintain schools which are dedicated to, and which regularly teach, the Catholic faith." It was therefore alleged that this practice would mean a "use of State power to support church schools contrary to the prohibition of the First Amendment which the Fourteenth made applicable to the states."

14:19   History was made in response to this objection. The Court said that "the First Amendment, as made applicable to the states by the

Fourteenth" in *Murdock v. Pennsylvania,* 319 U.S. 105 (1943), commanded that a state, too, "shall make no law respecting an establishment of religion, or prohibiting the free exercise thereof." This, the Court reasoned, had been said to keep anyone from promoting "government favored churches." So far so good. Then came the controversial passage. "The 'establishment of religion' clause of the First Amendment means at least this: Neither a state nor the Federal Government can set up a church. Neither can pass laws which aid one religion, aid all religions, or prefer one religion over another." Negatively, "neither can force nor influence a person to go to or to remain away from church against his will or force him to profess a belief or disbelief in any religion." Nearer the point of *Everson,* "neither a state nor the Federal Government can, openly or secretly, participate in the affairs of any religious organizations or groups and *vice versa.*" All this was dry legal language; what was written to wake up those who read the decision was the fateful introduction of Thomas Jefferson's metaphor in the sphere of constitutional language where it had never been before. "In the words of Jefferson, the clause against establishment of religion by law was intended to erect 'a wall of separation between church and State.' " After elaborating, the Court concluded: "The First Amendment has erected a wall between church and State. That wall must be kept high and impregnable. We could not approve the slightest breach." Almost as an afterthought, it ruled, "New Jersey has not breached it here."

One of the most controversial features of this ruling was the phrase which stated that there must be no laws to "aid all religions." Some asked: did not the government regularly aid all religions through military and institutional chaplaincies, presidential proclamations of sacred holidays, and the like? Princeton professor Edward S. Corwin was among those who responded at once. In the Catholic magazine *Thought* in 1948 Corwin claimed that to anyone rereading the materials of the 1780s it would be clear that the "historical data support its last clause, but rule out its middle clause." Which meant that so long as there was no "preference to any religion, or any denomination," there could be government support of religion. A whole school of legal scholars, historians, and publicists agreed with Corwin. Black's three-word phrase, "aid all religions," came to be one of the most important and most controverted of modern Supreme Court statements on the First Amendment.   14:20

Justice Frankfurter now allied himself with Justice Jackson in   14:21

dissent. "Is it constitutional," he asked, "to tax this complainant to pay the cost of carrying pupils to Church schools of one specified denomination?" Simply: no. Jackson quoted Roman Catholic canon law to show that the schools were out-and-out Catholic and religious. But then he introduced a sectarian-sounding shocker of his own: "Our public school, if not a product of Protestantism, at least is more consistent with it than with the Catholic culture and scheme of values." But what about Catholic schools? "We cannot have it both ways." Religious teaching cannot be a private affair in cases where the state tries to impose regulations which infringe on it indirectly, "and a public affair when it comes to taxing citizens of one faith to aid another, or those of no faith at all." Catholics, Jackson thought, might find his language harsh, but he reminded them that it was the same Constitution, here interpreted, that also protected them.

14:22   Justice Wiley Rutledge went even further in supporting Court language about absolute separation of church and state. He was sure that the New Jersey statute in question allowed for exactly what founders James Madison and Thomas Jefferson had originally fought to rule out. "The great condition of religious liberty is that it be maintained free from sustenance, as also from other interferences, by the state. For when it comes to rest upon the secular foundation it vanishes with the resting." Rutledge's most startling reading on separation of church and state, in the eyes of many in 1948, rested on what he claimed was Madison's and Jefferson's goal: "to create a complete and permanent separation of the spheres of religious activity and civil authority by comprehensively forbidding every form of public aid or support for religion." The *wall* metaphor was born rigid: "Neither so high nor so impregnable today as yesterday is the wall raised between church and state by Virginia's great statute of religious freedom and the First Amendment, now made applicable to all the states by the Fourteenth."

14:23   Catholics welcomed one aspect of the ruling while opposing much of the reasoning and many of the implications. Cincinnati archbishop John T. McNicholas, responding for the National Catholic Welfare Conference, replied to a notable Protestant manifesto against the ruling. "We are confident that the framers and signers of this manifesto do not speak for the great body of Protestants," he wrote, "nor for informed Jews and God-fearing Americans having no religious affiliation." The conference's leadership denied that the Catholic bishops were "seeking a union of church and state." They tried to be reassuring: "If tomorrow Catholics constitute a majority in our country, they would not seek a union of church and state." They would continue instead to uphold the Constitution and all the amendments. "The First Amendment is being distorted today, especially by those who advocate secularism in education and in every department of our government." Now and henceforth to such Catholics, not Protestantism but secularism was the enemy.

It was Protestants, however, at the moment not opposing secu-   14:24
larism but Catholicism, who responded angrily. Among them, the Methodist bishops resolved that the ruling was "a departure from the American principles of the separation of church and state and carries with it a serious threat to our public educational system which is a bulwark of democracy." Methodists in any case, they announced, would "resist all attempts by the Roman Catholic hierarchy to secure public support for such schools and other religious enterprises," basing their resistance "on the ground of the separation of church and state." Then in the not-nice language often used at the time between these communions, they added a question: "Are our Roman Catholic brothers, with whom we desire the friendliest of relations and for whom we demand the same religious liberties we insist upon for ourselves, to push their demands so far that we must in self-defense take steps that will protect our liberties and those of our children?" The Baptist Joint Committee on Public Affairs spoke for three Baptist bodies who were hardly on speaking terms with each other on many other issues. The majority opinion, they said, was "turning back the hands of the clock as far as religious liberty and the separation of church and state are concerned in these United States." The committee was convinced that the ruling "will divide the people of the nation at a time when unity is greatly needed." As Baptists, they were "resolved that the struggle for religious liberty, in terms of the separation of church and state, must be continued. Having lost the battle, we have not lost the war."

It was the *Everson* ruling that, more than anything else, in-   14:25
spired the formation of the militant group momentarily called the National Council of Citizens on Church and State. Founders quickly incorporated it on January 11, 1948, under the name Protestants and Other Americans United for Separation of Church and State. Liberals like Edwin McNeill Poteat, who headed the Bap-

tists' Colgate-Rochester Divinity School, and Methodist bishop
G. Bromley Oxnam joined *Christian Century* editor Charles Clayton Morrison in leadership, but they also welcomed support from
the more fundamentalist wings. The manifesto they issued announced that they would "resist every attempt by law or the administration of law further to widen the breach in the wall of separation of church and state."

14:26   Catholics, as mentioned, liked the outcome of *Everson* but not
the reasoning about the wall of separation set forth by the Court
minority. John M. O'Neill, a Catholic and a leader of the American Civil Liberties Union, was upset enough by Justice Rutledge's
most rigorous separationist interpretation of the First Amendment
in *Everson* that in 1949 he published *Religion and Education under the Constitution.* O'Neill opposed the application of Jefferson's
"wall of separation" metaphor to this issue. He thought it "difficult
to find another set of arguments of similar length from any responsible source containing so many instances of ignoring and misin-
terpreting relevant facts of history and the language of pertinent
documents." But even the majority "indulged in false history and
biography, garbled quotations, and fallacious reasoning." O'Neill
vehemently criticized Black for his "clear attempt to insert into the
Constitution a vague, figurative principle which is new as a constitutional provision. No Congress, no President, no Supreme Court
decision, had ever recognized or promulgated 'the complete separation of Church and State' as a principle operative, until February 10, 1947." The Court's magnification of Jefferson's wall was
"fantastic. It has no relation to any reality of either law or fact. No
such wall has existed for a single day in any state in the union or
in the United States as a nation."

14:27   O'Neill was only warming up to take on the dissent of Justice
Rutledge, in which three other justices concurred. An "almost incredible document," he thought it must be, adding acidly that perhaps it was the result of "bad punctuation or a printer's error,"
so far off the mark it was. He cited many exceptions to the notion
that the First Amendment was to rule out support to "all religions." Rutledge "simply wants to put into the Constitution of the
United States a doctrine which the responsible representatives of
the people have (apparently without protest or reproof) officially,
publicly, definitely refused many times to allow in the Constitution!" There would be misrule on the First Amendment until there
were a majority of justices on the Supreme Court "who are thor-

oughly competent in understanding, interpreting, and writing the English language, and who know American history, especially constitutional and Supreme Court history." That time would be long or short depending on whether the American people "express pleasure or displeasure at the substitution of life under a dictatorship for democracy and constitutional government."

What O'Neill called dictatorship then struck, thanks to another   14:28 Court action, only a year after *Everson*. The new decision shows how little Catholics had won. O'Neill never liked to see the modern divisions posed between two faith communities. The "current campaign to subvert the First Amendment," he charged, was accompanied by "a widespread attempt to make this a Catholic *vs.* a Protestant fight." One headline the professor had despised after *Everson* read, "Protestantism Takes a Licking." Yet the "licking was administered with interest a year later," he said, "in the McCollum case." After that case, two dozen distinguished Protestant clerics and educators issued a press release to restate and affirm the constitutional "interpretation of the American doctrine of separation of church and state," as they put it, "and to protest against the interpretation that has been formulated by the Supreme Court." "Protestants Take Catholic Line," read the headline to a *Christian Century* article concerning the twenty-four. What lay behind these confusions?

If supporting the busing of children to parochial schools with   14:29 public tax moneys was a Catholic strategy to counter secularism, the main new Protestant approach was through programs they called "released time." Protestants, it was becoming clear, could no longer control the content of public school education. So they feared that religion in the schools would be either not their own kind of faith or a watered-down expression. So they wanted to have children released to go to churches or synagogues for lessons. Others provided for religious instruction on school property itself. The test case that addressed this practice was *McCollum v. Board of Education* 33 U.S. 203 (1948). One of the cities to have a released-time program was Champaign, the home of the University of Illinois. There the religion classes were being held on public school territory. Resident Vashti McCollum, whose husband was employed by the university, protested the use of tax-supported property for the religious education given to her ten-year-old son. Champaign school authorities always did what they could to accommodate dissent like hers and also to be attentive to the sen-

sibilities of the larger public that wanted religion. But nothing satisfied Mrs. McCollum or the American Civil Liberties Committee.
They pressed the case and lost in circuit court. Mrs. McCollum
and the American Civil Liberties Union somehow worked the case
up to the United States Supreme Court, which took it up in October 1947.

14:30   McCollum was a militant person who took pleasure in being branded "a wicked, godless woman, an emissary of Satan, a
Communist and a fiend in human form," just as she was being
hailed by others as "a courageous heroine, a champion of American liberty, a true pioneer, democrat, and patriot, and 'a woman
George Washington would have been proud to know.'" McCollum thanked Lutherans and Baptists, Quakers and Jews, Christian
Scientists and Unitarians, Seventh-day Adventists and Jehovah's
Witnesses for having helped her. She was less an "atheist," she
said, than a "Humanist." She enjoyed making much of her biblical
name, from the Book of Esther, and would say, "My mother was
fond of saying that Vashti was the 'first exponent of woman's
rights.'" Baptized in a Lutheran church and nurtured in a Lutheran
Sunday school, she was urged by her freethinking father to think
for herself. He even wrote a pamphlet, "Rationalism vs. Religious Education in the Public Schools," which was quoted in the
McCollum case. His influence won out.

14:31   The civil liberties experts claimed not to be opposing religious
education but insisting that it occur in private space. If America
bought the Champaign version of the plan, it "would be flooded
with sectarian publications, crowded with religious teachers, many
in clerical garb. Pupils would be classified and segregated according to their diverse beliefs or lack of belief. There would not be
enough rooms to hold all the classes." Then "the public school
system for all practical purposes would cease to exist and its ideal
of secular education would be a mockery." The ACLU attorneys
further argued that "religion is not a civil function or a public matter. An education which includes religious teaching is a private
matter and function." The "wall separating church from state"
demonstrated that. The "public ideal of secular education and the
inspired concept of separation of Church from State should not be
tarnished by compromise. They invade the religious rights of no
one. They assure freedom for all."

14:32   By now a Protestant party of "strict separationists" had
emerged to link with the rationalists and civil libertarians. Co-
alescing were the Joint Baptist Committee on Public Affairs, the

Seventh-day Adventists, the Synagogue Council of America, and more. They cheered when by an eight-to-one majority the Court ruled against the Champaign approach to on-premises religious teaching. Justice Black went to the heart of the case: "This is beyond all question a utilization of the tax-established and tax-supported public school system to aid religious groups to spread their faith." The Court blithely quoted its own *Everson* ruling, as if unaware of negative responses to it. The justices did not agree that "historically the First Amendment was intended to forbid only government preference of one religion over another, not an impartial governmental assistance of all religions." No, "the First Amendment rests upon the lofty premise that both religion and government can best work to achieve their lofty aims if each is left free from the other within its respective sphere." And there was that wall again, metaphorically ready: "As we said in the *Everson* case, the First Amendment has erected a wall between Church and State which must be kept high and impregnable." The Champaign case, they made clear, was "not separation of Church and State." Other ways of deciding the issue were preferable.

Justices Frankfurter, Jackson, Rutledge, and Burton concurred, 14:33
but they added themes which they hoped might keep the decision from becoming a precedent to be used against different kinds of released-time programs. "The secular public school did not imply indifference to the basic role of religion in the life of the people, nor rejection of religious education as a means of fostering it." But the "non-sectarian or secular public school" had been invented to prevent misuses of religion in the public sphere. In Champaign, "the courses do not profess to give secular instruction in subjects concerning religion. Their candid purpose is sectarian teaching." Back to *Everson:* "We renew our conviction that 'we have staked the very existence of our country on the faith that complete separation between the state and religion is best for the state and best for religion.'" Instead of a wall, Frankfurter spoke of a fence: "If nowhere else, in the relation between Church and State, 'good fences make good neighbors.'"

This time it was the Catholics' turn to react in frustration and 14:34
anger, while the old dissenters against *Everson* cheered. Both camps retreated behind their church and synagogue walls, there to defend the constitutionality of off-campus released-time religious education. Increasingly one heard language about the need to defend the "Judeo-Christian" version of public faith, which the government should help nurture. Opposing Vashti McCollum was

O'Neill, still protesting Court folly, as he saw it. "The opinions of the Supreme Court justices in this case are in some ways worse, in their disregard of the history and meaning of the First Amendment, than those in the Everson case." He rejected a footnote by Justice Frankfurter to the effect that "the fathers put into the Constitution the principle of complete 'hands off,' for a people as religiously heterogeneous as ours." Interpreting it thus was bad history. This ruling, O'Neill claimed, was "the *first decision* in our Supreme Court history in which the first clause of the First Amendment has been used to interfere with the freedom in religion or education of the people of the states—a freedom which the First Amendment was specifically written to preserve."

14:35   There remained a third decision to complete the midcentury argument, *Zorach v. Clauson* 343 U.S. 306 (1952). This second released-time case slightly modified the harshness of *McCollum.* It still allowed for released-time religious teaching but only off the public school grounds. The drafters of the decision kept using the "wall of separation" metaphor and argued that the Constitution forbade aid not only to *a* religion but to *all* religion. They used the Fourteenth Amendment to apply the First. Strange alliances had formed by then. In New York Charles H. Tuttle, attorney for the Protestant Council, and Porter Chandler, attorney for the Roman Catholic archdiocese, found themselves united against the American Civil Liberties Union, the New York Board of Rabbis, B'nai B'rith, the American Jewish Committee, and the American Jewish Congress. At issue was a New York statute that said children could be enrolled for religious teaching only by "a duly constituted religious body." Who would judge what "duly constituted" implied? Tessim Zorach of Holy Trinity Episcopal Church in New York charged that the very administration of the system involved the time of public school leaders, and this meant that the state was subsidizing religion. Meanwhile, Tuttle feared that the system would promote divisiveness.

14:36   The majority of the Court said that released-time programs meant no more than that the public school "close its doors or suspend its operations as to those who want to repair to their religious sanctuary for worship or instruction." But separationists did not like this language. To release some pupils meant not to release others, so there would inevitably be tax-supported administrative costs accompanying the practice, just as there would necessarily be discrimination between two types of students. The six-judge majority, however, ruled that released-time religious education off campus did not imply any form of informal establishment of religion. Some of the handwriting was on the wall which would lead to ever more "separation of church and state," segregation of religion from republic, and reduction of faith from public to private spheres. That was becoming obvious. In dissent, Frankfurter, as was his wont in such cases, turned sarcastic: the "unwillingness . . . to dispense with such use of the public schools betrays a surprising want of confidence in the inherent power of the various faiths to draw children to outside sectarian classes." That evidenced "an attitude that hardly reflects the faith of the greatest religious spirits." And Justice Jackson wrote that if released time turned out to work better than other, more voluntary, religious education, this would be "due to the truant officer who, if the youngster fails to go to the Church school, dogs him back to the public school room." Meanwhile the school "serves as a temporary jail for a pupil who will not go to church. It takes more subtlety of mind than I possess," Jackson added, "to deny that this is governmental constraint in support of religion." Why call on the help of Caesar in things of the spirit?

Justice Douglas, often thought by the pious to be a secularist, in the *Zorach* ruling surprised everyone by describing the national piety positively. In making the case for the New York plan, he remarked, "We are a religious people whose institutions presuppose a Supreme Being." The first half of his proposition was being demonstrated to be defensible again in its own ways during the revival of interest in religion at midcentury. The second half of the phrase was not obviously supportable. "We guarantee the freedom to worship as one chooses. We make room for as wide a variety of beliefs and creeds as the spiritual needs of man deem necessary." But to use public schools to make religious participation difficult would "show a callous indifference to religious groups. That would be preferring those who believe in no religion over those who do believe." There was "no constitutional requirement which makes it necessary for government to be hostile to religion and to throw its weight against efforts to widen the effective scope of religious influence." The Court majority, Douglas went on, "cannot read into the Bill of Rights such a philosophy of hostility to religion." While theologians and jurists argued over the Supreme Court rulings on religion from 1940 through 1951, the people kept trying to find out in what ways they were a "religious people," and how to express their religiousness beyond the sanctuary after the public school had become a problem, no, a battle site. Many feared that the Court

14:37

trend showed the secularists to be winning in what should have been a "religious people's" finest hour. There might turn out to be One Nation, but it would not be so Under God, because religious belief was to be kept private and enclosed behind a wall while secularists ranged freely through the republic and its institutions.

15

"Men and Women Should Own the World as a Mutual Possession"

P ublic argument over the role of religion in One Nation, Indi-   15:1
visible, was largely in the hands of "public men." To have spoken
of "public women" at midcentury would have been insulting; the
word then connoted the woman of private, not public affairs, as
with the French *femme publique*. In any case, few women had or
gained platforms and outlets comparable to those of men in public
discourse in the fifteen years after the war. To characterize the few
participants who did break into the conversations and debates,
there was no agreed-upon positive term. *Feminism* was used now
and then, but it usually had pejorative connotations. What came to
be called modern feminism—the liberation of women, the change
in women's consciousness, a new stage of struggles for women's
rights—became a public theme after the Eisenhower-era "revival
of interest in religion." Women, of course, made up the majority
of church membership and were commonly observed outnumbering men at public worship. They dominated in religious education, whether as nuns in Catholic parochial schools or directors of
religious education or volunteer teachers in Judaism and Protestantism. Many of the elements of life closest to religious meanings—conceiving, giving birth, nurturing, providing care, interpreting illness, educating, making sense of the passages of life—were
the monopolies of women or at least were connected more with
women than with men. Their auxiliaries and independent wom-

en's organizations were among the main agents of denominational activity. No doubt many women were discontented with circumscribed public roles, and the uncovering of diaries and reminiscences will show ever more how much dispiritedness and rage were hidden from view.

15:2   For all that, in the specifically public roles, it was men who were "locked in argument," as Thomas Gilby, O.P., and John Courtney Murray, S.J., defined the discourse that went on in civilization. On the national level, there was one woman senator, one representative, no high court justice, no governor of a state. While some women had voices in religious journalism, only one or two were tenured in theological schools, and not many taught in religious studies departments, even in women's colleges. Tens of thousands found honored but limited places in Catholic religious orders, and Protestant deaconesses were important, but they did not have much voice in the public forum. Outside the Pentecostal bodies and the Salvation Army, where they had preaching parity—and thus in religious groups seldom turned to for contributions to the public argument—few women were ordained, even in the liberal Protestant denominations. Those who were, usually had to be so preoccupied with parochial duties that they had little opportunity to get into the national debates. The bibliographies of works on religion and public life, church and state, and ecumenism include very few women's names in the fifteen or twenty years after the war.

15:3   The literary energies of a number of best-selling authors at midcentury went chiefly into legitimating the role of women as wives and mothers. Having a woman as author or coauthor did little to change a book's thrust. Thus a best-selling book that was taken seriously on this subject around the middle of the century was coauthored by Ferdinand Lundberg and Marynia Farnham, *Modern Woman: The Lost Sex*. In a later time that would have been a perfect title for feminist advocacy. But not in 1947. While the coauthors found little advocacy against which to face off, they still swung wildly at any evidences of it. They contended that such argument would deprive women of distinctively feminine virtues and turn them into pseudomales. The popular anthropologist Ashley Montagu put his science to work as late as 1958 to say: "I put it down as an axiom that no woman with a husband and small children can hold a full-time job and be a good homemaker at one and the same time." This axiom did not lead him to urge some women to take on full-time jobs. No, a woman should fulfill herself in "the most important of all occupations in the world" and become "a good wife, a good mother, in short, a good homemaker." Lynn White, Jr., a pioneer ecologist, in 1950 published *Educating Our Daughters.* Because he was president of Mills College in California, a prestigious women's institution, one would have expected him to prescribe curricula for careers. But he derided such efforts: "The tragedy is not that our career-minded higher education has diverted some girls from marriage," he said, but that it had "prevented them from flinging themselves with complete enthusiasm and devotion into the pattern of life which they had chosen," which was homemaking. Emphatically, "secular man" was no more ready to advocate enlarged roles for women than were religious leaders.

College was not necessarily the place to go to experience femi-   15:4
nist breakthroughs. In 1949 the *New York Times Magazine* surveyed the opinions and fortunes of women who had graduated fifteen years before, in 1934. Of these respondents, 82 percent were married, and of them 88 percent believed that marriage was more important than career, and almost as many argued that marriage and career could not mix except in truly extraordinary circumstances. Mildred McAfee Horton, former president of Mount Holyoke College, whose husband Douglas was a Congregationalist and ecumenical leader of note, tried to balance the two: "College failed to teach these women that most people accomplish most in the world by working through established social institutions, and that the family is entirely respectable as a sphere of activity." It should be noted, however, that nine years later Horton was advocating additional roles, including the ordination of women in ministry: "The crucial questions about the place of women in the church is whether or not the church will accept the pattern of the secular society (with which most women are fully content) or will take the lead within its own life demonstrating the truth of its age-old teaching that human personality is of ultimate worth, whether it be male or female."

With such sentiments abroad in the place where the secular and   15:5
churchly worlds met, it would not be likely that the somewhat more conservative church leadership would say or hear much that would break the old boundaries. What was changing, then, was not the argument of intellectuals but the entry of women into the workforce outside the home. World War I, coinciding with the first women's suffrage movement, saw many enter that force, only to have to return home to make room for the returning military men, who were supposed to be the breadwinners. Many suffrage advo-

cates, feeling they had won much by winning the vote, sat back to enjoy victories but they underestimated the power of backlash; the feminism that had helped produce women's suffrage seemed spent in the period following. World War II, without any organized movement or cause such as suffrage, again found hundreds of thousands of women drawn into the labor force as men were called into the military, and this time there were women military. They kept their roles during the Korean War and after, but again in general the men outranked or displaced the women. The cultural ethos created the expectation that women would marry and have children and not think often of profession or career. As for mothers with children under six years old, 10 percent worked outside the home in 1940; despite the wartime changes, that figure had grown by only 2 percent by 1950.

15:6   One of the first rays of light thrown on women in public church life in the first years after the war, one of the first ponderings of why there were not more, came from the international ecumenical scene but had considerable bearing on the American situation. In 1952 Kathleen Bliss, one of the most highly placed women in the World Council of Churches, exercised her leadership and wrote *The Service and Status of Women in Churches*. Bliss was aware of the American scene and paid attention to *Male and Female* by pioneer anthropologist Margaret Mead. In Europe she encountered the very controversial *Le Deuxieme Sexe* by French existentialist philosopher Simone de Beauvoir. Bliss knew that these authors were read "because they seek to enter into the total experience of women in the modern world and to provide some signposts in a bewildering scene." Not much missed Bliss's scrutiny, but she found Christian writers "silent except for the quantities of practical little books" that were valuable only within their limited range. They dealt with marriage and home life. Bliss had nothing against this except when it circumscribed "the total experience of women." One cannot picture her placing such practical little books where the gaze of a Mead or a de Beauvoir would fall upon them.

15:7   Take Bliss as a distant early warning to men who opposed the growth of women's roles, a signal from Great Britain at the beginning of the Eisenhower-era religious revival and the beginning of the baby boom. Who else asked, as she did, why churches lacked "prophetic imaginative writing?" As an ecumenist, she knew that the churches were still apart on this issue. They were in this case "deeply divided in what they think about the place of women in the modern world and in the Church." Of course, there was a special niche for "the woman who accepts the judgment of men on most subjects, who is happy in the small practical tasks to be found in every congregation and seeks protection from the harsh problems of the modern world." But she also knew that others were discontented with such a role. "The woman of an independent cast of mind who has earned her own living and perhaps that of dependents and is accustomed to taking her share in decisions without diffidence usually finds it difficult to be at home in the church." Such a person had to judge that woman was being treated as "a secondary being, an agent enabling and completing man: probing will uncover the existence of ancient taboos about women's impurity, still lurking in most unexpected places." When churches desperately lacked manpower, they put women to work. But when the situation eased, "theological reasons against women doing this kind of work are at once raised." Such an approach, said Bliss, debased theology and was unjust to women. Interestingly neo-orthodox dogmatician Karl Barth, a European man, was one of the few who was calling for opportunities for women to "show what they can do."

Bliss wrote for world Protestantism and paid little attention to   15:8
Roman Catholicism, where some signals of change were beginning to appear. The creation of the Women's Auxiliary Army Corps (WAAC) in 1941 was a challenge to Catholicism. If the church discouraged Catholic women from enlisting in this military agency, some would suspect their patriotism. But many leaders could not encourage them, either. Thus Bishop J. J. O'Hara, a delegate to the armed forces military vicar, spoke against the idea of service-women, appealing to his own concept of gender roles. He was sure that his audience of policemen would, if they were in service, prefer "for the sanctity of the home, . . . to peel potatoes and darn your own socks rather than have women in the army." But as a group the bishops backed off from the suggestion that they should formally oppose this change in the roles of women. About 25 percent of the WAAC, later the Women's Army Corps (WAC)—an auxiliary no more—were believed to be Catholic, a number at least as high as the percentage of Catholics in the population.

Some editors were grudging. The diocesan *Brooklyn Tablet* ar-   15:9
gued that the army corps would degrade women "by bringing back the pagan, female goddess of de-sexed, lustful sterility." Given such grumblings and accusations, the military went out of its way to make room for Catholic opinion and employed public relations people, for instance, to counter charges that the corps distributed

contraceptives. A Catholic chaplain was sure that the charges were "a gigantic nationwide plot instigated by Axis agents," and the story about distributing condoms was an "insult to womanhood." Because the condom charge issued from the fevered imagination of a newspaper columnist, Catholic magazines were soon attacking attackers of the corps. An early opponent, the Jesuit weekly, *America,* came around and asserted that the corps was a "tremendous contribution to the war effort" and "a lasting contribution to women's place in our national life." Eventually even Bishop O'Hara was won over.

15:10   If a front-rank secular college like Mills was hearing its president counseling domesticity, one can hardly fault Catholic women's colleges for limiting the concept of women's role. Thus in its curriculum at midcentury the College of New Rochelle in New York scorned careers for women in industry or science or anything that would pull women from their "all-out career of Catholic wife and mother." Touted for more than a decade was another typical offering, this by Brescia College of the Ursuline Sisters in Kentucky. They had a "pink room" where "the Eternal Woman" could be taught submission to the man as "an expression of all creation to its Creator." The approach was both deconstructive and holistic: "In figure, face, hair, posture, voice, vocabulary, styles, grooming, the whole woman is taken apart and put back together." But such curricula no longer matched life experience, and if anything, ideology had trouble catching up with practice. Thus in the middle of the war years, Ruth Reed in the Jesuit *America* wanted the church to be realistic: "The belief that all women can remain in the security and leisure of a protected home environment is a genteel middle-class assumption which has never applied to the masses of women."

15:11   Individual women of power emerged; Dorothy Day was by no means alone. In Boston, Frances Sweeney led the fight against Catholics who occupied the far right, "the anti-Semites, the Christian Fronters, and the fanatical isolationists." Her founding of the *Boston City Recorder* gave her a place to reproduce the "News about Bigots, Racism, and Work Accomplished against Them That Is Not Printed Elsewhere." For example William Cardinal O'Connell threatened in his archdiocesan newsletter to excommunicate Sweeney for her attacks on fascist-leaning clergy, but she charged ahead anyway. Better known was a convert of Bishop Fulton J. Sheen, actress Clare Boothe Luce, who served in Congress but announced retirement from politics in February 1946: "I just wanted to be home." She did not stay there; soon she was taking up anti-communist causes, running for the United States Senate, and serving from 1953 to 1957 as ambassador to Italy. Mrs. Luce walked gingerly in the post, being the first Catholic ambassador to that nation. But the rest of the time, whatever she did she did boldly, and she served as an exemplar or object of envy to many Catholic women who wanted more than just "to be home."

A good way to glimpse the Catholic woman "between the   15:12 times" is to look at her organizations, one of the most experimental being the Grail. This small but influential Dutch movement, imported in 1940, allowed somewhat expansive but still limited roles for Catholic women. Although the Grail centered on the communal life of single women who did not join religious orders, the ideal was to oppose the idea of seeing women work also outside the home. Just as Protestant women kept being given the ideology of submission to males, so these Grail Catholics heard maternal

Among the expressions of vitality among Catholic lay women at mid-century was a movement called the Grail. Thoughtful, disciplined women experimented with communal living and offered new models of spirituality in the decade before the fuller-fledged Catholic feminism was to emerge. Here at Grailville in Ohio the Grail Singers produced four recordings and from Grailville they went on concert tours, incidentally spreading word of the movement. (Photo: U.S. Center for the Grail, Loveland, Ohio.)

roles or virginity exalted. One of the most gifted of the leaders in America, Lydwine van Kersbergen, argued that "in the Divine plan, Eve, the lover and helpmate, is destined to safeguard the Godward direction of mankind." Van Kersbergen and her colleagues attempted to establish themselves in the Chicago archdiocese, where much experiment went on, but were frustrated there and eventually settled on a farm near Cincinnati, Ohio. Their intensity and anomalous character raised suspicion, but they wanted to be perfectly orthodox contributors to a "Catholic revival," in this case, on somewhat utopian grounds. In short, they saw themselves in the avant-garde of those who would restore some sort of united order. In 1950 van Kersbergen said it boldly: "We must work for a new Christendom."

15:13   The early Grail ethos perpetuated an emphasis on the value of suffering. Thus one of the American leaders, Joan Overboss, wrote in 1943 that as Ladies of the Grail they were finding "with the young women in America" that "once they discover the beauty of suffering," of course "in union with Christ's suffering, their whole lives seem to change." Janet Kalven, a Jew who converted to Catholicism at the University of Chicago, linked with Overboss to help take the Grail message on the road. They connected with the liturgical movement and the National Rural Life Conference. On first hearing, Kalven seemed ready to make a break with perceived traditions. Thus she faulted the Protestant Reformation and the Industrial Revolution for having relegated women to church, kitchen, and nursery, "Kirche, Küche und Kinderstube," in the interest of protecting male values. Yet curiously she did not ask women to leave those sites. She instead wanted them to develop more positive images of their roles. They were unfortunately learning the worst habits and aspiring to the worst in America, "a culture of the self-assertion of man; of man's reason and scientific method in the intellectual sphere; of man's will to power and conquest in business and world affairs; of man's independence of God in all aspects of life." Kalven quoted Catholic journalist G. K. Chesterton, finding, she said, more than a witty pun in his observation that "twenty million women rose to their feet with the cry: 'We will not be dictated to' and proceeded to become stenographers." No, "men should be manly, the women womanly." Woman was to "be for mankind a living example of the spirit of total dedication to God." As spouse, mother, nun, or religiously dedicated single person, woman transmitted "the fundamental heritage of civilization, the traditions of culture and religion, to a new generation." It was superficial "to think as women that we must be in the forefront of public affairs, politics, or business to influence the course of the world."

The ideal of Christendom was an integrating one; church and world were to come together, and womanhood played its part. One Grail brochure said that "on the one hand here is the richness and beauty and meaning of the Church. And on the other is the life of the Church leading to order and peace." The Grail would use art, music, drama, and writing, to "bridge the gap between the Church and the people." They would help "bring forth from the crucible of the times" a demonstration that "the life of the Church and the life of the people are one. Our task is one of integration." The lay apostolate became the grand theme as they promoted liturgical life, conceived world mission, and started other small centers. Some of the time the Grail attacked Protestantism for having watered down doctrine and formed a "union with the forces of secular humanitarianism." But more infuriating was apathetic Catholicism. "Has the Catholic Church renounced her goal of winning the world?" asked a Grail pamphlet.   15:14

The Grail, an outlet for women and in a way a liberator of women, was also a gathering force of opposition to feminisms. Thus when Simone de Beauvoir's book appeared, van Kersbergen wrote *Woman, Some Aspects of Her Role in the Modern World*. She scored de Beauvoir for a "deep-seated, misogynous aversion for everything connected with the specific womanly role in love and motherhood." Beauvoir's book was also dangerous because it spread the notion that "the achievements which our society designated as masculine are the only really valuable achievements." The author was somewhat happier with Margaret Mead, and she also cited people like journalist Dorothy Thompson and psychologist Helene Deutsch, who noted the limits of fulfillment for women in the workforce beyond the home. Yet they could but offer partial vision. Only Christian theology could take women to the "ultimate metaphysical meaning of womanhood" through the current "unparalleled opportunity for Christian thinkers to take the initiative in the work of integration." This is not the place to follow the path of the Grail to disintegration, as ecumenism and feminism prospered. Ever adaptive, however, Janet Kalven and other Grail leaders did an about-face and signed on with feminism when that movement emerged, recognizing that new days called for a new ethos and theology.   15:15

While Catholic women stood no chance at all of being ordained   15:16

to the priesthood, Protestant denominations at midcentury began to move toward enlarging women's ministerial role. The issue of ordination, ordinarily a churchly issue, has a bearing on this story of public religion and argument. It will be clear to any reader of this whole book that, for all the contributions by laypeople, ministers and priests and rabbis had more immediate and convenient access to the forum. So one must keep an eye on women's ordination. One good case study is that of the Presbyterian Church in the U.S.A., the largely northern, somewhat more liberal but typical mainstream group. In that body, one level of recognized ministry was eldership. In 1940 only 6.6 percent of the Presbyterian churches that responded to a survey reported having women elders, and fifteen years later it was learned that denomination-wide only 4.5 percent of all elders were women—3,000 out of 65,744. During clergy shortages of World War II, one might have expected a breakthrough of women into other orders of ministry. A few small congregations put women to work in such roles, but they lacked denominational sanction. Thus in 1943 the presbytery of Cedar Rapids, Iowa, ordained Elizabeth Brinton Clarke, because she wanted to be a chaplain in the Women's Army Corps. Her theological training was meager, but the presybtery acted on the understanding that she would not thereby obtain rights to pastoral duties in congregations. Aware that wars eventually end and that the church would have a problem on its hands with this thereupon civilian woman cleric, the national body a year later revoked the action by Cedar Rapids. Few women were yet rebelling against national policy on the ordination of women, and little happened to change the scene.

15:17 One dramatic incident, however, did force that church to know it had a problem and an opportunity on its hand and sooner or later would have to act. The first Japanese civilian to be allowed to visit the United States a year after the war was Tamaki Uemura, an alumna from prewar times of Wellesley College in Massachusetts. She had become an ordained and fully authorized minister in the Church of Christ of Japan. The potential for high drama was here: what was designed to be a sign of concord could easily become an occasion of conflict, and it did. The Presbyterian Women's Organization was to be her host. As a sign of reconciliation of the nations, the group did not want her visit to go by without a communion service. The women wanted to follow protocol, so they asked William Lampe, the moderator of the General Assembly, to preside, with laywomen assisting. Lampe invoked church law and said no. So the women of the organization came to his office to challenge Lampe and the interpretation of the stated clerk, William B. Pugh. (Lampe was a person of contradiction, living under stress. A year before, during a controversy on the subject, he reportedly had agreed that it was hypocritical to keep women out of ministerial roles but maintained that there was a book of rules, something a good Presbyterian would not transgress. He had thrown the rule book across the room while declaiming all this.) The Presbyterian women came back and asked on what grounds American Presbyterians could in effect take away the meaning of ordination rites of someone in another church, in this case, of the Reverend Uemura.

The women produced a lawyer, who introduced a jarring reso-   15:18
lution: "We record it as the unofficial view of the General Council, that it would be a calamity in this day, if arrangements could not be made whereby our Japanese friend might participate in the communion service." Again, it was counseled, with an "unofficial view" they had found "a way whereby it can be done." All the groundwork was laid, but precedent was not to be broken: Pastor Uemura, thanks to travel difficulties, arrived a day late. Nevertheless, evidently stung or prodded by the incident, Lampe joined the women in sending overtures to presbyteries asking for support for the ordination of women. The next moderator, Frederick W. Evans, read more signs of the times and told commissioners, who did indeed pass the motion, that if they did not do so, they "might have to give a hard accounting to their wives." By then, only one Presbyterian woman was recorded as speaking up for tradition. Mae Ross Taylor, an unordained antiordination staff member at Chicago's Fourth Presbyterian Church, said: "no lone woman could ever know and meet the needs of a community, could ever in the fullest sense of the word be a pastor." Eastern presbyteries massively opposed change, and the measure lost. A minister got on record thanks to a *New York Times* report. He said, "women get what they want," so in time they would "get the privilege of the pulpit and the pastorate." He knew they would win, "and God bless them. But also, God keep too many of them from taking up this new field all at once."

The *Christian Century,* inspired by advocacies like that of Kath-   15:19
leen Bliss, began to publish articles that were intended to show the public that women were conspicuously involved in American church life. A United Church Women study embarrassed the mainstream church leaders, who had hoped to have more to show by

midcentury. As of 1950, 6,777 American Protestant women were ordained, which meant one in 25 of the nation's ministers, whereas a decade earlier it had been only one of fifty who were women. In 1951 the *Yearbook of the American Churches* offered the best data it could, with no ideological reasons to promote or oppose ordination. It could account for only 2,896 women pastors and 5,791 licensed (not ordained) women ministers. But only 608 of these, fewer than a tenth of the whole, served in the moderate and liberal bodies that made up the National Council of Churches. The Church of God, the International Church of the Foursquare Gospel, and Christ Unity Science denominations accounted for three out of five of them.

15:20   In the mainstream, Methodism's numbers were slightly more precise and cheering to women than elsewhere. Methodists had long traditions of involving women in social movements like abolition, temperance, and suffrage. On the far left, Winifred L. Chappell, with her mentor, Harry F. Ward, advanced communist causes at Riverside Church through World War II years. She was associate director of a People's Institute of Applied Religion, which trained leaders in religion to serve as labor organizers and leaders of struggles against the poll tax, racial discrimination, and other repressive elements in the social order. In her institute post, Chappell used biblical motifs to inspire radical action; she kept doing this, despite chastenings, until 1946, by which time the Cold War had begun and she lost influence.

15:21   Much more representative and influential was the single woman teaching on mainstream Protestant theological faculties. Georgia Harkness was an ethicist and a mystic of sorts, well trained by the Boston "personalist" schools to keep a focus on the question of God. Centering her work in the concept of the love of God, Harkness carried on a lifework devoted to reconciliation and made peace her cause. She became one of the more visible pacifists right up to the outbreak of World War II, and even wartime did not dim her commitment. In 1941 she tried to pay income tax through a system that would keep her funds from supporting the defense effort, a system that was, of course, denied. Harkness's role in movements of support for the ordination of women reached back to the 1920s, and by the time southern and northern Methodists merged in 1939, she was on record supporting it even if it rendered more complex the movements toward Christian unity that she also favored. Throughout she opposed "the last stronghold of male dominance" that she thought the church had become. On May 4, 1956, her moment of triumphal participation occurred, when her church formally voted "full clergy rights for women." Yet through it all she worked mainly behind the scenes, wanting to read and change the mind of the church more than to force anything. But later Methodist feminists found little of her work formally dedicated to legitimating feminism; she gave no support, for example, to efforts to refer to God in feminine terms. She more or less simply lived out a Methodist role model as a teacher after 1939 at Garrett Biblical Institute in Chicago and later at the Pacific School of Religion. Still, a delegate to the General Conference, after the vote was taken to ordain women, asked the conference to applaud the person who for many years had done most to advance "this valiant fight."

A third instance in our Methodist case study is Dorothy Rogers   15:22
Tilly. Tilly's father was a Methodist minster who was quite aged when the civil rights struggle came to a point a few years after World War II. But the daughter was in the advance guard, after a long career as a volunteer and activist in standard Methodist causes promoting justice and peace. In 1945 President Truman named her to the Commission on Civil Rights, the only southern woman to be so appointed. A year later she was investigating a race riot in Columbia, Tennessee, and observed the consequences of the lynching of two black couples; in both cases there was, of course, flagrant injustice. So she helped form an interracial movement, the Fellowship of the Concerned, in 1949, five years before a Supreme Court decision helped give impetus to the civil rights movement, a decision she supported with a pamphlet citing biblical reasons for doing so. Her fellowship called attention to the lynchings and may have helped reduce their number.

The notion of accepting a Supreme Court decision hardly   15:23
sounds radical, but it appeared to be so in some southern Methodist circles, where some women shunned Tilly and she had to hear the standard charge that she was procommunist. When critics phoned, she would play a loud recording of the Lord's Prayer to silence or outlast them. When the Ku Klux Klan threatened, she endured. When her meetings became dangerous settings because of threats, women attended without notifying their husbands. To others the meetings were not dangerous but boring: good Methodist that she was, Tilly allowed no alcohol to be served at them. Practices like these got her typed a conservative, and she was progressively dismissed by the emergent black leaders in the Southern Regional

Council. Despite her own extremely cautious views on the roles of women, she felt shunned by male leaders, but not before she had become a pioneer in civil rights causes.

15:24   Without movements of feminism in the churches, one turns to gifted writers to gain individual visions. Here the spectrum is broad. Thus Nobel Prize-winning novelist Pearl Buck, of a missionary family and herself religiously informed, tried to break some of the boundaries. She did so in a little-noticed work in 1941, *Of Men and Women*. An essay on morality, it was not specifically religious in outlook, but it addressed precisely the concerns to which the churches were applying themselves: motherhood, spousehood, and family life. Buck offered a challenge: "Let woman out of the home, let man into it, should be the aim of education. The home needs man, and the world outside needs women." Not antagonistic about men and women, she stressed mutuality: "Men and women should own the world as a mutual possession," something that could not happen within existing arrangements. Buck even saw women as victims of prejudice on a broader scale than what blacks experienced. "Profound as race prejudice is against the Negro American, it is not practically as far-reaching as the prejudice against women." Under the gloss of national life, "women suffer all the effects of a minority." She rejected what she called the "angel myth" placed alongside the "home myth." Think of women as angels, and they will be delicate and dependent. Women had failed thus to keep the world pure through their limited roles. With war coming, she wrote: "to continue to bear children only to have them slaughtered is folly." She wanted women to enter public life in order to help end the slaughter. As for now: "A man is educated and turned out to work. But a woman is educated—and turned out to grass." Strong words, these, but, as is often said of such words, "before their time."

15:25   *Of* their time, very much of their time, were the words of Catherine Marshall, probably the best-known Protestant woman of her day. In the economy of American religion, the spouse of the pastor played important local and often national roles. That there were strains in the relations between pastors and wives or between expectations extended to both and the inability or unwillingness of either or both to live up to them is evident from the record of the growing body of literature devoted to the subject. One scholar counted twelve books of prescription for ministers' wives in the fifteen years after World War II, whereas only three or four had been published in the previous century. Most were scripts of lighthearted encouragement, in which authors pictured and called for sunny faith on the part of spouses and families, mutuality in ministry, and exemplarity as in *The Care and Feeding of Ministers* or *How To Be a Preacher's Wife and Like It.*

Marshall was the spouse and the widow of Peter Marshall, chaplain of the United States Senate and pastor of the New York Avenue Presbyterian Church. He died suddenly of a heart attack at the crest of his career in 1949. Needing to support herself and a son, she published Marshall's sermons and followed up with a biography in 1951; *A Man Called Peter* became a popular film. Six years later she pondered the death and its aftermath in *To Live Again.* The author, a Presbyterian minister's daughter and an Agnes Scott College graduate, had married Marshall in 1936 and devoted the next thirteen years to him. She heard his sermons expressing the male ethos of Protestant ministry at midcentury. When women achieved equality with men in this century, he preached, "she copied the vices of men—in the name of progress!" The liberated woman thus lowered her moral standards and lost her ideals along with her "essential femininity." He was typical in advising that, after this loss, "to be sweet is far better than to be sophisticated" and that "America needs young women who will build homes" where "harassed husbands may find peace." The woman should devote full time to her home, husband, and children in a life's work wherein she will "know that she is carrying out the plan of God" and becoming "a partner with the Sovereign Ruler of the universe." As for daughters, they should not "seek to make a place for themselves by themselves." Marshall rang many changes on these few notes, and his widow edited and published them, with evident consent to their outlook. 15:26

Peter Marshall's death forced a career on Catherine. She was without resources. In the bed she had once shared with Peter she now wrote his life story. God, she was convinced, had told her: "Use the creative energy that I've given you for My purposes for the book." That Peter had been young was an asset: as she wrote, she became convinced that had an older person preached such a view of "woman on a pedestal" it would not likely have appealed to the "most modern young women." Was it possible that "under the stimulus of his thinking," career-seeking women "were seeking emancipation from their own God-given natures, and so were merely reaping inner conflict?" Maybe God had created women so that ideally they would "achieve greatest happiness and greatest character development" through their husbands' careers. She was 15:27

not sure, but "it was worth pondering deeply." One senses through these assertions mixed with ambivalences that there was some strain in her role. Catherine seemed resentful over the circumstances in which she and her kind had been placed. She was angry over Peter's occasional neglect of her while he gained fame and served others. She knew that some women in every congregation saw their minister through a romantic haze and somehow became rivals; Peter was a handsome, charismatic figure, so it is not hard to see how she might personalize this. Eight years after his death she was still complaining about having been left out of the financial planning. A week before his death as they drove home from church, he spoke romantically of her being his valentine; she responded: "Oh, sure! I'll be your valentine, having a gay time all by myself here in Washington while you're in Des Moines," where he would be on February 14. But for all the ambivalences, revealing as they were of her restless and sometimes resentful nature, she always came home at the end to accept the status of dependency that she advised for others. Through a second marriage and more accomplishment, she kept advising domesticity for others.

15:28   There were more radical advisers of role-changing than Buck and of role-retention than Marshall, but most of the diaries, novels, magazine articles, short stories, devotional literature, and prescriptive writings about the roles of women in Catholicism and Protestantism moved between the poles these two represented. Still, they were individuals, and one wishes to get glimpses of what went on in the organized life of religious bodies. Here, too, one must say that leadership lived, in words made popular by theologians, "between the times."

15:29   Notable among these bodies was the role of United Church Women (UCW), which occupied an often ambiguous status. Three organizations merged to form it, coincidentally in the week of Pearl Harbor. A statement prepared for a meeting at Atlantic City, December 11–13, 1941, urged that "the future is thrilling to contemplate." The authors, mistakenly equating the women in conciliar Protestantism with all of Protestantism, and thus overlooking the evangelical and fundamentalist portion, captured the sense of urgency in the new moment: "What a group of women—almost the total force of womanhood in the Protestant churches—can do if they set their minds to it! This really *can* transform the world." But, the statement added, "They must be prepared to share the grimmer reality this world has come to mean." War was declared even as they met. So the peace-minded delegates in their first act sent a telegram to the president: "The newly constituted United Council of Church Women, representing ten million women of seventy Protestant communions, pledges its loyalty to the highest ideals of our nation in this hour of grave crisis." Much of what followed is the history of bureaucratization, complex organization, conventions, dealing with routine business, and representing churchly causes, after the model of the Federal Council of Churches itself. Surprisingly little of the energy seems to have gone into questions of the consciousness of women or what in a later period is called "women's liberation." The council took for granted that black women's participation was as welcome as that of whites. In general, the council followed policies that would be called progressive.

Finally in 1948, after the ecumenical study by Kathleen Bliss   15:30
had appeared, the council took up *The Service and Status of Women in the Churches* and prepared its own report, *Women in American Church Life*. It reported that 583 men and 63 women were on the board of the Federal Council of Churches, as chosen by the denominations. In the International Council of Religious Education, the figure was 313 men and 41 women. Women were rarely disqualified from boards but rarely were chosen. Yet their influence was growing. In December 1950, when the new National Council of Churches was forming, the United Council, on the basis of almost unanimous voting, was present. In tribute to the council women, it must be noted that they were often in the vanguard at mid-century on issues of world affairs, civil rights, human rights, employed women—a growing trend—and ecumenism, just as they put energies into spiritual activities such as the World Day of Prayer. But as for leadership in the self-conscious development of women in religion and promotion of the ordination of women— agenda items that would be called "women's issues"—these had to wait for a later time. "Public Woman" in religion was just on the point of emerging as the decade of the sixties unfolded.

16

"The Dominant Currents . . . Have Been Centripetal"

16:1 It was natural for many of the religiously and racially divided citizens of the United States to dream of realizing One Nation in One World. They had had to overcome or obscure what temporarily looked like secondary issues while they fought for survival during World War II. After that war many of them, aware of how the world was split in two by the Cold War found new reasons to promote the idea of One Nation, Indivisible. How could they endure and eventually prevail if citizens indulged in the luxury of fighting with each other instead of amassing their moral resources to face the Soviet Union and its satellites? The cynic could say that in neither case was much thought given to the terms of domestic peace; that the prevalent language supporting unity and oneness was superficial and illusory. It was an expression of bad faith. The practical politician would say that in both cases the action and language promoting national unity were only strategic. Such language camouflaged the religious and racial conflicts within the nation, battles that, to be sure, were usually fought by other means than gunpowder. These still drained energies from the powers that wanted to influence and dominate in American spiritual life. The idealist, on the other hand, could say that the drive for unity, at least in the minds of the Christian majority—eight or nine out of ten Americans were self-described as Christian—had to be seen as being in its own way supernatural. That is, its sources were drawn

248

from divine revelation, from ancient scriptures; its development depended upon gifts of God to which faithful humans responded. In other words, American religious leadership in mid-century as never before pictured the boon to the One Nation in the One World if Christians became part of a church unity movement. Great benefits would accrue to the world, they promised, if these citizens and believers then shared the ecumenical spirit that was to attract Christians around the *oikoumene,* the whole inhabited world. For the task of understanding the force of such a national and then an international movement, no naturalists, cynics, or pragmatists need apply.

The middle years of what publisher Henry Luce was teaching   16:2
the nation to call the American Century were times of formal ecumenical advance unmatched in previous centuries. From the formation of the National Association of Evangelicals in 1942, the World Council of Churches in 1948, and the National Council of Churches in 1950 to the Second Vatican Council beginning in 1962, there were unequaled opportunities for Americans of almost every Christian stripe to respond to what they considered divine mandates and promises about the unity of believers. So privileged did ecumenical language become over denominational or sectarian defense and so consistent was the rhetoric favoring unity that one might appropriately say that the supernatural vision came naturally. To capture some of the exhilarating, almost intoxicating, affirmations expressed at least by leaders in the postwar moment is difficult in a later time when spiritual conflict rages. They seem especially remote in a time when discourse about churchly unity sounds weary or obsolete and when the artifacts of the unity movements look shopworn. One can best grasp or sense the headiness that characterized the advocacy of Christian unity by listening to advocates and apologists, some of whom stated their cases in books that quickly came to look archaic.

Henry Pitney Van Dusen is a thoroughly qualified candidate for   16:3
our attention. He spent much energy at the podium during the year the war ended and the year following. Van Dusen delivered lectures that became his book *World Christianity: Yesterday, Today, Tomorrow.* By now a familiar character in these pages, Van Dusen was a professor at and later president of Union Theological Seminary in New York, where Reinhold Niebuhr, John Bennett, and other Christian realists taught. Union was the flagship seminary in the ecumenical fleet, the focal theological academy of the times in the American Century moment. Being a vital place, Union experi-

enced considerable internal controversy. Yet people who look for representativeness in the Protestant—and hence, again, the majority camp within divided Christianity—will find it as readily in Van Dusen's book as anywhere. The mainstream Protestant blue blood lectured and wrote because he knew that new times needed new words. Arguing that his generation was experiencing a spiritual gestation on a cosmic scale comparable to childbirth on the intimate level, Van Dusen made an effort to coin a word; he spoke of "worldbirth," because, he contended, "for the first time in the long millennia, a global age has wrapped all mankind within a single garment of destiny and has willed for them a common fate."

16:4   Van Dusen was not alone among church leaders in sounding such a triumphal note as he surveyed the scene. He gloried in the fact that the Second World War revealed the Christian Church to have been the "one indomitable, invincible champion of human rights," "the one omnipresent, dauntless ministrant to human need," and now, "the one invulnerable, indestructible world community." While the world may not have been aware of all this on its own, *Life* magazine, a publication of the Henry Luce empire that was friendly to Van Dusen and Union, was alert, as the seminary president reminded his readers. He quoted someone identified as a representative of a major publishing firm that had spotted a new market: "There is a mounting interest in interdenominational understanding, if not Unification." Such notice inspired Van Dusen to reach for a wide brush to apply to his large canvas: "The record may be summarized in a single sentence: In Christian co-operation and unity, the five years of the second World War have been the most notable quinquennium in Christian history."

16:5   Five features from the war years' record stood out as Van Dusen grabbed his figurative pointer. First, the record of cooperation was achieved by *churches* and not individuals. "Only a great corporate reality can struggle effectively against demonic corporate might." Next, this was a record of "all Christian churches alike, conservative and liberal," a record of "*Christian Churches united.*" The reference here to conservative churches was exceptional: Van Dusen more than most liberals gloried in the unitive impulses that he was among the first to discern in rapidly expanding Pentecostal and evangelical circles. Third, he could point to a record of churches speaking "within a *world community*"; only a "*world church*" proved adequate amidst planetary strife. To all this, observers should add a vision of "*practical daring* and *spiritual renewal,*" which had gone hand in hand. Everywhere, he gloried, "the Chris-

tian Church has stood unshattered, uncorrupted, and undaunted."
Finally, all this activity had been made possible because for a
hundred and fifty years Christians had been working together, at
least on their world mission. True, one cloud above it all appeared
in a footnote about a "mighty exception" to the Church's moves
toward unity. Van Dusen's reference was to the more than half of
Christianity that was Roman Catholic. There was, he knew, "no
realistic prospect of participation by that Church as a world body
in what is termed 'ecumenical Christianity.'" No prospect at all.

Van Dusen, though friendly to what were then called sects, the   16:6
small intransigent groups, was not a sectarian. He liked to show
how at home the ecumenical movement was in secular circles. Ernest Barker, a British political scientist, was in the cloud of witnesses Van Dusen invoked from the London *Times*. Barker opined
that the present century "has its sad features. But there is one feature in its history which is not sad. That is the gathering tide of
Christian union." Similarly, from within the church came voices
like that of retired Methodist bishop Francis J. McConnell, who
projected that a hundred years hence church historians would call
the forming of the World Council of Churches the most significant
event of the twentieth century.

After quoting others, Van Dusen added his own witness in the   16:7
form of an image that could well describe the main forces chron-
icled in this book: "The dominant currents in the life of the Church
in the past half century have been centripetal." Looking at the tactical cooperation of forces around the church, the Union professor
found that "the centripetal forces in the world's life were superficial and ineffectual"; attaching Christian union to them would be
ineffective as a strategy. Future historians might single out as one
of the most significant features of the epoch the fact that "while
the centripetal trends within Christendom originated in part from
broader centripetal tendencies within the general culture," they
"*continued* with even more determined effort and significant result
after the general cultural drift had suffered radical reversal and
more powerful centrifugal forces than the earth had ever before
witnessed were loosed upon mankind."

Once the -*petal* and -*fugal* images captured Van Dusen, he   16:8
made the most of them. At the moment, the centripetal currents in
the age were too weak to determine the world's course, but these
might strengthen and resume their flow with multiplied power to
"bring into actuality that community of peoples and nations which,
patently, is the true destiny of mankind in our era," he thought. A

visionary but no fool, Van Dusen wanted to see believers devote practical attention to the Christian cause. It would be foolish, he said, to rely simply on a natural outcome of a merely pragmatic sort. Centrifugal counterforces always threatened the convergent ones. He had heard and could still hear people saying that "unity sacrifices essence" or "we meet only on the least common denominator" or "ecumenism has gone too far." But this was not the moment for Christians to back off: "To an age destined to survive, or to expire, as 'one *world*', we bring a *world Church.*"

16:9   The nitty-gritty follow-up work that accompanied such visions on the ecumenical scene fell to undramatic but steadfast executives of the church unity councils. Among them John R. Scotford stood out. He later became an employee of the emergent National Council of Churches, but in 1948 the Congregationalist minister and religious journalist busied himself writing a book for seminarians and young ministers in the denominations. Scotford also wrote for "the intelligent layman who yearns for a greater unity in Protestantism—and wonders why it is so long in coming." Scotford's credentials: he had worked as a journalist for all major denominations. His office for sixteen years had been under the same roof as offices of both the Federal Council of the Churches of Christ and the American office of the World Council of Churches that was coming to be in the year he was writing. He had served his own denomination and could speak of "living experience" in it after working with four hundred congregations. Having also been close to the Christian unity movement that he considered to be "definitely accelerating," the ecumenist rejoiced to think that his book would be out of date by the time it reached the public: "That is one of the most hopeful signs concerning American Protestantism today. It is not merely 'in a state of transition'; it is really changing."

16:10   "The man on the street has always believed that 'the churches should get together,'" observed Scotford as a person of the people. He dismissed hypocrites who gave "merely verbal tribute to the idea of a union." Among these were "many Fundamentalist freelance congregations and not a few community churches," which held a condescending attitude toward the denominations. Overlooking the branches of Protestantism—perhaps half of its membership by then—that were not favorable to mainstream ecumenism, he reported for all to read that ordinary church members were "overwhelmingly" for anything that "smacks of union." The larger the group to which negotiators for union submitted their proposals, "the fewer," he claimed, "are the voices that dare speak out in the negative." Although it is hard to picture anyone being rabid about unity, Scotford felt it important to answer critics who said that "emotional hysteria or the operation of the mass mind" drove Christians to support unity efforts.

The ecumenist's eye discerned four roots of the common but   16:11
strong desires for unity. The automobile, the printing press, the movie, and radio had provided a common culture "which makes our Protestant divisions seem a bit silly." Score one, then, for "the circumstances of modern life [that] minimize the divisive elements in American society and magnify those trends which unite us." With all other observers, Van Dusen paid tribute to the war and the United Nations: "If it is desirable for the nations to get together, why should each denomination cling to its pretensions to religious sovereignty?" Now that "for the first time the ideal of 'one world' has become a part of the mental furniture" of all intelligent people, he insisted, intelligent church people should match this cooperative endeavor. Practically, small congregations and denominations needed each other in order to survive. Larger congregations and denominations would become more efficient and effective when united. Ideology should also matter, added Scotford. American settlers escaping Old World churchly domination had set up and then jealously guarded their new organizations. But now theologians were developing a new concept. The church was not "something which men can set up and take down like a tent." Instead, it was an "age-old, world-wide institution devoted to ends which transcend the thoughts of finite man." The church had moved to a "higher bracket" in the minds of the thoughtful.

Scotford compromised this idealism with the realistic note that   16:12
haunted Protestant ecumenical talk. There was a dirty little secret that motivated the Protestant unity movement: "the emergence of the Church of Rome as an active element in American life." It is hard to account for the Protestant push for unity and the relative later decline of the mainstream Protestant councils and denominations unless one notices how much enmity against and fear of Rome motivated them. Catholicism had once been mysterious, "socially 'on the other side of the tracks,' ministering to an immigrant clientele," as Scotford remembered or read about it. Back then Protestants shuddered at Catholic practices but did not tremble before church power. Now, however, Catholicism was moving into the mainstream, its members becoming social peers of Protestants. "Its priests are American-born, American-trained, and well acquainted with the arts of public relations and political pres-

sure." With his peers, Scotford pictured Catholics as geniuses in self-promotion.

16:13　　Protestant Scotford looked at large Catholic churches crammed with communicants attending one of the multiple masses, and then in contrast he sadly surveyed the "job lot of ill-assorted congregations trying to uphold the faith of the Reformation." Alert Protestants knew that they needed to re-form "in a more imposing manner." Journalist Scotford knew that Roman Catholics had advantages when dealing with the media. Cardinals "trooping across the front page" of their favorite newspaper impressed ordinary church members. Were the editors converts to Catholicism? No, most of them were "merely Protestants out to sell their paper," and they knew that Protestant proceedings were not photogenic, while Protestant constituencies were too small to match the drama of Catholics. His advice: "Get together—and then do something striking." The chaplaincy in the recently completed war had boosted Catholic reputations. "The Catholics acted as a unit, and we did not." The government all but had to set the Protestant house in order on its own if it wanted to get anything done; "it could not be bothered with the minutiae of our setup."

16:14　　Since ecumenists were so sure that everyone wanted unity but so little was evidenced, it takes imagination to see the world as these advocates saw it; imagining is made easier if one listens to their own account of resistances to the centripetal movement. People held to their denominations as "a matter of ancestor worship," finding more emotional than theological reasons to remain attached. Of course, there had been union of denominations during the past century, after the immigrant and frontier separations. Scotford's selective reading of Protestant history led him to think of only one important unhealed schism in a century, that between Unitarians and Congregationalists. Slavery policy, as he reviewed it, had split Methodist, Presbyterian, and Baptist bodies on regional lines. But Methodists reunited in 1939. Presbyterians were working on merger. That left only the Baptists—the largest cluster, by the way—who showed no signs of merger talk. Of course, Scotford had to notice the marginal groups, the Church of the Nazarene, the Church of God, and "various other ecstatic and pietist groups" that issued from the impulse to innovate. On higher social and economic levels there developed the novelties of Christian Science, New Thought, Unity, and the new Buchmanite movements. But the real strength of Protestantism, he insisted, was in thirteen bodies with over a million members each. Today, he observed accurately, "there is surprisingly little contention between the Protestant denominations."

The important tensions of 1948 were within, not between denominations. A few High Church Episcopalians, humanistic Unitarians, and militant fundamentalists went and would continue to go their own way. But the passage of time would lead others that now stood aloof to become more tolerant; Scotford must have been breathing utopian air when he wrote that that process would probably affect even groups "which are now strongly set in their views—such as the Christian Scientists and the Missouri Synod Lutherans." The really important "standard brand" denominations fought over polity, less regularly over theology or doctrine. Yet even polity made little difference in almost every case; whether in episcopal or congregational patterns, leadership found modern life to be leveling: bishops had to deal with democracies, as did congregations when they elected officers. "The practical difference between these two systems is largely a matter of words—except, of course, to the sacerdotalist," who evidently counted little in matters ecumenical.

Those wishing to peek over the sociologist's shoulder to glimpse some social dimensions of mainstream Protestantism are well served when they listen to Scotford, a gifted amateur in the field. He used his expertise to elaborate. Social distinctions still divided Protestants. Episcopal, Presbyterian, Congregational, and Unitarian bodies, for example, were the "society churches." Methodists, Baptists, Disciples of Christ, and Lutherans represented "the churches of the common people." The Church of God, Nazarene, Pentecostal, and foreign-speaking groups were "the 'other-side-of-the-tracks.' " Scotford was nettled that class had mattered so much in this accounting of church life, but he shared the widespread belief of his day that America was converging and becoming middle class. Postwar distinctions were blurring. Thus "Lutherans have crossed the tracks into polite society; in another generation they will be firmly established 'on the avenue.' " What about recalcitrant aristocrats among the denominations, people who presumably would rather not consort intimately with those who were not of their kind? Scotford reassured them: "The union of denominations does not of itself impose large-scale social contacts."

Bureaucrat that he was, Scotford knew the bureaucratic mind. He was too sunny in outlook to think of his ministerial colleagues as selfish; in any case, in that remote mid-century world he was confident that denominations would see to pastors' needs. They

16:15

16:16

16:17

simply each had emotional interests in the status quo. Names like Congregational, Methodist, and Presbyterian were "essentially silly, and yet they have become holy to many." Certainly there could be tactful ways to guide the members of denominations to church union. They also had to see the problem of competing for too-small markets. He shared belief in "comity" arrangements, cooperation in planting new churches or merging declining ones. The "standard brand" groups did work together, "but the Missouri Synod Lutherans, the Southern Baptists, and the Fundamentalist and Pentecostal groups will move in next door to anybody's church if they feel the call to do so." These villains aside, people should be expected to improvise "union churches," "federated churches," or "community churches" so long as denominations remained in competition, even those whose improvisations were vulnerable and ineffective because they were such small minorities.

16:18   Scotford was realist enough to know that no sane person could expect that "by some sudden alchemy 'one big church'" could take shape. But he argued that it was useful to envision a direction for current piecemeal efforts. The church was currently experiencing "like with like" unions; next would come "union of unlike bodies, present and presumptive," as Christians had seen such mergers form in Canada, South India, and elsewhere. The railroad provided an image: "A modern Diesel pulls a heavier load with the same crew but with a much less relative expenditure of energy than does a switch engine." The tireless Scotford argued that "American Protestantism has had altogether too many switch engines chuffing up and down its tracks, and too few streamliners going places."

16:19   Typical of assessments then and valuable still for its portrayal of a lost world was Scotford's review of denominations; they merited and merit notice because they made up the "standard brand" group that in so many ways had dominated in the culture and were now yielding their privileged place. Thus "as the church of culture and fashion, the Protestant Episcopal communion has prospered enormously in recent years." Unfortunately, its participation in union ventures was "exceedingly spotty." Another group that represented bullish investments of hope? "Strength marks the Presbyterians in nearly every aspect of church life: financial wealth, social prestige, numbers, a closely knit organization." And at least the northern wing had given "unflagging support to Protestant cooperation in every area." The bettor on standard-brand churches at mid-century would have stood with Scotford in assessing that "the Methodist Church is the strongest Protestant organization yet to arise" and that it was still "organized for action." Methodists might often be self-centered, but they carried their load ecumenically. The Congregational Christian churches were leaders in interdenominational activity. They were "emotionally and intellectually mature," but "the acids of modernity have eaten deeply into the faith of many of their churches," so one must welcome even smaller signs of recovery. The Disciples of Christ were disappointing: "They have talked more about union than any other group— and done less."

At the fringes were other groups. Northern Baptists were   16:20
"simple folk, modest in their pretensions, and willing to walk in brotherly love with most anybody," but, though internally divided, they were closer to the ecumenical movement than were the Southern Baptists. These "dominate the South," Scotford noted, but "have developed a tendency to move northward," though without ever carrying a word such as "co-operation" in their vocabulary. They were, Scotford saw, "an imperious company who look down on other churches, cooperate rarely, and who assume that the salvation of the world pretty much depends upon them." He liked the Evangelical and Reformed, who were ready to merge into a United Church of Christ. What the Lutherans did, they did well, but they remained hesitant about unity, and their Missouri Synod remained aloof. "Time will undoubtedly bring the Lutheran bodies closer to one another and to organized Protestantism." Not one line in his denominational review was given to African American Protestants, though they numbered in the millions and wore standard-brand labels such as Baptist and Methodist. Scotford gave no signs of racism to match his sense for class; he simply joined most mainstream Protestant branders in overlooking fellows in faith if they were of another color. Also not part of the centripetal forces were the Church of God, the Church of the Brethren, the Friends, the Universalists, the Unitarians, and the like.

"The future of co-operative Protestantism is bright," thought   16:21
the ecumenical bureaucrat, if one looked to councils and federations. As for organic union, the Protestant Episcopal Church "will remain as it is." Methodists might absorb the Evangelical United Brethren Church, "but that is all." Presbyterians and Lutherans would set their own houses in order. That left four "well-defined and distinctive Protestant denominations." Did Scotford realize how his accounting diminished the force he thought was prime? A United Church of Christ, then being formed, might some day in-

clude the Disciples and Northern Baptists. The result would not be "one big church" but a more effective and integrated Protestantism. Why did Scotford care about practical moves? "The ultimate incentive for church union is the desire to meet the needs of the world." Catholicism did carry on good works, but "its day-to-day business," Scotford reminded all, was "the assuring of salvation to individuals through the medium of the sacraments." Its church was too exclusive to work with others. As for the other huge cohort, the fundamentalist, pentecostal, and ecstatic sects, each had "its own road map to heaven, and therefore cannot co-operate with anyone else."

16:22   The almost inevitable scaling down of the hopes of Van Dusen to the practical evidences of Scotford must have disheartened leaders then as it bemuses those who today try to connect ecumenical rhetoric with denominational reality. The One Church in the One Nation for the One World came down to a matter of small local councils of churches and timid interactions. In 1960 sociologist Ross Sanderson reviewed "the Expectant Forties" for the Association of Council Secretaries, a then rather strategic group. Sanderson had to see global significance in intimate events. His first subhead read "Planet Shrinks, Councils Consolidate." If the council secretaries' group was strategic, its scope was also limited. In Conference Point, Wisconsin, at its meeting the week Hitler invaded Russia, 84 persons were present to appraise a budget balance of $252.59. But they also had the thrill of listening to keynote speaker Dr. Toyohika Kagawa, "the Japanese Albert Schweitzer," as some called him, because of his good works and his aim to reconcile people—this a half-year before Pearl Harbor.

16:23   The council secretaries saw the war years as a time that inspired their movement to be the agent for the birth of new forms. At the 1943 meeting, Church Federation of Greater Chicago head John W. Harms told the secretaries: "The whole matter rests on the assumption that territorial councils are as valid ecclesiastical bodies as the national denominational bodies." That would have looked like hubris to denominationalists, but Harms thought the future belonged to the new forms. Sanderson, quoting a desk encyclopedia, did his own elaborating: just as a "chief positive result of the war was the formation of the United Nations," so "the cooperative unifications of the denominations, at least as difficult a matter, already begun, was to be accelerated by international happenings." Both depression and war as worldwide events "were making it crystal clear that a parochial or sectarian type of organized religion was outmoded on our shrinking planet." For that reason, in the perspective of Sanderson, when an Inter-Council Committee on Closer Relationships met in April 1941, "to prophetic minds and spiritual insight the meaning of the world drama was clear, but now a whole series of ecclesiastical chores must be patiently accomplished."

Only those who love bureaucratic language could appreciate the stated goal of the Association of Council Secretaries in 1941, but coded in its practical language were signals of a larger world: "The central purpose (of the ACS) to be progressively realized: to achieve a functional unity in the development and projection of a comprehensive strategy for Protestant and non-Roman Catholic Christianity in America." Through the war and Cold War years, progress promoting such unity was slow but real, and the local councils grew in number. Those were times, Sanderson remembered, of the "disruption of normal life," "turmoil," "economic readjustment, moral laxity, political corruption, spy-hunting, religious uncertainty, and the rise of militarism." But over against all these was the prospect of "new heights of prosperity," and the year 1950 was the beginning of a great new ecumenical impetus, the start of "still greater state and local cooperation in American Protestantism." 16:24

One World needed a World Council and One Nation a National Council, and at midcentury the world and the nation got both. John Scotford had pointed to the relief strategies of the World Council of Churches even before it was formally organized. "A common dedication to a common cause" united people; "the theory is sound and the practice ultimately irresistible." But the World Council had more than works of love in mind. Twelve years after its founding, Paul G. Macy entered into the record an appropriate review of its early years. Macy had been an American secretary of the provisional World Council organization and an insider at its assemblies, and he was the first secretary of the "Friends of the World Council of Churches, U.S.A., Inc." Although Macy benefited from some hindsight, when he first wrote, the Council was still too young to have veered far from its origins. Macy faced at once the problem of selling the strange word *ecumenism.* He quoted Ross Sanderson's complaint that it is "phonetically execrable and psychologically questionable," but it was "etymologically incontestable, theologically estimable, and pragmatically inevitable!" 16:25

Horror over World War I helped lead to the beginnings of the 16:26

World Council. The world in 1914, falling apart, needed "holding together." So the Church did *"nothing."* Two-thirds of a billion Christians made up a church that "was powerless to hold the world together. It did not even hold its own members together. Church members slew church members—even members of the same communion fought each other." The sense of unity in Christ had "utterly vanished." Suppose someone *had* wanted to do something; what agency was there? "None." Christians of conscience thereupon began to change, but the world took little notice of the positive turn. Thus on May 12, 1938, the Council of the League of Nations met in Geneva to debate the fate of member-nation Ethiopia. The press gave it good coverage. The League collapsed. Almost no press in the world told of another meeting that very day at Utrecht, Holland. There eighty leaders of Christendom, "representative of all the great communions save Rome" (Macy and other World Council types decided which ones were "great") completed plans for an organization that might do what diplomats and politicians had failed to do, to "hold the world together" through the Church of Christ. They thereupon held together *"without a single dissenting voice"* to complete the plan for the World Council. On May 11, 1938, "at Geneva it was a *counsel of despair;* at Utrecht, a *council of hope."*

16:27 In postwar retrospect Macy could score points by reminding readers just who had been opposed to the council. The leaders of the pro-Hitler "German Christian" movement were the ones who attacked "every supranational or international Church structure, whether in the form of Roman Catholicism or of World Protestantism," seeing in them a *"political denaturing of Christianity."* The Nazis were enemies of the World Council approach, as evidenced in a wartime pamphlet that appeared with Nazi approval: *The Reich as a Task.* It opposed the "idea of the universal church as the idea of a community which has to stand above the nations of the world." Instead, "National Socialism has had to assert itself over against both these ideas." The Nazis for a long time saw things going their way: "The idea of humanity has been overcome comparatively quickly," said the propaganda pamphlet, "by the outburst of national consciousness which is almost comparable to a natural force." As for international Christianity, the writer contended, "We must continually work with gigantic patience and equally gigantic caution until the men in our Reich finally recognize in its true significance the natural and accordingly divine superiority of membership in a nation to the arbitrarily selected membership in a confession." The lesson was clear: the World Council attracted despicable enemies.

Macy brought back to America the language of the First World 16:28 Conference of Christian Youth, which met in Amsterdam in 1939, one month before the European war began. Its report included a line for Macy and his readers to cherish: "Just at the time that the nations of the world are falling apart, the Churches of the world are coming together." In the spring of 1945 as the war ended, the council was ready. Its main agent, Dr. Willem A. Visser 't Hooft, visited New York to tell of ecumenical wonders. Why had council work prospered? He argued that it had because the churches had discovered that worldwide participation in the work of the Church of Christ was "not just a holiday activity of people who like to go to conferences in Switzerland." They learned instead that the Church "is an absolute essential, that a sense of universality and world-wide community is essential to the fulfillment of the voca-tion of the Church." The World Council symbol was a sailboat representing the church as the ark of God. "*We've had the wind of God in our sails.*"

Americans were a strong presence at Amsterdam in August 16:29 1948 when the World Council people met to discuss "Man's Dis-order and God's Design." There eighty-three-year-old American Methodist John R. Mott, who thirty-eight years earlier had chaired the pioneering World Missionary Conference at Edinburgh, gave a forward-looking address. (Catholics were not present at the found-ing, even as official observers, and priests had been forbidden to go on their own. Likewise, the Soviet government prevented Rus-sian Orthodox delegates from attending.) Much of the meeting was drudge work, but some comments on the social scene drew fire from the American right, and Macy was well aware of the hazards of a World Council which said that "the Christian churches should reject the ideologies of both Communism and *laissez-faire* capital-ism, and should seek to draw men away from the false assumption that these extremes are the only alternatives." Some American sup-porters of free enterprise thought the council treated the systems of the Cold War enemies as equivalent evils, and they targeted it as a leftist organization, a dangerous label in a time when anything left of center was suspect in America.

Although Catholics could not travel to the council meeting, 16:30 its social program attracted some spiritual fellow-travelers in America. Father Edward Duff, S.J., completed a book-length ap-praisal of World Council social thought by 1954 and published it in 1956. Not permitted to make a positive theological appraisal, Duff concentrated on the social themes that gave American reporters at Amsterdam something to "write home about." Duff grasped the mid-century ecumenical ethos well, noting that "in such a situation the judgment of religious groups is accorded a more attentive hearing." He knew that "the very survival of organized religion whose disappearance was so confidently prophesied by the more sanguine spokesmen of the gospel of Progress a century ago, indeed its increasing vitality, have engendered at least a grudging respect." Duff was ungrudging in praise of Protestant ecumenism's move from the "sentimental, essentially subjective, conception of religion as affecting merely personal relations at most and, at its highest, as satisfying private needs" to a search for church unity and the pursuit of "the social consequences of religious truth."

16:31   Duff was perceptive about American uneasinesses, the "vague fear that the World Council of Churches represents the foreshadowing of a spiritual imperialism" and development of a party line in economic and political fields. The limited resources of the Geneva secretariat and the unresolved tensions within the ecumenical family would prevent that. "Any such alarm should be readily quieted by a candid consideration of the relative impotence of religious forces in the shaping of modern society" in this "post-Christian era." Duff quoted Columbia University sociologists who, after observing some Akron, Ohio, citizens, came to the conclusion that "religious teachings had small impact on their judgments in concrete social situations." He quoted Emil Brunner of Switzerland, who had put Amsterdam delegates in their place: "Among the outstanding leaders of human society in recent generations, we find few Churchmen; other voices have possessed greater power of conviction and other minds more prophetic vision." Still, Duff did not want anyone to underestimate the vitality of the ecumenical movement and its churches. He quoted French journalist André Siegfried, a frequent visitor to and reporter on America. Siegfried watched the World Council as it formed and saw the body representing "in the history of Protestantism and indeed of Christianity in general, an event of capital importance, a manifestation of the aspirations perhaps of the necessities of our age."

16:32   Americans, who subsidized 85 percent of the fledgling council's budget, were often given the snob treatment by European theological elites, but they contributed much to the effort. An American even took credit for having named the council. Samuel McCrea Cavert, a more notable church council leader than Macy, remembered having been asked at an ecumenical service, "What name shall we now give the child?" Timidly Cavert answered the question with a question: "How about World Council of Churches?" The archbishop of Canterbury replied: "Why not? That's what we really need and want." So "World Council of Churches" it came to be, thanks to packaging by an America experienced in pluralism and hopeful for Christianity at home and abroad. Cavert, looking back on the eve of the Second Vatican Council in 1961, remembered the Amsterdam meeting as "unquestionably the most widely representative gathering of the churches that had ever been held." He was cheered to see delegates from communist countries, people whose presence led American rightists to attack the council for communist leanings. Cavert saw the coming together as being motivated by "the growing recognition of the significance of the church as a corporate community in our modern world." But corporateness in other parts of the world had also brought "the rise of secular totalitarianism, which, in the form of both national socialism and Communism, threatened the entire Christian tradition." Now the Christians seized the instrument of the enemy for sacred purposes.

While Americans supported the World Council, the National   16:33 Council of Churches was their own product. Since 1908 the standard-brand Protestant churches had cooperated through a Federal Council of Churches and correlate organizations. That council had given general support to the New Deal, a fact that irritated members of affiliated churches whose economic views better matched those of the Republican Party. The Depression hit the council denominations hard, and the ecumenical organization became both more timid socially and more prudential about using its energy on the condition of the churches rather than society. A National Preaching Mission, for instance, had been designed to regather members for the churches after they had experienced some losses. Between 1926 and 1936 fifteen of the twenty-two denominations had experienced decline. During the Second World War the council efficiently worked for the Protestant churches in support of the war effort. No matter how cautious its leadership might be, however, the extreme right faulted it for communist leanings. But it stood up to examination, and John Foster Dulles, hardly a liberal by 1949, led a committee that pronounced its "full confidence that the Federal Council functions with complete fidelity to Christian ideals." It even made some bids to be open to evangelicals in the major denominations.

16:34   During the war several interdenominational bodies began to cooperate, and by 1949 seven of the eight voted to link up; the eighth
cast its "aye" in April 1950. In November of that year, in Cleveland, sixty delegates voted into existence a new National Council
of Churches of Christ in the United States of America. The fledgling council was cumbersome and hardly ready to meet expectations. Its organizational chart resembled that of American corpo-
rations, which did it no good when corporate leaders attacked the
stated economic and social policies of its task forces and elites. In
retrospect, the council at first followed what looked like moderate
policies and worked to build up the churches. By 1950, some in it
were noting a nascent revival of interest in religion. In 1940 only
49 percent of the American people had been listed as church members, but by 1950 that figure had risen to 57 percent. The timing
was right for a forward-looking council, and the National Council was born during a great snowstorm as the Korean War started.
The startup date was precisely at mid-century, on New Year's
Day, 1951.

16:35   While the National Council was to care most for One Nation, it
kept a global view. On May 16, 1951, its general board pronounced
that "the churches have special responsibility and a special contribution to make to the world and to the nation in its relations with
other nations." There was to be no idolatry of nation, no introver-
sion: "As the instrument for God's purposes they are concerned
with peace, freedom and justice for all peoples." Their missionary
agencies "contribute to the strengthening and upbuilding of a living world community and they gain an insight and perspective that
should be brought to bear on American foreign policy." Missionaries were not sent out merely to save souls. Their work was "a
powerful expression of faith in God's purpose in history and of
practical concern of the needs of men everywhere."

16:36   Of course, with Roman Catholicism as a competitor, the denominations in the National Council, to stay in the running, sensed
that they had to evangelize, to convert Americans. The *Christian
Century,* a friendly critic of the council, cheered its efforts to that
end. In 1954 the editors wrote that "the task of converting and
churching America is too big to be accomplished by a divided Protestantism." Through the Division of Home Missions, the council
members would set out "to evangelize the fearful or the small
minded and to preach in season and out the principle and practice
of cooperation." In that area, the National Council was demonstrating that the member churches could "rise above sectarianism

and achieve wholeness." Always with one goal in mind, the editors applauded: "Toward the winning of America a beginning has been made."

Cavert introduced the council in the 1951 *Yearbook of the American Churches.* "It is the instrument through which American churches now work together in all common tasks." The new movement was born to face communism, materialism, and the "secularized temper of the times." Cavert counted 29 denominations with 143,959 local congregations and 32 million members in its scope. Key words in the names of the combining groups indicated their reach: foreign missions, home missions, religious education, missionary education, higher education, church women, stewardship, church world service, interseminary, film, radio. Here was "a great effort to represent the *wholeness* of the Christian task." While the council could not delve into dogmas, it did insist that "all Churches which share the basic faith in Jesus Christ as Divine Lord and Saviour" were eligible for membership, a fact that kept Unitarians out and should have ruled Catholics in. But Catholicism stayed aloof, and Cavert did some verbal skimming when he said that the council numbered "more people within its circle than any other religious body in America." To its friends and enemies, was it a "body" for any purpose except statistical comparison?   16:37

Realists had to point out to the enthusiasts one great limitation: not one denomination ever surrendered any of its autonomy to this "body." Cavert used this fact to advertise that the council, having "no authority over the denominations," was "in no sense a super organization." In fact, he stressed, "as the Council was officially created by the Churches, so also it is wholly responsible to them." It linked with 875 city, county, and state councils, all of them also products of denominations. Affiliates included 1,720 councils of church women and 2,000 associations of local ministers. Henry Smith Leiper, a missionary leader, caught the mood in his final line in the *Yearbook:* "All the experience of the past leads to the confident prediction that this new relationship will be highly productive of understanding cooperation, a spirit of good will, and a better symbolized ecumenical fellowship."   16:38

While the National Council was to acquire a reputation for liberalism in social policy, the moderately conservative Episcopal editor Peter Day, who reviewed the "pronouncements" of the first conciliar decade, found them merely glib. "Beginning with a lifeless theological generalization," he judged, "they go on to confess the sins of lay members of the constituent churches, dividing deli-   16:39

cately between the 'some,' the 'many' and the 'all.' " Then they
wind up, complained Day, with "a bold proposal for solving the
problems of the year before last." He found as a result nothing
enshrined by forty-nine pages of hierarchical vision: "The unique
contribution of the NCC to the American Christian scene is its
bigness."

16:40   Day was snide but powerless. However, as quickly as the council formed it picked up very powerful enemies among conservatives in the standard-brand Protestant churches. All the apologies
and claims by Van Dusen and Cavert or Macy and Sanderson
would have prepared few for the vehemence, skill, and resource-
fulness of the enemy within. Few of these critics and counterorgan-
izers wanted to leave the council or its denominations. They simply
wanted a more militant voice in the Cold War, consistent defense
of laissez-faire free enterprise economics as the sole Christian pattern, and theological conservatism to counter the liberal tendencies
of the council's leadership. Even while the organizational merging
was still going on, its leaders were blindsided by the formation of
the conservative National Lay Committee. Before the council ever
spoke, it was being spoken against. The council leaders brought in
an overly ambitious budget and knew they needed support from
the very laypeople of means who feared "progressivism." Among
these the loudest voice was that of J. Howard Pew of the Sun Oil
Company, who offered his services on July 6, 1950. He led a
family that ranked in America's wealthy "Top Ten," and he could
have put his contacts to work to make the council solvent. Instead
he became part of a group of eighty-five men and women, most
of them Presbyterian and Episcopal, who wanted to correct the
council and keep it from "social and political matters," fearing
the worst.

16:41   Liberal clergy and lay leaders were not originally aware of the
status that was sought and won by the National Lay Committee.
But as they became alert, they soon showed how conscious they
were of the predispositions of Mr. Pew and friends. While Cavert
did not mention the situation in the 1951 *Yearbook of the American
Churches,* he had to cope with it when he became the first general
secretary of the council. The Pew people did not simply walk into
position. Liberal Methodist bishop G. Bromley Oxnam, for instance, opposed giving such "overarching" privileges to the lay
committee, and people like Oxnam succeeded in reducing the Pew
group to advisory status on March 28, 1951. The committee did
get to place five women and five men at seats on the general board,

but they had no vote; this infuriated Pew, who felt commitments were being broken. Still, he and his group did try to raise $600,000 that year for council activities. The first president, Episcopal presiding bishop Henry Knox Sherrill, for a time shuttled deftly and worked sincerely trying to effect a bridge between Pew's people and the rest of the council. Thus when a panel was ready to go with a liberal statement, Sherrill cautioned "go slow"; Pew pronounced "go not."

The time for compromise and concessions had arrived. The 16:42 board said it would "limit the number of occasions" on which it would "make a pronouncement in the name of the churches" and would confine such judgments to matters in which there was "an unmistakable ethical or religious concern and which seem to require an utterance by the church." Pew had a hard time seeing when that could ever be. Yet others in the council were on the mark and set to go in the pronouncement field. Through 1951 the Pew element seemed to be winning the major encounters, yet some liberal agency spokespersons found ways to work around the lay committee. Pew sensed this counterforce even as he was amassing power, including voting rights for four of the general board's members. When the oil company executive held retreats for his personnel, he stocked the program with noteworthy conservatives such as Minnesota congressman Walter H. Judd and *Christian Economics* editor Howard E. Kerschner. The latter used this occasion to come out in support of legally authorized Bible reading as a devotion in the public schools and the gold standard in economics.

Liberals countered Pew's moves by preparing a report called 16:43 "Basic Christian Principles and Assumptions for Economic Life." It became raw meat for the retreatants to tear apart. *Christian Economics* judged that "there is no 'Christian economic system' that is suitable for all situations." The plenary lay committee, calling the report socialist, voted 47 to 0 against it. The members said they wanted a report that would honor the American free enterprise system for the contributions it had made "to human welfare, to the establishment of freedom, justice and order and in the implementation of Christian principles." Pew felt he was coming out on top in a showdown on March 17, 1954. Two months later a "Lay Affirmation" argued that "the furtherance of the coming of the Kingdom of God . . . through worship and evangelism" was the only legitimate *Christian* activity. The liberals in their turn began to listen to and promote some more moderate lay voices, like those of J. Irwin Miller, a Christian humanist of note and a maker of diesel engines—a man with impeccable credentials as an industrialist; lawyer Charles P. Taft, whose late brother Senator Robert A. Taft had been a conservative politician; and economics professor Kenneth E. Boulding. With such figures on stage, defenders of the council in effect were asking how the lay committee could claim that no competent laypeople disagreed with their archconservatism. Other moderates subsequently began to crawl from under cover to oppose the lay committee, even as the Sun Oil Company president decreased his financial contributions to the National Council of Churches. That September the general board parted company with the lay committee, making clear its awareness that the council could not survive as a house consistently divided against itself.

16:44   In the final set-to J. Howard Pew was absent by choice, but his representative, B. E. Hutchison, reacted furiously to charges by Presbyterian cleric Eugene Carson Blake that the position of the lay committee was "heresy." Another critic charged that the committee itself was "illegitimate." Hutchison, upon hearing the term, fumed that "this was the first time anybody found a way to call me a bastard!" Blake, in his turn, reacted against Hutchison's choice of the word *hierarchy* to characterize the council. Blake responded: "I would say basically we have been struggling for four years with a problem of distrust. I think it is mutual." On January 19, 1955, as Blake became council president, he wrote Pew a letter that could be seen as a disbanding of the lay committee. Pew thereupon took his money and energy and ran to evangelical opponents of the council. Part of the dream of being representational therefore evaporated in the first five years of the council.

16:45   Pew may not have considered the National Council to be an illegitimate invention, though he certainly thought it had developed malignly. He and his group believed that it was not reliably American, that it leaned leftward, and that in its own way it was less devoted to the One Nation than it should have been. Almost at once one could see the ironic situation of a council that would represent One Church in One Nation and One World, though it was organized against the Catholic one-fourth of America, paying little attention at first to African American denominations, being opposed by the anticonciliar fifth of the American population, and finding its own denominations riven over theology and economics alike. But the council did give new visibility to other elements in the ecumenically minded churches and did recognize their growing power.

The National Council was never the only place Americans put   16:46
ecumenical energies. In 1954 American leaders had their finest
moment connecting with the World Council of Churches as it met
in Evanston, Illinois, for the first assembly after its formation in
Amsterdam in 1948. Robert S. Bilheimer, the American employed
by the council to engineer its events, gloried in the scope of Evanston. He remembered that the assembly's printing needs consumed
seven tons of mimeograph paper, a high figure for that day. The
regular audiences at the assembly numbered 7,000 people. A pag-
eant celebrating Christian themes attracted 135,000 people to Chicago's Soldier Field, while 25,000 more were outside the arena.
The Art Institute of Chicago featured Christian art, and the
Chicago Symphony Orchestra let European theologian Karl Barth
pick a Mozart symphony for a special ecumenical concert. Coverage, according to the council reports, "surpassed all previous religious events in attention from the US mass media," as ecumenical
leadership connected with Main Street. The theme of the event was
"Christ—the Hope of the World." One European essayist under-
scored the theme and showed how centripetal was the intention:
"We dedicate ourselves to God anew, that He may enable us to
grow together." Although no denomination surrendered autonomy,
and there were deep divisions over Israel, racial tensions, the role
of Orthodoxy, and historic theological themes, still, no one would
give up on the notion that "Christ—the Hope of the World" would
and could draw Christian churches and people together.

For all the federating and conciliar action; for all the merging   16:47
of organizations and inventing of new ones; for all the rhetoric
advancing Christian unity, there was precious little motion at mid-
century toward merging denominations and creating the organically united church that was the goal of many ecumenists. Henry
Pitney Van Dusen in his book on ecumenism admitted that he
found many denominational meetings at the forming of the World
Council in Amsterdam in 1948 to be "dull, wearisome, and fruit-
less." The one exception, "the gathering of delegates from 'united
churches,'" was "live, thrilling and immensely valuable." The
Church of South India and the Church of Christ in Japan were
there, as was the United Church of Canada. "Next in inclusiveness
and significance," but reduced to a footnote for Van Dusen, was
such a United Church of Christ in the United States. In an appen-
dix Van Dusen included a chronology of modern ecumenical moments. He noted 88 of these in the 1950s, with 14 having occurred
in the United States. Three had to do with ecumenical organiza-

tions; others were in-house: Unitarian-Universalist, Friends, Evangelical Free Church, Free Methodist. Two showed Presbyterians tidying up their divided house, and three dealt with the Lutherans. None of this was very exciting.

16:48   In 1951, however, representatives of eight denominations met in Cincinnati to consider a plan of union that proposed a "United Church of Christ." This body was born in 1957 when the Evangelical and Reformed Church and the Congregational Christian Churches merged. That was the decade's *only* real merger to go "outside the intimate family," the only step toward the fulfillment of the dream of transcending denominations. One strain in the merger was continental, Germanic, now mainly midwestern; the other went back through New England congregationalism to the descendants of English Puritans who had migrated there. Theologian Walter Douglas Horton, a regular at all things ecumenical, said of the day the new denomination was formed, June 25, 1957, that it was "electric with a sense of great event, for all knew there had never been a meeting just like it in the history of the Christian church in this country." At last boundaries were being overcome; here were "representatives not merely of two parts of a single church family" but "of two different church families." The less easily moved Reinhold Niebuhr, who had roots in the Evangelical and Reformed body, called the new church "a landmark in American religious history." For him, it offered "a particularly vivid example of the kind of mutual invigoration which is proceeding in the whole range of American Protestant pluralism, and it offers some hope of order out of what is chaotic in that pluralism." The *Christian Century* exulted over the events at Cleveland Music Hall. The radical significance of the new church was "that in it American Protestantism turned a corner. A trend that had run in one direction for 300 years was reversed."

16:49   Critics always talked about the ecumenists' thirst for bigness, while leaders of the union movement played that down. Yet Horton could not resist mentioning that the baptized members, including children, added up to three or four million, "which is not far from the corresponding total of the citizens of the United States in 1776," when "the original thirteen colonies . . . by union became the United States of America." Horton did not fail to mention some aspects of the pluses of bigness. In 1957 he wrote in the *Christian Century* that "the most obvious advantage of the union is the least important and has been the least frequently mentioned": its "out-and-out benefit to the business life of the two communions." Usually a voice for the spiritual, Horton here had a different orientation: "All the features of denominational life which depend upon what is commercially the size of the market or the breadth of the financial base will be profited." He vastly underestimated the expense and overestimated the imagination of the bureaucracy in a uniting church and did not foresee the membership decline that began almost at once.

While Christians had thought theology kept them apart, Horton   16:50
paid attention to the "apparently untheological human category." Playfully he turned culinary: "The New England boiled dinner and Pennsylvania sauerkraut had to come to terms with each other." Furthermore, some of the Evangelical and Reformed leaders were cigar smokers, "and smokers of cigars plainly have not the spiritual sensitivity (thought some) of the smokers of cigarettes!" Polity became an issue; Horton said "Congregationalists had to gulp more than once before swallowing the idea of naming the ranking body of the new United Church, the General Synod." Some dissident Congregationalists, proud of the old heritage, went to court to win their way. The court decided against this faction. Union, said Horton, "hung on a thread of gossamer." The Reverend Ben M. Herbster, an Evangelical and Reformed leader, asked the right question when faint hearts and turned stomachs were on the point of prevailing: "What is the mind of Christ about this union?" Confident that they knew Christ's mind, and that it promoted unity, delegates elected Herbster the first president and set to work.

In the years to follow no more churches joined. The Christian   16:51
Churches (Disciples of Christ) were friendly but did nothing. Community churches were inquisitive and conversational, but it ended there. Horton never tired of keeping the ecumenical question alive, however. He asked whether it was not true, as many Western leaders thought, that "real Christianity" was the only force that could hold the world together. But now in America, "where the stream of the Gospel is divided into more than two hundred and fifty denominational rivulets," he asked, "how can one expect to see real Christianity?" There were good unitive signs, but Horton had to add, "we must regretfully admit that to the ordinary community the work of these councils might as well be in the stratosphere."

Despite the discouragements, ecumenical leaders worked on,   16:52
never tiring of projecting their image of the centripetal force of Christianity as dominant. The ecumenical movement would help believers address issues of One Church, One World, and, yes, One

Though its critics on the right saw the National Council of Churches as leaning to the left in its social pronouncements, its nationalist predilections were clear at the beginning. In December 1950, when the council met for the signing of its covenant, "This Nation Under God" was the grand slogan above the dais. (Photo: National Council of the Churches of Christ in the U.S.A.)

Nation. After all, the National Council *was* a *"national"* council! On the eve of his election as its first president, Bishop Henry Knox Sherrill made clear its purposes. The council, he affirmed, "marks a new and great determination that the American way will be increasingly the Christian way, for such is our heritage. . . . Together the Churches can move forward to the goal—a Christian America in a Christian world." Again, the imagery signaled what the standard-brand leadership was aspiring to represent. In the Cleveland auditorium where the council was born in mid-century, the Christian flag and the flag of the United Nations were displayed, but so also was the United States flag. The commemorative volume produced for the occasion, called *Christian Faith in Action,* published a picture of the scene. "Above the proscenium in great shining letters was the theme phrase of the convention and the Council—'this nation under god.'" The council leaders could not, however, agree among themselves about what "nation" and being "under" meant or, some would say, even about the character and charter of "God."

Part Three

"Under God" during
the Eisenhower
Presidency,
1952–1960

17

"The American Way of Life Is the Operative Framework"

Revivals, revivalists, and revivalism were standard features of the American Protestant past. No one spoke of religious revivals in Judaism, Catholicism, or, by definition, in secularism. But after a dozen years of world war and Cold War experience, the public religion of America came to be routinely referred to as "Protestant, Catholic, and Jewish," and people looked for common experiences in the larger faith communities. So webbed together were the fates of each of the big three that low morale or misfortune in one was increasingly seen as affecting all. The American ethos, the American character, the American Way of Life—all concepts that were being given more religious attention than before—provided a penumbra around the various religious groups and led them to be seen as sharing a common destiny. Thus during the economic depression of the thirties, those who thought religion prospered as a solace for people in hard times had expected to find an increase of religious devotion. But most of them saw decline into a religious depression. Participation in the war effort and then in the Christian crusade against atheistic Communism led to some increase in the fortunes of those who touted faith: the spiritual communities and religious institutions. The word *revival*, almost unbreathed outside the circle of Protestant evangelical revivalists for a century, began to describe religious trends in America at the end of the Roosevelt-Truman era and by the time Dwight D. Eisen-hower took office in 1952.

17:2   "Is there a revival of religion?" Precisely at mid-century, just before Thanksgiving in 1950, the *New York Times Magazine* asked this question of Protestant-Catholic-Jewish-secular America's most notable public theologian, Reinhold Niebuhr. His answer was an only slightly qualified "Yes, there was a revival," and the subtitle to his article gave an editorial condensation of his plot: "A time of historic crisis brings out again manifestations of man's deep per-plexities." Whether a generalized revival was going on became a subject of debate, especially among sociologists. Not all of them agreed on what cultural indicators should be observed or what data counted if one was assessing the spiritual temper and practice of the nation. No matter, or not much matter, said the cultural histo-rians, who were recording among other things what mass commu-nicators, academic observers, and representatives of the public thought. Still, despite the almost universal talk about the existence of an interfaith revival of religion, one brings suspicion to the claims. Therefore, the story of the mid-century religious revival has to begin with a revisiting of the argument over whether there was one and what its character was.

17:3   In this period, for the first time, cultural assessors and religious strategists regularly used the opinion poll to measure the religious climate. Although reports on religion had been available from the United States census every ten years since well back into the nine-teenth century, these included too few questions on religion to be of much use. Polling on religion included mainly spotty, sporadic, and localized attempts at interviewing and counting. For example, sociologists Helen and Robert Lynd pioneered when they probed the religious views and practices of high school students and homemakers in Muncie, Indiana, as part of the research for their book *Middletown* in 1924. In 1943 Hadley Cantril made a one-question inquiry and Louis Bultena a one-city stop (in Madison, Wisconsin) to ask about religion, but only a few readers of social-scientific journals could have noticed them. Perhaps the most public breakthrough occurred when the American Institute of Pub-lic Opinion sampled the intensity of religious faith for the *Ladies Home Journal* in 1947. Even so, not much notice seems to have been paid to this pioneering effort beyond the scope of that popular magazine's readership. Nor was much of cultural import seen in a sampling by the Episcopal church the year President Eisenhower was elected. The Eisenhower-era pollsters virtually started from scratch.

The new era began when Ben Gaffin and Associates in June and July 1952 asked religious questions of 2,987 American adults. The *Catholic Digest* carried reports of their findings, and their work came to be referred to quite simply as "The *Catholic Digest* poll," even though far more than Catholic interests were at stake. George Gallup, Sr., of the American Institute of Public Opinion, remembered that in addition to the *Ladies Home Journal* sampling in 1947 he also had made little stabs in the direction of religion in the two previous decades. But these were all highly focused; they asked, for example, whether there should be a moratorium on preaching; how popular was the Bible; how the clergy should support the war; or whether Christianity and communism could mix. Polling had not become regular, nor were the results frequently cited. Questions surface, of course, concerning how reliable polls were or how honest citizens were in their answers, but addressing and settling such questions are very technical operations. The issue for us here is what opinion-makers, church leadership, and the public at large made of the findings and how the findings themselves contributed to talk about a religious revival.

17:4

Curiously, to anyone who had put faith in Gallup's summary of opinion about affiliation in 1947, the polls of 1952—usually seen as a base line from which to measure revival—should have suggested instead a decline. In the earlier assessment about 75 percent of the respondents said they were church members, and in 1952 only 73 percent did—the same figure that turned up after the episode was all over, in 1965. What is startling, however, is the jump in the number of people who remembered or claimed that they "happened" to have worshiped in the previous seven days. That increased from 37 percent in 1940 and 39 percent in 1950 to 46 percent in 1954 and 49 percent in 1958, the peak times in the history of polling. Did this figure reflect an actual jump? Or did a change in cultural mood induce more people than before to "remember" differently how they had spent the weekend? If the former, it was impressive evidence that there was practical revival; if the latter, it was similarly support for the notion that church attendance was a good thing, something respectable citizens supported, a practice one would report to pollsters and have them report to the public.

17:5

The *Catholic Digest* survey, the state of the art in 1952, provides

17:6

the best access to opinion about opinion. "By the way, what is your religious preference—Protestant, Catholic, Jewish, or what?" was an apparently casual question that carried a strong thrust. The answers: over 68 percent said Protestant, over 22 percent said Catholic, and between 3 and 4 percent said Jewish, while only 5.5 percent indicated "other" or "no preference." Astonishingly, only about 1 percent called themselves atheists or made the point to interviewers that they did not believe in God. If citizens were religious, however, they were not any longer trying merely to avoid brimstone and fire in the life to come. Of the 58 percent who believed there was a hell where unrepentant sinners would be punished, only one of eight regarded it as a possible future alternative for themselves. Only 17 percent of the people thought it was most important for the church to convert people to a spiritual belief so they could earn a happy life after death. Forty-nine percent, however, focused on teaching people "how to live better every day with all other people," while another third answered "both." Reports like these began to prompt critics to say that if there was revival, it had little theological depth or communal scope: the culture-religion revealed superficiality and self-satisfaction in the populace.

17:7   While articles by notables like Niebuhr reached part of the public, the scholars immediately raised their suspicions about the genuineness of the revival. (Raising suspicions is exactly what scholars should do, at least in the company of other social scientists.) A frequently reprinted paper by California sociologist Charles Y. Glock at the end of the decade showed him pondering the difficulty of determining what had happened. Revivals of religion never are incidents the way declarations of war, signings of treaties, or earthquakes are. They represent names given complex sets of incidents, notions, expressed opinions, and subtle trends, and in the nature of the case cannot be identified precisely.

17:8   In the case of the Eisenhower-era revivals, the projection of images and the talk about a renewal or revival themselves revealed something important in national life. For instance, all signs indicate that in the more secularized segment of life represented in the academy, there was little expectation of religious surges or resurgences. Europe, on which the culturally lagging United States presumably depended for signals to follow, had seen and was seeing religious decline. Later in the period of the Eisenhower-era revival of interest in religion, Oxford psychologist Michael Argyle in fact had to point to drastic "decline in religion in Britain," even while he saw signs of revival in the United States. What occasioned the evidences for religious renewal, he asked, since few comparable signs had come with the Depression? "Since the war," Argyle thought, "the churches have become both more secular and more liberal, hence appealing to the prosperous middle class." He saw significance chiefly in this burgeoning class. As for the visible and increasingly mentioned of "rise in the small sects," this, the Britisher thought, was "simply a social movement among the underprivileged" and thus was "typical of the beginnings of all religious movements."

Argyle presented his contrasts by employing data gathered be-   17:9
tween 1948 and 1952 in Britain and, for America, used the Gallup polls taken during the 1950s. He could hardly conceal his surprise at the results for an America that sociological determinists thought should have been joining Great Britain and the Continent in increasingly abandoning religious practice. At mid-century 57 percent of Americans claimed church membership, while only 21.6 in Britain, despite its surviving established church, did so. In the United States 43 percent claimed weekly worship attendance, compared to only 14.6 percent in Great Britain. More of the British claimed to pray daily than did Americans, and 61 percent of them could name the four Gospels, while only 35 percent of the less biblically literate Americans could do the same. "Religion is not taught in American schools," Argyle explained, while the British got some basics there. "A real difference in character between religion in the two countries," however, was evident. Why? "Religious people emigrate there," meaning to the United States, some explained, but not to his satisfaction. He joined virtually all explainers in saying that "the sociological scene encourages religion" in the United States. Scores of pundits and scholars spent energies pondering that scene through the decade.

The perspective of the Oxford scholar informs surveys of the   17:10
American scene. He tried out the whole range of theories to account for the apparent revival of religion in the United States: parental attitudes, war experience, religion and age, sex differences, individual personality traits, mental disorder, marriage, social class, sociological factors, minority groups, urban-rural differences, social disorganization, economic prosperity: the whole catalog gave him little that was conclusive. So he tried out some signals relating to his own specialty: "Theories of Religious Behaviour and Belief." Argyle's subheads included "Religion as a Response to Frustration," "The Theory that God is a Fantasy

Father-figure," "The Obsessional Neurosis Theory," and "Cognitive Need Theories." Some of these helped explain why people were religious, but few helped indicate why Americans were, or saw themselves to be, more so.

17:11   "Social Disorganization": that might be the cause! But Argyle dropped that explanation as soon as he picked it up: "There is little evidence that religious activity varies with the degree of social disorganization." Glock himself, with partner Rodney Stark, reached instead for the deprivation theory, citing a sociologist named Kingsley Davis, who gave a summary: "The greater his [the person's] disappointment in this life, the greater his faith in the next. Thus the existence of goals beyond this world serves to compensate people for frustrations they inevitably experience in striving to reach socially acquired and socially valuable ends." But Argyle, looking on from Britain, dismissed that notion, too: "There is very little relation between religion and economic prosperity and if anything there is more religious activity during times of prosperity." Since America was becoming "the affluent society," according to the deprivation theory it should be seeing less religious interest, not more.

17:12   Most puzzling was the social-class scene. Argyle almost had to overlook the renascent fundamentalist, evangelical, Pentecostal, and conservative church movements that contributed to talk of the revival in America. He thought the expanding middle class and the middle-class churches were the main beneficiaries, observing that "liberalism has become more widespread in the U.S.A. since 1900, and that it is more common in the churches of the upper and upper middle class" than elsewhere. That assessment forced him to rule out frustration theories. "In a sense," he concluded, "liberals are simply less religious" than the other types he considered, but they did continue to hold to certain basic beliefs and humanitarian concerns. Therefore, he added, "one possible explanation" of the religious revival across class lines was that "liberal churches primarily reflect the outlook and ideology of the prosperous middle class, expressed in terms of traditional religion, and combined with a good deal of purely secular activity." Therefore they were instruments of a different sort of class experience and need. Following such a conclusion, one would expect revival talk to be a virtual monopoly of the standard-brand and mainstream churches, where the other trends Argyle noticed were so strong.

17:13   The most notable promoter of the revivalist impulse and best-known user of the term, however, did not speak out of the sphere of those churches: evangelist Billy Graham also was remarking on the revival. Of course, it is the business of revivalists to predict revivals. Evangelists always have the difficult task of pointing to a people's state of spiritual decline that demands revival and then proclaiming that revival has begun with them. One year before the Niebuhr article with its generalizing about revival, Graham was quoted in *Time* magazine voicing a standard particular claim: "We are standing on the verge of a great national revival, an old-fashioned, heaven-sent, Holy Ghost revival that will sweep the nation." While Graham dealt with a species of the revival genus that Niebuhr, Glock and Stark, and Argyle were noticing, he drew on the theories of disorganization and deprivation to get launched. "The human mind cannot cope with the problems that we are wrestling with today." When intellectual leaders admit they do not know answers, and when masses in the street find this out, "then they are going to turn somewhere. They will turn to all sorts of escapisms. Some will turn to alcohol. Others will turn to religion in the want of security and peace—something to hold onto." Graham thus introduced some spiritual themes; he was an agent of revival but not a reasoned analyst of it. His critic Reinhold Niebuhr better serves in that role.

"The evidences of a contemporary revival of religion are not   17:14 conclusive," said the dialectical-minded Niebuhr in the *New York Times Magazine* piece. The Union Theological Seminary professor noticed two types; the first was Billy Graham's, with its accent on mass conversions, aroused emotions, elicited commitments, all now back on the scene in more visible form than they had been since Billy Sunday's prime, two generations before. Niebuhr cared more, however, about evidence that in the culture at large there was "a receptivity toward the message of the historic faiths which is in marked contrast to the indifference or hostility of past decades." In that culture, revival was moving far beyond the sawdust trail and the tents of the Bible Belt. Niebuhr pointed to prominent writers, artists, and cultural leaders who were converting to religious faith. In the academic communities where he was at home there was an increase of interest in religious problems. "For obvious reasons the 'secular' spirit of the age" had been most pronounced there, but all of a sudden colleges and universities were themselves creating or enlarging departments of religious studies. Before World War II their courses had been apologetic or defensive, timid surveys of "the Bible as literature." But now teachers and students plumbed scriptures "guided by a conviction of the importance and relevance of the 'message' of the Bible."

17:15   Niebuhr had to cover some of the bases touched by sociologists Glock and Stark and psychologist Argyle. Maybe the judgment that there was a national revival, he thought, rested on an a priori notion that this was an age of crisis and that religion was expected to be appealing at such a time. Niebuhr joined some critics in connecting the idea of revival to concepts like "failure of nerve," "hysteria," or "escapism" and then found some signs of these all around, notably in the renewed response to mass evangelists like Billy Graham. But Niebuhr speculated that the secular worldlings who analyzed the cultural moment too readily dismissed faith by their act of seeing it as nothing but escapism from tragic realities. Such criticisms, he charged, came with ill grace from a culture that offered every type of secular salvation and then could not deliver on its offerings. A prudential culture like the American one of that moment all too readily spoke of escape in respect to experiences which provide "a sense of life's meeting above and beyond the chaos of the day," and as such might become a resource "for doing our social and historic duties." In that sentence the theologian almost sounded like Billy Graham.

17:16   Niebuhr argued that in some senses there never were irreligious ages or individuals: "Every age and every person has some sense of the meaning of life. That is its or his religion." In the previous century the religion of the age had tried to deny sin and promote belief in progress. Now that faith had failed. "From the standpoint of the historic faiths, an age of crisis is more explicitly 'religious' in the sense that it tends to refute the quasi-religious schemes of meaning by which men have lived in times of stability and ease," he noted. The "so-called 'credulities' of the great historic faiths are really quite sophisticated compared with the credulities of an 'age of reason,'" because the latter were superficial, and they promised too much. Among these faiths was Marxism; Niebuhr remembered that three decades before, when he was getting his start, the "socially sensitive members" of the generation had been "in revolt against the social irrelevance of the religious faith of their fathers." But they made a mistake of turning an economic program into what he called a "scheme of salvation." Out of their venture came cruelties and fanaticisms, not utopia but "a real hell—on earth."

17:17   "Some aspects of the current religious 'revival,'" of course, would be "no more than manifestations of the general hysteria and disillusionment" of the times. And other aspects, Niebuhr added, would of course be irrelevant. But he was curiously upbeat: "Those of us who are devotees of the great historic faiths have the right to hope and believe that there will be aspects of the revival which will represent a profounder awareness of the depth and height of our human existence, of the mystery and meaning of the divine power which bears it." Those dimensions of the revival, he hoped, would contribute to the "renewals of life which are possible if destructions and frustrations are appropriated with contrition rather than bitterness." He did not neglect the search for international concord when he envisioned what a revival of profound faith could achieve: "Such a religious faith could contribute to the 'healing of the nations.'"

Niebuhr often drew upon the broad experience of ordinary   17:18
people, but as a theologian he spoke most of the time to cultural elites, and he may have been more concerned with expressions by intellectuals and literary figures than were pollsters or evangelists. The evidence from them was indeed ambiguous and often self-contradictory, he knew, but Niebuhr could adduce some documentation when he spoke of the concept of "failure of nerve" among these intellectuals. Earlier in 1950, the very year in which he was writing, for instance, a prominent journal of the left, *Partisan Review,* invited contributors from the presumably most secular, most religiously alienated sectors of the culture to participate in a symposium titled "Religion and the Intellectuals." Jewish sociologist and theologian Will Herberg five years later looked back on the venture by twenty-nine writers, "most of them of radical background," and ran up the score. As he saw it, half were still hostile to religion, five gave explicit testimony to faith, and ten were friendly but remained uncommitted. Herberg quoted Asher Byrnes, who reviewed the articles which became a book: "The startling thing about the collection is the size of the middle group, the fellow travelers of faith." Byrnes believed that such fellow travelers who now were "mixing and merging with those for whom faith has a much deeper meaning" were "increasingly giving the tone to the more advanced intellectual life of the nation."

Herberg was struck with the importance of the *Partisan Review*   17:19
symposium and elaborated in a footnote. That that journal "should have come around to running such a symposium, in which the attitude of intellectuals to religion is regarded as something susceptible of more than one kind of answer," was of real significance.

Some years earlier its symposium on a similar set of subjects had been titled "The Failure of Nerve." Back then it was "devoted exclusively to the lamentations and explanation of anti-religious intellectuals confronted by the rising tide of religious interest among the cultural elite." Now Herberg could quote the editorial introduction to the new symposium: "One of the most significant tendencies of our time has been the turn to religion among intellectuals and the growing disfavor with which secular attitudes and perspectives are now regarded in not a few circles that lay claim to the leadership of culture." He stopped short of quoting further confirming words: "There is no doubt that the number of intellectuals professing religious sympathies, beliefs, or doctrines is greater now than it was ten or twenty years ago, and that this number is continually increasing or becoming more articulate." The editors tried to put the trend in perspective: "the first decades of this century begin to look like triumphant naturalism; and if the present tendency continues, the mid-century years may go down in history as the years of conversion and return."

17:20   H. Stuart Hughes, an astute observer of intellectual trends, one year later concurred with the *Partisan Review*. Ten or fifteen years ago "no self-respecting 'enlightened' intellectual would have been caught dead with a religious interpretation of anything." Only Catholics thought in those terms—Hughes implied that no Catholics must have been enlightened intellectuals back then—"plus a scattering of Protestants whom we dismissed as harmless eccentrics." The rest of "us" were either " 'idealistic' Socialist-radicals or skeptical, hard-boiled Freudian-Paretans." Being of any other sort and thus holding any other attitude would have been "a betrayal of the avant-garde." Now students were sending different signals up to their college teachers, and Hughes had to conclude: "The avant-garde is becoming old-fashioned; religion is now the latest thing."

17:21   It was Will Herberg who, to use his own term, now best engaged in "mixing and merging" the worlds of intellectual fellow travelers and popular travelers on the road to revival, the worlds of elites and common folk alike. In 1955, in the high years of the talk about religious revival, he published *Protestant-Catholic-Jew,* a description of the current ethos. While by no means all who read that description agreed with Herberg's main explanatory thesis, they regarded the account itself as generally reliable. The author was not off the point when he noticed almost instantly after its appearance, and not without pride and glee: "It is obvious that the book is making something of a sensation." He claimed to have intended no more than that it should "contribute to a better understanding of both religion and society in mid-twentieth century America." Herberg reached further than had Argyle and others who were merely observing the new prosperity of churches and synagogues. He was instead engrossed with the broader role of religion in the One Nation, Indivisible, that had survived the world war and was now in the midst of the Cold War. Religious renewal belonged now to the whole community: "it is the American Way of Life that supplies American society with an 'overarching sense of unity' amid conflict." Religious groups had once been the intolerant agencies. But, he claimed, now "it is the American Way of Life about which Americans are admittedly and unashamedly 'intolerant.'" He saw citizens assigning this way of life the status of religion, of faith. "It is the American Way of Life that provides the framework in terms of which the crucial values of American existence are couched." To a convert from Marxism to prophetic Judaism, this apparently superficial attachment had to look idolatrous, but there it was: "By every realistic criterion the American Way of Life is the operative faith of the American people."

Herberg came to these observations and judgments partly in autobiographical terms. He was himself one of those intellectuals who started reading Niebuhr as part of a turn toward a new set of questions. In fact, Niebuhr could have used Herberg as Exhibit A to illustrate the company of those who once had made a faith out of Marxism. In 1947 and 1948 Herberg confessed that in an earlier day Marxism had been "a religion, an ethic, and a theology; a vast, all-embracing doctrine of man and the universe, a passionate faith endowing life with meaning, vindicating the aims of the movement, idealizing its activities, and guaranteeing its ultimate triumph." Economics, of course, was "the invisible god of the Marxist faith." But it started to fail Herberg at a certain point, and "vaguely and almost fearfully," he said, he came to the "stunning realization" that he was having his "first authentically religious experience." Perhaps, he thought for a time, biblical themes would make him a better Marxist. That did not happen. Momentarily he dabbled with Catholicism and then with Niebuhrian Protestantism; but Niebuhr, Herberg claimed, urged that he renew his ancestral Judaism. The seeker read the great modern Jewish thinkers Franz Rosenzweig and Martin Buber. Then, shunning Zionism as a form of nationalism and thus a perversion of biblical faith, he identified with Jews who saw themselves as being a "People of the Book."

17:22

Such Judaism was a sign of an "already emerging" *post*-modern mind, secular modernity having failed.

17:23   By 1951, with *Judaism and Modern Man,* Herberg showed that his conversion was decisive. Niebuhr called the book a likely "milestone in the religious thought of America." While Herberg was not a professional theologian, significant numbers of the professionals in Judaism did take note. Herberg employed Niebuhrian realism to begin a long move beyond Niebuhr toward the political and cultural right. Along the way he chided other ex-communists who did not move as far or as fast from their old identifications as he did. Eventually a self-described "neoconservative," he signaled the drama of his change early on when he praised Whittaker Chambers, an ex-communist now anticommunist, who fingered a favorite of many liberals, Alger Hiss, in the most dramatic loyalty issue of the day. Herberg joined the lecture circuit, picking up impressions from audiences wherever he went. Having made his living in labor organization and journalism on the old left, he now looked for a spot in the academy and eventually joined the faculty of the largely Methodist Drew University School of Theology. Like Niebuhr, Herberg appeared to be one of the last rare academics who made it through a theological school career without a Ph.D. degree, though he claimed to have had one. As he was making his way, he turned his back on his old company. To justify this turn, he quoted Herbert W. Schneider, an authority on the subject: he found but a "dwindling band of radical secularists" and only a "few remaining militant atheists or freethinkers" in the cultural elites.

17:24   Herberg was especially attuned to the voice of President Eisenhower as someone who read the culture well. But Eisenhower had *under*stated the case when he said that "contrary to what many people think, the percentage of our population belonging to churches [has] steadily increased." Herberg corrected the president: "In a hundred years, that percentage has multiplied more than three times." Here amateur sociologist Herberg could pile on statistics. Sunday schools, for example, were booming. From 1947 to 1949 Sunday schools had grown by 3 percent. By 1953, 35,389,000 children and adults were said to be on the rolls, and Sunday school became a weekend event for the masses. As never before, congregations were building new churches and synagogues. A grateful body of Methodist bishops in 1954 collectively sighed: "A new spirit has fallen upon our people," and Herberg was there to listen for such sounds. Clergy now had a good name. Pollster Elmo Roper found that 40 percent of the people thought ministers were "doing most good" and were most to be trusted among the professions. Roper concluded that no other group "came anywhere near matching the prestige and pulling power of the men who are the ministers of God."

If the American Way of Life mattered more than mere church   17:25
statistics, Herberg had to keep his eye on public life, on politics. Only one of 95 senators at the time reported no religious affiliation. Foreign observers were right: "in no other modern industrial state does organized religion play a greater role" than in the United States. And with Niebuhr and Hughes he had to keep his eye on intellectuals. Herberg let Herbert W. Schneider do some of his spotting on this scene: as recently as 1920, said Schneider, "faith was taken as a sign of intellectual backwardness or imbecility." But now "that age has disappeared almost without a trace, and the generation that has arisen since finds it well-nigh impossible to imagine what those days were like, so remote from our consciousness have they become." Herberg similarly invoked London's *Times Literary Supplement,* where a writer had argued that in America "the intellectual climate for religious thinking and the social climate for religious living" were "more congenial than they were in the twenties and thirties." Herberg with pleasure cited *Publishers Weekly* as its editors talked about trends in 1954: "The theme of religion dominates the non-fiction best sellers in 1953, as it has in many of the preceding years." Religious Christmas cards were popular. People read Søren Kierkegaard, Jacques Maritain, Reinhold Niebuhr, Martin Buber, Paul Tillich, Nicolas Berdyaev, and Simone Weil, and Herberg liked their tastes. That religion in general was on the upswing was clear from evidence "unequivocal beyond all possibilities of error."

Herberg's main energies went into reflecting on the American   17:26
Way of Life in the One Nation, Indivisible. This was interesting, and indeed problematic, because he saw this nation religiously divided three ways, into Protestant, Catholic, and Jewish subcultures. He addressed this situation by concentrating on the issues of identity and belonging. Returning to an old metaphor, the Jewish thinker argued that America had not turned out to be a melting pot for identities and a merger for belongers. It had instead three melting pots, "three great sub-communities." Therefore, "to find a place in American society increasingly means to place oneself in one or another" of these broadly defined communities. He agreed with the then immensely popular sociologist David Riesman that Americans were "other-directed." They took signals not from their

traditions or inner strivings but from their peers. Religion helped them become "adjusted" to the surroundings: "being religious and joining a church is, under contemporary American conditions, a fundamental way of 'adjusting' and 'belonging.'" In the spirit of the times Herberg additionally saw citizens responding to the "demonic threat of Communist totalitarianism," the fear of the hydrogen bomb, and the "contemporary crisis of Western civilization." In the face of these, religion became "synonymous with peace," which everyone wanted.

17:27   From the global scene Herberg turned to the local and intimate zones. He noted the sudden rise of the birth rates; the postwar "baby boom" had begun. It was in daily occupations that religion helped people ward off the "depersonalizing pressures of contemporary life." There, Herberg further observed, they found an "inexpugnable citadel for the self in a world in which personal authenticity is threatened on every side." Having said good-bye to science and progress as saviors, humans still needed "faith, a total, all-embracing faith, for living." And religion rescued them from having to come up with the satisfying explanation that also eluded Argyle and all others: "Religion, touching as it does man's ultimate relation, in the end escapes all explanatory categories."

17:28   Still, if religion was elusive, belonging was not. To address the theme of affiliation, Herberg's main and still controversial theory came into play. America, he reminded readers, was a nation of immigrants. Many millions of citizens were heirs of people who had arrived in the decades before 1924, when immigration was drastically reduced by law. Herberg snatched a line from historian Marcus Lee Hanson's observation about the generations of immigrants: "What the son wishes to forget, the grandson wishes to remember." Children, he observed, cannot remember or recover the setting or language of grandparents. The most portable and revivable aspect of the grandparental world was religion, and to this feature of the older life the grandchild could return. This return benefited religious institutions, promoted adherence and affiliation, and bred "conformism"—a big theme in cultural analysis of the 1950s. Now Herberg claimed he could explain "the characteristically American device of 'interfaith' endeavor," which in his eyes was "not secularistic or indifferentist but in its own way quite religious." So "to be a Protestant, a Catholic, or a Jew are today the alternative ways of being an American." Herberg overlooked the great differences within Protestantism. African Americans, though they numbered in the millions, did not show up in his book, and the conservative churches received attention only in a few lines. Herberg's accounts of Judaism paid but the slightest attention to Israel and the Holocaust; its "suburbanization" was his theme. Herberg may have overworked his third-generation thesis, but reviewers, except for some professional sociologists who dismissed him as an intuitive but amateur essayist, tended to agree with Nathan Glazer: Herberg's analysis of the "religion of religion" and the "religion without faith" was brilliant.

Report piled upon report following Herberg's precedent and often quoted him. The most notable of those studies coming from the growing academic world was *The Surge of Piety in America* (1958), by A. Roy Eckardt. The Lehigh University professor, having had three years more time during which to gain perspective, backed off from the normative judgment that religious revival was under way. He contented himself with the safer and probably more accurate notion that there had been "a manifest upsurge of *interest* in religion." One new note came with Eckardt's observation of "some signs that the crest of the recent flood of religious interest may already have passed" and that the new piety "is becoming a little old." Eckardt joined all the other observers in making cautious use of church statistics, all of which were "up." He spent energies watching politicians, entertainers, and advertisers vie to sidle up most readily to the religious cause. For an example, the group named Religion in American Life had (or dared show) no interest in particular churches or doctrines. It was part of a mass endorsing movement that would "emphasize the importance of all religious institutions as the foundations of American life and . . . urge all Americans to attend and support the church or synagogue of their individual choice." Choice was becoming an ever more important element.

With many other theologically informed analysts, Eckardt disdained many signs of popular religion and was uneasy about others. The identification of American religion with an anticommunist cause or the defense of free-enterprise capitalism (through groups like Spiritual Mobilization) was worrisome: the god of such folk religion had to be "on the side of certain persons or a particular community or a particular nation." Eckardt cited F. Ernest Johnson of the National Council of Churches, who pointed to a paradox in the American pattern. Religion was encouraging radical individualism and was drawing upon elements of it in the American psyche. But some compensatory impulses were also at work, born of "the necessity of co-operation in implementing the values that

17:29

17:30

support American society as a collective entity." In this sphere idolatry became the great temptation.

17:31   Many sociologists were less sure than theologians or journalists that there was a statistically observable and unambiguous revival. Seymour Martin Lipset, for example, stressed that America had always been religious, so he saw no changes in *formal* religious affiliation and practice. But in the eyes of Herberg, people like Lipset paid too little attention to changes in cultural tone. "There Is a Religious Revival!" he thundered. Charles Y. Glock, who was most cautious and precise about defining the elements of a revival, stood between the two. He faulted clergy, church administrators, theologians, and journalists who made too much of the secularization hypothesis. They paid too much attention to the fate of the religion that went on in specifically religious institutions and consequently overlooked the ways the culture in general bore religious meanings. But Glock found selective changes in the religious temper going on. Yes, he admitted, "there has been post-war growth in religious affiliation and observance," but it was accompanied by "an increase of interest in ideas and commodities having a religious content." Sociologist Lipset found less doctrinal rigidity than before, along with a growth in tolerance, a readiness shown by more Americans "to accept the validity of faiths other than their own." Then Lipset crossed his fingers again in caution, sure that something was going on but reluctant to give social-scientific endorsement to notions that were too generalized.

17:32   A popular revival deserved popular notices. Plenty of these were provided; they are typified by journalist Claire Cox in *New-Time Religion.* The author took a roll call of those thought to be indicators of the culture, meanwhile throwing in some of the clichés that had been developed by the cultural critics of the decade; they deserve entry into the record: "The Organization Man, the Man in the Gray Flannel Suit, the White Collar Girl, the Working Mother, the Suburban Housewife, the Farmer, the Retired Bank Clerk, the Factory Hand, the Widow, the Status Seeker, the Egghead, all," Cox said, "are four-square behind the upsurge in religious interest." She also catalogued names for the event: "It has been labeled a 'revival,' a 'renewal of interest', an 'upsurge of piety,' 'a spiritual aspirin tablet,' 'religiosity,' 'corporateness,' 'a cult of reassurance,' 'faith in faith,' and even a 20th Century reformation. Whatever 'it' is," Cox judged, "religion is fashionable beyond a doubt."

17:33   Critics in the spirit of Seymour Martin Lipset and Charles Y.

Glock would have grumbled about the imprecision and the breathlessness of Cox's account, but there were good reasons for them to agree with her summary that "superlatives are almost endless when it comes to describing the big boom in religion." "Never," she wrote, "has religion had it so good, to rework an election campaign slogan used successfully by President Eisenhower." And "never has religion been so institutionalized, so conspicuous, so public. Never has churchgoing been so acceptable, so much 'the thing to do.'" Cox's sense of the times met general approval: "This new-time religion has taken shape since World War II." She looked at Europe and compared what she saw with her own nation: "Nowhere else is religion prospering as in America." Everything following that judgment confirmed the first line of her book: "There is a new-time religion in the land." Because so many people believed that to be the case, in a way, there was.

18

"A Civic Religion of the American Way of Life"

18:1   T̲he "new-time religion" in the land had to do with the nation itself. Of course, believers practiced their old-time religions in old and new ways in church and synagogue, at home and work and military camp. But after the Second World War and during the Cold War, the new-time religion of Protestants, Catholics, Jews, and many secularists was in new ways a religion not only of the American Way of Life but of America itself. Although such a religious outlook and practice had a prehistory reaching back for centuries, the emergence itself turned out to be a peculiar mid-century development. In 1955 the Jewish theologian Will Herberg, while busy defining the American world of Protestants, Catholics, and Jews, worked his way through a thesaurus of terms to give an appropriate name to what he was finding. His book *Protestant-Catholic-Jew* included notions of a "common faith," "democracy as religion," "the democratic faith," and "the common religion," among others. Such a faith or religion was inevitable, he thought, and had its creative side. But representing as it did "a radical break with the fundamental presuppositions of both Judaism and Christianity," he thought that to those who professed biblical faith "it must appear as a particularly insidious kind of idolatry." Herberg settled on the term *civic faith* or a "civic religion of the American Way of Life" to describe this.

18:2   With all others who spelled out this civic faith or this civic reli-

294

gion, Herberg found its chief priest in the person of a Cold War–era United States chief executive, Dwight D. Eisenhower. Should historians of American religion use presidencies to mark periods of development in the faith of the public? Ordinarily one might answer no. No one speaks of the Harding-Coolidge-Hoover-era civic religion, and few would write of Roosevelt's or Truman's elaboration of civic faith as representing a period of special development. But something new came in 1952, and it is certainly proper to speak of "the Eisenhower era" as a period and its fabrications as an incident in the unfolding of American creeds, liturgies, and practices. This contention may seem strange and hard to sustain, since the much-liked "Ike," the easily victorious general-turned-president for two terms between 1952 and 1960, seemed hardly a charismatic sort, not a likely exemplar of a faith. Reporters liked to collect his bland and meandering sayings—for instance, "Things are more like they are now than they have ever been before."

Herberg was not wasting his time or ruining his focus, however,   18:3
when listening to Eisenhower's use of the bully pulpit that was the White House or when watching the thirty-fourth president meander through civic rituals. Herberg, himself turning ever more politically conservative through these years, was not offended by the administration of Ike. But he had to be wary when he read the Republican National Committee's official resolution of February 17, 1955, which said that the president "in every sense of the word, is not only the political leader, but the spiritual leader of our times." *The* spiritual leader. Such a fusion of political and spiritual leadership in the person of an elected leader in a republic, Herberg said, was "in accord with neither the American democratic idea nor the tradition of Jewish-Christian faith." Yet few seemed to mind, and many welcomed that fusion. The political exploitation of the "President's religion" aroused little comment. If religion was the "spiritual" side of being an American, Herberg asked, "why should not the President of the United States be hailed as the 'spiritual leader of our times'?"

America's spiritual leader could have gotten nowhere had the   18:4
president come across to anyone as a rival to the leadership of church and synagogue. Even a popular president would have been in trouble had his faith been perceived by ordinary citizens as a competitor of the faiths professed by men, women, and children in the new suburbs, the changing cities, the old-time towns and country. Herberg even reported on Eisenhower's delighting in and

bragging about church religion. In 1954 the president told the Evanston, Illinois, assembly of the World Council of Churches, and thus religious leaders far beyond America, that "contrary to what many people think, the percentage of our population belonging to churches [has] steadily increased. In a hundred years, that percentage has multiplied more than three times." Yet Eisenhower was not needed in the crowded rank of ministers, priests, and rabbis within formal religious institutions and organized religion. His priesthood was part of his role as leader of a "crusade," as he called it, against "godless Communism" abroad and "corruption and materialism" at home. Not since Woodrow Wilson had such language of crusading idealism in the name of faith been heard in the White House. "The things that make us proud to be Americans are of the soul and of the spirit," Eisenhower declared. And being American, for a president who was baptized and who joined a church for the first time after having been elected, meant being a theist. For the American Legion's "Back to God" campaign in 1955 Eisenhower argued that "Recognition of the Supreme Being is the first, the most basic, expression of Americanism. Without God, there could be no American form of government, nor an American way of life."

18:5   Should theism be a part of the law of the land? What council could provide the creed or code to spell it out? The final arbiter was the United States Supreme Court, speaking for the judicial branch of government. And define it did. Ironically, it was this Court that for a moment at mid-century had made a theistic reference in the very years when many church members thought it was turning too humanistic. But just as Eisenhower was broadening Woodrow Wilson's notion that America was a "Christian nation" to his own claim that it was a "religious nation," so the Supreme Court was also instinctively widening its claims. In 1931 in *United States v. Macintosh* their predecessors had written for a last time, "We are a Christian people." Now in 1952 a dictum of Justice William O. Douglas, seen as a humanist and secularist by Court critics, was included in a ruling concerning "released-time" religious instruction and public schools, *Zorach v. Clauson:* "We are a religious people whose institutions presuppose a Supreme Being."

18:6   In many respects, however, that line in *Zorach* was misleading, because the Court itself was moving away from a custodial or priestly role during the Eisenhower years. Thus another 1952 ruling, in *Kedroff v. St. Nicholas Cathedral,* gave supporters of civic religion little to go on. Two factions of the Russian Orthodox church were battling over the use of the Russian Orthodox Cathedral in New York. The patriarch of Moscow and his American followers had a claim on the sanctuary, while another element, split from this jurisdiction after 1917, also wanted a share. There must have been a temptation in the Cold War for the Court to rule against the heritage of the Moscow faction. Yet Justice Stanley Reed argued for the majority that it would violate the separation of church and state for the United States government to interfere with the patriarchate's historic claims, even though there might be some risks along the way of the infiltration of "atheistic or subversive influences." And Justice Frankfurter reinforced this notion of risk: "Under our Constitution it is not open to the governments of this Union to reinforce the loyalty of their citizens by deciding who is the true exponent of their religion."

Another instance that would have given the Court an occasion   18:7
to decide on democratic dogma affecting religion was *Burstyn v. Wilson*. This dealt with a case involving a film by Roberto Rosselini. In it, an Italian girl, impregnated by a stranger, confuses him with Joseph and herself with the Virgin Mary. The New York Board of Regents in 1950 found an exhibitor of the film guilty of sacrilege. When the New York appellate courts agreed, the Supreme Court took up the case. Justices Tom Clark and Felix Frankfurter agonized their way around the concept of *sacrilege*. Then they decided, in Frankfurter's words, that what might be considered sacrilege could not be the business of a society that separated church and state: "Conduct and beliefs dear to one may seem the rankest 'sacrilege' to another." Clark showed that the Court was recognizing the ever-growing pluralism in American life: "It is not the business of government in our nation to suppress real or imagined attacks upon a particular religious doctrine, whether they appear in publications, speeches, or motion pictures." Orthodoxy could not be coerced. The Court unanimously declared that censorship of the sort involved in the case of *Burstyn v. Wilson* was unconstitutional.

Dissents by Justices Hugo Black and Robert H. Jackson re-   18:8
vealed uneasiness with what Douglas had said in *Zorach v. Clauson*. Yes, Black agreed, Americans in 1789 and 1952 alike were "a religious people." But the First Amendment was designed to prevent the government from involving itself with religion and thus jeopardizing both the equality and the freedom all citizens now enjoyed. "The choice of all" to worship, they said, "has been as

free as the choice of those who answered the call to worship moved only by the music of the old Sunday morning church bells." The spiritual mind has been free. But "the First Amendment has lost much if the religious follower and the atheist are no longer to be judicially regarded as entitled to equal justice under law." Jackson's dissent was less romantic, more militant. A religious person himself, who sent his children to privately supported church schools, he was angered at the implication that to challenge the Court on this subject was an "antireligious, atheistic, or agnostic" act. "My evangelistic brethren confuse an objection to compulsion with an objection to religion." So Jackson was worried: "The day that this country ceases to be free for irreligion it will cease to be free for religion—except for the sect that can win political power." Religion had to belong to the voluntary realm, encouraged by rhetoric or example. This in his own way Eisenhower was prepared to supply.

18:9   What other agency than the White House or the Supreme Court could have set forth that creed; what company of theologians might have codified that dogma? The Congress was the best-poised candidate to act in that way, but the First Amendment of the United States Constitution certainly gave Congress no license to do so. To be sure, there had been sporadic attempts from time to time, naturally revived in the Eisenhower era, to amend the Constitution to correct what some thought had been an oversight in the vision of the nation's founders. Vermont senator Ralph Flanders tried to give Christian specificity to the civic faith by a constitutional amendment that would recognize the authority and law of Jesus Christ. For a time during the Cold War government postal cancellation stamps asked citizens to "Pray for Peace," without directing to whom to pray. But in the years when not Christianity but interfaith, specifically tri-faith religion was coming to the center, the proposal of New Jersey congressman Peter Rodino seemed to make more sense. He wanted citizens to "join together, Protestant, Jew, and Catholic," in his case to support a theistic addition to the Pledge of Allegiance to the flag. And Michigan congressman Louis C. Rabaut was appropriately vague when he argued that it was good to show "our dependence upon God" and "our faith in His support," a demonstration motivated by "the ever increasing attacks upon us by forces of godlessness and atheism."

18:10   Though the Christian Amendment got little backing in the Senate, one legislative affirmation of theism moved faith from the persuasive to the coercive zones of life. On the thousands of pages of

the *Congressional Record,* one could find frequent courtesy in-
clusions of religious material; many references to God cropped up
in the speeches and writings of lawmakers. But only an event in
1954 made God a part of the law of the land. A nation which had
stressed to itself and others during the war and the Cold War that it
was One Nation, Indivisible, had coerced the saluting of the flag,
along with a pledge of allegiance to it. Jehovah's Witnesses early
in the war years had had a hard time avoiding that salute and
pledge. Still, something seemed to be missing: God. The original
pledge had appeared on September 8, 1892, in the *Youth's Companion:* "I pledge allegiance to my flag and to the Republic for
which it stands; one nation indivisible with liberty and justice for
all." A former Baptist minister, Francis Bellamy, had drafted it to
promote the four-hundredth anniversary observance of Columbus's
discovery of America. In 1945, during World War II, Congress saw
fit to recognize a by-then slightly revised version. During debates
over Jehovah's Witnesses dissent, in *West Virginia State Board of
Education v. Barnette,* Justice Frankfurter resorted to casuistry
when he argued that the flag salute was not akin to oath tests in
government, which would have been simply unconstitutional. It
differed, he said, because saluting the flag did not suppress belief
or curb it. In *Barnette,* students were exempt from saying those
words. But later rulings argued that teachers were not exempt from
leading the pledge. That would not have been much of a problem
to any teacher outside groups like Jehovah's Witnesses, because
the pledge was in no formal sense religious. Until 1954.

It may seem strange to find a secular Congress supplementing a   18:11
pledge invented decades before by a religious person in a religious
magazine, but few things done by the 83rd Congress were more
popular than changing the Pledge. On February 7, 1954, the Reverend George M. Docherty, pastor to many in Congress, preached
at New York Avenue Presbyterian Church in Washington, on the
topic of the pledge. His tones reflected the mood of the Cold War.
He conjured images of "little Muscovites" who could "repeat a
similar pledge to their hammer-and-sickle flag," since they also
claimed to support liberty and justice in *their* republic. Insert the
words "under God" into the sacrosanct American pledge, he argued, and you would have a distinctive one, not utterable by those
Muscovites. Living "under God" was a "definitive factor in the
American way of life." The preacher surmised that some "honest
atheists" in the United States might have some trouble with this,
but then he gave his own peculiar reading of the First Amendment:

"It is not, and never was meant to be, a separation of religion and life." He went on to rule out atheists from first-class citizenship: "An atheistic American is a contradiction in terms." It is important to note that Docherty was no extremist; he spoke from the center of the core of the mainstream establishment. In fact, Mr. and Mrs. Eisenhower were in the congregation, and that evening the president joined some Protestant, Catholic, and Jewish clerics on the radio to say, "Whatever our individual church, whatever our personal creed, in our fundamental faith we are all one. Together we thank the Power that has made and preserved us a nation." Churches climbed aboard a cause that brought some people in Congress more mail than they had had for any other legislation. The Unitarian Ministers' Association of Boston was almost alone in sending resolutions opposing the change, but few listened to them at a time when veterans' organizations, newspaper chains, fraternal organizations, and labor unions were "getting religion" and joining the cause. The Unitarians said the change was "an invasion of religious liberty," but this was not the kind of case most other religious groups wanted to challenge.

18:12   Motion toward law had begun, and Representative Rabaut, eager to be on the popular side, seconded the motion. "You may argue from dawn to dusk about differing political, economic, and social systems," he said, "but the fundamental issue which is the unbridgeable gap between America and Communist Russia is a belief in Almighty God." Rabaut had introduced a bill to insert those words a year earlier, in April 1953, but no one noticed until the Presbyterian pulpiteer took up the issue. Similarly ignored had been sixteen other like resolutions in the House. Now Michigan senator Homer Ferguson picked up the cause and sent a resolution to the Senate on May 11, 1954. Rabaut resented the Senate's aim to get credit for godliness and presented his own bill. The House was so eager to claim credit that it broke protocol and passed Rabaut's proposal, which differed from Ferguson's version by only a comma. Flag Day, June 14, was near at hand, so Ferguson asked his colleagues to overlook the House's bad manners this one time. Thereupon the Senate passed the House resolution unanimously on June 8, and the bill went to the Eisenhower White House for ready signature. The president saw here a charter for daily proclamation by schoolchildren of the "dedication of our Nation and our people to the Almighty." Here was a sign of "our country's true meaning," an affirmation of "the transcendence of religious faith in America's heritage and future." As always, those "little Muscovites" were in mind as a foil, because they were pictured doing their pledging, but in the context of the "materialistic philosophy of life" of Communism.

Rabaut reminded the people: "You and I know that the Union   18:13
of Soviet Socialist Republics would not, and could not, while supporting the philosophy of communism, place in its patriotic ritual · an acknowledgment that their nation existed 'under God.'" And Senator Ferguson said that the passage of a resolution inserting the two words would enable the United States to "strike another blow against those who would enslave us." Warming up to his task, he reinforced the claim: "I believe this modification of the pledge is important because it highlights one of the real fundamental differences between the free world and the Communist world." And Louisiana congressman Overton Brooks relished the way the new pledge would show how belief in God was the one thing distinguishing "free people of the Western world from the rabid Communist." The change in the pledge showed that "we in effect declare openly that we denounce the pagan doctrine of communism and declare 'under God' in favor of free government and a free world." Rabaut and Ferguson made peace between themselves and the houses of Congress for this holy cause, and, after hurried passage of the legislation, together read the new pledge with the words "under God" on the Capitol steps on Flag Day. CBS carried the proceedings so the nation could hear it. Adding "In God We Trust" to the national motto in 1956 was a logical follow-up. Not a single member of the House or the Senate voted against the idea.

Will Herberg cited philosophers and scholars who had pro-   18:14
moted attempts to relate religion to democracy on liberal terms, but who knew of them? Yet Americans heard and supported Eisenhower. In fact, ex-presidents now could also be invoked. Herbert Hoover in these Cold War times called for "a definite, spiritual mobilization of the nations who believe in God against this tide of Red agnosticism." He was even ready to turn the nation's back on the United Nations, because of its religious and nonreligious mixtures, and link up with the God-fearing nations: "And in rejecting an atheistic other world, I am confident that the Almighty God will be with us." Such a sentiment, perhaps held by the Quaker president in early Depression days, had not been invoked back then— it had not been needed. Only now in the face of internal insecurity and external threat did the nation have to reassure itself at home and define itself abroad with the "under God" reference. President Harry S. Truman had said of communism that "it denies the exis-

tence of God and, wherever it can, stamps out the worship of God," while "our religious faith gives us the answer to the false beliefs of Communism." And he used "chosen people" language that had recently been shunned by his predecessor. "I have the feeling that God has created us and brought us to our present position of power and strength for some great purpose." But Truman, though better informed in religion and a faithful church member long before Eisenhower, made no formal moves to see theism become part of official legal language.

18:15   Eisenhower was a different case. A war hero with parental influence out of sectarian roots that included some River Brethren pacifism, he was schooled in the Bible by his parents. He said that as supreme commander of the Allied Expeditionary Forces in Europe he had engaged in some soul-searching. He then let his newfound piety show in a prayer he wrote and read at his inauguration, two weeks before he was baptized. Soon Eisenhower was trying to get legislative support for a national day of prayer, attending annual presidential prayer breakfasts, and appointing a minister to a new special presidential post for religious matters. His rhetoric, however, had the most appeal. Critics who came at him from what Will Herberg would have called a "Jewish-Christian prophetic" angle lunged at words like these from 1948: "I am the most intensely religious man I know." Eisenhower's talking about faith did not ally him to denominationalism, he insisted: "That does not mean that I adhere to any sect." But "a democracy cannot exist without a religious base. I believe in democracy." No one knew anything about Eisenhower's creed except for the first two words: he once quoted a song that, he said, "made a great impression on me, and it has a title that has been rather a motto for me ever since I got into politics. And it was this: 'I Believe.' "

18:16   One of the widely read critics was William Lee Miller, who kept a running commentary on Eisenhower in the *Reporter* magazine and then summed things up in a book, *Piety Along the Potomac*. Miller spoke for those who were amused by Eisenhower's syntax and bemused by his "aboveness," his ability to live beyond criticism. Miller picked up on a 1954 *Reader's Digest* article by Eisenhower speechwriter Stanley High. The author there spoke of a "revival of moral and spiritual faith in America" as being Eisenhower's goal. Miller suspected that High was writing sentences for Eisenhower like "religion and the 'godly virtues' account for America's beginning and growth," and that these were necessary for the future. And he quoted the Reverend Edward L. R. Elson,

Eisenhower's baptizer, who said of the president, "It may not be too much to say that through his personal conduct and expression he has become, in a very real sense, the focal point of a moral resurgence and spiritual awakening of national proportions."

Fortunately for the nation, thought Miller, Eisenhower had the kind of personality and mien that made it possible for him to announce a crusade without becoming a crusader, a zealot. "What was the cause? Who was the infidel, where the Holy City?" Ike, to be sure, had first pronounced Washington corrupt, but that was not a new theme. Such was an American tradition, and the Eisenhower associates themselves were soon contributing to the life of that tradition. Was public adulation an escape from politics? During the Eisenhower period came the Hungarian Revolution and the Suez Crisis in 1956; the Russians' lead in the space race after Sputnik in 1957; the racial crisis at Little Rock, Arkansas; and a cooling economy in 1958 while the Berlin crisis shocked America; a U-2 spy embarrassment came in 1959, the same year a summit went bad and the Japanese rioted against American ties. And here was a president remaining popular while uttering mere and simple pieties.   18:17

Miller monitored Eisenhower early and for a long time. On July 7, 1953, he was already deciding that the president was sincere but inauthentic. "Although he won votes with it, Mr. Eisenhower plainly did not employ the 'God stuff,' as Franklin Roosevelt is reported to have called it, simply as a political device." Sincerely, Eisenhower grounded his program in a "deeply felt religious faith." Miller caught attention with an apt phrase: "President Eisenhower, like many Americans, is a very fervent believer in a very vague religion." And, fortunately for the interest in Miller's book, it also caught the other side of pious Washingon. Miller knew an irreverent story that ended, "Dammit, we forgot the opening prayer." Also irreverent was commentator Elmer Davis, who wrote that the president on one Independence Day had called the public to a day of penance and prayer and then "himself caught four fish in the morning, played eighteen holes of golf in the afternoon and spent the evening at the bridge table."   18:18

The laughs were there, and easily gotten, but Miller cried, or cried out, as well. "The faith is not in God but in faith; we worship our own worshiping." The critic did not know whether to call all this "the semi-secular religion or the semi-religious secularism" that marked the nation, but he did see in all of it a utilitarian view of religion. "Officialdom prefers religion which is useful for national purposes, but undemanding and uncomplicated in itself. It   18:19

President Dwight D. Eisenhower exemplified and embodied many dimensions of "the religious revival" in the generation after World War II. On October 12, 1958, he took part in the cornerstone laying at the Interchurch Center in New York, an event attended by ecclesiastical dignitaries and a congregation of 30,000 people. (Photo: National Council of the Churches of Christ in the USA.)

also wants religion which is negotiable to the widest possible public." Miller moved on to score the public. In 1954 he wrote that "the press says that the United States is having a religious revival now, but one wonders whether those are quite the words to describe what is going on." He was convinced that "there is an increase in religious behavior, but it is not clear that this quantitative increase represents any qualitative change in the nation's religious life." Of course, intellectuals were reading Kafka and Kierkegaard, Berdyaev and Maritain, but the theological renewal born of all this appeared "to bear little relation to the revival of religious interest in the broad mass of the people." Where now were the profound revivalists like Jonathan Edwards and Walter Rauschenbusch of the American past, who had fused piety and public prophecy? The combinations now of "religion and Americanism, God and country, Cross and flag" left America in a tradition "geared to arouse enthusiasm and passion, not to produce wisdom and patience"; that tradition was "more at home with single, simple, moral choices, than with complex, continuing political problems."

Billy Graham, the evangelist who in Miller's view should have   18:20 worn but did not wear the mantle of people like Edwards and Rauschenbusch, vaulted to Eisenhower's defense. He said he had met the general in 1952 when Ike was still commanding forces near Paris. Hard-drinking, poker-playing Texan Sid Richardson urged Graham to promote Eisenhower, so Graham, while claiming to be above politics, wrote the future president an encouraging letter. Eisenhower later asked Richardson: "Who was that young preacher you had write me? It was the darndest letter I ever got." Richardson responded: "I want to send this young fellow over [to talk to you] who's stirring up the country so. . . ." The two talked; in fact, at one time during the campaign Eisenhower whispered to Graham, "I don't believe the American people are going to follow anybody who's not a member of a church." When Graham learned that Eisenhower was of River Brethren lineage, the evangelist showed more savvy about denominational prestige than comparative dogma when he recommended Presbyterianism to Eisenhower because it was "fairly close" to River Brethren.

The record of the 1952 campaign found Graham saying in the   18:21 spring, "the people are hungry for a moral crusade, and they need a Moses or a Daniel to lead them in this hour." Eisenhower might take on the aspect of such a biblical figure. Graham talked twice with Eisenhower and reassured others that he sensed "a dependence upon God." The candidate told the evangelist "on both occasions that the hope of building a better America lay in a spiritual revival." If all that was not sufficiently explicit for Graham's constituency there was more: "Another thing that encourages me about Mr. Eisenhower is that he is taking advice from some genuine, born-again Christians." After election the new president summoned Graham to a New York hotel to ask advice about "bringing something spiritual, some spiritual note and tone into the inauguration ceremony." Graham answered, "General, you can do more to inspire the American people to a more spiritual way of life than any other man alive!" After the ceremonies Graham said he was sure that "the overwhelming majority of the American people felt a little more secure realizing that we have a man who believes in prayer at the helm of our government at this crucial hour." And Eisenhower told Graham, according to the evangelist, "Billy, I believe one reason I was elected President was to lead America in a religious revival." He did.

18:22　　For the record, Eisenhower's opponent in both elections, Adlai Stevenson, was a Unitarian, a liberal, a divorced man, and thus in that climate (for these reasons and others) unelectable. But he presented a cautious and more liberal version of the civic faith himself. More eloquently than Eisenhower, he preached to the nation: "Your salvation is in your own hands; in the stubbornness of your minds, the tenacity of your hearts and such blessings as God, sorely tried by His children, shall give us." In the crisis times, redeemed America "cannot lose, and will pass from darkness to the dawn of a brighter day than even this thrice-blessed land of ours has ever known." Like Eisenhower, Stevenson the intellectual could draw on the two primal nostalgic images of the day: "People are smarter than some may think—'There's still a God's plenty left in people of the little red schoolhouse and the little white steeple.'" Stevenson when pressed by Senator Joseph McCarthy for being "soft on Communism" could quote Catholic bishops against "dishonesty, slander, detraction and defamation of character" as "truly transgressions of God's Commandments" in political life. He could connect Mormonism in a Salt Lake City speech with the American Way of Life: "Let us recall that our basic faith in liberty of conscience has an ancient ancestry. We can trace it back through Christian Europe, and through pagan Rome, back to the Old Testament prophets." But he was against exclusivism: this faith "is by no means exclusive with us. It is in fact our bond of unity with all free men. But we are its ordained guardians today."

18:23　　Liberals as well as conservatives, Democrats as well as Republicans, knew the need to address the Cold War spiritual contrast. At Alamo Plaza in San Antonio in October as the campaign of 1952 was ending, Stevenson paid attention to Texans, with "many men of Spanish blood" among them, and reminded them of the foe they had faced long ago at the Alamo, "an enemy who offers no quarter." But the new enemy is more threatening, "for his aim is total conquest—not merely of the earth, but of the human mind. He seeks to destroy the very idea of freedom, the concept of God Himself." And he could speak of divine election, a call, a covenant: "God has set for us an awesome mission: nothing less than the leadership of the free world." God gave power and opportunity and expected the nation to be good stewards. Stevenson was aware of the vivid pluralism of the nation. To campaign volunteers in Boston that month he said on a Sunday, "Some of us worship in churches, some in synagogues, some on golf courses," and added, "I don't know whether there are any Mohammedan Volunteers who worship in mosques." For now, "we are all children of the same Judaic-Christian civilization, with very much the same religious background basically." He did not want citizens to "forget about the religious sources of democracy." In the Cold War "our people will triumph, because of the fact that they express eternal truths and because of the fact that the communists embrace eternal wrongs in their meanings." Generous social programs would be the best way of waging the Cold War: "The first answer to communism is not a lesser, but a fuller application of Judaic-Christian ethics to the neighborhood of nations around us." Stevenson lost the election, but he promoted the common faith "under God" with as much passion and more theological precision than Eisenhower: "We vote as many, but we pray as one," said Stevenson. Giving such attention to a losing presidential candidate could be out of place, except that it helps amplify the picture of a religious revival including bipartisan civic faith.

Stevenson's fellow Illinoisan, University of Chicago historian   18:24
Daniel Boorstin—typed as a "consensus historian" in the time when the One Nation formula was so important—listened in on Stevenson and found him religious but indifferent about denominations. Boorstin quoted the candidate of 1952: "If it's true that politics is the art of compromise, I've had a good start; my mother was a Republican and a Unitarian, my father was a Democrat and a Presbyterian. I ended up in his party and her church." Boorstin, more conservative than William Lee Miller, observed some of the same theological trends in the candidates and the country. America was a two-party political system reinforced by "nondenominationalism" in religion. Religions had to be *instrumental* for governmental purposes. That is, "they commend themselves to us for the services they perform more than for the truths which they affirm." Religion in such a context had to be *personal;* it should not intrude on public affairs but must perform services "subordinated to the need of the individual personality." And it must be *nondenominational.* On this third rubric he cited Eisenhower. Boorstin saw all sides promoting "interfaith" activities to demonstrate the "vitality of religion in general."

Not since the days when Roman emperors were worshiped,   18:25
Boorstin thought, had there likely "been a comparable submersion of separate religious beliefs in a common generalized religion." Yes, it was true, there were denominations, hate move-

ments, Know-Nothings, the Ku Klux Klan, and the anti-Catholic proclamations of Paul Blanshard as counterevidence. But America was being kept from the worst religious strife because of its "ability to produce a kind of elixir, sometimes vapid and always unpungent, a blended distillate of all our different religions," a religion without dogmas. It was neither pantheism nor humanism but the "lowest common denominator of all presently accepted and respectable institutional religions found within the borders of our country." All this made it difficult for Americans to communicate with cultures that did not mix religion and politics in this way.

18:26   Boorstin pointed all this out in *The Genius of American Politics,* published in 1953. At its heart was a chapter titled "The Mingling of Political and Religious Thought." The Chicago professor compared the instrumental religion of America to that which the great historian Edward Gibbon had seen in the age of the Antonines in Rome. Gibbon wrote: "The various modes of worship which prevailed in the Roman world were all considered by the people as equally true; by the philosopher as equally false; and by the magistrate as equally useful. And thus toleration produced not only mutual indulgence, but even religious concord." In that climate, Boorstin noted, "religion is of enormous importance," while "theology and religious studies languish." The boom in these latter was just beginning and could still be almost overlooked in 1952 when Boorstin was writing. But the historian also noticed a trend among some in his time to make "the un-American demand for a philosophy of democracy" to use "as a weapon against Russia and a prop for our own institutions." Citizens wanted something salable that could compete with Russia's approach in the world market. The threat to this development came not from the religious right but from the left, where people were puzzled that America had not yet come up with a philosophy. "They are," Boorstin said, "even frightened at what they might find—or fail to find—when they open the *sanctum sanctorum* of national belief." These creedalists of democracy on the left were dangerous friends who, finding the national Holy of Holies empty, would refuse to admit this and would develop an idolatry, making "their own graven image." Boorstin cautioned both camps against this: "We must refuse to become crusaders for liberalism, in order to remain liberals," and "we must refuse to become crusaders for conservatism, in order to conserve the institutions and the genius which have made America great."

18:27   Instinctively one turns to the right to look for the other kind of people who made Boorstin nervous, conservatives this side of Senator Joseph McCarthy who wanted to invent ideology for Cold Warfare. But it was voices on the liberal left, though less frequently heard and less noisy, who would make much of Eisenhower's simply stated faith, "I believe in democracy." At mid-century these voices drew on the influence of philosopher John Dewey, who in 1934 had published *A Common Faith;* the book's substance matched Eisenhower's but differed in its dismissiveness of church religion. One of the most articulate of the Deweyites was Mount Holyoke College chaplain and professor J. Paul Williams, a Methodist-reared Congregational cleric who was also a member of a Friends Meeting. In 1952 he wrote *What Americans Believe and How They Worship,* a work whose last chapter outlined a religion of democracy on Deweyan lines.

How did Williams come to talk about the common faith in a book whose main subject was the many faiths? He catalogued and discussed "an astonishing number of religious sects" that flourished in the United States. But the encyclopedic treatment of their peculiarities served to show—as Boorstin had shown, though against "certain sections of the American intelligentsia"— the presence and utility of religion. "A man's religion is whatever he does to relate himself to what he believes is the supreme reality in the universe. Religion in this sense is basic to all high living." And "religion is essential also to the welfare of societies. Every society is at bottom a spiritual entity. Every society is founded on some kind of religion." For that reason, "the thing most worth knowing about any people is the actual status of their religious thinking." Even though "more than one-third of the American people are members of no church or synagogue," they too were religious as Williams had defined religion. 18:28

For four hundred pages Williams tried to give fair-minded treatment to denominations that turned out to be for him irrelevant. To him a form of nationalism was what mattered. "Probably no man can be a successful politician in America today unless he does obeisance to nationalistic gods, certainly not if he attacks them." The college chaplain quoted the favored liberal columnist Walter Lippmann from World War II days: "we must consider first and last the American national interest." Over against church religion, "we shall succeed in so far as we can become fully enlightened American nationalists." In a chapter appended to the 1962 edition, "The Role of Religion in Shaping American Destiny," Williams revealed what the whole book had led up to. The 1962 edition—in 18:29

perfect elaboration of the logic of the 1952 volume, but written at a time when he thought the religious revival was "about over" — gave him a chance to cite statistics of denominations, but he found denonimational religion less important than either private religion or societal religion. Societal religion was the most important: now, it "would be shared with the members of a whole society." He quoted J. Robin Williams, a sociologist of religion who argued, following Emile Durkheim, that "every functioning society has to an important degree a *common* religion." Thus "a society's common-value system—its 'moral solidarity'—is always correlated with and to a degree dependent upon a shared religious orientation." Eisenhower and Stevenson found this in Judaic-Christian roots. Williams had to go further.

18:30   Williams in 1962 cited essays that historian Sidney E. Mead had published at the height of the Eisenhower-era revival. Mead wrote of a late-nineteenth-century emergence, a religion of "the American way of life." Now there were two religions, one of the denominations and the other "the religion of the democratic society and nation." Other worthies were also writing in support of republican religion and democratic faith. Williams saw that such faith could oppose the quasi-religion of communism. "The peril of our position is increased by the fact that the devotees of Communism evidence all the earmarks, not merely of religious dedication, but of religious fanaticism." He was dangerously critical of the churches. "Like most institutions churches strive to expand the area of their control. Thus they seek dominion over the whole of religion. They tend to religious imperialism" and thus violate society's "*common* religion." Where could one locate the generating center of such a nonimperial faith? For Williams and his kind, the answer was in the government. But even Walter Lippmann's recent work, *The Public Philosophy,* Williams thought, did not go far enough; because Lippmann spoke of values as being *ultimate,* Williams thought he himself ought to be blunt and call for religion.

18:31   The Mount Holyoke chaplain was only more blunt and clear than others about this common faith not based in churches or in the Judaic-Christian lineage. His societal religion, his common faith, in an America that was spiritual to the core, urged that "democracy must become an object of religious dedication. Americans must come to look on the democratic ideal (not necessarily American practice of it) as the Will of God or, if they prefer, the Law of Nature." The articulators of this religion of democracy had to be

systematic about spiritual integration, or they would be as haphaz-
ard as the churches. Of course, once they were in command, they
should mobilize churches and synagogues. Their leaders had experience, skill, personal integrity, and the loyalty of multitudes.
"Many church and synagogue leaders already make the teaching
of democracy a major objective."

Was not such a humanistic religion a sect of its own? Was it not   18:32
too narrow, as its critics claimed, while they were ecumenical? No,
argued Williams, democracy was "a way of life for all men."
Would not teaching democracy as religious dogma, as "the Will
of God," pull religion down to "mere ethics?" No, such an accusation made too much of eternal salvation, mystical experience,
and the like. Churches and synagogues when they counterattacked
his kind were exclusivist and imperialist. Williams collected names
used by the exclusivists in order to stigmatize his position: " 'a
fourth faith,' 'a form of nationalism,' a 'conspiracy' against Catholicism, Protestantism, and Judaism, 'a vague and somewhat
sentimental religious syncretism,' a 'superreligion,' 'a particularly
insidious kind of idolatry.' " No: it was simply a religion of democracy.

How could this civic religion be institutionalized? "The State   18:33
must be brought into the picture," Williams said. "Governmental
agencies must teach the democratic ideal *as religion*." In fact,
"systematic and universal indoctrination" in the values on which a
society is based was essential "if that society is to have any per-
manence or stability." Now he sounded protective: "the only way
we can preserve our liberties in private and denominational religion is to forgo some liberties in societal religion." And he was
programmatic: use the public schools as if they were established
churches. They should promote the religion of democracy with
"metaphysical sanctions" and "ceremonial reinforcement." They
must be dogmatic, indoctrinating the young with the notion that
"the democratic ideal accords with ultimate reality," whether that
reality is seen in naturalistic or supernaturalistic terms. The ceremonies should glorify the values, calling for self-appraisal and rededication. Nazis and Japanese knew how to do all this for evil
ends; why not have American societal religion do it for humane
purposes? Williams, of course, had no following like that of President Eisenhower and Governor Stevenson in the center, or figures
on the right as mild as Will Herberg and as mean as Joseph R.
McCarthy. But his appearance here shows that civic religion had

advocates who could articulate from the liberal left an anticommunist prodemocratic vision to support a version of the American Way of Life in Cold War times. Across the spectrum, then, the religious revival quickened civic faith and public religion on unprecedented scales.

19

"The Popular Religious Revival Is . . . Tied to a Popular Patriotism"

According to all evidence, the Americans who welcomed
the religious revival for the encouragement it gave to civic faith and
public religion continued to devote most of their spiritual energies
to personal faith and private religion. Of course, the two larger
spheres of expression intersect, overlap, and transform each other.
The revival of interest in civic religion, nurtured under the pulpit
of a Dwight Eisenhower in the White House, colored the elabora-
tions of faith within little white churches, most of them featuring a
United States flag in the chancel, just as it colored the character of
new suburban synagogues and inner-city congregations. And the
readiness of citizens to respond to symbols on any level made it
easier for civil leaders to make appeals to religion. A national revival of interest in religion has to be by definition popular. There
can be a recovery of formal theology in the seminaries, and there
was around mid-century. There can be ecumenical committees and
movements for social action on the part of elites. But unless millions are swept up or at least lured by a cause, it is not likely to be
called a revival or experienced as one. Once upon a time revivals
were measured by the size of the camp meetings and tent-service
crowds or by the numbers of souls gathered at the river for baptism.
At mid-century, for the new-time religion, the measurers used
opinion polls, lists of best-selling religious books, and assessments
of the size of audiences for biblical films or radio and television

19:1

evangelism to gain a sense of the scope of change. Thus the same Will Herberg who documented the civic faith also pointed to what he called a "cult of faith," a "faith in faith," which took on both introvert and extrovert characteristics.

19:2   The introvert version offered the promise of mental health and peace of mind, the dissipating of guilt and anxiety, and the translation of the individual soul "to the blessed land of 'normality' and 'self-acceptance.'" To critic Herberg the entire effort appeared to be a debasement of psychoanalysis. Through it, all people drawn to the movement seemed to be synthesizing religion and psychiatry. Meanwhile, the extrovert form showed up in efforts to promote throughout the culture the modes and moods of "positive thinking" and "affirmation" over against "negativity" and "skepticism." Moved as he was by prophetic biblical faith, Will Herberg was able to find little authentic faith in anything, "certainly not the theocentric faith of the historic religions"; the only thing present was faith itself, or the attitude of having faith. Here the sociologist would be the smasher of idols; in popular religion, he said, one saw the "inner disintegration and enfeeblement of the historic religions; the familiar words are retained, but the old meaning is voided." Given the title of his own book, *Protestant-Catholic-Jew,* plus the author's preoccupations and the engrossments of many others in that decade, it is not surprising that Herberg's illustrations from the world of best-sellers were Protestant, Catholic, and Jewish: Norman Vincent Peale's *Power of Positive Thinking,* Fulton Sheen's *Peace of Soul,* and Joshua Loth Liebman's *Peace of Mind.*

19:3   If Protestant minister Peale represented the peak of the popular revival, Rabbi Liebman, writing immediately after the war, was the pioneer who anticipated many of the themes in the time when "faith in faith" was becoming dominant. Liebman was somewhat more assertive about facing problems in the social order than were his Christian counterparts, and he included more notes of realism than did Protestant Peale. Liebman said he wanted to separate the fears of such enormities as the new atomic bomb from the everyday fears that need not be quite so horrifying. But the pursuit of inner peace was the rabbi's theme, too. No dogmas bound him, and he offered very free and expansive interpretations of Jewish history. These enabled Liebman to reach far beyond Judaism for a clientele. Before the war his market would have been limited to Jews. His book drew on Jewish tradition but broadened it so effectively that it saw thirty printings before the publisher chose to put out a cheap paperback version to enlarge the market further in 1955. Liebman readily quoted philosophers and theologians, among them Alfred North Whitehead. The presence of such a philosopher on those pages contributed to the sense that Liebman was dealing with the place where science and religious thought met. Having undergone psychoanalysis, he brought psychological insight to his Reform rabbinate at Temple Israel in Boston. To him, atheism was a neurosis, and religion was designed to address psychological fears. Liebman's proposal, hardly modest in his statement, was "A New God for America." America was a civilization that, he said, "has little of the father complex in it." He thought the nation was finding it "increasingly difficult to submit to the idea of a dominant Father." Rather than an all-powerful, threatening God, his was a benign affirmer, as the many thousands who bought his books testified.

Liebman was a harbinger of the new trend in popular religion   19:4 that appeared markedly different from prewar, Depression-era modes. As soon as it appeared, the psychologists and sociologists, now prospecting in veins of rich subject matter, were on the scene. They analyzed the revival, argued with its promoters, and pondered what it meant for the culture. Thus sociologists Louis Schneider and Sanford M. Dornbusch observed much of what at least middle-class America meant by religion in the Eisenhower decade. They studied the words of New York's Norman Vincent Peale, the immensely popular master of soothing and reassurance at Marble Collegiate Church. That congregation had ties to the Reformed Church in America and its pastor had grown up in Methodism, but neither of these lineages did much to color the message; popular religion was becoming increasingly nondenominational. The co-authors of the study dipped into a coauthored Peale book and quoted some samples, including: "Here is a text from the Scriptures. Take it. . . . Conceive of it as a medicine dropping into your mind, and it will spread a healing influence that will give you an immunity from [your] fear." But the Schneider and Dornbusch tandem did not content themselves with medicinal palliatives from the "big three" faiths. At hand for their observation were many more figures, such as George W. Crane, M.D., dispensing cures: "Religion produces more serenity than all the phenobarbital and reserpine and other drugs we shall ever discover," he promised. Being a scientist, Crane thought he should support that claim with evidence, and he did so by arguing that active church people lived longer and suffered less from stress diseases than did those who never worshiped.

19:5   While civic faith was addressed to the corporate body of Americans in their One Nation, Indivisible, popular religion was assigned the task of serving the individual. Schneider and Dornbusch, having read thousands of pages of popular religious literature, deduced that in it the human "scarcely lives in a society or culture at all." Of course, there had to be some references in the material and in their study to one social form, the intimate circle of the family, which was advertised strenuously as a religious support. The company of friends, employees, and neighbors sometimes got mentioned as well. But the literature avoided most intimations of larger surrounding frameworks, and this feature, to the professional observers, seemed "a crucially important gap." One more institutional exception was the local religious gathering. The idea that "belief in God" suffices for a full life was then qualified by the almost unanimous prescription: "participation in *some* (any) church is necessary." Authors of religious self-help literature advised people to attend church, read scriptures, and consult a personal spiritual counselor. When large numbers of people took such advice, did this mean that a real "religious revival" was going on? Schneider and Dornbusch were not so sure, because they observed that the accent on church participation as such did not have to be particularly religious. It was part of a "broad cultural movement" exemplifying what sociologist David Riesman called "other-directedness."

19:6   Any canvass of the surviving popular religious literature of that period is likely to turn up what Schneider and Dornbusch found; most of it was designed to advance personal and private energies. The same Robin Williams who was then observing and claiming that each complex society had, and had to have, a common faith, also assessed the increasing privatism in religion that coexisted with common faith in the minds and lives of citizens. The two modes blurred into each other. How could they be sorted out? Williams produced a catalog in 1951 that turned up terms like the following as being central in the mix of goals: "achievement and success, activity and work, moral orientation, humanitarian mores, efficiency and practicality, progress, material comfort, equality, freedom, external conformity, science and secular rationality, nationalism-patriotism, democracy, individual personality, racism and group superiority." But Williams's list, long as it was, according to Schneider and Dornbusch, was notable for what it didn't include. Almost completely absent at mid-century was an earlier preoccupation: "the Social Gospel trend of thought." What had happened to causes that would have produced a better social world? "That movement might virtually never have existed as far as the preoccupations of our writers are concerned." The other-directed individual was now the center of the popular religious universe.

Because the neo-Reformation, neoscholastic, and shall we say   19:7
neorabbinic schools of thought dominant in the seminaries differed vastly from popular religious obsessions, a gap between intellectual centers and lay religion widened. Another (somewhat
more easily bridged) gap was that between official religion, which
stressed ritual, dogma, action, practice, and intellectuality, and
popular religion, which was almost wholly given over to "the drive
to raw experience." The mainstream churches and synagogues
were not necessarily denying such experience, but they did not
promote it effectively, so the church members and the public smuggled it in through the inspirational religion that was becoming a
large market item. Significantly, those best at promoting "raw experience" did try to mediate and encourage the growth of institutional religion, but they failed to stimulate any outside their own
congregations partly because the communal expression of faith
was such a secondary matter. Joshua Loth Liebman, the rabbi who
met his millions with *Peace of Mind*, had to have been popular
with congregational rabbis for the way he stressed that "church
and synagogue have created what might be called 'strategies of
solace,'" including comforting rituals for the poignant hours of
crisis. Schneider and Dornbusch spoke of this as an "integrative"
trend, typical of life in that period.

While those two authors were equivocal about a revival, plenty   19:8
of analysts of the same literature, media expressions, and material
evidences were clear in their minds. Thus William Lee Miller, so
caustic about President Eisenhower's civic faith, found the popular
religion of the day equally wanting. As noted in the previous chapter, he agreed with the press in 1954 about "an increase in religious
behavior, but," as he put it, "it is not clear that this quantitative
increase represents any qualitative change in the nation's religious
life." Intellectuals were "reviving" by reading Kafka and Kierkegaard, Berdyaev and Maritain, the Niebuhr brothers and Tillich.
Try to sell these gloomy and heavy writers to the revivalists'
crowds, Miller taunted, as he listened across the gap between elites
and the popular. Two centuries earlier and again a half-century earlier, when theologian Jonathan Edwards and Social Gospel leader
Walter Rauschenbusch had led the revivals, both intellect and heat

were produced. Miller invited readers to find evidences of intellectual force in Dr. Peale, Bishop Sheen, or evangelist Graham. The implication was clear that it was not there to be found. Instead mass media packaged the revival themes and made no appeal to the thoughtful. Films based on biblical stories but without artistic merit were popular, as were religious novels. Religious and inspirational lyrics were juke box selections. Magazines like *Reader's Digest* brought messages of reassurance to the millions. Such a message came on the market as "salable" religion, always "helpful" and "useful," while formulas for "self-help" were most marketable. Was this what religion was supposed to have been about? asked Miller.

19:9   Miller and his kind deftly connected individual with cultural criticism on some issues. Thus Miller noticed the obvious ties between "peace" and "power" that were not central in the work of Peale or in the observations of Schneider and Dornbusch. These ties appeared most vividly in *Peace of Soul* by Catholic bishop Fulton Sheen but also in the writings of Peale, even though the Protestant preacher generally tried to avoid overt comment on public and political life. "The popular religious revival," wrote Miller, "is closely tied to a popular patriotism, of which it is the uncritical ally: religion and Americanism, God and country, Cross and flag." So the faiths of many individuals played their part in promoting the One Nation, Indivisible, in Cold War times. "There are crusades all across the country," he wrote, in the "period of popular religiosity." As for the individual, so it was for the nation: an "illusion" of omnipotence was present, a notion that "America can do whatever she wants to." The revivalist heritage had long suggested that, and the unfolding new American religious tradition enchanced it, being "geared to arouse enthusiasm and passion, not to produce wisdom and patience; it is more at home with single, simple, moral choices, than with complex, continuing political problems." As with Sheen, so with Peale. If you have read one Peale book, said Miller, you have read them all. Shuffle paragraphs, transpose the chapters of each, and the single message would survive. Peale's attraction was "his constantly reiterated single theme," so typical of and popular in the times: "The idea is that affirmative attitudes help to make their own affirmations come true." So Peale could always say what the people wanted him to say, but being the Reverend Doctor Peale, he could call down the blessing of God on goals people had already set for themselves.

19:10   Miller was not envious but awed. Peale "has the ability—and

the nerve—to fit his message precisely to the exacting requirements of mass popularity." Peale affirmed old American roots in a
new culture, stressing what his critics called "our self-confidence
and optimism, our worldly practicality, and our individualism and
striving for success, concerned more with private career than public problems." But whatever had once been sound in the tradition
was now being reduced and refined away. Miller judged that even
Christianity in these works and in the lives of their users now
became "a simple yet scientific system of successful living that
works," while the Bible was "a book which contains a system of
formulas and techniques designed for the understanding and treatment of human nature." Even the teachings of Jesus had to be sold
as "workable." And "in place of any Holy of Holies there is the
bathroom mirror, on which you are to paste the latest slogan." But
again, piety connected with power. Peale did not resist all ties to
political power. In 1952, for example, he had proposed a "prayer
plan" to select *the* man God wanted to be president. Miller: "God
seems regularly to answer Dr. Peale's own prayers with the Republican candidates," one of whom won in 1952. Peale insisted that
ministers ought ordinarily to stay out of politics, unless there was
a *moral* issue. Then they should speak up—which meant in support of Eisenhower and Nixon.

The popular pianist Liberace, scorned and derided by all critics,   19:11
became famous at that time for saying he "cried all the way to the
bank." The authors of best-sellers could have done the same. But
Peale was easily hurt and wrote regular apologies. He was surrounded by admirers who claimed that content analysis of Dr.
Peale's sermons and books would show him to be closer to basic
biblical themes than were his critics. Thus Allan R. Broadhurst,
one of the first to use the new invention, the computer, on sermon
content, thanked Michigan State University for the help its computer named Mystic gave him as he wrote *He Speaks the Word of
God.* Broadhurst, despite the trappings of the computer, was no
more objective than was Miller on the other side. He defended
Peale for his belief "that doctrine and dogma should be mini-
mized and Christianity made a practical, usable faith for a modern
world." To Broadhurst, politics was a villainous tempter that on
occasion almost distracted Peale from his mission. At one stage,
the analyzer pointed out, Peale "went through the experience of
engaging himself and his congregation in needless controversy because he had not been able to distinguish between a real principle
and marginal custom." Even through World War II Peale kept

clinging to the belief that the cleric "had not only the right but the duty to speak out on political affairs, presidential elections, social issues, etc." Before he learned better, Peale supported General Douglas MacArthur and then Governor Thomas Dewey against President Truman in 1948, until he noticed that he was alienating some in his congregation. So one day he got up to say, "I've been wrong." He had hurt his ministry. "Believe me, from this point on, if the country were collapsing, and a committee were formed to save the Republic, I wouldn't join it!" Not until the issue of religious freedom led him to foresee collapse did Peale reenter politics, taking part in a brief-lived Protestant movement to oppose the presidential candidacy of Catholic John F. Kennedy in 1960. On that urgent occasion he did "join" in.

19:12   Broadhurst moved from politics to theology, to state the case for and against Peale. How did he answer charges of Reinhold Niebuhr and others that all this was "easy religion," "quasi-Christianity," designed to mislead, distort, or confuse? Niebuhr disturbed Peale's apologist most when he objected that "the basic sin of this new cult is its egocentricity. It puts 'self' instead of the cross at the center of the picture." And Liston Pope, dean of Yale Divinity School, kept returning to the scene because he saw Peale's work as an attempt to redefine the Christian faith itself: "This criticism of the new religion of peace of mind is no theological quibble." Similarly, on the denominational front Franklin Clark Fry, president of the United Lutheran Church of America, said "there is nothing more sinister . . . than that instrumentalization of religion—the use of God to accomplish a specific aim." This, he charged, "positive thinking" set out to do. Methodist bishop G. Bromley Oxnam added to the controversy when he wondered "whether [Peale's] message is a Christian message" at all, however helpful it may have been to some.

19:13   Peale, as Broadhurst understood him, sometimes seemed to be killing the critics with kindness, pleading that he was only simplifying truths, not challenging them. Broadhurst's computer showed that Peale did touch on many orthodox measures. In 97 percent of the dissected sermons "the God/Christ Theme" showed up: "In God and Christ man finds the key to wholeness of his mental, physical, spiritual, and emotional faculties." And in 63 percent "the Prayer Theme" was present: prayer "is the basic method for problem solving." "the Faith Theme" was in 58 percent of the sermons, while "the Problem Theme" appeared in 57 percent of them. Then came "the Interpersonal Relations Theme," which was in 50 percent of the sermons, while the same number applied to "the Defeat/Fear Theme." None of this looked like a departure from orthodoxy, and Broadhurst took snippets of Peale out of their contexts to make them appear creedal. But Peale's patent was "the Thought Theme," "the message that thoughts and mind attitudes determine the situation of a person's life. Thus, a person becomes what he thinks." Peale drew on the Bible, Marcus Aurelius, Ralph Waldo Emerson, Dr. Karl Menninger, and William James, it was said, but on the basis of what he read he invented a "realizable wish" formula. It was this that got Peale into trouble, because, said critics, it "subordinated God to the will of man." Maybe it sounded that way, but listen to the way Peale wed it to the other six themes in most sermons, Broadhurst advised.

Between the attacks of people like Miller and the defenses of   19:14
Broadhurst and associates, were historians who tried to locate the popular religious revival and its leaders in the longer traditions of American religion. Thus Donald Meyer picked up on one theme that defender Broadhurst recognized, Peale's sources in people like Ralph Waldo Emerson and "New Thought." But Meyer gave Peale credit for innovation. "Did Norman Vincent Peale simply ride the postwar (especially the post-Korean War) 'revival of religion' to its crest? Or had he been in part responsible for its surge?" Peale was riding a wave, but it became in a sense "his" wave. Peale's primal insight matched the new times: "There is resident in you an immense reservoir of force; the power of the subconscious mind. Faith releases this power." But to the notion that a certain kind of thinking could become "automatic" and an individual was "conditioned," Peale added theistic terms that his partner, Freudian psychiatrist Smiley Blanton, did not promote: "When you put your trust in God, He guides your mind so that you do not want things that are not good for you or that are inharmonious with God's will." But, said Meyer, "Peale's ideas about God were minimal." Meyer used very technical terms to assess Peale's psychology: in it, "a superego super-consciousness inducing automatic behavior through the medium of an autohypnotized sub- or unconscious, the superambient realm of authority, beyond criticism and even comment, had more definite social and economic than divine features." The people who bought millions of copies of Peale's works probably would not have recognized themselves in the portrait, and we are free to picture the people's helper crying all the way to the bank.

A decade after the Eisenhower election Meyer reviewed the   19:15

Peale record in public life and found some surprises. Miller had said that Peale's psychology moved him "less into a theology than into a politics or, better, a non-politics." *Was* his popular religion all that nonpolitical? Meyer found that Peale had supported the right-wing Committee for Constitutional Government. He had endorsed a book that called Franklin Delano Roosevelt a dictator. On the economic right were the Spiritual Mobilization movement and the Christian Freedom Foundation, both favored by him. But Meyer took seriously Peale's attempt after 1948 to turn from these commitments because he was losing some constituents. So Peale told listeners and readers to think only of themselves, not of the political or economic order. Along the way, Meyer made a discovery: Peale was not teaching people how to be successful but "prescribing for those still unhappy in their success." He was teaching them not about how to live life in the thick of things but about how to avoid life in the thick of things.

19:16   As the revival of religious interest took a different character late in the fifties, Peale seemed to sense a need to be more "tough-minded." The preacher admitted that he had made it too easy to join the church. But he employed the forum of *Reader's Digest* to swing back at his despisers. "It's all very well for our divinity students to stretch their minds wrestling with the concepts of our tremendous theologians." But while doing so they lost the common touch. The "great postwar return to religion" was now declining, Peale thought. Why? Because, he charged, the seekers were alienated when they "found preachers offering intellectualized sermons on social problems." And though Peale was one of the great blurrers and amalgamators of ideas and congregations, he swung further at the "amalgamation of denominations, the whole ecumenical movement." Insofar as he represented the popular religion of the Eisenhower era, and it would be hard to find his match in sales and audiences, he turned out to be equivocal, too. The minister broke religion down into the smallest component, individual life, while building up Marble Collegiate Church and One Nation, Under God, Indivisible—skipping over or disdaining the institutions of religion and government that sustained both. If religious institutions prospered after mid-century, they were not where Peale put his energies most years. Peale contributed greatly to what came to be called the "privatizing" of American religion.

19:17   To complete the triangle of Protestant, Catholic, and Jew, Americans regularly ranked Bishop Fulton Sheen with the best of the avatars of that day. Sheen offered psychologically informed treatments of Catholic dogma in beguiling ways, also to non-Catholics. For the first time, a Catholic priest became a celebrity, and one acceptable beyond Catholicism at that. His motif was "peace of soul," which the priest connected with Catholicism. Here was orthodox dogma offered as healing. Sheen had a gift for reading the discontents of middle-class Catholic Americans and ministering to them. More than Peale, Sheen blamed the turmoil in the souls of Americans on the responsible self. Donald Meyer summarized this part of Sheen's message: "The tormented minds of today are not the effects of our tormented world; it is our upset minds that have upset the world."

Paul Blanshard, redoubtable publicist and attacker of all things   19:18
Catholic, including popular counsel, paid Sheen tribute by making him a target. Networks were not supposed to be criticizing particular bodies, but Sheen regularly and violently attacked "religious liberalism—the group that embraces Unitarianism, Universalism, liberal Congregationalism, and liberal Judaism." How could the bishop get away with sentences like "Protestantism in great part has ceased to be Christian?" He grew furious when Sheen connected Catholicism and patriotism. During the war Sheen had argued that America had a special connection with the Virgin Mary, "the Woman to whom God gave the power of crushing the head of the serpent." Sheen reminded his audience that in 1846 the hierarchy had "consecrated the United States to the Immaculate Conception of Our Blessed Mother," and he showed how America's entry into the war, V-E Day and V-J Day, the ends of the European and Japanese wars, and other wartime events matched Marian events. To Blanshard this was showing a "reliance on necromancy or astrology" in the name of religion. Sheen did stretch things so far that Blanshard did not even have to be discerning. Thus his critic heard him saying "On September 1, 1945, the first Saturday of the month which our Lady of Fatima asked should be consecrated to Her, General MacArthur accepted the surrender of Japan aboard the *Missouri*." And on September 8, the birthday of Our Lady, the first American flag flew over Tokyo, with MacArthur intoning: "Let it wave in its full glory as a symbol of victory for the right." If Blanshard thought that pointing out such excesses would offend the public, he read it all wrong. Sheen's popularity took off precisely in the years he was thus speaking.

Sheen prospered also with the rise of television. Networks were   19:19
supposed to donate public-service time. Mike Gallagher, producer of Catholic programs, was aware of the auspices: "I have a rather

cynical attitude towards the networks. They're just using religious shows to fulfil their FCC [Federal Communications Commission] obligations." But religious groups seized on the opportunity. Billy Graham spread his revival message on televison. Conservative denominations like the Lutheran Church—Missouri Synod, the Southern Baptists, and the Seventh-day Adventists invested heavily in dramatic programs. More mainstream were other efforts also not built around celebrities: "Lamp Unto My Feet" (CBS), "Directions" (ABC), "Frontiers of Faith" (NBC), and "Look Up and Live" (CBS), favorites in the years of revival, often used the new and inexpensive panel format. But everything changed when commercial sponsorship and the star system were born, and Fulton J. Sheen was focal in both. He dressed in clerical garb and played the role of the professor, using a blackboard as his prop. It was said that even in many bars the proprietors or drinkers switched from viewing athletic events to watching the bishop during his prime time between 1952 and 1957. Admiral Corporation footed the bill. But mainstream Protestantism and Catholicism were never able to hold their place after religious groups had to pay for time and after Sheen, the last Catholic television celebrity, began to decline and be less welcome around 1957.

19:20   Television became virtually universal in American households within a decade after the war, a fact that led religious leaders to explore its effects on the ethos. For some, television virtually became a substitute religion, and the set served as a familiar altar and icon-bearer. Some Protestants who wanted to study the impact of mass media on religion therefore commissioned a team headed by Everett C. Parker to learn what it could by monitoring one city, New Haven, Connecticut. What "need system" drew people to the set, and what "interest groups" made up the audiences? The team learned from interviews that in value-ranking, family and home came first; social status was second; preoccupation with self was third. Whatever met those interests was most likely to succeed in popular religion, where "need systems" were the whole focus. In the New Haven study, "social responsibility" was far down the scale, and "formal religion" even lower. Because religious television then was ordinarily the projection of establishment religion, whoever depended on these last two elements, as mainstream churches did, had to be in trouble.

19:21   Fulton J. Sheen as bishop certainly represented "formal religion," and he used his cassock and the trappings of churchly office to make the point. But Parker and his colleagues learned that Sheen

Monsignor Fulton J. Sheen was the pioneer religious television celebrity. He transcended the role earlier assigned priests and had an appeal that went far beyond Roman Catholicism. Here he participates in a telethon with comedian Milton Berle and New York Mayor Vincent R. Impellitteri. (Photo: Courtesy of the Society for the Propagation of the Faith.)

masterfully used implied authority to address "need systems." With his television audience, "the largest by far," Sheen was a natural topic for interviews. Mr. and Mrs. Richardson were one Congregationalist couple who watched Sheen. "His" preoccupation was "work," and "hers" was "social status." They represented "class conventionality" in their upper-class congregation. Mrs. Richardson remembered having first tuned in to Sheen on television accidentally. The children, momentarily repelled by the priest's cassock, soon came under the spell. "I listened to the entire program even though I am not a Catholic, and I don't believe in the Catholic religion." What did she see and hear? Nothing of what Paul Blanshard thought got transacted. To her the program was neither restricted to Catholicism nor "purely religious"; in the mood of the decade, it was "more of a general religion," the preaching of "goodness." Mr. Richardson chimed in with a yes: "It's hard for me to explain but I don't think in the programs that I saw that he made any reference to one religion or the other. It's just more or less generalized." A Catholic Broadhurst who might have used a computer on Sheen's message would have found in it perfect particular orthodoxy. But the bishop came across as a general preacher of goodness.

19:22   The Parker folk dropped in on the Kevin Boyle family. Kevin did own up to a preoccupation with "formal religion" and attachment to "family and home." The well-off Boyles were active Catholics and thus found Sheen's dogmatic system congenial. But they were also unsettled. Mrs. Boyle, for instance, was in turmoil over motherhood and vocation. She showed no awareness of ideas, concepts, abstractions, theological themes; she did believe in prayer and in a moral code backed by mystical authority. In her eyes, Sheen successfully ministered to turmoil using Catholic resources. She told the interviewer, when asked about Sheen as an interviewer, that "when the Catholic Church believes in one thing and you read about something else, then I will question those things. And he'll inevitably come out with it" and clear things up. But the Boyles twisted the dial anyhow, or stayed with "Frontiers of Faith" as it worked through the three-faith cycle. "We listen to the Protestant part. And the Jewish. My goodness; a lot of the time you'd swear that you were listening to your own." Catholic pride and prejudice led them to stay with Sheen, but Mrs. Boyle emphasized, when speaking of Sheen, "He's not preaching the Catholicity of everything." And speaking of his sort, she went on: "When they get up they don't, uh, definitely stay with one religion. They're just talking about God and the whole, and His principles." Religion in general.

19:23   The Parker company stayed around also to assess Norman Vincent Peale's hold on typical New Haven Congregationalist John West, who had heard the New York preacher in person. He responded, when asked, that he could not "recall anything he said. It was a cumulation"; it was Peale's general philosophy that moved him. West spread Peale pamphlets among employees: "I think they enjoy them thoroughly, for there's so many things applicable to a businessman and his church in Dr. Peale's sermons—*why we're both dealing in people.* They're different paths but I think their reaction is about the same." Thanks to Peale's urgings, West and his employees even read the Bible: "It *builds business because they reflect to the customer that we're—uh, a good Christian firm and that our dealings are based on the Christian faith.*" Parker added: "Emphasis supplied."

In 1955 New Haven provided only a "small but significant au-   19:24
dience" for Billy Graham. The interview team visited the Lutheran Nels Swensons, who watched and heard the evangelist's televised rallies. Using the designated scales, Parker said that Nels's pre-occupation was "Self" and his wife's was "Self." They brought Lutheran loyalties from Sweden to their local church. Then what about Catholic Sheen? "As far as he preaches you wouldn't know that he was a Catholic" was the response. Mrs. Swenson provided the characteristic gloss of all the televised religious figures, "They are all trying to get to the same place eventually," but by "different roads." Her husband added: "The way he preached last week was almost like Lutheran ministers would preach." But for the Swensons, Billy Graham was their mainstay. He sounded like their own Lutheran preacher, except "he [Graham] don't preach long enough, that's the trouble." The New Haven team visited only one family that shared Graham's background, but like the Swensons, its members also believed that all the television religious people were trying to "get to the same place eventually," if by "different roads."

Oberlin sociologist J. Milton Yinger tried to make sense of the   19:25
changes going on in best-selling and televised popular religions and came up with a fresh twist. "Many interpreters," he said, "have spoken of the growing interest in religion in the very context of apparent secularization," just as there seemed to be an "increasing discussion of religious separatism in the very context of ecumenicity." Some called this situation a paradox, but Yinger had a simpler explanation. He agreed with those who witnessed a "revival of an interest" in religion after a lag from 1900 to 1940. Now there was "a strong increase in religious activity and interest." Now "local, state, and national political processes have steadily acquired more religious symbols and practices." He thought that Peter Berger, another sociologist, did well to speak of a religious establishment, "in a nontechnical sense of the word." And Will Herberg, who thought he was chronicling mere secularization, unwittingly provided Yinger with a theme when the latter unconsciously defined secularization thus: "persons acting religiously in a way that does not express directly the faith they profess." The two processes, of secularization and religious change, were not identical. In the pattern of secularization people carry on life's

decisions with no reference to religion. In the latter, the style of Americans during their revival, they simply redefine religion "while disguising or obscuring the process, by holding, somewhat superficially, to many of the symbols of the earlier religious system." Change in these circumstances was latent but dynamic. In America this all meant producing through religious symbols what Peter Berger called "the O.K. world," defined as the support of the dominant values and institutions of society.

19:26   Yinger aptly summarized what the revival had been about. Religion was "highly relevant to the process of supporting the basic institutions and values of the society." Berger and Herberg wanted its spokespersons to be "prophetic," but there was little chance that a prophetic message would be heard. "The churches of those who are comfortable in a society are almost always well accommodated to that society." Was this secularization? No, said the sociologist; what the people were coming up with made a package that fulfilled one of the most persistent functions of religion. "Those of us who share sectarian religious tendencies—who want religion to stand in constructive tension with society," he said, had to be aware of their own values when they spoke of secularization. There was a danger that observers would confuse it with religious change. The religious "boom" of the recent past, then, had not been a superficial covering for religious decline; "what we are witnessing" instead, Yinger wrote, "is the development of new religious forms." Middle- and upper-class urban Americans were undergoing novel experiences and had to be religiously inventive, even if their inventions repulsed religious professionals. The popular religious figures—Liebman, Sheen, Peale, and to some extent Graham, in our instances—and the people were making use of the old stories, the traditional symbols of Protestantism, Catholicism, and Judaism. For that reason, "the changes are being obscured by the continuity of symbols," but "a new religion is developing at the hands of laymen"—or, as Parker had shown, laywomen—right under the noses of the clergy. The invention was not churchly but "*church-like.*" The religious professionals were spending the years responding more to catastrophes and cruelties, the threat of future war, and the capacities for hostility. "These developments" among intellectuals "also support the religious revival," but attention to them, thought Yinger, created a kind of schism between elites and devotees of popular religions. Theologians were less sensitive than the popular leaders to the "new crises of affluence, mobility, and anomie."

Yinger's analysis throws interesting light on Billy Graham,   19:27
the most paradoxical figure of all. If Sheen suppressed some of
the Catholic particularities, Graham never obscured the points of
latter-day fundamentalism, now called neo-evangelicalism. His
message, in classical biblical terms, should have been a "scandal"
to non-evangelicals and non-Christians—recalling that the Greek
word *skandalon* meant something one trips over or falls into. Yet
"everyone" except a few intellectuals seemed to like Graham. His
first serious biographer, William McLoughlin, never tired of ac-
centing Graham's scandalous message. The evangelist had been
converted by a notoriously racist and anti-Semitic revivalist. He
grew up in a culture suspicious of Judaism, even though fundamentalism's millennial theme made him friendly to the state of Israel. McLoughlin cited a sermon by Graham from 1948, "The Sin
of Tolerance." The evangelist there defined tolerance as broadmindedness; it meant one was "willing to put up with beliefs
opposed to one's convictions." Graham used a vivid metaphor:
"When we come in for the landing in the great airport in heaven I
don't want any broadmindedness. I want to come in on the beam
and even though I may be considered narrow here, I want to be
sure of a safe landing there." Even McLoughlin had to follow this
up with a footnote: "This does not mean that Graham indulges
in anti-Semitism or anti-Catholicism. He does not." But, noted
McLoughlin, when people at rallies came forward after Graham's
appeal, the people assigned to counsel them backstage after the
event were instructed to try to proselytize Catholics or Jews.
His biographer thought that practice would make them despise
Graham. "Nevertheless Graham has been so friendly toward the
Roman Catholic church that some of his original supporters among
the fanatical fundamentalists have attacked him for betraying their
cause."

Graham wanted to be "a rallying center around whom all   19:28
people interested in good things may gather," but soon he was in
danger of being all things to all people. "He is accused of being
too liberal by the fundamentalists and too fundamentalistic by the
liberals." But it happened that the vast public was itself located
between the extremes. McLoughlin tracked Graham through the
paths of paradox. Anyone who knew orthodoxy would have found
great differences between Graham and Peale, but in Graham's New
York crusade, when people who made a "decision for Christ" indicated a preference, Peale's church had more such votes than any
of the other 1,500 cooperating congregations. "The pietistic fun-

damentalist and the mystical modernist meet in the realm of hope and miracles."

19:29   The most puzzling paradox was in Graham's preaching an imminent fiery end of the world while being perceived as an affirmer of the American Way of Life. He could fairly shout that "America at this moment is under the pending judgment of God, and unless we have a spiritual revival now, we are done as a nation. The hour is far later than we think." Yet while preaching dependence on God, Graham wanted America to take its own defense into its own hands. "Christianity needs a show of strength and force." This meant "we must maintain the strongest military establishment on earth." The best antidote to atheistic communism was "old-fashioned Americanism." At times Graham almost echoed Senator Joseph McCarthy: "Communism is far worse than we realize. With termites in America and barbarians outside, we are beginning to crumble apart." For all the apocalypticism, however, Graham came across to the public as a prophet of peace, a unifier. He wrote a best-seller in symmetry with the others, *Peace with God.* Graham cited "peace of conscience, peace of mind, and peace of soul," peace on earth, peace in the face of the crises of life as desiderata. But the Bible taught most of all peace with God. The "solution" was to be "born again," through repentance and belief in God.

19:30   Jews could not accept a Gospel centered in Jesus Christ. Catholics could not accept a Jesus Christ apart from the Catholic church. Yet, while elites among them joined Protestant grumblers, their publics were generally welcoming when Graham came to town. While doom was part of his analysis in *Peace with God,* the evangelist brought cheer, golfed with presidents, won favor with businesspeople, and assured Americans that all was, or could be, well. As Yinger would say, Graham took the old symbols of non-change in religion and appealed to people who needed continuity in a changing world. But he would change the effect of these apocalyptic and prophetic symbols so that they matched the needs and interests of a changed audience and populace. Thus, with all the popular religionists of his time, he also helped effect the "new religion" of the day, the popular faith that was a singular version of the plural civic faith in the One Nation, Under God.

20

"Men Locked Together in Argument"

Both developing civic faith and popular religion in the mid-   20:1
century decades marked the efforts of Americans to create for their
time "One Nation, Under God." Yet because they knew that One
Nation included people of many faiths, citizens popularized the
word *pluralism* to describe their society. They also knew that they
did not experience *mere* or *utter* pluralism, a chaos of plotless sects
and rootless individuals. People came together in denominations,
ecumenical and interfaith forces, voluntary associations, racial and
ethnic clusters. How could those who would describe the society
and interpret its moves bring some plot to the patterns of these
groupings? How could they find the roots and boundaries of the
faith commitments of millions? The mid-century decades saw two
especially inventive efforts to simplify the pattern and provide
some coherence. One was the argument that the American Way of
Life was expressed in three large communities: Protestant, Catholic, and Jew. The other was the contention that the society was
formed and informed by a particular religious tradition of moral
discourse and pious practice. The word *Christian,* still used by
the Supreme Court in 1931, had come to be too exclusive. The
word *religious,* the adjective used to describe the American people
in a 1952 Supreme Court decision, was too inclusive and vague.
Somewhere between these two was developed the concept of "the
Judeo-Christian tradition," an entity unknown in Europe, where

both Jews and Christians had lived for centuries. The notion had hardly been thought of in the United States for most of the three centuries after Jews arrived in 1654.

20:2   President Dwight D. Eisenhower advanced the latter terminological cause by his frequent references, beginning in the campaign of 1952, to "Judeo-Christian" religion. One does not picture him or his speechwriters spending evenings with dictionaries compiled, as the *Oxford English Dictionary* puts it, "on historical principles." If they had, they would have found one reference to this term dating as far back as 1899. But it certainly did not enter the argot of America until World War II. Then it was occasionally useful first over against rightist antisecular or sometimes anti-Jewish movements that fought to call the nation "Christian America." In 1949 at the Conference on Science, Philosophy, and Religion, Cornell professor Arthur E. Murphy summarized the case: "It is in 'our Judeo-Christian heritage,' the culture of 'the West,' or 'the American tradition,' that our spiritual leaders look[ed] for the moral foundations of our democratic ideals." Of course, anti-Semitic people could argue that the hyphenated word seemed to give parity to a community representing 3 percent of the population alongside one that attracted varying degrees of loyalty from between 80 to 90 percent. Against such a charge, Christian leaders could point to the Jewish roots, in the Bible and the synagogue, of the Christian tradition. In any case, Jews did quickly seize on and promote the term. Thus in 1951 at a National Federation of Temple Brotherhoods meeting, speaker Roger Straus found the term useful when posing a contrast with the Cold War enemy. Straus pictured a "world-wide clash of two divergent beliefs: the Judeo-Christian philosophy and the crass materialism of communism."

20:3   Will Herberg used the term *Judeo-Christian* at the end of his classic *Protestant-Catholic-Jew* in 1955 when he wanted to speak of a "fundamental religious affirmation and commitment held in common by Judaism and Christianity." In 1953 Father John M. Oesterreicher devised an Institute of Judaeo-Christian Studies at Seton Hall University, in a sign of Catholic commitment. The most prominent Protestant theologians also found the concept congenial. Reinhold Niebuhr identified himself with the sources out of which others were patenting the name Judeo-Christian, though he preferred another term: "I have, as a Christian theologian," he wrote in wartime, "sought to strengthen the Hebraic-prophetic content of the Christian tradition." In his major book at the time of *Protestant-Catholic-Jew, The Self and the Dramas of History,* Niebuhr stressed the Hebraic as opposed to the combined Hebraic-Hellenic roots of Christian faith. Paul Tillich, the German refugee who had come to fame also at Union Theological Seminary, in 1952 titled an article "Is There a Judeo-Christian Tradition?" and answered an unsurprising "Yes." Waldo Frank, a Jewish writer who was a friend of Niebuhr, cited both Niebuhr and Tillich as "religious minds who read the great stories of both Testaments" to reach deeper truths. Of course, all Christians this side of "Aryan" and anti-Semitic Nazism were thus reading both Testaments, but it was in America that a new political use was made of the reading.

Some critics saw the invention of the hyphenated term as a 20:4 blending designed to promote civic religion. Thus figures from World Council of Churches in their conference in Evanston in 1954 backed off from attempts to proselytize Jews, because attempts at conversion "would embarrass them in their relationships with their Jewish friends." Jewish scholar Seymour Martin Lipset perceived in such gestures not only etiquette but a kind of failure of nerve on the part of these mainstream Protestants. Fundamentalists and evangelicals, not represented at Evanston, by the way, would not have worried about such embarrassment, even though many of them for reasons based in their millennial belief needed, and were friends of, the State of Israel. And in Lipset's eyes, another set of believers was unready to make good use of the term: "the Catholics, of course, [who] are 'un-American' in this sense, since no good American should believe in the superiority of his own religion." Now in contrast, Lipset further observed, the mainstream Protestants, who were yielding their old claims to monopoly or hegemony and learning to share space and power with others, evidently began to use Judeo-Christian language in order to sound American and to abandon claims for superiority.

Catholics, however, more than Lipset noticed at the moment, 20:5 were entering the argument over naming and conceiving pluralism in precisely those mid-century years. While any number of figures worked on the theme alongside Father Oesterreicher, one looks to the most profound and influential of the thinkers, Father John Courtney Murray. Although he did not need the term, he was fighting off any concept of a Judeo-Protestant (and secularist) culture. Murray was indeed "un-American" in Lipset's terms, because he did share the orthodox Catholic belief that *extra ecclesiam nulla salus,* "outside the church there is no salvation." This belief made Murray sound more ambivalent about pluralism than did Herberg or Niebuhr, but the priest was finding ways to make Catholicism more acceptable and less "un-American" to non-Catholic America. He spent the years establishing grounds to justify a place for Catholicism in pluralism. The agenda for all this was being set by outsiders, such as Harvard sociologist Talcott Parsons, then in his prime. How, Parsons often asked, could one at the same time be at home with pluralism, civic religion, the Protestant-Catholic-Jew and Judeo-Christian formulas, so long as official Catholic teaching against tolerance remained on the books? Catholicism, said Parsons, "does not believe and never has believed in principle in religious toleration in the specific American sense; it accepts it, because being in a minority status it has no alternative."

20:6   The concept *Judeo-Christian,* when thought of doctrinally, looked like a formula for letting tolerance win out over Catholic truth. Monsignor Joseph Fenton, editor of the *American Ecclesiastical Review* and one of Murray's two most persistent enemies, attacked Murray frontally on this point. "Neither the Church nor the faithful teachers of the Church try to understress any section of Catholic doctrine, simply because it happens to be unfashionable or happens to be abused by anti-Catholic agitators at the time." A similar criticism was leveled by Murray's other critic, Father Francis J. Connell, but Murray rejected it: "Father Connell credits me with the intention of trying to 'smooth the way toward a better understanding of the Catholic Church on the part of non-Catholics in America' by a process of compromising Catholic principles, or concealing them, or understating them." No, Murray said, he was using precisely those principles to justify new civil relations with other "conspirators," people who "breathed with" you, in the republic. Murray wrote essays that he collected several years later in a major work, *We Hold These Truths.* During those years he made the requisite *Time* magazine cover appearance and became a religious celebrity of sorts.

20:7   Murray, a forceful person with an aristocratic mien, could sound off-putting. At times wearing the hat that identified him with Catholic doctrinal exclusivism, he could say that Protestants and Catholics were not two of one kind. Nor did the invoking of a Judeo-Christian tradition succeed in making Catholic truth less than uniquely true. When, however, the religious groups "conspired," they did this not only on the grounds of sentiment but by drawing on something much deeper. Murray argued that argument was basic to the life of a republic; and he quoted Dominican Thomas Gilby to make his point: "Civilization is formed by men locked together in argument. From this dialogue the community becomes a political community." But, the priest went on to argue, argument could not occur unless people who were in contention also shared something of the same worldview. He called this basis a civil consensus. This meant "an ensemble of substantive truths, a structure of basic knowledge, an order of elementary affirmations that reflect realities inherent in the order of existence."

Murray knew that such argument would be difficult to prose-   20:8
cute. "As we discourse on public affairs, on the affairs of the commonwealth, and particularly on the problem of consensus, we inevitably have to move upward, as it were, into realms of some
theoretical generality—into metaphysics, ethics, theology." But
how could consensus be found up there? Instead of consensus,
Americans demonstrated "confusion" because Protestants, Catholics, Jews, and secularists lived in "a plurality of universes of
discourse. These universes are incommensurable." Jews, he noted,
often allied with secularists to fend off Christian aims at dominating. Protestants and Catholics distrusted each other. The secularist
opposed the other three. "In secularist theory there can be only one
society, one law, one power, and one faith, a civic faith that is the
'unifying' bond of the community, whereby it withstands the assaults of assorted pluralisms." The secularist would push religion
aside into irrelevance, conceiving it to be a "purely private matter."
Or secularist theory might support what Murray dismissed in a
sneer, "religion-in-general, whatever that is."

Murray never came to a full defense of pluralism, but he repeat-   20:9
edly told why he put energy into it. "Religious pluralism is against
the will of God. But it is the human condition; it is written into the
script of history. It will not somehow marvelously cease to trouble
the City," by which he meant society, a republic. Then he set out
to trouble it marvelously. He argued against the secularist. Using
the new official terminology, the Jesuit declared that America was
indeed a "nation under God," a God who was sovereign over
nations as over individuals. Murray welcomed the Supreme Court
statement of 1952 about Americans: "We are a religious people
whose institutions presuppose a Supreme Being." Human rights in
America, he liked to stress, were grounded in natural law. Advocates of these rights witnessed that their source was in God, "the
Creator of nature and the Master of history." But now, Murray
mourned, that ground and source were being obscured, lost, or
forgotten, in pluralism. Here Murray sounded most negative about
the situation: "The truth is that American society is religiously pluralist. The truth is lamentable; it is nonetheless true." Americans

believed in many false things. Yet government could not decide which of these were true or false. Curiously, Catholicism thrived in this climate. "It has been good for religion, for Catholicism, to have had simply the right of freedom," the American priest asserted, with one eye on Europe and another on Fathers Connell and Fenton.

20:10   Murray was critical of civic faith and popular religion alike, and he did the worrying for many others, not Catholics alone, when he looked at the unfolding pluralism around him. In a remarkable passage he asked: "How much of the pluralism is bogus and unreal? And how much of the unity is likewise bogus and undesirable?" And then he added two more questions: "How much pluralism and what kinds of pluralism can a pluralist society stand?" The converse also needed to be asked: "How much unity and what kind of unity does a pluralist society need in order to be a society at all, effectively organized for responsible action in history, and yet a 'free' society?" Murray was one of the first to use the term *postmodern* to describe the situation into which America was moving. In such a moment his questions were especially urgent. The unfolding ecumenical movement showed him that divided Protestantism "now feels its own inner discordant pluralisms as no longer an unqualified glory but as something of a scandal." Meanwhile, Catholicism remained too sure of its past unities, confined by its old inherited European mold. Murray did his own simplifying of the scene. "There may indeed be some three hundred religious bodies in America," he agreed, but there were generically only three *styles* of these—the Protestant, the Catholic, and the Jewish. Only natural law tradition, he argued, stood any chance of grounding the discourse of these three.

20:11   To his credit, Murray showed awareness that he could not easily sell his version of that tradition. For an instance: Presbyterian theologian Robert McAfee Brown, a pioneer in conversing with Catholics, was well known to Murray. For Brown, said the priest, "the whole doctrine of natural law is a challenge, if not an affront, to his entire style of moral thought and even to his religiosity." As a typical Protestant, Brown misunderstood and distrusted natural law argument. It was true that for Brown and his kind, "Catholic appeals to natural law remain a source of friction rather than a basis of deeper understanding" because such critics mistakenly thought they were based on distinctively Roman Catholic presuppositions. Murray argued the negative of this proposition: natural law's "only presupposition is threefold: that man is intelligent; that reality is intelligible; and that reality, as grasped by intelligence, imposes on the will the obligation that it be obeyed in its demands for action or abstention." Everything was supposed to be as simple as that. Yet ironically Murray's search for common ground in natural law made Catholicism appear to be an island apart from the worlds of non-Catholics. Despite all the problems, however, Protestants and Jews were so happy to find such a clarifying and ready voice in Murray that they were glad to pick up the conversation with him, or to take up what he preferred to call more accurately not a conversation but an argument over the republic.

Most Jews in the debate found it easier to move toward the cen-   20:12
ter of national life through reference to the Judeo-Christian tradition than to natural law. But like Murray and the Catholics, or like every kind of serious Protestant, they also had to draw on their own resources in order to find rationales for their place within pluralism. To advance this project, they had to retrieve texts and meanings from the Jewish past. A theological debate demanded theological awareness. It happened that a rebirth, one might almost say a birth, of Jewish theology was then in process. Jews had not often spoken of having a theology at all, since the very concept was Greek. But in Europe Franz Rosenzweig and Martin Buber had been engaging in profound reflection about the human condition in Jewish terms, and what they voiced found resonance in America. So strong was the emphasis on such reflection that some Jews worried about its potential effects. Would not theology tear Judaism apart, just as it had produced pettiness and factionalism in other religious communities? Since theology was traditional and referred to the supernatural, would it not distract Jews from their goal of becoming truly modern? Judd Teller in 1958, arguing as a self-named secularist Jew, feared that a Jewish theology would inevitably be otherworldly in accent. Thus it would work against the worldly good in pursuit of which Judaism had won a good name at last, and its expression might inspire new outbursts of anti-Semitism, because it had to be particular. Teller as a matter of fact underestimated the earthiness of Jewish theology and the interest Christians were showing in Buber, Rosenzweig, immigrant survivors of Nazism like Abraham Joshua Heschel and Emil Fackenheim, and a home-grown set of thinkers.

A controversial turn in the conversation within Judaism came   20:13
when in 1949 the notable scholar Milton Steinberg was invited to state the case for theology to the conservative Rabbinical Assembly of America. Judah Goldin had to read the address for the ter-

minally ill Steinberg, who could not attend. The Steinberg argument began with this call: "a need exists" for theology, "a great and crying need." Without it, Judaism would be a wasteland, or thoughtful Jews would turn to Christian communions, "which do furnish the required spiritual nutriment." Will Herberg, in response to Steinberg, sounded benedictive: "May this discussion here today mark the beginning of a new creative effort on the part of American Jewry" to meet and fulfill the need for a search for the word of God. Not much further happened by way of immediate response, but through the subsequent decade many rabbis and professors picked up on Steinberg's cue. Herberg himself in those years employed Hebraic and Judaic sources in order to criticize the civic faith and popular religion of the Eisenhower era. In his eyes, both Rabbi Joshua Loth Liebman and the Reverend Norman Vincent Peale did their formulating largely outside the "theocentric faith of the historic religions." "Positive thinking," as they developed it, represented the "inner disintegration and enfeeblement of the historic religions." Herberg dismissed Billy Graham and the revivalists from the public argument because, "for all the power and fervor of their crusades," they still spoke in the "language of individualistic piety, which in lesser men [than the admired Graham] frequently degenerates into a smug and nagging moralism." Within mainstream Protestantism, he further charged, there was "not much difference between the 'churched' and the 'unchurched.'" Herberg recalled better days: "It was very different when Protestantism meant 'the sovereignty of God, the kingship of Christ, and the coming kingdom,' the transformation of life and the promise of salvation." Herberg pronounced his prophetic judgment: "So the Protestant movement has not been resumed." In revisiting the critiques of Herberg and those who follow, I do not mean to say that all criticisms were just or, as Abraham Joshua Heschel was to say in derision, that they could all be checked out by social-scientific measures. The purpose in adducing them here is to treat the assertions, taken together, as an event: this happened. This is how the theologically informed critics looked at the American spiritual situation during the years of the revival. More, then, from Herberg.

20:14   As the newcomer from Marxism to Jewish theology surveyed the other partners in pluralism, the Catholics, he watched as they "began to regard their church as one of the three great American religious communities and themselves as devotees of religion in one of its three American forms." While holding officially and canonically to the claim that they held unique and exclusive truth, Catholics demonstrated a "deep-lying, though often unarticulated, conception of American social reality." Thus an alert Catholic, Herberg thought, could not close his eyes to the intrinsic pluralism of American society and to the way his church had to operate and be regarded as only one among several communities. Catholics were learning "to operate with a double vision," seeing themselves first as a "self-enclosed microcosmic community within their own church" and second as a member of the "tripartite macrocosm" of Protestant, Catholic, and Jewish subcommunities that were busy promoting one American faith. Now at last, having displayed "openness to the outside world," he observed, the Catholic church "speaks to, and is heard by, the entire nation." Now, he further argued, when the hierarchy blasts "secularism" and "atheistic materialism," its voice does not sound sectarian but is regarded as a general religious pronouncement to the nation. At last, no matter what theologians thought, the Catholic church was "recognized as a genuinely American religious community." Catholicism had become one of the three great "religions of democracy." It was at home, though not heard as the Universal Church; it had paid a price for the place it had gained.

While defining pluralism, Herberg put major energies into a critique of Judaism. Disappearing or gone, he thought, were such ideologies and causes as social radicalism and militant Zionism. In their place, "serious works dealing with Jewish faith and destiny" were beginning to find "interested readers precisely among the most American segments of the Jewish community," such as in Reform. But—and now his nervousness showed—he had to ask, "What was the shape and form of the religion of the Jewish community in mid-twentieth century America?" Jews had adopted Christian forms, and "old-line secular Judaism is obsolescent," he pronounced, while religious Judaism had become secularized. As ambivalent as Murray in the end, he also saw two contradictory pulls within his community. Herberg made virtually no reference to the Holocaust or the birth of Israel as constitutive of modern Judaism in the United States. The American Jew could establish his Jewishness "not apart from, nor in spite of, his Americanness, but precisely through and by virtue of it." Now when it had become the third of the "religions of democracy," he had to observe that "there was perplexity and restlessness." This provoked Herberg to ask without providing a clear answer: "Was this all there was to Judaism after all? Had it no higher purpose or destiny?"

20:16   What did rule? "The fundamental unity of American religion, rooted in the American Way of Life" was now in place, but even in its presence conflict and tension remained. Perceptively Herberg read the heart and mind of Protestants. They were experiencing "the sudden realization that Protestantism is no longer identical with America," so they presented the "anomaly of a strong majority group with a growing minority consciousness." Jews also suspected that Catholics had an imperial design on America. But Herberg wanted to reassure non-Catholics: they should not be "unduly disturbed lest the growing religio-communal pluralism disrupt the unity and subvert the foundations of American society." No matter what the tensions, he thought, it was "the American Way of Life" that would prevail. And then, as quickly as always, he would apply his prophetic Jewish perspective: "It is only too evident that the religiousness characteristic of America today is very often a religiousness without religion," a contentless form of sociability or "belonging" and not a reorienting of life to God. Where were the ties to "Christian or Jewish faith rooted in the prophetic tradition?" As for the "civic religion of the American people," which at some moments and for some functions Herberg viewed positively, in this context he thought it was a sanctification of the society and the culture it reflected, "and that is one of the reasons why Jewish-Christian faith has always regarded such religion as incurably idolatrous." The new religiousness, as he saw it, reinforced national self-righteousness and self-will. He quoted Protestant A. Roy Eckardt, "The God of judgment has died."

20:17   Herberg, at midcareer, was not without company as an advocate of Jewish theology and social criticism. Jews of the younger generation also began to be heard during the Eisenhower years. Thus Arthur Cohen, publisher, novelist, and theologian, reported on trends and spoke up himself both in a later book, *The Myth of the Judeo-Christian Tradition,* which drew on viewpoints shaped during those years but was written in 1962, and in *The Natural and Supernatural Jew.* Cohen took off from an essay published by Mordecai Kaplan in 1947, "Towards a Philosophy of Cultural Integration." For the critical portion of his book he cited Will Herberg, A. Roy Eckardt, and William Lee Miller as authors of full-fledged critiques. He also summoned "an expanding group of writers, including John Courtney Murray, S. J., Reinhold Niebuhr, Martin E. Marty, William Clancy, and the present writer," who together had addressed themselves to a "criticism of precisely the 'soteric' [meaning "pertaining to salvation"] unity of religion and the democratic way" praised by, among others, Kaplan and his Reconstructionist Jewish colleagues.

Cohen then picked up on and revised Steinberg's writings, be-   20:18
cause Steinberg, he thought, was moving away from being a lover of Jewish civilization apart from God and toward affirmation of God, ideas of transcendence, and Jewish theology. It was true that "the God of Milton Steinberg was a philosopher's God," to whom it was difficult to pray. But Steinberg at least saw that "the deepest problem of human life is not the survival of the group but the survival of individual conscience and private intellectual and religious integrity." At the very end of his life Steinberg recognized that Judaism "has the daring to admit that while man can know little, very little, about God and himself, he can and does know something."

There Cohen took off. In the midst of American pluralism,   20:19
much as Niebuhr had done for Protestants and Murray for Catholics, now, by analogy, Jews must work: "Unless the vocation of the Jewish people, that which encumbers it with supernatural charge and obligation is reaffirmed," Jewish thought had no future. Of course, all Jewish theologians, including Cohen himself, agreed that the *sine qua non* of Jewish life was the "necessity of the existence of the Jewish people." But mere survival was not enough; Cohen cared that "the supernatural Jew shall survive." The modern Jew must now ask: "Can he believe? What does he understand his belief to be? What obligations does his belief confer?" The renewal of the Jewish vocation was then "not a fact of history but an article of faith." Cohen spent little time on sociology; he was God-intoxicated. Talk about God, or theology, is "the science of sacred history. It sets itself but one task: to apprehend and interpret the presence of God in time and history." Cohen then stood against the face of popular Judaism. "The role of Judaism, therefore, is not to create culture *as such,* but to be the critic of culture—to make culture the partial consummation of history and the anticipation of the Kingdom of God." In the new America, the task of religion in culture was not to conserve the vision but "to dislocate those who pretend to institutionalize *less* than the vision." Cohen could sound as critical as Herberg when he looked at the "religion of democracy" advocated by some Jewish leaders only a few years earlier. In the America on which he sweepingly commented, "there is no religion; there is only religious sentiment." There was neither vision nor the loss of vision, only "ambiguity and the abyss." Therefore, "in a disintegrating culture the task of religion is prophetic."

20:20   Jews in Judeo-Christian America, or in the Protestant-Catholic-Jewish nation, needed a theologian and critic to match Christians Niebuhr and Murray, someone to match the others as a *Time* cover subject. (Protestants, as a larger group, got two: Paul Tillich was a similar Luce magazine celebrity in theology.) Abraham Joshua Heschel, Cohen's teacher, a "rhetorician of faith," came to occupy that place for Cohen and for many others in the public sphere. For Heschel, God was an "ontological presupposition," which meant that the "experience of God presupposes the reality of God." On that presupposition Heschel could be an articulator of Cohen's "supernatural Judaism" and at the same time a judge of both civic faith and popular religion. Cohen used Heschel to make his own point about contemporary America: "Ardent and profound belief is dead and conventional belief and practice dull and weary both believer and nonbeliever." Jews had known plenty of sages; now they needed a prophet. Heschel, a refugee from Hitler who started teaching at Jewish Theological Seminary in 1945, seemed a misfit in the conservative camp. He was rooted in Hasidism, a movement that looked esoteric in postwar America. It was at home with biblical and mystical references. Heschel imported and transmitted currents of Judaism that ran counter to the adapted Judaism that had made the Jewish people and their civilization, not the God of Israel, central to Jewish life.

20:21   Heschel expressed shock as he spoke to the Rabbinical Assembly of America in 1953. "I have been in the United States of America for thirteen years. I have not discovered America, but I have discovered something in America. It is possible to be a rabbi and not to believe in the God of Abraham, Isaac and Jacob." Heschel was already American enough to back up his observation about disbelief with surveys. But the rabbi was met at first not with shock but with impassivity, except among a few of the younger theologically minded rabbis. One scholar who later appraised the moment heard in Heschel an analogous word to one that Protestant Paul Tillich had uttered in 1948: "The first word, therefore, to be spoken by religion to the people of our time must be a word spoken against religion." And Tillich had provided a charter for this: "It is the word of the old Jewish prophets spoken against the priestly and royal and pseudo-prophetic guardians of their national religion." Conservative rabbis, Heschel knew, were not yet ready to be thus confronted and challenged.

20:22   Heschel shared a platform with Niebuhr, Murray, and Tillich at a notable "Protestant-Catholic-Jew-secularist" engagement in May

1958 at the World Affairs Center in New York. The Fund for the Republic there convened notables to discuss "religion in a free society." Heschel used his time to denounce civic faith and popular religion alike, employing generalizations that were vast and stated without allowance for exceptions. "Little does religion ask of contemporary man," he began. "It is ready to comfort; it has no courage to challenge. It is ready to offer edification; it has no courage to break the idols, to shatter the callousness." In less than four lines Heschel condensed his analysis of Judeo-Christian America. "The trouble is that religion has become 'religion'—institution, dogma, securities. It is not an event anymore." The rabbi grasped well the mood of the religious revival. Religion's acceptance, he said, "involves neither risk nor strain. Religion has achieved respectability by the grace of society, and its representatives publish as a frontispiece the *nihil obstat* signed by social scientists."

By paragraph two Heschel was delivering on Cohen's promise   20:23
that one must talk of faith with an object. "There is no substitute for faith, no alternative for revelation, no surrogate for commitment." Americans "define self-reliance and call it faith, shrewdness and call it wisdom, anthropology and call it ethics, literature and call it Bible, inner security and call it religion, conscience and call it God." All of that Heschel called counterfeit and considered perishable. Believers liked to blame secular science and antireligious philosophy for their plight, but it would be more honest to blame religion for its own defeats. "Religion declined not because it was refuted, but because it became irrelevant, dull, oppressive, insipid." Heschel's critical diagnosis of the spiritual condition of mid-century America inspired rhetorical flourishes: "Needs are looked upon today as if they were holy, as if they contained the totality of existence. Needs are our gods." And religion adjusted to the modern temper "by proclaiming that it too is the satisfaction of a need." This concept was "surely diametrically opposed to the prophetic attitude," thought Heschel, and the absence of prophecy contributed to the "sterilization of religious thinking." The mind of the prophets, he reminded, "was not religion-centered." They dealt with public and religious shortcomings. Where was their kind of transcendent justice proclaimed in America?

In the fashion of the decade, Heschel distinguished religion   20:24
from faith. "Religion has become an impersonal affair, an institutional loyalty," which survives on activities, not commitment. When Jewish intellectuals measured faith using social scientific instruments, he said, religion fell "victim to the belief that the real is

only that which is capable of being registered by fact-finding surveys." It lacked soul. But Heschel offered a prescription: "Religion's major effort must be to counteract the deflation of man, the trivialization of human existence." And he could toss an occasional bouquet: "Our religious traditions claim that man is capable of sacrifice, discipline, of moral and spiritual exaltation, that every man is capable of an ultimate commitment." And, in prophetic style, Heschel relied on the presence of a faithful remnant: "Surely God will always receive a surprise of a handful of fools," and "there will always remain a spiritual underground where a few brave minds continue to fight." Speaking in New York, surrounded by tall towers of the United Nations and competitive commerce, the rabbi expressed his concern: not "how to worship in the catacombs but rather how to remain human in the skyscrapers."

20:25   The development of Jewish theology as a part of the religious revival, a response to neo-Protestant theology, and a contribution to pluralism (needed in a Judeo-Christian or a Protestant-Catholic-Jewish culture) was not always welcomed, nor did it go unchallenged. At the end of the decade, for example, the influential editor of the *Jewish Spectator,* Trude Weiss-Rosmarin, blew a whistle in an editorial that signaled the beginning of a change from support of religion in general toward Jewish particularism. The fact that theology was a word of Greek origin was not what disturbed her. "It is born when religious belief as emotion asks questions. Theology is the reflective revaluation of belief." Her problem was with the dominance of neo-Protestantism in American culture and the way it was so consistently being used as a model. "The oft-repeated platitude that Judaism has no theology, too, is a result of the notion of the existence of a theological norm by which the 'theological' nature of religious reasoning is to be determined." Too many Jews took their signals from the Niebuhr brothers and Paul Tillich.

20:26   Weiss-Rosmarin named names and sometimes connected them with sneers, as in "Will Herberg is not the only would-be theologian of Judaism who thinks in the categories of Reinhold Niebuhr and thus, inevitably, distorts Jewishness by making it conform to a Protestant theological norm." But Herberg seemed simply beyond redemption to Weiss-Rosmarin. It was more of a "melancholy commentary on the lack-and-loss of Jewish theological independence," she went on in her indictment, that the late Milton Steinberg ten years earlier had presented "The Theological Issues of the Hour" at a Rabbinical Assembly convention, and made his main reference to figures like Niebuhr, Tillich, "and their schools." Of course, he criticized them, but then he said that he, for one, owed "a considerable debt of gratitude to the neo-Reformationists, Reinhold Niebuhr in particular." Such thinkers had caused him to see a truth he had somehow missed in the surrounding world, though its evidences were everywhere. Steinberg had often encountered this in the rabbinic tradition, but, "being a creature of modernity," he had denatured it. This truth had to do with the depth and tenacity of evil in human nature. "If a Milton Steinberg could fall in this type of thraldom to neo-Protestantism," said his critic, it was no wonder that younger rabbis fell further. She attacked among them David Wolf Silverman, who in another paper at the Rabbinical Assembly in May 1949 spoke on "current theological trends" only by reference to neo-Protestant theology and in his bibliography included not one Jewish title.

Silverman's rattling off of Jewish names gave particularists like 20:27 Weiss-Rosmarin a rogue's gallery: Will Herberg, Arthur Cohen, and ten others did not classify for her as *Jewish* theologians. Why had Silverman overlooked one Max Kadushin, "the only Jewish theologian in America who has created an original system of Jewish theology," which was "not a reaction or answer to neo-Protestant theology." Kadushin was not, like Heschel and his imitators, "a tender-minded mystic and a poet-ecstatic expositor of Jewish sentiment"; he *was* someone who worked "altogether independent of the Barth-Niebuhr-Tillich wave of the present." Judaism, Weiss-Rosmarin argued, was *sui generis,* "unique and without analogy," and so must its theology be. Hers was the signal that not all could be subsumed under the hyphen in Judeo-Christian. "If a *Jewish* theological renaissance is to bloom in this country, it must be rooted in *Jewish* theological thought. It must base itself on *Jewish* theologians and philosophers," among whom she listed the Kantian Hermann Cohen and the modernist Leo Baeck. (There seemed to be no way for even *her* Jews to be *sui generis.*) The perplexed Jewish generation needed guidance on how to believe and how to understand belief, but, she insisted, "as Jews, we want to walk by the light of our heritage, not by the illumination borrowed from Kierkegaard and Niebuhr." But Weiss-Rosmarin's voice anticipated the Jewish turn that would come several years later; during the revival of religion in the Eisenhower period, the voices of the Niebuhrs and Paul Tillich set many of the terms.

We have already seen Reinhold Niebuhr as a Cold Warrior writ- 20:28

ing *The Irony of American History,* with its criticism chiefly of Soviet communism and secondarily of the United States for identifying "a particular force in history with the final purposes of the God of history." For Niebuhr the United States had seemed somewhat remote from the historical turns of the time, but now at midcentury, he wrote, "we are drawn into an historic situation in which the paradise of our domestic security is suspended in a hell of global insecurity." He had to question the reality of the paradise and did so by comparing the national scene to *Don Quixote:* "Of all the 'knights' of bourgeois culture, our castle is the most imposing and our horse the sleekest and most impresssive. Our armor is the shiniest," and "the lady of our dreams is the most opulent and desirable," for she has been turned into "prosperity." Sometimes, Niebuhr charged, Americans disguised knowledge of the world around them from themselves; that is where President Eisenhower fit in: "the Eisenhower myth is partly dependent upon the desire of the American people to forget their anxieties and troubles."

20:29   When Niebuhr wanted to find fault with the emergent religious scene, however, he characteristically criticized fellow Christians, most notably those who followed positive thinker Norman Vincent Peale or evangelist Billy Graham, the quintessential ministers for Americans' prosperities and anxieties. In 1955 in an editorial in *Christianity and Crisis* Niebuhr turned on the National Council of Churches for supporting Norman Vincent Peale and for contributing to the general superficiality of the times. Modern religiosity of this sort, he thought, expressed "various forms of self-worship." The popular leaders of the Christian church offered this self-worship, regarding it not "as a substitute but as an interpretation" of the Christian faith. Jesus' word, "Repent ye, for the kingdom of heaven is at hand," came to be reduced to the "power of positive thinking." This religiosity promoted self-esteem, but profound secularists now had to take up the task of stating responsibilities. "One must come to the conclusion that religion per se and faith per se are not virtuous, or a cause of virtue." The question had to be: what was the object of worship? Niebuhr insisted that so long as such superficiality reigned, citizens could "take no satisfaction in the pervading religiosity of our nation." Much of it aggravated more than it mitigated the problems of successful people.

20:30   As for evangelist Billy Graham, who got a free ride from most public commentators, Niebuhr wrote for the *New York Times* that among signs of a revival was "the evidence of 'mass' conversions under the ministrations of popular evangelists who arouse the religious emotions and elicit religious commitments with greater success than at any time since the days of Billy Sunday." Niebuhr had Graham in mind and probably could not have named a second such evangelist of his own time. By 1957, as Graham neared his prime, the theologian had grown more critical than at the beginning. Much of mainstream Protestantism in New York was backing Graham's forthcoming crusade. How could the New York City Protestant Council be a sponsor, asked Niebuhr, and the ministers be turned into "ballyhoo helpers," given "all the high pressure techniques of modern salesmanship" and "all the arts of the Madison Avenue crowd?" The theologian found Graham indeed to be "personable, modest and appealing," but Niebuhr had to "dread the prospect" of that New York crusade because the evangelist had "wedded considerable dramatic and demagogic gifts with a rather obscurantist version of the Christian faith."

That year Niebuhr published *Pious and Secular America,* a   20:31
book that found him siding with "responsible and discriminating secularists" against Graham. Now Niebuhr used the ironic perspective, finding it ironic that Graham's gospel gave "even simpler answers to insoluble problems" than did the secularists. "It cuts through all the hard antimonies of life and history by the simple promise that really good people will really be good." But there was pathos, too: "It does this at the precise moment when secularism, purged of its illusions, is modestly ready to work at tasks for which there are no immediate rewards and to undertake burdens for which there can be no promise of relief." Mainstream Protestants critical of the revival sided with Niebuhr, but they were outnumbered and hardly listened to, given the popularity of Graham, who treated Niebuhr with respect and even claimed to have taken seriously some of Niebuhr's counsels. And, in turn, some who would have sided with Niebuhr on most affairs came to champion Graham. Thus Princeton Seminary dean Elmer G. Homrighausen, himself a "neo-Protestant," asked in a *Christian Century* article what Niebuhrian-style faith was accomplishing. Was it not "hesitant and weak in calling persons to a positive faith?" Why had mainstream Protestantism been unable "to lead the way in the revival or rebirth or restoration of a relevant Protestantism in the local church?" Yet a National Council of Churches commission, of which Homrighausen was a part, turned in a report in May 1957 that was more Niebuhrian than Grahamite. Revivalism could be-

come a "gross caricature," because, he said, it "involves both possible values and very real perils for evangelism." Graham and the evangelicals found the evangelistic path clear.

20:32   In 1960 Niebuhr looked back on the decade and told Union Seminary students that it took him longer than it should have "to realize that no religion can guarantee personal integrity." Paraphrasing novelist Mary McCarthy, who had said "religion is a good thing for good people but a bad thing for bad people," he said, "religion is a good thing for honest people but a bad thing for dishonest people." This outlook reflected his thought in this period when he suggested that Americans, like the ancient Athenians in the account of the book of Acts, were "very religious." But "our religiosity seems to have as little to do with the Christian faith as the religiosity of the Athenians." The "unknown god" in America was faith itself, and politicians were those who admonished people to have such faith, which had to be an idol. "We are so sure of ourselves, of our power and of our virtue, and yet we are not sure of our destiny at all." And again at the end of the decade, Niebuhr confided in a letter to Supreme Court Justice Felix Frankfurter that this piety "has been reduced to triviality," whether at Union Seminary or in the whole church. "You can imagine my state of mind after having devoted all these decades to the religious enterprise." The great ironist now sounded the note of pathos.

20:33   Other witnesses also bid seriously for the nation's ear with their critical voices. Trude Weiss-Rosmarin and other critics conventionally spoke of "the Niebuhrs," for Reinhold had a brother, H. Richard Niebuhr, a Yale Divinity School power from 1931 until his death in 1962 and usually regarded to be a more profound and systematic theologian than Reinhold. He eschewed the journalism on which his brother thrived and was much more the classroom teacher than the circuit-riding lecturer. Though never a *Time* cover celebrity, he was memorialized with a magnificent portrait by Alfred Eisenstaedt featured in *Life* magazine. Through two generations of students and some closely reasoned books he had indirect impact through the clergy on mainstream Protestantism as it made its way between secularism and revivalism. In 1956 he took part in the most ambitious study of the ways theological education was setting out to meet the challenge of the times, and he published his own perspective on it, *The Purpose of the Church and Its Ministry.* Niebuhr kept his eye on America, having stated the thesis in 1937 that "American Christianity and American culture cannot be understood at all save on the basis of faith in a sovereign, living, loving God."

Three statements by this Niebuhr—the report of 1956, a book   20:34
on monotheism in 1960, and the earlier classic *Christ and Culture*—show the vantage from which he looked on church and
world, since he did not provide journalistic coverage of the events
of the revival decade. *Christ and Culture,* published in 1951, was
a work of typology, which showed five ways in which "Christ"
and all that Christ means were related to "Culture" and much
of what it meant. H. Richard Niebuhr rejected the oppositional
"Christ against Culture," shown by sectarians, or the "Christ of
Culture," in which the culture absorbs Christ, church, and faith;
his brother would have located Norman Vincent Peale there.
"Christ above Culture" placed Christ above the turmoil of real
life and was out of the question to anyone who took a prophetic
stance. Two categories remained, and Niebuhr saw something in
both. One was "Christ Transforming Culture," the standard Reformed Puritan Protestant approach, out of which had come movements like the Social Gospel. The other was "Christ and Culture
in Paradox," for it said both "yes" and "no" to elements in the
culture.

This Niebuhr brother observed the battle between "Christ's"   20:35
people and the secularists, especially in the field of public education. He wanted to distance himself from the secularists, through
the proclamation of a vigorous monotheism. Christian faith in this
one God beyond the gods was "intolerable to all defenders of society who are content that many gods should be worshiped if
only Democracy or America . . . receives its due, religious homage." Here he evidently had in mind John Dewey and articulators
of common faith like J. Paul Williams. They attacked particular
Christianity because, they contended, it "imperils society by its
attack on its religious life; it deprives social institutions of their
cultic, sacred character; by its refusal to condone the pious superstitions of tolerant polytheism it threatens social unity."

During the high years of the religious revival H. Richard Nie-   20:36
buhr, especially in a series at the University of Nebraska in 1957,
lectured on themes he collected in 1960 in a book called *Radical
Monotheism and Western Culture.* He reminded Americans that
there were no Golden Ages for them to look back to for escape. He
had in view the nostalgia of many Protestants for the more homogeneous society they had once dominated, but which in a time of

pluralism they were learning to share; one was closed, the other open. "When we examine our longings we often discover that what we yearn for is the security of the closed society with its social confidence and social loyalty." The present-day temptation was to misuse "organized religions" of Judaism and Christianity. Niebuhr sounded a note rare in the public advocacy of mainstream Protestantism when he criticized Judaism and Christianity for not being "really religious in the narrow sense of that term." Yes, piety was important, but what people normally called religion—"such as activities of prayer, of reverence for the holy, of expiation"— was not evident in the activities of organized religion. For Christians, instead, the temptation had been to establish and conduct "Christian states, Christian nations, Christian schools, Christian families, Christian economics, and Christian philosophies as well as Christian cults." What the Yale professor found was "a total ethos, not merely a piety."

20:37   In one of the more profound comments on the stance of the nation during the revival of interest in religion, Niebuhr found Americans torn between its civic religion and monotheism. "National faith is forever being qualified by monotheism. It will not do, to be sure, to say that the American nation is intensely God-fearing in a monotheistic sense of God." There was too much contrary evidence. But then Niebuhr described a charter for the public churches and saw signs of hope. God-fearing "is present among us and is in almost daily conflict or tension with our large and small social faiths." Niebuhr noticed bargaining going on to corrupt the scene in which prophetic judgment should occur: "so long as people can be counted on to make national loyalty supreme, they may be allowed to follow any religion." So it had been in the Roman Empire, and now so it was with America and its civil faith. Over against such faith, Jews and Christians ought to protest: "Loyalty to God is prior to every civic loyalty." Civil religions tended to obscure such protest. So H. Richard Niebuhr said both yes and no as he analyzed the two religions of America, civic faith and monotheism proclaimed in synagogue and church.

20:38   Always mentioned by those who, like Trude Weiss-Rosmarin, wanted to summarize the thought of the times as "neo-Protestant" were "the Niebuhrs" and Tillich. Paul Tillich, a refugee from Hitler's Germany, made little mark in the United States before or during World War II but then was ascendant after mid-century. Henry Luce's *Time* did give him cover treatment and had him speak at the magazine's fortieth anniversary dinner before a company of the magazine's cover subjects. He came to be a familiar if not often easily understood celebrity on the campus circuit. Tillich taught alongside Reinhold Niebuhr at Union Theological Seminary, and, after Niebuhr's stroke, came to be a regularly consulted and quoted commentator on American culture. Several years after the war the ambitious theologian wrote a German friend: "Harvest time is here; indeed I am now gathering in my harvest." His essentially American comment began with *The Protestant Era* in 1948. A stream of books issued through the subsequent years, including *The Courage to Be,* published in 1952, which showed how he was turning from the political interests that had occupied him in Germany to the psychology of the therapy-minded age. He put most energy into a three-volume *Systematic Theology* begun at Union, developed in a first retirement at Harvard Divinity School, and completed at the University of Chicago, his last academic home.

Tillich provided an epigram used by many to relate faith to the   20:39 surrounding world: "Religion is the substance of culture, culture is the expression of religion." He could speak positively of the America which became home to him as a displaced person at the age of forty-seven. "I saw the American courage to go ahead, to try, to risk failures, to begin again after defeat, to lead an experimental life both in knowledge and in action, to be open toward the future, to participate in the creative process of nature and history." But he also saw the danger of this courage, noting the anxiety it generated, especially among the young. A lay philosopher, Theodore M. Greene, pondered the meaning of Tillich in the secular culture. He found it astonishing to hear a systematic theologian say that the "first word" to be "spoken by religion to the people of our time must be a word spoken against religion." Greene made much of a basic Tillichian distinction, one that matched the two sides of the thought of the Niebuhrs. One was "the Protestant principle," which referred less to churchly Protestantism than to the prophetic note. The Protestant prophet "declares his opposition to all absolutizing of the relative, that is, to all idolatry, and also to all relativizing of the Absolute, that is, to all forms of relativistic nihilism." The supporter of "Catholic substance" was devoted to all genuine human creativity and discovery and could embrace much of the achievement of modernity.

Tillich applied the vision of both the Protestant principle and   20:40 Catholic substance to postwar America. He provided a context by comparing the Germany in which he had grown up after World War I with the America he inhabited after World War II. European thinkers, in the darkness of that earlier hour, did sense a *kairos,* the Greek term for an especially weighted and pregnant moment. "There is no such ecstatic experience after the Second World War, but a general feeling that more darkness than light is lying ahead of us." If the first time there had been "utopian hope," now there was "cynical realism." Tillich was writing before commentators were speaking of an affluent society, a prosperous time, an era of good feelings in the Eisenhower years. In the earliest postwar years he called on Protestantism, at the end of its era, to fulfill an important function. He wrote that "the Protestant principle judges both cynical realism and utopian hope. It justifies the hope, though destroying its utopian form; it justifies the realism, though destroying its cynical form." So Tillich could both negate and affirm as revival came: "In the spirit of such a realism of hope," he said, "Protestantism must enter the new era, whether this era will be described by later historians as a post-Protestant or as a Protestant era." The Protestant principle, not the era, was what was lasting.

20:41   In *The Dynamics of Faith,* Tillich took his dialectical vision to the new culture. One of the things he feared was new nationalism. In the present century of nationalisms, "everything is centered in the only god, the nation—a god who certainly proves to be a demon, but who shows clearly the unconditional character of an ultimate concern." Tillich worried about "the ultimate concern with 'success' and with social standing and economic power," which challenged authentic ultimate concern. "It demands unconditional surrender to its laws even if the price is the sacrifice of genuine human relations, personal conviction, and creative *eros.*" The church had a role in such a culture. It evangelized "to show to the people outside the Church that the symbols in which the life of the Church expresses itself are answers to the questions implied in their very existence as human beings." For the moment, only fringe movements at the edges of the church, "sectarian and evangelistic movements of a most primitive and unsound character," were vital and had great success. The church could not take such a route, but it could not remain inert; it was needed for "its prophetic role," for in that role "the Church is the guardian who reveals dynamic structures in society and undercuts their demonic power, by revealing them, even within the Church itself." So the church had to listen to voices outside itself.

20:42   Tillich would, he said, "fight against any groups working for American provincialism," and he went on to pledge: "we shall work for an America in which every provincialism, including

theological and philosophical provincialism, is resisted and conquered." In a sermon of the period he saw danger in a moment
"when religious propagandists use the fear of the approaching end
to preach new forms of old religious conformisms"; was Billy
Graham specifically in his mind? In a kind of thank-you note
to America in 1953 he expressed gratitude for the openness to
"worldwide horizons" that he was seeing. But he also worried
about the narrowing of that vision. After two decades in the United
States he had to ask, "Will America remain what it has been to us,
a country in which people from every country can overcome their
spiritual provincialism?" It was possible to be a political world
power and a spiritually provincial people, and Tillich wondered,
"Will the emphasis on the 'American way of life' produce such a
situation?" He sounded like Will Herberg: "There is a serious
danger that it will." On that theme Catholics like Murray, neo-
Protestant or neo-Jewish Jews, and "the Niebuhrs and Tillich" for
the Protestant mainstream agreed.

21

"Is There a Pink Fringe?"

21:1 The postwar revival of interest in religion inspired critics of both civic faith and popular religion. They united in prophesying against the dangers of nationalism as an idolatry of the nation, and of provincialism as a form of being closed off to the larger world. These critics were sometimes allies of those who, to ward off such tribalisms, advocated ecumenical Christianity, Judeo-Christian interfaith movements, and general support of the human family through agencies like the United Nations. But those who stressed these centripetal instruments in postwar international and national life alike did not have the field entirely to themselves. For a significant minority of Americans the call came to reject all such ecumenical and international ventures. For them One Nation, Under God, meant a closed society, one filled with suspicion of dissenters and dedicated to a single form of public expression. The record of these revival years would be incomplete without reference to this significant counterforce, one that often took malign forms for anticommunist crusading at home, to match the anticommunism that united almost all citizens when they looked at threats abroad. The name given to most of the self-advertised patriotic and often quasi-religious outbreaks of suspicion was McCarthyism, after Wisconsin Senator Joseph McCarthy. But other outgrowths in right-wing Christian anticommunist crusades and in groups like the John

Birch Society survived after McCarthy himself met disgrace in the early Eisenhower years.

Senator Joseph McCarthy began to occupy center stage, where   21:2
he would remain for three years, with a speech to the Republican Women's Club dinner in Wheeling, West Virginia, on a February night in 1950. Some of the diners might at first have responded by nodding politely or in boredom, so familiar was much of the religious Cold War rhetoric voiced by the visiting senator. First, he said: "The great difference between our western Christian world and the atheistic Communist world is not political, ladies and gentlemen, it is moral." He expounded: "The real, basic difference" between the two systems lay "in the religion of immoralism," invented by the Marxists on one hand and by the Christian world on the other. "This religion of immoralism, if the Red half of the world wins—and well it may—this religion of immoralism will more deeply wound and damage mankind than any conceivable economic or political system." Second: "Today we are engaged in a final, all-out battle between Communistic atheism and Christianity. The modern champions of Communism have selected this as the time. And, ladies and gentlemen, the chips are down— they are truly down." Some of the ladies and gentlemen may have begun to perk up, especially when McCarthy brought the third point home. "As one of our outstanding historical figures once said, 'When a great democracy is destroyed, it will not be because of enemies from without, but rather because of enemies from within.' "

Who could these enemies from within be? McCarthy made   21:3
news when he suggested that he knew exactly who some of them were. "I have here in my hand a list of 205—a list of names that were made known to the Secretary of State as being members of the Communist party and who nevertheless are still working and shaping policy in the State Department." Playing to popular anti-intellectualism, he said that the subversives were not the less fortunate or members of minority groups who have been selling this nation out. Instead it was those "who had all the benefits that the wealthiest nation on earth has had to offer." That was "glaringly true in the State Department. There the bright young men who are born with silver spoons in their mouths are the ones who have been worst." The tough-talking forty-one-year-old senator had a way of transfixing audiences when he made charges like these. He had made no mark in the Senate until then and may not have planned

to cause a sensation in Wheeling. A Washington newsman had simply ghostwritten the talk, and McCarthy even claimed not to have followed a text as he spoke. Later when he inserted a transcription into the *Congressional Record* his number of subversives had dropped from 205 to 57, the number he had used in a Salt Lake City speech a day after the Wheeling event. The figure shifted constantly from speech to speech. No matter: the point was not the precise number but the sense that there must be a precise number of such people—even though McCarthy had no names and no persons in mind to serve as documentation for the sensational charges.

21:4   Other senators on the right had been making charges similar to McCarthy's, but none had suggested that they had numbers and names to back what they said. McCarthy always spoke in menacing tones and with the demagogue's gift for attracting a following on a topic so controversial that he all but brought some expressions and endeavors of the Truman adminstration to a halt in its last years and complicated the life of Dwight D. Eisenhower in the first years of his. To gain fame and credibility McCarthy had exaggerated his war record. Misrepresenting the source of a knee injury, he advertised himself as "tail-gunner Joe" and, as the wearer of a Purple Heart for war wounds, he took on and defeated the progressive Robert M. LaFollette, Jr., in the 1946 Wisconsin Republican primary. Once in the Senate, the ambitious but directionless young man looked for a cause. According to Jack Anderson and Ronald May in their popular biography of McCarthy, the senator had been advised to make the St. Lawrence Seaway his issue in speeches like the one at Wheeling, but he dismissed that suggestion: "That hasn't enough sex." His biographers credit or debit Georgetown University's Father Edmund Walsh for planting the idea of communist-hunting as a cause, so McCarthy decided to get his speechwriters busy and "hammer" at communists.

21:5   Anti-McCarthy anti-Catholics made much of Catholic support for McCarthy; it was mixed, but strong where it appeared at all. For the most part, if there were many Catholics in a region, he had the same percentage of support as he did in regions where there were few. Not on the popular level but among the arguing elites one could best isolate Catholic voices. By no means did all his fellow Catholics favor either his way of dividing the nation and the world or his techniques for pressing his claims. For example, one of his nemeses was another Senator McCarthy, this one named Eugene. This critic, a strong Catholic, made the most vigorous response to the Wisconsin senator the day after the Wheeling

Senator Joseph McCarthy, most notorious of the communist-hunters, discredited
for having distorted the records of his enemies, for a time was favored by some
Catholic leaders. They saw in him an ally because they shared his anti communism,
but most later broke with him because of his extremism. Here he is pictured in
April 1954 at a Holy Name Society communion breakfast in New York; Monsignor
Joseph McCaffrey and Francis Cardinal Spellman joined him at the head table.
(AP/Wide World Photos.)

address. But Eugene McCarthy made his case on liberal political grounds, not religious grounds. Soon the issue did move into
churchly zones. On May 25, 1950, the Catholic Press Association
asked the Wisconsin senator to address its meeting at Rochester,
New York, in mixed company that included some of his foes.
Bishop Matthew Ready of the National Catholic Welfare Conference anticipated the speech with an attack of his own, on unnamed
people, clearly including McCarthy, "who lately and hysterically
identify themselves as the sole defenders of the nation." McCarthy
hit an interfaith note in his reply. Communists wanted to destroy
"all the honesty and decency that every Protestant, Jew and Catholic . . . [had] been taught at his mother's knee." Then he jabbed at
"Protestants, Jews, and Catholics" who he claimed were servants
of the communist cause. On a later occasion he prophesied that
an attack on him would fail "in its attempts to inject religious
bigotry into this fight," but here he played to the Catholic editors:

"You have been engaged in what may well be that final Armageddon foretold in the Bible—that struggle between light and darkness, between good and evil, between life and death, if you please." That roused the audience to warm applause; he was winning them over or at least neutralizing them. Only one or two diocesan papers and the liberal lay *Commonweal* grumbled in their responding editorials.

21:6   The Catholic bishops showed more discretion and courage at their meeting in November 1951, when they spoke up knowing that the public would see McCarthy as their focus in a critical statement: "Dishonesty, slander, detraction, and defamation of character are as truly transgressions of God's commandments when resorted to by men in political life as they are for all other men." A gathering of Protestant clerics was uncharacteristically friendly when they applauded this "direct slap" at the senator. While Joseph McCarthy kept gaining political power during the end of the Truman administration, he stayed on as a major distraction when Eisenhower, a president from McCarthy's own party, took office and tried to change the agenda. The popular "Ike" tried to be above the battle, but he had to be aware of how divided the nation was becoming on this issue. The division was not on Catholic-Protestant lines; less than two percentage points now separated Catholic and Protestant populations when polled on this subject. Thus in March 1953 a Roper poll found 56.6 percent of the Catholics having no opinion about McCarthy and the charges, while 16.6 percent indicated that they were pro-McCarthy and 17.4 percent con. But leaders began to exploit McCarthyism for their various Catholic-versus-Protestant battles.

21:7   Some Catholic editors, concerned about the texture of the society they shared with Protestants in pursuit of truth, were in a good position to become defenders of the Protestant clerical reputation when rabid anticommunist Catholics swung too widely. *Boston Pilot* editor Father Francis Lally, for instance, complained in print that many Catholic editorials were strident and misguided when they suggested that "Protestantism seems to take on a kind of pink hue" and that "if the Reds are not in the pews they are at least in the pulpits." No, countered Lally, the record of Protestants against communists was too impressive to ignore. But some other Catholics did use Protestant opposition to McCarthy in their anti-Protestant campaigns. Thus when the *Christian Century* asked the bishops to spurn McCarthy, *Ave Maria* editors fired in return: "Haven't you been telling us how keen you are for complete separation of Church and State? Well, just what are you for?" Such a condemnation would clearly violate the line of separation.

No one could keep the continuing religious cold war between   21:8
Catholics and Protestants out of the hotter political war over Mc-
Carthyism. The bruises of battle worsened when Senator McCarthy and his Senate committee employed a former Methodist minister, J. B. Mathews, who had also some years before been an
enthusiastic Stalinist. He had now turned on communism with an
apostate's passion and set out to take revenge on his own spiritual
past while trying to settle old scores. In the summer of 1953 Mathews published an article, "Reds and Our Churches," in *American Mercury.* His opening line sounded as vivid as McCarthy's "I
have in my hand" charge. "The largest single group supporting the
Communist apparatus in the United States today is composed of
Protestant clergymen." Such a charge, if true, would have been
devastating in the climate of the day. Mathews slightly qualified
this by saying that "the vast majority of American Protestant clergymen" were loyal, but they were embarrassed "by the participation of the minority in the activities of the most sinister conspiracy
in the history of the world." He had numbers, too: during "the last
seventeen years the Communist Party has enlisted the support of at
least 7,000 Protestant clergymen" as "party members, fellow trav-
ellers, espionage agents, party line adherents and unwitting dupes."

Reaction to this charge came quickly, as in a telegram to Presi-   21:9
dent Eisenhower from Father John A. O'Brien, Rabbi Maurice
N. Eisendrath, and Dr. John Sutherland Bonnell. This Catholic-
Jewish-Protestant troika said that such attacks would mean "de-
stroying the trust in the leaders of Protestantism, Catholicism, or
Judaism by wholesale condemnation" and weakening "the great
American bulwark against atheistic materialism and Communism."
Eisenhower telegraphed right back to the National Conference of
Christians and Jews, expressing agreement with the message he
had received. "The churches of America are citadels of our faith in
individual freedom and human dignity," it read. Such faith was
"the living source of all our spiritual strength." And that strength,
the president said, was "our matchless armor in the worldwide
struggle against the forces of godless tyranny and oppression."

Crocodile tears over the Protestant clergy then came from *Ave*   21:10
Maria, which deplored both telegrams and wished for "careful and
calm study" of the Mathews article. (Evidently the editors had not
read the piece carefully; they consistently spelled the name "Matthews.") The editors did their own calculating: since there were

257,000 Protestant clerics in the United States, 7,000 of these would represent only about 3 percent of the whole, "a relatively small group." Many in even this small group were no doubt "un-witting dupes" of the alien cause. *Ave Maria* editors, not born the day before, had to know that in the current climate of suspicion even seven Protestant clerical communists would have represented a crisis. But they still tried to score some points: they did not wish by the statement about unwitting dupes "to minimize the gravity of the situation wherein some Protestant ministers, professedly teaching Christianity, have gone over to the communist conspiracy while belonging to the body of the Protestant clergy." They named no names of the accused but cited J. Edgar Hoover, head of the Federal Bureau of Investigation, who said he had apprehensions "so long as communists are able to secure ministers of the Gospel to promote their evil work and espouse a cause that is alien to the religion of Christ and Judaism." Hoover also did not name names, nor, in what could have provided support for *Ave Maria*'s guessing, did he even single out Protestants. *Ave Maria* went on, however, to disagree with people overseas who saw Americans becoming hys-terical about the issue. "Actually the people of this country are very cool, calm, and collected about the communist conspiracy that would like to take over their country." The anti-anticommunists and the anti–Senator McCarthy people were the hysterics. And the Catholic editors rubbed salt in mainstream and ecumenical Protestant sores by seeing a "refreshing note" in the defense of Mathews and McCarthy that was coming from Carl T. McIntire, the "head of the Protestant organization known as the International Council of Churches," a man who was seen, in the eyes of all but his followers, to be at least as irresponsible as Mathews and McCarthy were, and whose minuscule organization was simply his mouthpiece.

21:11   Protestants could also be as uncool, uncalm, and uncollected as were such Catholics. Princeton Seminary's John A. Mackay, who had long fought Catholicism on every front, thought that McCar-thyism lurked behind Mathews as "the Twentieth Century Ameri-can version of the Sixteenth Century Inquisition." Yet Catholics did give people like Mackay ammunition to use against them. Fran-cis Cardinal Spellman, who aspired to be the voice of the hierarchy from his New York base, tried to score points. In August 1953 he came out for McCarthy; the senator, Spellman said, "is against communism and he has done and is doing something about it." The cardinal rarely spoke thus, but he was so prominent that his words

were welcomed by Protestants who wanted to collect some inflammatory remarks from Catholics to use in their own campaigning.
Meanwhile, Father George Ford, a popular Columbia University
chaplain who often differed with Spellman, teamed up with Rabbi
Nathan Perlman at Freedom House. There they showed a film that
undercut the claim that Catholics had a near-monopoly on anticommunism and that Protestants favored the communist side. In
any case, the battle between elites seemed not to exacerbate the
popular level of tensions between Catholics and Protestants. Polls
of the time showed less than 1 percent of the people any longer
fearing Catholicism as a threat to the country. In 1953 a poll found
only 4 percent expressing such fear, and in November 1954, in
McCarthy's prime, this figure dropped to 2 percent. That month
80 percent of those polled said they had heard no talk against
Catholics in the previous six months. The editors and other leaders
were fighting over domains in ways that the mass of church and
synagogue members did not recognize as their important personal
battle.

McCarthy made his fatal mistake when he took on the United
States Army and later, in more indirect fashion, President—and
former General—Eisenhower. Televised hearings exposed Mc-
Carthy to the public, and he went down to Senate censure on
December 2, 1954, by a vote of 67 to 22. One of only two ab-
stainers, besides McCarthy himself, was a young Massachusetts
senator, John F. Kennedy. Kennedy may have ducked the Mc-
Carthy issue out of respect for his father, Joseph P. Kennedy, a
McCarthy devotee. Or he may have been constrained by a partly
pro-McCarthy constituency. After the censure McCarthy retreated,
sulked, took solace in alcohol, and died suddenly on May 2, 1957,
having seen his cause move to slightly more moderate hands.
Curiously, at the McCarthy funeral, the Protestant chaplain of the
Senate, the Reverend Frederick Brown, as if wanting to let bygones
be bygones but becoming shrill himself, spoke in affirmative tones:
"And so this fallen warrior, though dead, speaketh, calling a nation
of freemen to be delivered from the complacency of a false security
and from regarding those who loudly sound the trumpets of vigilance and alarm as mere disturbers of the peace." Other Protestant
ministers would more likely have agreed with a contemporary analyst and biographer, Richard Rovere: "McCarthy, though a demon
himself, was not a man possessed by demons. His talents as a
demagogue were great, but he lacked the most necessary and awesome of demagogic gifts—a belief in the sacredness of his own

21:12

mission." Rovere also quoted longshoreman-philosopher Eric Hoffer: "Faith in a holy cause is to a considerable extent a substitute for the lost faith in ourselves." McCarthy never had, or early lost, faith in himself and did not even learn how to make his cause holy.

21:13   The demise of McCarthyism did not mean that this strongest defensive impulse against the dream of uniting Americans in their One Nation, Under God, had disappeared. All through the decade an American Right, often a Christian Right, kept developing and changing strategies. A number of authors isolated this movement in *The New American Right,* a book which appeared in 1955 and stayed current enough to reappear retitled and updated in 1963 as *The Radical Right.* The analysts observed the elements of this Right picking up themes of the populist revolts of the 1930s, back when men like Father Charles E. Coughlin, evangelist Gerald L. K. Smith, and Louisiana governor Huey Long had set the tone and the terms. Some saw social class and ancestry playing a part in the lineup of forces. Thus social philosopher Seymour Martin Lipset, writing in the thick of things, found that Jews and African Americans opposed McCarthy most consistently and that the senator was "generally opposed by descendants of old American Protestant families, and he drew disproportionately from Catholics of recent immigrant background."

21:14   This did not mean that well-off and educated old-stock Protestants always distanced themselves from factory-town Catholics or backwoods and hill-country Protestants. A glimpse of one of many struggles on the congregational level comes from the record of a potent Methodist church in Houston. Methodism was home to many liberals, some of whom came to be billed as being "soft on Communism." Its elites did include people who had spoken well of socialism, and some of these had influenced the left-leaning Methodist Federation for Social Action. Action begetting reaction, a Committee for the Preservation of Methodism formed in Texas. This was a good setting for drama because Methodism was at that time the largest national Protestant body and was outnumbered even in Houston only by Southern Baptists. In 1947 the *Houston Press* drew attention to local Methodist tensions. Bishop A. Frank Smith, himself a liberal who was being nettled by laity on the right, thought he could pacify the congregations by keeping the Methodist Federation at a safe distance, say in New York and Washington. He intended his words for Houston consumption but forgot that federation people would be listening as he used typical Cold

War language: "Any group calling themselves 'Methodist' . . . that might discredit American democracy and exalt atheistic communism, or any other totalitarian philosophy is to be deplored, and has my unreserved condemnation." There, that ought to quiet Texas! But it caused disquiet at federation headquarters.

Keeping home fires damped became more difficult after journalist Stanley High, for reasons best known to himself, published an article titled "Methodism's Pink Fringe" in *Reader's Digest.* The article seemed to confirm the suspicions of conservative Methodists. W. Kenneth Pope, the moderate pastor of Houston's First Methodist Church sought middle ground as Bishop Smith had been doing and met with the objectors who believed the popular magazine more than the disclaimers in the Methodist press. Bishop Smith later said he knew that High's charges and similar ones from the then-powerful House Committee on Un-American Activities were "too preposterous." But, speaking of the laity, he said, "these men read that stuff, and they thought their church had sold them down the river." Pope wanted to avoid confrontation with the lay leaders who were both misguided and his good friends. "No, I will not denounce them. These are good men who love the church, and we are going to save them for the church." In suburban Houston the more liberal pastor Grady Hardin was more assertive in his lecture "Stanley High Hitting Low." And he received surprising lay support even when he spoke *ad hominem:* "Stanley High will do anything for a dollar." Despite counterattacks like that one, the subject remained on the agenda.

21:15

With such a spectrum of responses in Houston it seemed to some leaders to be the time for drafting a conciliatory statement. But the Methodist Federation for Social Action leaders, not reading well the climate in Houston and elsewhere, and being too sure of themselves, ignored the statement and pursued a course that the arch-conservatives among the laity chose to label procommunist. In this setting, on December 19, 1950, some locals organized the Committee for the Preservation of Methodism, a lay gathering whose members came from a number of prestigious congregations. The federation people could often issue boilerplate statements and go almost unnoticed, but when they named specific localities, they drew return fire. The committee published the booklet *Is There a Pink Fringe in the Methodist Church?* and circulated it nationally. They demanded that Houston congregations "exercise renewed vigilance in searching the background and beliefs of writers,

21:16

speakers, teachers, and church leaders." These Houstonites believed that they were the ones who had to exercise vigilance in
respect to the federation and other Methodist leaders.

21:17   From the distance of Chicago the *Christian Century* spread
word of the tense situation. The editors chose to criticize authors
and promoters who, they said, were "self-styled 'circuit riders'
whose calluses if any come from riding Cadillacs" as they profit-
ably pursued "the intimidative techniques of the Red Hunt." Such
words did anything but quiet the agitated element in the Houston
laity, who kept finding conspiracies closer to home. Their committee then reprinted an article titled "The Communists Are After
Your Church!" Handbills appeared: "Subversion in the sanctuary
is no scare cry—it's happening! Ruthless Communists—in clerical garb and out—are 'using' unsuspecting church members in a
vicious assault on . . . religion." Now Bishop Smith began to back
off in the face of unreason and the use of such language, and a
note of pathos colored his summary of people on the committee:
"These were good men, men who were young with me, and we
had grown old together here, and I had looked forward to the time
when they would be our leaders in the church—and they had gotten led off by this 'Pink Fringe' business."

21:18   Why did Smith mention only the men? The most formidable
attack came from the local chapter of the Minute Women of the
U.S.A. Inc., organized in Houston in 1951. This often anti-Semitic
extremist group, which made Joseph McCarthy look moderate,
experienced numbers of defections and schisms, after the manner of such groups, but by the time of the controversy it still held
five hundred members. They charged that Catholic bishop Robert L. Lucey, Rabbi Hyman Judah Schachtel, and other high clergy
were members of "Communist fronts." On "Race Relations Sunday," when African American Rufus E. Clement, the president of
Atlanta University, was invited to speak at an interfaith service at
the First Methodist Church, the Minute Women and the Committee
for the Preservation of Methodism, guilty of misidentifying targeted figures as they often were, protested in one circular: "Must
a Church Select a Speaker with Communist-Front Record?" Those
interested in "the preservation of Americanism and Christianity,"
it said, dared not support "an individual with a Communist-front
record presiding over their Brotherhood services." The condemn-
ers did not know that this target, President Clement, was a conservative who, like almost every other black leader, could not have
been active in public life in those decades without having some-

where been listed with the wrong company for no good reason. Pastor Pope at First Methodist held a meeting designed to pacify the attackers. Given the suspicion Clement roused, Pope was asked, could he not personally pay for Race Relations Sunday and move it to Houston City Auditorium? The time for some heroism had arrived. Pope replied, "I can not, in good conscience, turn my back on having the service in our sanctuary and I can not, therefore, and will not, preside over the service at the auditorium."

A third partner to the assault, the local American Legion's Americanism Committee, then threatened to picket the service. Fearing violence, Pope smuggled Clement in to face a standing- 21:19

The Minute Women in Houston attacked religious, civil, and educational leaders alike in the early years after they organized in 1951. They were capable of mobilizing hundreds of militant women who opposed liberal movements in church and state. Four leaders, Virginia Hedrick, Mrs. H. W. Cullen, Norma Louis Barnett, and Anne L. Harrison were marked by a captioner at a school board meeting on July 15, 1953. (Photo: Courtesy of the Houston Research Center, Houston Public Library.)

room-only crowd, with the hostile people packed into the front rows. This was a religious service, reminded the pastor, who also served notice that any disruption would be illegal. Someone from the floor thereupon demanded a hearing for charges against Clement. But Pope simply read letters of support from people like Brigadier General Elbert P. Tuttle, past commander of the Atlantic American Legion post. He called Clement "an outstanding American." Clement, following this and staying in character, attacked communism and supported the American Way of Life. Pope triumphed, but he always remembered the day as his most trying in Houston. He also admitted that thereafter he played things cautiously, knowing that the "reactionary element wouldn't have minded tearing down the church." These critics claimed that "there was a Communist under every pew and behind most of the pulpits anyhow." The group never turned up a single Houston Methodist fellow traveler.

21:20 The committee and the Minute Women, busy on many fronts in Houston and undeterred by their failure to find anything wrong with Clement, made one more attack on Methodist citadels. Taking advantage of a climate created by the charges made against national Methodist leaders in Washington, they tried to have Pope, Hardin, and three other Houston Methodists removed. Three local moderates, some would have said conservatives, also came into their line of fire for allegedly favoring premarital counseling, an almost universal clerical practice which the radical right somehow connected with communism. Their Washington victim was to have been G. Bromley Oxnam, who was guilty of being a friend of Bishop Smith and who was innocent of charges that flew wildly in the House Committee on Un-American Activities. On May 26, 1953, Oxnam accepted an invitation to defend himself in Houston, but he did himself no good because he came in a spirit of scorn and with a tongue of fury, alienating even his supporters. The committee, however, also found no basis for its local charges and began to tire of the national battle. The Methodist Texas Conference criticized it in a mild resolution, and the communist-hunters decided to put energies into better causes than the Methodist front, where it had successfully intimidated people without catching anyone.

21:21 The Houston incident, early in the anticommunist crusade and a classic case, typified the encounters between church leaders and the religious radical right. While the local clashes were the most vicious and personal, more generalized national attempts to divide the One Nation, Under God, were also made. Two groups that attacked from the right, the fundamentalist American Council of Christian Churches and its kin, the Church League of America, both antedated and outlasted the McCarthy era. A third, the Christian Anti-Communist Crusade, for a time bridged the communities of church and the larger public. A fourth, the John Birch Society, arose late in the 1950s alongside the Crusade; it was not churchly—its leader favored an evolutionary philosophy at variance with conservative Christianity—but acquired a quasireligious cast. And, for a moment, there was the personal evangelistic crusade of Billy James Hargis. These all professed a common desire to pose their kind as the only true representatives of the One Nation, Under God, against atheistic communism and all other comers from the left. Claiming to want to unite all the God-fearing citizens, they merit notice because they disrupted unity and brought mixed emotions to the era of Eisenhower-bred good feelings.

Carl McIntire, whom *Ave Maria* had named a credible Protestant, was a survivor of the fundamentalist-modernist wars in the America of long ago and a participant in two Presbyterian schisms thereafter. We have met him as the founder of the American Council of Christian Churches and the International Council of Christian Churches, two steadfastly fundamentalist groups. By mid-century McIntire had become a constant picket at ecumenical gatherings, especially the World and National Councils of Churches, both Antichrists in his book. He wrote against the World Council as the "modern tower of Babel." John Mackay, president of Princeton Theological Seminary, in striking back, brought several of his own prejudices into the light and showed how religious Cold War rhetoric begot more of the same: "While being concerned about Communism," Mackay said of the American Council, "it carries on work with Communist technique." And of its leaders, he added, "They act without the slightest interest in truth and with terms of a Jesuitical ethic."   21:22

McIntire lumped together everything on his left, beginning with the staunchly conservative evangelical magazine *Christianity Today.* The New Jersey firebrand claimed that even its editor, Carl Henry, had demonstrated "a soft hand in dealing with Communism." McIntire also drew upon and fed sources to J. B. Mathews and Joseph McCarthy. He teamed with Verne Kaub, founder of the American Council of Christian Laymen to write a pamphlet that made much of Mathews' claims: */How Red Is the National Council of Churches?* He counseled: "Don't give it one dollar. The National Council receives large sums from various Jewish and other   21:23

Dr. Samuel McCrea Cavert watches Dr. Roy G. Ross press the button that will start the printing of the new RSV Bible in 1952. (Photo: National Council of the Churches of Christ in the USA.)

non-Christian groups." The Madison, Wisconsin, author thought that "only an organized movement of laymen" like his own could reverse the trend of clergy choosing to be duped by communism. His own mailing list was not large, but he found ways to be quoted and have his influence spread.

21:24   McIntire, however, put his main energies into attacking clergy and councils of churches. In the Eisenhower years that meant he had to choose vivid causes connected with the National Council of Churches. He found the ideal one in the council's project to produce the Revised Standard Version of the Bible. Not liking some lines of the new translation, he called the book "the work of Satan

and his agents." (In their desire to be faithful to the original manu-
scripts the translators had in places deviated from the King James
Version in English, on which some doctrines preached by McIntire
were dependent.) He and other fundamentalists named it "Stalin's
Bible" and praised those who burned a version of it in 1952. He
would not put a torch to the book, but, he said, "I'm kind of glad
that old boy down in North Carolina did."

It was McIntire who in 1953 promoted action by the House   21:25
Committee on Un-American Activities against Bishop G. Bromley
Oxnam. McIntire distributed a characteristic pamphlet, *Bishop
Oxnam, Prophet of Marx.* Oxnam, "as perhaps no other man," it
said, "represents the popular, radical, pro-communistic element in
religious circles in America." While in some contexts McIntire
made the astonishing charge that Oxnam was pro-Catholic, a claim
that would fire up fundamentalists, in this pamphlet he did not
do so, perhaps hoping for Catholic support against the Methodist
leader. Oxnam—somewhat the worse for the wear after the committee's treatment but innocent of its charges or able to explain
away others—was no longer a valuable target. That left the National Council of Churches itself, "the strongest ally of Russia
and the radical labor movement within the U.S." And John Foster
Dulles, whose credentials as a Cold Warrior satisfied everyone
else, should not be appointed secretary of state, McIntire said in
1952, because Dulles had been "long associated with extremely
radical and pacifist leaders in the Federal and World Councils."
McIntire seemed to have been born for making innuendos that
even his best enemies could not match: "Do we actually have in
the WCC an effective powerful instrument for pro-Soviet propaganda for the destruction of the West?" The reader was left with
no doubts about the answer, and McIntire for years worked on its
premises.

Every year there seemed to be some cause that demanded a   21:26
fight. Not long after the bonfires of Revised Standard Version
Bibles had died, the World Council of Churches held the largest
North American ecumenical gathering to date, in Evanston, Illinois, in 1954. This was the moment in which to show the rest of
the Protestant and Orthodox world how mature America could be
in helping to lead movements of reconciliation around the One
World. The mention of Orthodoxy signals that Russian Orthodox
clergy were in Evanston. This was all McIntire needed to charge
that at last he had found "Red clergy" and that they were right
under the roof of a Methodist sanctuary in Illinois. Even the Red-

baiting *Chicago Tribune* of those days found these attacks to be too virulent, the publicity too damaging to Chicago; its editors not only criticized McIntire's charges but also chose to be of help to WCC leaders in Chicago and suburbs. The ecumenical forces at mid-century seemed too strong for even the obsessive Carl McIntire, who was reduced to picketing and picking up little headlines wherever he could. With the decline of Senator Joseph McCarthy, that year should have represented the end of the era.

21:27   Far-right groups still kept appearing, however, almost as if called to be sure that someone would go against consensus. It was hard to find leaders in the Eisenhower administration or the churches who really were, as advertised, "soft on Communism." Frustration and vague discontent about existence in a world that the United States could not control and that the far right could not direct inspired some of the inventiveness behind the creation of these new anticommunist fronts. One old organization, the Church League of America, founded in 1936, had a new moment in the sun under "Captain" Edgar C. Bundy. A regular witness at congressional committees whenever they went out to pursue communists, Bundy also identified with Senator McCarthy, trying to work up lists of religious leaders he could label as communist or leaning toward communism. Not trusting the government to keep tabs on suspicious persons, he would do so and provide others on the right with materials for attack. In his *Collectivism in the Churches* the fundamentalist urged separation from all entangling alliances with nonfundamentalist churches. But for all the archivist energies and pack-rat instincts of its founder, the Church League of America never became much more than a filing system turned noisy, a nettler of liberals, a voice that suggested that the ecumenical forces could not alone own the day.

21:28   How, then, could Bundy create any stir? He took the posture of the informed intellectual. Instead of following the revivalist trail and techniques of earlier demagogues, he polished a lecture-circuit style. He brought along footnotes and academic trappings that shrouded his inability to provide hard data or credible attacks. John A. Mackay at Princeton, a conservative in almost anyone's book, was to him "a Presbyterian Red," for no reason at all. Protestant modernism was "the most potent and subtle means of bringing in Communism in its full form." Bundy posed Scriptures against "scriptures": "Having done away with the infallible Word of God and the authority contained therein, they [the modernists] have substituted the teachings of Marx and Gandhi for the teachings of Holy Writ." In doing so, they rejected evangelism and were "calling for a Protestant Vatican which will attack the economic and political problems of the world in general." In advertisements, for example, one in the Wichita Falls, Texas, *Record* in 1953, Bundy announced three speeches sponsored by twelve fundamentalist churches: "*How Are the Communists Invading the Churches?* Congress says they are! Mr. J. Edgar Hoover says they are! Captain Bundy will tell how they are." His punch line: "Moscow's dearest friends discovered in pulpits and seminaries in the USA."

In the second wave of radical right anticommunists, Dr. Fred C.   21:29
Schwarz posed as the respectable leader, leaving evangelist Billy James Hargis to be the rough-and-tumble exemplar. Schwarz, a physician from Australia, at one time spoke on McIntire radio programs. But to become respectable he later distanced himself and in 1952 organized the Christian Anti-Communist Crusade. In May 1957 he neared the edges of the national spotlight when he met with Richard Arens, staff director of the House Committee on Un-American Activities. Though his testimony was marginal for the committee's purposes, it became the core of Schwarz's book of 1960, *You Can Trust the Communists (To Be Communists)*. It sold a million copies. Schwarz had a way of attracting industrialists, including leaders of the Schick Safety Razor Company, Richfield Oil Corporation, and others who must have felt a stake in enlarging the definitions of socialism and communism. While Schwarz used the seminar and lecture model to attract a following on the West Coast, he failed to keep the audience when he took the program to New York. It seems easy to dispense with such figures and programs in a paragraph, decades later; but those who lived through attacks and insinuations by the likes of Schwarz testified that in his prime he forced them to expend great nervous energy fending off his assaults in a suspicious society.

Billy James Hargis replicated the demagogic style of Depres-   21:30
sion-era evangelists and seemed a throwback, a mutation in the Eisenhower years. A Disciples of Christ minister long identified with fundamentalist causes, Hargis started circuit riding in 1950. Like Carl McIntire, he made use of radio to spread his message. In McCarthy style he set out to build what he called "a force for God and against Communism." He said, "I consider it my Christian responsibility to fight Godless, atheistic Communism because I want to save this nation." His Christian Crusade prospered at the expense of less colorful agencies as he set up shop with his Hargis

Anti-Communist Leadership Schools. He also favored the kind of book title that ended with a question mark: *Communist America— Must It Be?* Answer: yes, unless you readers join my crusade. Hargis swung so wildly that in his eyes even American Nazi Party leader George Lincoln Rockwell had been "a front, a stooge for liberals." The way to produce "salvation from satanistic Communism," he said, was through an "immediate return to the faith of our Fathers in Jesus Christ, Son of God."

21:31   While waiting for Christ to return, Hargis in 1958 published a pamphlet titled "The National Council of Churches Indicts Itself on Fifty Counts of Treason against God and Country." But Hargis did not make it to the front page of the newspapers until in 1960 a United States Air Force training manual favorably quoted him. The Air Force was quickly given enlightenment concerning the suspect sources it was using and withdrew the manual. But followers on the right henceforth used it to gain some measure of credibility. Carl McIntire, who had helped inspire Hargis, also drew on Hargis's use of the Air Force manual. The evangelist sold Nutri-Bio products, vitamin pills, to stay profitable. With McCarthy he spread suspicion about American life: "Moscow has set a date for our conquest, and the greatest problem facing us today is taking care of communism internally." Somehow the evangelist successfully lured to his platform people like former Utah governor J. Bracken Lee and Major General Charles A. Willoughby, former member of General Douglas MacArthur's staff. Hargis seemed unassailable—until sex scandals ended his career in its prime.

21:32   Eventually Kaub, Bundy, Schwarz, and Hargis receded into footnote status and were all but forgotten. But the John Birch Society matched all competitors on the scene toward the end of the Eisenhower era. Its founder was a New England candy maker, Robert Welch. He aimed for influential people, and when they showed interest he tried to turn them into a very cohesive group, almost, in the language of the day, like a cult. While evangelists worked the church circuit, Welch moved where civic faith was most attended to. After 1958, from his base in Belmont, Massachusetts, he published *American Opinion,* a digest of conspiracy theories, most of them generated by Welch himself. That year he drew to himself in Indianapolis eleven seasoned businessmen, who with him made up a company of twelve apostles against the Reds; the twelfth of these led the apostolate for anticommunism. Out of this meeting came the society's "bible," *The Blue Book.* A drab document, it did have one line that helped it and its author gain attention: "My firm belief that Dwight Eisenhower is a dedicated, conscious agent of the Communist conspiracy is based on an accumulation of detailed evidence so extensive and so palpable that it seems to me to put this conviction beyond any reasonable doubt." There must have been reasonable doubt about the propriety of publishing such lines, because in later editions it was edited out.

The Blue Book was the sacred canon for John Birch Society   21:33
members. The language about a polarized world matched that of the churchly crusaders: "This is a *world-wide* battle, the first in history, between light and darkness; between freedom and slavery; between the spirit of Christianity and the spirit of anti-Christ in the souls and bodies of men." The battle would be won "by alertness, by determination, by courage, by an energizing realization of the danger," and, if necessary, with lives. No fundamentalist, but brought up as one, founder and leader Welch believed that the loss of fundamentalist-type faith meant the undercutting of civilization itself. He wanted to embrace the many creeds of his followers on the basis of a substructure. This was his sense that there was a common belief in "an ennobling conception, equally acceptable to the most fundamentalist Christian or the most rationalistic idealist," one that would have been acceptable to a Baptist like John Birch, a conservative Catholic, or "the agnostic Thomas Jefferson." When Welch did get around to setting forth details of his religion, he devised a creed no fundamentalist could have accepted. His text came from Alfred Lord Tennyson: "For I doubt not through the ages one increasing purpose runs." On that ground he described an evolutionary faith. Then he cited someone named Harry Kemp: "Thou hast put an upward reach in the heart of man." The orthodox Protestants in his camp would have called this a Pelagian heresy. "To make us truly religious," he elaborated, "we do not need to know anything more about God, man, and man's relationship to God than is given by a reverent understanding of that line."

Nor were Welch's views of democracy in any way orthodox. For   21:34
example, he spelled out the nature of his organization: "*The John Birch Society will operate under completely authoritative controls at all levels.*" It was simply too late in world history, he said, to form a collection of debating societies: "We mean business every step of the way." Debating evidently did not mean business. Only through such an agency as he was devising, he thought, could he celebrate John Birch, whom he described as the first victim of

World War III. A fundamentalist Baptist missionary, Birch was killed ten days after V-J Day in 1945 by Chinese communists. The incident was never clearly explained, nor were the reasons for Welch to seize upon his memory carefully expounded. Since Welch considered the death to be a murder calculated by communists, it fit his view of history.

21:35 Years after McCarthy was off the scene, and with only the more woebegone followings of Dr. Schwarz and evangelist Hargis busy with the cause, Welch remained ominous to civil libertarians. He busied himself with the secular details of organizing, publishing, forming cells, and attacking political leaders. He trained his members to keep their eyes on local leadership of all religious organizations, because Welch conceived that they would be propagators of communist teaching. His members were not particularly attached to churches; the society served as surrogate for the church for many. But religious leadership was highly aware of the John Birch Society. The National Council of Churches was a natural object for the society's attack. In *The Blue Book,* Welch, without identifying a church, said of the clergy that "some actually use their pulpits to preach outright Communism, often in very thin disguise if any, while having the hypocrisy as atheists to thank God in public for their progressive apostasy."

21:36 Far-right church movements, though uneasy with the John Birch Society, formed linkages with it and used what was called evidence gathered by this organization that was more prosperous than theirs. Edgar C. Bundy and Carl McIntire, for instance, could not have accepted Welch's creed, but they spoke positively of his political viewpoint. McIntire even named a room at his hotel, the Christian Admiral, "The John Birch Room." Had the Christian right been consistent, it would have been attacking John Birch for its departures from orthodoxy as much as it attacked the National and World Councils of Churches.

21:37 Between the Wheeling speech of Senator McCarthy in 1950 and the election of President John F. Kennedy in 1960, the radical right, churchly or quasi-religious, enjoyed a decade of expression. Its leaders exploited the Cold War fears that led many Americans to wonder why their nation could not rule the world. The frequency of rightist attacks on the councils was a compliment to the power of the churches. It was no compliment to these critics that they came up with so little to substantiate their charges. Their accomplishment was to present a counterforce against which those who worked for tolerance and interfaith cooperation had to push. The

American Way of Life may have represented a huge canopy over national existence, but some citizens wanted to push out from under the canopy those whose ideology did not match theirs or satisfy them. The only effective alliances in which they were involved linked them with right-wing pundits and politicians who, apart from the strategic value of coalitions, would have seen no assets in organized religion. And, taken together, the challengers from the right did not prevail. They too spoke of One Nation, Under God, but their God or gods were too small to serve the larger purposes of America in Cold War times.

22

"True Integration Will Be Achieved"

22:1   T̲he ideal of One Nation, Under God, Indivisible, seemed beyond the reach of millions of Americans at mid-century. African Americans, then usually called Negroes, lived largely segregated existences. No matter what their vast contributions to or modest gains in World War II, no matter how loyal they were to the American project in the Cold War, they seemed fated to live apart. In the South, formal Jim Crow legislation kept them from realizing their role as full partners in the One Nation. In the same South, where legislation did not do so, ethos kept them out, or down. But if the radical right worked to disintegrate the nation by ruling people out, Negro and other minority leadership worked to integrate it, to find themselves ruled in. In the course of time, more and more white leaders joined their cause.

22:2   If anything illustrates the centripetal ideal, the notion that disparate elements of the human family and nation should converge, it is this late but developing devotion to racial integration. Because Christian churches were the main nongovernmental institutions serving the black community and among the chief bastions of segregation in the white population, they were on the spot. Yet changes began to occur, and those who resisted racial integration came progressively to be put on the defensive. Robert Spike, who in the course of the civil rights struggle assumed leadership of the National Council of Churches program to address the racial issue,

376

summarized the situation for the white churches at the end of the decade: "There are many kinds of racial and cultural barriers in our national life, erected by Anglo-Saxon majorities against Negroes, Jews, Indians, Mexicans, Puerto Ricans, and to a lesser extent now the Orientals." But he knew a *kairos,* a moment of special urgency and decision, was there: "The crucial issue today, through which we shall discover whether we can conquer our prejudices, is how we shall behave during the period of the extinction of injustices against Negro Americans."

In the eyes of Spike, as in those of many other leaders after a   22:3
decade of only modest gains, the condition of white Christians was well described in his book title, *Safe in Bondage.* He knew he could assume that the church was generally prospering during the religious revival: "Religion is enormously successful," and, more significantly, "many Americans are again interested in religious problems with great seriousness." Yet "a suspicion that the religious renewal in America is superficial" had begun to grow near the decade's end. The resistance to racial integration fed that suspicion. Like almost everyone else alert to the issue at the time, Spike regarded the United States Supreme Court decision of 1954, *Brown v. Board of Education,* to be the first and strongest legal sign that a new day was coming. It would "stand in our history along with the Emancipation Proclamation as a significant step toward racial justice." The world was watching, and the issue had become national: "Northern white people have no ground of moral superiority on which they can stand to berate their Southern brothers." Spike also knew that integration by itself solved too little: "It would be unfair to create the impression that the racial crisis can be fully understood in terms of integrating Negro individuals into a white society." No, a whole society had to change, and that meant for whites to listen to Negroes, to learn to know them and receive their gifts. Still, integration of churches and neighborhoods represented a first move. "The battle for church integration may be long, but the victory will have important consequences for the whole Church of Christ."

Brown v. Board of Education can be seen as an episode in legal   22:4
history, but churches often served as organizing centers for civil rights activities, and *Brown* altered the circumstances for the churches. The court decision dealt with a compulsory aspect of American life, schooling; it had a bearing on voluntary aspects, like churches. No longer would "separate but equal" serve in schooling; what would the churches have to leave behind? *Time*

magazine knew how intimate the schooling issue was: "In its 164 years the court had erected many a landmark of U.S. History," but none except the Dred Scott case a century earlier "was more important than the school segregation issue," because "none of them directly and intimately affected so many American families." Spike and others knew how intimate the church issue was, as well: any change affecting one person's sharing of a pew, a communion cup, a church supper, or a prayer circle with another "directly and intimately affected" millions.

22:5   Religious figures were part of the drama of *Brown*. The Reverend J. A. DeLaine was minister of an African Methodist Episcopal Church in Clarendon County, South Carolina. He also served as one of 300 county schoolteachers. At the head of their system was the Reverend L. B. McCord, a white Presbyterian minister. "He is a capable man," wrote the local newspaper, "with a keen perception of fairness to all, and the best interests of the school children of Clarendon are close to his heart." DeLaine had learned not to create troubles and to serve quietly under McCord. As of 1947, said DeLaine, "I was one of McCord's good niggers." But they came into conflict about rights. The presence of ministers on both sides of cases that made their way to the Supreme Court suggests how webbed were the fates of religion and public life in the culture of the mid-century South, and this presence deserves some notice.

22:6   DeLaine, first. A minister's son, he remembered the hardships of his childhood and was aware of how meager his early education was. He remembered the deep wounds that most of his peers suffered along with him. For instance, he recalled the time years before when a white boy had shoved DeLaine's sister off a sidewalk. In angry response, he had pushed the boy. The young avenger was then condemned to suffer twenty-five lashes, a punishment he avoided only by leaving for Atlanta. Before long he was preparing for a career in ministry, but he and his wife, Mattie, had to teach in public schools in order to survive the Depression. They enjoyed teaching but also found a cause in civil rights and drew on specifically Christian norms to help make their case. DeLaine, Sr., had trained his son to be submissive and law-abiding. The younger man wanted to combine Christian hope with practical action, but he quickly learned that he and his colleagues could achieve little by remaining docile or passive. His personal awakening came in the summer of 1947 when at summer school he heard James M. Hinton, the state head of the National Association for the Advancement of Colored People, prod the audience to pursue justice more vigorously—and to use the schools to do so. Inspired, the young minister agitated for better access to school and better schools, but to no effect. His situation became dangerous, so he had to work quietly, receiving help from black lawyer Thurgood Marshall of the NAACP, who was soon to become a Supreme Court justice. Notwithstanding such help, the NAACP was thwarted at every turn by the white elite. By 1949 the couple saw that they could no longer withhold their talents, and they agreed to work publicly to represent black citizens. Their ministerial colleagues became teammates; their song became "Together Let Us Sweetly Live, Together Let Us Die."

Twenty signatures were necessary for a court challenge to the   22:7
old ruling that "separate but equal" circumstances would satisfy legal requirements. Those who gave their signature took considerable risk, and some lost their jobs. But the black clergy by and large persisted in supporting the cause. At St. Mark's African Methodist Episcopal Church the Reverend J. W. Seals spoke for many: "We ain't asking for anything that belongs to these white folks. I just mean to get for that little black boy of mine everything that any other South Carolina boy gets—I don't care if he's as white as the drippings of snow." In the face of such defiance, the Ku Klux Klan began to threaten DeLaine during this "getting" controversy. Then frivolous but also ominous court citations distracted the minister during the year before the case, which ultimately involved twenty-eight plaintiffs, reached trial as *Briggs v. Elliott. Briggs* was soon to be linked with four other cases. As threats grew against DeLaine, his denomination wanted to relocate him, to protect him physically, but the minister, teacher, and now plaintiff stayed with the case. In October of that year his house, probably after a torching, burned while the local Summerton fire department stood by because, as they said, it was located a hundred feet outside the town limits, which was true enough.

Despite such setbacks, DeLaine stuck with his part of the case.   22:8
The 1924 Democratic presidential candidate, John W. Davis, represented the state's case for segregation over against lawyer Marshall. As the cluster of cases made their way in 1952 from the district court to the Supreme Court, *Briggs* fell by the way, while its associated case, *Brown,* was to be argued. Thurgood Marshall saw to it that *Briggs* was not denied in the district court and that it came to be reassociated with *Brown.* While the latter therefore took prominence over *Briggs,* DeLaine had the satisfaction of knowing that his instance represented the first school-desegregation case to

make it to the highest court, and subsequently he could enjoy the legal victory, though in Summerton it did not have full immediate impact. That town had a low school budget and could not quickly adapt, and white citizens dragged feet, so little changed in the actual circumstances of schooling during DeLaine's years.

22:9   The United States as a whole had never lived up to its promise of assuring equality. The move of Negroes to the North and whites to the suburbs, taking their churches with them, meant that most churches everywhere kept their patterns of segregation and thought they could evade the hard issues. The Earl Warren court made it ever harder for them to do so, however, especially when in the decision of 1954 it ordered school districts to provide integrated education "with all deliberate speed." Deliberation at best, and stalling, not speed, marked the systematic response. Mississippi senator James Eastland, saying he knew that "strife and turmoil" would follow any efforts to enforce the ruling, said that the South would simply "not abide by or obey this legislative decision by a political court." No matter how resistant the Eastlands of the South might be, a long process of adapting had begun, and churches came necessarily to be involved all along the way.

22:10   Sometimes a voice from the secular surroundings serves to jar the religious community. One of the best of these times was the word of black psychologist Kenneth B. Clark who, a year after *Brown,* wrote a book called *Prejudice and Your Child.* He knew that the school issue affected children on the front lines most of all, and that, as they grew, they would shape the next generation. Where were the churches as exemplars? "Nearly ninety million Americans are enrolled in some church," Clark noted, and "nearly thirty million American children are enrolled in Sunday schools," which were nurseries for citizen behavior. But in church and Sunday school Clark could discern only "general vagueness" on the issue of race. Why? "The major difficulty in the translation of these moral and religious ideas into social reality lies in the fact that churches themselves are predominantly segregated institutions." Here they could not lead. Worse, psychologist Clark went on, studies showed that "individuals who profess strong religious affiliations or attend church frequently are more likely to be prejudiced than those who do not." Therefore until ministers, priests, and religious educators met their challenge, "religion as generally practiced in America" had to be seen as "another passive force which kept prejudice alive."

22:11   Clark was at home with church experience. He devoted a whole chapter to it, citing pro-integration statements from "as early as 1946" by the Federal Council of Churches. He knew that the council's Department of Racial and Cultural Relations had prodded local congregations, recognizing the "pattern of segregation in race relations as unnecessary and undesirable and a violation of the gospel of love and human brotherhood." Clark admired the department's goal of working for a "non-segregated church and a non-segregated society." But little had happened. Only a half million of the seven million black Protestants were affiliated with denominations that had some predominantly black as well as some predominantly white congregations, and a mere tenth of these, or 50,000 members, were in predominantly white denominations. Less than one-half of one percent of black Protestants regularly worshiped in nonsegregated congregations. Clark was no enemy, indeed he was a friend, of African American churches, but he knew what their segregation also represented. He admitted that blacks often now desired segregation, but this preference resulted from the experience of oppression in slavery days, from snubs in Reconstruction times, and, more positively, because a congregation served well "not only as a source of religious inspiration but also as a social center." Middle-aged blacks therefore, would not pursue the dissolution of Negro churches into the mass of white congregations. But younger blacks would likely have a different vision and end in view.

Clark kept an eye out for change. He applauded some Roman   22:12
Catholics for having worked to desegregate their parochial schools, but he thought that formal resolutions and Sunday school literature did little to hasten the churchly cause of support for integrated public schools. The psychologist admired a lesson he read in a Presbyterian program that urged readers, with respect to action on controversial racial issues, to "be sure you decide as a *Christian,* not as a person who wants above all else to be popular, or to avoid criticism." But was day-to-day behavior changing in white Christian America? The psychologist saw the churches acquiescing to society's standards, and he thought it a judgment on the moral claims of the church that the secular court had lived out ideals to which many of them gave only lip service.

In the South, efforts, however tardy, by a minority of churches   22:13
were regularly frustrated. An all-too-typical instance occurred in connection with the execution of Mississippian Willie McGee in 1951, after he was accused of the rape of a white woman, an act of which he was almost certainly innocent. Mississippi whites could

not conceive that Mrs. Willamette Hawkins could have encouraged a black man and then forced him into a relation that he was trying to sever when he was accused. Mississippi Supreme Court Chief Justice Harvey McGehee sealed their opinion with his own: "If you believe, or are implying, that any white woman in the South, who was not completely down and out, degenerate, degraded and corrupted, could have anything to do with a Negro man, you not only do not know what you are talking about, but you are insulting us, the whole South." And then: "You do not know the South, and do not realize that we could not entertain such a proposition; that we could not even consider it in court." Had the churches put all their energies into confronting racism, it is not likely that they could have achieved much immediately in such a setting.

22:14   Those who did speak up for McGee, though threatened with violence, were undeterred. On May 5, 1951, hundreds of blacks gathered on the Capitol lawn at Jackson, hoping to stage a "sunrise prayer meeting." They hoped that they might influence the judge to prevent the execution. Two dozen outstate white women were to have joined them, but the police kept them from the place and prevented the whole gathering from occurring. Such a climate could easily have produced violence against these prayerful blacks and the white women who wished to stand up to the most profound human hatred. It is appropriate to locate the moment by tying it to Cold War themes. Thus, for example, a black journalist quoted the *Jackson Daily News:* "Why the hell go to Korea to shoot Communists when the hunting is good on home grounds." McGee was not spared. He faced the electric chair singing, "Only the Father, He'll understand. The Father alone, he knows why. When I see Jesus, he'll know the reason. Only the Father, he'll understand."

22:15   Dwight D. Eisenhower, who was not popularly elected, or psychologically prepared, to promote integration, named California's Earl Warren to be chief justice in what he later called "the biggest damfool mistake I ever made." When Warren (and Eisenhower) took office, there were 16 million blacks in America. As a group they were on the bottom rungs of American ladders of opportunity, if they could find ladders of any sort to climb at all. At that time 68 percent of the blacks still lived in the South, a figure that would decline to 60 percent within the decade. Eisenhower came to see that he had on his hands a national issue that he could not evade. At a public occasion he could remind citizens that to protect civil rights was "a sacred obligation binding upon every citizen." But the president was reluctant to live up to the obligation, and he only weakly followed up the *Brown* decision. "I don't believe you can change the hearts of men with laws or decisions," he said to console himself. Eisenhower told Warren that enemies of school desegregation were concerned about governmental actions; "their sweet little girls are not required to sit in schools alongside some big overgrown Negroes." And when foreseeable violence occurred, the president acted late and did too little. Little Rock, Arkansas, in 1957, was the place and time where, because of a threat of violence, Eisenhower had to act; he did so in a sequence of actions whose details belong by themselves in political histories. What interests us here are the rationales that developed to reinforce and impel the African American religious community in this time of creativity and stress.

The choice of one of those rationalizing and motivating voices,   22:16
that of the classic civil rights leader, the Reverend Martin Luther King, Jr., needs not even one line of defense. In the public eye and the history books he came to be and remains more identified with the program of integration than anyone else. Less well known, but a towering spiritual figure at the time both within the black community and beyond it, was another cleric, Howard Thurman. There is no way to do justice to the range and variety of African American church leadership at the time, and no one can credibly make the case that Thurman was typical among the ministers. But in quiet ways he fed the spiritual hungers of his congregants, hearers, and readers, and he exemplifies as well as anyone the use of convergent, uniting terms in religious life during a time of great racial divergence and separation. By the time of the civil rights struggles, Thurman had several decades of ministry behind him, including a dozen years at Howard University in Washington, where, as dean of the chapel, he influenced young black elites, Washingtonians, and others.

Disappointed with his experience of the particularism of   22:17
American religion, including its black manifestations, Thurman early in his journey began looking for what he called "common ground" among world religions. He studied Hinduism and other Asian religions and met Mohandas Gandhi while on a trip to India, Burma, and Ceylon before 1944, when he founded the Church for the Fellowship of All Peoples in San Francisco. He carried the search for common ground from there to the deanship of Marsh Chapel at Boston University. The year of the *Brown* decision Thurman was speaking about God as the all-including Creator, a theme that had obvious if indirect relevance to the integration struggle.

The individual who experiences God, he said, finds that experience "to be inclusive of all the meaning of life—there is nothing that is not involved." But evil, the destructive principle that worked against harmony, wholeness, and, yes, integration of the person with himself or herself and with community, always threatened.

22:18   Thurman, anticipating a choice made by King and importing the notion, as King did, from India and Gandhi, promoted nonviolence as the means of realizing community in the face of disruption caused by evil. He was impatient with the church but did not despair of its potential as an instrument for effecting nonviolent change and reconciliation. The preacher spoke of "the Jesus idea" that was entrusted to the churches, but he found that it was frustrated in the denominations. "The separate vision of a denomination *tends* to give the one who embraces it an ultimate particularized status, even before God." So when denominationalists and dogmatic people fought over their unique holds on truth, it was "like dogs that fight over bones in the backyard." In 1963 in *Disciplines of the Spirit* Thurman detailed the view of community that he had developed consistently through the years of his prime. Few American thinkers of any race pushed so persistently the animating vision of integrality: "If life has been fashioned out of a fundamental unity and ground, and if it has developed within a structure, then it is not to be wondered at that the interest in and concern for wholeness should be part of the conscious intent of life." Thurman found this drive to be "more basic than any particular conscious tendency toward fragmentation."

22:19   While Thurman thus displayed an expansive religious vision, when he dealt with issues of his time and place and race he often focused on the Jesus proclaimed in the black churches. In 1949 he wrote that the "striking similarity between the social position of Jesus in Palestine and that of the vast majority of American Negroes is obvious to anyone who tarries long over the facts. We are dealing here," he argued, "with conditions that produce essentially the same psychology." He drew on spirituals from the slave era to illumine struggles in his own time. The miracle of the achievement of "these slave singers," which gave them a place "alongside the great creative religious thinkers of the human race," was that "they made a worthless life, the life of chattel property, a mere thing, a body, *worth living*." It did not take much translating to see the relevance of all this for those who suffered in segregated, "separate," but never equal American circumstances.

22:20   Like Kenneth B. Clark, Thurman struck out at churchly complicity in segregation. "It is to the utter condemnation of the Church that large groups of believers all over the United States have stood, and, at present, stand on the side of a theory of inequality among men," one that "causes the Church to practice in its own body some of the most vicious forms of racial prejudice." Segregation was "a complete ethical and moral evil," because "whatever it may do for those who dwell on either side of the wall, one thing is certain; it poisons all normal contacts of those persons involved." He knew the landscape of hatred: "The bitter truth is that the Church has permitted the various hate-inspired groups in our common life to establish squatter's rights in the minds of believers because there has been no adequate teaching of the meaning of the faith in terms of human dignity and human worth." The spiritual writings of Thurman left their mark on the more practical work of the younger minister, King, who acknowledged Thurman's influence.

No modern religious figure in America has had such a wide   22:21
public influence as King, the prime figure in the efforts to integrate the races and help produce a racial One Nation. The son of a prominent African American pastor in Atlanta, and thus a person of relative privilege in his community, Martin was well schooled in the ways of black church life. After graduating from Morehouse College in Atlanta he joined a small company of black students in the largely Baptist Crozer Theological Seminary in Chester, Pennsylvania, to train for ministry. The liberal Protestant message taught there was no longer current in "neo-Protestant" circles, but King learned at Crozer still to draw on the thought of the Social Gospel liberal, Walter Rauschenbusch. Onto that heritage he grafted elements of the Christian realism taken from Reinhold Niebuhr, whose *Moral Man and Immoral Society* King read in the autumn of 1950. To Niebuhr, Thurman would have been too utopian, too mystical, while Rauschenbusch held to a progressive vision that helped shape Niebuhr but that he largely left behind. King fused teachings of all three, plus themes from Paul Tillich and Gandhi. He summarized: "Niebuhr's great contribution to contemporary theology is that he has refuted the false optimism characteristic of a great segment of Protestant liberalism." Niebuhr did this—and now King referred to European neo-Protestants also then in favor—without falling into the antirationalisms or semi-fundamentalism favored on the other side of the Atlantic.

King had to find his own way; he needed to fashion a pattern of   22:22
ideas that would give him resources for leadership and that would

reach wide segments of the African American community without alienating potential followers. He was not an original philosopher, and by anyone's reckoning was a flawed human being, but he was also imaginative and courageous. All students of King stress the context of his life, including the Atlanta childhood where, he said, he had "grown up abhorring not only segregation but also the oppressive and barbarous acts which grew out of it." His father was not in the forefront of any movements to change the racial situation, but his stance did not protect him or his family from experiencing white antipathy. Young King read Henry David Thoreau and began fashioning a philosophy of freedom. At Crozer he sampled but dropped Marxism for its materialism (though right-wing critics persistently tried to connect King with communism, and he did have some admirers to his left). At Crozer he was drawn to but rejected the pure pacifism expounded by veteran A. J. Muste. He needed something more assertive and found it, as some other black leaders were beginning to do, in Gandhian *satyagraha,* which meant the force of love and truth. King could not accept Niebuhr wholesale because, he thought, Niebuhr's realism and impatience would not permit him to pursue sustained nonviolence.

22:23   In 1951 King enrolled at Boston University School of Theology, the school where Thurman was dean of the chapel; there he wrote a thesis on Paul Tillich, who seemed more remote from civil rights struggles than was Thurman. The creatively eclectic young seminarian while there also adopted elements of a philosophy or theology called *personalism,* taught there by three senior professors, including King's original adviser, Edgar Sheffield Brightman. From him King took the notion that "the clue to the meaning of reality is found in personality" and that "only personality—finite and infinite—is ultimately real." From this he was able to witness to "the idea of a personal God" and "the dignity and worth of all human personality." King's was always a God-centered philosophy which resonated in the minds and souls of many American believers who would not have been moved otherwise. While many thought that his dissertation subjects, Henry Nelson Wieman and Paul Tillich, could not or would not elaborate on a personal God, King stayed with personalism. "I am convinced of the reality of a personal God." This is "a living reality that has been validated in the experiences of everyday life." For him, "God is a living God. In Him there is feeling and will, responsive to the deepest yearnings of the human heart: *this* God both evokes and answers prayer."

22:24   King had to forge his philosophy in the face of some African

American leaders who were keeping the motif of black particularism alive and even enhancing it. King could not believe that one
race, no matter what its experience, had a special hold upon divine
agency and favor. Yes, the Negro had to affirm blackness, but this
was a tactical, not a metaphysical, matter, useful for leverage because of "the white man's crimes against him." King developed a
personal notion of human or social solidarity. People live in webs
of mutuality. In King's view, all people were to ask of each significant action how it affected everyone who came within the scope of
its consequences. Over against the tribalism that struck him as in-
version and self-worship, he progressively moved toward a vision
that he articulated only in his last years but that was emerging already by 1963. Shortly before his death he called "for a world-
wide fellowship that lifts neighborly concern beyond one's tribe,
race, class and nation" and that would be "in reality a call for an
all-embracing and unconditional love for all men." He also picked
up the language of "the beloved community" as his ideal.

An instrumentality of that community, though not the only one,   22:25
was the Christian Church, to which King remained devoted. It was
not to be an exclusive, bounded reality but a dynamic respondent
to divine love and an agent of transmitting it and then putting it to
work. The Baptist preacher kept his churchly roots and some years
later summarized: "I am many things to many people; Civil Rights
leader, agitator, trouble-maker and orator, but in the quiet recesses
of my heart, I am fundamentally a clergyman, a Baptist preacher."
Much of his power base in the civil rights movement lay where the
recesses of his heart took him. "This is my being and my heritage
for I am also the son of a Baptist preacher and the great-grandson
of a Baptist preacher. The Church is my life and I have given my
life to the Church." Yet the same man could also be "greatly disturbed by the Church" and "confused by the so-called un-christian
Christian in our midst." He often quoted Yale Divinity School dean
Liston Pope: "It is appalling that the most segregated hour of
Christian America is eleven o'clock on Sunday morning, the same
hour when many are standing to sing, 'In Christ there is no East or
West.'" And it was appalling to him, and to others who shared the
realization, that the most segregated school was the Sunday school.

King's philosophy was not fully developed when he left Boston;   22:26
he forged it more in his pastoral activities. After graduation there
followed a pulpit at Dexter Avenue Baptist Church near the state
capitol in Montgomery, Alabama, where he was immediately
drawn into controversies over civil rights. Only two weeks into his

ministry there the Supreme Court ruled against segregation in *Brown v. Board of Education.* Though the ambitious King had designs on being a theological leader, the young minister instantly found himself plunged into the battles for integration and civil rights. He became active with the National Association for the Advancement of Colored People, whose local secretary was Rosa Parks, a quiet woman who came to acquire mythic status for a single courageous act. She simply refused to move to the back of a public bus, as law and ethos required. "I was just tired from shopping. I had my sacks and all, and my feet hurt," was her understated explanation.

22:27   To protest Parks's arrest, blacks organized a boycott of the bus system. Two months after it began, when King was indicted for conspiracy, he explained himself, therewith enlarging the terms of the struggle. The audience heard, "this is not a war between the white and the Negro but a conflict between justice and injustice. This is bigger than the Negro race revolting against the white." Already he showed that he had found his life theme: reconciling nonviolence. "We must use the weapon of love. We must have compassion and understanding for those who hate us."

22:28   The civil rights leaders, with King gaining stature among them, outlasted Montgomery's resistance in the case of the bus boycott and learned from it the need to outlast those enemies who had pledged to outlast it. Through it all King kept pressing the theme of the integrative spirit. Blacks had to go forth into the conflict "with an understanding of those who have oppressed us and with an appreciation of the new adjustments that the court order poses for them." For him the test was always the field of direct action, but he liked to ground the cause in the Hebrew prophets, the gospel of Jesus, and the American constitutional tradition. "If we are wrong, the Supreme Court of this nation is wrong," he said as soon as he thought it judged rightly. "If we are wrong, the Constitution of the United States is wrong. If we are wrong, God Almighty is wrong." And a tinge of messianism could creep in: "If we protest courageously, and yet with dignity and Christian love, when the history books are written in the future, somebody will have to say, 'There lived a race of people, of black people, of people who had the moral courage to stand up for their rights. And thereby they injected a new meaning into the veins of history and civilization.' "

22:29   Neither political party had done much to address the racial situation, but by 1956 the party platforms began to change. Even the merely prudential or overly opportunistic partisans set out to win

the support of blacks and, in some cases, to explore their own consciences. King worked on such consciences, targeting churches,
including the evangelical ones that dominated in the South. He
came very informally to terms with evangelist Billy Graham, who
had been converted by a white racist and who carried the legacy of
segregated churches. To a Reinhold Niebuhr, Graham would have
looked remote and retrogressive on issues of race. But it took some
courage for the evangelist to integrate his southern rallies and some
risk for King to accept the evangelist's invitation to say a prayer at
a Graham Crusade meeting in New York in 1957. Graham, incidentally, was one of the few whites who felt privileged to call King
by the nickname for his original name, Mike. For one moment
King pictured joining forces with Graham on a kind of crusade of
their own, but Graham was wary of the Social Gospel and feared
backlash among his southern supporters. The two leaders kept in
occasional quiet touch behind the scenes.

The African American churches did not pursue change and inte-   22:30
gration on a massive and united front, at least not at first. The Reverend Joseph H. Jackson, who headed the multimillion-member
National Baptist Convention, rebuffed all efforts for cooperation
with King, made clear his opposition to King's policies, courted
conservative white America, and showed his envy of his rival in
many ways. Other black religious and secular leaders to King's
right and left also opposed him. But the public for good reasons
regarded him as the prominent voice for black America at a time
of sudden change.

After setbacks, depression, and power struggles, King and his   22:31
associates saw the movement enter a new stage when on February 1, 1960, four new students at North Carolina Agricultural and
Technical College in Greensboro went to lunch. They chose to do
so at a segregated lunch counter in the local Woolworth's. Their
courage inspired others, until hundreds and then a thousand "sat-
in" near the counter. They used their technique to build solidarity
and to impress on the larger community their commitment to
progress and integration. Many students credited a sermon by King
at Shiloh Baptist Church as their great motivator. Soon thereafter
Vanderbilt Divinity School students in Nashville, under the leadership of recent expellee James Lawson, were advancing the cause.
Lawson also promoted the integrating philosophy of nonviolence:
"Such love goes to the extreme; it remains loving and forgiving
even in the midst of hostility." Out of these moves came the Student Nonviolent Coordinating Committee; before long a song

The towering leader of the civil rights movement and a world-renowed leader
with roots in and ties to African-American Christianity in particular and American
religion in general, Martin Luther King, Jr., was used to addressing huge rallies
but he also stayed in touch with small gatherings of followers who could produce
various sizes of congregation whenever he would stop to speak, as he does here
with a random audience. (Photo: Courtesy of the Bettman Archives.)

united the demonstrations: "We Shall Overcome." And a presidential race between Richard M. Nixon and John F. Kennedy portended further change in the situation of beleaguered blacks.

22:32   It was two years into the Kennedy administration when King summarized the views of integration that he had developed and practiced through the early years of the civil rights movement; they showed a remarkable consistency. Speaking to church leaders at Nashville on the "ethical demands for integration," he showed how much the concept of being part of the One Nation, Indivisible, meant to him, however much he was also dedicated to internationalism and the concept of a reconciled human family. Now he spelled out most clearly why the negative concept of *desegregation* was unsatisfying, "empty and shallow." "The parallel thrust of the *integration* process" was what he and his movement were about. Whereas desegregation was "eliminative and negative," he remarked, "integration is creative, and is therefore more profound and far-reaching." Integration is "genuine intergroup, interpersonal doing," and must become "*the ultimate goal of our national community*" [emphasis mine]. King argued all this on the basis of the Declaration of Independence, which proclaimed the "sacredness of human personality" as no other sociopolitical document had done. He drew on a range of witnesses including black leader Frederick Douglass, philosopher Immanuel Kant, and Jewish thinker Martin Buber. But the "oughtness" of integration, he argued, was rooted most of all in the Hebrew-Christian tradition, which insisted that the human was made in *the image of God.* Coming back to African American participation, King insisted that "only by establishing a truly integrated society can we return to the Negro the quality of 'thouness' which is his due because of the nature of his being." Then the preacher reached from the particularism of African America toward the humanly universal. Integration was an ethical demand because it was a "recognition of the solidarity of the human family. Integration seems almost inevitably desirable and practical because basically we are all one." When the apostle Paul had declared that God "hath made of one blood" all nations of the world, he was stating what was "more anthropological fact than religious poetry." Because "all men are caught in an inescapable network of mutuality," King stressed that "at the heart of all that civilization has meant and developed is 'community'— the mutually cooperative and voluntary venture of man to assume a semblance of responsibility for his brother." King referred to a distinction stated by Harry Emerson Fosdick. Desegregation, as King applied Fosdick's terms, was an "enforceable" obligation. On the other hand, integration was "unenforceable," which meant it was voluntary, a purer expression of the human communal ideal. "True integration will be achieved by true neighbors who are willingly obedient to unenforceable obligations." Whether or not the legislators of 1954 had all that in mind when they promoted the notion that the United States was "one nation, under God, indivisible," King more than anyone else in his time taught millions that the implications of the concept went far beyond tribal identification of God with America.

King's career came to be poised between forces resisting integration, or at least integration on his model. On one side loomed figures like Joseph H. Jackson; on the other, the more secular

22:33

thinkers like W. E. B. DuBois, and, in the end, the Nation of Islam. DuBois was in a company of secular leaders, many of them politically radical, who pioneered in civil rights causes long before *Brown v. Board of Education*. On the right, Jackson well symbolized the old black church establishment which had settled for its place in segregated America and had grown somewhat complacent in it, while serving seriously the needs of its members in their communities. Jackson was a crowd-pleaser, the pastor of the largest Baptist church in the nation, and president of the National Baptist Convention. He supported conservative political causes and backed Richard M. Nixon, the Republican in the 1960 presidential campaign, while most of the black civil rights leadership courted and was courted by Democrat Kennedy. The Kings and the Jacksons knew each other well; the senior King in Atlanta helped Jackson, who was an occasional guest in their home, get elected president of the National Baptist Convention in 1953. Young Martin assisted in that cause. The Chicagoan showed up to celebrate the bus boycott victory in Montgomery but pointedly made almost no reference to this new successful tactic. Yet his very presence before eight thousand people gave tacit support momentarily to King, who was soon to be Jackson's rival for Baptist leadership. But in 1957, when Jackson was supposed to retire from the presidency on constitutional grounds, he manipulated the rules and kept King from leadership. A Jackson aide simply jumped up and asked that the rules be suspended so Jackson could exceed the term and remain in office. By acclamation, he stayed, to exclude King and his people and to oppose the movement. King was left with the small Southern Christian Leadership Conference. The larger public became more aware of the latter than of the convention, and King reached out progressively beyond the African American churches, some of whose leadership often frustrated him and the cause.

22:34   If Jackson represented the right, another senior figure still exerted influence on the left, the far left—W. E. B. DuBois, one of the pioneer and premier African American intellectuals. DuBois appreciated the black churches but left them behind, though he learned partly from them a language of prayer through which on occasion, at least in his earlier years, he expressed himself. DuBois moved into Marxism and even joined the Communist Party, but he never completely dismissed the nonviolent dimension of the movement as King developed it. In 1957 when King led a prayer pilgrimage at Lincoln Memorial in Washington, the aged DuBois paid some attention in order to write a magazine article. King, speaking for the first time to a national audience, was hearing cries of "Black Power." But he kept articulating his vision of integration and cooperation. Civil rights was for him "an eternal moral issue which may well determine the destiny of our nation in the ideological struggle with Communism." Even in that moment of triumph, DuBois heard King saying that he did not want to be satisfied "with a court 'victory' over our white brothers." Instead, he said, "we must act in such a way as to make possible a coming together of white people and colored people on the basis of a real harmony of interest and understanding. We must seek an integration based on mutual respect."

DuBois and his wife had written a letter of support for the   22:35 Montgomery bus boycott. With strategy in mind, he was cheered to see that King was no extremist and thus could not satisfy the attempts of "Red-baiters" to find him flawed in this respect. DuBois was dumbfounded that at the Washington event about which he was writing the article, President Eisenhower could "sit silent through this meeting and 'never say a mumblin' word.'" DuBois was a realist; he reminded readers of the awesome power of resistance in the white South and warned that the movement could go no further than it had unless blacks everywhere received the vote; the South would "never allow eligible Negroes" to get this "if they can help it." King could consider the article by the aged leader both an agenda and an endorsement. DuBois had also been changing through the years. In an interview at that time he said, "there was a time when I thought that the only way in which progress could be made in the world was by violence." He had also thought, he said, "that the only way the darker people were going to get recognition was by killing a large number of white people." Now he saw it differently: "the violence that accompanies revolution is not the revolution." King could have said the next line: "The revolution is the reform, is the change in thought, is the change of attitude [in] the people who are affected by it." He also connected King positively with Gandhi. Now he hoped blacks would become free "under the leadership of another Gandhi."

None of this meant that DuBois could be placed in the nonvio   22:36 lent camp. Two years later, when King was posed over against a challenger in the black community, North Carolinian Robert F. Williams, who in certain circumstances and toward special goals would advocate violence, DuBois expressed lingering doubts whether the "slavery and degradation of Negroes in America has not been unnecessarily prolonged by the submission to evil." And he was moved to ask what program King and his followers had in place to offset southern white resistance. Yet DuBois did not despair of King, who through it all was stepping up his endeavors. King had been reacting to a word from Williams, who had suffered much from the Klan and had consequently armed himself: "Since the federal government will not bring a halt to lynching in the South," Williams said, "and since the so-called courts lynch our people legally, if it's necessary to stop lynching with lynching, then we must be willing to resort to that method. We must meet violence with violence." Given such inflammatory language as this, it was politic for the NAACP to let Williams go, and he also did some backing off.

22:37   King certainly understood Williams's agony and rage but found that he had to respond. When people are frustrated, King said, they can, as Williams did, produce "a confused, anger-motivated drive to strike back violently, to inflict damage" in a pattern that was "punitive—not radical or constructive." Or they could build "a wholesome social organization" to counter the enemy. King argued that "there is more power in socially organized masses on the march than there is in guns in the hands of a few desperate men. Our enemies would prefer to deal with a small armed group rather than with a huge, unarmed but resolute mass of people." King knew that Williams spoke a truth when he said that most white people had "no idea of the violence with which Negroes in the South are treated daily—nay, hourly," and all that with condonement by the authorities. These authorities had permitted violence in "unceasing and unremitting" fashion for centuries. King could not deny that Williams was in his own way right: "The South is not a civilized society; the South is a social jungle"; but King could not finish such a sentence with the radical line that Williams used: "so in cases like that we had to revert to the law of the jungle."

22:38   King's encounter with Williams was brief. The enduring pressure from a more radical front came from the Nation of Islam, the Black Muslims. They came to public notice in July 1959, when CBS produced a special, "The Hate that Hate Produced." The Nation's leader had been Elijah Muhammad, but by 1959 Malcolm Little, now called Malcolm X, was coming to leadership to challenge King's integrationist movement. Muhammad and Malcolm X were ready to use violence in the face of violence. Elijah Muhammad was to say, "We must return to the Mosaic law of an eye for an eye, and a tooth for a tooth. What does it matter if ten million of us die? There will be seven million of us left, and they will enjoy justice and freedom." But such remarks were made mainly for effect; the Nation of Islam largely wanted to pursue nonviolent courses. The main difference in this period was between the Black Muslims' demand for separation, for a segregated space in the United States—for example, the states of Alabama and Mississippi—while King still promoted integration in the One Nation.

The Black Muslim taunters were ready when King moved his   22:39
headquarters from Montgomery to Atlanta. As the *Los Angeles Herald-Dispatch* reported it, "In February, this same Reverend Martin Luther King, the Darling of the South, Honey Boy of the North, is now moving his headquarters from the increasingly hostile atmosphere of Alabama to the more lucrative haven of Atlanta." Was that not a retreat? "Has his philosophy developed from 'turn the other cheek' to 'turn and run away'?" King and the Southern Christian Leadership Conference knew that a generation of disaffected and ambitious younger blacks enjoyed such sneers and were looking for more dramatic and provocative approaches. The Black Muslims demanded attention. They received this when C. Eric Lincoln in 1961 published his doctoral dissertation, *The Black Muslims in America,* which amounted to a report on the movement to almost that date. Lincoln coined the name "Black Muslims"; followers of Chicagoan Elijah Muhammad had called themselves "Temple People" or "the Nation of Islam."

Lincoln remembered how as a student at Clark College in At-   22:40
lanta he had been shocked to read a term paper by a gifted young Muslim minister which argued that "The Christian religion is incompatible with the Negro's aspirations for dignity and equality in America." It went on, "Christian love is the white man's love for himself and for his race. For the man who is not white, Islam is the hope for justice and equality in the world we must build tomorrow." But the Islam that Lincoln discovered was not the orthodox Qur'anic Muslim faith; it was a made-in-America brand that reflected American realities. Psychologist Gordon Allport wrote a foreword for Lincoln's book. "Peaceful integration is not the Negro's goal," Allport heard Black Muslims saying, and then asking, "why integrate with a dying man?" Allport was personally dismissive of Elijah Muhammad's claims, seeing them taken together as nothing but a "historical monstrosity," but he had to pay attention because of the new prophet's compelling way. Muhammad's movement rested on an "absolute and inflexible dichotomy of white-Negro, or, more accurately, white-non-white. White is evil; non-

white is good." So Allport invoked the ultimate comparison: "This erroneous slicing marks the thought of all racists—of Hitler, of the White Citizens Council, of the Black Muslims." And the psychologist had to ask: "Will educated Negroes find it possible to subscribe to an absurd ideology as did many German intellectuals under Hitler?"

22:41   By the time his book was published in 1961, according to Lincoln's estimate, the movement numbered 100,000 militant men and was "probably America's fastest growing racist sect." He knew of sixty-nine temples in twenty-seven states, places where followers heard Elijah Muhammad's call for an "ultimate demand—that Black Men be allowed to set up a separate state within the United States, occupying as much as one-fifth of the nation's territory." The Nation of Islam claimed divine revelation, developed a mythology, and showed a genius for organization. It generated an ethos and propagated a doctrine that countered the ideology of the period when it called for "absolute separation of the black and the white races." Significantly, the word *so-called* kept creeping into Muslim speech: "Those so-called Negroes who seek integration with the American white man are, say the Muslims, unrealistic and stupid." Why blend with the dying white world, asked Muhammad. "Any man who integrates with the world must share in its disintegration and destruction."

22:42   It was clear that Muslims targeted black Christians for conversion. Until 1959 many Negro Christian churches had regarded the Muslims benignly and loaned them their churches, but then the doors began to close. Jews largely ignored them, though the Nation of Islam verbally attacked Jews: "The Jew is a white man." Orthodox Muslims, when made aware of the movement that shared part of their name, almost unanimously repudiated it. They repudiated the extreme racial views, the militancy, the unhistoric and heretical teachings. And the white community responded negatively. Lincoln, the scholar who paid the most attention and a "so-called Negro" to Black Muslims, found the movement divisive. "For most of us, there is no value quite so exalted as that implicit in being 'American.' All other values are subsidiary—religion, political affiliation, even moral consciousness." According to Lincoln, most citizens agreed that "to be an American means to be associated with a great civilization, a unique civilization." They may share certain values, for example of religion and art, with the rest of the world, but "only *we* are Americans." Still Lincoln could speak as a black, for the blacks: " 'American' also has an implication of color," he said; most of the world and other citizens here regarded it as a "white man's country," and it was that attitude that made Black Muslims credible to many.

Arnold and Caroline Rose in 1948 wrote *America Divided*, which Lincoln now quoted with favor. Group identification, they said, had assets for those who suffered discrimination and prejudice, but it also brought perils. It "frequently promotes chauvinism and nationalism, which voluntarily separates the group from the broader opportunities and contacts that it presumably is fighting to secure." Most groups did not need to identify overmuch with their own kind alone. For instance, Jews could and did pass into the dominant white group. Some Japanese Americans, having suffered in the war, had to organize on group identity lines. Spanish-speaking Americans, "the second largest unassimilated ethnic group in the country," were organizing. But "it is the Negroes, then, more than any other minority, who find a corporate release in social, protective and protest organizations." And they were expressing "a new sense of *urgency.*"

Lincoln built on these words of 1948 to report on what he had found in the years following. He revisited his own earlier writings that dealt with the "excruciating anxiety" produced by the word *integration* in the ears of many people. So he did some defining. *Integration* referred "to the freedom of a minority to participate in the total life of the community without necessarily merging with the majority group." It could retain its own identity and cultural values. *Assimilation,* on the other hand, he said, "refers to the merging of a minority into the general community and the gradual disappearance of its identity and its unique cultural values." Thus in an assimilated society, a minority group does not, and is not forced to, cling together. "Its members flow into the general community, accepted and fully mobile in every area of social and cultural intercourse." There was no reason for the Negro to be "troubled by the possibility of assimilation into the mainstream of American life." Integration was the plausible route, and the Negro was "intensely serious about integration." So long as integration was the ideal, with Joseph H. Jackson's passivity remaining powerful but belonging to the past, King had an advantage over Du-Bois, Williams, Muhammad, and Malcolm X. White America was giving it lip service and, increasingly if selectively, more heart service than before. However hard it was to advance the cause, even

22:43

22:44

after *Brown v. Board of Education,* African Americans on by now almost instinctive Christian grounds responded to the call to seek liberty and pursue racial integration. This, they felt, gave them their best chance to make their way in the One Nation, Under God, that appealed as strongly to them as to those who had more immediate access to its liberties.

23

"In Unblushing Competition for the American Soul"

When C. Eric Lincoln was writing *The Black Muslims in* 23:1
America, he had to take up the discussion of the way minorities, or
for that matter any peoples, related to the national whole. He may
have been hyperbolic about the place of devotion to the nation in
his time, but only slightly. We recall reading his observation that
"for most of us, there is no value quite so exalted as that implicit
in being 'American.'" Prophetic types might not like the sociologist's observation that "all other values are subsidiary—religion,
political affiliation, even moral consciousness," but they could not
easily argue with it. Lincoln immediately recognized that such an
exaltation of national identity could easily promote "chauvinism
and nationalism." Then he contrasted the ways four peoples—
Negroes, Spanish-speaking Americans, Japanese Americans, and
Jews—related both to their own people and to the reality of being
American. In Lincoln's reckoning, Jews had the easiest time, because they could pass into the dominant white group, America being so often thought of as a "white man's country." He poised each
of these peoples between the concepts of *integration* and *assimilation.* Integration, we recall, meant to him that a minority could
participate in the total life of the community without necessarily
merging with the majority group. Assimilation meant such merging along with the "gradual disappearance of [the group's] identity
and its unique cultural values." The members of such a minority

group, he said, "flow into the general community, accepted and fully mobile in every area of social and cultural intercourse."

23:2   Jews at mid-century found themselves poised between these twin ideals, whether all of them would have used these terms or not. Curiously, the Nazi murder of the Jews and the birth of Israel, the two most profound events of modern Judaism, did not serve as the main markers of identity at the time. Many works on Judaism and by Jews referred to the Holocaust not at all or else with perfunctory treatment in a paragraph or two. The founding of Israel in 1948 occasioned an intense debate about whether Zionism might mean dual loyalty for American Jews and might lead non-Jews to suspect Jews of belonging to two nations. But while issues associated with Zionism did not die during the Eisenhower period of revived interest in religion, a canvass of literature from that time shows that Jews who were part of the public argument and conversation had a very different agenda from the Zionist preoccupation. Within a score of years a population group numbering less than 3 percent of the nation achieved a kind of equal status in the developing concept of "Judeo-Christian" America. Or it acquired at least one-third of the weight of terms in the other new coinage, "Protestant-Catholic-Jewish" America. While anti-Semitism survived (along with anti-Catholicism and many kinds of anti-Protestantism), that achievement suggested that Jews were now integrated; should they also be assimilated?

23:3   Survey research and opinion polling developed so rapidly in the midcentury years that their sophistication has to be regarded as much an important event in itself as well as a means of measuring events and trends. Jewish scholars took to these sociological devices with zest. In 1957 Marshall Sklare, presenting a major social-scientific study, quoted Louis Finkelstein, then head of Jewish Theological Seminary. Finkelstein had complained only a few years before that while a hundred or more professionals were equipped to tell about Jews in Jerusalem in the first century, "there does not seem to be one who has the same duty to the Jews of New York in the twentieth century." During the period just before 1957, however, that circumstance changed, thanks chiefly to the dispersal of Jews out of the thickness of urban ghettos into the diffusion of suburban pluralism. One way to assess meanings of the move is to take close-up looks. Rabbi Albert I. Gordon, a student of Finkelstein's who turned his mentor's observation about neglect of the contemporary into a challenge, concentrated on the suburb where he served, Newton, Massachusetts. He left a telling picture of Judaism poised between integration and assimilation.

In the time when the American Way of Life came to be treated   23:4
with capital letters, Gordon spoke of suburbanism also as a "way of life," a "state of mind," much as pioneer sociologist Robert Park had once called the city a state of mind. As the rabbi saw it, Jews, typically urbanites, in making the sudden suburban move wanted "the best of both worlds." In the process they had "changed the location and often the character of Jewish community life in America." Gordon checked out this claim by gaining information from rabbis in eighty-nine suburbs from coast to coast. He claimed to know more than 90 percent of the Jewish communities in America, thanks to his travels while serving as the executive director of the United Synagogue of America, the agency of Conservative Judaism.

The suburb was, to Gordon and his generation, the new frontier   23:5
in the "nation of nomads." Between 1940 and 1956 the suburban population, he noted, had grown three times faster than that of central cities. Between 1950 and 1955 the population of suburbs grew almost seven times as fast. Such a change had to affect Jews more than most, since two-thirds of the nation's 5.5 millions Jews lived in or near ten of America's largest metropolises, and most of the rest were also in sizable cities. Motives for the move were many: inexpensive governmentally insured loans for military veterans were available; there were assets for people in families who desired to be near green plants, "growing things"; people sought and the suburbs often offered new status and prestige; most of all, perhaps, Jews, along with other whites, took flight from blacks and Puerto Ricans who moved into Jewish neighborhoods, while along the way, as sociologist David Riesman put it, they were engaged in "a tremendous but tacit revolt against industrialism." Gordon saw some irony in the dislocation. Jews had long protested the segregation of the ghetto but were now helping form economically fortified suburban ghettos.

The suburban move brought perplexity. Many Jews could pass   23:6
as Gentiles outside the ghetto. At the very least, they could escape the demands of Jewish community life, but only for a time. Soon more Jews would arrive in their new suburb of choice, Jewish identification would grow, and escape "became almost impossible in the suburb." And Gordon knew, for all his comment on the irony of resegregation, that most Jewish suburbanites did not want to

recreate the ghetto or form too close a community. "They *fear* segregation, in contrast to their parents, who in many cases sought it." Some kept old temple ties in the city for a while, but eventually most built suburban synagogues. Interestingly, in those secular times, Gordon observed, "these Jews are *not* irreligious." But they were different: "the uniqueness of present-day Jewish suburbanites, then, is associated with the fact that they, unlike their fathers' generation, feel 'at home' and secure in their Americanism." The economy of the postwar years made it hard for people to go scapegoat hunting as they did in Depression times, so there was less virulent anti-Semitism than ever before. Most Jews were middle-class, no longer cramped by economic necessity in the ghettos. They were free.

23:7   The family, a basic Jewish institution, was being recast in the fresh setting. After reckoning with trends for three decades, Gordon found the new suburban Jewish community to be a matriarchy, headed by Jewish women in the "new position of executive leadership." Most suburban women were married; their husbands were engrossed in business affairs at some distance, and the wives acquired new status, even when it came to religious choice. He quoted representative women: "I am the one who decided which temple to join." Another: "I'm the one who said that [my Orthodox husband] would simply *have* to get home earlier on Friday evening in order that we could have a family Sabbath meal. I light the Sabbath candles and try my best to make the Sabbath Eve beautiful." Gordon showed himself to be caught between generations when he made an observation that ten years later would have been typed as chauvinist: "Judaism requires that its lay leaders . . . possess specific and even detailed knowledge of the basic texts and rituals of Judaism. The Jewish woman is unfortunately not prepared as yet for this kind of leadership." The notion that they would soon be prepared to serve as rabbis was not even foreseen.

23:8   Many Jews regarded each suburban location as a *temporary* home. Mobility and rootlessness kept them from settling and building institutions. Yet the synagogue, a center of both spiritual and secular or worldly life, did prosper. In 1956–57, when the National Council of Churches estimated that national church affiliation drew 62 percent of the people, 60 percent of the Jews were committed enough to sign up on synagogue rolls, with many of the synagogues now in the suburbs. What went on in the temples? What characterized belief and practice there? Here comparisons to Christianity were helpful to the Newton rabbi. In the suburbs neither fundamentalist churches nor Orthodox temples were numerous. There was a decline of interest in creeds, denominationalism, or literal views of the Bible. For Protestant and Jewish suburban communities alike, "each, functioning within the framework of its own distinctive religious tradition, is increasingly emphasizing the neighborhood, the community, the ethical, moral and social values associated with religion, and the needs of living people." As this was so, "theological and denominational differences," Gordon judged, were "seemingly less important. The rapid growth of the ecumenical movement in the church today offers support for this thesis." Jewish families might associate with Conservative, Reform, or Orthodox temples in the same community, and then interact, in a kind of Jewish ecumenism.

While Gordon made less than did C. Eric Lincoln of what "being 'American' " meant in the religious scheme, he did agree with journalist and poll-taker Max Lerner that suburban religion meant worship of the "five great goals in American civilization which make for happiness." Jews were uniting in homage to "success, prestige, money, power, and security." Some synagogue-goers even saw the act of contributing to the synagogue to enhance all these. Many treated the temple as a plant, a business, an industry, believing that "everything, including religion, can be bought." And when in the act of buying, Jews sought moderation. Both Orthodoxy on the right and Reform on the left seemed a bit extreme; therefore, "in most cases since 1946, the first synagogue in a new suburban community is Conservative," which meant moderate, judged Gordon. Strong ideology seldom was a factor in choice; "the interest of the total Jewish community" was what mattered. After making their choice, most of the affiliated seemed satisfied. In Gordon's survey, 83 percent said their congregations were "doing a good job," and only 7 percent had basic complaints.

Where was the God of Israel, of Judaism, in all this? Faith had been a key element in the Jewish story through the ages, and in a time of theological renewal leaders were looking for it. Many suburban rabbis, however, expressed concern that the congregations were seeking an easy, relaxed, country-club atmosphere. Where was the positive philosophy of Jewish life, "with a strong belief in God and His purposiveness at its very center?" Gordon often heard apprehensions expressed that "though the synagogue is the formal symbol of a religion-centered way of life, it may very easily become a completely secularized institution if it limits its program to nonreligious activities and interests rather than to deep-rooted

23:9

23:10

spiritual needs." The rabbi was somewhat reassuring: "The synagogue is not now and never was *only* a house of worship." Conservative Judaism and its Reconstructionist movement had invented the "synagogue-centers" some years before and now saw them proliferate: "They offer each Jew the opportunity to come to know his own rich heritage and to live his life as an American Jew." This norm would hardly have satisfied the evokers of prophetic Judaism, like the Herbergs or Heschels, the Kadushins or Weiss-Rosmarins, but it had precedence.

23:11   Worship clearly was not at the center of most suburban synagogue life. A Gallup poll in 1955 had found that while 74 percent of Catholics and 42 percent of the Protestants claimed to have attended worship on a weekend about which they were questioned, only 27 percent of Jews did, and only 12 percent claimed to attend weekly. Gordon found this response "rather anemic," as one supposes a rabbi would. Why did people attend? The largest group, 26 percent of these, said "it gives me a good, peaceful feeling." A 1958 study by Marshall Sklare had not found a single respondent saying that prayer and worship were important motivations for attending. Yet 92 percent of the Jews questioned said they believed in God, even though most were doubtful about the role God played in the lives of people. Here for once and at last came a show of Holocaust influence: "These young men and women, recipients of college educations, are deeply moved and disturbed by the Nazi holocaust and the annihilation of six million Jews," said Gordon. Then he added that the same people were aware of problems science raised for belief. They did appeal to a personal God in crisis but felt no urgency when "things are normal." Overwhelmingly, they signed up at a suburban synagogue for purposes of "belongingness" as part of what rabbis uncertainly defined as a "religious revival."

23:12   If the Holocaust was in the back of the suburban synagogue-goer's mind, what was in front? "Most suburban Jews have a friendly, though at times uneasy, feeling about the State of Israel," thought their observer. They avidly read about it. They were aware that their Hebraic tradition and even Torah were directly associated with it. Jews were proud of Israeli courage and achievements. Yet few suburban men enrolled in Zionist organizations, though their wives were a bit more involved. They bought Israel bonds and hoped to visit Israel "sometime." But Gordon foresaw confusion: "What the attitude may be should Israel suffer any reverse in the years ahead, it is difficult to say." At the moment sentiment was pro-Israel because "everyone loves a winner."

Was belongingness the whole story? Many rabbis agreed, said   23:13
Gordon, that "it is 'congregationalism' rather than faith which is experiencing a revival." But the Newton rabbi cited psychologist Erich Fromm to suggest that something deeper was also at stake. Affiliation helped the Jew "relate himself to [a] system which would give meaning and direction to his life." Religious fellowship was the great positive element. Therefore, said the author, "the up-surge we are witnessing today may not be a completely unqualified revival of religion. It is, rather, a quest—a search for the meaning of human existence," and, to put a happy face on it all, suburban Jews were leading this search.

There were also reasons for scowls in the suburban way of life   23:14
for Jews, and one had to do with their experience in public schools. The Protestant Christian majority made use of the school calendar to do their own version of celebrating holidays; they included two in which Jews especially could not take part, Christmas and Easter. Yet "Jewish children were expected to accept the standards of the majority." Now that situation was beginning to change in many places. For Jews, religious freedom meant that moral teaching based on different religions and thus not acceptable to everyone had to be eliminated; such teaching based on Bible reading, re-leased-time programs, and the like were divisive. Gordon and his respondents were not even happy with released-time programs sponsored by and beneficial to Jews: did Americans really want such parochialism to be administered through public schools? Real trouble was ahead: "The fuse has already been lighted. Only major statesmanship and continued mutual respect can reduce the effect of the explosion which may result," he thought, if particular reli-gions overplayed their hands as majorities.

Rabbi Gordon would not have been a person of his times had   23:15
he not rued conformity and conformism. He cited Arthur Schlesin-ger's crack about "the bland leading the bland" to score suburban synagogues for their colorlessness. With psychologist Abraham Maslow he worried about the issue of too much adjustment and asked, with Maslow, adjustment to what? A sick culture? Once again, Gordon was a soft critic. For the vast majority in the sub-urbs, "it may be said that the basic values upon which their lives and families are founded are indeed sound." While Gordon feared, along with others, that Jews could be "ghettoized" in "gilded

ghettos" in the suburbs, and saw problems with the "isolation and segregation of Jews in suburbia," something that could "hardly be looked upon approvingly by Jews or Christians," he saw strong counterforces. "Not only is brotherhood good in its own right, but the American ideal assumes that, out of such interchange of ideas and interplay of personalities, a culturally superior American people will develop." Belongingness and congregationalism meanwhile were clearly the dominant motifs: "not all students of the suburban scene may agree that a true revival of religion has taken place, but there *is* agreement that American Jews are actively affiliated with their religious institutions and centers."

23:16   If Gordon presented the most ambitious and detailed assessment of suburban Jews, sociologists Eugene J. Lipman and Albert Vorspan only slightly later—in 1960, at the decade's end—were testing this "brotherhood" in ten cities. Their report, *A Tale of Ten Cities,* reflected regional and metropolitan differences wider than the differences from suburb to suburb in Gordon's account. Their approach to American pluralism zooms in more closely than the broad-brush approaches of people like Will Herberg. For instance, readers of the report learned that as recently as 1959 Richard Cardinal Cushing of Boston, who had a reputation for manifesting good will, could still express his views of Jews in cultural stereotypes. In some articles in the *Boston American,* Boston's top cleric referred to Jews as "International Bankers," erroneously said that Leon Trotsky's real name was Leonard Bernstein, and relied for his opinions on militant anti-Zionist and far-right-wing publications and advisers. But the authors could also report on change and happy endings. Cushing was operating out of naiveté, and when the Jewish Community Council protested, Cushing's response was "prompt and unequivocal. He apologized humbly." The cardinal said that while he was in the hospital, speechwriters had prepared the script for him. "I am truly very sorry. Please believe me." Clearly, something new was going on in pluralist America; once upon a time such an accused figure would have stood his ground rather than apologize. That year Cushing became the *Boston Jewish Advocate*'s "Man of the Year."

23:17   Cooperation between Protestants and Jews, said Lipman and Vorspan, was "continuous, firm, and cordial." While Protestants wore the mantle of champions of civil rights and civil liberties, "the robe is large enough to admit the vibrant Jewish community." The coauthors even had the luxury of being a bit snide: "One powerful segment of Boston opinion-shapers has reared a cult of interfaith banquetry and headtableship as a charm for warding off any suggestion that relationships are less than harmonious. Boston has not one, but two leaders of Christians and Jews." And the local branch of the National Conference of Christians and Jews, they said, "churns away at the traditional educational approach to tolerance." Meanwhile, a "Massachusetts Committee, Catholics, Protestants, and Jews" was "the front runner in the contest for bigger and more spectacular good will banquets."

One incident in Boston showed how progress was being made. 23:18 Not many years before, Father Leonard Feeney, the ultraist leader of the Slaves of the Immaculate Conception, had blasted at Jews: "It is imperative that American Catholics wake up to the fact that the Jews, as an organized force, are the implacable, declared enemies of Christianity—of its tenets, its traditions, its moral code, its very culture." The Slaves despised Archbishop Cushing for his moderation while the Feeneyites themselves showed "special contumely for the Jews of Boston." The coauthors were glad to give Cushing credit for having Pope Pius XII excommunicate the extremist Father Feeney in 1953 and then to ignore the dwindling company of his followers. Score another victory for pluralism, brotherhood, growing harmony, and Jewish blending into the larger community.

If Gordon saw Protestant-style prayer in public schools cloud- 23:19 ing his scene of suburbia, Lipman and Vorspan, dealing with Massachusetts, took note of several other issues as well. Non-Catholic Massachusetts had a more immediate and irritating issue: birth control information. Massachusetts was one of only two states— Connecticut being the other—which forbade doctors to prescribe contraceptives. In the nineteenth century, Protestants had put the laws against contraception on the books, but now, with Jews at their side, they were trying to clear the books. Israel was also an irritant. The Catholic *Pilot* regularly attacked Israel for "nationalistic intoxication" and the "most predatory type of modern nationalism." Not everything was yet harmonious, but Lipman and Vorspan saw gains, as more and more Bostonians were adopting the advice of a Chinese missionary: "We must agree to differ by resolve to love."

Another sample city was Cleveland, where Jews had virtually 23:20 evacuated this sixth most Jewish metropolis and headed for the suburbs. "Cleveland proper is almost literally a city without Jews," Lipman and Vorspan found; some suburbs had become virtual ghettos. Contact with non-Jews, where it existed, was generally positive but not profound. Leading ministers and rabbis scarcely knew one another, but laypeople had considerable contact. Ironically, "vital interreligious relations seem to result *least* out of directly religious concerns." These tended to be out of bounds, and only social issues could come up across faith lines. In Cleveland as elsewhere the tension was greatest over public education and religion. As for ghettos, "the Roman Catholic community is the most isolated of the three major faith groups."

23:21   Los Angeles, having the second largest Jewish community, merited more study; with its 425,000 members, it had doubled its size since 1941. A certain amount of self-segregation marked Jewish life; one Christian minister in a "not unkindly fashion" thus called Beverly Hills "Hebrew Hollow." Jewish children often experienced "denominationally sheltered environments." But relations between Jews and Christians were "generally good on a superficial level." In Los Angeles, Jews stood almost alone in opposing Bible reading in the public schools and had to face a coalition of Catholic and Protestant groups that favored the practice. Here as so often different issues produced different kinds of coalitions: "Only some Seventh Day Adventists, humanists, and Masons joined the Jewish community in opposing [a pro-school prayer] bill publicly." Fundamentalists were supposed to have been separatists worrying about other worlds, but not in the scene Lipman and Vorspan confronted. "Fundamentalist spokesmen stood on the undisguised platform that this is a 'Christian nation,' and that 'godlessness' was at the heart of our current plethora of immorality and crime."

23:22   In Los Angeles it was Catholic-Protestant tensions that were strained and worsening. Once again, the crazy quilt of coalitions was positive: most Protestants and Jews could often work together in causes wherein Catholics were self-excluded or to which they were opposed. Thus the Catholic archdiocese, said the authors, "eschews cooperation" with the National Conference of Christians and Jews. One labor official denounced the conference for " 'selling brotherhood for $25.00 a plate' while others were putting brotherhood into action." Yet the conference helped produce minor breakthroughs, such as the development of a University Religious Conference at the University of California at Los Angeles. Here as everywhere, Jews had to be alert on the church-state front, because, it was noted, "most of the encroachments are Christological in character." This meant they had to oppose the placing of Christian symbols on tax-supported public places. "Efforts to involve Jewish and Christian leaders in serious discussion of separation of church and state have invariably fallen flat," noted the coauthors. And here as everywhere, they said, it was "deep religious rifts over public education" that "should jar Los Angeles religious leaders into more forceful action in building freeways of cooperation."

A fourth sample came from Nashville, the "Athens of the South," whose mere 3,000 Jews were no match for 14,000 Catholics and 183,000 Protestants. The county had 600 churches, most of them Protestant; "more religious literature is printed in Nashville each year than anywhere else in America," and most of it was Protestant. With three synagogues, one Orthodox, one Conservative, and one Reform, Nashville's Jewish community was regarded as "one of the most active and affluent in the south." The issue that plagued other cities arose in Nashville as well; school leadership took for granted that public-school religion was Protestant Christian. Each year the schools invited outstanding athletes to "speak for Christianity" in the schools. One year the committee invited Vanderbilt hero and ex–Los Angeles Ram football veteran Herbert Rich. "I will be glad to speak," he said, "but I will speak for the Jewish way of life. Didn't you know I was Jewish?" They had not known. He did not speak. When a rabbi in a seminar at Peabody College Graduate School spoke up to urge the elimination of sectarian religion, an important high school principal interjected: "The only religion that I will permit in my high school is my religion. I'm not a Jew or a Catholic so you know what religion that will be!" Such evidence was anecdotal, of course, but it was consistent enough to carry weight. Here, as always, however, Lipman and Vorspan saw signs of cheer among those who, they said, were "quietly working for justice, for harmonious race and religious relationships, for community progress, and for brotherhood in action." Nashville was "making progress—agonizingly slow progress it sometimes appears, but progress nonetheless."   23:23

Next was the very Catholic Philadelphia. "Protestants and Jews—in the city as in the suburbs—usually get along better together than either group does with Roman Catholics," according to the reports that reached Lipman and Vorspan. Catholics were self-isolated, and their social doctrines often collided with those of others. As always, adjudged the authors, "the most tender problem in the area of interreligious relations has to do with separation of church and state, and specifically the question of religion in the public schools." Here "the usual Protestant-Jewish cooperation breaks down," the authors observed, and Jews were joined only by   23:24

a "small group of humanists, secularists, and liberal Protestants" in their protest. On the intimate level things worked best. Another anecdote illustrated this. A Catholic mother, exasperated by Jewish opposition to Christian carols in the schools, dropped in to complain at the Philadelphia Fellowship Commission. As the coauthors reported it, "A Protestant staff member calms her down by asking, 'Look, you are a Catholic, I am a Protestant. Would you allow your children to sing "Jesus is *not* the Son of God?" Well, that is the dilemma of the Jewish mother when we sing carols in the public schools that say "Jesus *is* the Son of God." '"

23:25   New York and its surrounding counties had more Jews than any other city in the world, including Jerusalem and Tel Aviv. There the mass media were models of good behavior. "Religions and religious institutions are rarely the subject of direct or overt public criticism or attack," and "the churches exercise a decorous restraint toward one another." This meant that "the city is probably a poor barometer of the deep theological and communication gulfs that separate Protestant from Catholic and Christian from Jew." The more one read Lipman and Vorspan, however, and the more apparent it became that the only consistently divisive issue was prayer in the public schools, the more one can picture how a foreign visitor, fresh from any place where religion motivated a kind of tribal warfare, would have rubbed her eyes to see harmony at all. Yes, the issue of Christian holidays in the public schools was "one issue of such extraordinary difficulty that even the vaunted skills and ingenuity of the Board of Education failed to measure up to its formidable challenge." The fact that Catholics were forbidden to discuss theology was an inhibitor that forced interfaith groups to produce programs that rarely went past "brotherhood for the sake of brotherhood." So Lipman and Vorspan asked, "Why gather around the conference table if there is no possibility of a meeting of minds in the area of faith?"

23:26   Minnesota's Twin Cities had a climate where "in general, relationships among all the religious groups are superficially calm and friendly." The generous-minded state legislature in 1957 bent so far forward that it passed a bill making the Greek Orthodox church the fourth major religious faith in the state. Curiously, noted Lipman and Vorspan, "there seems to be no record of bills having been passed declaring the other three major faiths officially major faiths in the state of Minnesota." But some interfaith problems had begun to appear, and it was noticed that clergy rarely participated in activities sponsored by the National Conference of Christians and Jews; they left the laity to do that. No surprise: "By all odds, the most frequent, the most prevalent, and most complex group of problems which arises to bedevil the interreligious relationships in Minnesota is the thorny problem of church-state relations." Public schools taught Jewish children to sing "I Have Room in My Heart for You, Dear Jesus," and "Jesus Loves Me, This I Know."

In 1957 Jews protested when the Minnesota Centennial Commission adopted an emblem containing the cross. When this issue came up, "opponents of the commission's position were accused of 'ritualistic liberalism' as well as agnosticism, unbelief, and pro-Communism." The cross stayed in the emblem, even though by then many Christians joined Jews in the call for the commission to be sensitive. Even State Senate chaplain C. A. Nelson said that "for the protection of minorities, this ought not to become an issue at this time." Archbishop William O. Brady argued that the cross had a historical referent. No, said Jews, "the emblem was not designed to represent the past." "If today's pressure forces the cross onto a state emblem as the only symbol of the spiritual and religious expression of all citizens of Minnesota, tomorrow's pressure will attempt to force it into our public schools and in other governmental areas." After the centennial, Archbishop Brady met and patched things up with the Minnesota Rabbinical Council. So Lipman and Vorspan could conclude: "There is a surprising amount of good will and understanding prevalent among the various religious groups that make up the state." 23:27

So plaguing was the school issue, *the* disrupter of efforts to integrate America or help groups be assimilated, that Lipman and Vorspan made a twenty-one-page case study of an incident in Plainview on Long Island, where half the people were Catholic and a third were Jewish and only 15 percent Protestant. Good relations broke down when in 1956 the issue of religious observances in the public schools came up. But Plainview citizens and their leaders laboriously worked out some guidelines that the coauthors thought might even be helpful in other communities. Thus they would learn how to "use inevitable interreligious differences as an opportunity for increased communications among citizens of all faiths, for an increased sense of community, and for increased opportunities to solve community problems amicably and creatively." 23:28

At the end of their ten-city tour, Lipman and Vorspan offered Jewish views of pluralism at the end of the Eisenhower years of religious revival. "*America is no longer a Protestant country.* Was it ever? It certainly was." Now there was talk of the "post-Protes- 23:29

tant age." Will the United States ever have a Catholic majority; would there be a "conquest by fecundity?" The authors were not overly concerned. They devoted themselves instead to reflection on the place of Jews in a pluralistic society and on pluralism itself, and did this so systematically and representatively that they merit some lingering attention. They were aware that not everyone welcomed even the idea of pluralism: "Implying as it does a kind of religious coexistence, the very concept is as repulsive to the consciences of some as is co-existence in the international sphere." But pluralism, the authors kept reminding themselves and their readers, was a fact of life, and in general Protestant, Catholic, and Jewish groups had accepted the new concept. The One Nation motif was strong here as elsewhere. In the observation of Lipman and Vorspan, the three religions were "in unblushing competition with one another not so much for the individual souls of Americans, but, in a sense, for the American soul, for the opportunity to shape American culture in the image of the religious ethic of each." So they could not cooperate except in the face of shared enemies, "secularism, materialism, apathy, intellectual superficiality, nihilism, and communism." As a result they developed "a many-splendored 'culture' in a state of kaleidoscopic flux." The inevitable second result was "interreligious tensions."

23:30   Jews, thought the authors of the ten-city study, could find comfort in the "plural culture-in-becoming" that prevented any religion from dominating. In 1958 even the body of Catholic bishops in America for the first time referred to *faiths* in the plural, they noted. "Pluralism in America means, inevitably, competitive coexistence among the faith groups and between the faiths and secularism." Jewry after World War II had been "jet-propelled from the periphery of American life, an immigrant, low-income, embattled, defensive group, to a rising middle-class status, in a community of highly-educated, mobile, culturally-advanced, predominantly native-born Americans." The old sense of "inadequacy, of diffidence, of defensive self-abnegation" had now declined. Jews represented only 3 percent of the population but, remarkably, "public deference to the balanced representation of 'the three major faiths'" (presumably outside Minnesota where, with Orthodoxy, there were four) "invests Jewry with respect and opportunities disproportionate to its numbers." The danger now was that the tradition was "being steadily diluted by pressure toward conformity to the conservative values of suburbia."

23:31   Lipman and Vorspan found what Rabbi Gordon and most other observers noted. Jewish synagogue worship was low, and even synagogue members seemed to be secularized. Yet, they said, "Jews are very conscious of their Jewish identity which is expressed in terms of a strong feeling for Israel, a sense of connection with other Jews throughout the world, an attachment to some Jewish cultural as well as religious traditions, and a tendency to self-segregation." Their goals were now American cultural values: "happiness, security, popularity, wealth, power, success, and status—more than the historic values of Judaism—piety, love of Torah, prayer, and ethical living under God."

Like the other observers, these coauthors also noted the shock   23:32
of religious advance at someone's expense—Protestants. "American Protestants have suffered a severe historic jolt. This is no longer 'their' country. The shock has been most painful in the cities," where in most places Protestants did not hold sway any longer. "Protestants have developed a minority response in many of the key cities in America." And Protestantism had lost much of its vibrant confidence in its own values. "The somber, simple, culturally-parochial, politically-provincial outlook of early Protestantism has been replaced by a complex culture, with radical experimentation in the arts and sciences, in world relationships, and in individual human contacts." So they were fighting last-ditch battles in their efforts to keep their religion in public schools. Only fundamentalists, they thought, seemed to invoke theology in a kind of atavistic attempt to hold power at the expense of Jews. "Interreligious cooperation is manifestly impossible when a Christian looks upon Judaism as an anachronistic atavism which isn't here to stay, particularly if he, the Christian, does a good enough selling job." The zealous fundamentalist did not worry about the "niceties of interreligious sensitivity" that others were learning. Meanwhile, a "triple ghetto" was forming wherein "millions of Americans— Protestant, Catholic, and Jewish—are living in homogenized white neighborhoods" where everybody was in the same racial, economic, "and—increasingly—religious grouping" despite the fact that they all lived in "a shrinking world of color and diversity." Could America lead in such a world?

A third means for assessing Judaism inside a pluralist One Na-   23:33
tion is available in Marshall Sklare's work of 1957, *The Jews: Social Patterns of an American Group*. Sklare timed the study to follow the tercentenary of Jewish arrival in America in 1654. In it Ben Halpern, a secular Jew who kept resisting Will Herberg's analysis of the triple melting pot of Protestant-Catholic-Jew and who saw

the concept of the Judeo-Christian tradition to be mere public relations that did not allow for Jewish particularism, was represented
by a reprinted essay, "America Is Different." Halpern noted that
"especially since Eisenhower's election, all America has been over-
whelmed with the feeling that now is our time of destiny, that this
is the American Century." *America was different* was the refrain
sung also by Jews, according to Halpern, "because it has no long-
established majority ethnic culture, but is still evolving a com-
posite culture to which Jews, too, are privileged to make their characteristic contributions." No longer was it simply a Protestant
domain. There were puzzles for Jews, however. Whereas Jews elsewhere had to face survival in the face of hostility, in America they
dealt with survival "in the face of a friendliness which threatens to
dissolve our group ties and submerge us as a whole by absorbing
us individually." Anti-Semitism was present, but not as government policy; it was a part of aimless hate-mongering, of unorganized impulses, as a "sociological or 'cultural' phenomenon." Reduced to aphorism: "In Europe, then, the stick; in America, the
carrot."

23:34   Halpern was in the rare company of those who framed suburbanization between the two determining events of modern Jewish
spiritual history: "The crucial difference which has been brought
about in the Jewish problem in the past generation is not only the
rise of the State of Israel, but perhaps even more the destruction of
European Jewry." Many would overlook it as negative, unpleasant.
But it did pose a new situation: "Now we live in a Jewish world
where, essentially, we see only two main constituents: ourselves—
American Jewry—and the State of Israel."

23:35   The time had not yet come for a full realization of what the
event of the Holocaust and the presence of Israel were doing to
suburban Judaism. For that moment, an article by Smith College
historian Arthur Mann was more apt. Whether or not he spoke for
the fundamentalists or the hyperorthodox Jews, Mann did have his
eye on the larger American scene that suburbia came to typify, including the way that, "in forging a conception of their own peoplehood, Americans learned to overlook doctrinal differences and
agree on moral fundamentals." With a historian's eye on the two
centuries since the nation's founding, he could conclude that what
the eighteenth-century Deists had hoped "to achieve without a
church has in large degree come to pass in the land of many
churches." The ethos of the One Nation, Under God, was indeed
powerful: "the idea that religion is handmaiden to democracy

has made such headway," said Mann, that "American Catholicism, American Protestantism, and American Judaism appear like parallel shoots on a common stock." And, everyone agreed, they were all prospering around mid-century in their One Nation, now Under God.

24

"Frontiers of American Catholicism"

24:1   Protestants, Catholics, and Jews in the 1950s were "in unblushing competition with one another," but not so much "for the individual souls of Americans," as many would have expected religious leaders to be. So observed Eugene J. Lipman and Albert Vorspan as they visited the three groups in ten cities. The competition instead was "in a sense, for the American soul." All three communities formed what Lipman and Vorspan called their three ghettos, and they competed "for the opportunity to shape American culture in the image of the religious ethic of each," as mainstream Protestants earlier had done from a privileged position. The soul of America was very much the target of mid-century Catholics, who, like Jews, were breaking out of their ghetto and carrying on the argument among themselves and with others over the place and role of the one-fourth of America that was Catholic. To tell the story of Catholic participants as being always and only defensive, as victims challenged by Protestants and secularists who wanted to keep them confined, is to miss the positive side, the inner dynamics, the self-advertising of a more confident and aggressive church than other Americans had seen before.

24:2   No Catholic intellectual at mid-century better exemplified the voice of Catholics speaking both defensively, with the memory of ghetto existence in mind, and aggressively, with the prospect of reaching the American soul, than Father John Tracy Ellis, the pre-

416

mier Catholic church historian of his day. In 1955 he concluded lectures delivered at the University of Chicago by reminding his public that Catholics had been in America for four centuries and that they had always shown maximum loyalty to the republic and its principles. "There are now nearly fifty million Americans whose religious faith and theological beliefs are—and will remain—those of the universal Church of Rome." It ought to have been obvious, but the priest-historian felt called to remind hearers and readers: "American Catholics are here to stay, and those who seem to make something of a career out of criticism of this largest of American religious groups might as well reconcile themselves to that fact." Father Ellis used the standard four-group model: "Protestants, Catholics, Jews, and men of no religious faith are here and will remain," and "they will, therefore, have to go on living together."

Not all of Ellis's reasons for such self-confidence grew out of the inner life of the church. One of the great events of modern Catholicism, seldom referred to in church histories, occurred on June 22, 1944, when President Roosevelt signed the "Servicemen's Readjustment Act," code-named the "GI Bill of Rights." Before World War II the fact that few Catholics went to college, and even fewer to non-Catholic colleges, helped keep the faithful in their figurative ghetto. Thanks to the GI Bill and what it did to bring higher education in reach of people who had once been excluded, Catholicism had produced a well-educated laity that was eager to use its knowledge and skill in the pluralist society about which it learned and in which it thrived in college and university settings. Like Jews, Catholics also relocated by the millions into middle-class suburbs, leaving behind much of their image as a church of immigrants, the upper lower-class, and blue-collar laborers. 24:3

Ellis stretched things a bit when he referred to 50 million Catholics, yet even cautious estimates saw the numbers double between 1940 and 1960, from 21 to 42 million. Catholicism added twelve of these millions between 1954 and 1963, thanks to high birth rates, intermarriages which led to Catholic gains, conversions, and immigrations (like airlifted populations from Puerto Rico and elsewhere). Celebrities like Fulton J. Sheen helped many to identify with the church that once had seemed a handicap to their aspirations. All the graphs charting leadership had lines curving sharply up on the right end. In 1954, 158,069 religious sisters ran hospitals and parochial schools. To replenish retirees among the 46,970 priests there were 32,344 seminarians, many of them there on the 24:4

GI Bill. Two-thirds of the laymen and three-fourths of the laywomen were said to attend mass regularly, in numbers that shamed Protestant and Jewish counterparts. Between 1949 and 1959, the Catholic parochial school enrollments jumped from 2,607,879 to 5,600,000, and there were 112,765 students at mid-century in Catholic colleges, 116 of them schools for women. The Jesuits alone ran 25 colleges, turning some of them into major graduate institutions.

24:5   Communications and action groups prospered. Through a network of 580 publications, Catholic leaders claimed 24,273,972 subscribers, a good proportion of whom no doubt read these newspapers and periodicals. The family needed support, and the church would provide it. In 1949 the hierarchy issued a pastoral letter calling a crisis in family living a "present danger more fearsome than the atomic bomb." An invention of the war years and after, Cana Conferences helped reinforce marital life; three-fourths of the dioceses had chapters. In 1949 Chicagoans Pat and Patty Crowley led thousands in forming a Christian Family Movement, which boasted 30,000 couples in its core membership late in the fifties. The Crowleys and their colleagues helped Catholics connect the intimate circle of home life with the larger surrounding world. Catholics were secure in the prospering movements of organized labor. A liturgical movement involved laypeople in the central acts of worship and helped explain the meaning of the mass to the people. On secular college campuses, gatherings at Newman Centers helped students connect Catholic faith and public learning and action. Ellis had good reason to swagger.

24:6   Although Catholicism was a hierarchical "top-down" body, the pulse of the church was in the local parish, suddenly and at last a favored subject of Catholic sociologists. The picture one gets from their study of parishes is not so much one of people contending for the "soul of America," though that was always a side effect or submerged theme. They were devoted to worshiping, building community, providing opportunities for nurture, and developing "belongingness." A revised Code of Canon Law, in effect since 1918, spelled out the role of the "irremovable pastor," the priest who served under the bishop and was a key to parish strength. Archbishop Richard J. Cushing spoke romantically but not inaccurately in 1947: "The Catholic parish, with its pastor and priests, its altar and confessionals, its pulpit and schools, its good works, its sinners, its saints—the Catholic parish so constituted is a microcosm, it is the whole Church in miniature and through the parish Christ does for a limited group what He founded the Universal Church to do for the whole world." To overlook the parish was to miss the concrete life of the Catholic church.

The visitor to the parish would find an array of "parish soci-   24:7
eties" to match the subgroups in Protestant and Jewish congregations. These were designed to foster loyalty and reinforce identities. The array of these societies in typical dioceses toward mid-century suggests something of the memory of the inherited church and the reach of the burgeoning one. For men there were the Holy Name Society, St. Vincent de Paul Society, Catholic War Veterans, Knights of Columbus, Knights of St. John, and more. Women worked through the Sodality of the Blessed Virgin Mary, Altar Society, Rosary Society, Altar and Rosary Society, Ladies of Charity, Christian Mothers' Society, and dozens like them. They provided morning-to-night, in-season and out-of-season, cradle-to-grave expressions so that Catholics could live in a kind of world within the world, what its critics called a ghetto. Sociologist Francis J. Engel saw these societies advancing "in Catholic solidarity and *esprit de corps,*" part of a "larger Catholic unity of which each (individual and society) is a reflection," so that the whole could be "the hope of the Mystical Body of Christ in America."

The already mentioned parochial schools pumped the pulse in   24:8
thousands of parishes. They helped habituate the young to the Catholic way of life inside the American Way of Life. As Catholics moved to suburbs with their large families, or to start them, they brought the practice of parochial education with them and built schools. Protestants and others viewed these with suspicion: were they not somehow un-American, since they kept Catholic children out of the great blender, the public school? Would the leaders succeed in getting tax funds for their sectarian purposes, at least enough to pay for school busing? Catholics in turn looked out from these schools and criticized the public schools for their secularism, their faithfulness to the inimical philosophies of people like John Dewey, who promoted "a common faith," as Dewey himself once put it in a book-length polemic against particular and parochial faith. Schools therefore became battlegrounds and bastions.

Women in orders dominated as administrators and teachers at   24:9
these schools, but laypeople were increasingly needed and welcomed, despite the strain they put on budgets because they needed living wages, as women in religious orders did not. Some leaders promoted lay teaching. In 1948 Cincinnati Catholic school superintendent Monsignor Carl J. Ryan stated the case: "I am quite con-

Dorothy Day dominated the Catholic social action scene through all the mid-century decades. Her World War II pacifism lost her some support, but she won it back as a voice of conscience during the Eisenhower years and even more after them. (Courtesy of the Marquette University Archives. Photo by Ed Lettau.)

vinced that our Catholic schools will never attain their goal of turning out Catholic men and women fully equipped to meet their religious, social, and civic obligations in these United States until we have a liberal supply of lay teachers on all levels." None of this was to occur at the expense of the vocation of women religious. In all cases, the schools had to show themselves poised to promote the American Way of Life, and they worked hard to do so.

24:10   The parish was ill-equipped to carry on all parts of what came to be called the apostolate, the public mission. One of the most gifted writers among the priests of the day, Joseph B. Gremillion, in 1943 headed to Louisiana to take up parish life. But first he schooled himself in the way apostolate movements worked in Europe and elsewhere. In 1954 Gremillion used military terms as he wrote of his Shreveport, Louisiana, parish, the "marshalling ground" for the church in society: "The fifteen thousand soldiers of Christ who are in the best position to bring Him into the marketplace have no program for training, no marshalling ground, no concerted plan of attack." There were big issues for which the parish was poorly equipped in the changing South: fighting against

racial discrimination and segregation and for civil rights, dealing with "labor-management teamwork, share-cropping, migrant
workers, the fading family farm, dislocations arising from heightened industrialization, 'the welfare state,' education without God,
corrupt politics," and the like.

For the move beyond the ghetto and the routines of the parish,   24:11
Catholics had to be ready with intellectual argument. Gremillion
had a rightful complaint: "The bill of fare offered by our parish
and organizational life tastes insipid to the average college man,
hopelessly flat and out of touch with boiling reality for the exceptional gifted person." Much of what went on was puerile. The
college graduate "finds no attraction in organizing benefits and
bingos"; youth work in the form of "athletics and talent nights and
teen-town parties" would not challenge trained people. The priest
tried to form Catholic Action units in the parish, but within four
years he was tired and spent, ready for new roles. He issued indictments that did not square with the comfortable pictures of Cushing
and the apologists: " 'Receive the sacraments and give a good example' is woefully inadequate in this age." The geographical parish was a place where "mere accident of residence determines its
composition. But does function, loyalty, and 'belongingness'?"
No, "The parish *is* not meeting our needs. CAN it do so?—I leave
[the matter] open to discussion, but personally I think not." Off
Gremillion went to Rome to pursue doctoral studies and a different
career in the Church.

The *apostolate* became the key term in evaluations of the mis-   24:12
sion of the church as it competed for the soul of America. Father
Francis B. Donnelly, speaking up for it, captioned his concern "*ad-
aptation and conquest.*" It was the latter concept that frightened
non-Catholic Americans. Donnelly quoted Pius XI, who in 1943
had said there were "new and important battles being waged all
along the way" on the "terrain opened up to us by the development
of civilization." Ghetto Catholicism was quaint, puzzling, and remote to non-Catholics, but post-ghetto Catholicism seemed encroaching. Sometimes Catholic advance came in the form of competition for individual souls and not only the soul of America. In
1951 Paul Hanley Furfey, thinking that the Catholic population of
the United States was at best one-fifth of the total, noted that this
would mean about nine thousand non-Catholics in a parish with
two thousand Catholic souls. "How much of the parish energy
should go to the care of the two thousand Catholics and how much
to the conversion of the nine thousand non-Catholics?" he asked.

Almost never did people like Furfey keep in mind that most of these non-Catholics would have to be converted not from secularism but from Protestant, Jewish, or other religious traditions. Fewer than 10 percent of the American people listed themselves as unbelievers or identified in the broadest sense with no faith. "Should we not consider the United States as being, quite factually, a missionary country?" asked Furfey in language which, when overheard, was capable of inducing fear or eliciting fury in what was left of Protestant America. Citing statistics from one year, when only 115,214 conversions were part of the church's net growth of 807,254—birth rates were high—Furfey wanted Catholics to be more aggressive for the "conversion of America."

24:13   Language such as Furfey's was intended to equip Catholics, but its echoes were heard afar, especially when he used military metaphors. "The situation appears promising," thought Furfey, for the development of the "role of a militant laity." "A *militant* is more than a fervent Catholic; a *militant* is one who is not only fervent but apostolic." Yet Protestants should not have worried; most parishes and parishioners did not look militant and were not. For example, late in the Eisenhower years, Joseph B. Schuyler, S.J., looked out of the window in the Bronx at Our Lady of Mercy Parish near Fordham University. He treated it as the stereotypical northern parish. The priest listed 8,570 parishioners as "fully recorded" in a parish of 14,000 Catholics. What were their practices? The school was the hub; Schuyler had "emphatic evidence" that its achievement was found in the "personalities of millions of parochial-school graduates who have been formed and socialized in their classrooms as American Catholics," just as non-Catholics feared there were and would be. Yet his claim was curious in the light of the statistical data his survey turned up. Non-Catholics who worried about the shaping power of Catholic schools need not have done so, despite what Schuyler had said in praise of them. One tentative conclusion, he thought, should disturb the Catholic educator. The 176 parishioners who had the benefit of Catholic schooling "did not show greater acceptance of Catholic attitudes toward religious, moral, and social issues than did all the 293 respondents to the questionnaire." Almost in resignation he added, "it suggests that there is much work still to be done in the schools and parishes."

24:14   Schuyler listened carefully and found otherwise. Overwhelmingly people did not crave an apostolate. They wanted the priest to be "preacher and teacher of God's word," with "counselor" and "father" next, followed by "liturgical leader" and "educational leader." While 276 polled people stressed the first of these roles, only 6 cited "leader" and 9 wanted "social leader." As for "least important" roles, "civic leader" was now in first place with 174 votes, while not one voted for "preacher and teacher of God's word" as being unimportant. A theologian could say that if priests got God's word right, they would be civic leaders and reformers, but their interpretation would not have matched that of most laity. Still, Schuyler used the language of Catholic advance: "Catholicism is catholic for many reasons, one of the more important being the universality of its mission. Its aim is to win the minds and hearts of all men everywhere, all kinds of men in all kinds of circumstances." The parish had many societies, but Schuyler found that only one-tenth of the members attended even the most important of these, and apathy seemed to be the rule.

In that last moment before the openings made visible by the   24:15
Second Vatican Council, Schuyler's listening ear turned up few signs of revolt against Catholic law. Should the church make exceptions to its laws on divorce and birth control in difficult cases? The poll showed that almost two-thirds of the respondents indicated that the church should make no exceptions in the case of divorce, and three out of five thought the same on birth control. Schuyler piously shelved his own sociological objectivity for a moment to add that apparently the respondents "who thought the Church should make exceptions (about 20 percent) do not know that it is not within the power of the Church to change those laws which it teaches are divine." Should the church allow for religiously mixed marriages? At that moment 83 percent definitely agreed with the church's stand against such marriages, and some among the remaining small percentage were not sure or had doubts about the stand. Fewer than 60 percent were even aware that the church had said that workingmen had a right to form unions. "Apparently the Church's teachings on industrial and economic life are not too well known," concluded Father Schuyler. The North had been untested racially, and while Father Joseph Fichter, a sociologist, found only 12 percent wanting integrated parishes, over 90 percent of the respondents in the Bronx parish showed "a wholesome Catholic attitude on the race question."

Lipman and Vorspan said that Protestants, Catholics, and Jews,   24:16
fighting "for the American soul," did not cooperate, but they did share enemies: "secularism, materialism, apathy," and the like. Schuyler could not have been reading those authors, but his con-

clusion could well have fed their assumption. "The Church's battle with undying materialism, secularism, and indifference to God" was decisive; it would "not be won by some master stroke of Vatican policy." The master stroke occurred in divine revelation and with the establishment of the Catholic church and its commission. "It but remains to implement that commission." Schuyler found Our Lady of Mercy Parish to be "a vitally functioning social system," but hardly the needed militant body to assault materialism, secularism, and indifference to God.

24:17   A somewhat more cheerful picture of the apostolate appeared when one moved from observing a single Bronx parish to a large and generally progressive archdiocese. Vincent J. Giese took such a look just before Vatican II at Chicago, a "booming, switches-open nerve center of Mid-America," a place which, he said, "literally has proliferating under her wings almost all the world's problems in microcosm." Half of Chicago's 3.5 million people were Catholic in 1956. They were served by 870 priests in 279 parishes, whose average population was 13,000, of whom Catholics averaged 6,000. Giese concentrated on the lay apostolate there and found "a rather wide-spread social awareness" and "a groundswell of lay responsibility." There is no substitute for suggesting the vitality but to catalogue with him the names of some of these movements: "The Christian Family Movement, the Young Christian Workers, the Young Christian Students, the Catholic Labor Alliance, the Catholic Interracial Council, the Catholic Guild for the Blind, Friendship House, Blessed Martin de Porres Center, Peter Maurin House, the Calvert Club of the University of Chicago, St. Benet Library and Bookshop, the Thomas More Association, Fides Publishers Association, Adult Education Centers, the Lay Auxiliaries of the Missions, Opus Dei, *Today* magazine, . . . the Cardinal's Committee for Spanish Catholic Action," and the two lay-controlled groups, "the Cana Conference of Chicago and the Confraternity of Christian Doctrine." Foreign and domestic observers alike were impressed at the work of Chicago's Samuel Cardinal Stritch and his lay, religious, and clerical workers.

24:18   Giese had no trouble showing that activism and intellectual endeavor both marked this apostolate, as he pointed to great annual events attracting thousands and to countless small-group meetings in homes, rectories, and parishes. Everywhere there was "genuine contact between priests and people and all this without any feelings of anti-clericalism on the part of the laity." Instead there were "real feelings of respect on the part of priests for the role of the layman in the Church." He pointed to surrounding educational institutions that fed the Midwest Catholic prosperity, Notre Dame in Indiana, St. John's in Minnesota, Marquette in Wisconsin, St. Louis University in Missouri. The diocesan press in Dubuque and the Grail Center for women in Cincinnati were other signs. "This is the great apostolic heritage which the Mid-west hopes to pass on to the Catholic Church in America." Significantly, nowhere in his long account did Giese even hint that the intention was to take over once-Protestant America. The whole accent was on natural expressions of Catholic faith.

If tension remained, it was on the church-and-state front, cov-   24:19
ered by the usually exuberant Notre Dame priest John A. O'Brien. In place of the old nativisms he could praise the National Conference of Christians and Jews. Since it did not touch theology, it was acceptable to Catholics. In fact, Brotherhood Week, the most visible symbolic creation of the conference, "was first conceived," said O'Brien, "by the late Father Hugh W. McMenamin, the universally beloved pastor of the Cathedral in Denver." Brotherhood Week, thought O'Brien, "promises to become as much a part of the American calendar as Independence Day or Thanksgiving Day." Despite postwar discontents, "the forces of religious antagonism" were "fighting a losing battle." Educated people were "sick and tired" of strife, and in the face of the changes, the Catholic church in America, he said, "today enjoys a freedom, vitality, prosperity and growth unsurpassed in any country." Sooner than some, he saw the end of "the bogey that any group, if it gained numerical preponderance, would wish to rescind" the separation of state and church.

O'Brien liked to quote statements of principles by interfaith   24:20
groups, including one fashioned by the National Conference of Christians and Jews and signed by Protestant, Catholic, and Jewish leaders. "In a year marking the 300th anniversary of friendly co-existence of Jews, Roman Catholics and Protestants in the United States," they said, "we are reminded again that on the basis of [the moral principle that all men under God are equal] we have built a nation of people from many lands who worship, according to the dictates of our conscience, in many religious groups." He constantly cited with favor how "together, we Protestants, Catholics and Jews" were working "in unity for the common good." True, some old Catholic teachings which sought privilege if not monopoly for Catholicism within specific polities were still on the books, but in practice American Catholics had always left

them behind and moved ahead. The interfaith policy was an instrument in the day's "struggle against the forces of Communism which threaten anew the foundations of freedom and brotherhood." O'Brien quoted *America* against the Catholics who wanted to be "more Catholic than the Pope" when it came to cooperation with non-Catholics. They did this out of a "vague fear" that collaborating to clear slums or spread civil rights "would contribute to the spread of religious indifferentism." Such worriers should listen to the pope, who called cooperation "necessary and urgent."

24:21   Statistics of parishes and dioceses can provide evidences of the actual posture of American Catholics, but the language of the visionary offers another picture of the argument over One Nation, Under God. Walter J. Ong, S.J., a Catholic humanist of note and a pioneer participant in interfaith conversation, published two perceptive if not fully systematic glimpses of a vision for Catholicism's place: *Frontiers of American Catholicism* and *American Catholic Crossroads*. These books by the accomplished St. Louis University Jesuit illustrate what forward-looking Catholics were coming to expect during the religious revival and what at the last moment before the surprise announcement of the Second Vatican Council would enlarge frontiers and create more crossroads. Ong was articulate and positive as few Catholics were about the notion that people across the world were "becoming more and more conscious of cultural pluralism and of the importance of cultural perimeters, past, present, and future," for developing the human in the universe. He saw American Catholicism to be "in a state of intellectual and spiritual crisis," self-conscious about its mission in America "seen precisely as America."

24:22   Ong was the celebrator of a Catholicism that was no longer defensive and reactive. The old posture in hostile America had led to a paradox: "a Catholic mentality which in many ways is the most conservative in the world set in the midst of the nation whose genius seems to be adaptability and change." The wary defined Catholicism as a European inheritance and rarely realized the resources of the American experience—such as the invention of the parochial school system. Catholics in his period often idealized medieval times, but "that the Church in America has in any way improved on the 'age of faith,'" he complained, remained "practically unthinkable" as a reality. Ong was aware of the sniping and blasting by the likes of Paul Blanshard but hurried past that tired topic to get to the issue of Catholic intellectuality. He was sure that the American intellectual, if confronted, would be "intrigued by learning what the Church in America has to do with the American experience: with the experience of the frontier, the spirit of enterprise and exploration, the process of expansion." Especially in a new day such intellectuals would be interested in the Catholic experience "with the forces at work in a mass, industrialized culture, and with the maintaining and interior development of personality in such a culture."

Father Ong's choice of zones for inquiry was itself surprising. 24:23 In the historic church of the laborer, he saw the development of middle-class and affluent America and wanted Catholics to engage in "an apostolate of the business world." The European Catholics had not prepared American fellow believers to see the "complete social acceptability of business in the United States." Historians traced the "*elan,* the sense of exaltation and expansiveness" from the dogma of optimistic evangelical Protestantism to a kind of self-generating sense of what might be possible. Catholicism could make a contribution in the face of such a culture's spiritual poverty: "The Church feels this milieu is not to be neglected, but redeemed." Nor should contemporary Catholics fear the technological frontier, which they too readily connected with "secularization." They had been told that the "age of the machine" had replaced the "age of Catholic faith," but Ong countered that faith in the technological age was "more apparently and unmistakably Catholic" than it ever was in the age of faith. Today Catholics were at last in every country on the globe and shared lines of communication. They should talk not of secularization but of the "hominization" of the world, the "taking over of our planet by mankind."

Another Jesuit, Pierre Teilhard de Chardin, who celebrated evo- 24:24 lution in the Christian scheme, had not yet been translated into English and so had not yet made his mark in the United States, but Ong cited him and then sang his own virtual hymn to evolution. Technology had to face "a kind of cosmic nostalgia, the desire somehow to escape from history," but this temptation was "an old pagan disease. There is nothing Christian in it." The Catholic church did "not dream of a Golden Age to which she longs to return." Instead, the church looks to the Second Adam, Christ, and is better off than with the first. The "elaboration of a Christology of an evolving universe seems to be the great task before modern [theologians] and in a particular way before American theologians." Ong wanted them to venture into the world of American intellectuality, citing philosophers Josiah Royce, William James,

Charles Sanders Peirce, and John Dewey along with Justice Oliver Wendell Holmes and Justice Louis D. Brandeis as figures Catholics should encounter. Unremarkable as all this sounded a few years later, it stood out in the years before the Vatican Council, especially when Ong urged Catholics to get over their "dominantly negative approach to Dewey" and others like him.

24:25   At the time Ong wrote, Catholic intellectuals were choosing as "their idols (the word is hardly too strong)" figures such as Britishers G. K. Chesterton, Evelyn Waugh, Graham Greene, and American journalist, playwright, and ambassador to Italy, Clare Boothe Luce. They, along with converted communists, "testify to the religio-intellectual charge at the borderline between the Church and her surroundings." Well and good. And these leaders also admired great French Catholics like Etienne Gilson and Jacques Maritain. But why admire these, unless Catholics had a deep emotional need to identify with the European-medieval context? Eighteenth-century rationalism, which had influenced America in the years of its founding, and nineteenth-century romanticism were more important. Emphatically, this did not mean that Ong was going to make his own idol of the One Nation, now Under God. "This is not to call for chauvinism or for a specialization in 'Americanology' based on the belief that this country is called by God to lead the rest of a benighted world to salvation." Ong was put off by Catholics who were now defining America in such jingoistic terms. No, not the demands of patriotism but those of intellectual maturity were at stake. Catholics needed a *mystique* supporting technology, science, and "the whole social surface which is a property of life in the United States." They needed, he further argued, mystiques of personalist philosophies of optimism. "Today," Ong wrote, "when our world perspectives are enlarging, so that America can be seen as part of the general movement of the human spirit through history, meaningful in terms of the over-all trajectory of history," he did not think the American Catholic intellectual would turn out to be a mere nationalist even if and as he succeeded in returning to "his roots in his own American world." Instead, thought the St. Louis Jesuit, "he will doubtless better succeed in thinking through his connections with the rest of mankind, and in living out his own tiny share of the total life of Christ."

24:26   In *American Catholic Crossroads* Ong invited Catholics to emerge from the ghetto to enjoy a walk with him through the "religious-secular dialogue in a pluralist society," as he experienced it through a Fund for the Republic conference on the topic in 1958. "Human society over the face of the globe develops toward greater unification," he stressed. Where would citizens get satisfactory models for dealing with American pluralism? Certainly not from the "romantic concept of medieval Europe" still favored by many Catholics. Certainly not from "Christendom," a once self-sufficient unity. "The ghetto was a typical medieval institution," Ong reminded; it thwarted communication. He wanted Catholics to regard pluralism as "basically an old human problem, not a recent one." He was sure of human confluences: "The age of geographical races," he said, "is *passé*." The human is "made to unite humanity."

While John Courtney Murray was promoting dialogue as part   24:27
of argument in a civil society, Ong developed a somewhat softer and more conversational style. He pictured how in earlier times, diagrams, spatial relations, and geographical manipulations had governed human action. Now in the age of communication one had to see church and state, religion and the secular, related not in diagrams but "in terms of dialogue, of voice, of speech" between humans. This insight matched the New Testament, which had nothing to offer about territory or areas of sovereignty. The gospel sayings of Jesus even personalized government: Jesus spoke not of the state but of Caesar. In America the line between the City of God and the City of Man did not follow neat spatial models such as that of the "wall of separation" but followed instead the dialogical terms of "I" and "Thou." There were interreligious meanings in Ong's call to rethink American history. "The prelude to war is to halt dialogue, to cease to talk, to break off diplomatic relations." On the other hand, "all communication, all dialogue, has this effect: it unites."

Ong never tired of calling Catholics to see that their name meant   24:28
not only something Latin, as in *universalis,* but also something derived from the Greek, *katholikos,* which meant "through the whole," with no hint of fencing in or being in a ghetto. Here was a different vision from the one lived out in Catholic polemics: "What is catholic floods being with itself. Let being grow, expand, as much as you will; what is Catholic will grow and expand with it, filling its every nook and cranny." So Catholic faith, hope, and charity would aim at the soul of America because they "have an expansive, positive quality as against the pinched, impoverished, forced, and quite unpersuasive 'universal' love for 'universal' mankind in this 'universal' frame of the universe which men of the Enlightenment liked to profess." One doubts whether a Paul Blan-

shard or Protestants and Other Americans United for Separation of Church and State read or would have understood the positive reach of a Walter Ong as being anything but a sneaky new mode of Catholic subversion. The Jesuit may not have been widely read or representative in his own time, but he anticipated many trends picked up not long after in the Second Vatican Council and its American appropriations.

24:29   The hour for people with Ong's expansive vision had not come, but he had plenty of company among bewailers of the present situation. John Tracy Ellis, the historian mentioned above, stated their case in the most remembered critique of Catholicism in the decade. He delivered it in Maryville College in St. Louis and published it at mid-decade in the prestigious journal *Thought*. If this picture was accurate, and most colleagues thought it was, Catholicism hardly yet looked like an ominous competitor for the American soul or mind. Ellis found "universal agreement" that the situation of the intellectual in general was then "deplorable." His colleagues agreed with historian Henry Steele Commager that intellectuals "have failed to enlist the great mass of their countrymen in the common cultural and intellectual enterprise necessary for the Republic's progress and security." Catholics were in no position to change that. He agreed with British wartime visitor D. W. Brogan that "in no modern Western society is the intellectual prestige of Catholicism lower than in the country where, in such respects as wealth, numbers, and strength of organization, it is so powerful." Little in the next fourteen years had changed to improve the situation.

24:30   Ellis did generalize about one zone in which Ong called for an apostolate. Catholics, he said, "have probably attained more distinction in the business world than they have in any other sector of American life." But success there did not spill over to the realm of the mind. Ellis quoted Archbishop Cushing, who had observed as recently as 1947 that "in all the American hierarchy, resident in the United States, there is not known to me one Bishop, Archbishop or Cardinal whose father or mother was a college graduate." Such words helped Cushing identify with the audience to which he was speaking, organized labor, but it showed why there was little sympathy for the life of the mind. Where was Catholic thought appreciated? Ironically, at non-Catholic schools like the University of Chicago, the University of Virginia, and Princeton University, where philosophers were promoting a revival of scholastic Catholic thought, while Catholics were not matching this "love of scholarship for its own sake," even in their own universities. Few Catholics by that late date were in *Who's Who,* and very few of those who were came from the sciences. "The picture in the sacred sciences, the liberal arts, and the humanities is no brighter." The one bright spot was Catholic women's colleges, which were producing scholars of distinction and which were highly ranked among liberal arts colleges; Ellis gave them due credit.

The villains in Ellis's indictment were not Protestants, Jews, or   24:31
secularists but Catholics themselves. The fault lay "in their frequently self-imposed ghetto mentality which prevents them from mingling as they should with their non-Catholic colleagues, and in their lack of industry and the habits of work." Ellis piled on loaded words when he quoted culture critic Peter Viereck: "Is the honorable adjective 'Roman Catholic' truly merited by America's middleclass-Jansenist Catholicism, puritanized, Calvinized, and dehydrated?" He also quoted a speech by Heinrich Rommen: Catholics "must irradiate their faith, informed by charity, into their own beleaguered democracy; a flight into a Catholic ghetto, into a catacombs, is a kind of treason today." But why bother to come out of that ghetto? Ellis said that America was soon to be engaged in a debate in which "religious and moral values" would once again be honored. There was a unique opportunity for the Catholic scholars in the United States, if they only took it up.

In the next two years dozens of Catholic journals and papers   24:32
reprinted the essay by Ellis, and he received hundreds of letters in support. Other educators took up the theme and made it their agenda. Most systematic was sociologist Thomas O'Dea of Fordham, who in 1958 spoke not of the ghetto but of the "American Catholic dilemma." O'Dea took Paul Tillich's word, spoken originally about Europe and applied it to America: for centuries Catholics, Tillich said, had been "fighting a defensive war directed equally against Protestantism on the one hand and autonomous civilization [self-sufficient secularism, said O'Dea] on the other." In America there was still a tendency "to segregate the American Catholic population, to hinder the participation of Catholics in the national life, and to make the development of a creative relationship between Catholicism and the national culture more complicated and difficult." While Ong had worked to achieve dialogue and dynamism, O'Dea found it necessary to report that there was still "the partial segregation of the Catholic community and the partial alienation of American Catholicism from important aspects of American secular culture."

24:33   Catholics could cheer about some things that had happened at mid-century. "The decline of intolerance and nativism is too evident to need any documentation." There was still one threatening spot, "the regrettable rise of new Catholic-Protestant tensions recently and the anxieties of those non-Catholics who imagine they see 'Catholic aggression' in this country today." But that could be overcome or ignored in *non-intellectual* areas; after all, Catholics were assimilated in the national milieu. A "considerable proportion of the diocesan press" at times revealed "serious hostility towards certain aspects of non-Catholic culture," but these attitudes were not gross enough to provide Catholics with an excuse for them not to engage America positively. Now Catholics should catch up. "The great Protestant and secular thinkers of America are not just men who made mistakes, like the 'adversaries' of the scholastic manual," he said of the old way argument had gone on. No, "they have positive things to say to those American Catholics who have neglected the [intellectual] search themselves." Sadly, Catholics were currently borrowing only the wrong things: "Outside the narrow moral sphere which American Catholicism has taken as its central province, the American Catholic is assimilated to the materialistic society about him in some of its most pernicious aspects." O'Dea's final judgment on that point was that "American Catholic middle-class life often tends to be more materialistic than is that of many Protestant and secularist groups." But the contemplative life, the activist life, movements connected with secular institutes, lay retreat houses, the Christian Family Movement, the liturgical movement were vital countersigns. It was the intellectual front that needed the development.

24:34   Many non-Catholics were still getting their picture not from figures like John O'Brien, John Tracy Ellis, Walter Ong, Thomas O'Dea, or the leaders of the apostolates but from Paul Blanshard and professional anti-Catholics. Or they would see the media of mass communications working not with such professors or workers in the inner city but with the most prominent church leaders, some of whom met all the terms Ong described as supporting chauvinism, nationalism, and jingoism. The best-known and most celebrated hierarch of the period was New York's Francis Cardinal Spellman, six of whose seven books dealt with the American theme. He said explicitly that he belonged to the "My country . . . right or wrong, my country" school. Spellman tried his hand at poetry: "America, Our America!/With dignity all sublime,/Thou art dedicated to Mary./Her mission is through thee." His prayers reflected on the flag and its colors: "*White* for the basic righteous-ness of our national purpose," he led off. America was the "last unfailing hope of embattled humanity struggling for survival against the menace of atheistic Communism that would desecrate and destroy both the flesh of man and man's spirit." And Spellman told readers why Catholics were such nationalists. "Leaders of a religion will espouse nationalism not simply to keep their church acceptable in the pluralist society, but out of the same need for identity and the sense of belonging that motivates all people in the given society." Fortunately for the given society of America, other voices less nationalistic were audible. They presented many varia-tions, but with surprising consistency they were playing the "One Nation, Under God" theme.

25

"The Ultimate Fate of Protestantism . . . Remains in Doubt"

In the competition for the souls of individuals and the soul of America, white Protestants had been the main and privileged contenders in the British colonies and the United States from 1607 until at least the middle of the twentieth century. Most of them feared a monolithic Catholic takeover or, later, a homogenized secularist takeover of their old realm. Yet Protestantism itself had never been monolithic or homogenized. It was broken into scores of denominations, a fact that Catholics brought up whenever the issue of the truth of faiths arose. Division also haunted the minds of ecumenically minded Protestants who wanted to unify their movement. Yet cultural fissures deeper than denominational ones had often plagued Protestants who looked for unity. Baptists, Methodists, and Presbyterians who were white had virtually nothing to do with their African American counterparts, and other denominations followed the same practice. Again, the largest denominations, the Baptists, Methodists, and Presbyterians, had split into Southern and Northern wings, and the two halves of each blessed the cannon on opposite sides in the Civil War. In the century after that war, however, the division that tormented Protestants in their claims on the American soul was not so much regional or ethnic as it was cultural and theological. The rise of a fundamentalist movement after 1920 and a neo-evangelical organization after 1942, because together they and their kind attracted millions with fierce loyalties, compromised efforts of the mainstream Protestants to assure that the One Nation, Under God, would be guided by their norms.

In 1943, one year after the National Association of Evangelicals   25:2
formed, its leaders set up an office in Washington. Why Washington, especially for Protestants who inherited a strong belief in the separation of church and state and who believed that the Kingdom of Jesus was "not of this world?" Why Washington for a movement that was critical of moderate and lay Protestants and all Catholics who wanted to influence government? According to James DeForest Murch, historian and apologist for the association, "God gives specific instruction as to the Christian's relationship with his government." The evangelicals wanted to be sure that Washington and the nation got this instruction from them, not from the kind of Protestants who made up the Federal and later National Council of Churches. Murch and the evangelicals perceived enemies on all sides. "First," he warned, "there are the efforts of the Roman Church to promote Church-State union with the Church dominant." The secularists, in his eye, represented the opposite flank of attackers. He wanted to thwart the "effort of the agnostics, atheists, and misguided zealots who misinterpret separation of Church and State, to take all religion out of government, to take Christ's teachings, ideals and witness out of government." While evangelicals supported the new nation of Israel because it had a role in their vision of the second coming of Christ, Murch indulged himself in critical comment on American Jews. They belonged to minorities who were "in the name of freedom of religion abusing their rights to restrict the majority." Here "in a few cases those of the Hebrew faith" opposed the "distribution of the New Testament to students on the grounds that it is a sectarian book." Writing just after the McCarthy era, Murch also threw in a separate charge that there were also "abuses committed by Communists and Socialists in the government," though he named none.

In the books and leadership programs of such evangelicals, it   25:3
was made clear that mainstream Protestants were not able to fend off such foes or impart God's specific instructions about government. Of these evangelicals, however, Murch could say, in an approach characteristic of many leaders, that unless evangelicals "let their voice be heard, their influence felt, a pagan conscience will prevail." He evidently did not include the Protestants of the National Council of Churches when he spoke of Christians: "Either Christians who love the Lord are going to take Christ into the political life of the nation or the increasing infiltration of Roman

Catholic power will take over." Murch boasted that in 1953 the National Association of Evangelicals had "reached an all-time high in cordiality" after eleven years of their organized life, when President Eisenhower received the leaders in the White House and discussed the moral and religious bases of American freedoms with them.

25:4   In the manner of the evangelicals in his time, the author insisted: *"Evangelicals do not want the Church in politics."* Then he bragged about how evangelicals were successful in politics. One illustration had to do with Native American affairs, because evangelicals had issued "pleas for religious liberty for non-Catholic Indians." Along with this, according to open records of advocacy, the nonpolitical evangelicals were political about civil rights, public schools, immigration, liquor sales, salacious literature, military chaplaincy policies, human rights, Catholic aggression in Italy, opposition to American ambassadorships at the Vatican, and several Cold War issues. One theme was of special importance to Murch: the "encouragement of investigations of subversive activities, anti-Communist propaganda," and the like. The other theme demanded a bit of an ideological leap: the evangelicals opposed statism and fascism, so they also voiced "opposition to governmental regimentation and bureacratic controls." Not being at home in the liberal World Council of Churches, Murch's group was taking steps to form a World Evangelical Fellowship. It would stand against communism and against "ever-resourceful Roman Catholicism," which, he said, "continues its relentless warfare against Protestantism, open where it has temporal power, underground where the use of force is impossible." Thus American evangelicalism opposed communism and Romanism because "both are absolutist. Both have concepts of freedom which are capable of enormous abuse."

25:5   Like all who call their troops to battle, Murch, heady from recent evangelical gains, worried about enemies closer to home. "Evangelicals had won a battle, but the war is still on," he insisted. For example, Protestant neo-orthodoxy was in vogue. This movement was beguiling to the truly orthodox but was religiously false because it did not begin with belief in an inerrant scripture. Similarly, the Christian realism in mainstream Protestantism was also deceiving. Both of these views represented a liberal "strategic retreat to newly entrenched positions where more subtly and (it is hoped) more effectively than ever the orthodox, evangelical, biblical position may be attacked." Most confusing and seductive of all was ecumenism, especially when invitations to Christian bodies came from movements that said they had Christ at the center, but did not focus on him sufficiently to satisfy Murch. "Never was cooperation *with compromise* more charmingly sought." But evangelicals had to be on guard. "We need to mobilize all our evangelical forces, endowments and personnel in the local churches, in inter-church agencies, in education, in evangelism, in journalism, in radio and television, in missions." All that organization taken together would form "a movement of such proportions that God can take it and use it to the accomplishment of His ultimate purposes." Evangelicalism would be the "vanguard of a movement" that would "turn the world upside down" in its "wholehearted determination to match and exceed the highest and the best that liberalism, humanism, and paganism have to offer," said its apologist.

Ecumenical Protestantism seemed to offer no better options   25:6
than liberalism, humanism, or paganism on this evangelical screen. When Murch listed all the divisions within historic Protestantism, he had to conclude that "the 'fly in the ointment' was liberalism." He called it "THE GREAT APOSTASY." It drew on the same sources, including scientific naturalism, rationalistic philosophies, secularism, and scientism, that "produced Karl Marx's *Humanist Manifesto* [*sic*] and World Communism." So there were two flanks to fight: "From without the churches were beset by the perils of atheism, humanism, communism and statism; from within by secularism, sectarianism, pharisaism and liberalism." Hence "the battle of the century" resulted, as the liberals formed the Federal Council of Churches and took over the denominations. "While vigorously opposing the political and ecclesiastical pretensions of Roman Catholicism the Council became a sort of neo-Catholic church 'embodying the best in Protestantism,'" Murch charged. While the vague creed of Dwight Eisenhower inexplicably did not offend Murch, he said he had been put off by the "essentially humanistic" outlook he discerned in Harry S. Truman. Murch remembered that in 1946 the council conventioneers sat without protest as they heard Truman speak, as presidents are wont to do, of the "worth and dignity of man" as "*the one basic principle* upon which both religion and democracy are founded." Where was God in that?

Murch's strongest attacks on "ecumaniacs" came when he and   25:7
National Association of Evangelicals leaders thought they saw the World Council cooperating with what could become "world socialism and world dictatorship." Murch was most explicit: "The

growing interest of Moscow in the use of the World Council of Churches, the National Council of Churches (USA) and UNESCO to further Communist aims needs to be watched carefully." But Murch also had to stand on the ramparts and warn "eager advocates of 'the new evangelicalism'" to be on their guard "lest they go too far in their quest for a wider fellowship" and themselves get too close to "the Super-Church."

25:8   The attack on Protestant conciliarism was at least as obsessive for Murch as was his critique of Catholicism and communism. He resented council officials for boasting that "Washington politicians knew they were not dealing with a paper organization," when transacting with them, or when *Newsweek* in 1941 said that the Federal Council had "a virtual monopoly" in American Protestantism. Remarkably, he found the council to be too soft in its opposition to Catholicism. The only cheer he took from the mainstream camp was the *Christian Century* coverage of neo-evangelicalism as early as 1943. The magazine's editors had said the National Association of Evangelicals was "giving sectarianism a new lease on life" by encouraging what Murch called the "reactionary and dissident wings of the great Protestant denominations." The same editor had also said that liberals should mark the rise of evangelicalism and take it seriously. Murch said that readers were "witnessing the beginning of an open, organized rift in American Protestantism which was bound to affect every Protestant denomination and institution in the land." Evangelicals also fought against their spiritual cousins, the fundamentalists. The two camps might agree on basic doctrines, but they differed over style and ethos. Murch explained that when the National Association of Evangelicals formed in 1942, it did so because of the "odious connotation" of fundamentalism in recent years, when "men with much zeal, enthusiasm and conviction, yet lacking frequently in education or cultural breadth," had taken over.

25:9   The evangelicals were causing a schism within the schism that produced the Protestant right wing. They were distancing themselves from harder-core fundamentalists, Protestants who defined themselves as "separatists" following biblical commands to "come out and be separate" from all others. And such fundamentalists, in turn, did not take well to the pretensions of their new rivals on the moderate right. Thus the intransigent leader John R. Rice saw evangelicals as "a bridgehead by which contacts may be made by modernists to get fundamentalists to come over to the modernists." The Billy Graham New York crusade of 1957 exposed this schism to public view. In his *Sword of the Lord* magazine, Rice looked at the goings-on in Madison Square Garden and chided Graham and evangelicals in general: "Old-time Bible-believing fundamentalists insist that the Bible clearly forbids yoking up with unbelievers, even though one's motives may appear to be good." The unbelievers were the ecumenical Protestants and the councils of churches whose backing Graham was then welcoming. As militant as Rice was Carl McIntire, who had organized the American Council of Christian Churches a year before the evangelicals got together. In the eyes of Rice the New York crusade by Billy Graham represented a "distinct defeat for the fundamentalists." He was irked because Graham had rebuffed fundamentalist efforts to get him to hold a separatist rally. Fundamentalist leaders John R. Rice, Bob Jones, Sr., and Carl McIntire thus simply dismissed Graham at the New York crusade for "selling out."

McIntire was the most consistent and noisiest enemy of ecu- 25:10
menism; his International Council of Christian Churches had been designed to promote "Bible Christianity" and to "awaken Christians everywhere to the insidious dangers of modernism and Roman Catholicism" alike. In the eyes of McIntire's group, the American members of the World Council were "fellow travelers with systems of totalitarianism and authoritarianism." J. Howard Pew, who two years later headed the National Lay Committee to protest, from within, trends in the new National Council, gave McIntire $50,000 to help him launch his campaign against the World Council, which was denounced as being made up of "conspicuous modernists" and "near-blasphemous unbelievers." The McIntire following passed resolutions against the "anti-Biblical, anti-evangelical, and un-Protestant" character of the World Council. When that council met at Evanston, Illinois, in 1954, McIntire found his great opportunity to picket and demonstrate, but he had been just as ready to oppose the National Council when it formed. It was to him "another mile-post on the road to a super-church," a "whistle-stop on the train back to Rome," a "twentieth century hybrid." The Eastern Orthodox, whom he despised, were in the council; for him they possessed "all the Babylonian admixture of truth and error found in the Church of Rome, universal in scope, and eventually leading up in the Romish abomination itself."

The *Christian Century,* looking back across the chasms, ordi- 25:11
narily refused to see much difference between old fundamentalism and neo-evangelicalism. In 1958, however, it published an article by Arnold W. Hearn not quite accurately titled "Fundamentalist

Renascence." Hearn kept an eye on the endeavor by evangelicals "to disentangle the core of concern for unqualified theological orthodoxy from the more objectionable traits which have heretofore seemed inseparable from fundamentalism," especially because of evangelicals' "capacity to make their case in terms more sensitive to the integrity of the modern mind." The editors were not always so friendly to this "parachurch dimension." Aged and blind editor emeritus Charles Clayton Morrison momentarily came out of retirement to make an effort to cast the new conflict in terms of the controversies of the 1920s, as he was being told of the "rising tempo of a powerful evangelical drive developing independently of the churches," and thus in an unfamiliar channel. He was disturbed when in 1957 the Protestant Council of New York cooperated with Billy Graham; it had thus opened an "access to a channel of official church life which had previously been closed" to fundamentalists. Morrison feared such an opening as much as did the militant fundamentalists. *Christian Century* editors also noted that evangelicals were consistently anticonciliar. In fact, the NAE said in its program that it "insists that its members must not only repudiate and denounce apostasy (i.e., the National Council) but also separate from it. The NAE settles for repudiation and denunciation."

25:12   By 1956 and 1957 the evangelicals came up with someone who matched Billy Graham's theology but wanted to give intellectual respectability to the evangelical cause as a theological movement. He was Carl F. H. Henry, a newspaperman converted to a conservative Baptist outlook. Henry became a seminary professor and editor of a Graham-inspired flagship periodical, *Christianity Today.* His "confessions," written thirty years after the birth of that magazine, may distort memories, as autobiographies tend to do. But they give access to the thought world that was associated with the rise of the neo-evangelicals. Henry recalled and revisited the founding of Carl McIntire's hastily organized American Council of Christian Churches; McIntire had heard rumors of "an organizational challenge to the Federal Council [later National Council] of Churches" being in prospect and jumped the gun in 1941. But the evangelicals went ahead with their own organizational challenge: "Conservative Christians felt increasingly that without some such effort they could not effectively confront the Federal Council's liberal orientation of theology and socio-political perspectives," and the like.

25:13   In the year of the New York crusade, Henry published *Evangelical Responsibility in Contemporary Theology.* In that book he criticized the centripetal tendencies of liberal religion. He complained that in order "to assail the Communist disparagement of religion as an opiate of the masses, the free world assumes more and more the brotherhood or essential kinship of all religions." But the efforts to advance brotherhood had degenerated: "in this placid climate of events," added Henry, "denominational debate, Protestant polemics, and competitive missions threaten to build the thunderheads of religious feuding." Favoring meteorological metaphors, Henry went on: "Within Protestantism itself, in our generation, the great barometer of church history is registering toward conciliation and union." Further, "the ecumenical forecast of pan-Protestant cooperation has sounded over our fast-moving century, to diminish the pressure of divisiveness that has vexed Protestantism since the Reformation." One of two forces driving all this was spiritually unifying: Jesus had, after all, prayed for his disciples and thus for his church "that they may all be one." The other drive had to do with "tactically competitive factors"—the same that drove the National Association of Evangelicals: "An added pressure is the specter of growing Roman Catholic political power in America." He read the signs well: "Intolerant of religious debate and fragmentation, the temper of the times is overtly predisposed to cooperation and concord."

The evangelicals were caught up with that concordant temper,   25:14
too, said Henry, who spoke to the "ecclesiastical mood and movement" toward unity. There were alluring questions. Should not Christians hope that in religion they "may find a way to resolve differences in a spirit of love?" Did not "the Hebrew-Christian religion" enjoin neighbor love? Then how could Christians not be "properly indignant over some warring chapters in the total history of Christianity?" Would not all believers wish to delete accusing paragraphs about disunity from the "indelible annals of our times?" But Henry's evangelical movement was not ready to give up its own separate struggles: "The ultimate fate of Protestantism, shadowed throughout the West by two generations of theological turmoil, remains in doubt." He said that he did not want to revive the fundamentalist-modernist controversy but to move ahead—yet never in company with mainstream ecumenism. "Ecumenical inclusivism rolls on; each passing year registers new mergers and numerical gains while the minority outside diminishes." Ministers ask: should they not stop being contentious and start joining ecumenical forces, or at least should they not move into an attitude of "quiescent indifference" rather than opposition? Henry knew that

"pugilistic spirituality" was not winning. Certainly "the spiritually illiterate" who were causing the "present upsurge in church attendance" would only be bewildered by a revisiting of the old controversy.

25:15   Henry saw no real signs of compromise among the old liberals. Harry Emerson Fosdick, the frontline liberal in the battles of the twenties, had just written his autobiography, a "highly readable" book that spun "a halo of self-justification over Dr. Fosdick's vagabondage and endeavors to vindicate the liberalism to which he raised an altar" so long before. Fosdick, said Henry, simply reprinted his earlier indictments of fundamentalism as a "retreat into hidebound obscurantism," as "the flare-up of a rear-guard action," as "bitter intolerance" and "out-dated thinking." Fosdick therefore was overlooking the new moderate evangelicals and acknowledging no validity in fundamentalist criticisms of his own camp. Henry thought the *Christian Century* was also eager to overlook the moderates and keep frozen the old fundamentalist picture. He seemed a bit nervous about the fact that the magazine was becoming a bit open to the right. The editors, he complained, would listen when fundamentalists criticize fundamentalists, "but unless they defect from evangelical Christianity to liberalism they are still unacceptable" to such liberals. Henry himself was critical of the "fundamentalist reduction." He was right to see it, he wrote, not as simple old-time religion; "the fundamentalist movement became a distinctly twentieth-century expression of Christianity" but failed to produce "a comprehensive world and life view."

25:16   Liberalism to Henry in 1957 presented only a "mirror of outdated prejudices" and "reflected the invasion of a secular spirit." But he now tried to call for equal rejection of the old parties that were its alternatives. If Fosdick was unrepentant about attacking fundamentalists, leaders as great as Europe's Karl Barth could get away with being savage in their criticism of modernism. "Should evangelical leaders as candidly admit the excesses of fundamentalism as neo-orthodox leaders have admitted the excesses of the prevailing liberalism?" The question answered itself: "They dare not do less." His indictment ended: "If modernism stands discredited as a perversion of the scriptural theology, certainly fundamentalism in this contemporary expression stands discredited as a perversion of the biblical spirit." Here clearly was a man trying to carve space for a new movement, as the Barths and Niebuhrs had done for the liberal movement toward neo-orthodoxy. Henry disagreed with these neo-orthodox critics chiefly because they lacked the "high view of inspiration" of Scripture needed for the new battles. It was not enough, however, to be merely uneasy over "the creedal vagrancy of the World Council of Churches."

Henry, Billy Graham, *Christianity Today,* and the National Association of Evangelicals found a new mission. "Many earnest evangelicals," Henry wrote, "are active in the World Council of Churches; many are active outside the National Association of Evangelicals and similar agencies." All these needed to be rallied, to win back initiative for the unifying of the church, an initiative which, in the public mind, the evangelicals had let the liberals take over. Then he spoke only to his camp: "We have a task to do, a task of apostolic awesomeness; let us rise to the doing. The hour for rescue is distressingly late." He was at the moment providing an apology for *Christianity Today,* the magazine the Graham forces and his own had started in 1954 to challenge the *Christian Century.* Graham, when approaching Henry on the subject, wanted to be sure that the newspaperman-theologian understood that "the new magazine's prime objective would be not to reach or please American fundamentalists but to lead confused and bewildered liberals to accept the authority of Scripture." Yes, Henry knew. Henry later told of the prehistory of this encounter. Graham had approached his father-in-law, L. Nelson Bell, a lay medical missionary, and through him got access to magnates such as Sun Oil Company head J. Howard Pew, who was fresh from his wars against the National Council of Churches and who could bankroll the experiment. Henry described the boundaries. The magazine aimed to be "(a) transcontinental, (b) interdenominational, (c) theologically affirmative, (d) socially aggressive and (e) irenic." 25:17

Autobiographer Henry later looked back on the founding years and explained why a socially aggressive magazine had ducked the religiously based civil rights movement, which was addressing the biggest social cause of its era. "We were not consulted when ecumenical leaders made their moves. If the ecumenical effort was 'Johnny come lately' in concern over national discrimination, evangelical engagement was admittedly 'Johnny come later.'" The magazine through those years did oppose the "disrespect for law implicit in mob demonstration and resistance," feeling, over against Martin Luther King, Jr., that a single well-publicized protest could have thrown the issue into the courts where justice issues were to be resolved. Graham's father-in-law, meanwhile, had been 25:18

assigned the task of assessing King's theology and had found it not "the gospel." The editors decided then that the race problem was not "the cutting edge of a dramatic social reformation."

25:19   Henry looked back on the heady days when the well-financed magazine began to make its mark. "In a single fortnight I had two hours with the religion editor of *Time,* lunch with the religion editor of *Newsweek* and left for Oberlin as an invited evangelical consultant to World Council study sessions on 'The Unity We Seek.' " The magazine was clearly establishing itself. "United States Information Agency libraries around the world began to display it alongside the *Century.*" A final sign of having achieved success occurred when in 1960 Republican presidential candidate Richard M. Nixon called Henry in: "Nixon clearly hoped that *Christianity Today* would endorse his candidacy, to offset the *Century*'s endorsement of Kennedy." The *Christian Century* in fact did not endorse either candidate, being forbidden by its tax-exempt charter to do so; but the editors were divided and wary over Kennedy's Catholicism. Nixon was correct, however, in his perception that the liberal Protestant magazine was not endorsing him!

25:20   To use the rivalry between the new little National Association of Evangelicals and the newer larger National Council of Churches or the magazine warfare between the new *Christianity Today* and the old *Christian Century* does not do justice to the degree of contention between two wings of Protestantism fighting for the right to gain access to the American soul. It was also fought out in the denominations and among them; in the congregations and among them; and in the power centers where ministers were preparing for Christianity in the next century, Christianity tomorrow: the seminaries. Evangelicals knew that liberals had taken over all the old prestigious interdenominational schools, at Harvard and Yale, Union and Chicago, Vanderbilt, some aspects of (largely Presbyterian) Princeton, and many more. There were fundamentalist Bible colleges and a few ministerial training centers plus some bona fide seminaries. But the time had come to found an interdenominational seminary to enter the competition. Evangelicals chose the West as the place from which to point to the future, Princeton Seminary as a (slightly too liberal) model, and, to run it, people generally congenial to leaders like Billy Graham and Carl Henry.

25:21   The Reverend Harold John Ockenga, pastor of Boston's Park Street Congregational Church, who commuted between there and Pasadena, California, for years, was cofounder of the new school with evangelist Charles Fuller, after whom the school was named. That the soul of America was at stake, in the eyes of the founders, was clear from Ockenga's opening convocation address at the Pasadena Civic Auditorium on October 1, 1947. The Bostonian's address was titled "The Challenge to the Christian Culture of the West," not meaning everything west of Boston Common or around Pasadena, but Western culture. It was a strongly nationalistic lecture on the American potential in the cultural recovery of a postwar world. Ockenga wore the mien of the elite: "ordinary Christians" could not do the task; there had to be experts who would "redefine Christian thinking" and prepare for the "rethinking and restating of the fundamental thesis and principles of a western culture." He defined Western civilization as "those great Christian principles, which have been infused into society over centuries, and which now are bearing their fruit." These included "the concept of the infinite value of individual man," of "responsibility to God," something resulting, said Ockenga, "in the moral fiber of our Christian thinking."

The Protestant Reformation, he reminded his audience, had produced much of this, and it was the evangelicals, now gathering, who were its legatees and custodians. "We have allowed Romanism to step in with a social program that will make Romanism the challenging religious factor in western civilization, and in particular the United States." But the other predictable enemy was worse: America, he said, was "experiencing today that inner rupture of its character and culture, that inner division with vast multitudes of our people following that secularist, rationalist lie of 'scientific naturalism' in the repudiation of God and God's law." Ockenga was challenging the fundamentalism that lay behind him, because it was separatist, while he spoke of "infusion." And the Boston pastor went on to challenge the Protestant mainstream, which already had a Presbyterian seminary in California—San Francisco Theological Seminary. Ockenga intended to insult when he said that "there is no outstanding seminary in the West" because "the testimony of most denominational seminaries has been vitiated by modernism." Aware of the anger of many California Presbyterians and their kind who resented a rival, Ockenga promised to be "ecclesiastically positive." The school would "repudiate the 'come-out-ism' movement" and its people would have no time for "negativism." 25:22

Carl Henry was on the founding faculty, busy that year publishing his landmark book *The Uneasy Conscience of Modern Fun-* 25:23

damentalism. In it he talked more about the soul of America. "For the first protracted period in its history," he charged, "evangelical Christianity stands divorced from the great social reform movements." Fundamentalism had been a "revolt against the Christian social imperative." Biblical allusion gave Henry impetus: "If the evangelical answer is in terms of religious escapism, then the salt has lost its savor."

25:24   How difficult bridge-building would be was demonstrated in an incident that shadowed Fuller Seminary in its earliest years. In Europe one could easily be both ecumenical and evangelical, and Bela Vasady, a Hungarian displaced person, was indeed both. He was a founder of the World Council of Churches in 1948, a fact that would not endear him to the natural Fuller constituency, though it was no problem for a European evangelical. Ockenga was impressed with Vasady, despite the Hungarian's friendliness to the World and Federal Councils, and thought that his presence on the Fuller faculty would lead West Coast Presbyterians to take Fuller more seriously. Unfortunately for public relations, Vasady along the way chose to attend a moderate Presbyterian church whose pastor was Vasady's friend, Eugene Carson Blake. He was typed as a liberal and his congregation of choice, to one Fuller faculty spouse, was a "hell-hole." In the fall of 1949 some of his critics found an article in which Vasady argued that Christians should develop a "one-church-consciousness" and that they should be seeing everything "through ecumenical glasses" as they concentrated on "one world" and "one church," two notions which, he claimed, "belong together organically."

25:25   Such language seemed to belong more in the camp of the enemy, so the Fuller faculty issued a statement that it did "not endorse the World Council of Churches, because of its present disregard of evangelical convictions," and insisted that faculty members must "avoid approval" of the council. Vasady, who had outlasted Hitler and who now wanted to help subvert communism, found such strictures too familiar: "In Europe, it is the method of totalitarian regimes to keep a secret about suspected individuals and to lay before them all the data when their services are not any more needed." Now he faced "an ecclesiastical pattern of a police-state." The faculty followed through with an attempt to force its definition of biblical "inerrancy" on him, and he did not survive to get a permanent appointment there.

25:26   Even Fuller presidents could be caught in the vise of contradictory expectations. Edward John Carnell, a serious evangelical

intellectual who began leading a generation of young fellow believers to places like Harvard Divinity School, where he took his
Ph.D., was a man on a mission. Carnell, a dour and troubled
scholar, in 1952 complained to Carl Henry of the "lukewarm re-
ception" given his largely unbought, unread, unreviewed, unnoticed A Philosophy of the Christian Religion. Carnell aspired to
straddle camps: "After pouring the fruit of my philosophic labors
into it, it has received little or no acclaim." He complained, "There
is a parochialism in evangelicalism from which I must withdraw."
He wanted "to command the attention of [Paul] Tillich and [John]
Bennett"; then he could be "in a better place to be of service to
the evangelicals. We need prestige desperately." Carnell would
bring repute to Fuller, whose board named him president in 1954.
Disaster came early. His thoroughly orthodox inauguration speech
in 1955 almost split the school and helped ruin his administration, because he elaborated "a Christian philosophy of tolerance,"
which was not precisely what many at Fuller thought their school
was there for. Students, he said, should be imparted "an attitude of
tolerance and forgiveness toward individuals whose doctrinal convictions are at variance with those that inhere in the institution
itself." The enraged wing of the faculty, backed by its kind of constituents, was in no mood to be tolerant or forgiving, and Carnell,
hardly a natural administrator, never could bring stability to the
post or the school.

The Graham Crusade in New York, which Fuller supported, was   25:27
the most public face neo-evangelicalism had yet shown. It was devastating to the flank that wanted to keep ties to separatist fundamentalism and liberating for those who promoted Ockenga's "new
evangelicalism." Graham's friendship with President Eisenhower
emboldened more of this party to move toward centrist Republican
politics, away from the far right. In 1956 Christian Life magazine
made a pronouncement with which Fuller was to live in the year of
the crusade: "Fundamentalism has become evangelicalism." Carnell, still president in 1958, evidently thought he could build on
this shift. In an address at Chicago that year he charged that fundamentalists had "forgotten the dictum that great ideas are going
to rule the world." Evangelicals, he charged, had surrendered their
leadership, insofar as they belonged to the fundamentalist camp.
Mainline secular publishers like Macmillan and denominational
houses like Westminster started to publish Carnell, and the Christian Century turned to him for reliable insider reports on the new
evangelicalism. He spoke at a forum with Karl Barth at the Uni-

versity of Chicago and named moderates like Britisher Geoffrey Bromiley, a translator of Karl Barth, to the faculty. But attacks on Carnell only grew, and he eventually had to resign. He was clinically depressed and died in mysterious circumstances—some thought as a suicide. But while he failed as an administrator, he had helped the school move into a more open evangelicalism and had helped poise the movement for a more open encounter with ecumenical Protestantism and the secular world surrounding it.

25:28   Not all of those who were uneasy with ecumenism joined the para-ecumenical National Association of Evangelicals, identified with *Christianity Today,* or became supporters of schools like Fuller Theological Seminary. Some belonged to large denominations whose leaders were well aware of the centripal motion of ecumenism, the vortex of secular and religious motion toward celebration of the common, in One World and One Nation, but were determined to resist it, for various reasons. When the World and National Councils of Churches were forming, ecumenist Samuel McCrea Cavert mourned that "conspicuously absent from the list of co-operating denominations" were the Southern Baptist Convention, on the way to being the largest Protestant body in the United States, and the Lutheran Church—Missouri Synod, a large body. They, together with evangelical, Pentecostal, and "sectarian" (ungraciously thus named, said Cavert) groups represented "vacant chairs in the ecumenical household," and their vacancy was "so significant as to call for sober reflection." Cavert thought that it was "important to understand why such earnest companies of Christian people were on the outside."

25:29   The Southern Baptists were the greatest embarrassment and enigma. In 1949 the *Baptist Standard* in Texas could boast that "Baptists have gained more rapidly in the past 10 years than in any single decade in our history. This is true throughout the Southern Baptist Convention," which listed 7,079,880 members in 1951 and 10,191,303 in 1962; no other denomination was as assertive or statistically successful during the years of the revival of interest in religion. In 1961 demographer and geographer Wilbur Zelinsky looked at the South, where 49 percent of *all* southern Protestants were Baptist, by far most of the whites among them being in the SBC. They were highly orthodox and had polls to prove it. Some of them were a bit more friendly than others to non-Baptists, including the Methodists next door, the second largest southern Protestant group and nationally still the largest. Francis Butler Simkins, a capable observer, in 1957 saw some increase in civility. It was "no longer good manners, in pulpit or parlor, to criticize a church other than one's own." Simkins must have used the Baptists as his model when he added: "Southerners adhere firmly to the Christian dogma that there is but a single road by which a person can be saved. Because each denomination believes that it has the right road to the Heavenly Kingdom, there is no room for compromise with those who claim other roads." Asked in 1950 whether they favored a merger of all Protestants into one church, 61 percent said no; that number grew to 70 percent during the next ten years, the presumably ecumenical decade. It has to be observed, however, that the jump in numbers nationally was from 39 percent to 64 percent in opposition to such a scheme, further evidence that the rhetoric and action promoting merger belonged to elites and not the broad memberships.

The Southern Baptist Convention was profiting from migration   25:30
into the South, as that region was converting from being "Dixie" to being the "Sunbelt." The Baptists specialized in evangelism, not ecumenism. They had no interest in seeing Christians come together; they were out to gain new ones through conversion. They would contribute to the centrifugal and competitive movements and shun the centripetal. In 1940, when the convention was invited to help form the World Council of Churches, it said that it "positively and definitely" declined. Leaders made clear that this attitude, as they put it, "continues to please our constituency with perhaps increased conviction." There were convention resolutions against any "compact or agreement . . . with any organization, convention, or religious body" that would compromise Southern Baptists. Of course, there dared be no "organic connection with the Federal Council of Churches of Christ in America"; all such ties would lead members to forget the "dangers of interdenominationalism and nondenominationalism."

Only mavericks withstood the anti-ecumenical push. Thus   25:31
Ernest F. Campbell, a notable preacher on the way to becoming pastor at Riverside Church in New York, spoke of the "sad blunder" his fellow Southern Baptist Convention members made when they refused to help form the World Council and exercise their influence there. Joining would have meant giving up nothing except, he said, "our selfishness, our complacency and our unholy ambition and conceit that make us feel we can save the world by ourselves alone." And Edward Hughes Pruden, pastor to President Truman in Washington, defended ecumenists who had in mind "nothing more dangerous than brotherly cooperation on a purely

voluntary basis." He also got no following. Cavert let his irritation show over this, for example, when he complained that the convention never hesitated "to establish competitive churches even in communities where there were already strong congregations affiliated with the American Baptist Convention."

25:32   The convention, being congregational in polity, officially turned down invitations with a phrase like this: "Our Convention has no ecclesiastical authority; it is in no sense the Southern Baptist Church." Cavert properly challenged the logic of this, since the convention was already a member of the Baptist World Alliance and similar groups. He argued that "in fact, a Council of Churches rests on the very principle of voluntary fellowship which Southern Baptists magnify." No, he assured, the World Council will not become "some sort of a 'Protestant Vatican.'" The anti-ecumenical majority in the convention, meanwhile, could always solidify their ranks by stressing their independent polity, their intense congregationalism. Trying to create a bridge was Southern Baptist Theological Seminary professor Theron D. Price, who knew the problem of selling one extreme. "It would be difficult to convince us that the visible reduction of the mystical body [of Christ] to one legal corporation would enhance the true unity of the church." But, he felt, "we Southern Baptists are in much greater danger, at present, of failing to make our witness to the whole Church by isolation than of losing the distinctiveness of that witness by association."

25:33   In a similar stance was the Lutheran Church—Missouri Synod. The Missourians were heirs of a Saxon immigration born of an impulse to resist "unionism." Originally that meant the Prussian Union or similar governmentally based forced mergers in Germany, but in America it became the Missourians' hallmark as they used the strategy to keep everyone else at a distance, including other Lutherans, with whom they refused to pray. The fact that the largest Lutheran body, the United Lutheran Church, was a member of the National Council of Churches only added to the impulse of Missouri Lutherans to shun ecumenism. While the majority of Lutherans in America were members of the World Council and their leaders were friendly to the National Council, while most were in a Lutheran World Federation and a National Lutheran Council, the Missouri Synod stood apart. While the theologians of other groups were trying to recapture the dynamism of Luther's Lutheranism, Missouri dogmaticians were staying with the seventeenth-century scholasticism that had helped them congeal as a doctrinal body. Cavert well understood the synod's "rigidity in doctrine" and was friendly enough to hear that the leaders were "not unconcerned with the unity of the church, but they have insisted that there must be agreement in the statement of doctrine as a prerequisite of either co-operation or union." He was cheered to see them sending friendly observers to some ecumenical events, like a 1957 conference at Oberlin, "The Nature of the Unity We Seek," and he heard more and more pro-ecumenical voices among Missouri Synod moderates.

One other group, as dynamic as evangelicalism (to whose genus   25:34
it was often seen to belong as a species) and as the Southern Baptist Convention, was the cluster of largely African American as well as white Pentecostal churches. Evidence from that period suggests that they were not yet participating much in the argument over religion and public life or competing for the soul of all America, but they were busy with and increasingly successful at winning "the souls" of Americans. Born at the turn of the century at the Holiness fringes of Wesleyanism, and thus sort of second cousins of now-staid Methodists, the Pentecostals had often been dismissed as backwoods, hill-country, holy-rolling people. Cavert saw them to be "a considerable sector of relatively new Protestant bodies" that had "only slight contact with mainstream Protestantism" and were "inclined to be very critical of the prevailing institutional forms of religious life." He knew that at the edges were "bizarre figures—shouting revivalists, sensational faith healers, and jazzy singers of sentimental gospel songs." Many met in storefronts, but Cavert saw them moving toward more conventional settings in groups, too long dismissed as "sects," called Assemblies of God, the Churches of God, and the Church of the Foursquare Gospel.

While the Pentecostals had few reasons to be involved with for-   25:35
mal ecumenism, they were almost too busy to be opposed to it. And people like Cavert wanted to be alert: "If the ecumenical movement is to represent the *wholeness* of the church, it will take fuller account of this type of churchmanship than it has thus far done." He took cheer from the fact that the Pentecostal Church of Chile was applying for membership in the World Council of Churches. Also David J. du Plessis, who called himself an "ecumenical Pentecostalist," had come to be at home with the World Council. The ecumenical movement, wrote Cavert, "may well ask itself whether it does not have lessons to learn from the Pentecostals." But in the United States there was little contact. Council liberals thought of Pentecostals as fundamentalists, though fundamentalists did not. Back in 1928 had come the first condemnation,

from the World's Christian Fundamentals Association. It wrote off "the present wave of modern pentecostalism, often referred to as the 'tongues movement'" and marked by "fanatical and unscriptural healing" as a "menace" that worked "real injury." So it went on record as "unreservedly opposed to Modern Pentecostalism," and the thirty intervening years had not led to a healing of the breach. Only when modern evangelicalism emerged could there be new ententes. By 1956 the Assemblies of God, the Pentecostal Church of God of America, the Pentecostal Holiness Church, and the Church of God of Cleveland, Tennessee, had brought their many hundreds of thousands of members into the National Association of Evangelicals, as a sign that they were on the move.

25:36   The Pentecostals in 1948, meeting in Des Moines, formed a Pentecostal Fellowship of North America that often criticized the National and World Councils, fearing a "combination of many denominations into a World Super Church" which would "probably culminate in the Scarlet Woman or Religious Babylon of Revelation." On such a scene, David du Plessis knew his work would be difficult. But in 1951, he said, he had had a conversation with God: "The Lord spoke to me and clearly told me to go and witness to the Leaders of the World Council of Churches." He was warmly received at its Second Assembly in Evanston in 1954. And he reported back to his fellow Pentecostals that "a sincere recognition of the work of the Holy Spirit among the top echelons of Protestantism" was a new signal of openness.

25:37   No survey of all the anti-ecumenical groups who would not buy conciliar models for the centripetal energies of the church and world would be complete without mention of by far the largest resistant group. This was the Roman Catholicism that, if anything, helped all other ecumenical groups organize themselves by providing the common target, the foil to those who would otherwise have stayed apart. The tension was acute in the United States. The Vatican allowed Catholics nowhere to have dealings with the World Council and left no room for experiment by American Catholics with the National Council. Pope Pius XI already in 1928, in *Mortalium Animus,* forbade all ecumenical contact but did acknowledge the positive intent of the movement: it has "never perhaps so taken hold of men's minds as in our time." But Cavert knew that the Catholics built only stone walls against ecumenical doings. Stephen C. Neill, an Anglican bishop with experience in world missions and now ecumenism, groused that Catholicism's attitude showed that it thought it had "everything to teach and nothing to learn." As late as 1961 Cavert could add, "There is no reason to expect that the Roman Church will retreat from this dogmatic position," though he sensed some possibility of "ecclesiastical summitry" because Pope John XXIII had called for a not yet convened ecumenical council.

The inhibition against contact in America was reinforced in 1949 by the Holy Office in Rome, which issued *Ecclesia catholica,* an "Instruction to Local Ordinaries." Never "without the previous sanction of the competent ecclesiastical authority," but sometimes with it, could Catholics have even limited participation in "mixed meetings" that deal with "matters of faith and morals." Saying the Lord's Prayer or some other approved prayer at the beginning or end of meetings was all that was ever licit. Now and then approved Catholics like pioneer ecumenist Father Gustave Weigel, S.J., or the Paulist editor Father John B. Sheerin were designated unofficial observers at events like the Faith and Order meeting in Oberlin, Ohio, in 1957. Hoping for more thaw in the religious "cold war," Cavert urged warmer relations of the sort he discerned in journals like *Commonweal, America,* and *Cross Currents* or in books like Father George H. Tavard's *Catholic Approach to Protestantism* and the Jesuit Edward Duff's *The Social Thought of the World Council of Churches.* Yet these crossings of barriers and signs of armistice were so recent, so timid, so rarefied that, said Cavert, "many American Protestants do not yet seem aware how the great change in their cultural situation is affecting the religious patterns." He noted that many of these Protestants still thought of America as Protestant, living still with André Siegfried's observation in 1927 that Protestantism was America's "only national religion." For these people, Catholicism was still an "alien intruder," to be treated "at best with a patronizing air and at worst with suspicious hostility." Therefore Catholics shut themselves off as "a beleaguered minority and tended to develop a ghetto mentality."

Only at the end of the decade could Cavert point to hopeful signs. In an unprecedented act, Father Weigel gave the Nathaniel William Taylor Lectures at Yale Divinity School, while Harvard Divinity School, then as Protestant as was Yale, invited Catholic historian Christopher Dawson to be a guest on its faculty. When the National Council met in San Francisco in December 1960, the Catholic *Monitor* there recognized that "the Council's overarching hope is Christian unity," that its motives were sincere, humble, and "transparently clear." But there was much work to do. Prot-

25:38

25:39

estants did not regard most Catholic efforts as sincere, humble, or transparently clear. Secularist Paul Blanshard feared that some liberal Protestants "would make almost any compromise with the hierarchy which would lead to the give-and-take of mutual adjustment." But not all Protestants were liberals. The Baptist *Watchman-Examiner,* which forty years before had given the name *fundamentalism* to the reactive movement, watched the new Pope John act in "pontifical majesty" in 1959 and blasted him. A National Association of Evangelicals writer saw the Catholic church as a "multi-billion dollar organization . . . looked upon with suspicion and resentment by millions of enlightened Americans." Robert J. St. Clair in *United Evangelical Action* was not amused or attracted when Pope John XXIII announced an ecumenical council, but he feared that liberal Protestants would be lured. "To minimize doctrine in favor of an ecumenical movement based on sentiment and good intention is to demonstrate a total refusal to face the avowed Romanist goal of state and social domination based on an inexorable pretention to be the sole guardian of all divine truth."

25:40   Not all Catholics were in the mood to make ecumenical gestures either. Thus Father John Hardon, S.J., judged harshly the World Council representatives at Evanston in 1954 who were "hoping to discover some vestige of unity among the member churches." He thought nothing of the "basic remedy for disunity proposed to the member churches," that of "blind self-surrender, 'even unto death.'" Did they not know that there was one simple path based on the simple logic of Roman Catholic faith? There was already a fully united Church which possessed the full truth. Come to it. The merger front meant only "doctrinal miscegenation." True, "Protestant ecumenism in America shows certain obvious merit," Hardon had to admit grudgingly. But "as a rule, churchmen who are most ecumenically-minded are the least conscious of dogma." In his observation, they supported American "'religion in general,' from which Protestants have least to expect and most to lose." The Jesuit's cultural comment was the most astute part of his analysis: "After generations of a virtual monopoly in forming the religious aspect of American culture and going beyond religion to inform the culture as a whole, Protestantism is being displaced by a temporalized national feeling."

25:41   Nor did all liberals overcome resistance to Catholics at the first sign of friendliness. At the University of Chicago Divinity School, church historian James Hastings Nichols in 1957 wanted to resist calls for entente: "to this day the Roman Church has never been able to keep itself free from spiritual and moral rottenness except in the presence of criticism from without." So: criticize. Two years later, the *Christian Century* reacted negatively to a European Lutheran who seemed to be a bit ecumenically friendly: "Must Protestants enter the discussion," it asked, "by granting in advance all that Roman Catholics need to make their claims and their empire complete, effective, and total?"

When Pope John XXIII called for the Second Vatican Council, even friendly Protestants thought it would represent only a "come home to Rome" approach. The *Christian Century* put most color into its expression of suspicion. "A meeting in the city of the popes, staged with imperial pageantry to show thousands of cardinals, archbishops, and bishops from all over the world worshipping, parading, and conferring in full medieval regalia—that is a public relation man's dream." Look for contrast, it advised, to the humble World Council of Churches, which had an assembly coming up: "We need entertain no doubt as to the conclusion history will reach when it compares the two meetings."

25:42

26

"The Boundless Community of the Best in the World-That-Is": Toward the New Frontier and the Great Society

Two events, one political with religious implications and one religious with political implications, climaxed American efforts in the two mid-century decades to promote convergences in national life. Both had to do with the place of Catholicism. One was the election of Catholic John F. Kennedy to the presidency in 1960, on the eve of the new decade. The other, the Second Vatican Council, announced in Rome in 1959 but not convened until 1962, had many implications for Americans. While there were numerous examples in Judaism and Protestantism to illustrate the theme of readiness for change, reformers in Catholicism at the end of the Eisenhower years demonstrated special new openness to the secular order and contributed to the reduction of tensions or removal of obstructions between groups. Historian Jaroslav Pelikan, in a prize-winning and, for the time, a daring book, *The Riddle of Roman Catholicism*, pointed to both of these developments. According to Pelikan, "most Americans," meaning the non-Catholic three-fourths of the citizenry, still looked at Roman Catholicism "with a mixture of suspicion and fascination" and asked "Can a Roman Catholic be a loyal President of the United States?" And they also looked forward to the ecumenical council, an event not announced as having a bearing on or promise for Protestantism: "Yet Protestants cannot be indifferent to the outcome of such a council," wrote the theologian, "even if it should turn out that they are not directly involved."

Robert McAfee Brown, a contemporary of Pelikan and another   26:2
wary but eager Protestant conversation partner in dialogues with Catholics, also looked back in 1959 to quote and agree with Harvard historian George Williams on a central point. In 1954 Williams had already noticed what militant Protestants in 1960 wanted to overlook, that "American Catholicism, far from being monolithic, is in fact, molten, susceptible of taking any one of a variety of possible shapes depending upon the outcome of the conflicting pressures, shocks, and strains of the present upheaval and realignment of forces in American society." At the turn between 1959 and the presidential election of 1960 that became clear, as did the reality earlier made evident to the Catholic magazine *Commonweal,* which Brown also cited: "There are legitimate and wide areas of freedom within the Church in which public disagreement between a layman and a member of the Church's hierarchy is possible, proper, and at times, even desirable."

The story of the role of religion in the Kennedy presidency be-   26:3
longs to a later period, but one glimpse of the campaign is illuminating here. While many Protestants fought Kennedy and Catholics in politics fervently—even mild Norman Vincent Peale was momentarily associated with an anti-Kennedy-as-President movement—a *Who's Who*'s-worth of Protestant, Orthodox, Catholic, Jewish, African American, and other leaders prepared a "Statement on Religious Liberty" on September 12, 1960. They did not deny the civic faith or public religious role of the nation's chief executive. "The President's participation in important national and community religious functions can be a fine symbol of the common concern for the spiritual welfare of the nation." But, aware that anti-Catholics were saying that a Catholic could not be president because sometimes such functions were unacceptable to his church, the statement went on: "But if for reasons of his own he feels that participation in a particular religious ceremony is not in order, it would be contrary to the civic character of the American Presidency for him to feel obligated to accept the invitation." After all, they said, something perhaps forgotten during the Eisenhower

When President Dwight D. Eisenhower (here with General Vernon Walters) met with Pope John XXIII in 1959, relations between Protestants and Catholics, including the pope, had begun to thaw, not least of all because of the outgoing personality and religious hospitality of the pope, who called a Vatican Council in 1958 and convened it in 1962. (Photo: Religious News Service.)

presidency with its priestly tone was that "participation in special religious ceremonials is an aspect of the Presidency that is secondary in importance to matters of constitutional responsibility."

26:4   The authors of the statement criticized Protestant and other opponents of a Catholic presidency so vigorously that, concurrently, any sense that Protestantism or Judaism were monolithic and not molten also had to disappear. Candidate Kennedy defused some attacks, won over some critics, and pacified millions after a highly publicized meeting of the Greater Houston Ministerial Association in Texas. Kennedy said he knew "he would not lose further from forthright and persistent attention to the religious issue, and could gain." He told the Protestants, "I believe in an America that is officially neither Catholic, Protestant nor Jewish," and where no pope, National Council of Churches, or any other ecclesiastical source would try to impose its will. The National Association of

Evangelicals, less won over at the time, still kept up a program of opposition, but was increasingly isolated and after the Kennedy election dropped its old opposition. By Reformation Sunday, October 30, a week before the election, in the large auditoriums where Protestants formerly lambasted the pope and Catholics in the public order, according to the headline in *Religious News Service,* "Religious Issue Plays Minor Role in Reformation Sermons."

The story of the Second Vatican Council also belongs in another   26:5
time, another narrative, but brief reference to its convocation provides some reference for those who would follow the trajectory of American religion at the turn of the decade. Protestants and Jews brought no, or very low, expectations to it, and even showed open disdain for the project when it was first called. Yet the council showed the Catholic church to be not monolithic, as votes by the bishops in Rome made clear, but instead surprisingly open to the secular world and ready for "hominization," "globalization," and friendlier relations with Protestant, Orthodox, and Jewish believers and also with people of no faith. No one inside or outside the church could have known or foreseen this as late as 1960. When the Vatican newspaper, *Osservatore Romano,* almost casually announced the council on January 26–27, 1959, Union Theological Seminary president Henry Pitney Van Dusen said he admired Pope John XXIII for his originality, but he said of the pope that it was "doubtful whether he could possibly reverse, even if he wished to do so, the direction that has dominated the church's thought for most of the past century." And the Episcopal *Living Church* focused on ecumenism: "It is tragic, but true, that Rome does not yet show any signs of being ready, at the official level, to take part in the ecumenical dialogue." The *Christian Century* foresaw a Catholic public-relations dream and an ecumenical nightmare. Evangelical editor Donald Grey Barnhouse in *Eternity* thought that "more great blasphemies will be promulgated as official Roman Catholic doctrine."

The *Christian Century,* however, soon joined some other non-   26:6
Catholics in extending a bit of hope for the council because of the character of Pope John: "For the first time in many generations a prelate sits on the papal throne whose kindness outshines the imperial splendor of Rome." His encyclical *Mater et magistra,* unnerving to many Catholic conservatives, was unsatisfactory to Protestants because of its firm support of Catholic policies against birth control. But a second encyclical, *Pacem in terris,* was very popular among liberal Protestants at least. The council was to pro-

ceed in general support of ecumenism, though without opening formal ties to the non-Catholic councils. It made some penitent moves toward Judaism. Very important in American eyes would be its Declaration on Religious Liberty, made under the influence of John Courtney Murray and politicked through the council past Vatican conservatives by American hierarchs like Chicago's Albert Cardinal Meyer. At last, Catholicism was on record as saying that the human person has a right to religious freedom and is to be immune from coercion in respect to religious freedom. Here was an indication that George Williams was right. Catholicism was molten, dynamic, and it could change; it was changing! The strongest weapon in the anti-Catholic armament in America after centuries was now weakened or lost: the charge that Catholic power based on Catholic doctrine *had* to mean a threat to democracy and the republic, to the religious and human rights of others, no longer would serve.

26:7   If the events of the 1960s await later telling, it is important for the point of this book to visit several schools of thought that reinforce the theme that American movements were largely centripetal, expressing a thirst for coherence, a belief that "everything that rises must converge"—and that spiritually and intellectually much was rising. *The Vital Center* was the title of the book Arthur M. Schlesinger, Jr., published in 1950. Remembered more for its title than its content, the theme of the book caught the historical moment well. That was "the McCarthy era," and the two opposing sides then contending might have wanted to speak of the vital right or the vital left. But "center" it was and has been in the retrospect of most who try to assess the spirit of the United States at midcentury. Ten years later not a historian but an economist, Canadian-born John Kenneth Galbraith, again in a book more memorable for its title than its content, spoke of the moment as *The Liberal Hour.* The end of the moderate Republican Eisenhower administration and the defeat in November 1960 of Republican candidate Richard M. Nixon, along with the absence of vital rightist movements—the John Birch Society was idiosyncratic more than it was indicative—would have kept assessors of the spirit from calling it "the conservative hour," though, in retrospect, it might well have been seen as a moderate one. Yet, whether viewed as description or prescription, as sign of hope or occasion for fear, the Galbraith title can stand for its brief moment: in the public religion as well as in the social ethos and political tilt, it was "the liberal hour."

26:8   To speak thus of religion in a liberal mode is not to imply that

Orthodox Jews were deserting their synagogues, traditionalist Catholics were crying out for vernacular masses, or fundamentalists and evangelicals and Pentecostals and Protestant conservatives were abandoning their sanctuaries and withdrawing their tracts—anything but that. It meant that in the national culture, where radio and television, films, magazines, and books offered depictions of where the nation was and should go spiritually, attention now turned to those people self-described and those movements prescribed as *liberal*. While such a word carries so many connotations that one cannot even begin to catalog them, several stand out. The liberalism of the brief-lived New Frontier of President John F. Kennedy or the Great Society of Lyndon B. Johnson's first two years implied that social planning held promise; much Protestant, Catholic, and Jewish religious leadership supported it. The liberal accent on equality and rights brought religious elites to advocate participation in the civil rights movement. Religiously, ecumenism was to be favored over sectarianism and standoffishness. The grand themes of the Enlightenment—reason, science, and progress—were features in religious vocabularies across a wide spectrum. A semisecular progressive or millennial—even utopian—outlook countered pessimistic premillennialisms in the favored theologies. One can think of counterforces and exceptions when mentioning each of these, but those who revisit the evidences left by cultural indicators at the end of the Eisenhower years generally concur that this was the liberal hour.

In public theology in those years, little notice was given to devotionalism and spirituality; mysticism and metaphysics, miracle and mystery seemed beside the point. Whereas ten years before and through much of the Eisenhower period, "the secular" and secularism were negative terms, now Catholic, Jewish, and Protestant theologians alike embraced them positively. *New Yorker* writer Ved Mehta, after visiting the theological centers and the theologians, wrote *The New Theologian*. Most of those described in his book had complaints about his journalistic account, but many of them gave him good reason to summarize his findings in a sentence like this: "The New Theologian set himself the old task of equating faith and theology with reason and secularism, and doing so without any sacrifice on either side—a task, in its way, no less tantalizing than squaring the circle." Such a sentence implies a context, a reference to many kinds of events and trends. While my account properly ends around the year 1960, the chosen story cannot end or make the sense it might if it ends too abruptly and if

26:9

there is no notice given the results of the momentum built up during the years when centripetal or convergent forces dominated. What follows, then, is part epilogue, part aftermath, and part a following of the turns in some spiritual trajectories.

26:10   Where should one begin? Those who try to capture bursts in the Zeitgeist turn to literary culture. While the proverbial "person on the street" does not read philosophy of history, philosophers of history do in part draw upon street currents and trends of the time, which they project into the future and onto the past. Some of such thinkers provide a framework. One thinks of Pierre Teilhard de Chardin, for instance; the Jesuit scientist and mystic had a momentary vogue at precisely this moment. He was attaining posthumous celebrity as his writings, long under suspicion by the Vatican, were being translated, published, sold, and quoted for their evolutionary optimism. Novelist Flannery O'Connor, not given to fascination with trends of the moment, did confess to a correspondent that she was "much taken with Pere Teilhard." She said, "I don't understand the scientific end of it or the philosophical," but "even when you don't know those things, the man comes through." Then she announced the title of her next collection of stories: "I've even taken a title from him—'Everything That Rises Must Converge.' " Her choice of phrase could well serve to describe the spiritual direction in the public theology and religion of America at about the time she wrote (1961). Teilhard coined phrases to capture a cosmic sweep, terms like *hominization* and *planetization,* to locate the human family in the material order, as part of an evolutionary convergence that would consummate in "Omega Point," the fulfillment in Christ, now projected into the future. One did not need to "understand the scientific end of it or the philosophical" to capture a sense of Teilhard's cultural appropriateness.

26:11   "Everything that rises must converge" is an epigraph that could summarize the integrative impulse of many a popular philosopher then in fashion. The literature by and about such figures is extensive. Someone who seeks to condense the prophecies does well to turn to a canvass and a digest by Warren Wagar. In 1963 he published *The City of Man,* in which, he said, he had made "no effort to conceal his solidarity" with the prophets of a world civilization. He believed with those on whom he reported "that the idea of an organic world civilization can become the great directive Myth of the century which lies before us." The One Nation myth was becoming a One World fulfillment at last! Wagar reviewed a half-century of endeavor under the rubric "The Search for Synthesis." Most of the thinkers he treated were Europeans well read in America, or refugees in and immigrants to the United States. All had seen what Carl Gustav Jung had meant when he said "everything seems desolate and outworn." Erich Kahler's complaint was that "everything is involved in perpetual change and dissolution." Paul Tillich thought Western civilizational anxiety had matched the mental climate of declining and falling Rome or the Middle Ages, when they were waning. "Cyclical" historians, who looked for recurrences—writers like Oswald Spengler, Pitirim Sorokin, or the current best-seller Arnold Toynbee—all had observed modern civilization going under, as had the teachers of a "theology of crisis" in Europe and America.

The old dogmas, Wagar and the thinkers he treated all knew,   26:12 would no longer serve: neither the doctrines of pure individualism nor those beliefs that produced Marxist-Leninist superstates; not "the old Western tribal gods of nationalism" still being sought for salvation in much of Asia and Africa; nor was "the only refuge" to be "the faith of their fathers, a return to the spiritual sources of life now in process of disintegration," which could "no more be put back together again than Humpty-Dumpty." But between and beyond these prophecies of disintegration, "flashes of authentic prophetic insight" which needed gathering up appeared. Let some dismiss what they would regard as the "overtones of old-fashioned Utopianism"; Wagar was confident that here was "the most vital vision in the thinking of our time." Marxist and Catholic and other "religious leaders of every faith" would find that such thought cut through the "blinkered imagination of bigotry." The thinkers to whom he called attention, Wagar was quick to say, were anything but antireligious; the secular imagination did not have the globe to itself. Indeed, "the Roman Catholic Church, the world communist movement, Islam, the Bahai [*sic*] Faith, and many other groups wedded to a particular creedal orthodoxy"—all had, "according to their peculiar and always lopsided genius, contributed prophets of a coming planetary society." Together they would supply the generations with "a life-orienting and life-fulfilling objective."

Wagar and evidently the readers of his kind of books found the   26:13 chosen thinkers important because they were realists who knew the limits of human nature. But they all transcended some of those limits and offered hope: "Wrestling on the precipice makes for profound dizziness, but also for a quickening of every sense." Wagar adduced the example of Albert Camus, the French novelist also then in vogue: "The struggle itself toward the heights is enough to fill a man's heart." Bringing it all closer to home: Wagar's America would be part of "cosmopolis," or "world-city," no place but a gathering, the "inevitably large spiritual and intellectual and administrative capital of a civilization, of the whole known civilized world." Of course, "a cosmopolis is not a utopia; it is not the best of all possible worlds, but the boundless community of the best in the world-that-is." Ethnocentrism, as of 1963, was the enemy, but it was doomed. "Out of the travail of empire-building, especially, comes revelation. The world opens out. Gods, morals, styles, world-views agglomerate and, under the best conditions, fuse to produce a richer, fuller way of life." Even in reactive moments when "a people cleaves unto itself again, as Jews, Germans, and Irishmen have often tried to do," they found they could not return to the "purity of the past." No "parochial *ersatz* religion" could fill the void of the times. Wagar quoted one of his favored thinkers, social philosopher Lewis Mumford: "Civilization is the never-ending process of creating one world and one humanity." Wagar dealt with international figures, but they were being read and appropriated, and their spirit was affecting the context in which an enlarged debate over One Nation, Under God— or "simply secular"—continued.

26:14   The philosophers quoted in *The City of Man* did not set a simple agenda for the progressive and utopian theologians-of-the-secular. They were contending with the very concept of the secular and the realities behind it. Wagar quoted philosopher William Barrett: "the central fact of modern history in the West" was the decline of religious faith. When humans lost religion, according to Barrett, they "lost the concrete connection with a transcendent realm of being" and were "bound to feel homeless in such a world." True, there was a religious revival going on, but, as Gerhard Szczesney's new book *The Future of Unbelief* contended: "Not even the recent flurry of reverent interest in Christianity awakened by modern man's sense of his inadequacy" had "altered the fact that the real content of the Christian doctrine of salvation, for a dominant type of modern man, has become completely unacceptable." So Wagar and his people turned to the testimony of scientists like the atheist Sir Julian Huxley, who was inspired by a line read long ago in Lord Morley, that "the next great task of science will be to create a religion for humanity."

26:15   Huxley was premature; he had trouble being taken seriously back in 1946 when he called for "some sort of comprehensive philosophy, based not on sectarian theologies or competing ideologies, but on the universal facts and methods of the natural sciences." Teilhard was not hobbled by such handicaps, because as a "mystic, a theist, a Jesuit, a scientist, an evolutionary humanist, and a prophet of world order" he would not be resisted by "a jaded century." In the spirit of the line favored by Flannery O'Connor, Teilhard had written: "There is only one way which leads upwards; the one which, through greater organization, leads to greater synthesis and unity." Wagar, whom I cite not because he was exceptional but because he was so representative of currents, argued that there had to be a breakthrough beyond the "broadening, but still far too restricted, circles of family, country and race. . . . The Age of Nations is past." It was time to build the Earth.

Arnold Toynbee, though British, was an American best-seller,   26:16
much touted by *Life* and *Time* and the Book of the Month Club and other agencies that helped bring celebrities to American attention. He was the best known of the then current prophets of "world integration." As he looked for synthesis, Toynbee considered Judaism to be tribal and fossilized. Wagar was unimpressed by the response to such a notion: "A few, notably Jewish scholars," he observed, had "all but descended to character assassination on behalf of their respective tribal gods." Notice, please, he directed, that Toynbee paid respect to "higher religions" like Hinduism, Zoroastrianism, Buddhism, Christianity, Islam, and even, for some of its features, the Judaism that he was also stigmatizing. For Toynbee, now, these religions disengaged the "spiritual presences higher than man" from the "highly integrated life of some particular local community" in order that the realm of God or absolute spirit might come "to be thought of as being coextensive, not with some local state or some regional civilization, but with the entire Universe, while its worshipers come to feel themselves members of a church that, in principle and in intention, embraces all men." Wagar paraphrased Toynbee: "Through the transfiguring power of the higher religions and much luck and perseverance, mankind may transcend the age of civilizations altogether and enter a wholly new phase of life."

Wagar's gallery of witnesses further included the aged Ameri-   26:17
can idealist Christian, William Ernest Hocking, who in 1956 prophesied a "coming world civilization." Hocking had said that "our present period is one of general and reciprocal osmosis of thought, technique, art, and law" and that "these processes can neither be stopped nor undone; the lines that have 'gone forth into all the world' cannot return to their origin." The human task was

now to transform "this human history into the pattern of a divine community." Over against such thinkers Wagar posed "doctrinaires," chiefly Catholics and Muslims. Each "demanded that the whole world submit to its particular idea of a theocratic world so-. ciety, and even its particular theology, ritual, and law." Both "still had devotees who dream of a world united under their sign, cross, or crescent." Wagar wrote this during the half-century when the number of Muslims in the world was increasing from one in seven to one in five. "A rejuvenated Islam astride half the world is no fantastic prospect." And Catholicism remained astonishingly vital. Wagar had to deal with particularist critics, enemies of the envisioned integrative world philosophy. Their favorite words for synthetic visions, he knew, were "mishmash," "syncretism," "eclecticism," and "hodgepodge." Many religionists still wrote in such terms. Countering their narrowness was the hunger of people for whom "nothing else matters so crucially to the organic wholeness of civilized life" as this integrative vision. "Practically everybody who has written recently on the subject of religion, for or against, agrees that the contemporary crisis in religion is radical, painful, decisive, and tragic."

26:18   World civilization clearly could not survive without some form of religion, some search for ultimate reality and ultimate unity. Wagar relied on Hocking to point some ways. For the Harvard philosopher, "radical displacement" of one faith or culture by another, as sought in missionary movements that attempted to convert, could no longer do. Surprisingly, given what one would have expected at this point, Wagar had to agree with Hocking that the "way of synthesis" took too long and led to artificiality, to "inorganic aggregates, not true religions." The only alternative was the third way, the "way of reconception." The existing faiths were all "wretched vessels," all "wrapped in sanctimony, dusty-eyed with self-satisfaction," their leaders not daring to engage in the "perilous task of *thinking*." Now they must think. Hocking foresaw no single, united global religion, even though the faiths were all "already fused together, so to speak, at the top." Now each would keep its integral identity. Toynbee thought that "all religions, while retaining their historic identities, will become more and more open-minded, and (what is more important) open-hearted, towards one another." Thus "the World's different cultural and spiritual heritages" would become, "in increasing measure, the common possession of all Mankind."

26:19   Wagar looked around at how candidates for this "open" approach were doing, in order to see how reconception was occurring. He was pleased by the ecumenism, for Catholics, of the current Vatican Council and also by Catholic-Buddhist dialogues. Paul Tillich among Protestants was offering visions of religions meeting. Historian-philosopher Franklin Baumer at that time discerned the outlines of a "Layman's Religion" that was impatient with clerisy and dogma. Ahead there had to be "an all-encompassing world faith." Wagar appended a bedeviling last chapter in which he asked the question that readers who followed him thus far had to have in mind: "Who Will Integrate the Integrators?" Here Lawrence Frank was his witness. The haunting idea of world order always gets compromised, Frank said, because "each proposal has demanded acceptance of the particular religion, philosophy, political organization, or military power of the proponent." The humanist Charles Frankel arrived on that scene and seemed to help somewhat when he said that "social integration in a liberal society does not come from integrating ultimate values. It comes from organizing secular institutions in such a way that men's 'ultimate' values—their consciences, their sense of the meaning of life, their personal dignity—do not become elements of public conflict." Of course, religious conservatives would be smart enough to dismiss this kind of thinking as secular humanism, as itself a sort of "particular religion" that, like all the others, demanded acceptance. And Wagar himself would go further than Frankel: "there will be no world civilization without a substantial measure of tentative agreement among its intellectual leaders" on several matters, including ultimate values. He regretted that the prophets themselves had set a bad example by working in isolation. That individualism or isolation would have to change, until what Karl Mannheim called "integrative behavior" would result.

Wagar was not a widely known intellectual, his book was a non-classic, and his register of world synthesizers included then-stellar but now out-of-fashion thinkers. Far from seeing him as intrusive or excursive in a book on American public religion around 1960, I am contending that he described well an ethos and an agenda picked up in highly diverse ways by Protestant, Catholic, and Jewish thinkers in the One Nation, Under God, that was America. From such a vantage, the conception of this period as "the liberal hour" makes sense, as do the components of this liberalism that verged on utopianism; some of the details need revisiting. First of all, one had to keep an eye on the new political ethos in the era when—as Lipman and Vorspan had put it—Protestants, Catholics,

26:20

and Jews had been "in unblushing competition with one another not so much for the individual souls of Americans, but, in a sense, for the American soul, for the opportunity to shape American culture in the image of the religious ethic of each." But whereas those two writers had been noticing that the three religious communities under study did share secularism as an enemy that could not quiet their "interreligious tensions," now the secular world was greeted as a potential ally, and genuine efforts to reduce tensions were proceeding. That was a novel argument in the Protestant and to some extent Catholic avant-garde, and some progressive Jewish thinkers argued that they had favored this openness to secularity for a long time.

26:21   The National Council of Churches continued into the new times, and its leaders used the ten-year-old organization to advance a program of advocacy and activism, especially on the civil rights front, in the war on poverty, and in international relations. With the National Lay Committee's opposition from within long gone and the moderates silent or silenced, the story of the National Council in these terms could have been written under the title *The Liberal Hour*. But council leadership was increasingly distanced from its constituency. Not many years later even General Secretary R. H. Edwin Espy allowed in public that "the National Council is 'tightly run by a small clique of bureaucrats.'" Liberal theologian Harvey Cox, a friend in general of the council, also now looked back on its development as being part of the "managerial revolution" of technically equipped experts who were out of touch with the people "whom they are supposed to represent." "Activist ministers," who must "frequently contend with the socially conservative laymen who sit on the boards and committees that rule the parish" lost sympathy for people like council leaders who were "more insulated from direct lay control."

26:22   Espy did not want the council to retreat. In 1961, in the headiest minutes of the liberal hour, he kept saying why religion and republic, church and state, council and government had to be close: "The nation and the world impinge on our lives in a degree unimagined two generations ago." Government was an impinger: "Whether we like it or not, big government is with us and is here to stay." Paradoxically, "at a time when the national government has penetrated our lives so deeply," he said, many citizens were "reluctant as a people to share in determining its policies." But the churches were "in contact increasingly and inescapably with the federal government" in the Kennedy years. "The church," wrote Espy, "must

Cynthia Clark Wedel represented the kind of ecumenical leadership that became prominent in the 1950s and shortly thereafter. In the course of her career she held leadership posts in Church Women United (as president, 1955–58), in the World Council of Churches, and the National Council of Churches. She was also an observer at the Second Vatican Council. (Photo: National Council of the Churches of Christ in the USA.)

skillfully and prophetically point its people to opportunities for Christian witness and service in the life of the community, both governmental and non-governmental." There was theological vision behind this: "God is the ruler of both the church and the state, as of all the affairs of men. His voice must be heard by the state." While the church "is not equated with God, it is expected by God to be a special instrument of his will." Espy even had evidence that "many of our government leaders expect and desire the church to speak in this sense—from the high plane of Divine perspective insofar as this is humanly possible."

The Vatican Council was to alter the situation of the World   26:23 Council of Churches, which also opened the decade with its every-sixth-year meeting in 1961 at New Delhi. Americans were brought close to the non-European ecumenical sphere as never before. But questions about the prospects for unity were beginning to be raised not just from Asia and Africa but from within the European and American spheres. Keith Bridston and Walter Wagoner coedited a critical book, *Unity in Mid-Career,* and in it ecumenist Ralph Hyslop observed: "Councils, councils, everywhere. But none to make us one." Presbyterian Lewis S. Mudge, Jr., said, "Never before has the World Council of Churches had more prestige, forged ahead more effectively on a multitude of fronts, or been more genuinely useful to its member churches," yet, he noted, the movement toward unity was virtually stalled. Mudge kept making the theological point: "Organic unity is something we seek primarily because the Gospel requires us to break one bread and confess one faith in each place." The emphasis was clear, even if the reality did not appear: "Where we are dealing with a single, organic unity of society, the unity of the Church must also be organic."

26:24   Bridston and Wagoner insulted the ecumenical organizations but never wavered in support of the ecumenical spirit. "The tides of Christian unity, moving wave on wave, for more than fifty years have been mounting and deepening," and they themselves would not resist the surge, nor could any human-made dikes. "The great spiritual tide of unity will prevail," they were sure, however much humans might try to divert or dam it." The critics said they had "deep affection" for the World Council, which was the "center of many of the most poignant ecumenical hopes" of the day. But movements of reformation and renewal gel; lava hardens. Bridston now saw the council in the light of Quaker economist Kenneth Boulding's *Organizational Revolution.* It was coming under iron laws of the "almost irresistible influence of oligarchical, hierarchical, and monopolistic forces in institutional evolution." It was an institution, and "the natural tendency of an institution is to remain at rest, to stay where it is, to be immobile," and, in this case, to be "a kind of ecclesiastical monstrosity." It needed shaking up: "the only real alternative to politics is bureaucratic domination," and it was becoming an instrument of such domination as older people ran it. Given "its size and prestige and ecclesiastical dignity," the council would henceforth "inevitably lack the spirit of heretical nonconformity, the mood of restless experimentation, the willingness (and ability) to risk failures, the passion for change, that are the indelible seals of youth."

26:25   If local, state, national, and world councils of churches were turning into hardened bureaucracies, expressing motifs of religious

activism in the liberal hour but losing touch with their constituencies, or being displaced in part by Catholicism's entrance on the
scene, this did not mean that the avant-gardes in synagogue and
church were giving up on ecumenism or interfaith ventures. Just
the opposite: they were bent on enlarging these, on finding new
and larger venues and surprising fresh allies. Now the attempt to
win the soul of America was to be marked by coalescences with
the open, softer, good-willed side of the old enemy, the representatives of the secular. Some in the religious avant-garde began to
speak of "secular ecumenism." The New Frontier and the civil
rights movement threw Protestant, Catholic, Jewish, and secular
persons together, in marches and demonstrations, in efforts to promote a welfare society and to capture idealism, as in the Peace
Corps. There was a sudden new openness to technology on the part
of theologians in churches where science, the industrial age, and
technology itself had been seen as preemptions of the divine,
"playing God," forming their own priesthoods, protecting their
own sacred cows. Technology was to be a friend, not the enemy.

Theological optimism, though it matched the technological   26:26
counterpart, was the proper language for religious radicals in the
brief liberal hour. Near its end in 1964, Americans imported
Bishop John A. T. Robinson's British best-seller *Honest to God,*
which offered a kind of Christian vision of a world with ever
greater measures of human mastery, and many theologians devoted
themselves to celebrations of German theologian Dietrich Bonhoeffer's concept of "religionless Christianity" for a "world come
of age." At the end of the liberal hour, at the last possible moment
in which one could credibly write in this mode, Protestant William
Hamilton, a "secular Christian" on the way to celebrity, wrote in
1963 and published in 1965 an essay that only said more clearly
what so many theologians were probing. The new believers in their
move from the cloister to the world did "not ask God to do for us
what the world is qualified to do. Really to travel along this road
means that we trust the world, not God, to be our need fulfiller and
problem solver, and God, if he is to be for us at all, must come in
some other role." Meanwhile, added Hamilton, "in the time of
waiting we have a place to be. It is not before an altar, it is in the
world, in the city, with both the needy neighbor and the enemy."
That place defined the faith. Hamilton conceived "our being in
the world, in the city" not only as "an obedience to the Reformation formula, from church to world," but "an obedience to Jesus
himself."

26:27   Thinkers like Hamilton, at home with the secular, had no need for the historic church. "The church is present whenever Christ is being formed among men in the world." Jesus Christ was "best understood as neither the object nor the ground of faith, neither as person, event or community, but simply as a place to be, a standpoint." This place, Hamilton said, "is, of course, alongside the neighbor, being for him," as with the Negro in the civil rights struggle. "He is also with all sorts of other groups: poets and critics, psychiatrists and physicists and philosophers," eager to be attentive "as a man and therefore as a theologian." Paul Van Buren, an Episcopal theologian influenced by Karl Barth, also promoted "secular Christianity." He was clear about the venture: "We are saying that it is possible today to be agnostic about 'otherworldly' powers and beings, but that people matter." The alternatives seemed to be "a sectarian secularism which ignores essential elements of the Gospel, giving us a faith without Christ or a Christ without Jesus, or a very orthodox but meaningless faith which refuses to enter the secular world." Van Buren hoped that this interpretation might "claim for a secular Christianity the full tradition of the faith."

26:28   Harvey Cox, meanwhile, was asking for people of faith to build the secular city. Secularization meant "the loosing of the world from religions and quasi-religious understandings of itself, the dispelling of all closed world-views, the breaking of all supernatural myths and sacred symbols." Yes, there were religious vitalities. But "the age of the secular city, the epoch whose ethos is quickly spreading into every corner of the globe, *is* an age of 'no religion at all.'" Cox urged others not to name nationalism, Nazism, or communism "religions." No, "secularization rolls on, and if we are to understand and communicate with our present age we must learn to love it in its unremitting secularity." His advice: "it will do no good to cling to our religious and metaphysical versions of Christianity in the hope that one day religion or metaphysics will once again be back." No, "they are disappearing forever and that means we can now let go and immerse ourselves in the new world of the secular city." One could make a hero, Cox thought, of the recently assassinated John F. Kennedy for his pragmatism. The pragmatist "does not ask religious questions because he fully believes he can handle this world without them." And he cited Albert Camus, who "did not allow his atheism to deteriorate in a fanatic anti-theism, which would have been a new religion"—yet who was an exemplar for a new time. Did the assassination of Kennedy

and the senseless death of Camus in an automobile accident compromise Cox's vision? "I think not," he said, for it was "still the
spirit of Kennedy which triumphs, not that of his murderer." There
were still darker currents in the day, and eruptions of irrationality,
but they need not triumph.

Cox criticized the civic faith of the period immediately pre-   26:29
ceding the liberal hour. He feared lest Protestants and their new
friends, Catholics and Jews, would link up in Brotherhood Week
fashion, urging that "after all we are all Americans and have
a common religious heritage." No, it was the secularization of
America, he argued, that brought about the emancipation of Jews
and thus of Protestants. The three faiths should not seek "a kind of
tripartite American religion." Instead, "Christians should continue
to support the secularization of American society, recognizing that
secularists, atheists, and agnostics do not have to be second-class
citizens." Now, Cox said for the whole population, "the secularists
of America may be God's way of warning us that the era of sacred
societies is over." Therefore, "the task of American Christians vis-
à-vis their nonreligious fellow citizens is not to browbeat them but
to make sure they stay secular."

In 1960, before Cox wrote thus, but discussing the world the   26:30
theologian described, economic historian Robert Heilbroner used
a different genre, speaking of the future as history in a book of that
title. He addressed the worldview of the optimist. "At bottom, *a
philosophy of optimism is an historic attitude toward the future—*
an attitude based on the tacit premise that the future will accommodate the striving which we bring to it." Thus "optimism is
grounded in the faith that the historic environment, as it comes into
being, will prove to be benign and congenial—or at least neutral
to our private efforts." William Hamilton wrote best in that mood,
too. He reviewed the fifteen years that had passed before he wrote.
Several figures and features stood out. Reinhold Niebuhr and his
Moral Man and Immoral Society had matched the mood of the
Depression and war. But "neoorthodoxy was in part a pessimistic
theology, even though many have made that point insensitively."
In its prime, neoorthodoxy "took psychotherapy, existentialism, I
and Thou in its stride," turning to the inner world of the human,
away from the outer world of politics. Born to oppose the bourgeois, it ironically became "one of the fashionable ideologies for
the Eisenhower period in American intellectual life." Hamilton
watched the neoorthodox Jew Will Herberg move to become religion editor for conservative William F. Buckley's magazine and

enter its orbit. The theologian's acid comment: "Old Niebuhrians tended to go to the back pages of the *National Review* to die." The tragic sense, thought Hamilton, "went along quite well with good manners, nice clothes, sensitivity to interpersonal relations, and a good conscience about the rat-race."

26:31   Now, however, neoorthodoxy would not work because during these years of the New Frontier and the Great Society it became clear that "this pessimism doesn't persuade any more." Hamilton thought that instead "optimism is a possibility for man and a necessity for some today in a way that has not been the case in America for some time." He marked January 4, 1965, the day of gloomy Christian poet T. S. Eliot's death and Lyndon B. Johnson's announcement of the forthcoming Great Society, as a date that could symbolize the change of sensibility. But even as Hamilton was writing, there was war in Vietnam. What about it? The theologian judged that "in spite of Vietnam today, America is not afraid, and it once more is beginning to take seriously the fact that it has a real future." America was sending supplies and consultants to South Vietnam to help ward off the increasingly pesky communist guerrillas and North Vietnamese invaders, but all that was far away. The legislative record of Congress that spring showed that "this shift we are charting from pessimism to optimism can also be described as a move from alienation to politics, from blues to the freedom song."

26:32   Hamilton pointed for an example of the trend to Quaker economist Kenneth Boulding, who in *The Meaning of the Twentieth Century* described a move "from a civilized to a post-civilized society," along the way shedding no tears for the civilized one. The postcivilized age was "the age of the mass media, of automation, of the constantly accelerating rate of change." Boulding worked at the Conflict Resolution Center in Ann Arbor, where the atmosphere was "one of a resolute confidence and optimism that even the really intractable problems that have marked our civilized period can be overcome, problems as apparently irreducible as war and mental illness." Hamilton also pointed to Marshall McLuhan, another celebrity who had great influence on Americans as he foresaw that in the media age "the process of knowing will very shortly be extended to the whole of human society, not merely to those we call educated in some limited sense." His was, like Boulding's, "an optimism about the future, and will remind some of the venerable doctrine of progress over which we have preached so many funeral orations." People like Boulding and McLuhan were still in a mi-

nority, thought the theologian, but, he said, they "see what is going
on, and invite us to responsible and excited participation." The
social science of such people gave "a radical 'yes' to this century."
The arts offered further evidence. Lionel Trilling had just pub-   26:33
lished a "difficult and beautiful essay" about "the new America in
which optimism is possible, the America in which the radical theology is trying to live." The music of John Cage rejected the modern tradition and offered a "play that affirms life." Robert Rausch-
enberg assembled ordinary things to produce "something gay and
beautiful." In popular music, the Beatles' sound was "part of this
mood of celebration and rejoicing." The civil rights movement was
the "most decisive piece of evidence." Why? "That there is a gaiety, an absence of alienation, a vigorous and contagious hope at the
center of this movement is obvious and this optimism is the main
source of its hold on the conscience of America, particularly young
America." The song "We Shall Overcome" leads one "into the
world of historical optimism, in which this world is the place, and
now is the time, for the making of the long-overdue changes." Jews
were part of all this. Hamilton showed Norman Podhoretz, editor
of *Commentary,* being Dionysian in mood and vision. A few years
earlier Podhoretz had worried about the premature adulthood of the
generation that emerged "before the civil rights movement and the
New Frontier rescued them from their inner preoccupation." And
now he quoted Podhoretz as an agent of the new optimism; he listened in as the Jewish editor said, "And something very wonderful may come about when a whole generation in its late thirties
breaks loose and decides to take a swim in the Plaza [Hotel] foun-
tain in the middle of the night." Hamilton saw the prediction of
Podhoretz coming true; "Pessimism—political, theological, cultural—is coming to an end. The Plaza pool is crowded these
nights."

What, Hamilton asked, "does theology make of this new opti-   26:34
mism?" In the immediately previous period of pessimism people
read Paul, Augustine, Kierkegaard. Who should they read now?
Writings about Jesus offered some clues. But others should look
up additional and new sources; the old orthodoxies and neoorthodoxy were devoted to the tragic sense of life. But now there are
"no tragedies around," because "there can't be tragedies." Why?
"Because the presence of tragedy requires the presence of God or
the gods, and the presence of the gods is just what we do not have."
What we did have was optimism: "I have been concerned," said
Hamilton, "to establish a new mood of optimism in American cul-

ture." Tragedy henceforth was "culturally impossible, or unlikely. We trust the world, we trust the future, we deem even many of our intractable problems just soluble enough to reject the tragic mode of facing them."

26:35   Postscript: In July 1965, after Hamilton wrote for his generation but before his article was published, President Lyndon B. Johnson committed large numbers of American troops to a land war in Southeast Asia. As for the domestic American scene, especially in respect to the gaiety, absence of alienation, and the optimism of the civil rights movement: after the passage of the civil rights legislation in early summer of that year, African Americans rioted in August and set fire to Watts in Los Angeles, portending a new stage in race relations and urban change in America. Such incidents render the climate of the period just before those incidents irretrievable. Theist and realist Langdon Gilkey, perhaps the best analyst of secular and radical theology in "the liberal hour" and one who could appreciate some of its expression, with the advantage that came with four years of retrospect commented on the thought of Hamilton and his kind: it was turning more optimistic, liberal, and humanistic "at the very moment when, ironically, the most 'with it' movements in secularism, the hippies, the New Left, and the ble.k power movement have precisely lost this faith in the possibilities of our democratic society." But they are part of another, later story. At the end of this one, they were signalling the arrival of a new America, one that divided the people—racially, ethnically, philosophically, esthetically, economically, in respect to gender, and not least of all in religion. These were citizens, most of whom through World War II and the postwar period had worked seriously and hoped profoundly that they were, in the world of surrounding insecurity and change, at least and at last realizing the vision of their One Nation, Under God, Indivisible.

Notes

Chapter One

1:1. See Martin E. Marty, *Modern American Religion,* Volume 1: *The Irony of It All, 1893–1919* (Chicago: University of Chicago, 1986).

1:2. Martin E. Marty, *Modern American Religion,* Volume 2: *The Noise of Conflict, 1919–1941* (Chicago: University of Chicago Press, 1991), 3–4.

1:3. Ibid., 334–45.

1:4. Frankfurter is quoted in Robert T. Miller and Ronald B. Flowers, *Toward Benevolent Neutrality: Church, State, and the Supreme Court,* 3d ed. (Waco: Markham Press Fund, 1987) in Minersville School District v. Gobitis 310 U.S. 586 at 596 (1940).

1:5. Frankfurter pleaded for common symbols in the case just mentioned. Later chapters of this book will enlarge upon the Judeo-Christian, Protestant-Catholic-Jew, and other convergent concepts mentioned in this paragraph.

1:6. As I shall mention at the end of this book, the period following the one covered here will not easily admit to the chronological treatment in these three volumes, each of which is independent of the others or which can be taken together. It will probably be a set of stories that help account for the religious roots of what has come to be called "multiculturalism" and will, in any case, describe the centrifugal impulses that dominated after the mid-sixties of the century.

1:7. Bernard Crick, *In Defence of Politics* (Baltimore: Penguin Books, 1964), 176, derides the whole notion of "consensus" in a diverse society like that of the United States; the only one he professed to find in that nation was "G. Marx's existentialist *cri de coeur:* 'Take care of me. I am the only one I've got.' "

1:8. Molly Haskell, *From Reverence to Rape: The Treatment of Women in the Movies* (New York: Penguin Books, 1974), 234; Brandon French, *On the Verge of Revolt: Women in American Films of the Fifties* (New York: Frederick Ungar, 1978), 154; both are quoted in Wini Breines, *Young, White, and Miserable: Growing Up Female in the Fifties* (Boston: Beacon Press, 1992), 1, 205. Breines brings together references to a considerable literature that questions stereotypes of sexual and other identities in the 1950s.

1:9. See chapter 20.

1:10. Chafe is quoted in Glenna Matthews, *The Rise of Public Woman: Woman's Power and Woman's Place in the United States, 1630–1970* (New York: Oxford University Press, 1992), 188, where Matthews's own comment appears; see also ibid., 3–4, 223. Matthews, 188, also quotes Chafe: "Mary Anderson [Chief of the Women's Bureau of the Department of Labor] concluded that the WAC [Women's Army Corps, originally WAAC, the other 'A' standing for 'Auxiliary'] had been created as a calculated device to put women 'off in a corner' while denying them any real power.' "

1:11. The literature on multiculturalism, with its critique of the culture of dominance, is enormous; it will be a major theme in the fourth volume of *Modern American Religion*. For now, one can gain access to it conveniently through an anthology edited by David Theo Goldberg, *Multiculturalism: A Critical Reader* (Cambridge, Mass.: Blackwell Publishers, 1994); the bibliography, pp. 429–41, is especially useful.

1:12. William Chafe records the arrival of the homogenizing era in television: "Two years after the war 7,000 TV sets were sold. Three years later the figure had leaped to 7 million. By the middle of the 1950s, 66 per cent of all homes boasted their own television. As Max Lerner declared, TV had become 'the poor man's luxury because it is his psychological necessity.' . . . Television altered the shape of the culture, bringing people from the most disparate backgrounds together in a common experience. . . . For the most part, television reinforced the conservative, celebratory values of the dominant culture. 'I Remember Mama' offered a vision of immigrant life designed to warm every American heart with its depiction of assimilation, upward mobility, and ethnic nostalgia. . . . Shows like 'Father Knows Best,' in turn reassured Americans that traditional male authority and female subservience offered the only way to true happiness." William Chafe, *The Unfinished Journey: America Since World War II* (New York: Oxford University Press, 1986), 128–30.

1:13. These three are quoted in ibid., 141–42, in a long sequence of citations reinforcing the theme of conformity, though Chafe also discerned signs from the "subsoil," countercultural signals coming from beatnik poets, existentialists, film stars like James Dean and Marlon Brando.

1:14. Stephanie Coontz, *The Way We Never Were: American Families and the Nostalgia Trap* (New York: Basic Books, 1992) devotes many pages to the 1950s; see also Wini Breines, *Young, White, and Miserable; W. T. Lhamon, Jr., Deliberate Speed: The Origins of a Cultural Style in the American 1950s* (Washington: Smithsonian Institution Press, 1990).

1:15. Marty, *The Noise of Conflict*, 6–8, elaborates on social, intellectual, and cultural history as here conceived.

1:16. Thomas E. Crow, *Painters and Public Life in Eighteenth-Century Paris* (New Haven: Yale University Press, 1985), 5.

1:17. Celeste Michelle Condit, *Decoding Abortion Rhetoric: Communicating Social Change* (Urbana: University of Illinois Press, 1990), 4.

1:18. Ibid., 5–7. Condit commends Bernard L. Brock and Robert L. Scott, *Methods of Rhetorical Criticism*, 2d ed., rev. (Detroit: Wayne State University Press, 1980) and James R. Andrews, *The Practice of Rhetorical Criticism* (New York: Macmillan, 1983) as introductions to this subject.

1:19. See Condit, *Decoding Abortion Rhetoric*, 9; she cites Jürgen Habermas, *Communication and the Evolution of Society* (Boston: Beacon Press, 1979) and Douglas Ehninger, "Argument as Method: Its Nature, Its Limits, and Its Uses," *Communication Monographs*

37 (June 1979). Condit elaborates her "double articulation" theory on 226 and cites Murray Edelman, *The Symbolic Uses of Politics* (Urbana: University of Illinois Press, 1964).

1:20. Peter Laslett, *The World We Have Lost* (New York: Macmillan, 1984) deals with a different past, but provides a provocative and relevant image concerning the difficulty of retrieving many elements and the impossibility of recovering all, especially when changes have been so sudden and drastic as they have been in the half century and more after 1941.

1:21. Douglas L. Wilson, "Imposing on the Past," *Illinois Issues,* January 18, 1994, 20.

1:22. Ibid., 21.

1:23. Martin E. Marty, *The New Shape of American Religion* (New York: Harper and Row, 1959), especially 67–68.

1:24. Ibid., 111, 113, 118–21; see chapters 7 and 8, "The Poise of the Parish" and "The Practice of the Parish," 134–57, for a view of congregating as a base for renewal.

1:25. Ibid., 166.

1:26. Ibid., 167–68. The reference is to H. Richard Niebuhr, *The Meaning of Revelation* (New York: Macmillan, 1951), 40–41.

Chapter Two

2:1. For reference to pacifism before the war and to opinion polls, see Lawrence S. Wittner, *Rebels Against War: The American Peace Movement* (New York: Columbia University Press, 1969), 3, 6–7; Hadley Cantril, ed., *Public Opinion, 1935–1946* (Princeton: Princeton University Press, 1951), 966, 978; Francis Sill Wickware, "What We Think About Foreign Affairs," *Harper's* 179 (September 1939): 404; Jeanette Rankin, "Two Votes Against War—1917, 1941," *Liberation* 3 (March 1958): 4–7.

2:2. Wittner, *Rebels Against War,* 3, 6–7; see also Vernon Howard Holloway, "American Pacifism Between Two Wars, 1919–1941" (Ph.D. diss., Yale University, 1949): 176–82, 200.

2:3. Peter Maurin wrote in the *Catholic Worker* 5 (July-August 1939); Thomas was quoted in Harry Fleischman, *Norman Thomas: A Biography* (New York: W. W. Norton, 1964), 195.

2:4. On the role of clergy, see Ray H. Abrams, "The Churches and the Clergy in World War II," *Annals of the Academy of Political and Social Science* 256 (March 1948): 111–19; Donald H. Meyer, *The Protestant Search for Political Realism, 1919–1941* (Berkeley: University of California Press, 1960), 350–54; Wittner, *Rebels Against War,* 30; Edwin Buehrer wrote in *Christian Century* 56 (May 17, 1939): 645.

2:5. Reinhold Niebuhr, *Christianity and Power Politics* (New York: Scribner's 1940), ix, 4; Harold E. Fey in *Christian Century* 57 (March 6, 1940): 325.

2:6. For reference to Federal Council of Churches activities, see Abrams, "The Churches and the Clergy," 111–19; Meyer, *The Protestant Search,* 350–54.

2:7. "Hitler's Victory," *Christian Century* 57 (June 26, 1940): 814–16; "Future of France," *Christian Century* 57 (September 25, 1940): 1167; "A Crisis in American Peace Policy," *Christian Century* 54 (October 20, 1937): 1286; Meyer, *The Protestant Search,* 382, shows how Morrison equated "church" with religious culture growing out of America's special character, and 384–85 develops the insight about the defense of Protestant culture.

2:8. *Christian Century* 58 (March 26, 1941): 415–17; Meyer, *The Protestant Search,* 360.

2:9. Meyer, *The Protestant Search,* 360; *Information Service* 19 (June 1, 1940):

8; *Christian Century* 58 (January 22, 1941): 134; Henry Pitney Van Dusen, "Irresponsible Idealism," *Christian Century* 57 (July 24, 1940): 924–25.

2:10. Charles Clayton Morrison, *The Christian and the War* (Chicago: Willett, Clark and Co., 1942), 60–61.

2:11. On the laws and administration, see Peter Brock, *Twentieth-Century Pacifism* (New York: Van Nostrand Reinhold, 1970), 171–74.

2:12. Wittner, *Rebels Against War,* 41; see also Vernon H. Holloway, "A Review of American Religious Pacifism," *Religion in Life* 19 (Summer 1950): 369.

2:13. Wittner, *Rebels Against War,* 45, gives statistics of Mennonite, Church of the Brethren, and Quaker conscientious objectors; for Rufus Jones's words, see "Quakers Affirm Peace Witness," *Christian Century* 57 (July 17, 1940): 909.

2:14. Guy L. Hershberger, *War, Peace, and Nonresistance* (Scottsdale, Pa.: The Herald Press, 1944), 188–89, 195, 197–200.

2:15. Wittner, *Rebels Against War,* 72–75.

2:16. Ibid., 83–84, 77–79; 86–96 is an ample accounting of organized resistance.

2:17. Brock, *Twentieth-Century Pacifism,* 174–75.

2:18. Ibid., 178.

2:19. *Catholic Worker* 9 (January 1942) and (March 1942); Dorothy Day, *Loaves and Fishes* (New York: Harper & Row, 1963), 63–64; Dorothy Day, *The Long Loneliness* (New York: Harper Brothers, 1952), 182, 258–59.

2:20. Mel Piehl, *Breaking Bread: The Catholic Worker and the Origin of Catholic Radicalism in America* (Philadelphia: Temple University Press, 1982), 196–97; *Catholic Worker* 7 (July-August, 1940): 1.

2:21. Nancy L. Roberts, *Dorothy Day and the Catholic Worker* (Albany: State University of New York Press, 1984), 123–30, discusses the FBI role; the offending editorial was by Louis Lee Lock, "Forget Pearl Harbor," *Catholic Worker* 9 (December 1942): 3; the quoted letter appears in Day, *Loaves and Fishes,* 62.

2:22. Piehl, *Breaking Bread,* 200–202.

2:23. Francis J. Spellman, *The Road To Victory* (New York: Scribner's, 1942), x.

2:24. "The Churches at War," *Time* (December 22, 1941): 67–68; Morrison, *The Christian and The War,* 58–61.

2:25. Morrison, *The Christian and the War,* 66–69.

2:26. Wittner, *Rebels Against War,* 101; he quoted Norman Vincent Peale writing to A. J. Muste, March 6, 1944, in a letter preserved in Fellowship of Reconciliation files; see Walter Lippmann, *U.S. Foreign Policy: Shield of the Republic* (Boston: Little, Brown, 1943), 53.

2:27. Wittner, *Rebels Against War,* 43–44, lists pacifist Protestants; the story of Tittle is well told in Robert Moats Miller, *How Shall They Hear Without a Preacher? The Life of Ernest Fremont Tittle* (Chapel Hill: University of North Carolina Press, 1971), 435–38.

2:28. Miller, *How Shall They Hear,* 435–38; the sermon, preached on September 24, 1939, appeared in *The First Church Pulpit* 8:1; Herbert Hoover, *An American Epic* (Chicago: Henry Regnery, 1964), IV, 1–73, gives the account.

2:29. Miller, *How Shall They Hear,* 444–47; the Methodist Church's *The Daily Christian Advocate* (May 7, 1940): 461–63.

2:30. Miller, *How Shall They Hear,* 448–49; *Christian Century* 58 (February 5, 1941): 178–80.

2:31. Miller, *How Shall They Hear,* 450–52; Niebuhr, *Christianity and Power Politics,* 33–34; the letter was from Tittle to T. T. Brumbaugh, June 11, 1940.

2:32. Miller, *How Shall They Hear,* 457; the sermon was "The Need for Spiritual

Adventure," *The First Church Pulpit* 4:7, preached December 14, 1941; italics are in the original; the letter was to Walter S. Coffman, December 28, 1942.

2:33. Miller, *How Shall They Hear,* 458–64, an account based on personal interviews and letters, along with *The Daily Christian Advocate* (May 3–8, 1944).

2:34. Wittner, *Rebels Against War,* 55, 57; Jo Ann Robinson, who wrote a dissertation on Muste, condensed its themes in Charles Chatfield, ed., *Peace Movements in America* (New York: Schocken, 1973), 81–85; see also *Time* (July 10, 1939): 37.

2:35. Wittner, *Rebels Against War,* 63–67, based chiefly on Fellowship of Reconciliation and Congress of Racial Equality archives.

2:36. Ibid., 59, quotes Fosdick to Muste, April 27, 1944, from Fellowship of Reconciliation files; see Harry Emerson Fosdick, *The Living of These Days: An Autobiography* (New York: Harper and Brothers, 1956); see also Vera Brittain, *The Rebel Passion: A Short History of Some Pioneer Peace-Makers* (Nyack, N.Y.: Fellowship Publications, 1964), 60; Robinson is quoted in Chatfield, *Peace Movements in America,* 81–84.

Chapter Three

3:1. Carsten Colpe writes on the etymology of "syncretism" in Mircea Eliade, ed., *The Encyclopedia of Religion* (New York: Macmillan, 1987), vol. 14, p. 218: "The term *synkreetismos* first occurs in Plutarch (*Moralia* 490ab). It was probably based on *sugkreetos* (Ionian form of *sugkratos,* "mixed together") and was explained by popular etymology or by Plutarch himself as referring to the behavior of the Cretans who, despite the discord habitual among them, closed ranks when an external enemy attacked them." Discussions of the term in ancient and in Renaissance humanist writings "are based on Plutarch's explanation, which was thus transmitted to the modern period."

3:2. An extensive literature dealing with the home front, the change in mores, and the role of women is developing. See for examples, Karen Anderson, *Wartime Women: Sex Roles, Family Relations and the Status of Women During World War II* (Westport: Greenwood Press, 1976); Richard Polenberg, *America at War: The Home Front* (Englewood Cliffs: Prentice-Hall, 1968); D'Ann Campbell, *Women at War with America: Private Lives in a Patriotic Era* (Cambridge: Harvard University Press, 1984); Leila J. Rupp, *Mobilizing Women for War: German and American Women in the 1940s* (Princeton: Princeton University Press, 1978); Susan M. Hartmann, *The Home Front and Beyond: American Women in the 1940s* (Boston: Twayne Publishers, 1982); John Costello, *Virtue Under Fire: How World War II Changed Our Social and Sexual Attitudes* (Boston: Little, Brown, 1985) which includes an extensive bibliography of works on these subjects published during the war itself. My examination of this literature reveals little attention to women and religion, a rich topic for future research. The most extensive treatment of religion in World War II is Gerald L. Sittser, "A Cautious Patriotism: The American Churches and the Second World War" (Ph.D. diss., University of Chicago, 1989); there are some references to women, family, and the home front in Chapter 6, "The War at Home."

3:3. Ellwood C. Nance, *Faith of Our Fighters* (St. Louis: Bethany Press, 1944), 302–3.

3:4. Ibid., 247–49.

3:5. Ibid., 263–64.

3:6. Ibid., 255, 260.

3:7. Louis J. Roehm, *Tract No. 20* (New York: American Lutheran Publicity Bureau): 23. Otto A. Geiseman, "We Are At War," *The Cresset* 5 (January 1942): 16–22.

3:8. "The Russian Terror," *The Cresset* 2 (June 1939); "Viewing the Polish Remains," *The Cresset* 3 (January 1940); "Finland: The Story," *The Cresset* 3 (January 1940); "Finland: The Lesson," *The Cresset* 3 (January 1940); Theodore M. Graebner, "The Russian Mystery," *The Lutheran Witness* 64 (September 11, 1945): 298.

3:9. Pastor A. M. Motter was answered by Professor E. E. Fischer in "Prayer for Nation's Victory," *The Lutheran* 23 (April 30, 1941): 8.

3:10. F. Ernest Johnson, "The Impact of the War on Religion in America," *The American Journal of Sociology* 48 (November 1942): 353–55.

3:11. Ibid., 354–55, 358.

3:12. Ibid., 359.

3:13. Ibid., 360.

3:14. Daniel A. Poling, *A Preacher Looks at War* (New York: Macmillan, 1943), dedication page.

3:15. Ibid., ix-x.

3:16. Ibid., x-xii, 17, 18.

3:17. Ibid., 18, 20, 26–27, 30–31, 62–66.

3:18. Details of Fosdick's career appear in rich detail in Robert Moats Miller, *Harry Emerson Fosdick: Preacher, Pastor, Prophet* (New York: Oxford University Press, 1985).

3:19. Ibid., 490–91, 517.

3:20. Ibid., 522–25.

3:21. Ibid., 527–28, comments on the company both sides kept and recalls the tone of the argument.

3:22. Ibid., 534–35.

3:23. Harry Emerson Fosdick, *A Great Time to Be Alive: Sermons on Christianity in Wartime* (New York: Harper & Brothers, 1944), 1–2, 8–9.

3:24. Ibid., 50, 146.

3:25. Ibid., 152, 150, 216–17.

3:26. Miller, *Harry Emerson Fosdick*, 536–47, 549, 553.

3:27. Niebuhr during the war years is the subject of "Wiser in Their Generation," Chapter 9, in Richard Wrightman Fox, *Reinhold Niebuhr: A Biography* (New York: Pantheon, 1985), 193–222.

3:28. Ibid., 194–96; see Reinhold Niebuhr, *Christianity and Power Politics* (New York: Scribner's, 1944), 47, 69.

3:29. Fox, *Reinhold Niebuhr*, 196–201; Reinhold Niebuhr, "The Christian Faith and the World Crisis," *Christianity and Crisis* 1 (February 10, 1941): 3; Reinhold Niebuhr, *Christian Realism* (New York: Scribner's, 1953), 17; Reinhold Niebuhr, "Anglo-Saxon Destiny and Responsibility," *Christianity and Crisis* 3 (October 4, 1943): 2; Reinhold Niebuhr, *The Children of Light and the Children of Darkness* (New York: Scribner's, 1944), 153–90.

3:30. Fox, *Reinhold Niebuhr*, 207–9, discusses the activities of the "snoopers." He quotes, among other sources, Frankfurter materials in archives at Harvard Law School.

3:31. Niebuhr, *Children of Light*, 1, 2, 11, 32, 5, 104, 117; Reinhold Niebuhr, "Just or Holy?" *Christianity and Crisis* 1 (November 3, 1941): 1; Reinhold Niebuhr, "The Bombing of Germany," in D. B. Robertson, ed., *Love and Justice* (Philadelphia: Westminster Press, 1957), 222–23; see also "Is the Bombing Necessary?" *Christianity and Crisis* 4 (April 3, 1944): 1–2.

Chapter Four

4:1. Mark Silk, *Spiritual Politics: Religion and America Since World War II* (New York: Simon and Schuster, 1988), Chapter 2, "A New Creed," 40–53, traces the development of the idea of a "Judeo-Christian Tradition"; the phrase about a curiosity becoming the third faith is drawn from a book title, Joseph L. Blau: *Judaism in America: From Curiosity to Third Faith* (Chicago: University of Chicago Press, 1976), which manages to tell a comprehensive story of American Judaism through the centuries without reference to the Holocaust or Zionism during World War II.

4:2. Two books on which we have relied for access to materials on the response to the Holocaust are David S. Wyman, *The Abandonment of the Jews: America and the Holocaust, 1941–1945* (New York: Pantheon, 1984) and Robert W. Ross, *So It Was True: The American Protestant Press and the Nazi Persecution of the Jews* (Minneapolis: University of Minnesota Press, 1980); for Goldenson and Gordon quotes, see Samuel H. Goldenson, "Jewish Moral and Spiritual Thinking," *Yearbook of the Central Conference of American Rabbis* 49 (Philadelphia: Press of the Jewish Publication Society, 1940): 346, and *Yearbook of the Central Conference of American Rabbis* 50 (Philadelphia: Press of the Jewish Publication Society, 1941): 273–74.

4:3. Philipson is quoted in *Yearbook of the Central Conference of American Rabbis* 47 (Philadelphia: Press of the Jewish Publication Society, 1937): 112–13; the resolution is on 98; see *Are Zionism and Reform Incompatible?* (New York: Central Conference of American Rabbis), 48–63; *Yearbook of the Central Conference of American Rabbis* 53 (Philadelphia: Press of the Jewish Publication Society, 1943): 93–94, vote tally on 98; for an account of the debates of these years, see David Polish, *Renew Our Days: The Zionist Issue in Reform Judaism* (Jerusalem: World Zionist Organization, 1976), esp. 231 on the subsequent life of the American Council for Judaism.

4:4. Michael A. Meyer, *Response to Modernity: A History of the Reform Movement in Judaism* (New York: Oxford University Press, 1988), 333–34, recounts the Houston story.

4:5. Wyman, *Abandonment of the Jews,* 162–64, 166–67, 170–77; see also Abba Hillel Silver, *Vision and Victory* (New York: Zionist Organization of America, 1949), 14–21.

4:6. *Yearbook of the Central Conference of American Rabbis* 54 (Philadelphia: Press of the Jewish Publication Society, 1944): 171.

4:7. "It Is Hard to Believe," *The Lutheran Companion* 46 (November 24, 1938): 1479.

4:8. "Terror in Germany," *Christian Century* 55 (November 23, 1938): 1422–23; "Demonic Germany and the Predicament of Humanity," *Christian Century* 55 (November 30, 1938): 1456–58.

4:9. A chronology of events appears in Ross, *So It Was True,* 122–23; "Horror Stories from Poland," *Christian Century* 59 (December 9, 1942): 1518–19.

4:10. Advertisement, *The Presbyterian* 111 (December 11, 1941): 2; "Persecution of the Jews: A Letter from the President of the Baptist World Alliance," *The Watchman-Examiner* 30 (December 24, 1942): 1261.

4:11. Wyman, *Abandonment of the Jews,* 112–22; Law is quoted in Arthur B. Morse, *While Six Million Died* (New York: Random House, 1968), 63; see *New York Times* (May 4, 1943): 17; Wyman cites a letter from Niebuhr, Daniel Poling, G. Bromley Oxnam, and others to Roosevelt, August 6, 1943.

4:12. *Christian Century* 59 (December 9, 1942): 1518–19.

4:13. Wyman, *Abandonment of the Jews,* 43–45, on the State Department relations to Wise, citing Paul T. Culbertson in a letter of August 13, 1942; 47, discusses Wise's efforts to get support for islands of refuge or food; 51 reports on the conversation with Welles; see Stephen S. Wise, *Challenging Years: The Autobiography of Stephen S. Wise* (New York: G. P. Putnam's, 1949), 275–76. Wise is quoted from his letter in the *Christian Century* 60 (January 13, 1943): 53.

4:14. Wise, *Christian Century* 60 (January 13, 1943): 53. Wise, *Challenging Years,* 274-79, for the rabbi's account; "A Return to Barbarism in Eastern Europe," *Christian Century* 60 (February 3, 1943): 125; "Polish Atrocities are Entered in the Books," *Christian Century* 59 (December 30, 1942): 1611.

4:15. Wyman, *Abandonment of the Jews,* 64, 102-3; *Commonweal* 37 (December 11, 1942): 204-5, and (December 18, 1942): 220; *World Alliance News Letter,* December 1942 and thereafter, kept promoting the cause; "Various Messages and Resolutions Adopted by the Council's Biennial Meeting," *Federal Council Bulletin* 26 (January 1943): 12; "Christian Concern for the Suffering Jews," *Federal Council Bulletin* 26 (February 1943): 4-5; "Observance of the Day of Compassion," *Federal Council Bulletin* 26 (June 1943): 6; Karl M. Chworowsky of the Flatbush Unitarian Church in Brooklyn, N.Y., wrote the letter "'Day of Compassion' Ignored," *Christian Century* 60 (June 2, 1943): 669; "The Chief Rabbi May Well Complain," *Christian Century* 60 (March 3, 1943): 253; "Britain to Transfer Jewish Children to Palestine," *Christian Century* 60 (March 10, 1943): 284.

4:16. Wyman, *Abandonment of the Jews,* 101, quotes a letter from Goldenstein to Clinchy, March 3, 1943, and a response the next day from Clinchy.

4:17. "Biggest Atrocity Story Breaks in Poland," *Christian Century* 61 (September 13, 1944): 1045; Ross, *So It Was True,* 203, continues the chronology in 1945; see also "Have Jews a Jewish Citizenship?" *Christian Century* 62 (January 3, 1945): 4-5; "Gazing into the Pit," *Christian Century* 62 (May 9, 1945): 575-76.

4:18. "The Jewish Problem," *The Watchman-Examiner* 33 (November 8, 1945): 1080.

4:19. Wyman, *Abandonment of the Jews,* 609, discusses restriction; 5-9 elaborate on anti-Semitism; see also David Wyman, *Paper Walls: America and the Refugee Crisis* (Amherst: University of Massachusetts Press, 1968), 10-14.

4:20. *Christian Century* 60 (March 10, 1943): 284.

Chapter Five

5:1. A generalization that awaits full-length documentation and development is in C. Eric Lincoln, *Race, Religion, and the Continuing American Dilemma* (New York: Hill and Wang, 1984), pp. 89-90: "The most crucial achievement of the World War II era was black ethnicity, and among the institutions most critically affected was the Black Church." African American military people during the war had seen the world; "They had discovered black ethnicity. For strength they turned toward each other, and the principal symbol of their inner strength was the Black Church, which had always been the reservoir of black togetherness and the affirmation of superlative value in being what God had designed them to be."

5:2. Gunnar Myrdal, *An American Dilemma: The Negro Problem and Modern Democracy* (New York: Harper & Brothers, 1944), viii.

5:3. Ibid., xix, 755-56.

5:4. Ibid., 997-98, 1002-4, 1006-7, 1010-11, 1014-15, 1022.

5:5. Ibid., 858-59.

5:6. Ibid., 862-63.

5:7. Ibid., 864-67.

5:8. Ibid., 868, 871-73; also quoting Edwin R. Embree, *Brown America: The Story of a New Race* (New York: Viking Press, 1931), 208-9.

5:9. Ibid., 872-78.

5:10. See the introduction by Richard Wright to St. Clair Drake and Horace R.

Cayton, *Black Metropolis: A Study of Negro Life in a Northern City* (New York: Harcourt, Brace, 1945), xvii–xxi.

5:11. Wright in Drake and Cayton, *Black Metropolis,* xxi, xxiii, xxv, xxvii–xxxii.

5:12. Drake and Cayton, *Black Metropolis,* 412–13, 415–16.

5:13. Ibid., 416–20, 422–24.

5:14. Ibid., 650–57, 677–79, 682, 710; "The Middle-Class Way of Life," Chapter 22, 658–715, details the new goal of Bronzeville.

5:15. Ibid., 745–55, 767.

Chapter Six

6:1. For a general introduction to the story of Japanese-American incarceration during World War II, see Roger Daniels, *Concentration Camps, North America: Japanese in the United States and Canada During World War II* (Malabar, Fla.: R. E. Krieger and Co., rev. ed., 1981).

6:2. Allen R. Bosworth, *America's Concentration Camps* (New York: W. W. Norton, 1967), 60, quotes McLemore from *San Francisco Examiner* files (January 29, 1942); Warren is quoted in Robert A. Wilson and Bill Hosokawa, *East to America: A History of the Japanese in America* (New York: William Morrow, 1980) 197, 209; the Lavery material is from a letter he wrote to President Truman, reported in *Pacific Citizen* (September 24, 1949).

6:3. See Hazel Takii Morikawa, *Footprints: One Man's Pilgrimage: A Biography of Jitsuo Morikawa* (Berkeley, Calif.: Jennings Associates, 1990). Hundreds of such family memoirs are available. I selected this one because of personal acquaintance with the subjects and thus some extra ability to judge perspectives on a still controversial incident.

6:4. Ibid., 29.

6:5. Ibid., 29, 38–46, tells of Morikawa's conversion, 46–53 deals with father-son relations and the furthering of his education, 54–63 with seminary and marriage.

6:6. Ibid., 54–64, esp. 64, recounts December 7 and aftermath.

6:7. Ibid., 65–67; DeWitt is quoted from Bill Hosokawa, *Nisei: The Quiet Americans* (New York: William Morrow, 1969), 260–61.

6:8. Morikawa, *Footprints,* 67, 70–79.

6:9. Ibid., 75–79.

6:10. Toru Matsumoto, *Beyond Prejudice: A Story of the Church and Japanese Americans* (New York: Friendship Press, 1946), 9, 10.

6:11. Ibid., 11–12, quotes Thompson; 14–15 describes DeWitt's response; see 25 for Tolan's remarks.

6:12. Ibid., 25–30, includes the report of the Susu-Magos and Pastor Thompson; see also 37–48.

6:13. Ibid., 49, comments on the magazines; 45–50 reproduces the Federal Council of Churches initiative; 99 prints the letter from Abe.

6:14. *Los Angeles Times* (December 8, 1941); Walter Lippmann, "Fifth Column on the Coast," *Washington Post* (February 12, 1942): 9; Murrow was quoted in a letter in University of Washington archives dated January 29, 1942; all are in Roger Daniels, *Asian Americans: Chinese and Japanese in the United States Since 1850* (Seattle: University of Washington Press, 1988), 200–201.

6:15. Daniels, *Asian Americans,* 202, 218, 221; Morton Grodzins, *Americans Betrayed: Politics and the Japanese Evacuation* (Chicago: University of Chicago Press, 1949), 408.

6:16. Grodzins, *Americans Betrayed,* 186; see also Ryo Munekata, ed., *Buddhist*

Churches of America, vol. 1, 75 Year History (Chicago: Nobart, 1974), 61; Tetsuden Kashima, *Buddhism in America: The Social Organization of an Ethnic Religious Institution* (Westport: Greenwood Press, 1977), 49–52, quoting items from the library of Reverend Tetsuro Kashima.

6:17. Kashima, *Buddhism in America,* 55–63; cites a publication of the Buddhist Brotherhood of America, *Buddhist Gathas and Ceremonies* (Los Angeles: The Buddhist House, 1943), 65–66; Kashima also cites a typescript by Paul Andrews on the youth movement, and "Relocated Buddhists," *Newsweek* (January 3, 1944): 62.

6:18. Sandra C. Taylor, "Fellow-Feelers with the Afflicted: The Christian Churches and the Relocation of the Japanese During World War II," in Roger Daniels, Sandra C. Taylor, and Harry H. L. Kitano, eds., *Japanese Americans: From Relocation to Redress* (Salt Lake City: University of Utah Press, 1986), 124–25; Taylor cites U.S. Congress, Select Committee Investigating National Defense Migration, *Fourth Interim Report,* 77th Cong., 2d sess. (Washington, D.C.: U.S. Government Printing Office, 1942), Part 30: 11607–9; Matsumoto, *Beyond Prejudice,* 15; Audrie Girdner and Anne Loftis, *The Great Betrayal: The Evacuation of the Japanese Americans During World War II* (New York: Macmillan, 1969), 126, 360; Girdner and Loftis cite a letter appearing in the *San Francisco Chronicle.*

6:19. Matsumoto, *Beyond Prejudice,* 121–22, on Ickes; 123–24 deals with terrorism and quotes the Hood River ministers.

6:20. Ibid., 135–37, on integration; 141 is an expression of his hopes for the future.

Chapter Seven

7:1. Fulton J. Sheen, *Philosophies at War* (New York: Scribner's, 1943), 1–2; and Fulton J. Sheen, *Seven Pillars of Peace* (New York: Scribner's, 1944).

7:2. Sheen, *Philosophies at War,* 4–5, 7–10, 13–15.

7:3. Ibid., 27–30, 34–37, 39–40, 43–45; cites Nicholas Berdyaev, *The Meaning of History* (New York: Charles Scribner's Sons, 1936).

7:4. Sheen, *Philosophies at War,* 50, 55, 58, 60–63, 67, 76–78.

7:5. Ibid., 176, 178–84.

7:6. Sheen, *Seven Pillars of Peace,* 9, 15–17.

7:7. Ibid., 20–27, 29–31.

7:8. Ibid., 33–34, 41, 38–39, 98–104, 109–12.

7:9. I am drawing on Charles DeBenedetti, *The Peace Reform in American History* (Bloomington: Indiana University Press, 1980), 144–45, about the rise of science's prestige at the expense of "the old vision of Protestant order." He also commented on the limits of Protestant clergy and women as critics since they had not effectively opposed mass bombings.

7:10. Ibid., 139–43; on the "first Protestant lobby," see E. Raymond Wilson, *Uphill for Peace: Quaker Impact on Congress* (Richmond, Ind.: Friends United Press, 1975), 13; see also Wendell Willkie, *One World* (New York: Simon and Schuster, 1943).

7:11. Roswell P. Barnes, *A Christian Imperative: Our Contribution to World Order* (New York: Friendship Press, 1941), v–vii.

7:12. Ibid., 12–15, 24, 31–33; Carleton J. H. Hayes, *Essays on Nationalism* (New York: Macmillan, 1926), 119.

7:13. Barnes, *A Christian Imperative,* 45–47, 94–100, 117.

7:14. See Mark G. Toulouse, *The Transformation of John Foster Dulles: From Prophet of Realism to Priest of Nationalism* (Macon: Mercer University Press, 1985), 47–59, 63–72, 81–82, an account on which I have depended that tells the story of Dulles' involvements from 1937 to 1945; see the *Federal Council Bulletin* 23 (January 1940): 3; others on the commission included Reinhold Niebuhr, John C. Bennett, Harvard's Professor William E. Hocking, Charles Clayton Morrison, John R. Mott, and Harry Emerson Fosdick; Toulouse collects comments from, among others, Reinhold Niebuhr, "American Power and World Responsibility," *Christianity and Crisis* 3 (April 5, 1943): 4; Henry P. Van Dusen, "The Six Pillars of Peace," *Christianity and Crisis* 3 (March 22, 1943): 1; Carl McIntire, *Twentieth Century Reformation* (Collingsworth, N.J.: Christian Beacon Press, 1946), 121, 129, 132; see John Foster Dulles, ed., *Six Pillars of Peace: A Study Guide Based on 'A Statement of Political Propositions'* (New York: Commission to Study the Bases of a Just and Durable Peace, 1943); "Christian Standards and Current International Developments," part 2 of "A Message to the Churches," from the Cleveland Conference of 1945, *International Conciliation*, no. 409 (March 1945), 142–49.

7:15. Toulouse, *Transformation of John Foster Dulles*, 72–82, 90–91, tracks Dulles as he gathered support for the proposals; cites John Foster Dulles, "Statement of Guiding Principles," *Biennial Report* (1942): 42–45, published by the Federal Council of Churches; Toulouse also cites Luman J. Shafer, "American Approaches to World Order," *The International Review of Missions* 33 (April 1944): 176.

7:16. John Foster Dulles, "The American People Need Now To Be Imbued With A Righteous Faith," *A Righteous Faith for a Just and Durable Peace* (New York: Federal Council of Churches, Commission on a Just and Durable Peace, 1943), 5–7, 9–11.

7:17. Everett R. Clinchy, "Christians Must Seek the Cooperation of Other Faiths," *A Righteous Faith for a Just and Durable Peace* (New York: Federal Council of Churches, Commission on a Just and Durable Peace, 1943), 32–35.

7:18. Walter Van Kirk, *Religion and the World of Tomorrow* (Chicago: Willet and Clark, 1941), 4, 8–9, 15, 37–56, 108–9, 126; Henry Luce's "American Century," *Life* 10 (February 17, 1941): 61–65.

7:19. Walter Van Kirk, *A Christian Global Strategy* (Chicago: Willet and Clark, 1945), 10–13, 24–44, 50, 52–55, 60–63, 69–71, esp. 42–44, 50, 55, 61, 63.

7:20. Ibid., 93–96, 101.

7:21. Ibid., 170, 177, 179, 197.

Chapter Eight

8:1. Just as the term "fundamentalism" was coined (1920) and came into use near the beginning of the period treated in the second volume of my *Modern American Religion, The Noise of Conflict, 1919–1941* (Chicago: University of Chicago Press, 1991), so "evangelicalism" acquired new meanings near the beginning of the time covered in this third volume, thanks to an act of organization in 1942 that signaled another development in conservative Protestantism. The literature on the movement is enormous; for access, see Edith L. Blumhofer and Joel A. Carpenter, eds., *Twentieth-Century Evangelicalism: A Guide to the Sources* (New York: Garland, 1990), and Norris A. Magnuson and William G. Travis, *American Evangelicalism: An Annotated Bibliography* (West Cornwall, Conn.: Locust Hill, 1990).

8:2. For the account of the turn on the part of some from fundamentalism to evangelicalism, see especially Joel A. Carpenter, *Revive Us Again: The Recovery of American Fundamentalism, 1930–1950* (New York: Oxford University Press, 1991).

8:3. James DeForest Murch, *Cooperation Without Compromise: A History of the National Association of Evangelicals* (Grand Rapids: Eerdmans, 1956), 41.

8:4. Ibid., 42–45, 48–50; he quoted the *Muskegon Chronicle* (February 8, 1945).

8:5. Murch, *Cooperation Without Compromise*, 53n; he quotes an International Council of Religious Education release, *Movement Toward Cooperation Among Conservative Christian Groups*, dated 1945.

8:6. A history of the second wave of fundamentalism and evangelicalism is Louis Gasper, *The Fundamentalist Movement* (The Hague: Mouton, 1963), 23; the "anti-modernist" quotation is from Carl McIntire, *Twentieth Century Reformation* (Collingswood, N.J.: Christian Beacon Press, 1946), 181; Gasper also cites *Which Council?*, a pamphlet published by the American Council of Christian Churches, 3.

8:7. Murch, *Cooperation Without Compromise*, 54–55, 59–61.

8:8. Ibid., 65–66, 69–70; Gasper, *Fundamentalist Movement*, 30, provides the statistic of one million members; "Sectarianism Receives a New Lease on Life," *Christian Century* 60 (May 19, 1943): 596.

8:9. *New York Times* (May 21, 1939): 3; see Lerond Curry, *Protestant-Catholic Relations in America: World War I Through Vatican II* (Lexington: University of Kentucky Press, 1972), 37; see R. A. Graham, S.J., *Vatican Diplomacy: A Study of Church and State on the International Plane* (Princeton: Princeton University Press, 1959), chap. 12; see also C. M. Cianfarra, *The Vatican and the War* (New York: Dutton, 1944).

8:10. John S. Conway, "Myron C. Taylor's Mission to the Vatican, 1940–1950," *Church History* 44 (March 1975): 88–93; he quotes Myron Taylor papers in the Roosevelt Library and a papal document in *Foreign Relations of the United States* 1 (1942): 129.

8:11. Conway, "Myron C. Taylor's Mission," 97–99, quoting a letter in a report of Taylor in December 1944; Harold E. Fey, "Can Catholicism Win America?" *Christian Century* 61 (November 29, 1944): 1378, provides the reference about the fifty cities; see also U.S. Department of Commerce, Bureau of the Census, *Historical Statistics of the United States: Colonial Times to 1957* (Washington, D.C.: U.S. Government Printing Office, 1960), 228–29; "Protestant Reorientation," *Christian Century* 60 (October 27, 1943): 1222–24.

8:12. Fey, "Can Catholicism Win America?" 1378; see also Harold E. Fey, "The Center of Catholic Power," *Christian Century* 62 (January 17, 1945): 76.

8:13. The standard history, including sources, is Ruth Rouse and Stephen Charles Neill, eds., *A History of the Ecumenical Movement, 1517–1948* (Philadelphia: Westminster Press, 1968); see Cavert in William Adams Brown, *Toward a United Church: Three Decades of Ecumenical Christianity* (New York: Charles Scribner's Sons, 1946), vii.

8:14. Brown, *Toward a United Church*, vii, ix–x, 1–2, 4–5.

8:15. Ibid., 190–92.

Chapter Nine

9:1. On the rise of Russophilia and Russophobia around 1945, see Randall B. Woods and Howard Jones, *Dawning of the Cold War: The United States' Quest for Order* (Athens: University of Georgia Press, 1991), pp. 24, 26, 33, 35, 39, 91.

9:2. For a view of Roosevelt's looking backward for precedent as he envisioned postwar America, see John Lewis Gaddis, *The United States and the Origins of the Cold War, 1941–1947* (New York: Columbia University Press, 1972), Chapter 1, "The Past as Prologue: The American Vision of the Postwar World," 1–31.

9:3. Ibid., 226–27, 229, quotes Dean from "Repressible Conflict?" *Time* (June 11, 1945): 24; Swing spoke with Archibald MacLeish, and a memorandum is in Department of State records where MacLeish also stated his own view.

9:4. Wittner, *Rebels Against War*, 126–27, quotes *New York Times*, August 20, 1945, and March 6, 1946, and especially the Federal Council of Churches, *Atomic Warfare and the Christian Faith* (March 1946), 11-12. See also Robert C. Batchelder, *The Irreversible Decision, 1939-1950* (Boston: Houghton Mifflin, 1961), and Robert W. Gardiner, *The Cool Arm of Destruction: Modern Weapons and Moral Insensitivity* (Philadelphia: Westminster, 1974).

9:5. Gaddis, *The United States and the Origins of the Cold War,* Chapter 8, "The Impotence of Omnipotence: American Diplomacy, The Atomic Bomb, and the Postwar World," 244-81, esp. 253, 258, 261.

9:6. Ibid., 284, summarizes 1946 developments; Truman's comment is quoted, 289, from a memorandum (which Secretary of State Byrnes, for whom it was intended, claimed never to have heard of) on January 5, 1946; 296-97 quotes Harriman, as recorded in the diaries of Forrestal; see Walter Millis, ed., *The Forrestal Diaries* (New York: Viking Press, 1951), 47.

9:7. George F. Kennan, "The Sources of Soviet Conduct," *Foreign Affairs* 25 (July 1947): 567-68, 571, 575 (Kennan wrote anonymously as "X"); see Harold H. Osmer, *U.S. Religious Journalism and the Korean War* (Washington, D.C.: University Press of America, 1980); Walter Lafeber, *America, Russia, and the Cold War, 1945-66* (New York: Wiley & Sons, 1967), 40-41; see *Life* (October 21, 1946): 65, 72.

9:8. The Truman speech is in *New York Times* (March 13, 1947); Gaddis, *The United States and the Origins of the Cold War,* 351, quotes *Public Papers of the Presidents of the United States: Harry S. Truman, 1947* (Washington, D.C.: U.S. Government Printing Office, 1963), 178-79; the White Paper is in *Documents on American Foreign Relations,* vol. 11: January 1-December 31, 1949 (Princeton: Princeton University Press, 1950), 538-546, esp. 546.

9:9. Truman's press release on this subject is in Harry S. Truman, *Memoirs, vol. 2, Years of Trial and Hope* (Garden City: Doubleday, 1956), 338-39; on "God is with us," see *Public Papers of the Presidents of the United States: Harry S. Truman, 1950,* (Washington, D.C.: U.S. Government Printing Office, 1965), 344; see *Commonweal* 53 (February 9, 1951): 438; see also Eisenhower's message to Congress, in *Documents on American Foreign Relations, 1953* (New York: Harper and Brothers, 1954), 19-20, esp. 20.

9:10. *America* 84 (December 30, 1950): 370; Osmer, *U. S. Religious Journalism,* 31-33; 38-41 reproduces opinions of denominational editors who, Osmer contends, basically paralleled *Christian Century* views; 41-43 cites *The Churchman* and *Friends Intelligencer* among the anti-military voices; 46-52 shows the massive support for the United Nations in most of the religious press; Osmer cites the periodical of the Knights of Columbus, *Columbia* (December 1950): 2, and the address by Supreme Knight John E. Swift, "Our Supreme Council Meets," *Columbia* (October 1950): 11; see Daniel Poling, "New Flag Over South Korea," *Christian Herald* 79 (September 1950): 16; *Christian Century* 67 (December 6, 1950): 1446, 1448; *Commonweal* 57 (February 6, 1953): 441; James A. Crain, "Goodwill on a World Scale," *World Call* (March 1953): 15.

9:11. Arthur M. Schlesinger, Jr., *The Vital Center* (Boston: Houghton Mifflin, 1949), 156; I owe the notion of clustering books on "The Vital Center" to Alonzo L. Hamby, *Beyond the New Deal: Harry S. Truman and American Liberalism* (New York: Columbia University Press, 1973), 279-81; see also Leland Stowe, *Target: You* (New York: Alfred A. Knopf, 1949), 164, 5, 10.

9:12. LaFeber, *America, Russia and the Cold War,* 129-35, poised Niebuhr between Hans Morgenthau and Senator Robert Taft, a candidate for the Republican nomination for president; see Morton White in *New Republic* 126 (May 5, 1952): 18-19.

9:13. These details are summarized from Richard Fox, *Reinhold Niebuhr: A Biography* (New York: Pantheon, 1985), 232, 234-42, esp. 232; see also "Editorial Notes," and "Democracy as a Religion," *Christianity and Crisis* 7 (August 4, 1947): 1-2; Barth's condensed address appeared as "No Christian Marshall Plan," *Christian Century* 65 (December 8, 1948):

133–32; Fox also cites a pamphlet published by the American Council of Christian Laymen, *How Red is the Federal Council of Churches?* (Madison, Wisc.: 1949).

9:14. Fox, *Reinhold Niebuhr,* 244–48, tells the story of the writing of *The Irony of American History* and of Niebuhr's stroke. On the titling of the book, Fox cites letters between Niebuhr and editor William Savage dated September 11, 1951, and December 5, 1951; Reinhold Niebuhr, *The Irony of American History* (New York: Scribner's, 1952), viii.

9:15. Niebuhr, *The Irony of American History,* 24, 28, 74, 2.

9:16. Ibid., 155, 165, 122, 150.

9:17. Mark Toulouse, *The Transformation of John Foster Dulles: From Prophet of Realism to Priest of Nationalism* (Macon, Ga.: Mercer University Press, 1985), 15; he quotes letters between Dulles and the pastor, Dulles's Princeton classmate Tertius Van Dyke, November 4 and 6, 1925; 57–58 describes the formation of the commission, citing Federal Council of Churches of Christ in America, *Annual Report, 1941:* 94; in a footnote on 65 Toulouse also quotes an interview he had years later with Samuel McCrea Cavert.

9:18. Federal Council of Churches of Christ in America, *Biennial Report, 1942,* 42, cited by Toulouse, *The Transformation of John Foster Dulles,* 66; Toulouse, 67 quotes Federal Council of Churches of Christ, *Annual Report, 1943:* 97; Niebuhr wrote on the subject in "American Power and World Responsibility," *Christianity and Crisis* 3 (April 5, 1943): 2–4; see Toulouse, 70–71, and for pacifist critiques, 82; see the response in defense by John C. Bennett, "Editorial Notes," *Christianity and Crisis* 5 (March 5, 1945): 2; Toulouse, 110–11; the Council statement of August 9, 1945, is in the Dulles papers; Truman wrote Samuel McCrea Cavert on August 11, 1945; the letter is in the Dulles files; Truman wrote Dulles on November 6, 1945 and Connelly wrote May 23, 1951; the letters are in the Truman Library; see Merlin Gustafson, "Religion and Politics in the Truman Administration," *Rocky Mountain Social Science Journal* 3 (October 1966): 127.

9:19. Toulouse, *The Transformation of John Foster Dulles,* 111, 134–35, 144–45, cites Dulles's speeches entitled "The Atomic Bomb and the Moral Law," given on November 15, 1945, "Acceptance of Appointment as General Adviser to the U.S. Delegation, San Francisco Conference," given April 5, 1945, and a speech entitled "America's Role in the Peace," all of which are found in the Dulles papers.

9:20. Ibid., 174–75; John Foster Dulles, "Thoughts on Soviet Foreign Policy and What to Do About It," *Life* (June 10, 1946): 120; "Freedom Through Sacrifice," *The Commercial and Financial Chronicle* 163 (May 30, 1946): 295.

9:21. John Foster Dulles, *War or Peace* (New York: Macmillan, 1950), 75; Toulouse, *The Transformation of John Foster Dulles's,* 176–77, cites Dulles' speeches including "Draft," March 11, 1948, and "Religion in American Life," November 4, 1951, found in the Dulles papers.

9:22. Toulouse, *The Transformation of John Foster Dulles,* 192, cites Dulles's speech "Principle versus Expediency in Foreign Policy," September 26, 1952, found in the Dulles papers; see also Dulles, *War or Peace,* 260.

9:23. Luther J. Holcomb, "Christian America's Contribution to World Peace," *Moody Monthly* 47 (October 1946): 98; see also Toulouse, *The Transformation of John Foster Dulles,* 198, who cites letters from Dulles to Charles R. Petticrew, January 20, 1950, and Allan B. Crow, May 31, 1950.

9:24. Toulouse, *The Transformation of John Foster Dulles,* 232, cites a radio address, "Universal Bible Sunday Broadcast," November 20, 1950, found in the Dulles papers; see also "U.S. Military Actions in Korea," *Department of State Bulletin* 23 (July 17, 1950): 92; for a view of Dulles which sees more continuity, less breach, in his thought and career than does Toulouse, see Ronald W. Pruessen, *John Foster Dulles: The Road to Power* (New York: The Free Press, 1982).

Chapter Ten

10:1. On the historical roots of Protestantdom's schism, which I have called "the Two-Party System," see Martin E. Marty, *Righteous Empire: The Protestant Experience in America* (New York: Dial, 1970), chapter 17, pp. 177–187, acknowledging the influence of Jean Miller-Schmidt.

10:2. Clarence W. Hall and Desider Holisher, *Protestant Panorama: The Faith That Made America Free* (New York: Farrar, Straus and Young, 1951).

10:3. Ibid., 3–4, 6; Taft is quoted from unnumbered introductory pages.

10:4. Ibid., 4, 6, 9, 14.

10:5. Ibid., 19, 20.

10:6. Ibid., 53, 55, 56, 60–61.

10:7. Ibid., 62, 63, 69–70.

10:8. Ibid., 91, 93.

10:9. Ibid., 95, 99–101.

10:10. Ibid., 103–6.

10:11. Ibid., 106–7.

10:12. Ibid., 119–20, 125, 127, 129–30.

10:13. Ibid., 134, 136, 145–46.

10:14. Ibid., 174–76.

10:15. Ibid., 99–101; Paul Hutchinson, *The New Leviathan* (Chicago: Willett, Clark, 1945).

10:16. Hutchinson, *The New Leviathan,* vii–viii, 21–27.

10:17. Ibid., 28–32.

10:18. Ibid., 40, 71, 73–74, 91–93.

10:19. Ibid., 106–16 discusses Hayek and his colleagues; 117–22 treats the papal letters.

10:20. Ibid., 125–40, on the world scene; 140–47, on Catholicism; Ryan and Boland receive treatment on 147 and 148; on Father Murray, see 151–52; 192–96.

10:21. Ibid., 197–203, 205–16.

10:22. Ibid., 227, 229–32.

10:23. Charles Clayton Morrison, *Can Protestantism Win America?* (New York: Harper and Brothers, 1948), vii, viii. Morrison matched his title to that of his colleague Harold E. Fey, who had just published articles in the *Christian Century* on "Can Catholicism Win America?"

10:24. Morrison, *Can Protestantism Win America?,* 1–3, 5–7, 10.

10:25. Ibid., 17–32, esp. 21, 25, 31.

10:26. Ibid., 33, 36–37, 39, 41.

10:27. Ibid., 60–62.

10:28. Ibid., 64–67, 72–73, 76–77.

10:29. Ibid., 81–89.

10:30. Ibid., 91–94, 97–99, 104–09, 112, 114–29, esp. 115, 117, 129.

10:31. Ibid., 149, 154, 158, 161, 169, 218–19.

10:32. Willard L. Sperry, *Religion in America* (New York: Macmillan, 1946), 159–60.

10:33. Ibid., 161.

10:34. On continuities between Billy Sunday and Billy Graham and on the rise of Graham, see William G. McLoughlin, *Revivals, Awakenings, and Reform: An Essay on Religion and Social Change in America, 1607–1977* (Chicago: University of Chicago Press, 1978), pp. 145–50; 186–93.

10:35. William Martin, *A Prophet With Honor: The Billy Graham Story* (New York: Morrow, 1991), part II, chapter 6, "Geared to the Times, Anchored to the Rock," tells the Youth for Christ story, esp. 92–93. In later editions Martin corrected a statement based on a familiar but inaccurate story: Graham was not converted on the date of Billy Sunday's death in 1935 but in 1936.

10:36. Ibid., 93–95, 101; *Charlotte Observer* (November 10, 1947, and November 23, 1947).

10:37. Martin, *A Prophet With Honor*, 104–5, 109; on revivals, see William G. McLoughlin, *Billy Graham: Revivalist in a Secular Age* (New York: Ronald Press, 1960), 50–51; see also Billy Graham, *Revival in Our Time* (Wheaton, Ill.: Van Kampen Press, 1950).

10:38. Martin, *A Prophet With Honor*, 115–16; see *Charlotte Observer* (October 2, 1948); Graham, *Revival in Our Time*, 124, 3 ; McLoughlin, *Billy Graham*, 47.

10:39. Martin, *A Prophet With Honor*, 636n., discusses whether Hearst issued exactly that order, along with speculations as to why he might have done so; see also 120ff., 131–33.

10:40. Ibid., 145–46.

10:41. Ibid., 146; Associated Press, February 4, 1952, included Graham's belief that he could be elected; on the "blocs," see McLoughlin, *Billy Graham*, 121; see also Charles T. Cook, *The Billy Graham Story* (London: Marshall, Morgan & Scott, 1954), 100.

10:42. Carl F. H. Henry, *The Uneasy Conscience of Modern Fundamentalism* (Grand Rapids: William B. Eerdmans, 1947), 9–10, 16–17, 20.

10:43. Ibid., 60, 64, 68, 69.

10:44. Ibid., 81.

10:45. Ibid., 86–87, 89.

Chapter Eleven

11:1. Something of the flavor of the Catholic counterattack against latter-day Nativism is preserved in John J. Kane, *Catholic-Protestant Conflicts in America* (Chicago: Regnery, 1955).

11:2. See Paul Blanshard, *Personal and Controversial: An Autobiography* (Boston: Beacon, 1973) for the author's self-description and his readiness to accept the charge of being an "anti-Catholic bigot," especially 213–22.

11:3. Ibid., 216–17.

11:4. Ibid., 217–19.

11:5. Ibid., 222, 220.

11:6. Paul Blanshard, *Communism, Democracy, and Catholic Power* (Boston: Beacon Press, 1951), ix, 43, 287, 295.

11:7. Ibid., 296–301.

11:8. Ibid., 227–33.

11:9. Ibid., 228–32, 307–9.

11:10. Francis E. McMahon, *A Catholic Looks at the World* (New York: Vanguard Press, 1945).

11:11. Ibid., ix, 15–19; he quoted Adolf Hitler, *Mein Kampf*, vol. 2 (New York: Reynal and Hitchcock, 1939), 677.

11:12. McMahon, *A Catholic Looks at the World*, 23–24, 26–30, 32, 37, 60.

11:13. Ibid., 37, 60, and all of the chapter "The Failures of Christians."

11:14. Ibid., 120.

11:15. Ibid., 120, 124–25, 130, 134–35.

11:16. Ibid., 136–37, 147, 151.

11:17. Ibid., 154–56, 178, 181.

11:18. Ibid., 184.

11:19. Ibid., 221–23, 225–28, 236.

11:20. Ibid., 274–81 on African Americans; 281–84 on Jews.

11:21. Ibid., 284–86, 288–92.

11:22. Ibid., 293–94, 310.

11:23. Ibid., 293–94; for biographical details, see Donald E. Pelotte, S.S.S., *John Courtney Murray: Theologian In Conflict* (New York: Paulist Press, 1976), esp. 6–7 regarding journals and societies.

11:24. Ibid., 12, quotes a letter of Murray to Zacheus J. Maher, S.J., the American Assistant of the Society of Jesus; see Francis Connell, "Discussion on 'Governmental Repression of Heresy,' " *Proceedings of the Third Annual Meeting of the Catholic Theological Society of America* (Chicago: Catholic Theological Society of America, 1948): 100.

11:25. Francis Connell, "Catholics and 'Interfaith' Groups," *The American Ecclesiastical Review* 105 (November 1941): 337–53, esp. 341; the response was John Courtney Murray, "Christian Co-operation: Current Theology," *Theological Studies* 3 (September 1942): 414; Pelotte, *John Courtney Murray,* 23 n.25 tells the publishing history of the Declaration; John Courtney Murray, "Current Theology: Intercredal [sic: "It was my own coinage," said Murray] Co-operation: Its Theory and Its Organization," *Theological Studies* 4 (June 1943): 274, 262.

11:26. Murray, "Christian Co-operation: Current Theology," 416; Francis J. Connell, "Pope Leo XIII's Message to America," *American Ecclesiastical Review* 109 (October 1943): 254–55.

11:27. Pelotte, *John Courtney Murray,* 17–18, discusses Murray's growing interest in secularism; see John Courtney Murray, "Reversing the Secularist Drift," *Thought* 24 (March 1949): 36–37; John Courtney Murray, "Paul Blanshard and the New Nativism," *The Month* 191 (April 1951): 216, my emphasis.

11:28. "Across the Gulf," *Time* (September 12, 1949): 48–53; the two articles were W. Russell Bowie, "Protestant Concern Over Catholicism," *American Mercury* 69 (September 1949): 261–73, esp. 261, and in the same issue, John Courtney Murray, "The Catholic Position—A Reply," 274–83, esp. 281; see also John Courtney Murray's "Letter to the Editor," *American Mercury* 69 (November 1949): 637; on the Yale experience, see Pelotte, *John Courtney Murray,* 31–34.

11:29. Richard Armstrong, *Out to Change the World: A Life of Father James Keller of the Christophers* (New York: Crossroad Publishing, 1984).

11:30. Ibid., 60.

11:31. Ibid., 65–69, deals with his contacts with the influential; the report on "fundamentals" is on 68.

11:32. Ibid., 72–74; cites Michael de la Bedoyere, "The Failures of Christianity," *The Catholic Mind* 39 (July 22, 1941): 14–15.

11:33. Armstrong, *Out to Change the World,* 78–79, quotes James Keller, "You Can Be A Christopher," *The Catholic World* 162 (January 1946): 316–25, esp. 316–17.

11:34. Armstrong, *Out to Change the World,* 80–83, deals with the new superior and the early days of the Christophers; the references to communism are quoted from *Christopher News Notes,* no. 4, 1946, no. 53, 1953, no. 12, 1949, and no. 43, 1952.

11:35. Armstrong, *Out to Change the World,* 85–90, on Keller's chafing; Walsh is quoted on 86; 91–92 on the writing of the book; McConnell's views were voiced twenty-five years later, in 1980, in an interview with Armstrong.

11:36. Ibid., 93–95; James Keller, *You Can Change the World* (New York: Longmans, Green, 1948), v, 328.

11:37. Armstrong, *Out to Change the World*, 96-97, 100; see also Edward S. Skillin, "Changing the World," *Commonweal* 49 (December 17, 1948): 253-54.

11:38. Armstrong, *Out to Change the World*, passim, for celebrity contacts.

11:39. The Feeney story is told in more detail in a book on which this account is dependent, Mark Silk, *Spiritual Politics: Religion and America Since World War II* (New York: Simon and Schuster, 1988), 70-73, and all of Chapter 4, "The Wages of Conversion (II)."

11:40. Ibid., 72-73, 74-78; Silk, 74, quotes Dulles from the first issue of *From the Housetops* (1946).

11:41. Ibid., 74-81; see Mark Amory, ed., *The Letters of Evelyn Waugh* (New York: Ticknor and Fields, 1980), 292-93.

11:42. Silk, *Spiritual Politics*, 81-83, 85-86; Catherine G. Clarke, "The Failure of Inter-Faith," *From the Housetops* 1 (December 1946): 46, discusses the rabbi, priest, and minister; Silk quotes Feeney's response to Ben Bagdikian in the *Providence Evening Bulletin* (April 20 and May 23, 1949).

Chapter Twelve

12:1. For background to this chapter, the story of prewar Zionism, see Melvin I. Urofsky, *American Zionism from Herzl to the Holocaust* (Garden City: Anchor Press, 1975), and David Polish, *Renew Our Days: The Zionist Issue in Reform Judaism* (Jerusalem: World Zionist Organization, 1976).

12:2. Franklin H. Littell, *The Crucifixion of the Jews* (New York: Harper and Row, 1975), 82, retells this story, and adds: "God bless the Southern Baptist Sunday school that trained Harry Truman as a boy!" for imparting such biblical knowledge to him. Having heard this story repeated several times, I checked the original copy of Truman's address on that occasion and found no such reference, nor is it recalled in seminary or other press reports of the occasion. Rabbi Jacob Finkelstein, the Jewish Theological Seminary president at that time and the president's host, in correspondence wrote that he could not recall such words having been said. So I have called the event a "legend," but one which suggests how religiously weighted the issue of Israel as Zion is. See Isaiah 45:1-4 for the Cyrus references.

12:3. Zvi Ganin, *Truman, American Jewry, and Israel, 1945-1948* (New York: Holmes and Meier, 1979), 80-81, quotes Silver and Truman from American Zionist Emergency Council Papers in the Zionist Archives, New York.

12:4. Louis L. Gerson, *The Hyphenate in Recent American Politics and Diplomacy* (Lawrence: University of Kansas Press, 1964), 95, includes the pro-Israel quotation; the memorandum of June 1, 1945, is in the President's Secretary's Files, *not* included in a quotation cited by William Hillman, ed., *Mr. President* (New York: Farrar, Strauss, and Young, 1952), 118, but quoted by Michael J. Cohen, *Truman and Israel* (Berkeley: University of California Press, 1990), 7.

12:5. Cohen, *Truman and Israel*, 3-18, on the Jacobson relation; Ganin, *Truman, American Jewry, and Israel*, 20, quotes David Ben Gurion to Bernard Joseph, April 14, 1945, in the Mapai Archive, Beit Berl, Israel.

12:6. Cohen, *Truman and Israel*, 36-37, from Truman's senatorial and vice-presidential files.

12:7. Ibid., 46-47, 50; Ganin, *Truman, American Jewry, and Israel*, 14-15.

12:8. Ganin, *Truman, American Jewry, and Israel*, 40, 101.

12:9. Cohen, *Truman and Israel*, 65, quotes the American Council for Judaism files in the American Jewish Archives.

12:10. Louis D. Brandeis, *The Jewish Problem: How to Solve It* (New York:

Zionist Essay Publication Committee, 1915), 9–13; Thomas A. Kolsky, *Jews Against Zionism: The American Council for Judaism, 1942–1948* (Philadelphia: Temple University Press, 1990), 42–43, tells of the conflict, relying on interviews with Jacob R. Marcus and Malcolm H. Stern; 47 cites correspondence in the Louis Wolsey papers.

12:11. Kolsky, *Jews Against Zionism,* 67, 69, 117–20; Elmer Berger, *The Flint Plan* (Flint, Mich.: Committee on Lay-Rabbinical Cooperation, 1942), 9–20; the "Digest of Principles" appeared in The American Council for Judaism's *Information Bulletin* (December 15, 1943): 4; see also L. J. Rosenwald, "Reply to Zionism," *Life* (June 28, 1943): 11; the Anglo-American testimony is reported in "Tiff Breaks Calm at Inquiry on Jews," *New York Times* (January 11, 1946): 2; see Melvin I. Urofsky, *A Voice That Spoke for Justice: The Life and Times of Stephen S. Wise* (Albany: State University of New York Press, 1982), 350–51; also Elmer Berger, *The Jewish Dilemma* (New York: Devin-Adair, 1945), 5.

12:12. Hertzel Fishman, *American Protestantism and a Jewish State* (Detroit: Wayne State University Press, 1973), 83–84; cites Henry Van Dusen, "I Support the American Council For Judaism," *Information Bulletin* (March 1, 1946): 1–2.

12:13. "The Sorry Story of Palestine," *Christian Century* 62 (November 28, 1945): 1311; "Germany's Regeneration," *Christian Century* 62 (June 13, 1945): 702.

12:14. *The Nation* 154 (February 21, 1942): 214–16, and (February 28, 1942): 253–55; Fishman, *American Protestantism and a Jewish State,* 68–70; see Reinhold Niebuhr in the Foreword to Waldo Frank, *The Jew in Our Day* (London: Victor Gollancz, 1944), 15–16.

12:15. Fishman, *American Protestantism and a Jewish State,* 72ff., drawing on archives of the Christian Council for Palestine, Zionist Archives in New York; see also Carl H. Voss, "Christians and Zionism in the United States," *Palestine Year Book* 2 (New York: Zionist Organization of America, 1946), 497.

12:16. Fishman, *American Protestantism and a Jewish State,* 76, 80; Fishman quotes a statement from the papers of the Christian Council on Palestine and the Zionist Archives in New York.

12:17. Ganin, *Truman, American Jewry, and Israel,* 5–6; Bergson to Weizmann, April 2, 1945, is quoted from the Hillel Silver papers.

12:18. Dan Tschirgi, *The Politics of Indecision: Origins and Implications of American Involvement with the Palestine Problem* (New York: Praeger, 1983), 61–62.

12:19. Virginia Gildersleeve, *Many a Good Crusade* (New York: Macmillan, 1954), 409, 184–85; Fishman, *American Protestantism and a Jewish State,* 209 n.15 quotes a press release from the committee, dated June 18, 1948, found in the Zionist archives in New York.

12:20. Robert J. Donovan, *Conflict and Crisis: The Presidency of Harry S. Truman, 1945–1948* (New York: Norton, 1977), 319; the Eleanor Roosevelt letter is quoted in Margaret Truman, *Harry S. Truman* (New York: William Morrow, 1973), 385; Ganin, *Truman, American Jewry, and Israel,* 157, quotes Oscar Ewing interview in 1969, from the Oral History collection at the Truman library.

12:21. Cohen, *Truman and Israel,* 87–100, for the State Department account, esp. 91, which quotes Max Lowenthal's diary entry of May 26, 1948, from the Max Lowenthal Papers at the University of Minnesota.

12:22. Ibid., 102–3, quotes Samuel Halperin, *The Political World of American Zionism* (Detroit: Wayne State University Press, 1961), 315; Cohen also quotes Thomas A. Kolsky, "Jews Against Zionism: The American Council for Judaism, 1942–1948" (Ph.D. diss., George Washington University, 1986), 15, 444; Joseph Proskauer, *A Segment of My Times* (New York: Farrar, Strauss, 1950), 199; Ganin, *Truman, American Jewry, and Israel,* 92, tells of Goldmann's meeting with Proskauer on August 7, 1946, as documented in Hadassah archives.

12:23. Leonard Dinnerstein, *America and the Survivors of the Holocaust* (New

York: Columbia University Press, 1982), 122; Cohen, *Truman and Israel,* 113–21, discusses the Displaced Persons lobby; see also Naomi Cohen, *Not Free to Desist: The American Jewish Committee, 1906–1966* (Philadelphia: Jewish Publication Society of America, 1972), 290.

12:24. Cohen, *Truman and Israel,* 122–46.

12:25. Ibid., 152, 157–58; Ganin, *Truman, American Jewry and Israel,* 125.

12:26. Ganin, *Truman, American Jewry, and Israel,* 174–78.

12:27. Cohen, *Truman and Israel,* 167–68, 170; quotes "Eddie Jacobson: Unofficial Envoy," *Kansas City Star* (May 13, 1965); also cites Jacobson diary for December 8, 1947, and the Granoff interview.

12:28. Cohen, *Truman and Israel,* 173–87, esp. 183,186–87; Kolsky, *Jews Against Zionism,* 181; see also Ganin, *Truman, American Jewry and Israel,* 154–56, who cites announcement of the formation of the Committee for Justice and Peace that appeared in the *New York Herald Tribune* (March 3, 1948); Jacobson's daughter, Elinore Borenstine, reported on the Weizmann and Silver incidents in a letter to William B. Silverman, July, 1968, preserved in the Silverman papers at the B'nai Jehuda Archive.

12:29. Ganin, *Truman, American Jewry and Israel,* 187–88.

12:30. "Middle East—Number One Danger Spot," *Christian Century* 68 (July 1951): 838; Fishman, *American Protestantism and a Jewish State,* 215 n.67; see *American Zionist* 43 (April 5, 1953): 10.

12:31. *Christian Century* 64 (September 17, 1947): 1100; see also *Christian Century* 67 (January 11, 1950): 36; on internationalization see Fishman, *American Protestantism and a Jewish State,* 113–23.

12:32. "Perils to America in the New Jewish State," *Christianity and Crisis* 9 (February 21, 1949): 9–10.

12:33. Stephen S. Wise, *Challenging Years: The Autobiography of Stephen S. Wise* (New York: G. P. Putnam, 1949), 140–41.

Chapter Thirteen

13:1. For background to church and state issues in this period, see the extensive bibliography and introductory essay by James D. Beumler, "America Emerges As a World Power: Religion, Politics, and Nationhood, 1940–1960," in John F. Wilson, ed., *Church and State in America: A Bibliographical Guide. The Civil War to the Present Day* (New York: Greenwood, 1987), 225–61.

13:2. This chapter draws on sources brought together comprehensively in Dorsey Milam Deaton, "The Protestant Crisis: Truman's Vatican Ambassador Controversy of 1951," a Ph.D. dissertation from Emory University, 1970.

13:3. "Religious Unity, à la President," Arizona *Baptist Beacon* 12 (November 29, 1951): 2.

13:4. Deaton, *Protestant Crisis,* 256, 226; see *Reference Manual on U.S. Diplomatic Representation at the Vatican* (New York: National Council of Churches of Christ in America, 1950), 14; "Blunder," *Churchman* 165 (November 15, 1951): 18; *Boston Herald* (October 22, 1951); Archer is quoted in *New York Times* (October 21, 1951): 30; see headline in *New York Times* (October 21, 1951): 1.

13:5. Deaton, *Protestant Crisis,* 5–6, 464; Short's statement is in *Public Papers of the Presidents: Harry S. Truman, 1951* (Washington, D.C.: U.S. Government Printing Office, 1965), 601; André Siegfried, *America at Mid-Century* (New York: Harcourt, Brace, 1955), 98.

13:6. Deaton, *Protestant Crisis,* 421; John Cogley, "Call It The Thing," *Commonweal* 55 (November 9, 1951): 110; Deaton cited Crapullo from a *New York Times* story; Weigel is in Robert McAfee Brown and Gustave Weigel, *An American Dialogue* (Garden City: Doubleday, 1961), 190–92.

13:7. For statistics, see Benson Y. Landis, "Trends in Church Membership in the United States," *Annals of the American Academy of Political and Social Science* 332 (November 1960): 7; the comment is in *Chicago Tribune* (October 23, 1951): 18.

13:8. Deaton, *Protestant Crisis,* 122, 194–95, found that during the first seven months of the Holy Year, the White House received on this subject 33,000 cards and letters, with an 85-to-1 ratio against ambassadorship. Deaton also reports on the Archer-to-Truman telegram of June 13, 1950, and points to the *New York Times* (June 21, 1946) for some substantiation of the Hitler accusation; "New Body Demands Church Separation," *New York Times* (January 12, 1948): 1, 12.

13:9. Deaton, *Protestant Crisis,* 196, found this letter of June 6, 1950, in the Truman Papers, Truman library; 211–14, Deaton interviewed Clark on March 6, 1969, and nowhere aside from his reminiscences is there a record of the transactions; see *Public Papers of the Presidents: Harry S. Truman, 1951,* 601, 603; "Nomination of U.S. Ambassador to the Vatican," *U.S. State Department Bulletin* 25 (December 3, 1951): 894.

13:10. Deaton, *Protestant Crisis,* 271–74; "The Politics Behind the Vatican Nomination," *Christian Century* 68 (October 31, 1951): 1244; "A Vatican Ambassador?" *Commonweal* 55 (November 2, 1951): 84.

13:11. Deaton, *Protestant Crisis,* 231–32, 293, 208–9; *Public Papers of the Presidents: Harry S. Truman, 1950* (Washington, D.C.: U.S. Government Printing Office, 1965), 759–60; *Public Papers of the Presidents: Harry S. Truman, 1951,* 549–50; Deaton cites *Zion's Herald* 124 (October 10, 1951): 6–7; Hugh D. Darsie, "N.C.C. Delivers Formal Protest," *Christian Century* 68 (November 14, 1951): 1326.

13:12. Deaton, *Protestant Crisis,* 296, 299; for the reminiscence, see Harry S. Truman, *Mr. Citizen* (New York: Bernard Geis Associates, 1960), 133; for the NCCJ speech, see *Public Papers of the Presidents: Harry S. Truman, 1949* (Washington, D.C.: U.S. Government Printing Office, 1965), 563; see also *Public Papers of the Presidents: Harry S. Truman, 1951,* 549–50.

13:13. Deaton, *Protestant Crisis,* 354–56, 361; *Boston Globe* (October 31, 1951); "A Time For Protest," *Christian Advocate* 126 (November 15, 1951): 1417; see especially "Poll Notes Heavier Protest on Clark," *Church and State Newsletter* 5 (January 1952): 1, 5.

13:14. Deaton, *Protestant Crisis,* 307–8, 374, 314, 223; Arthur M. Schlesinger, Jr., "Relations With the Vatican: Why Not?" *Atlantic Monthly* 189 (January 1952): 55; *Congressional Record.* 82nd Cong., 2nd sess., 1952. Vol. 98, pt. 3: 3546; see also *Congressional Quarterly Almanac* 8 (1952): 112–13; *New York Times* (October 21, 1951): 26; *St. Louis Post-Dispatch* (October 23, 1951); F. William O'Brien, "General Clark's Nomination as Ambassador to the Vatican: American Reaction," *Catholic Historical Review* 44 (January 1959): 435; "Along the Way," Boston *Pilot* (January 19, 1952).

13:15. Deaton, *Protestant Crisis,* 330, 417; George Lindbeck, "Should the U.S. Send Ambassador to Vatican?" *Foreign Policy Bulletin* 31 (December 15, 1951): 6, 4.

13:16. Deaton, *Protestant Crisis,* 421–22, makes reference to G. Bromley Oxnam's statement to the Council of Bishops of the Methodist Church, December 10, 1951; also 202–3 for Deaton's references to Oxnam and Pruden's request for the meeting with Truman; "Storm of Objections Rise In Face of Church-State Issue," *Presbyterian Outlook* 133 (November 12, 1951): 3; "President Surrenders to the Pope," *Christian Century* 68 (October 31, 1951): 1243.

13:17. Deaton, *Protestant Crisis,* 467, 323, 327; Robert Lee, *The Social Sources of Church Unity* (Nashville: Abingdon Press, 1960), 128; see chapter entitled "Protestantism," in Willard L. Sperry, ed., *Religion and Our Divided Denominations* (Cambridge: Harvard

University Press, 1945); "An Ambassador at the Vatican?" *Christian Century* 68 (November 7, 1951): 1272–75; on de facto recognition, see F. William O'Brien, *Catholic Historical Review*, 431; "What They're Saying," *Christian Advocate* 126 (November 15, 1951): 1418.

13:18. Deaton, *Protestant Crisis,* 341, 343; Mark De Wolfe Howe, "Diplomacy, Religion, and the Constitution," *The Nation* 174 (January 12, 1952): 29; Henry Pitney Van Dusen, "Should U.S. Send Ambassador to Vatican?" *Foreign Policy Bulletin* 31 (December 15, 1951): 5; W. E. Garrison, "Vatican Embassy—A Personal History," *Christian Century* 68 (November 14, 1951): 1309.

13:19. Deaton, *Protestant Crisis,* 426; "Correspondence," *Christian Century* 68 (November 14, 1951): 1312; Deaton cites "Readers Write," *Zion's Herald* 129 (1951): 1058; John C. Bennett, "The Vatican Appointment," *Christianity and Crisis* 11 (November 26, 1951): 154, 148.

13:20. Deaton, *Protestant Crisis,* 365–68, bases his view of Clark's attitude on an interview with Clark; *New York Times* (January 14, 1952): 1.

13:21. Deaton, *Protestant Crisis,* 368, 429–30, 435; "Truman and the Vatican," *New Republic* 125 (October 29, 1951): 6–7; *The Churchman* 161 (November 15, 1951): 19; "Issue to be Settled by Senator or by Ballot," *Christian Century* 68 (October 31, 1951): 1244.

13:22. Arnold S. Nash, ed., *Protestant Thought in the Twentieth Century* (New York: Macmillan, 1951), 3–13; "Pluralism—National Menace," *Christian Century* 68 (June 13, 1951): 701–3.

Chapter Fourteen

14:1. In addition to an anthology edited by Robert T. Miller and Ronald B. Flowers (see note 14:5), I commend John T. Noonan, Jr., *The Believer and the Powers That Are: Cases, History, and Other Data Bearing on the Relation of Religion and Government* (New York: Macmillan, 1987), as a well-introduced collection of decisions. The American Civil Liberties brief from the *McCollum* case and including the words that form the title for this chapter are quoted in Donald E. Boles, *The Bible, Religion, and the Public Schools* (Ames: Iowa State University Press, 1965), 174.

14:2. For an introduction to Jehovah's Witnesses history, valuable for understanding these cases, see M. James Penton, *Apocalypse Delayed: The Story of Jehovah's Witnesses* (Toronto: University of Toronto Press, 1985).

14:3. On expectations extended to Frankfurter and on the reputation he brought, see H. N. Hirsch, *The Enigma of Felix Frankfurter* (New York: Basic Books, 1981), 127–37. Hirsch employs a psychoanalytic model for interpreting Frankfurter.

14:4. Anson Phelps Stokes, *Church and State in the United States,* volume 2 (New York: Harper & Brothers, 1950), 602; Stokes is citing William G. Fennell, *Compulsory Flag Salute in Schools* (New York: Committee on Academic Freedom, American Civil Liberties Union, 1936), 8, 9.

14:5. *Cantwell v. Connecticut,* 310 U.S. 296 (1940), 300–311; reproduced in Robert T. Miller and Ronald B. Flowers, *Toward Benevolent Neutrality: Church, State, and the Supreme Court,* 3d ed. (Waco: Markham Fund Press, 1987), 60–63.

14:6. *Cantwell v. Connecticut,* 310, 311; Miller and Flowers, *Toward Benevolent Neutrality,* 63.

14:7. The full rendering of the flag-salute issue, on which this account draws, is David Roger Manwaring, *Render Unto Caesar: The Flag-Salute Controversy* (Chicago: University of Chicago Press, 1962), 2–11, and for a bibliography of critical articles by educators, see 257–58, nn. 60–66; see also Mary Tierney Coutts, "How the Flag Pledge Originated," *Journal of Education* 125 (1942): 225–27; "The Flag Salute," *National Education Association Journal* 32 (December 1943): 265–66; also see Pub. L. no. 829, c. 806, para. 7, 56 STAT. c. 1077 (December 22, 1942); the revision was Pub. L. no. 396, 68 STAT. c. 297 (June 14, 1954).

14:8. On other religious groups, see Manwaring, *Render Unto Caesar,* 11–16, in which he also catalogs sporadic oppositions; on Pennsylvania enforcement, see Manwaring, 76–88; he cites legal documents including "Complainant's Brief on Motion to Dismiss," *Minersville School District v. Gobitis,* 21 F. Supp. 581 (E.D. Pa 1937), 4; Lucille B. Milner, memorandum for files, "Flag Saluting: General," ACLU Archives 872 (January 31, 1936); 2 Pitt. L. Rev. 206 (1936) to document the expulsions and the beatings; see also Manwaring, 277 nn. 186, 190; Manwaring, 30–32, examines the Witnesses' case.

14:9. *Minersville School District v. Gobitis,* 310 U.S. 586 (1940), 591–601, esp. 591, 593–94; Miller and Flowers, *Toward Benevolent Neutrality,* 82–87, esp. 82–83; Hirsch, *Enigma of Felix Frankfurter,* 128, 238 n. 73.

14:10. *Minersville v. Gobitis,* 594, 596–97; Miller and Flowers, *Toward Benevolent Neutrality,* 83–84.

14:11. Hirsch, *Enigma of Felix Frankfurter,* 150–52; see also Stone's dissent in *Minersville v. Gobitis,* 601–6, esp. 606; Miller and Flowers, *Toward Benevolent Neutrality,* 86; see also Joseph Lash, ed., *From the Diaries of Felix Frankfurter* (New York: Norton, 1975), 68–72.

14:12. See pamphlet by the American Civil Liberties Union, *The Persecution of Jehovah's Witnesses* (January 1941): 3, 22; see also Stokes, *Church and State,* vol. 2, 603; Manwaring, *Render Unto Caesar,* passim; "The Flag Salute Case," *Christian Century* 57 (June 19, 1940): 791; Alpheus T. Mason, *Harlan Fiske Stone: Pillar of Law* (New York: Viking Press, 1956), 532; *Jones v. Opelika,* 316 U.S. 584 (1942), 623–24; Miller and Flowers, *Toward Benevolent Neutrality,* 63–74.

14:13. Hirsch, *Enigma of Felix Frankfurter,* 162–67, esp. 167; *Martin v. Struthers* 319 U.S. 141 (1943).

14:14. Harlan B. Phillips, *Felix Frankfurter Reminisces* (New York: Reynal and Hitchcock, 1960), 290–91.

14:15. *West Virginia State Board of Education v. Barnette,* 319 U.S. 624 (1943), 625–70, esp. 633, 638, 641–42; Miller and Flowers, *Toward Benevolent Neutrality,* 88, 90.

14:16. *West Virginia State Board v. Barnette.,* 646, 662, 653; Miller and Flowers, *Toward Benevolent Neutrality,* 92, 94–95.

14:17. Context set in Miller and Flowers, *Toward Benevolent Neutrality,* 378–82, 452–58.

14:18. Stokes, *Church and State,* vol. 2, 702; quotes New Jersey Laws, 1941, c. 191, p. 581; see *Everson v. Board of Education* 330 U.S. 1 (1947), 6; Miller and Flowers, *Toward Benevolent Neutrality,* 462.

14:19. *Everson v. Board of Education,* 8, 15–16, 18; Miller and Flowers, *Toward Benevolent Neutrality,* 464–65.

14:20. Edward Corwin, "The Supreme Court as National School Board," *Thought* 23 (December 1948): 669, 673; Anson Phelps Stokes, *Church and State in the United States,* volume 3 (New York: Harper & Brothers, 1950), 814; see J. M. O'Neill, *Religion and Education Under the Constitution* (New York: Harper & Brothers, 1949), 11, 91.

14:21. See Jackson dissenting in *Everson v. Board of Education,* 21, 23–24, 27; Miller and Flowers, *Toward Benevolent Neutrality,* 466–67.

14:22. See Rutledge dissenting in *Everson v. Board of Education,* 29–63, esp. 53, 31–32, 29.

14:23. Stokes, *Church and State*, vol. 2, 715–16; quotes *New York Herald-Tribune* (January 26, 1948).

14:24. Richard E. Morgan, *The Supreme Court and Religion* (New York: The Free Press, 1972), 93; "Bus Decision," *Churchman* 161 (March 1, 1947): 18.

14:25. Stokes, *Church and State*, vol. 2, 714–15; quoted in *New York Times* (January 12, 1948).

14:26. O'Neill, *Religion and Education*, 189–90, 197, 200.

14:27. Ibid., 201–2, 205–6, 217–18.

14:28. Ibid., 31; "Protestants Take Catholic Line," *Christian Century* 65 (June 30, 1948): 643.

14:29. *McCollum v. Board of Education*, 333 U.S. 203 (1948), 204–56; Miller and Flowers, *Toward Benevolent Neutrality*, 382–89; Vashti Cromwell McCollum, *One Woman's Fight* (originally Garden City: Doubleday, 1951; taken from rev. ed., Boston: Beacon Press, 1961).

14:30. *McCollum v. Board of Education*, 9–15.

14:31. Stokes, *Church and State*, vol. 2, 516–17; quotes "School Religion," *Churchman* 162 (January 1, 1948): 18.

14:32. *McCollum v. Board of Education*, 210–12; Miller and Flowers, *Toward Benevolent Neutrality*, 383.

14:33. *McCollum v. Board of Education*, 226, 231–32; Miller and Flowers, *Toward Benevolent Neutrality*, 384–87.

14:34. Miller and Flowers, *Toward Benevolent Neutrality*; O'Neill, *Religion and Education*, 220, 238–41.

14:35. *Zorach v. Clauson*, 343 U.S. 306 (1952), 308–25; Miller and Flowers, *Toward Benevolent Neutrality*, 393–97; for background to the case, see Morgan, *Supreme Court and Religion*, 129–30; see also Leo Pfeffer, *Church, State, and Freedom* (Boston: Beacon Press, 1967; rev. ed. of 1953 work), 414–28; quotes "Released Time Reconsidered: The New York Plan is Tested," *Yale Law Journal* 61 (March 1952): 405–16, and affadavits from the file in the County Clerk of Kings County in the case of *Zorach v. Clauson*, Index no. 10327/1948.

14:36. *Zorach v. Clauson*, 314, 323, 325; Miller and Flowers, *Toward Benevolent Neutrality*, 394, 396–97.

14:37. *Zorach v. Clauson*, 313–15; Miller and Flowers, *Toward Benevolent Neutrality*, 394–95.

Chapter Fifteen

15:1. On "public woman," see Glenna Matthews, *The Rise of Public Woman: Woman's Power and Woman's Place in the United States, 1630–1970* (New York: Oxford University Press, 1992), 3–11.

15:2. John Courtney Murray, *We Hold These Truths: Catholic Reflections on the American Proposition* (New York: Sheed and Ward, 1960), p. 6. Murray refers to Thomas Gilby, O.P., *Between Community and Society* (New York: Longmans, Green, 1953).

15:3. This account draws significantly on Carl Degler, *At Odds: Women and the Family in America from the Revolution to the Present* (New York: Oxford University Press, 1980), 439–40; see Lynn White, Jr., *Educating Our Daughters: A Challenge to Colleges* (New York: Harper & Bros., 1950), 101; Ashley Montagu is quoted in William H. Chafe, *American Woman: Her Changing Social, Economic, and Political Roles, 1920–1970* (New York: Oxford University Press, 1972), 206–7; Ferdinand Lundberg and Marynia Farnham, *Modern Woman: The Lost Sex* (New York: Harper, 1947).

15:4. John Willig, "Class of '34 (Female) Fifteen Years Later," *New York Times Magazine* (June 12, 1949), 53, quoted in June Sochen, *Movers and Shakers: American Women Thinkers and Activists 1900–1970* (New York: Quadrangle, 1973), 174. Sochen does not follow Horton's trail to see how in many ways she was in the advance guard of those who argued for fulfilment of women also outside the home as, for example, she became an advocate of women's ordination. See Mildred McAfee Horton, "Second Class Citizens or Partners in Policy?" *Presbyterian Life* (June 15, 1958): 26–27 and 42. Lois A. Boyd and R. Douglas Brackenridge give Horton credit in *Presbyterian Women in America: Two Centuries of a Quest for Status* (Westport: Greenwood, 1983), 155–56.

15:5. Degler, *At Odds,* 418–27.

15:6. Significantly, Bliss was commenting on findings of a survey of American churches more than she was commenting on the European scene in which she worked. For her report, see Kathleen Bliss, *The Service and Status of Women in the Churches* (London: SCM Press, 1952), 172–75, 184–87, 197–99, made convenient to American readers through an excerpt in Barbara J. MacHaffie, *Readings in Her Story: Women in Christian Tradition* (Minneapolis: Fortress, 1992); I am quoting from p. 202.

15:7. MacHaffie, *Readings,* 202–3.

15:8. James J. Kenneally, *The History of Catholic Women* (New York: Crossroad, 1990), 178–81; O'Hara was quoted in *New York Times* (March 22, 1942).

15:9. Kenneally, *History of Catholic Women,* 178–81; Baltimore's *Catholic Review* (July 2, 1943); *Catholic Citizen* (January 15, 1944); "Draft of Women," *America* 70 (February 26, 1944): 575.

15:10. Kenneally, *History of Catholic Women,* 176–78; see Mary Berenice, O.S.U., "Training All-Out Mothers," *Catholic World* 158 (October 1943): 79–81, esp. 80; Ethel Marbach, "The Eternal Woman," *Catholic Digest* 28 (October 1964): 79–81; Ruth Reed, "Women in War Jobs: A Social Evaluation," *America* 69 (July 31, 1943): 454.

15:11. Kenneally, *History of Catholic Women,* 182, 192–93; the author based his views in part on an interview with Mary K. Fitzgerald Phaneuf; see also "Frances Sweeney," *Commonweal* 40 (August 18, 1944): 427; Luce gave her reasons for conversion in "The Real Reasons," *McCall's* 74 (February to April, 1947); see also "Footnote to Mrs. Luce," *Ave Maria* 115 (April 12, 1947): 451–52; on her career, see Wilfred Sheed, *Clare Boothe Luce* (New York: E. P. Dutton, 1982), and Alden Hatch, *Ambassador Extraordinary: Clare Boothe Luce* (New York: Henry Holt, 1956).

15:12. Kenneally, *History of Catholic Women,* 189–90; Lydwine van Kersbergen, "Toward a Christian Concept of Woman," *Catholic World* 182 (October 1955): 6–11, esp. 9; Alden V. Brown, *The Grail Movement and American Catholicism, 1940–1975* (Notre Dame: University of Notre Dame Press, 1989), 59, 100, 101 n.12; Brown cited brochures by Elsa Chaney, "Writing and Being," (July 12–17, 1949), and by Elsa Chaney and Donna Myers entitled "Towards a World Vision—An Apostolic Program" (Grailville, 1954), as well as a brochure by Lydwine van Kersbergen entitled "The Normal School of Sanctity for the Laity," 37–38.

15:13. Brown, *The Grail Movement,* 38, 53–55; Janet Kalven, *The Task of Woman in the Modern World* (Des Moines: National Catholic Rural Life Conference, undated), 15, 2, 17, 1, 3, 11.

15:14. Brown, *The Grail Movement,* 100–101.

15:15. Ibid., 107–8; Lydwine van Kersbergen, *Woman, Some Aspects of Her Role in the Modern World* (Grailville, Loveland, Ohio, 1956): 14, 16–17.

15:16. A 1953 typescript is quoted by Lois Boyd and R. Douglas Brackenridge, *Presbyterian Women in America: Two Centuries of a Quest for Status* (Westport: Greenwood Press, 1983), 140, 142; see "Women's Status in the Protestant Churches," in the Federal Council of Churches Bulletin, *Information Service* (November 16, 1940): 8; Boyd and Brackenridge also cite "Minutes of Cedar Rapids Presbytery of the United Presbyterian Church of North America," July 2 and 4, 1943 and *General Assembly Minutes: United Presbyterian Church of North America*, Vol. 21, *May 31 to June 5, 1944* (Pittsburgh: United Presbyterian Board of Publication and Bible School Work, 1944): 43.

15:17. Boyd and Brackenridge, *Presbyterian Women*, 144–45; they based the story on interviews with Margaret Shannon Meyers and on typescripts and memos dated January 25, 1946, and May 10, 1946, involving Lampe.

15:18. Ibid., 144–46; they also cite "General Council Minutes" (March 13, 1946): 22–23 and (May 21, 1946): 6; see also the *Presbyterian Tribune* 61 (May 1946): 6–7; *General Assembly Minutes Presbyterian Church U.S.A.*, Vol. 8, Pt. 1, 187; *Presbyterian Guardian* 15 (July 10, 1946): 204; Mae Ross Taylor, "Why I Do Not Wish to Be Ordained," *Presbyterian* 117 (July 5–12, 1947): 8; see also Lyman Richard Hartley, "Women As Ministers: The Pros and Cons," *New York Times* (April 13, 1947).

15:19. For report on the the *Christian Century* and for these statistics, see Boyd and Breckenridge, *Presbyterian Women*, 147–48; see also the National Council of Churches of Christ in America's, *Information Service* 33 (March 6, 1954): 1.

15:20. Miriam J. Crist, "Winifred L. Chapell," in *Women in New Worlds: Historical Perspectives on the Wesleyan Tradition*, vol. 1, Hilah F. Thomas and Rosemary Skinner Keller, eds. (Nashville: Abingdon Press, 1981), 362–78, esp. 362, 365, 375–78.

15:21. On the participation of Georgia Harkness in contention over the ordination of women in Methodism, see Rosemary Radford Ruether and Rosemary Skinner Keller, eds., *Women and Religion in America*, vol. 3, *1900–1968: A Documentary History* (San Francisco: and Row, 1986), 299–303.

15:22. Arnold M. Shankman, "Civil Rights, 1920–1970," *Women in New Worlds: Historical Perspectives on the Wesleyan Tradition*, vol. 2, Hilah F. Thomas and Rosemary Skinner Keller, eds. (Nashville: Abingdon Press, 1982), 227–33, esp. 227, 229–30; see also Dorothy Tilly, *Christian Conscience and the Supreme Court Decision on Segregated Schools* (Atlanta: Southern Regional Council, [1954]); William Allred, "The Southern Regional Council" (M.A. thesis, Emory University, 1966), 121; Southern Regional Council Minutes (January 26, 1959), Josephine Wilkins Papers, box 2, Emory University.

15:23. Shankman, "Civil Rights, 1920–1970," *Women in New Worlds*, 231; see also Margaret Long, "Mrs. Dorothy Tilly: A Memoir," *New South 25* (Spring 1970): 46–48.

15:24. Pearl S. Buck, *Of Men and Women* (New York: John Day, 1941), 184, 183, 170, 123–36, 143, 86.

15:25. This account of Catherine Marshall draws on Paul Boyer, "Minister's Wife, Widow, Reluctant Feminist: Catherine Marshall in the 1950s," in Janet Wilson James, ed., *Women in American Religion* (Philadelphia: University of Pennsylvania Press, 1980), 253–71; see 258.

15:26. Ibid., 255–56; Catherine Marshall reprinted excerpts of Peter Marshall's sermon "Keepers of the Springs" in her *A Man Called Peter* (New York: McGraw-Hill, 1951), 54–55.

15:27. Boyer, "Minister's Wife," 262, 265; see Catherine Marshall, *To Live Again* (New York: McGraw-Hill, 1957), 144 and chap. 7, "The Walk in Wistfulness," 102–23; *A Man Called Peter*, 55–56, 116–18, 47; and, again, *To Live Again*, 12–13, 95.

15:28. Shelley Davis Finson, *Women and Religion: A Bibliographic Guide to Christian Feminist Liberation Theology* (Toronto: University of Toronto Press, 1991), includes many pages of references to women in Christian history, 26–50; most remarkable is the paucity of books and articles published during the mid-century decades about women in those two decades.

15:29. This account depends on Gladys Gilkey Calkins, *Follow These Women:*

Church Women in the Ecumenical Movement. A History of the Development of United Work Among Women of the Protestant Churches in the United States (New York: National Council of Churches, 1961), 58–70.
    15:30. Ibid., 75–76.

Chapter Sixteen

16:1. Since this chapter connects American church unity movements to the world Christian scene, access to reference materials on ecumenism is valuable. A one-volume source is Nicholas Lossky et al., *Dictionary of the Ecumenical Movement* (Grand Rapids: Eerdmans, 1991). It includes excellent bibliographical advice at the end of each entry; see also 101, the entry on "Bibliographies."
    16:2. For familiarization with the language, style, and practical elements of ecumenism, see the publication *Alive Together: A Practical Guide to Ecumenical Learning* (Geneva, Switzerland: World Council of Churches, 1989); no author is named.
    16:3. Henry P. Van Dusen, *World Christianity: Yesterday, Today, Tomorrow* (Nashville: Abingdon-Cokesbury, 1947), 11, 13.
    16:4. Ibid., 16, 30–31.
    16:5. Ibid., 32–34, 39.
    16:6. Ibid., 66.
    16:7. Ibid., 177–78.
    16:8. Ibid., 178–79, 251.
    16:9. John R. Scotford, *Church Union: Why Not?* (Boston: Pilgrim Press, 1948), vii–ix.
    16:10. Ibid., 1–2.
    16:11. Ibid., 2–7.
    16:12. Ibid., 7–8.
    16:13. Ibid., 8–10.
    16:14. Ibid., 11–19.
    16:15. Ibid., 19–30, esp. 20 and 26.
    16:16. Ibid., 30–33, esp. 32.
    16:17. Ibid., 31–35, also chapters 3, "The Co-operative Impulse," 36–51, and 4, "Where There Are Too Many Churches," 52–74, present these themes; see esp. 57, 59–60.
    16:18. Ibid., 75–83, esp. 76, 78, 83.
    16:19. Ibid., 85–86, 88, 92, 94–95, 97.
    16:20. Ibid., 100–9, 121–22.
    16:21. Ibid., 107–9, 121–22.
    16:22. Ross W. Sanderson, *Church Cooperation in the United States: The Nationwide Backgrounds and Ecumenical Significance of State and Local Councils of Churches and Their Historical Perspective* (Hartford: Finlay Brothers, 1960), 182–83.
    16:23. Ibid., 182–83, 187.
    16:24. Ibid., 188, 202–3.
    16:25. Scotford, *Church Union,* 122–23; Paul Griswold Macy, *If It Be Of God: The Story of the World Council of Churches* (St. Louis: Bethany, 1960), 23; Henry Smith Leiper introduced Macy, 7–10.
    16:26. Macy, *If It Be Of God,* 29, 59.
    16:27. Ibid., 65, 72; Macy cites *Christus Victor: The Report of the World Conference of Christian Youth, Amsterdam, 1939* (Geneva, Switzerland: World Conference of Christian Youth Headquarters, 1939), 237.

16:28. Macy, *If It Be Of God*, 67, 79–80.

16:29. Ibid., 87, 103–4, 110–11, 114–15.

16:30. Edward Duff, S.J., *The Social Thought of the World Council of Churches* (New York: Association Press, 1956), 1, 6.

16:31. Ibid., 14–16; he cited Alfred Winslow Jones, *Life, Liberty, and Property: A Study of Conflict and Measurement of Conflicting Rights* (Philadelphia: Lippincott, 1941); Brunner was in the World Council of Churches report, "The Church and the Disorder of Society," found in *Man's Disorder and God's Design* (New York: Harper & Brothers, 1948); André Siegfried, *Les Forces Religieuses et la Vie Politique* (Paris: Librairie Armand Colin, 1951), 218.

16:32. Duff, *Social Thought*, 11, 45–46; *Christian Century* 65 (September 22, 1948): 980; Samuel McCrea Cavert, *On the Road to Christian Unity: An Appraisal of the Ecumenical Movement* (New York: Harper & Row, 1961), 24–26.

16:33. Henry J. Pratt, *The Liberalization of American Protestantism: A Case Study in Complex Organizations* (Detroit: Wayne State University Press, 1972), 27–29; see also John A. Hutchinson, *We Are Not Divided: A Critical and Historical Study of the Federal Council of Churches of Christ in America* (New York: Round Table Press, 1941).

16:34. Pratt, *Liberalization of American Protestantism*, 31, 32; Samuel McCrea Cavert, *The American Churches in the Ecumenical Movement, 1900–1968* (New York: Association Press, 1968), 189–90, 195–96, 203–4, 206.

16:35. "The National Council of Churches Views Its Task In Christian Life and Work" (May 16, 1951), Pronouncements Issued By the National Council of Churches of Christ in The United States of America, Through February 1961, sections 9.1–6.

16:36. Pratt, *Liberalization of American Protestantism*, 36; "N.C.C. in the U.S.A.," *Christian Century* 69 (November 26, 1952): 1374–75.

16:37. Samuel McCrea Cavert, "Introducing the National Council of Churches," in George F. Ketcham, ed., *Yearbook of American Churches, 1951 Edition* (New York: The National Council of Churches, 1951): 1–2.

16:38. Ibid., 3, 15.

16:39. Pratt, *Liberalization of American Protestantism*, 19; quotes Peter Day, "The National Council of Churches: An Evaluation," *Christianity and Crisis* 20 (May 16, 1960): 67.

16:40. Pratt, *Liberalization of American Protestantism*, 84–88; cites *Fortune* 56 (November 1957): 177.

16:41. Pratt, *Liberalization of American Protestantism*, 89–91.

16:42. Ibid., 89–93, quoting General Board Minutes (November 28, 1951); on Judd and Kirschner, see *Christianity and Crisis* 12 (May 12, 1952): 63.

16:43. Pratt, *Liberalization of American Protestantism*, 93–94, 96–99, citing Pew's report.

16:44. Ibid., 99–104, citing Pew's report and an interview with Blake in March of 1969; for Miller's views at the end of this period, see *Christian Century* 77 (December 21, 1960): 1505–7, and *Christian Century* 78 (October 25, 1961): 1286.

16:45. It should be noted that the then four largest African American denominations were members of the council from the beginning; these were the African Methodist Episcopal Church and the African Methodist Episcopal Zion Church, the National Baptist Convention of America, and the National Baptist Convention, U.S.A., Inc. In 1966 the Progressive National Baptist Convention, Inc., joined it. Annual listings of current council members appear in Kenneth Bedell, ed., *Yearbook of American and Canadian Churches* (Nashville: Abingdon, 1993), 32. Among the larger African American denominations, those of Pentecostal outlook, e.g., the Church of God in Christ, identify more with evangelicalism and are not members of the National Council of Churches.

16:46. Robert S. Bilheimer, *Breakthrough: The Emergence of the Ecumenical Tradition* (Grand Rapids: Eerdmans, 1989), 67–68; cites *The First Six Years—1948–1954: Report of the Central Committee of the World Council of Churches on Activities of the Departments and Secretariats of the Council* (Geneva, Switzerland: World Council of Churches, 1954), and *The Christian Hope and the Task of the Church: Six Ecumenical Surveys and the Report of the Advisory Commission on the Main Theme* (New York: Harper & Brothers, 1954); see H. Krueger, "The Life and Activities of the World Council of Churches," in Harold E. Fey, ed., *The Ecumenical Advance: A History of the Ecumenical Movement*, vol. 2, *1948–1968* (Philadelphia: Westminster Press, 1970), 39–42, citing W. A. Vissser't Hooft, *The Evanston Report: The Second Assembly of the World Council of Churches, 1954* (New York: Harper & Brothers, 1955), 91, 70 ff.

16:47. Henry P. Van Dusen, *One Great Ground of Hope: Christian Missions and Christian Unity* (Philadelphia: Westminster Press, 1961), 123, 45 n. 30, 180–85.

16:48. Ibid., 180–85; Douglas Horton, *The United Church of Christ: Its Origins, Organization, and Role in the World Today* (New York: Thomas Nelson, 1962), 17–18; Louis H. Gunnemann, *The Shaping of the United Church of Christ: An Essay in the History of American Christianity* (New York: United Church Press, 1977), 13; cites Reinhold Niebuhr, "A Landmark in American Religious History," *The Messenger* (June 18, 1957): 11–23; see *Christian Century* 74 (July 17, 1957): 863.

16:49. Horton, *United Church of Christ*, 18–19; see also Douglas Horton, "Now the United Church of Christ," *Christian Century* 74 (June 12, 1957): 131.

16:50. Horton, *United Church of Christ*, 20–27.

16:51. Ibid., 275–76.

16:52. *Christian Faith in Action: Commemorative Volume: The Founding of the National Council of Churches of Christ in the United States of America* (New York: National Council of Churches, 1951), 13, 11.

Chapter Seventeen

17:1. Reporters on the revival of interest in religion in the 1950s generally concurred with what a major interpreter of revivals through American history later wrote in summary: "Great awakenings (and the revivals that are part of them) are the results, not of depressions, wars, or epidemics, but of critical disjunctions in our self-understanding." William G. McLoughlin, *Revivals, Awakenings, and Reform* (Chicago: University of Chicago Press, 1978), 2.

17:2. Reinhold Niebuhr, "Is There a Revival of Religion?" *New York Times Magazine* (November 19, 1950): 13.

17:3. Theodore Caplow et al., *All Faithful People: Change and Continuity in Middletown's Region* (Minneapolis: University of Minnesota Press, 1983), 20, renders the judgment that the Lynd surveys of 1924 were "the first sociological surveys of religious belief and practice in the United States." See Hadley Cantril, "Educational and Economic Composition of Religious Groups: An Analysis of Poll Data," *American Journal of Sociology* 48 (March 1943): 574–79, and Louis Bultena, "Church Membership and Church Attendance in Madison, Wisconsin," *American Sociological Review* 14 (June 1949): 384–89. Caplow et al. curiously neglect to mention the *Catholic Digest* poll of 1952 (see below); George Gallup, Jr., *Religion in America 50 Years: 1935–1985*, an issue of *The Gallup Report*, No. 236 (Princeton: The Gallup Report, May 1985), 5–6, reviews these early attempts; see also Lincoln Barnett, "God and the American People," *Ladies Home Journal* (November 1948): 37, 230–40.

17:4. Gallup, *The Gallup Report*, No. 236, 5–6; Barnett, "God and the American People," 37, 230–240.

17:5. Gallup, *Religion in America,* 41,43; on the validity of polls, see Jackson W. Carroll, Douglas W. Johnson, Martin E. Marty, *Religion in America: 1950 to the Present* (San Francisco: Harper and Row, 1979), 5–6.

17:6. John L. Thomas, S.J., *Religion and the American People* (Westminster, Md.: Newman, 1963), 18, 27–28, 51, 60–61, 66. Thomas interpreted the 1952 materials eleven years after the fact. Unfortunately, the original data cards have been lost, a fact that limits the usefulness of the survey in subsequent comparative work.

17:7. In order to treat the talk about the revival as part of the revival, I shall restrict myself to citations from articles written in the period, before there was the benefit of hindsight. Charles Y. Glock, "The Religious Revival in America?" was in Jane Zahn, ed., *Religion and the Face of America* (Berkeley: University Extension, University of California, 1958), 25–42. For a controversial retrospect on revivals, see William G. McLoughlin, *Revivals, Awakenings, and Reform.* Curiously, creatively, and in the eyes of some, eccentrically, McLoughlin does *not* treat the Eisenhower era revival among the—in his eyes—four "Great Awakenings." Instead it represents the "Nativist Phase" of the Fourth Great Awakening, which he dates after 1960 and foresees extending into the 1990s; 186–93. For a critique of the very notion of Great Awakenings, see Jon Butler, "Enthusiasm Described and Decried: The Great Awakening as Interpretive Fiction," *Journal of American History* 69 (September 1982): 305–25.

17:8. Michael Argyle, *Religious Behavior* (Glencoe: The Free Press, 1959), 28, 34.

17:9. Ibid., 35, 36, 38, Contents, vii, viii and the data passim, particularly in chapter-ending sections each time marked "Explanation" or "Summary." Note the discrepancy between the Gallup figures (7:5) and those in Argyle. Gallup used opinion polls and Argyle used the more realistic figures gatherd by denominations.

17:10. Ibid., 38.

17:11. Ibid., 137, 139. While Glock and Stark employed the deprivation theory in the 1950s, a summary of its sufficiencies and lacks appears later, in Charles Y. Glock, Benjamin B. Ringer, Earl R. Babbie, *To Comfort and to Challenge: A Dilemma of the Contemporary Church* (Berkeley and Los Angeles: University of California Press, 1967), 210–12; see also Kingsley Davis, *Human Society* (New York: Macmillan, 1948), 532; for a later, extensive critique of deprivation theories, one which saw Glock and Stark along with Argyle among its rare defenders (it "has received only a modicum of support, while most of the research has directly contradicted it"), see Dean R. Hoge and David A. Roozen, "Research on Factors Influencing Church Commitment," in Dean R. Hoge and David A. Roozen, eds., *Understanding Church Growth and Decline: 1950–1978* (Philadelphia: Pilgrim Press, 1979), 48–53.

17:12. Argyle, *Religious Behavior,* 176–77.

17:13. *Time* (November 14, 1949): 63; the "escapism" quotation is from *U.S. News and World Report* (August 27, 1954): 87.

17:14. Niebuhr, "Is There a Revival?" 13.

17:15. Ibid., 13, 60.

17:16. Ibid., 60, 62–63.

17:17. Ibid., 63.

17:18. Will Herberg, *Protestant-Catholic-Jew: An Essay in American Religious Sociology* (Garden City: Doubleday, 1955), 68, discusses the *Partisan Review* symposium and quotes Asher Byrnes, "Religion More or Less," *The Freeman* (October 30, 1950).

17:19. Ibid., 82–83; "Religion and the Intellectuals," *Partisan Review* 27 (February 1950), (March 1950), (April 1950); quote taken from (February 1950): 103.

17:20. Herberg, *Protestant-Catholic-Jew,* 67–68; see H. Stuart Hughes, "On Social Salvation," *Saturday Review of Literature* 34 (March 3, 1951): 14; "Paretans" were named after Vilfredo Pareto (1848–1923), the Italian economist and sociologist.

17:21. Herberg is quoted in the most ambitious if controversial study of his career,

Harry J. Ausmus, *Will Herberg: From Right to Right* (Chapel Hill: University of North Carolina Press, 1987), 136; Herberg, *Protestant-Catholic Jew,* 7, 88.

17:22. Ausmus, *Will Herberg,* 230–32 n.12, discusses the complicated question of the relative degree of intimacy between Herberg and Niebuhr, an acquaintanceship which was evidently more vivid in Herberg's mind than in Niebuhr's, and draws on archives including contemporary lectures; 69–70 traces Herberg's conversion to Judaism and relative degree of retention of Marxism and quotes a lecture by Herberg, "From Marxism to Judaism: Jewish Belief as a Dynamic of Social Action," found in *Commentary* (June 1947): 25–32, and a lecture delivered at Union Theological Seminary, April 29, 1948, from Ausmus collection; see also 80–82 on Rosenzweig, Buber, and the critique of Zionism, which also draws on Herberg Archives at Drew University, Madison, N.J.; Ausmus, 88 (and footnotes on 233), recalls the "post-modern" notion.

17:23. Ausmus, *Will Herberg,* notes that most of this material is from Herberg Archives; 106–7 for the Niebuhr comments; 116 on the campus scene; 126–29 on neoconservatism and Chambers; Herberg, *Protestant-Catholic-Jew,* 59–60; see Herbert Wallace Schneider, *Religion in 20th Century America* (Cambridge: Harvard University Press, 1952), 31–32. Ausmus discusses and provides reference for the fact that Herberg faked his advanced degrees in *Will Herberg: A Bio-Bibliography* (Westport: Greenwood, 1986), 3, 33.

17:24. Herberg, *Protestant-Catholic-Jew,* 61–66; Eisenhower was quoted in *New York Times* (August 20, 1954); the Methodist reference was in a May 1, 1954, release of *General News Service of the Methodist Church* (Commission on Public Relations and Methodist Information.); the Roper Poll was reported on NBC "Newsweek Documentaries," December 27, 1953.

17:25. Herberg, *Protestant-Catholic-Jew,* 64–66, 69–70; the senators were cited in *Information Service* of the National Council of Churches of Christ, December 27, 1952; Schneider, *Religion in 20th Century America,* 16, 33; see also *Publishers Weekly* (January 23, 1954); *Christopher News Notes,* no. 62 (November 1954); *Times Literary Supplement* (September 17, 1954): 64.

17:26. Herberg, *Protestant-Catholic-Jew,* 59, 69–73; he cited David Riesman, *The Lonely Crowd* (New Haven: Yale University Press, 1950) and Elmo Roper in NBC "Newsweek Documentaries," December 27, 1953.

17:27. Herberg, *Protestant-Catholic-Jew,* 74–77; Herberg drew on population statistics from the Population Reference Bureau, *Boston Daily Globe* (June 10, 1954).

17:28. Herberg, *Protestant-Catholic-Jew,* 43, 273–75; see Marcus Lee Hansen, *The Problem of the Third Generation Immigrant* (Rock Island: Augustana Historical Society, 1938), 9; Ausmus, *Will Herberg,* 150–51, reviews the reviews; see Nathan Glazer, "Religion Without Faith," *New Republic* 129 (November 14, 1955): 18.

17:29. A. Roy Eckardt, *The Surge of Piety in America: An Appraisal* (New York: Association, 1958), 17, 19, 22–26.

17:30. Ibid., 30, 42–49, 58, 128–29; see F. Ernest Johnson, ed., *Patterns of Faith in America Today* (New York: Harper and Brothers, 1957), Introduction, 2.

17:31. Charles Y. Glock, "The Religious Revival in America?" (see above, note 17:7), 32–42; He quoted Seymour Martin Lipset, "Religion in America: What Religious Revival?" *Columbia University Forum,* 2, no. 2 (Winter 1959); Herberg, "There Is a Religious Revival!" *Review of Religious Research* 1 (1959–60): 45–50. I have not chosen to begin in this volume the story of movements dating from very late in the decade that anticipate new religious expressions more characteristic of the 1960s. They are not without significance because they tested the conformist patterns of the religious revival of the 1950s, but in their own time were seen as part of the literary more than the religious scene, and were considered to be highly experimental outbursts of "fringe" literary circles. Included were the beat poets, the devotees of Zen, and the like. The literature on these movements is extensive. An excellent bibliography enhances some synthetic essays in Gregory Stephenson, *Essays on the Literature of the Beat*

Generation (Carbondale: Southern Illinois University Press, 1990). See also W. T. Lhamon, Jr., *Deliberate Speed: The Origins of a Cultural Style in the American 1950s* (Washington: Smithsonian Institution Press, 1990), which also has an important bibliography.

17:32. Claire Cox, *The New-Time Religion* (Englewood Cliffs: Prentice-Hall, 1961), 2, 3, 1.

17:33. Ibid. 5–7, 2.

Chapter Eighteen

18:1. Will Herberg, *Protestant-Catholic-Jew: An Essay in American Religious Sociology* (Garden City: Doubleday, 1955), 101–2. Among other authors he cited for these phrases were J. Paul Williams and Horace M. Kallen.

18:2. Eisenhower is quoted without reference in an anthology, Art Spiegelman and Bob Schneider, *Whole Grains: A Book of Quotations* (New York: Douglas Links, 1973), 64.

18:3. Herberg, *Protestant-Catholic-Jew,* 281, citing *New York Times* (February 18, 1955).

18:4. Herberg, *Protestant-Catholic-Jew,* 92–93, using quotations from Paul Hutchinson, "The President's Religious Faith," *Christian Century* 71 (March 24, 1954): 362–69; also Herberg, 274–75, quotes an Associated Press dispatch in "Eisenhower Urges Nation to Join 'Back to God' Drive," *New York Herald Tribune* 114 (February 21, 1955).

18:5. The Court cases are quoted by Philip E. Hammond, "Religious Pluralism and Durkheim's Integration Thesis," in Allan W. Eister, ed., *Changing Perspectives in the Scientific Study of Religion* (New York: John Wiley, 1974), 130–31; Hammond has an important discussion of "The Religion of the Legal System: A Disappearing Rhetoric," 129–35; the entire *Zorach v. Clauson* decision is reprinted in Robert T. Miller and Ronald B. Flowers, *Toward Benevolent Neutrality: Church, State and the Supreme Court,* 3d ed. (Waco: Markham Press Fund, 1987), 393–97.

18:6. *Kedroff v. Saint Nicholas Cathedral* 344 U.S. 94 (1952) appears in Joseph Tussman, *The Supreme Court on Church and State* (New York: Oxford University Press, 1962), 292–303; Frankfurter's comments are on 298–301; see Jackson's quotation on 303.

18:7. *Burstyn v. Wilson* is reproduced in Tussman, *The Supreme Court on Church and State,* 275–91; see 275 for Clark quotation.

18:8. Justice Black's dissent appears in Tussman, *The Supreme Court on Church and State,* 268–72; 273–74 for Justice Jackson's dissent.

18:9. Mark Silk, *Spiritual Politics: Religion and America Since World War II* (New York: Simon and Schuster, 1988), 99–100, quoting *Congressional Record,* 83d Cong., 2d sess., 1954, vol. 100, pt. 6: 7764; *Congressional Record,* 84th Cong., 1st sess., 1955, vol. 101, pt. 6: 7532–33.

18:10. Miller and Flowers, *Toward Benevolent Neutrality,* 87–96, includes Frankfurter's dissent; *West Virginia Board of Education v. Barnette* 319 U.S. 624 (1943).

18:11. Paul A. Carter, *Another Part of the Fifties* (New York: Columbia University Press, 1983), 114–16, tells the story of "Under God"; see "Put God in Flag Pledge of Allegiance," *Washington Post* (February 8, 1954): 12; see also Gerard Kaye and Ferenc M. Szasz, "Adding God to the Pledge of Allegiance," *Encounter* 34 (Winter 1973); *New York Times* (May 5, 1954) as quoted by Silk, *Spiritual Politics,* 96; Silk, 98, quotes the Eisenhower signing remarks from the *Congressional Record,* 83d Cong., 2d Sess., 1954, vol. 100, pt. 7: 8618.

18:12. *New York Times* (May 5, 1954); quoted by Silk, *Spiritual Politics,* 96, 98; see Kaye and Szasz, "Adding God to the Pledge," 52–55; *Congressional Record,* 83rd Cong., 2d sess., 1954, vol. 100, pt. 7: 8618.

18:13. Silk, *Spiritual Politics*, 98–99; Kaye and Szasz, "Adding God to the Pledge," 55; on "In God We Trust," see Douglas T. Miller and Marion Nowak, *The Fifties: The Way We Really Were* (Garden City: Doubleday, 1977), 89.

18:14. Herbert Hoover, *Addresses upon the American Road, 1948–1950* (Stanford: Stanford University Press, 1951), 66–67; see the critiques which quote Truman, "Mr. Truman's Spiritual Blindness," *The Christian Century* 67 (June 28, 1950): 728; *Public Papers of the President of the United States: Harry S. Truman—1951* (Washington, D.C.: U. S. Government Printing Office, 1966), 210, 548–49.

18:15. There is an excellent bibliographical essay on Eisenhower in Robert F. Burk, *Dwight D. Eisenhower: Hero and Politician* (Boston: Twayne, 1986), 191–99; Eisenhower's religion is set in context by Richard G. Hutcheson, Jr., *God in the White House: How Religion Has Changed the Modern Presidency* (New York: Macmillan, 1988), 50–52, and, with less favor, by Robert S. Alley, *So Help Me God: Religion and the Presidency, Wilson to Nixon* (Richmond: John Knox Press, 1972), 82–91; on "I Believe," see "The President Believes," *Christian Century* 75 (March 24, 1954): 362.

18:16. William Lee Miller, *Piety Along the Potomac* (Boston: Houghton Mifflin, 1964), 18–19; Miller was quoting Stanley High, "What the President Wants," *Readers Digest* 62 (April 1953): 1–4; and Edward L. R. Elson, *America's Spiritual Recovery* (New Jersey: Revell, 1954), 53.

18:17. Miller, *Piety Along the Potomac*, 21–22, 28–29.

18:18. Ibid., 32, 34, 41–45.

18:19. Ibid., 41–45, 125–31.

18:20. Marshall Frady, *Billy Graham: A Parable of American Righteousness* (Boston: Little, Brown, 1979), 232, describes Richardson and 255–57 tells of the developing relation with Eisenhower; see also Billy Graham, "God Is My Witness," *McCall's* (June 1964): 64; John Charles Pollock, *Billy Graham, Evangelist to the World: An Authorized Biography of the Decisive Years* (San Francisco: Harper & Row, 1979), 165.

18:21. The Moses or Daniel reference is quoted in Charles T. Cook, *The Billy Graham Story* (Wheaton, Ill.: Van Kempen Press, 1954), 100; on Eisenhower's dependence on God and the advice of the born-again, see William McLoughlin, *Billy Graham: Revivalist in a Secular Age* (New York: Ronald Press, 1960), 96; McLoughlin, 117, quotes Graham on the inaugural prayer, the helm, and "respite" from a radio message, "Three Minutes to Twelve," (1953) published by the Billy Graham Evangelistic Association and the program "Hour of Decision" (February 8, 1953, and April 19, 1953); that Eisenhower was to lead a religious revival is quoted in McLoughlin, 128; on Eisenhower's request for help and the ensuing conversation, see Frady, *Billy Graham: A Parable of American Righteousness*, 257, and Pollock, *Billy Graham, Evangelist to the World*, 96.

18:22. Adlai E. Stevenson, *Major Campaign Speeches of Adlai Stevenson* (New York: Random House, 1953), 197–98, 213, 218–19, from a speech at the Masonic Temple in Detroit, October 7, 1952; 245, 250 quotes from the Mormon Tabernacle address, October 14, 1952.

18:23. Ibid., 260–62, 282–84; see 319 for his concession speech of November 5, 1952.

18:24. Daniel J. Boorstin, *The Genius of American Politics* (Chicago: University of Chicago Press, 1953), 137, quoting Stevenson in *Time* (January 28, 1952): 16; Boorstin, 141–46, quoting the *Chicago Daily News* (January 12, 1952): 1; Boorstin, 146–47, 160.

18:25. Ibid., 146–47, 160.

18:26. Ibid., 135, 137, 184–85, 189; Boorstin quotes Chapter 2 of Edward Gibbon, *The History of the Decline and Fall of the Roman Empire*, vol. 1 (Philadelphia: Henry T. Coates, 1900), 73–74.

18:27. J. Paul Williams, *What Americans Believe and How They Worship,* rev. ed. (New York: Harper & Row, 1962), 13.

18:28. Ibid., 1, 8–9.

18:29. Ibid., 469–70, 475–78; he quotes Walter Lippmann, *U.S. Foreign Policy* (Boston: Little, Brown, 1943), 137; see also Robin M. Williams, Jr., *American Society* (New York: Knopf, 1951), 312, 342.

18:30. Williams, *What Americans Believe,* 478–79, 482–84; see Sidney E. Mead, "American Protestantism Since the Civil War. I. From Denominationalism to Americanism," *The Journal of Religion* 36 (January 1956); "American Protestantism Since the Civil War. II. From Americanism to Christianity," *The Journal of Religion* 36 (April 1956): 67; see also A. Powell Davies, *Man's Vast Future* (Farrar, Strauss and Cudahy, 1951), 27 f.; Williams also cited Walter Lippmann, *Essays in the Public Philosophy* (Boston: Little, Brown, 1955), 96–97, 101–4, 113–14, 181.

18:31. Williams, *What Americans Believe,* 484–85.

18:32. Ibid., 484–86; the names he cited were from Martin E. Marty, *The New Shape of American Religion* (New York: Harper & Row, 1959), 85 f., and Herberg, *Protestant-Catholic-Jew,* 102.

18:33. Williams, *What Americans Believe,* 488–90, 492; for the public school argument, Williams referred to his own earlier work, *The New Education and Religion: A Challenge to Secularism in Education* (New York: Association Press, 1945).

Chapter Nineteen

19:1. Will Herberg, *Protestant-Catholic-Jew: An Essay in American Religious Sociology* (Garden City: Doubleday, 1955), 102–3.

19:2. Ibid., 102–4.

19:3. Joshua Loth Liebman, *Peace of Mind* (New York: Simon and Schuster, 1946), 171–73; see especially pages 202, 173, 199; for locating Liebman in a movement, see Mark Silk, *Spiritual Politics: Religion and America Since World War II* (New York: Simon and Schuster, 1988), 33 ff.; Donald Meyer, *The Positive Thinkers: A Study of the American Quest for Health, Wealth and Personal Power from Mary Baker Eddy to Norman Vincent Peale* (Garden City: Doubleday, 1965), 327–28, develops the Liebman themes.

19:4. Louis Schneider and Sanford M. Dornbusch, *Popular Religion: Inspirational Books in America* (Chicago: University of Chicago Press, 1958), 1–2, 6–7; see Norman Vincent Peale and Smiley Blanton, *The Art of Real Happiness* (New York: Prentice-Hall, 1950), 16; Dr. George W. Crane, "Vitamin R(eligion) Doesn't Cost a Penny," *Boston Daily Globe* (July 18, 1956): 22; see also E. Stanley Jones, *The Way to Power and Poise* (New York: Abingdon-Cokesbury, 1949), 357.

19:5. Schneider and Dornbusch, *Popular Religion,* 24, 37; their critique of the very notion of "religious revival" is on 57–58.

19:6. Ibid., 43, 54, 25, 45; see Robin M. Williams, *American Society* (New York: Alfred A. Knopf, 1951), 390–440, for the value orientations he found.

19:7. Schneider and Dornbusch, *Popular Religion,* 49, 54–56; see Liebman, *Peace of Mind,* 82.

19:8. William Lee Miller, *Piety Along the Potomac* (Boston: Houghton Mifflin, 1964), 125–27.

19:9. Ibid., 126–37.

19:10. Ibid., 137–43.

19:11. Allan R. Broadhurst, *He Speaks the Word of God: A Study of the Sermons of Norman Vincent Peale* (Englewood Cliffs: Prentice-Hall, 1963), 47–51; the quotation about the Republic is from a contemporary biography, Arthur Gordon, *Norman Vincent Peale: Minister to Millions* (Greenwich: Fawcett Publications, 1964 reprint of 1958 edition), 187–88.

19:12. Broadhurst, *He Speaks the Word of God*, 53–59; Niebuhr was quoted from William Peters, "The Case Against 'Easy' Religion," *Redbook* 105 (September 1955): 22, 92, as were Liston Pope, Franklin Clark Fry, and G. Bromley Oxnam, 92–93.

19:13. Broadhurst, *He Speaks the Word of God*, 59–64, 81–86, 91; Peale was quoted in Arthur Gordon, "The Case for 'Positive' Faith," *Redbook* 105 (September 1955): 25, and in "Issue of Dr. Peale," *Newsweek* (February 21, 1955): 86.

19:14. Meyer, *The Positive Thinkers*, 262–68, 278–80; the reservoir quote is from Norman Vincent Peale, *Stay Alive All Your Life* (Englewood Cliffs: Prentice-Hall, 1957), 252; the trust in God quote from Peale's *The Power of Positive Thinking* (Englewood Cliffs: Prentice-Hall, 1952), 106.

19:15. Meyer, *The Positive Thinkers*, 278–87.

19:16. Ibid., 287–89; Peale's attacks were in "Can Protestantism Be Saved?" *Reader's Digest* 71 (September 1962): 49–54.

19:17. Meyer, *The Positive Thinkers*, 331–32; see Fulton J. Sheen, *Peace of Soul* (New York: McGraw-Hill, 1949).

19:18. Paul Blanshard, *American Freedom and Catholic Power*, second edition (Boston: Beacon Press, 1958), 238, 43, 160, 267–86; the reference to Protestantism was from Fulton J. Sheen, *The Mystical Body of Christ* (New York: Sheed and Ward, 1935), 2; on the Blessed Mother, Blanshard was citing Sheen's *Communism and the Conscience of the West* (New York: Bobbs-Merrill, 1948), 216.

19:19. Peter G. Horsfield, *Religious Television: The American Experience* (New York: Longman, 1985), 5, 7–8; Horsfield's source for the Gallagher quote was Roger Kahle, "Religion and Network Television," M.S. Thesis, Columbia University, 1970, 2:3–4; Horsfield credits Sheen with the breakthrough, calling attention to Fulton J. Sheen, *Treasure in Clay* (Garden City: Doubleday, 1980); see also Jeffrey K. Hadden and Charles E. Swann, *Prime Time Preachers* (Reading: Addison-Wesley, 1981), 81–83.

19:20. Everett C. Parker, David W. Barry, and Dallas W. Smythe, *The Television-Radio Audience and Religion* (New York: Harper and Brothers, 1955), 233, 235–36.

19:21. Ibid., 294, 296, 300–301.

19:22. Ibid., 302–3, 306–7, 313.

19:23. Ibid., 323–26.

19:24. Ibid., 348–50, 355.

19:25. J. Milton Yinger, *Sociology Looks at Religion* (New York: Macmillan, 1963), 67–71; the material first appeared in Yinger's H. Paul Douglass Lecture in 1962, where he paid attention to Peter Berger's *The Noise of Solemn Assemblies* (Garden City: Doubleday, 1961), 15.

19:26. Yinger, *Sociology Looks at Religion*, 71–74.

19:27. William McLoughlin, *Billy Graham: Revivalist in a Secular Age* (New York: Ronald, 1960), 214–15, 257 n.27, 209; he cites "The Sin of Tolerance," published in 1957 by the Billy Graham Evangelistic Association.

19:28. Ibid., 257 n.27, 209, 219; citing *New York Times* (January 26, 1958): 61.

19:29. Ibid., 70–80 condenses Graham's gospel citing Graham's *Peace With God* (Garden City: Doubleday, 1953), 90, 106–7, 155–56; Marshall Frady, *Billy Graham: A Parable of American Righteousness* (Boston: Little, Brown, 1979), 236–38; Frady cited the *Charlotte Observer* (June 22, 1951); Richard T. Stout for the *Chicago Daily News* World Service, in *Charlotte Observer* (June 16, 1960); *Charlotte Observer* (December 6, 1951).

19:30. Mark Silk, *Spiritual Politics*, 68–69, sees Graham as an agent of "adhesion" in the republic; Silk cites Arthur Darby Nock for his use of the term; see Arthur Darby Nock, *Conversion: The Old and the New in Religion from Alexander the Great to Augustine of Hippo* (New York: Oxford University Press, 1933), 7.

Chapter Twenty

20:1. Arthur Cohen, *The Myth of the Judeo-Christian Tradition* (New York: Harper & Row, 1969), xix–xxi, is a description of the critique of the "myth," elaborated upon at many places in the collection of essays that follow.

20:2. Mark Silk, *Spiritual Politics: Religion and America Since World War II* (New York: Simon and Schuster, 1988), 40–44, develops the Judeo-Christian concept through history; for comment on Eisenhower, see Patrick Henry, " 'And I Don't Care What It Is': The Tradition-History of a Civil Religion Proof-Text," *Journal of the American Academy of Religion* 49 (1981); Arthur E. Murphy, *Science, Philosophy, and Religion* 10 (1950), 460; for the Straus comment, see *New York Times* (October 29, 1951): 26.

20:3. Silk, *Spiritual Politics*, 45, 47–53; Will Herberg, *Judaism and Modern Man* (New York: Farrar, Straus and Cudahy, 1951), ix, xi; Will Herberg, *Protestant-Catholic-Jew: An Essay in American Religious Sociology* (Garden City: Doubleday, 1955), chap. 11, 254–72; Jacques Maritain discussed the theme extensively in *Moral Philosophy* (New York: Scribner's, 1964), 75–91; notice the Statement of Purpose by the editor of Oesterreicher's yearbook, *The Bridge* (New York: Pantheon, 1955), 9; Silk drew on Niebuhr, Tillich, and Frank; see Reinhold Niebuhr's Introduction to Waldo Frank, *The Jew in Our Day* (London: Victor Gollancz, 1944), 9; Reinhold Niebuhr, *The Self and the Dramas of History* (New York: Scribner's, 1955), 44; Paul Tillich, "Is There a Judeo-Christian Tradition?" *Judaism* 1 (1952): 107; Frank, *The Jew in Our Day*, 181–82.

20:4. Reinhold Niebuhr, *Pious and Secular America* (New York: Scribner's, 1958), 86; see "Second Round Table Conference," at Tercentenary Conference on American Jewish Sociology in *Jewish Social Studies* 17 (July 1955): 236; a critical review of the Niebuhr turn appears in John Murray Cuddihy, *No Offense: Civil Religion and Protestant Taste* (New York: Seabury, 1978), chap. 3, "Protestant: The Reinhold Niebuhr–Will Herberg 'Treaty'," 31–48.

20:5. John Courtney Murray, "Governmental Repression of Heresy," *Proceedings of the Third Annual Meeting of the Catholic Theological Society of America* 3 (Chicago: June 1949), 86; see Cuddihy, *No Offense*, 65; see also John Courtney Murray, "Separation of Church and State," *America* 76 (December 7, 1946); Talcott Parsons, "Sociology and Social Psychology," in Hoxie N. Fairchild, ed., *Religious Perspectives in College Teaching* (New York: Ronald Press, 1952), 326.

20:6. "The Status of a Controversy," *American Ecclesiastical Review* 124 (June 1951), 458; "For the Freedom and Transcendence of the Church," *American Ecclesiastical Review* 126 (January 1952), 43; Cuddihy, *No Offense*, 75, makes much of this "smoothing" issue; John Courtney Murray, *We Hold These Truths: Catholic Reflections on the American Proposition* (New York: Sheed and Ward, 1960), 11, 22, 41.

20:7. Murray, *We Hold These Truths*, 22, 6, 9; see also Thomas Gilby, O.P., *Between Community and Society* (New York: Longmans, Green, 1953), 93.

20:8. Murray, *We Hold These Truths*, 15, 19, 21.

20:9. Ibid., 22–23, 28–30, 37, 41, 74, 76.

20:10. Ibid., 130–32, 138.

20:11. Ibid., 17, 109; on Murray's battles with Rome and American Catholic authorities, see Donald E. Pelotte, S.S.S., *John Courtney Murray: Theologian in Conflict* (New York: Paulist, 1976), chap. 2, "Opposition and Rebuke: 1950–1959," 27–73.

20:12. Robert G. Goldy, *The Emergence of Jewish Theology in America* (Bloomington: Indiana University Press, 1990), 4–5, 12–13. Goldy locates Jewish thought as a postwar phenomenon; see also Joseph Zeitlin, *Disciples of the Wise: The Religious and Social Opinion of American Rabbis* (New York: Teachers College of Columbia University, 1945); see also Judd Teller, "A Critique of the New Jewish Theology from a Secularist Point of View," *Commentary* 25 (March 1958): 251; Marshall Sklare, *Conservative Judaism* (Glencoe: The Free Press, 1955), 43–65; Jakob Petuchowski, "The Question of Jewish Theology," *Judaism* 7 (Winter 1958): 53; Eugene Borowitz, "The Jewish Need for Theology," *Commentary* 34 (August 1962): 138–44.

20:13. Goldy, *The Emergence of Jewish Theology in America*, 18–20; see also Will Herberg, "Theological Problems of America," *Proceedings of the Rabbinical Assembly of America* 13 (1949): 411; Milton Steinberg, "Theological Problems of America," *Proceedings of the Rabbinical Assembly of America* 13 (1949): 404; Herberg, *Protestant-Catholic-Jew*, 103–4, 111, 134–35, 138—he was quoting H. Richard Niebuhr on the past glories of Protestantism.

20:14. Herberg, *Protestant-Catholic-Jew*, 166–67, 175–76.

20:15. Ibid., 203, 205, 211, 213.

20:16. Ibid., 247, 250–58, 276–80; he quoted A. Roy Eckardt, "The New Look in American Piety," *Christian Century* 71 (November 17, 1954): 1396.

20:17. Arthur Cohen, *The Natural and the Supernatural Jew: An Historical and Theological Introduction* (New York: Pantheon, 1962), 218; Arthur Cohen, *The Myth of the Judeo-Christian Tradition* (see note 20:1).

20:18. Cohen, *The Natural and the Supernatural Jew*, 222, 224, 230–31, 233; Steinberg, "Theological Problems of America," 213.

20:19. Cohen, *The Natural and the Supernatural Jew*, 279–82, 304, 307–9.

20:20. Ibid., 246, 251, 257–59; "ontological presupposition" is in Abraham Joshua Heschel, *God in Search of Man* (New York: Farrar, Strauss and Cudahy, 1955), 114–24; Goldy, *The Emergence of Jewish Theology in America*, 21–22; see also Abraham Joshua Heschel, "The Spirit of Prayer," *Proceedings of the Rabbinical Assembly of America* 17 (1953): 159.

20:21. Ibid., 21–22, 106; Goldy deserves credit for the linkage with Tillich; see Paul Tillich, *The Protestant Era* (Chicago: University of Chicago Press, 1948), 185–86.

20:22. Abraham Joshua Heschel, "The Religious Message," John Cogley, ed., in *Religion in America: Original Essays on Religion in a Free Society* (New York: Meridian, 1958), 244.

20:23. Ibid., 244–45, 247, 251–53.

20:24. Ibid., 256–57, 267–71.

20:25. Trude Weiss-Rosmarin, "Jewish Theology," *Jewish Spectator* 25 (November 1960), 5–6.

20:26. Ibid., 6.

20:27. Ibid., 6–7.

20:28. Reinhold Niebuhr, *The Irony of American History* (New York: Scribner's, 1952), 155, 7, 15–16; Richard Wrightman Fox, *Reinhold Niebuhr: A Biography* (New York: Pantheon, 1985), 259–65, advances the story of Niebuhr in the fifties; the Eisenhower quotation is on 265; see also Reinhold Niebuhr, "The Gospel in Future America," *Christian Century* 75 (June 18, 1958): 715, and "The Quality of Our Lives," *Christian Century* 77 (May 11, 1960): 571.

20:29. Reinhold Niebuhr, "Religiosity and the Christian Faith," *Christianity and Crisis* 14 (January 24, 1955): 185–86.

20:30. *New York Times* (November 19, 1950): 13; Fox, *Reinhold Niebuhr*, 265–66, describes Niebuhr's attitudes during the revival; for Niebuhr on Graham, see "Literalism, Individualism, and Billy Graham," *Christian Century* 73 (May 23, 1956): 642; "Proposal to Billy Graham," *Christian Century* 73 (August 8, 1956): 921; "The Billy Graham Campaign," *Messenger* (June 4, 1957): 38; *New York Times* (June 2, 1957): 38; Mark Silk, *Spiritual Politics*, 101–7 details Niebuhr's response; see *Christianity and Crisis* 16 (March 5, 1956): 18, and ibid. (April 2, 1956): 40.

20:31. Reinhold Niebuhr, *Pious and Secular America*, 5, 11, 21–22, 91; see Fox, *Reinhold Niebuhr*, 322 n. 14, for Graham's response to Niebuhr on the race question; see *Christian Century* 73 (1956): 640–42, 848–49, 921–22, 1197–99 for the debates over Graham; Silk, *Spiritual Politics*, 103–4, reports on the National Council of Churches' General Board's Commission to Study Evangelism.

20:32. June Bingham, *The Courage to Change: An Introduction to the Life and Thought of Reinhold Niebuhr* (New York: Scribner's, 1961), 397, quotes the Union address, "Religiosity and the Christian Faith," *Christianity and Crisis* 15 (January 24, 1955), reprinted by D. B. Robertson, ed., in *Reinhold Niebuhr: Essays in Applied Christianity* (New York: Meridian, 1959), 63–68; Fox, *Reinhold Niebuhr*, 267, quotes Niebuhr to Frankfurter in a letter of May 26, 1960.

20:33. H. Richard Niebuhr, *The Social Sources of Denominationalism* (New York: Henry Holt, 1929); H. Richard Niebuhr, *The Kingdom of God in America* (Chicago: Willett, Clark, 1937); with Wilhelm Pauck and Francis P. Miller, *The Church Against the World* (Chicago: Willett, Clark, 1935); *The Meaning of Revelation* (New York: Macmillan, 1941); *The Purpose of the Church and Its Ministry* (New York: Harper and Row, 1956); for a sample of his ecumenical work, see "The Disorder of Man in the Church of God," in *Man's Disorder and God's Design*, vol. 1, *The Universal Church in God's Design* (New York: Harper and Brothers, 1949), 78–88. This volume relates to the first World Council of Churches meeting at Amsterdam in 1948; quote is in H. Richard Niebuhr, *The Kingdom of God in America*, xiv.

20:34. H. Richard Niebuhr, *Christ and Culture* (New York: Harper and Brothers, 1951).

20:35. Ibid., 1–2, 8–9.

20:36. H. Richard Niebuhr, *Radical Monotheism and Western Culture* (London: Faber and Faber, 1960), 31–32, 60, 62.

20:37. Ibid., 69–70.

20:38. Fox, *Reinhold Niebuhr*, 257–59, describes the friendship and rivalry of Niebuhr and Tillich, chiefly over matters of sex and sensuality; on the provenance and reputation of *The Protestant Era*, see Wilhelm and Marion Pauck, *Paul Tillich: His Life and Thought*, vol. 1: *Life* (New York: Harper and Row, 1976), 219–21; for the publication events of the decade, see 225–45.

20:39. Paul Tillich, "Autobiographical Reflections," in Charles W. Kegley and Robert W. Bretall, eds., *The Theology of Paul Tillich* (New York: Macmillan, 1961), 20–21; the quotation on culture is from Paul Tillich, *The Protestant Era* (Chicago: University of Chicago Press, 1948), xvii; Theodore M. Greene, "Paul Tillich and Our Secular Culture," in Kegley and Bretall, 52; *The Protestant Era*, 185.

20:40. Tillich, *The Protestant Era*, xxvii–xxix.

20:41. Paul Tillich, *The Dynamics of Faith* (New York: Harper and Row, 1957), 2, 3; Paul Tillich, *Theology of Culture* (New York: Oxford University Press, 1959), 49–51.

20:42. Tillich, *Theology of Culture*, 169, 176.

Chapter Twenty-one

21:1. "McCarthyism" and the John Birch Society are the two extreme right-wing movements of the 1950s and early 1960s to have survived in national consciousness. Thus Robert Hendrickson, *The Dictionary of Eponyms: Names That Became Words* (New York: Stein and Day, 1973), 210–11, includes McCarthyism as an eponym and dates the invention of the term to April 5, 1950, when Max Lerner coined it in a column. "A host of other *isms* have arisen since the senator's time, including . . . *Birchism.*"

21:2. *Congressional Record*, 81st Cong., 2d sess., 1950, vol. 96, pt. 2: 1954, on the morality of his crusade; Richard Rovere, *Senator Joe McCarthy* (New York: Harcourt, Brace, 1959), 249–54; David H. Bennett, *The Party of Fear: From Nativist Movements to the New Right in American History* (Chapel Hill: University of North Carolina Press, 1988), 293–94.

21:3. *Congressional Record*, 81st Cong., 2d sess., 1950, vol. 96, pt. 2: 1954, for the McCarthy quotation; Bennett, *The Party of Fear*, 293–94, 466. n.19 provides bibliographical access to the controversy over the origin and content of the speech, and there is some controversy concerning the details of the speech; see Robert Griffith, *The Politics of Fear: Joseph R. McCarthy and the Senate* (Lexington: University Press of Kentucky, 1970), 48–51.

21:4. Donald F. Crosby, S.J., *God, Church, and Flag: Senator Joseph R. McCarthy and the Catholic Church, 1950–1957* (Chapel Hill: University of North Carolina Press, 1978), 47–52, 257, discusses the probably fictional elements in the story of McCarthy's speeches. Crosby documents his careful research, including interviews with intimates of Father Walsh. His book is the most elaborate and reliable discussion of religious issues associated with McCarthyism.

21:5. Ibid., 53, 257, cites an interview with Eugene McCarthy (February 3, 1972); 64–65, and 258 cites the *New York Times* (May 18, 1951): 25; *Chicago Tribune* (May 26, 1950); a release from Religious News Service (New York: National Conference of Christians and Jews, May 26, 1950).

21:6. Crosby, *God, Church, and Flag*, 84–85, 260 cites the bishops' statement from the archives in *National Conference of Bishops Papers* (Washington, D.C.: United States Catholic Conference, 1951) and *Madison Capital-Times* (November 20, 1951); also 119, 263, uses a Gallup poll No. AIPO 513 (March 1953) and a poll by Roper Public Opinion Research Center, Williamstown, Mass., in which 15.9 percent of Protestant and 17.8 percent of national opinion was against McCarthy.

21:7. Francis Lally complained in the *Boston Pilot* (June 6, 1953); see Crosby, *God, Church, and Flag*, 125–26, 264–65; *Christian Century* 70 (May 6, 1953): 531; "McCarthy in the White House?" *Ave Maria* 77 (May 30, 1953): 675.

21:8. "Reds and Our Churches," *American Mercury* (July 1953): 3; "Generally Speaking," *Ave Maria* 78 (August 1, 1953): 4–5.

21:9. "Generally Speaking," *Ave Maria*, 4.

21:10. Ibid., 4–5.

21:11. *New York Times* (July 12, 1953): sec. 10, 3; Crosby, *God, Church, and Flag*, 130, 265; Spellman is quoted by Crosby, 134, 265, from *Madison Capital-Times* (August 6, 1953); Crosby cites interviews with George Ford, 139–40, 143–44, 266; Hazel G. Erskine, "The Poll: Religious Prejudice, Part I," *Public Opinion Quarterly* 29 (Fall 1965): 489, 491.

21:12. *New York Times* (June 10, 1954): 10; *Congressional Record*, 83d Cong., 2d sess., 1954. vol. 100, pt. 12: 16329, 16335–36, 16340, 16370, 16380–81, 16392, give an accounting of the Senate vote; see also Crosby, *God, Church, and Flag*, 216, 274; on Kennedy and McCarthy see Crosby, 77, 105–6, 205–16; Rovere, *Senator Joe McCarthy*, 250–54.

21:13. Daniel Bell, ed., *The New American Right* (New York: Criterion, 1955);

Seymour Martin Lipset, "Three Decades of the Radical Right," in Daniel Bell, *The Radical Right* (Garden City: Doubleday, 1963), 407.

21:14. Much of this narrative draws upon Don E. Carleton, *Red Scare! Right-wing Hysteria, Fifties Fanaticism and Their Legacy in Texas* (Austin: Texas Monthly Press, 1985), a somewhat strident, but in this instance at least, reliable history; see 104–5, which cites Norman W. Spellman, *Growing a Soul: The Story of A. Frank Smith* (Dallas: Southern Methodist University Press, 1979), 361–63.

21:15. Carleton, *Red Scare!* 106–7.

21:16. Ibid., 108–9; *Is There A Pink Fringe in the Methodist Church? A Report to Methodists from the Committee for the Preservation of Methodism* (Houston, April 1953), 2–3.

21:17. *Christian Century* 69 (April 23, 1952): 487; Herbert Philbrick, "The Communists Are After Your Church!" *Christian Herald* 76 (April, 1953): 18–20, 92–95; for Smith quote, see Carleton, *Red Scare!* 111 and Spellman, *Growing A Soul,* 368; Carleton, 337–38, cites archives with the handbills and circulars from 1953.

21:18. Carleton, *Red Scare!* 129, 341, tells the story of the Minute Women in Houston on the basis of interviews; 143, 342 draws upon and cites archival material, letters from Jesse Jones to Rufus Clement, and interviews with Kenneth W. Pope and others concerning this open attack; see also 144, 342.

21:19. Ibid., 145, 151, 342–43, again based on interviews with Pope and others and newspapers of the day; see also *Time* (May 25, 1953): 96; for Pope's reminiscence, see Spellman, *Growing A Soul,* 369.

21:20. Carleton, *Red Scare!* 205–7; Carleton relies on interviews with Pope, Hardin, and others for a description of the Oxnam meeting; see also the *Houston Chronicle* (May 27, 1953) and *Journal of the Fifteenth Annual Session of the Texas Annual Conference of the Methodist Church, June 1–5, 1953,* 110–11.

21:21. Bennett, *The Party of Fear,* chap. 14, "The New Red Scare and After, 1946–1968," 239–272, provides the general background for the era.

21:22. Carl McIntire, *Modern Tower of Babel* (Collingswood: Christian Beacon Press, 1949); John Mackay was cited in Ralph Lord Roy, *Apostles of Discord : A Study of Organized Bigotry and Disruption on the Fringes of Protestantism* (Boston: Beacon, 1953), 195, taken from *The Christian Beacon* (January 5, 1950): 5.

21:23. Erling Jorstad, *The Politics of Doomsday: Fundamentalists and the Far Right* (New York: Abingdon, 1970), 51. I drew on Jorstad for access to other material in this chapter; the attack on Henry is in Jorstad, 44, citing *The Christian Beacon* (May 3, 1962): 3; see also Roy, *Apostle of Discord,* 244–50.

21:24. Roy, *Apostle of Discord,* 204, citing *Denver Post* (December 10, 1952): 29; Jorstad, *The Politics of Doomsday,* 55, citing *The Christian Beacon* (October 1952 and November 1952), which tracks the story of the Revised Standard Version.

21:25. On Oxnam, see *Christian Century* 70 (November 4, 1953): 1273, and (August 5, 1953): 885; Roy, *Apostle of Discord,* 244, 238, 240; John R. Rice's magazine, *Sword of the Lord* (May 29, 1953) reprinted the entire pamphlet; Religious News Service reported the attack on Dulles in a release of November 1, 1945; see also *Christian Beacon* (November 6, 1952): 8; McIntire's question is in the *Christian Beacon* (November 22, 1951).

21:26. See the extensive coverage of the World Council event in *Christian Century* 71 (March 24, 1954): 356; (April 28, 1954): 107–8; (May 5, 1954): 550; (May 19, 1954): 603.

21:27. Jorstad, *The Politics of Doomsday,* 69; see also Eckard V. Toy, "Ideology and Conflict in American Ultraconservatism, 1945–1960," (Ph.D. dissertation, University of Oregon, 1965), 94; see especially Edgar C. Bundy, *Collectivism in the Churches* (Wheaton: The Church League of America, 1958).

21:28. Roy, *Apostles of Discord*, 241-42, quotes the Wichita Falls *Record* and speeches delivered in Latin America in 1951 and reprinted in *Militant Truth* 10, nos. 10, 9, 51, 50.

21:29. Bennett, *The Party of Fear*, 328-29; Fred C. Schwarz, *You Can Trust the Communists (To Be Communists)* (New York: Prentice-Hall, 1960), 164-82; for a contemporary report on Schwarz, see Richard Dudman, *Men of the Far Right* (New York: Pyramid, 1962), 114-23.

21:30. Bennett, *The Party of Fear*, 329-30, introduces Hargis; see Billy James Hargis, *Communist America—Must It Be?* (Butler, Ind.: Highley Huffman Press, 1960), esp. 21-39, 96-97.

21:31. Jorstad, *The Politics of Doomsday*, 70-73, tells of the Air Force training manual incident; Harold H. Martin, "Doomsday Merchants of the Far Right," *Saturday Evening Post* (April 28, 1962): 24; Dudman, *Men of the Far Right*, 82-91.

21:32. An early survey is J. Allen Broyles, *The John Birch Society* (Boston: Beacon, 1964); the Eisenhower attack was first reported in *Christian Science Monitor* (April 1, 1961); see Broyles, 7; Robert Welch, *The Blue Book of the John Birch Society* (Belmont, Mass.: Western Islands, 1959).

21:33. Welch, *The Blue Book*, 10-11, 39, 63, 149-50.

21:34. Ibid., 152; Broyles, *The John Birch Society*, 22-26, reviews the career of John Birch.

21:35. Welch, *The Blue Book*, 59.

21:36. Jorstad, *The Politics of Doomsday*, 111-13.

21:37. It is significant that movements of the right that grouped or regrouped at the time of the presidential campaigns of Barry Goldwater in 1964 and Ronald Reagan in 1980 still had some ambiguity about the record of the extreme right of this earlier period. Goldwater welcomed "Birchers" into his campaign. See Barry Goldwater, *With No Apologies: The Personal and Political Memoirs of United States Senator Barry M. Goldwater* (New York: Morrow, 1979), 119, 189; he also spoke generously of McCarthy in a eulogy in 1957; see Jack Bell, *Mr. Conservative: Barry Goldwater* (Garden City: Doubleday, 1962), 102. A scholarly effort to pursue continuities and innovations in the record is William B. Hixson, Jr., *Search for the American Right Wing: An Analysis of the Social Science Record, 1955-1987* (Princeton: Princeton University Press, 1992), 299, where Hixson points out that the George Wallace campaign of 1968 was "run by right-wing activists, notably those belonging to the John Birch Society." A "New Christian Right" had replaced Birchers and the other relatively few people and movements who kept the McCarthy flame going until the time of Reagan.

Chapter Twenty-two

22:1. A good glimpse of Negro problems in the postwar era just before the Supreme Court decisions and the civil rights movement altered some circumstances is Rayford W. Logan, *The Negro and the Post-War World: A Primer* (Washington, D.C.: The Minorities Publishers, 1945).

22:2. Robert W. Spike, *Safe in Bondage: An Appraisal of the Church's Mission to America* (New York: Friendship Press, 1960), 127.

22:3. Ibid., 4, 128-31.

22:4. Richard Kluger, *Simple Justice: The History of Brown v. Board of Education and Black America's Struggle for Equality* (New York: Knopf, 1976), reviews the entire school segregation issue and provides a discussion of integration on which this account draws; Kluger quotes *Time* on 709; see "The Nation: To All on Equal Terms," *Time* (May 24, 1954): 21.

22:5. Kluger, *Simple Justice*, 3, 8, 10–11.

22:6. Ibid., 10–11, 12–21, recounts the details of DeLaine's awakening.

22:7. Ibid., 23–26, 329.

22:8. Ibid., 525–540, traces DeLaine and the *Briggs* case; 778 tells of DeLaine's death in 1974 when Summerton public schools had 3,000 black students and one white one.

22:9. Ibid., 710–11, quotes Eastland.

22:10. Kenneth B. Clark, *Prejudice and Your Child* (Boston: Beacon, 1955), 33–34.

22:11. Ibid., 104–5, 110–12.

22:12. Ibid., 106–9.

22:13. Charles H. Martin, "Black Protest, Anti-Communism, and the Cold War: The Willie McGee Case" (paper delivered at 1980 meeting of the Association for Study of Afro-American Life and History), 8, as quoted in Herbert Shapiro, *White Violence and Black Response: From Reconstruction to Montgomery* (Amherst: University of Massachusetts Press, 1988), 395–96.

22:14. Shapiro, *White Violence and Black Response*, 398–99, discusses the Communist charges and describes the prayer-meeting incident; Carl Rowan quoted the *Jackson Daily News* in his *South of Freedom* (New York: Knopf, 1952), 177; Shapiro, 401, quotes the hymn from a report in the *Jackson Daily News* (May 8, 1951).

22:15. The statistics are from Walter T. K. Nugent, *Modern America* (Boston: Houghton Mifflin, 1973), 300; Eisenhower is quoted in Peter Lyon, *Eisenhower: Portrait of a Hero* (Boston: Little, Brown, 1974), 563, 555; see "State of the Union Address, February 2, 1953," *Public Papers of the Presidents: Dwight D. Eisenhower, 1953* (Washington, D.C.: Government Printing Office, 1960), 30; William H. Chafe, *The Unfinished Journey: America Since World War II* (New York: Oxford University Press, 1986), 154–55; on Eisenhower's opinions, see Emmet Hughes, *The Ordeal of Power* (New York: Atheneum, 1963), 201; Earl Warren, *The Memoirs of Earl Warren* (Garden City: Doubleday, 1977), 291–92, reports on the conversation with Eisenhower.

22:16. The bibliography on Thurman is vast and increasing; of special interest for the present topic is Walter E. Fluker, *They Looked For a City: A Comparative Analysis of the Ideal of Community in the Thought of Howard Thurman and Martin Luther King, Jr.* (New York: University Press of America, 1989).

22:17. Ibid., 29, summarizes the career in "common ground" terms. The term appears in one of his book titles, Howard Thurman, *The Search for Common Ground: An Inquiry into the Basis of Man's Experience of Community* (New York: Harper and Row, 1971); Howard Thurman, *The Creative Encounter* (New York: Harper and Row, 1954), 28, 20; on evil, Fluker, 48, quotes a Thurman typescript, "What Can I Believe In?" at Boston University.

22:18. Thurman, *Creative Encounter*, 137, 140; Fluker cites a later oral comment on "dogs," 74, 225; Howard Thurman, *The Disciplines of the Spirit* (New York: Harper and Row, 1963), 104–5.

22:19. Howard Thurman, *Jesus and the Disinherited* (Nashville: Abingdon-Cokesbury, 1949), 34; Howard Thurman, *The Negro Spiritual Speaks of Life and Death* (New York: Harper and Brothers, 1947), 56.

22:20. Howard Thurman, "Fascist Masquerade," in Randolph Crump Miller, ed., *The Church and Organized Movements* (New York: Harper and Brothers, 1946), 97–98; Thurman, *Jesus and the Disinherited*, 98.

22:21. For the biographical details on the Crozer years, see Taylor Branch, *Parting the Waters: America in the King Years, 1954–63* (New York: Simon and Schuster, 1988), 68–79; Martin Luther King, Jr., *Stride Toward Freedom: A Leader of His People Tells the Montgomery Story* (New York: Harper and Row, 1958), 99.

22:22. King, *Stride Toward Freedom,* 90–100.

22:23. Ibid., 100; Martin Luther King, Jr., *Strength to Love* (New York: Harper and Row, 1963), 141–42; Branch, *Parting the Waters,* 102–19.

22:24. Martin Luther King, Jr., *Where Do We Go From Here?: Chaos or Community* (New York: Harper and Row, 1967), 97, 43–44; King, *Strength to Love,* 64, 81; Martin Luther King, Jr., "The American Dream," *Negro History Bulletin* 31 (May, 1968), 15.

22:25. Martin Luther King, Jr., "The Un-Christian Christian," *Ebony* 20 (August, 1965), 77; King, *Stride Toward Freedom,* 207.

22:26. Rosa Parks is quoted, among other places, in Henry F. Bedford, *Trouble Downtown: The Local Context of Twentieth-Century America* (New York: Harcourt, Brace, Jovanovich, 1978), 141; see *Time* (January 3, 1964): 14–15.

22:27. Anthony Lewis, *Portrait of a Decade: The Second American Revolution* (New York: Random House, 1964), 74.

22:28. Ibid., 72; King, *Stride Toward Freedom,* 171–73, 51; see Lerone Bennett, Jr., "When the Man and the Hour Are Met," in C. Eric Lincoln, ed., *Martin Luther King, Jr.: A Profile* (New York: Hill and Wang, 1970), 16–17; see also Stephen B. Oates, *Let the Trumpet Sound: The Life of Martin Luther King, Jr.* (New York: Harper and Row, 1982), 70–71.

22:29. Michael Barone, *Our Country: The Shaping of America from Roosevelt to Reagan* (New York: The Free Press, 1990), 273; Branch, *Parting the Waters,* 227–28, tells of the Graham entente.

22:30. Branch, *Parting the Waters,* 56–57, 101–2.

22:31. Chafe, *The Unfinished Journey,* 165–70, is a narrative of the sit-in movement.

22:32. Martin Luther King, Jr., "The Ethical Demands for Integration," *Religion and Labor* (May 1963): 1, 3–4, 7–8; reproduced in James Melvin Washington, *A Testament of Hope: The Essential Writings of Martin Luther King, Jr.* (San Francisco: Harper and Row, 1986), 117–25.

22:33. Branch, *Parting the Waters,* 228–30, 56–57, 101–2, 195–96.

22:34. Philip S. Foner, ed., *The Voice of Black America* (New York: Simon and Schuster, 1972), 919–24, esp. 922–23, quotes from King's speech entitled "Give Us the Ballot—We Will Transform the South."

22:35. W. E. B. DuBois, "Watchword for Negroes: Register to Vote," in Julius Lester, *The Seventh Son,* vol. 2 (New York: Random House, 1971), 652–53; 702–3 reprints the New York television interview of June 4, 1957; see also W.E.B. DuBois, "Gandhi and the American Negroes," *Gandhi Marg: A Quarterly Journal of Gandhian Thought* 1 (July 1957): 175–77.

22:36. W.E.B. DuBois, "Crusader Without Violence," *National Guardian* 12 (November 9, 1959): 8; see Robert F. Williams, *Negroes with Guns* (New York: Marzani and Munsell, 1962), 53–57; James Forman, *The Making of Black Revolutionaries* (New York: Macmillan, 1972); Williams, 14, quotes Martin Luther King, Jr., "The Social Organization of Non-Violence."

22:37. Williams, *Negroes With Guns,* 12–15, quotes King; see also 40–41, 63, for Williams's own statements.

22:38. On public notice of the Nation of Islam, see E. U. Essien-Udom, *Black Nationalism* (Chicago: University of Chicago Press, 1962), 73; for the Muhammad quotation, see C. Eric Lincoln, *The Black Muslims in America* (Boston: Beacon Press, 1961), 205.

22:39. Lincoln, *The Black Muslims in America,* iv, 153, picks up the Muslim taunts from the *Los Angeles Herald-Dispatch* (January 9, 1960).

22:40. Ibid., iii, ix–xi.

22:41. Ibid., 4, 10–12, 87–89.

22:42. Ibid., 155, 165, 227–29.

22:43. Ibid., 230–33; Arnold and Caroline Rose, *America Divided* (New York: Alfred A. Knopf, 1948), 218–19.

22:44. Lincoln, *The Black Muslims in America,* 239; see also C. Eric Lincoln, "Anxiety, Fear and Integration," *Phylon: Journal of Race and Culture* (September 1960); Lincoln also wrote a definitional footnote: "Whether assimilation presupposed amalgamation is, I believe, purely academic. Amalgamation is a biological phenomenon, and in the United States it is also a well documented social fact. Further, amalgamation is cognizant of neither 'integration' nor 'assimilation'; it is oblivious of both."

Chapter Twenty-three

23:1. C. Eric Lincoln, *The Black Muslims in America* (Boston: Beacon Press, 1961), 227–29, 231–33, 237–39; Arnold and Caroline Rose, *America Divided* (New York: Alfred A. Knopf, 1948), 218–19; see also C. Eric Lincoln, "Anxiety, Fear and Integration," in *Phylon: Journal of Race and Culture* (September 1960).

23:2. Marshall Sklare, *The Jews: Social Patterns of an American Group* (Glencoe: The Free Press, 1958).

23:3. Ibid., v; Albert I. Gordon, *Jews in Suburbia* (Boston: Beacon Press, 1959).

23:4. Gordon, *Jews in Suburbia,* xvii-xviii, xxiv; he quoted Sylvia Fleis Fava, "Suburbanism as a Way of Life," *American Sociological Review* 21 (February 1956): 34–37; Robert Park, *The City* (Chicago: University of Chicago Press, 1925), 1; and on "state of mind," see David Riesman, "The Suburban Dislocation," *The Annals of the American Academy of Political and Social Science* 314 (November 1957): 133.

23:5. Gordon, *Jews in Suburbia,* 1, 6, 8–9, 11–12; statistics from the U.S. Census were reported in *U.S. News and World Report* (August 10, 1956); see also Riesman, "The Suburban Dislocation," 130.

23:6. Gordon, *Jews in Suburbia,* 11–12, 16–18.

23:7. Ibid., 59–63.

23:8. Ibid., 85–86, 88.

23:9. Ibid., 91–92, 97, 119.

23:10. Ibid., 126–27.

23:11. Ibid., 148–53.

23:12. Ibid., 224–26.

23:13. Ibid., 155, 161, 166; see Erich Fromm, *Escape from Freedom* (New York: Rinehart, 1941), 21–22.

23:14. Gordon, *Jews in Suburbia,* 192–94.

23:15. Ibid., 195–98, 200, 207, 209, 231–32; he quoted Arthur Schlesinger, Jr., "Liberalism," *Saturday Review of Literature* 40 (June 8, 1957); Max Lerner, *America as a Civilization,* vol. 1 (New York: Simon and Schuster, 1957), 260–63; Paul Tillich in *New York Times* (June 12, 1957): 36; Fromm, *Escape from Freedom,* 185–206; Abraham Maslow, *Motivation and Personality* (New York: Harper and Brothers, 1954), 338.

23:16. Eugene J. Lipman and Albert Vorspan, *A Tale of Ten Cities: The Triple Ghetto in American Religious Life* (New York: Union of American Hebrew Congregations, 1962), 22–23.

23:17. Ibid., 16, 19–20.

23:18. Ibid., 23–24.

23:19. Ibid., 29–31, 40.

23:20. Ibid., 46–47, 59, 63–64, 67–68, 75–76.

23:21. Ibid., 78–79, 83–84, 86–87.

23:22. Ibid., 87, 90–91, 95, 97, 110.

23:23. Ibid., 141–42, 162–63, 165.

23:24. Ibid., 218, 222–24.

23:25. Ibid., 169, 171, 189–90, 201–2; they cite *New York Herald Tribune* (January 4, 1959): 1.

23:26. Ibid., 262–63, 273–76, 287.

23:27. Ibid.

23:28. Ibid., 231–52.

23:29. Ibid., 294–99.

23:30. Ibid., 300, 302–3, 307–9.

23:31. Ibid., 310–11.

23:32. Ibid., 311–13, 329, 334–35, 338–39, 341–42.

23:33. Ben Halpern, "America Is Different," in Marshall Sklare, ed., *The Jews: Social Patterns of an American Group* (Glencoe: The Free Press, 1958), 23–27, 31.

23:34. Ibid., 38–39.

23:35. Stuart E. Rosenberg, *America Is Different: The Search for Jewish Identity* (New York: Nelson, 1964), 33, 35; see Arthur Mann, "Charles Fleischer's Religion of Democracy," *Commentary* 17 (June 1954): 557.

Chapter Twenty-four

24:1. Eugene J. Lipman and Albert Vorspan, *A Tale of Ten Cities: The Triple Ghetto in American Religious Life* (New York: Union of American Hebrew Congregations, 1962), 298–99.

24:2. John Tracy Ellis, *American Catholicism* (Chicago: University of Chicago, 1956); I will use the second edition, revised in 1969, which is substantially the same except for a long chapter on post-Vatican II events; see 161–62.

24:3. On the GI Bill and other changes, see James Hennesey, S.J., *American Catholics: A History of the Roman Catholic Community in the United States* (New York: Oxford University Press, 1981), 283.

24:4. Ibid., 286–87, 296, provides these statistics.

24:5. For an assessment of the social face of Catholicism in the 1950s, see Jay P. Dolan, *The American Catholic Experience: A History from Colonial Times to the Present* (Garden City: Doubleday, 1985), chap. 14, "Religion, Education and Reform, The golden age of devotional Catholicism, the expansion of the educational network, and move toward social reform," 384–417.

24:6. Joseph H. Fichter, S.J., was a pioneer in parish studies, and one of his works came to be seen as a classic, *Southern Parish*, vol. 1: *Dynamics of a City Church* (Chicago: University of Chicago Press, 1951); this work was complemented by Joseph B. Schuyler, S.J., *Northern Parish: A Sociological and Pastoral Study* (Chicago: Loyola University Press, 1960). Another work which gathered the talents of several scholars and helped set the terms is C. J. Nuesse and Thomas J. Harte, C.Ss.R., *The Sociology of the Parish: An Introductory Symposium* (Milwaukee: Bruce, 1951); Philip M. Hannan, "The Development of the Form of the Modern Parish," in Nuesse and Harte, 41, quotes canon law; John D. Donovan in Nuesse and Harte, 77, quoted Cushing from the *Boston Morning Globe* (December 27, 1947).

24:7. Francis S. Engel, "Parish Societies," in Nuesse and Harte, *The Sociology of the Parish*, 196, 202.

24:8. Harold A. Buetow, *Of Singular Benefit: The Story of Catholic Education in the United States* (New York: Macmillan, 1970), 225, 235; on Dewey, see George Johnson, "The Activity Curriculum in the Light of Catholic Principles," *Education* 61 (March 1941): 418.

24:9. Buetow, *Of Singular Benefit*, 250–53; Carl J. Ryan, "The Lay Teacher in the Catholic School," *The Homiletic and Pastoral Review*, 49 (May 1948): 575.

24:10. R. Scott Appleby, "Priesthood Reconsidered: Presence Beyond the Parish, 1954–1962," in Jay P. Dolan, R. Scott Appleby, Patricia Byrne, and Debra Campbell, *Transforming Parish Ministry: The Changing Roles of Catholic Clergy, Laity, and Women Religious* (New York: Crossroad, 1989), 45–46; see also J. B. Gremillion, *Journal of a Southern Pastor* (Chicago: Fides, 1957), 19–20.

24:11. Appleby, "Priesthood Reconsidered," 46–49; Gremillion, *Journal of a Southern Pastor*, 69–72.

24:12. Francis B. Donnelly, "The Pastoral Ministry in Transition," in Nuesse and Harte, *The Sociology of the Parish*, 285–86; Pius XI was quoted from "Lettre à Mgr. Swireskas et aux Eveques de Lithuanie, December 27, 1930," in E. Guerry, ed., *L'Action Catholique* (Paris: Desclée de Brouwer, 1936), 32, while Pius addressed the alumni of the Papal College of Anagni, April 29, 1949; also see Paul Hanley Furfey, "The Missionary Role of the Parish," in Nuesse and Harte, 305–6.

24:13. Furfey, "The Missionary Role of the Parish," 309–12; Schuyler, *Northern Parish*, 75, 106, 165, 271, 278–79.

24:14. Schuyler, *Northern Parish*, 175, 215, 248–49.

24:15. Ibid., 263–64, 267, 269–70.

24:16. Ibid., 282.

24:17. Vincent J. Giese, "The Lay Apostolate in Chicago," in Louis Putz, C.S.C., ed., *The Catholic Church, U.S.A.* (Chicago: Fides, 1956), 358–61.

24:18. Ibid., 372–74.

24:19. John A. O'Brien, "The Catholic Church and Religious Freedom," in Putz, *The Catholic Church, U.S.A.*, 289–93, 295–97.

24:20. Ibid., 297–300.

24:21. Walter J. Ong, S.J., *Frontiers in American Catholicism: Essays on Ideology and Culture* (New York: Macmillan, 1957), vii, 2–3, 7–8; also *American Catholic Crossroads: Religious-Secular Encounters in the Modern World* (New York: Macmillan, 1959).

24:22. Ong, *Frontiers in American Catholicism*, 2–3, 7–8, 17–23.

24:23. Ibid., 24–25, 31, 34, 86–88, 101–3.

24:24. Ibid., 101–3, 106–10.

24:25. Ibid., 111–25.

24:26. Ong, *American Catholic Crossroads*, 16–23.

24:27. Ibid., 25–45, passim.

24:28. Ibid., 63–65.

24:29. One of the many reprintings of John Tracy Ellis, "The American Catholic Church and the Intellectual Life," was in Putz, *The Catholic Church, U.S.A.*, 315–57; see especially 316–17, citing Henry Steele Commager, "Why Are We Mad at Teacher?" *The Reporter* 11 (October 21, 1954): 41, and D. W. Brogan, *USA: An Outline of the Country, Its People and Institutions* (London: Oxford University Press, 1941), 65.

24:30. Ellis, "The American Catholic Church and the Intellectual Life," 330–31, 334, 341, 344, 346, 348–49; cites Cushing in the *Boston Pilot* (October 17, 1947).

24:31. Ellis was quoting a speech by Heinrich Rommen at the golden jubilee of the College of New Rochelle during the 1953–54 academic year. Ellis, ibid., 355–57; see Peter Viereck, *The Shame and Glory of the Intellectuals* (Boston: Beacon Press, 1953), 49.

24:32. For a summary of the response and effect through the decades, see John

Whitney Evans, "American Catholics and the Intellectual Life: Thirty Years Later," in Nelson H. Minnich, Robert B. Eno, SS, and Robert F. Trisco, *Studies in Catholic History in Honor of John Tracy Ellis* (Wilmington: Michael Glazier, 1985), esp. 367; Thomas F. O'Dea, *American Catholic Dilemma: An Inquiry into the Intellectual Life* (New York: Sheed and Ward, 1958), 81, 84, 88; see also Paul Tillich, *The Religious Situation* (New York: Meridian, 1956), 182.

24:33. O'Dea, *American Catholic Dilemma*, 90–92, 112, 117–18, 163; see Leo Ward, C.S.C., "The Church in America," *The American Apostolate* (Westminster: Newman, 1952), 2.

24:34. For an understanding of Spellman as American nationalist, see Dorothy Dohen, *Nationalism and American Catholicism* (New York: Sheed and Ward, 1967); p. 1 cites Spellman on the "my country" theme as late as Christmas of 1965 in Vietnam War days, quoting *New York Times* (December 24, 1965); see Francis Cardinal Spellman, *What America Means to Me* (New York: Scribner's, 1953), 15, 4, 23.

Chapter Twenty-five

25:1. Before the Second Vatican Council (1962–65), Catholic writers on Protestantism characteristically published the longest lists of Protestant denominations and called attention to the fissiparousness of non-Catholic Christianity as a mark of its departure from truth. Thus John A. Hardon, S.J., *The Protestant Churches of America* (Westminster: Newman, 1956), points to the tension and conflict within Protestantism, a study of which "gives those who possess the fulness of revelation a sympathetic understanding and a desire to share the true faith with those who are still searching for the truth."

25:2. James DeForest Murch, *Cooperation without Compromise: A History of the National Association of Evangelicals* (Grand Rapids: Eerdmans, 1956), 135–38.

25:3. Ibid., 139–52.

25:4. Ibid., 139–52, 179, 183–84, 207–8.

25:5. Ibid., 210–12, 214–15.

25:6. Ibid., 15–17, 19–21, 28, 31–43.

25:7. Louis Gasper, *The Fundamentalist Movement* (The Hague: Mouton, 1963), 44–46, details these attacks; see James DeForest Murch, "God's Word and the Church's Witness," *United Evangelical Action* 8 (April 1, 1949): 13–16; "Spirit of Revival Marks Indianapolis Meeting," *United Evangelical Action* 9 (May 1, 1950): 5; James DeForest Murch, "In the Pattern of Peaceful Coexistence," *United Evangelical Action* 15 (May 1, 1956): 9; James DeForest Murch, "Trends in Protestantism," *United Evangelical Action* 17 (March 1, 1958): 7.

25:8. Murch, *Cooperation without Compromise*, 19–21, 44–47, 70; he cited "Sectarianism Receives a New Lease on Life," *Christian Century* 59 (May 19, 1943).

25:9. Gasper, *The Fundamentalist Movement*, 119–20; see John R. Rice, "Don't Be Fooled," *The A.G.C. Reporter* (September 1958): 2, 10; Gasper quotes a statement by Graham on television, June 22, 1957; see John R. Rice, "Billy Graham's New York Crusade," *Sword of the Lord* (April 19, 1957): 1–2 is the source of the attack; Gasper, 142, cites "About Billy Graham," *Christian Beacon* (April 11, 1957): 1 and (April 25, 1957): 3; see also the editorials "Is Evangelical Theology Changing?" and "Is Evangelical Christianity Changing?" in *King's Business* (1957): 16, 23.

25:10. Gasper, *The Fundamentalist Movement*, 44–54; McIntire quoted in *New York Times* (August 21, 1948): 16; see Carl McIntire, *Modern Tower of Babel* (Collingswood, N.J.: Christian Beacon Press, 1949), 230–31; Samuel McCrea Cavert, *On the Road to Christian Unity: An Appraisal of the Ecumenical Movement* (New York: Harper and Row, 1961), 100–101.

25:11. Arnold W. Hearn, "Fundamentalist Renascence," *Christian Century* 75 (April 30, 1958): 528; "Needed: Evangelism in Depth," *Christian Century* 74 (June 26, 1957): 782–83; "Fundamentalist Revival," *Christian Century* 74 (June 26, 1957): 749–51; "N.A.E. Welcomes Probe of Clergy," *Christian Century* 70 (May 6, 1953): 550; "N.A.E. Expanding Scope of Action," *Christian Century* 68 (April 25, 1951): 536.

25:12. Carl F. H. Henry, *Confessions of a Theologian: An Autobiography* (Waco: Word, 1986), 105–7.

25:13. Carl F. H. Henry, *Evangelical Responsibility in Contemporary Theology* (Grand Rapids: Eerdmans, 1957), 9–10.

25:14. Ibid., 10, 15–18.

25:15. Ibid., 18–20, 33–37.

25:16. Ibid., 29–30, 43–47, 65, 77–82.

25:17. Ibid., 79–82, 86; Henry, *Confessions of a Theologian*, 140–41, 144–45.

25:18. Henry, *Confessions of a Theologian*, 158–59, recalls the magazine's position on civil rights.

25:19. Ibid., 163, 173–76, 179, 196.

25:20. A superior seminary history is George M. Marsden, *Reforming Fundamentalism: Fuller Seminary and the New Evangelicalism* (Grand Rapids: Eerdmans, 1987), esp. 3, and on the Princeton model, 21–25.

25:21. Ibid., 3, 21–25, 61–63.

25:22. Ibid., 61–65.

25:23. Marsden cites Carl Henry, *The Uneasy Conscience of Modern Fundamentalism* (Grand Rapids: Eerdmans, 1947), 36, 66.

25:24. Marsden, *Reforming Fundamentalism*, 98–108, is the basis for this account; Bela Vasady, "Through Ecumenical Glasses," *Religion in Life* (Fall 1949): 1.

25:25. Marsden, *Reforming Fundamentalism*, 109, 111, 115.

25:26. Henry, *Confessions*, 137, quotes Carnell; see also Marsden, *Reforming Fundamentalism*, 147–50.

25:27. Marsden, *Reforming Fundamentalism*, 153–57, 162–69, 172–75, 181–85, 188, 193–95; see especially "Is Evangelical Theology Changing?" *Christian Life* (March 1956): 16–19; Marsden quoted "What Is The New Fundamentalism?" tape recording from the Union League Club, Chicago (October 10, 1958); there is a fine biography of Carnell by Rudolph Nelson, *The Making and Unmaking of an Evangelical Mind: The Case of Edward Carnell* (New York: Cambridge University Press, 1987).

25:28. Samuel McCrea Cavert, *On the Road to Christian Unity: An Appraisal of the Ecumenical Movement* (New York: Harper and Row, 1961), 94.

25:29. George F. Ketcham, ed., *Yearbook of American Churches, 1951 Edition* (New York: National Council of the Churches of Christ in the United States of America, 1951): 24–27; the 1962 statistic is from Benson Y. Landis, *Yearbook of American Churches, 1964* (New York: Harper and Row, 1964), 254, 58; Kenneth W. Bailey, *Southern White Protestantism in the Twentieth Century* (New York: Harper and Row, 1964), 152, quotes the Dallas *Baptist Standard* which, in turn, was cited in Birmingham *Alabama Christian Advocate* (July 12, 1949); John Shelton Reed, *The Enduring South: Subcultural Persistence in Mass Society* (Chapel Hill: University of North Carolina, 1974), 63, 81, cites surveys on opposition to merger; see "'The Bible Belt': Southern Religion," chap. 6; Reed cites polling data on 57–60; see also Wilbur Zelinsky, "An Approach to the Religious Geography of the United States: Patterns of Church Membership in 1952," *Annals of the Association of American Geographers* 51 (June 1961): 139–39; Simkins is quoted by Louis D. Rubin and James Jackson Kilpatrick, eds., *The Lasting South: Fourteen Southerners Look at Their Home* (Chicago: Henry Regnery, 1957), 97–98.

25:30. *Annual, Southern Baptist Convention, 1914* (Nashville: Marshall and Bruce Company, 1914), 77–78, quoted in Raymond O. Ryland, "Southern Baptist Convention (U.S.A.)," chap. 7, in James Leo Garrett, ed., *Baptist Relations with Other Christians* (Valley Forge: Judson Press, 1974); see Ryland in Garrett, 79, citing the *Annual, Southern Baptist Convention* (1948): 58; (1949): 53; (1950): 37; (1951): 36; (1953): 51.

25:31. Ernest F. Campbell, "Southern Baptists and the World Council of Churches," *Religious Herald* 113 (July 11, 1940): 9, 24; Edward Hughes Pruden, "Brethren, Let's Be Fair," *Biblical Recorder* 117 (July 28, 1951): 9, 16, cited George D. Kelsey, *Social Ethics Among Southern Baptists, 1917–1969* (Metuchen: Scarecrow Press, 1973), 31–32; Cavert, *On the Road To Christian Unity,* 95–96; he referred to James R. Sampey, from an address at Oxford in 1937.

25:32. Cavert, *On the Road To Christian Unity,* 95–97; Theron D. Price, "A Southern Baptist View on Church Unity," in J. Robert Nelson, ed., *Christian Unity in North America* (St. Louis: Bethany Press, 1958), 86–88.

25:33. Ketcham, *Yearbook of American Churches, 1951 Edition,* 237, gives statistics on 21 Lutheran denominations, most of them small. The United Lutheran Church in America had 1,954,342 members, Missouri was second with 1,674,901, while two groups on their way to merger (in 1960), the American Lutheran Church and the Evangelical Lutheran Church of America numbered 813,837; for the prehistory of modern Lutheran ecumenism, see E. Clifford Nelson, ed., *The Lutherans in North America* (Philadelphia: Fortress Press, 1975), 495–98; Nelson, 498–508, follows the complex unity moves; for the history of involvements with the World Council, see Dorris A. Flesner, *American Lutherans Help Shape World Council: The Role of the Lutheran Churches of America in the Formation of the World Council of Churches* (Dubuque: Lutheran Historical Conference, 1981); Flesner deals with the period up through 1948 and pays no attention to debates over membership in the 1950s; Cavert, *On The Road to Christian Unity,* 98–99.

25:34. Cavert, *On The Road to Christian Unity,* 106–8, 111–13.

25:35. Ibid., 107–8, 111–13; the rejection was quoted by *The Pentecostal Evangel* (August 18, 1928): 7, cited in Vinson Synan, *The Holiness-Pentecostal Movement in the United States* (Grand Rapids: Eerdmans, 1971), 206; Synan, 208, tells of the formation of the Pentecostal Fellowship of North America; membership lists of the National Association of Evangelicals in 1956 appear in Murch, *Cooperation without Compromise,* 202–3.

25:36. William Menzies, *Anointed to Serve* (Springfield, Mo.: Gospel Publishing House, 1971), 221; Steve Durasoff, *Bright Winds of the Spirit: Pentecostalism Today* (Englewood Cliffs: Prentice-Hall, 1972), 87–89; David du Plessis, *The Spirit Bade Me Go* (Plainfield: Logos International, 1961), 12, 25.

25:37. Pope Pius XI, "The Promotion of True Religious Unity," trans. Rev. R. A. McGowan, in *Sixteen Encyclicals of Pope Pius XI* (Washington, D.C.: National Catholic Welfare Conference, 1937), 1; Cavert, *On The Road to Christian Unity,* 115–16; Stephen C. Neill, *Brothers in Faith* (Nashville: Abingdon Press, 1960), 48.

25:38. Cavert, *On The Road to Christian Unity,* 120–23, 127; he cited George H. Tavard, *The Catholic Approach to Protestantism* (New York: Harper and Brothers, 1955), Edward Duff, S.J., *The Social Thought of the World Council of Churches* (New York: Association Press, 1956), and Thomas F. O'Dea, "The New America," *Pulpit Digest* 40 (November 1959): 29–34, 102.

25:39. Cavert, *On The Road to Christian Unity,* 133–34; Eugene C. Bianchi, *John XXIII and American Protestants* (Washington: Corpus Press, 1968), 34–35, 79–80; Paul Blanshard, *American Freedom and Catholic Power,* revised edition (Boston: Beacon, 1958), x, 325; see *Watchman-Examiner* 47 (January 22, 1959): 70; Don Hillis, "Will Rome Rule the

World?" *United Evangelical Action* 18 (April 1959): 3, 6–7; Robert J. St. Clair, "A Protestant Council on Roman Catholicism—Talks and Talks and Talks," *United Evangelical Action* 19 (June 1960): 17.

25:40. John A. Hardon, *Christianity in Conflict: A Catholic View of Protestantism* (Westminster: Newman, 1959), 224–29; he cited the Commission on Evangelism of the Congregational Christian Churches, *What the Church Has to Offer* (Boston: Pilgrim Press), 13.

25:41. Bianchi, *John XXIII*, 59, quotes but miscites Nichols; see James H. Nichols, *Primer for Protestants* (New York: Association Press, 1950), 49; *Christian Century* 76 (September 16, 1959): 1044.

25:42. Bianchi, *John XXIII*, 72–75; *Christian Century* 76 (February 18, 1959): 189.

Chapter Twenty-six

26:1. Jaroslav Pelikan, *The Riddle of Roman Catholicism* (Nashville: Abingdon, 1959), 11, 170.

26:2. George H. Williams, "Issues Between Catholics and Protestants at Mid-Century," *Religion in Life* (Spring 1954), 171; *Commonweal* (September 17, 1954), quoted by Robert McAfee Brown, "The Issues Which Divide Us," in Philip Scharper, ed., *American Catholics: A Protestant-Jewish View* (New York: Sheed and Ward, 1959), 101.

26:3. On the anti-Kennedy meeting, see Douglas Cater, "The Protestant Issue," *Reporter* (October 13, 1960): 3–32; "A Statement on Religious Liberty in Relation to the 1960 National Campaign" is reprinted in Patricia Barrett, *Religious Liberty and the American Presidency: A Study in Church-State Relations* (New York: Herder and Herder, 1963), 152–60.

26:4. Barrett, *Religious Liberty,* 19–20, 25; "'Religious Issue' Plays Minor Role in Reformation Sermons," *Religious News Service* (October 31, 1960): 1.

26:5. Eugene C. Bianchi, *John XXIII and American Protestants* (Washington, D.C.: Corpus, 1968), 72–73, 75, 79, quotes Henry Pitney Van Dusen, "American Catholicism: Grounds for Misgivings," *Christianity and Crisis* 19 (August 3, 1959): 116; *The Living Church* 139 (September 13, 1959): 10; *Christian Century* 76 (February 18, 1959): 189; Donald Grey Barnhouse, "What's Behind the Pope's Ecumenical Council?" *Eternity* 10 (December, 1959): 47.

26:6. *Christian Century* 76 (November 4, 1959): 1267.

26:7. Arthur M. Schlesinger, Jr., *The Vital Center* (Boston: Houghton Mifflin, 1949) and John Kenneth Galbraith, *The Liberal Hour* (Boston, Houghton Mifflin, 1960).

26:8. The story of religion in the administrations of Presidents Kennedy and Johnson falls beyond the chronological scope of this story; readers who would like to anticipate some of the detail will find Robert E. Ellwood, *The Sixties Spiritual Awakening: American Religion Moving from Modern to Postmodern* (New Brunswick: Rutgers University Press, 1994) of interest. Ellwood titles his comment on the Kennedy years, "The Fifties Under Pressure," and the years 1964–66, the time in which several writings that we are using as retrospect on the earlier period, as "The Years of Secular Hope." As for transitions, he cites with approval the comment by Martin E. Marty, "Protestantism Enters Third Phase," *Christian Century* (January 18, 1961): 72–75, "Inauguration Day 1961 can serve symbolically as marking the end of Protestantism as a national religion and its advent as the distinctive faith of a creative minority." See Ellwood, ibid., 70.

26:9. Ved Mehta, *The New Theologian* (New York: Harper and Row, 1965), 209.

26:10. Flannery O'Connor to Thomas Stritch, September 14, 1961, reprinted in Flannery O'Connor, *Collected Works* (New York: The Library of America, 1988), 1152; "Everything that Rises Must Converge" appeared in *New World Writing*, no. 20 (New York: Mentor Books, October 1961). On Teilhard's exile years in America, where he gave new expression to some of his ideas on convergence and found a new audience, see Mary Lukas and Ellen Lukas, *Teilhard the Man, the Priest, the Scientist* (Garden City: Doubleday, 1971), 304 – 44.

26 : 11. W. Warren Wagar, *The City of Man: Prophecies of a World Civilization in Twentieth-Century Thought* (Boston: Houghton Mifflin, 1963), vii, 3 – 4.

26 : 12. Ibid., 6 – 10.

26 : 13. Ibid., 10, 15 – 16; he cited Albert Camus, *The Myth of Sisyphus* (New York: Knopf, 1955), 123.

26 : 14. Wagar, *The City of Man*, 53 – 55, 74; he cited as well William Barrett, *Irrational Man* (Garden City: Doubleday, 1958, rev. ed., 1962), 24 – 25; Gerhard Sczcesny, *The Future of Unbelief* (New York: G. Braziller, 1961), 12; Julian Huxley had written of Morley in *Religion Without Revelation*, rev. ed. (New York: Harper & Row, 1957), 82.

26 : 15. Wagar, *The City of Man*, 76 – 78, 80; Teilhard de Chardin, *The Phenomenon of Man* (New York: Harper and Row, 1959), 88 – 89; Teilhard de Chardin, *Building the Earth* (Paris: Editions du Seuil, 1958), 24 – 28.

26 : 16. Wagar, *The City of Man*, 85 – 87; Arnold Toynbee, *A Study of History* (London: Oxford University Press, 1946), 12, 83.

26 : 17. Wagar, *The City of Man*, 99 – 100, 112 – 13, 153, 155 – 56; see William Ernest Hocking, *The Coming World Civilization* (New York: Harper, 1956); Christopher Dawson, *The Historic Reality of Christian Culture* (New York: Harper, 1960); Christopher Dawson, *The Dynamics of World History* (New York: Sheed & Ward, 1956); Hugh Trevor-Roper, *Men and Events* (New York: Harper, 1957).

26 : 18. Wagar, *The City of Man*, 159 – 65; Hocking, *The Coming of World Civilization*, 148 – 49, 170; Arnold Toynbee, *Christianity Among the Religions of the World* (New York: Scribner, 1957), 103 – 4.

26 : 19. Wagar, *The City of Man*, 170 – 72, 239, 247, 249, 252, 258; Franklin Le Van Baumer, *Religion and the Rise of Scepticism* (New York: Harcourt, Brace, 1960), chap. 5; Lawrence Frank, *Society as the Patient* (New Brunswick: Rutgers University Press, 1948), 389; Charles Frankel, *The Case for Modern Man* (New York: Harper & Row, 1956), 83; Karl Mannheim, *Freedom, Power and Democratic Planning* (New York: Oxford University Press, 1950), 201.

26 : 20. Eugene J. Lipman and Albert Vorspan, *A Tale of Ten Cities: The Triple Ghetto in American Religious Life* (New York: Union of American Hebrew Congregations, 1962), 298 – 99.

26 : 21. Henry J. Pratt, *The Liberalization of American Protestantism: A Case Study in Complex Organizations* (Detroit: Wayne State University Press, 1972), 111, cites a reference to Espy in *Christianity Today* (17 March 1967): 42, and Cox from "The 'New Breed' in American Churches," *Daedalus* 96 (Winter 1967): 1 – 2.

26 : 22. Pratt, *American Protestantism*, 155 – 56, quotes Espy from the council's *Information Service*, 17 February 1962, pp. 2 – 3.

26 : 23. Keith R. Bridston and Walter D. Wagoner, eds., *Unity in Mid-Career: An Ecumenical Critique* (New York: Collier-Macmillan, 1963), 86, 195, 106.

26 : 24. Ibid., 1 – 3, 33, 40, 43.

26 : 25. Among all these changes, one of the most interesting had to do with the new attention shown technology in the religious communities. The subject is vast and would carry us far afield; there is an excellent bibliography, Carl Mitcham and Robert Mackey, *Bibliography of the Philosophy of Technology* (Chicago: University of Chicago Press, 1973); 123 – 41 are "Religious Critiques," many of them affirmations of technology.

26 : 26. William Hamilton makes reference to and summarizes the thrust of Bishop

John A. T. Robinson and Dietrich Bonhoeffer in "The Death of God Theologies Today," in Thomas J. J. Altizer and William Hamilton, *Radical Theology and the Death of God* (Indianapolis: Bobbs-Merrill, 1966), 23–50, especially 40, 41, 49.

26:27. Altizer and Hamilton, *Radical Theology,* 91–93; Paul M. van Buren, *The Secular Meaning of the Gospel Based on an Analysis of Its Language* (New York: Macmillan, 1963), 195, 200.

26:28. Harvey Cox, *The Secular City: Secularization and Urbanization in Theological Perspective* (New York: Macmillan, 1965), 2–4, 63, 70, 78.

26:29. Ibid., 98–100.

26:30. Robert L. Heilbroner, *The Future As History* (New York: Harper, 1960), 17; Altizer and Hamilton, *Radical Theology,* 157–58.

26:31. Ibid., 159–60.

26:32. Ibid., 161–62.

26:33. Ibid., 162–65.

26:34. Ibid., 165, 168.

26:35. Langdon Gilkey, *Naming the Whirlwind: The Renewal of God-Language* (Indianapolis: Bobbs-Merrill, 1969), 115–24, especially 120.

Index

Note: In a book on modern American religion the words "modern," "American," and "religion" appear too frequently to be indexed, as do such terms as "Christian," "Catholic," and "Protestant."